OCR Anthology for Classical Greek AS and A-level

D1477030

**OVERNIGHT
LOAN**

The following titles are available from Bloomsbury for the OCR specifications in Latin and Greek, first teaching September 2016

Cicero *Pro Milone*: A Selection, with introduction by Lynn Fotheringham and notes and vocabulary by Robert West

Ovid *Heroides*: A Selection, with introduction, notes and vocabulary by John Godwin

Propertius, Tibullus and Ovid: A Selection of Love Poetry, with introduction, notes and vocabulary by Anita Nikkanen

Seneca Letters: A Selection, with introduction, notes and vocabulary by Eliot Maunder

Tacitus *Annals* I: A Selection, with introduction by Roland Mayer and notes and vocabulary by Katharine Radice

Virgil *Aeneid* VIII: A Selection, with introduction, notes and vocabulary by Keith MacLennan

Virgil *Aeneid* X: A Selection, with introduction, notes and vocabulary by Christopher Tanfield

OCR Anthology for Classical Greek GCSE, covering the prescribed texts by Homer, Herodotus, Euripides, Lucian, Plato and Plutarch, edited by Judith Affleck and Clive Letchford

OCR Anthology for Classical Greek AS and A-level, covering the prescribed texts by Aristophanes, Homer, Plato, Sophocles, Thucydides and Xenophon, with introduction, notes and vocabulary by Malcolm Campbell, Rob Colborn, Frederica Daniele, Benedict Gravell, Sarah Harden, Steven Kennedy, Matthew McCullagh, Charlie Paterson, John Taylor and Claire Webster

Supplementary resources for these volumes can be found at
www.bloomsbury.com/OCR-editions

Please type the URL into your web browser and follow the instructions to access the Companion Website. If you experience any problems, please contact Bloomsbury at contact@bloomsbury.com

OCR Anthology for Classical Greek AS and A-level

Selections from

Thucydides, *Histories*, Book 4

Plato, *Apology*

Xenophon, *Memorabilia*

Homer, *Odyssey* 9 and 10

Sophocles, *Antigone*

Aristophanes, *Acharnians*

With introduction, commentary notes and vocabulary by
Malcolm Campbell, Rob Colborn, Frederica Daniele,
Benedict Gravell, Sarah Harden, Steven Kennedy,
Matthew McCullagh, Charlie Paterson,
John Taylor and Claire Webster

Bloomsbury Academic
An imprint of Bloomsbury Publishing Plc

B L O O M S B U R Y
LONDON · OXFORD · NEW YORK · NEW DELHI · SYDNEY

Bloomsbury Academic
An imprint of Bloomsbury Publishing Plc

50 Bedford Square	1385 Broadway
London	New York
WC1B 3DP	NY 10018
UK	USA

www.bloomsbury.com

BLOOMSBURY and the Diana logo are trademarks of Bloomsbury Publishing Plc

First published 2016
Reprinted 2016 (twice)

Introductions, notes and vocabularies © Malcolm Campbell, Rob Colborn, Frederica Daniele, Benedict Gravell, Sarah Harden, Steven Kennedy, Matthew McCullagh, Charlie Paterson, John Taylor and Claire Webster, 2016

Malcolm Campbell, Rob Colborn, Frederica Daniele, Benedict Gravell, Sarah Harden, Steven Kennedy, Matthew McCullagh, Charlie Paterson, John Taylor and Claire Webster have asserted their rights under the Copyright, Designs and Patents Act, 1988, to be identified as Authors of this work.

British Library Cataloguing-in-Publication Data
A catalogue record for this book is available from the British Library.

ISBN: PB: 978-1-47426-602-4
ePub: 978-1-47426-603-1
ePDF: 978-1-47426-604-8

Library of Congress Cataloging-in-Publication Data
A catalog record for this book is available from the Library of Congress.

Typeset by RefineCatch Limited, Bungay, Suffolk
Printed and bound in Great Britain

CONTENTS

General Preface vii

Thucydides, *Histories*, Book 4: 11–14, 21–23, 26–28, 29–40 1

Introduction 3
Text 27
Commentary Notes 37
Vocabulary 87

Plato, *Apology*, 18a7–24b2, 35e–end 99

Introduction 101
Text 121
Commentary Notes 133
Vocabulary 193

Xenophon, *Memorabilia*, Book 1: II.12–II.38 205

Introduction 207
Text 225
Commentary Notes 229
Vocabulary 247

Homer, *Odyssey* 10: 144–399 and *Odyssey* 9: 231–460 253

Introduction 255
Text to *Odyssey* 10: 144–399 281
Commentary Notes 287
Vocabulary 311
Text to *Odyssey* 9: 231–460 319
Commentary Notes 325
Vocabulary 357

Sophocles, *Antigone*, 1–99, 162–222, 248–331, 441–525, 531–81, 891–928, 998–1032 365

    Introduction 367
    Text 385
    Commentary Notes 397
    Vocabulary 437

Aristophanes, *Acharnians*, 1–203, 366–92 447

    Introduction 449
    Text 463
    Commentary Notes 471
    Vocabulary 499

GENERAL PREFACE

The text and notes found in this volume are designed to guide any student who has mastered Greek up to GCSE level and wishes to read these selections in the original.

The editions are, however, particularly designed to support students who are reading the set texts in preparation for OCR's AS and A-level Greek examination from June 2017 to 2019. (Please note this edition uses AS to refer indiscriminately to AS and the first year of A level, i.e. Group 1.)

Thucydides, *Histories*, Book 4
　Introduction, commentary notes and vocabulary by John Taylor with Malcolm Campbell
　AS: 11–14, 21–23, 26–28
　A-level: 29–40

Plato, *Apology*
　Introduction by Steven Kennedy
　Commentary notes and vocabulary by Benedict Gravell
　AS: 18a7–24b2
　A-level: 35e–end

Xenophon, *Memorabilia*, Book 1
　Introduction, commentary notes and vocabulary by Charlie Paterson
　A-level: II.12–II.38

Homer, *Odyssey*
　Introduction by Frederica Daniele
　Commentary notes and vocabulary for Book 10 by Claire Webster
　Commentary notes and vocabulary for Book 9 by Rob Colborn
　AS: Book 10: 144–399
　A-level: Book 9: 231–460

Sophocles, *Antigone*
　Introduction, commentary notes and vocabulary by Matthew McCullagh
　AS: 1–99, 497–525, 531–81, 891–928
　A-level: 162–222, 248–331, 441–96, 998–1032

Aristophanes, *Acharnians*
　Introduction, commentary notes and vocabulary by Sarah Harden
　A-level: 1–203, 366–92

Each edition contains a detailed introduction to the context of the ancient work. The notes aim to help students bridge the gap between GCSE and AS or A-level Greek, and focus therefore on the harder points of grammar, word order and idiom. At the end of each edition is a full vocabulary list for all the words contained in the prescribed sections, with words in OCR's Defined Vocabulary List for AS Level Greek flagged by means of an asterisk.

Thucydides, *Histories*, Book 4

Introduction, Commentary Notes and Vocabulary by John Taylor with Malcolm Campbell

AS: 11–14, 21–23, 26–28

A-level: 29–40

Introduction

Life of Thucydides

Thucydides is one of the greatest Greek historians, perhaps the greatest. Most of what we know about him is what he tells us himself (a much later compilation of biographical material survives, but is of dubious reliability). Thucydides is in general self-effacing, but his name is the first word of his only known work, whose opening sentence formed a sort of title page: 'Thucydides, an Athenian, wrote up the war of the Peloponnesians and Athenians, how they fought against each other . . .' (1.1.1). The war itself is usually referred to (from an Athenian viewpoint) as the Peloponnesian War, and this name – or 'The history of the Peloponnesian War' – is also often given to his work by modern scholars and translators. The war lasted (with a gap in the middle) from 431 to 404 BC. Thucydides lived through it, and fought as an Athenian general in 424/3 (the year of office ran summer-to-summer) – so in our terms he is writing about current affairs rather than history.

Military service took Thucydides to Thrace, the area north of Greece, where he had existing connections. In Book 4 he describes himself (again in the third person) as 'Thucydides son of Olorus, the author of this account' (4.104.4), and says he was deployed there because 'he owned the rights to work the gold mines in that part of Thrace, and therefore had powerful influence with the inhabitants' (4.105.1). As it happens, we know of another Olorus and another Thucydides, to whom he was almost certainly related. Miltiades, who commanded the Athenians at Marathon in 490 (in the first round of the Persian Wars), married the daughter of a Thracian king called Olorus (Herodotus 6.39.2). If a daughter of theirs was mother of the historian's father, he would be great-grandson of the first Olorus (male names were reused in families, but usually not in the next generation). A man called Thucydides son of Melesias (Greeks were identified by their father's name), who was the main rival of the great Athenian statesman Pericles in the 440s, belonged to the same family ([Aristotle] *Athenian Constitution* 28.2), probably by marriage to another daughter of Miltiades. If their daughter was the historian's mother, he would be grandson of the first Thucydides. At any rate, he was well-connected, presumably wealthy (most ancient authors were aristocrats), and related to people at the centre of Athenian public life.

The minimum age to serve as one of the ten annually elected generals was probably thirty, so Thucydides cannot have been born later than 454. In another autobiographical passage (5.26.5) he tells us he was of an age to understand events when the war broke out: he would scarcely say that if he were already middle-aged, so he is unlikely to have been born before about 460. The opening sentence in Book 1 goes on to say that he 'began' (not necessarily to write anything that survives, but perhaps at least to make notes and gather material) as soon as the war started, 'believing it would be a great war and more worth recounting than any previous one'. Thucydides here boldly claims for himself as a young man the foresight he admires in statesmen he writes about: Themistocles (who foresaw a second Persian invasion and persuaded Athens to build up her fleet), and above all Pericles. He will have come to adulthood in the years when Pericles dominated Athenian politics, and though the elder Thucydides had opposed him, the historian expresses warm admiration for the democratic leader who was also a top-notch aristocrat, describing Athens in his time (perhaps with some exaggeration) as 'in name a democracy, but in fact tending to become the rule of the first citizen' (2.65.9). This comes in the course of an obituary tribute when in 429 Pericles dies of the great plague which afflicted Athens in the early years of the war. Thucydides has earlier told us (2.48.3) that he caught the plague himself, but recovered.

The obituary of Pericles contrasts him with his successors, seen by Thucydides as men of inferior stamp, and rabble-rousing demagogues (2.65.10–11). Prominent among them was the demagogue Cleon (who has an important role in our set text). Thucydides' objection to him is ideological: despite his admiration for Pericles, his enthusiasm for (at least extreme forms of) democracy seems qualified. But there may also be a personal grudge. Though Thucydides appears to have been a competent general, he failed to prevent the northern city of Amphipolis from falling into Spartan hands (because of bad luck, and because he faced an unusually able enemy leader, Brasidas). For his failure he was punished with exile. Such decisions were taken by the democratic assembly in Athens (which all adult male citizens over eighteen could attend). Cleon was at this time the dominant figure in the assembly, and the later biographical tradition may be right in portraying him as the prosecutor of Thucydides.

The historian describes the events which caused his exile in dispassionate third-person style. But later (in a passage rounding off his description of the first section of the war, and saying it was at that stage far from over) he says: 'it happened that I was in exile from my country for twenty years after the Amphipolis campaign and thus had time to study affairs more closely, not least those of the Peloponnesians' (5.26.5). His eventual return will have followed an amnesty at the end of the war. So although he has told us that he began work earlier, exile was perhaps the real making of him as an historian. As he says, it gave him leisure, and access to both sides (at several places in the set text he seems to depend on Spartan informants). It probably also gave him some distance in his description of Athens, as well as a tendency to idealize the city's pre-war life. Thucydides' predecessor Herodotus spent most of his life away from his native Halicarnassus; it is more generally true that literal or metaphorical exile has been the experience of many great historians.

Thucydides certainly lived beyond the end of the Peloponnesian War in 404. Many individual passages show that he knew the outcome, and readers have sensed a pervasive sense of tragedy and impending doom for Athens (despite the presence also of passages which predate his realization that events over the course of twenty-seven years formed a single war). Yet his narrative breaks off abruptly in describing the events of autumn 411. He was probably still working on it when he died, perhaps around 400. It is unlikely that he did write an account of the rest of the war, and that it was subsequently lost, because within a few years Xenophon wrote his *Hellenica* ('Greek events'), beginning exactly where Thucydides had left off (and going on to cover Greek history down to 362). We know that at least two other historians, whose works are now lost, took the same starting-point. Thucydides may well have had draft material relating to the later years of the war, but if so it appears never to have been made public. His work is unfinished in this obvious way, but also in the sense that what does survive has numerous (if usually minor) loose ends and inconsistencies, and whole stretches which seem to lack a final polish. Few readers have doubted the brilliance and power of Thucydides' narrative of the Peloponnesian War, but what we have is a work in progress.

The Peloponnesian War

Origins

Greek history in the fifth century BC is dominated and defined by two major conflicts. In the Persian Wars of 490 and 480–479, chronicled by Herodotus, two Persian invasions of Greece were successfully fought off. To confront the second and greater expedition under Xerxes, most of the Greek city states formed an uneasy alliance under Spartan leadership, but with Athens making a major contribution. In the Peloponnesian War of 431–404, chronicled by Thucydides, Athens and Sparta, by now heading rival power blocs, fought each other; Sparta was eventually victorious.

The Peloponnesian War had its roots in the Persian Wars. When the Persians withdrew from Greece in 479, no peace was made and it was not clear that they would not invade again. Many Greek cities in Ionia (modern western Turkey) were and remained under Persian control. The Spartan commander Pausanias, operating in Cyprus and Byzantium, behaved arrogantly and made himself unpopular (away from the repressive militarism of their home city, Spartans often went off the rails). More generally, the ongoing ambition of Sparta was to dominate the Peloponnese (not least in order to control the helots, a large serf population), operating overseas only when necessary. Conversely, Athens had, over the previous century, increasingly developed trading interests in the Aegean world, and in 478/7 emerged as leader of a new alliance, known to modern scholars as the Delian League (from its headquarters on the sacred island of Delos). Its declared purpose was to continue the war against Persia, with members required to contribute ships or pay *phoros* (financial tribute). It was a full and lasting alliance, each member having one equal vote, but with executive power (notably to assess the tribute) vested in Athens. The League grew quickly, with members drawn particularly from Ionia and the Aegean islands, and at first anti-Persian objectives were vigorously pursued. Sparta and the other Peloponnesian states did not join, but apparently did not initially feel threatened. Their own looser grouping went back to the previous century, and continued now: it is known to modern scholars as the Peloponnesian League, but the ancient sources more accurately say 'Sparta and her allies'.

Over the following decades the Delian League changed gradually into an Athenian empire. From about 470 we have records of city states either being forced to join or prevented from leaving. Members were pressurized to contribute money rather than ships (soon only the large islands Chios, Samos and Lesbos were providing ships). Objectives beneficial to Athens were increasingly pursued. In 454 the League treasury was moved from Delos to Athens, ostensibly for security. The Persians had been driven from the Aegean, and by about 450 the war the League had been founded to fight was at an end (in practice if not by formal treaty). This must have been clear to League members: we learn from inscriptions that Athens around this time faced a great deal of opposition, in the form of withholding payment of tribute, from allied (now effectively subject) states. The Athenian response was not to disband the League, but to tighten control of it.

Meanwhile, from about 461, Athens had also been expanding in central mainland Greece, effectively controlling the region of Boeotia for about ten years. This involved her in a series of skirmishes with her trading rival Corinth, sometimes supported by Sparta – modern scholars have called this conflict the 'First Peloponnesian War' (in contrast to the second or main one described by Thucydides). In 447/6 these mainland subjects also rebelled, and a Peloponnesian army under the Spartan king Pleistoanax invaded Attica. He turned back before attacking Athens, but this led to the Thirty Years' Peace of 446/5: Athens gave up her possessions on the mainland, but her domination of the Aegean though the Delian League was recognized. This was superficially a victory for Sparta, but the instability of the settlement was quickly revealed as Athens continued to expand her interests, now in southern Italy, Thrace and the Black Sea region.

This is the context for Thucydides' repeated assertion that the real cause of the outbreak of the main Peloponnesian War was Sparta's fear of the growing power of Athens. The first mention of this 'truest reason' (1.23.6) describes it as 'least acknowledged', and carefully contrasts it with a series of lesser but 'openly proclaimed' grievances in the late 430s. Two are described in detail at this point, both involving Athens and Corinth. Corcyra (modern Corfu) was a colony of Corinth, but was of interest to Athens because it possessed the third largest fleet in Greece (after Athens and Corinth), and because it was an important calling-point on the shipping route to southern Italy and Sicily. Corcyra had joined Corinth in founding Epidamnus, further north on the mainland. Civil strife (a recurrent Thucydidean theme) in Epidamnus led to the exile of some aristocrats; they joined local non-Greeks in attacking the city. Epidamnus appealed for help, unsuccessfully to Corcyra (presumably friendly to the exiles) and successfully to Corinth (already at odds with Corcyra). The Corinthians were subsequently attacked and defeated in a naval battle by the Corcyreans. Epidamnus capitulated to Corcyra; Corcyra (hitherto neutral) appealed to Athens; Corinth tried to dissuade Athens; Athens (hoping to weaken Corinth but avoid a direct breach of the Thirty Years Peace) gave limited aid, but accepted Corcyra as an ally.

In the second case, Athens put pressure on Potidaea in northern Greece, a member of the Delian League, but maintaining strong links with Corinth by whom it had originally been colonized; Potidaea revolted (mainly because of an increase in tribute not mentioned by Thucydides), leading to a battle in which Athens fought Corinth, and Athens began a long siege of Potidaea. Subsequent debates also allude to trouble between Athens and Megara (the state between Athens and Corinth), and between Athens and Aegina (an island earlier forced to join the Delian League). In discussions among members of the Peloponnesian League, Corinth takes the lead in putting pressure on Sparta to go to war against Athens, on the grounds that the terms of the Thirty Years Peace have been breached. After describing the Spartan vote for war, Thucydides says that they were 'influenced not so much by the speeches of their allies as by their fear of increasing Athenian power, when they could see so much of Greece already subject to Athens' (1.88). This leads into a famous digression, the 'Pentecontaetia' ('period of fifty years' – more accurately forty-eight, i.e. 479–431) where Thucydides gives a selective account of the period between the Persian and Peloponnesian wars, focused on the build-up of Athenian power.

The Archidamian War

The first decade (431–421) of the main Peloponnesian War is by convention named after the Spartan king Archidamus who, despite having voted against hostilities, led several annual invasions of Attica. This strategy, of marching into enemy territory hoping to entice them from their fortifications to conflict, was traditional in Greek warfare and reflected Sparta's strength as a land power. But the strategy of the Athenian leader Pericles was to stay inside the fortified area created some decades earlier by the Long Walls joining the city to the harbour town of Piraeus, rather than trying to defend the farms of Attica. Athens retaliated by launching naval expeditions against the Peloponnese, but these were of limited effect because Sparta and other important Peloponnesian cities lay inland. There was thus an element of stalemate in the first years. Athens was a naval power, starting the war with large financial reserves; the agricultural communities of the Peloponnese were short of ships and cash but strong in soldiers, Sparta supremely so. Yet even Athens used up funds at an alarming rate, and had to resort to taxation of wealthy citizens.

Naval battles in the Gulf of Corinth in 429 revealed the Athenians' superior skill. Pericles died in that year, but his policy of keeping a firm grip on the empire continued. The revolt of Miletus and other cities on Lesbos was dealt with harshly (though less so than initially intended), and a Spartan attempt to support the rebels ended in fiasco. Both sides tried to support allies in north-west Greece, the Athenians already with an eye to Sicily, where they attempted to intervene in 427. A bitter civil war in Corcyra lasted two years before the pro-Athenian democrats were victorious. In 426 the Athenian Demosthenes, based at Naupactus on the Corinthian gulf, launched an expedition into Aetolia, though he became trapped and had to retreat.

In 425 a run of Athenian successes began. Demosthenes effectively broke the stalemate of the early years of the war by building a fortress in enemy territory at Pylos (this initiative and its consequences are the main subject of the set text). Spartan ships arrived and landed men on the island of Sphacteria, but the action of Athenian reinforcements left them trapped there. In negotiations for a truce, the populist Athenian leader Cleon took a hard line. He was cornered into accepting command himself and took more troops to join Demosthenes; together they succeeded in capturing most of the Spartans on the island. A threat to kill them put a stop to invasions of Attica – another major change in the conduct of the war. The Athenian commander Nicias increased pressure on Sparta by installing a garrison at Methana in the north-east Peloponnese and capturing the island of Cythera off its southern tip.

After this, the Athenians did less well. They had been regularly attacking Megara, but a plot by Megarian democrats to betray the city to Athens misfired and the city ended up in the hands of pro-Spartan oligarchs. A planned rising of pro-Athenian cities in Boeotia failed through poor timing; after occupying Delium a large Athenian force was attacked and defeated. The talented Spartan commander Brasidas accepted an invitation from local leaders to take a force of mercenaries and helots to the north Aegean, where many cities were members of the Delian League. He set about winning them over, and had a notable success with the Athenian colony of Amphipolis which Thucydides was too late to save.

After Pylos, many Spartans were anxious for peace, and in spring 423, a year's truce was negotiated. The city of Scione went over to Brasidas before news of it arrived, so war continued in the north; elsewhere the treaty held, and was extended until the end of the following summer. When it expired, Cleon was sent north with an Athenian force. He made a good start, but while risking a reconnaissance march towards Amphipolis was caught off guard by Brasidas and defeated. Both leaders were killed in the fighting, and Athens never recovered Amphipolis. Cleon and Brasidas had both strongly favoured continuing the war; after their deaths, Nicias in Athens and king Pleistoanax in Sparta were more inclined to make terms. The Peace of Nicias in spring 421 represented, in effect, a return to the situation of 431. It was supposed to last for fifty years. If successful, it would have fulfilled Pericles' aims, because in ten years of fighting Sparta had not significantly weakened the Athenian empire. But her allies Corinth, Megara and Elis refused to observe it. Anxiety about the prisoners taken on 'the island' (i.e. Sphacteria) was a main Spartan motive for accepting the peace; but in giving them up, the Athenians too readily trusted an insecure treaty.

The Peace of Nicias and the Sicilian Expedition

In an already unstable situation, a thirty-year peace treaty between Sparta and Argos came to an end. Corinth, in alliance with Argos, built up a group of city states disaffected with Sparta. Meanwhile in Athens the talented but unstable Alcibiades, offended that he had been given no role in negotiating the peace, tried to wreck it by allying Athens to Argos and its Peloponnesian neighbours Mantinea and Elis. Athens for the first time faced the prospect of fighting Sparta by land in the Peloponnese. After a Spartan attempt to attack Argos had come to nothing, the Argive alliance moved to Mantinea, to attack Tegea to the south. The Spartans under king Agis went to support Tegea. He was caught unprepared, leading to the battle of Mantinea (418), the biggest hoplite conflict in the Peloponnesian War, but the Spartans were victorious: the challenge to their dominance had failed. Argos, under oligarchic leaders, put out feelers to Sparta for shared control of the Peloponnese, but pro-Athenian democrats quickly returned to power, and the alliance with Athens was renewed.

In 416 Athens captured the Aegean island of Melos, the only one still outside its orbit. Thucydides gives us a dialogue between representatives of the two sides: the Athenians talk the language of power politics, asserting without compromise that 'might is right'; the Melians appeal (pathetically and in vain) to justice, the gods and the Spartans. The episode ended with the men of Melos killed, and the women and children enslaved.

Meanwhile in Sicily, Egesta, allied to Athens, was fighting Selinus, supported by Syracuse (the leading Sicilian city, on good terms with Sparta). Egesta appealed to Athens for help. Alcibiades was eager to exploit an opportunity to expand Athenian influence in the western part of the Greek world, whilst Nicias predicted that Sicily, even if conquered, would be hard to control. In the event they were appointed as two of the three commanders when Athens launched a major expedition, but Alcibiades was quickly recalled to face prosecution for religious offences, though he escaped to Sparta. In Sicily the Athenians were unable to follow up success in an early battle. In 414 they established themselves outside Syracuse and started building walls to blockade it, but had not got far when a Peloponnesian fleet arrived, commanded by the Spartan Gylippus. The Athenians sent another substantial force under Demosthenes. After a night attack on the fortress of Epipolae ended in failure, the Athenians were decisively defeated in a naval battle in the Great Harbour of Syracuse, with serious losses of ships and men.

The end of the war

In 413 the Peloponnesians, led by the Spartan king Agis, established a fortress at Decelea in northern Attica (a counterpart to Pylos), denying the Athenians access to their silver mines and much of their countryside. Athens fought on despite the Sicilian disaster, and indeed recovered to a remarkable extent, but the war now began to move in new directions. Sparta was approached both by rebellious members of the Athenian empire and by the Persian satraps (provincial governors) Tissaphernes and Pharnabazus. The Athenians established a naval base at Samos. Alcibiades (now out of favour in Sparta where he had earlier taken refuge) intrigued with Tissaphernes and held out to Athens the possibility of Persian support for them instead of Sparta if they switched from democracy to oligarchy, and allowed his own return. There was a brief oligarchic coup in 411 – the rule of the 'Four Hundred', soon replaced by the more moderate 'Five Thousand' – but Persian support was not forthcoming, instead being reaffirmed for Sparta. In autumn 411 the Spartans missed a chance to attack Athens while it was weakened by political turmoil. Their fleet moved to the Hellespont; the Athenians followed and defeated it at Cynossema.

At this point Thucydides breaks off, leaving us dependent on the thinner and conflicting accounts of other authors (mainly Xenophon and Diodorus). Alcibiades joined the Athenian fleet and in the next few years the Athenians won a number of naval encounters in the northern Aegean and Hellespont area. A peace offer from Sparta was rejected, and full democracy restored. In 407 Alcibiades finally returned to Athens, was cleared of all charges, and was given a unique position as commander-in-chief. Sparta made headway in negotiation with Persia, her admiral Lysander establishing a friendship with the Persian prince Cyrus. Alcibiades went once more into exile to avoid prosecution after the Athenian fleet suffered a defeat when he had left a subordinate in charge. A new Spartan admiral, Callicratidas, took his fleet to Lesbos; the Athenians under Conon followed him, but were blockaded at Mytilene. Athens equipped and manned another fleet, and defeated Callicratidas at Arginusae

(406), a group of small islands off Lesbos, but the victory was tainted when a storm prevented the generals recovering shipwrecked survivors and dead bodies.

In a subsequent battle at Aegospotami in the Hellespont (405) the Athenians were decisively defeated. The Spartans under Lysander blockaded Athens by land and sea. In spring 404 Athens accepted Sparta's terms: the Athenians had to demolish the Long Walls and the Piraeus, give up their overseas possessions and all but twelve ships, take back exiled oligarchs (from the 411 coup) and become a subordinate ally of Sparta. The demolition of the walls was hailed as the beginning of freedom for Greece. With the end of the Athenian empire, Sparta had achieved the aims for which she had gone to war.

Summary analysis of Thucydides

The division into eight books is ancient but post-dates Thucydides (other divisions are known to have existed). Each book was probably intended to fit on a single scroll. This summary is based on the fuller one in the Oxford World's Classics translation (see Further reading). Only the main events are included here. Famous and important passages that could profitably be read in English are indicated in **bold**.

Book 1 *Introduction and background*

Preface, and claim that the Peloponnesian War was greater than any previous war; **'Archaeology'** (1.2–19) justifying this claim by describing the growth of Greek power (especially sea power) from early times; **account of Thucydides' methods and difficulties in writing (1.20–3)**; causes of the war, distinguishing the real reason (Spartan fear of Athenian power) from grievances and disputes (Corcyra/Epidamnus and Potidaea); account of first meeting in Sparta; **'Pentecontaetia' (1.89–118)** justifying Thucydides' judgement of the real reason by describing the growth of Athenian power after the Persian Wars; congress of the Peloponnesian League in Sparta, with digressions on controversial past figures featuring in propaganda; Athenian response to Spartan pressure.

Book 2 *Formal beginning of the war, and events from the first summer (431) to the third winter (429/8)*

Thebes (pro-Sparta) attempts to seize Plataea (pro-Athens); the Peloponnesians invade Attica; the Athenians in response raid the Peloponnesian coast; the public burial in Athens of casualties in the first season is marked by **Pericles' Funeral Speech (2.34–46)**, describing the city's life and ideals; this is quickly followed by the devastating **plague in Athens (2.47–54)**; Pericles is attacked then reinstated, but soon dies (of the plague); laudatory **obituary of Pericles (2.65)**; Potidaea capitulates, the Thebans continue to besiege Plataea, and naval battles take place in the Gulf of Corinth.

Book 3 *Events from the fourth summer (428) to the sixth winter (426/5)*

The Peloponnesians continue to invade Attica annually; Mytilene in Lesbos revolts from Athens; Athens suffers financial difficulties; some of the Plataeans escape from their besieged city to Athens; **Mytilenaean debate in Athens (3.36–49)**, initially condemning the Mytilenaeans to death, but at a second assembly deciding on less harsh measures; description of **civil strife in Corcyra (3.69–85)**; the plague breaks out again in Athens; there is extensive campaigning in north-west Greece.

Book 4 *Events from the seventh summer (425) to the ninth winter (423/2)*

The **Pylos and Sphacteria campaign (4.1–41)** is described in detail, Athens establishing a fortress in enemy territory and capturing Spartan prisoners, interspersed with events in southern Italy and Sicily; Athens undertakes a series of campaigns in Boeotia; campaigning successfully in the north-east, **Brasidas marches against Amphipolis and Thucydides fails to prevent it falling into Spartan hands (4.102–16)**.

Book 5 *Events from the tenth summer (422) to the beginning of the sixteenth winter (416/5)*

Brasidas continues to campaign in the north-east, but the Peace of Nicias shortly follows; **second preface, about the unity of the twenty-seven year war (5.25–6)**; Argos develops an alliance to counter Sparta; various intrigues follow, and it becomes clear that the treaty is not being observed; Sparta attacks Argos; Athens attacks Melos, leading to the **'Melian Dialogue' (5.85–113)** in which the Athenians defend their right to exercise their superior strength, and Melos surrenders.

Book 6 *Events from the sixteenth winter (416/5) to the beginning of the eighteenth summer (414)*

Athens plans a major expedition to Sicily led by Nicias and Alcibiades; **departure of the fleet is overshadowed by religious scandals (6.26–9)**, for which Alcibiades is recalled, but he escapes to Sparta; the Athenians reach Sicily and begin to besiege Syracuse; the description of the Sicilian campaign is interspersed with accounts of fighting in mainland Greece.

Book 7 *Events from the eighteenth summer (414) to the nineteenth summer (413)*

The Spartan leader Gylippus arrives in Sicily; Nicias sends a letter to the Athenian assembly asking for further help; the Peloponnesians establish a fortress at Decelea in Attica; the Athenian general Demosthenes sets sail for Sicily; the description of the Sicilian campaign is again interspersed with accounts of fighting in mainland Greece, including an **attack by Thracian mercenaries on Mycalessus (7.29)**; Demosthenes arrives in Sicily, dismaying the Syracusans, but a **night attack on the fortress of Epipolae (7.43–4)** fails; Demosthenes now favours leaving, but an eclipse of the moon causes the superstitious Nicias to insist on staying; **naval battle in the Great Harbour (7.69–72)** in which the Athenians are defeated; the miserable **Athenian withdrawal (7.73–87)** is described.

Book 8 *Events from the end of the nineteenth summer (413) to the twenty-first summer (411) – unfinished*

News of the disaster is greeted with dismay in Athens (8.1); Chios leads a revolt against Athens in Ionia; Sparta negotiates with Persia, making several treaties and obtaining funds; after intrigues involving Alcibiades, the oligarchic revolution of the Four Hundred takes place in Athens, though democracy is quickly re-established by the Athenians on military service in Samos; the Peloponnesian fleet sails to the Hellespont, where campaigning takes place; the Four Hundred are replaced in Athens by the more moderate Five Thousand; campaigning in the Aegean and Hellespont continues – and Thucydides' narrative breaks off abruptly.

The literary and intellectual context

Homer and Herodotus

Thucydides had two great predecessors: Homer (to the Greeks just 'the poet'), and Herodotus (the 'father of history'). All three of them wrote about great wars: the Trojan War, the Persian Wars, the Peloponnesian War. In asserting the importance of his own subject, Thucydides in effect puts himself in competition with these chroniclers of earlier wars. Whether for a verse epic about the distant past or for a prose history about more recent events, a great subject was the necessary (though not, of course, the sufficient) condition for a great book. When Thucydides asserts that his was the greatest war, there is an unspoken hint that his is also the greatest book.

Homer was probably writing about 500 years after the traditional date of the Trojan War, put at about 1200 BC: whether that war 'really happened' is highly controversial, but Troy (controlling access to the rich resources of the Black Sea) was a real place, destroyed and rebuilt several times – each activity must have been worth someone's while, and the archaeology indicates two major destructions at approximately the right period. Herodotus was writing about fifty years after the Persian Wars. Thucydides (as reporter, note-maker and participant) might, on average, have been writing about any given event something like five years after it took place. So there is a progressive narrowing of the distance in time between subject and author. This is mirrored by a progressive distancing of the divine. In Homer, the Olympian gods (with both good and bad human characteristics magnified) are important characters in the story. In Herodotus, direct intervention has receded (visions of gods are rare, and reported indirectly), but the hand of 'the divine' is everywhere seen, and oracles and prophecies are taken seriously. In Thucydides, the gods have been edited out: they have no role in historical causation, and those who appeal to them are usually desperate and doomed.

In the *Iliad*, Homer used the events of a few weeks in the tenth year of the Trojan War to give a sense of the whole conflict. When his poem ends, the climactic events (the death of Achilles and the fall of Troy) still lie ahead, though they are clearly foreshadowed. Thucydides accidentally emulated Homer by leaving his narrative unfinished, so that the disaster in Sicily reads as a prefiguration of the defeat of Athens. But deliberately and repeatedly, Thucydides uses the Homeric device of a representative slice, or one example standing for many. When Pericles gives his Funeral Speech for the Athenian war dead, Thucydides tells us such a speech was delivered every year (2.34.6–7), but gives us only this (no doubt untypically elaborate) example. When he describes the *stasis* (civil strife) between oligarchs and democrats in Corcyra, he explicitly describes it as a shocking first example of something that subsequently convulsed most of the Greek world (3.82.1), but he alludes only in passing to instances elsewhere. Thucydides generalizes from the Corcyrean experience: everywhere, democrats sided with Athens and oligarchs with Sparta. The war between city states was, therefore, constantly accompanied by war between factions within them: this too echoes the *Iliad*, which describes conflict both between Greeks and Trojans, and within the Greek camp.

The plague in Athens in Book 2 has for Thucydides an entirely secular explanation: the crowding of the population within the city and Long Walls as a result of Pericles' war strategy, though his description echoes the plague sent upon the Greeks by Apollo at the beginning of the *Iliad*. He shows how it brought an alarming moral disintegration, and he sees this again in the Corcyrean *stasis*, prompting broader observation: such things 'will continue to happen as long as human nature remains the same . . . in peace and prosperity, states and individuals observe a higher morality . . . but war is a harsh teacher' (3.82.2). This links closely with Thucydides' general claim for the usefulness of history (1.22.4). He commends traditional moral values, despite his disregard for their religious underpinning. The notion of war as a harsh teacher is another echo of the *Iliad*, where war functions as an intensified symbol of human life.

The *Iliad* is remarkable for its humane portrayal of both warring sides. Some of the most sympathetic figures are Trojans, above all Hector, who almost eclipses Achilles as the main character. This even-handedness descends to Herodotus, with his lively interest in other cultures and moments of sympathy even for the Persian king Xerxes, and we find it again in Thucydides. We have seen that his exile allowed him the opportunity to interview participants on both sides, and the set text repeatedly shows how much he had been able to glean about Sparta, normally veiled in almost impenetrable secrecy. He admires individual Spartans, above all Brasidas. The presentation of him in Book 4 (both at Pylos and later in the north) has been likened to an *aristeia* in the *Iliad*: an extended stretch of narrative where an individual hero (who may be from either side) is the narrative focus, and seems to carry all before him. Inevitably it has been noticed too that the historian has a vested interest here: the more positive the portrayal of Brasidas, the less shameful is Thucydides' defeat at his hands. Literary models and contemporary concerns combine to produce the finished account, a phenomenon that we can trace throughout Thucydides, and indeed in most Greek authors.

The history of Greek literature has itself a clear narrative shape because different genres dominated successive periods (making a particular type of literature the natural thing to write), yet all of them were strongly influenced by Homer. The age of epic was succeeded by that of lyric poetry (of which little survives), and in the immensely productive fifth century BC (particularly in Athens) the legacy of epic was divided between historiography and drama: we shall see in the next section that Thucydides has significant affinities with Greek tragedy. Herodotus, who came from Halicarnassus in Ionia but seems to have spent much of his life in Athens, was the first major historian and the first important writer of prose. His work (in nine books) is aptly described as a prose epic. Because he sees the conflict between Greece and Persia as the expression of a fundamental divide, more than half of the *Histories* (forming a vast introduction) explores the Mediterranean and Near Eastern world over a century or so before his own time. The account is loosely organized around the theme of the build-up of Persian power, but Herodotus has great interest in foreign cultures and customs for their own sake, and is happy to digress – most spectacularly with a whole book devoted to Egypt, which becomes relevant at the point where the Persians conquer it.

Herodotus aimed to show that wars of the recent past had a heroic grandeur comparable to those of the distant (we might say mythic) past. We can trace this impetus elsewhere. In a poem by Simonides on the battle of Plataea in 479 (fragments of which have been found on papyrus and published only in recent decades), a hymn to Achilles introduced a narrative of the recent campaign. The 'Painted Stoa' in the Athenian Agora juxtaposed pictures of the Trojan and Persian Wars. Thucydides in effect adds a third layer to this existing equation by advancing the claims of an even more recent war. Both Homer and Herodotus dealt with the clash of east and west, and the Persian Wars certainly involved more people than the Peloponnesian War. Though Thucydides has a trump card in its sheer length, his war is, in one sense, parochial in comparison. Yet within a more limited compass, the theme of cultural contrast is every bit as important as in Herodotus: Athens (innovative, intellectual, adventurous and democratic) is in every respect opposite to Sparta (traditional, militarist, cautious and authoritarian).

Herodotus described his work as *historie* ('enquiry', with no implication yet of the study specifically of the past), and he does indeed enquire into a vast range of things. Thucydides never uses the word: he is in his own way no less diligent an enquirer, but his focus is much narrower. It is largely because of Thucydides that later historians concentrated on war and politics, both in the ancient world and beyond. Thucydides has few female and few non-Greek characters. He rarely digresses. This austerity is clearly self-imposed, but he was clearly conscious that readers might prefer his predecessor. Thucydides never refers to Herodotus by name, but he sometimes corrects him, and may have him in mind in a famous passage in Book 1:

The lack of the element of fable (τὸ μυθῶδες) will perhaps make it less pleasing to the ear, but I shall be content if it is judged useful by those who will want a clear understanding of what happened and – human nature being what it is – will happen again in the same or similar ways. It was composed as a possession for all time (κτῆμα . . . ἐς αἰεί) rather than a showpiece for a single hearing. (1.22.4)

Here again is the emphasis on essentially unchanging human nature, and with it an aspiration to abiding relevance.

Herodotus does indeed make more attractive reading in the sense that you can open his work anywhere and begin reading with immediate interest. The best parts of Thucydides have an incomparable grandeur, but it is not hard to find passages which are dry, tedious or difficult to follow. In the past Herodotus was often seen as an amiably naïve storyteller, and Thucydides as a serious 'scientific' historian. Both assessments are now rejected. The diverse material in Herodotus is arranged with great sophistication, and his habit of reporting several different versions or explanations (sometimes himself inclining to one we know to be wrong) is seen as attesting a more genuinely scientific approach. It is now acknowledged that an objective account of the past is unattainable: simply by selecting material and arranging it in a particular order, every historian necessarily interprets and judges. Thucydides gives an impression of magisterial authority, but this is an effect deliberately created, and it is reasonably pointed out that we cannot know what other versions or explanations he has silently, and perhaps wrongly, rejected. We know, too, that his account can be challenged or supplemented on particular points by inscriptions and other evidence; we are conscious of the many things he has left out, even on his own restricted terms (notably any adequate account of the economics of warfare). Despite all this, his narrative remains impressively detailed. It attests diligent research and penetrating intelligence. Overall it is still regarded as highly trustworthy, and it is, by far, the most important source for the period.

Medicine, rhetoric and tragedy

A link between Thucydides and ancient science has been seen in his treatment of medical matters, notably the plague in Athens. The famous physician Hippocrates of Cos was a contemporary, and associated with Athenian intellectuals: important treatises by him or his associates survive (making much use of the concept of *historie*). Thucydides may have gained particular details about disease and its treatment from this milieu, but the real point of interest is the analogy with his own working methods. The Hippocratic doctor is interested in causation: he makes general deductions from the observation of many individual cases, and he predicts the course a disease will take from past experience. All these seems close to what Thucydides says about the point of studying history, and to his own working methods; it also chimes with his admiration for foresight. The treatise *On the Sacred Disease* (i.e. epilepsy, seizures being traditionally interpreted as divine possession) robustly begins by saying it is neither more nor less sacred than any other disease, but has a rational explanation: this again seems close to the way Thucydides approaches and interprets historical events.

An even more important influence is that of rhetoric, not least because of its relevance to the speeches Thucydides puts into the mouths of people in his narrative. The fully democratic, prosperous and imperialist society of Athens had created a new demand for skills in public speaking: young men aspired to make their way in the city by speaking impressively and persuasively in the assembly or law-courts. They sought expert training, and travelling higher education teachers (many from the periphery of the Greek world) gravitated to Athens to provide it. Ranging from serious and original thinkers to charlatans seeking a quick profit, they are collectively called Sophists: σοφιστής was originally a neutral term ('wise man'), but – like δημαγωγός – came to have a specific and derogatory application. In this case it was because of a generalized association with a doctrine of relativism (associated particularly with the leading thinker Protagoras), the idea that there are no fixed values other than those agreed in a particular society. The public-speaking exercise of learning to argue both sides of a case equally well was regarded as suspect, in putting aside the question of right and wrong.

Much in all this is relevant to the speeches in Thucydides. In Book 1 he describes their use. Observing that he and his informants found it difficult to remember exact words, he tells us his policy has been, while keeping to 'general gist' (ξύμπασα γνώμη) of what was actually said, to make speakers say 'what in my opinion was called for by each situation' (1.22.1). This sentence has been much discussed, and is perhaps deliberately ambiguous. The commonsense view is that the speeches are on a sliding scale from reasonably close record (e.g. of a public speech in Athens that many people would remember) to almost complete invention (e.g. of the pep talk given by a general in Sicily to troops before a battle in which most of them were killed). Scholars in the past were disconcerted by the idea of the sober Thucydides putting made-up speeches into the mouths of real people, but we must allow for the conditions of a world with no recording equipment; the problem recedes when we acknowledge that his whole work is a literary construct (which is not, of course, to say that it is fictitious).

The speeches in Thucydides are a legacy from Homer and Herodotus, as well as a link with tragic drama, and with political life in democratic Athens. They are a source of human and psychological interest, raising the issue of individual character as a factor in history, and emphasizing the emotional undercurrents beneath an apparently dry and dispassionate narrative. The speeches (and passages of analysis, such as the account of the Corcyrean *stasis*) are in a different, more difficult and elaborate style compared to ordinary narrative, but this style is Thucydides' own (all the speeches are similar), not an attempt to reproduce the manner of any particular speaker. Speeches are often paired (there are several examples in Book 1, as the Peloponnesians debate the merits of going to war), the second answering the first with unrealistic neatness. Even more tellingly, speeches can seem to answer each other when delivered on different occasions: Pericles' first speech urging the Athenians to go to war (1.140–4) seems like a reply to what the Corinthians had said earlier in Sparta (1.68–71). Likewise, Cleon or Nicias can echo something Pericles said years earlier. In cases like these it seems clear that the speeches are slanted in this way to make a point to the reader. Some speeches may be regarded as psychological X-rays, telling us what, in Thucydides' view, the speaker was thinking, rather than what he would realistically have said. Thus Athenian politicians are presented as franker about the tyrannical nature of their empire than might have been prudent in practice. Indeed the very preoccupation of so many speakers with the nature of Athenian power surely reflects the historian's own interest in the question.

The Melian Dialogue (5.85–113) provides a stark example of the language of Athenian power politics. Its content takes us back to the Sophists, and the 'might is right' doctrine espoused by speakers we meet in the works of Plato (Callicles in the *Gorgias*, Thrasymachus in the *Republic*). Its probably experimental form, as a direct dialogue set out with speakers like a play, also seems to foreshadow Plato, but is more obviously indebted to tragic drama, in particular the cut-and-thrust arguments of many tense scenes (which often accelerate into *stichomythia*, where speakers fire single lines at each other). The dialogue comes just before the Athenians decide to launch the expedition to Sicily. Elaborate preparations are described: often in Greek literature this portends disaster. We are surely intended to sense that Athens is over-reaching herself, 'reaching out for more' in defiance of Pericles' advice not to extend the empire during the war, and will suffer for it. A similar pattern can be seen in Book 2, when the plague follows immediately after Pericles' glorification of Athens in the funeral speech. It might, of course, be said that Thucydides simply follows the order of events (though in this case it was his choice to give us the speech), but perhaps the order itself prompts a presentation irresistibly reminiscent of the many tragic dramas where pride precedes a fall.

For the tragedians, such a sequence of events involves the action of the gods. In his secularized world Thucydides perhaps intends only than that we should reflect on the unpredictability of life, and the destructiveness of war. What is beyond doubt is that behind his unemotional narrative is a pervasive awareness of tragedy, in a broader sense, of the pity and pathos of war, and its cost in human suffering. A famous example comes in Book 7, where some Thracian mercenaries no longer required by the Athenians rampage through Boeotia and attack the small city of Mycalessus.

> They fell upon a school, the biggest in the place, when the boys had just gone in, and slaughtered them all. So disaster struck the whole city and was the worst ever suffered, more sudden and terrible than any other. (7.29.5)

Comedy

Finally something completely different. A few months after the Pylos campaign, three of the main participants (Cleon, Demosthenes and Nicias) were represented, in thin disguise, in a play by the comic poet Aristophanes. *Knights* (or 'Cavalrymen', named after the upper-class young men who form its chorus) was performed at the Lenaea (one of two annual competitive drama festivals) in January 424, where it won first prize. Aristophanes is the only writer from whom we have complete plays in the genre called 'Old Comedy', which mercilessly satirized politicians of the day, as well as tragic playwrights and anyone else in the Athenian public eye.

Knights takes the form of an allegory about an old man called Demos ('The People'): he represents the citizens of Athens, and his household the city. He has two loyal slaves who (though never named) almost certainly stand for Demosthenes and Nicias. The household has recently been thrown into turmoil by the arrival of a new slave, loud and vulgar in style, who by gross flattery has won the confidence of the old man, but (the other slaves claim) is exploiting his privileged position by cheating and extortion. The new slave is known as the Paphlagonian, in line with the custom of naming foreign slaves from their place of origin (Paphlagonia is the area south of the Black Sea), but also punning on παφλάζω ('I bluster', i.e. shout in a boastful or threatening but hollow way). We are left in no doubt that the Paphlagonian represents Cleon, and his behaviour in the house that of Cleon in the assembly. By comic logic, the other two slaves decide the only way to outwit him is to find someone even more vulgar, so they recruit a sausage-seller from the street, who does indeed win a slanging-match with the Paphlagonian. Demos ends up wiser, and (thanks to a boiling by the sausage-seller) rejuvenated into a worthy personification of the 'violet-crowned' Athens once celebrated by the lyric poet Pindar.

Aristophanes appears (from this and other plays) to have had a similar view of Cleon to that of Thucydides, presenting him as a warmonger and a demagogue. Playwright and historian seem to share a generally conservative outlook (though fragmentary plays by other writers of Old Comedy suggest this may have been a convention of the genre: new ways of doing things are a natural target for satire). Like Thucydides, Aristophanes may have had a personal grudge against Cleon as well as ideological opposition: Cleon is said to have tried to prosecute him for an early play (now lost) called *Babylonians*, which seems to have portrayed the subject states in the Athenian empire as Babylonian slaves in a treadmill. Indeed Aristophanes and Cleon both came from the deme (city district) of Cydathenaeum, so their enmity might go back to the playground.

At any rate, we should exercise caution. An identifiably new style of politician does seem to have emerged after Pericles, but much of the satire directed at the so-called demagogues is no more than social snobbery. Aristophanes repeatedly refers to Cleon as a tanner (someone making raw hide into usable leather), when the truth is probably that his father was the wealthy owner of a tanning factory. But nor was 'new money' necessarily objectionable: Nicias, treated with gentle respect by both Thucydides and Aristophanes, was not a landed aristocrat but derived his wealth from gangs of slaves hired out to work in the Athenian silver mines. In the end it is perhaps a matter of style and personality. It is hotly debated how much political impact Old Comedy had or aimed to have. The audience of *Knights* no doubt enjoyed seeing Cleon taken down a peg after his triumph at Pylos, but the Athenians seem to have been happy to go on supporting him in the Assembly until he (together with the Spartan Brasidas) was killed fighting at Amphipolis in 422. In the following year's play *Peace* (perhaps planned to advocate, but by the time of its production able to celebrate, the Peace of Nicias), Aristophanes wrote of Cleon and Brasidas as two pestles now removed from the mortar of war in which the Greek city states were being crushed.

Reading the Pylos narrative

The language of Thucydides

The Greek used by Thucydides varies in difficulty, but narrative passages (describing events such as the account of the Pylos campaign) are generally more straightforward than speeches and passages of analysis.

His Greek has a few distinctive features:

- He uses the forms θαρσέω (I am confident), θάλασσα (sea) and usually ἤν (if – i.e. εἰ + ἄν), rather than θαρρέω, θάλαττα, and ἐάν which are used by most Attic prose authors and in Attic inscriptions.

- He used ξύν (with) rather than σύν, both as a preposition and as a prefix in compounds, e.g. ξυντρίβω (I smash).

- He makes prepositions work hard, so e.g. κατά with the accusative has a very wide range of possible meanings. He often uses a preposition and noun instead of an adverb, e.g. διὰ τάχους (with speed, i.e. quickly).

- He makes very full use of compound verbs, and often double compounds (with two prefixes), e.g. ἐπικαταβαίνω (I go down to face [the enemy]).

- He makes very full use of abstract nouns, and particularly likes those ending -ις, e.g. ἔκπληξις (panic), and -μα, e.g. ἀδίκημα (injustice). He often makes an abstract noun from the article with a neuter adjective, e.g. κατὰ τὸ αἰεὶ παρεῖκον τοῦ κρημνώδους (*literally* by what at each point offered a foothold on the precipitous part).

- He often sandwiches a preposition phrase or words giving other additional information between the definite article and its noun, e.g. τὸ κατὰ τὸν λιμένα τεῖχος (the wall by the harbour). He does the same with the articular infinitive, e.g. διὰ τὸ αἰεὶ ἐν τῷ αὐτῷ ἀναστρέφεσθαι (because they were constantly wheeling round in the same place).

- He likes expressions of paradox or reversal, e.g. ἐκ γῆς ἐναυμάχουν (they were fighting a naval battle from the land), μᾶλλον πολιορκούμενοι ἢ πολιορκοῦντες (being blockaded rather than blockading).

Themes and characters

Some questions to think about as you read:

- Why, do you think, did Thucydides decide to devote so many pages to his account of Pylos and Sphacteria?

- How important in the story is the physical setting of Pylos and Sphacteria? How well is it described (imagine you were an ancient reader who had not been there and probably had no map available)?

- Herodotus was described by an ancient critic as 'most Homeric'. Could this description be applied to Thucydides in the Pylos narrative? How is Brasidas portrayed?

- How good is the Pylos narrative as an adventure story? Does Thucydides hold the attention of a reader who may not be particularly interested in ancient warfare?

- How far do the events at Pylos illustrate the role of chance and the unexpected? Are there reasons for thinking Thucydides plays down the element of deliberate planning in the campaign? How is Demosthenes portrayed?

- How far does the Pylos narrative illustrate the contrasting characteristics and strengths of the Athenians and Spartans?
- How effectively does Thucydides move backwards and forwards between events in Pylos and elsewhere?
- What do we learn from Thucydides' account of the Pylos campaign about political life in Athens? How is Cleon portrayed? Is this in line with what we learn from other sources (especially Aristophanes' comedy *Knights*)? How does Thucydides make the most of the clash in the assembly between Cleon and Nicias (chapters 27–8)?
- The establishment of an Athenian fortress at Pylos and the capture of the Spartan prisoners on Sphacteria have often been seen as a turning-point in the Peloponnesian War. Does Thucydides' account justify this verdict?

Glossary

Achaea	region of the north Peloponnese.
Aetolia	region north of the Corinthian Gulf unsuccessfully invaded by Demosthenes in 426.
Amphipolis	city in the north Aegean which surrendered to Brasidas in 424.
Asine	place in the south Peloponnese from which the Spartans obtain timber.
assembly	decision-making body which in Athens all adult male citizens could attend.
Athens	one of the two leading Greek cities, situated in Attica in central Greece, governed by direct democracy, head of the Delian League.
Attica	the territory of Athens.
Brasidas	Spartan commander at Pylos in 425.
Chios	large island off Ionia and a prominent member of the Delian League.
city state	*polis*: a city and its surrounding territory, one of many in Greece and other parts of the Mediterranean colonized by Greeks.
Cleon	Athenian demagogue (populist leader), prominent after the death of Pericles, given command at Pylos when he criticizes Nicias.
colony	Greek city founded outside Greece from the eighth century BC onwards, maintaining links with its mother city.
Corinth	important city near the isthmus joining central Greece to the Peloponnese, ally of Sparta and trading rival of Athens.
demagogue	'people-leader', an originally neutral term used to describe populist politicians seen by their critics as irresponsible rabble-rousers.

Delian League	alliance formed in 478/7 against Persia, with headquarters on Delos but led by Athens, which gradually changed into an Athenian empire.
Delos	small island in the central Aegean traditionally sacred to Apollo.
Demosthenes	Athenian general who occupied Pylos in 425.
Epitadas	Spartan commander on Sphacteria.
Eurymedon	Athenian general, joint commander of fleet sailing to Sicily.
general	*strategos*: one of ten (usually one representing each 'tribe' of the citizen body) elected annually to command both land and sea forces.
helot	member of serf population controlled by Sparta.
herald	messenger between enemies, carrying distinctive staff, regarded as inviolable and protected by the god Hermes.
Herodotus	historian of the Persian Wars and much else, a generation older than Thucydides.
Hippagretas	second Spartan commander on Sphacteria.
Homer	epic poet, author of the *Iliad* and *Odyssey*, perhaps late eighth century BC.
hoplite	heavy-armed soldier, with helmet, breastplate, greaves, and circular shield, usually fighting in close formation.
Imbros	island in the north-east Aegean supplying soldiers to Athens.
king	obsolete in most of Greece, but Sparta had two (from different families, as part of a 'mixed' constitution), who often led armies.
Laconia	the territory of Sparta in the south-east Peloponnese.
Lemnos	island in the north Aegean supplying soldiers to Athens.
Megara	city state between Athens and Corinth.
Messenia	the south-west Peloponnese, controlled by Sparta; after a rebellion, some Messenians had been settled by Athens at Naupactus in 455.
Naupactus	city on the north side of the Corinthian gulf.
Nicias	Athenian general and politician, opponent of Cleon.
Nisaea	eastern harbour of Megara.
oligarchy	'rule of the few', usually wealthy and/or aristocratic, the main alternative to democracy in Greek city states.
outrigger	structure built out from the side of a trireme to accommodate rowlocks.
Pegae	western harbour of Megara.
Peloponnese	the large peninsula of southern Greece, dominated by Sparta.
Peloponnesian League	an alliance of Sparta and her allies (not all in the Peloponnese), dating back to the sixth century BC.
peltast	light-armed soldier with small shield and javelin, fighting not in formation but as skirmisher from a distance.
Prote	small island near Pylos.
Pylos	rocky peninsula in the south-west Peloponnese at the north end of modern Navarino Bay.

Sicily	large island south of Italy, with many Greek colony cities (often siding with Athens or Sparta).
Sophocles	Athenian general, joint commander of fleet sailing to Sicily – not to be confused with the tragic playwright of the same name.
Sparta	one of the two leading cities in Greece, situated in the southern Peloponnese, governed by mixed constitution, militarist and secretive, head of the Peloponnesian League.
Spartiate	Spartan with full citizen rights (a minority of the population).
Sphacteria	long thin island adjacent to Pylos, running north-south and almost closing off modern Navarino Bay.
Styphon	third Spartan commander on Sphacteria.
Theagenes	Athenian chosen to go as observer with Cleon to Pylos.
Thermopylae	mountain pass in central Greece where Spartans under Leonidas made a heroic stand against the invading Persians in 480.
Thrasymelidas	Spartan admiral at Pylos.
trierarch	captain and/or sponsor of an Athenian trireme; captain of any trireme.
trireme	long, fast warship with three banks of oars and 170 oarsmen, with a strong beak for ramming enemy ships.
Troezen	city in the north-east Peloponnese.
trophy	monument claiming victory, usually consisting of post with placard and captured enemy armour.
Zacynthus	island off north-west Greece.

Further reading

Athens and Sparta, S.C. Todd, (Classical World Series) Bloomsbury 2013

Aristophanes: Knights, any translation (for another view of Cleon)

The Athenian Trireme, J.S. Morrison and J.F. Coates, Cambridge University Press 1986

The Greek and Roman Historians, Timothy E. Duff, (Classical World Series) Bloomsbury 2013

Thucydides, W. Robert Connor, Princeton University Press 1984

Thucydides: The Peloponnesian War, translated by Martin Hammond, with introduction and notes by P.J. Rhodes, (Oxford World's Classics) Oxford University Press 2009

Thucydides, P.J. Rhodes, (Ancients in Action) Bloomsbury 2015

Thucydides: The Reinvention of History, Donald Kagan, Penguin 2010

Acknowledgements

The notes on the Greek text are adapted and expanded from those of Malcolm Campbell in *A Greek Prose Reading Course: Unit 4* (BCP 1997). I have depended heavily throughout on P.J. Rhodes *Thucydides: History IV.1 – V.24* (Aris and Phillips 1998), a masterpiece of lucid compression; I have also drawn on his *Short History of Ancient Greece* (I.B. Tauris 2014) in the Introduction. Simon Hornblower *A Commentary on Thucydides: Volume II* (OUP 1996) and A.W. Gomme *A Historical Commentary on Thucydides: Volume III* (OUP 1956) have been useful sources of reference. School editions of Book 4 by T.R. Mills (OUP 1909) and A.W. Spratt (CUP 1912), and of the Pylos narrative by J.H.E. Crees and J.C. Wordsworth (CUP 1919), have also given valuable help. I am grateful to an anonymous reader for comments, and to Alice Wright and Miriam Davey at Bloomsbury for their assistance and encouragement.

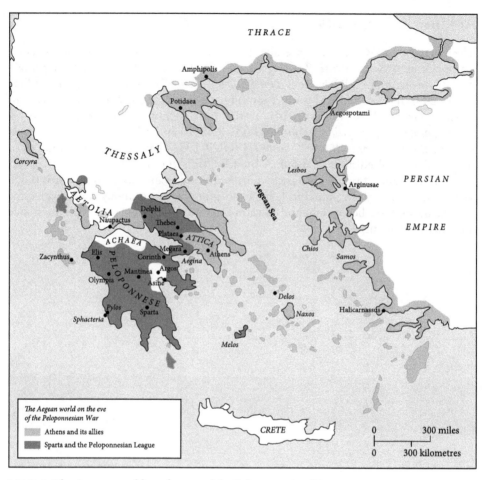

MAP 1 *The Aegean world on the eve of the Peloponnesian War*

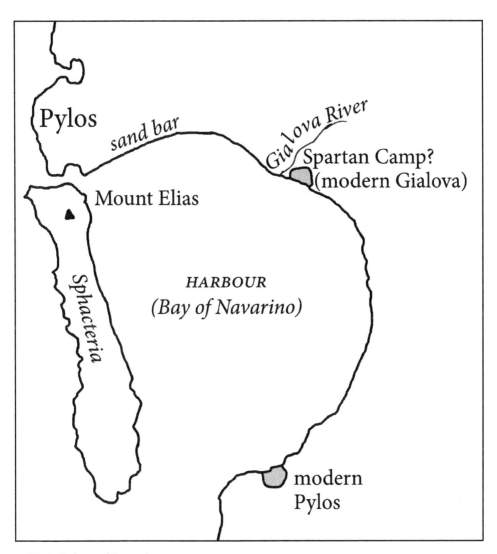

MAP 2 *Pylos and its environs*

Text

Chapters 1–10 describe the building of an Athenian fortress at Pylos, and the Spartan response.

11

τοσαῦτα τοῦ Δημοσθένους παρακελευσαμένου οἱ Ἀθηναῖοι ἐθάρσησάν τε μᾶλλον καὶ ἐπικαταβάντες ἐτάξαντο παρ᾽ αὐτὴν τὴν θάλασσαν. [2] οἱ δὲ Λακεδαιμόνιοι ἄραντες τῷ τε κατὰ γῆν στρατῷ προσέβαλλον τῷ τειχίσματι καὶ ταῖς ναυσὶν ἅμα οὔσαις τεσσαράκοντα καὶ τρισί, ναύαρχος δὲ αὐτῶν ἐπέπλει Θρασυμηλίδας ὁ Κρατησικλέους Σπαρτιάτης. προσέβαλλε δὲ ᾗπερ ὁ Δημοσθένης προσεδέχετο. [3] καὶ οἱ μὲν Ἀθηναῖοι ἀμφοτέρωθεν ἔκ τε γῆς καὶ ἐκ θαλάσσης ἠμύνοντο· οἱ δὲ κατ᾽ ὀλίγας ναῦς διελόμενοι, διότι οὐκ ἦν πλέοσι προσσχεῖν, καὶ ἀναπαύοντες ἐν τῷ μέρει τοὺς ἐπίπλους ἐποιοῦντο, προθυμίᾳ τε πάσῃ χρώμενοι καὶ παρακελευσμῷ, εἴ πως ὠσάμενοι ἕλοιεν τὸ τείχισμα. [4] πάντων δὲ φανερώτατος Βρασίδας ἐγένετο. τριηραρχῶν γὰρ καὶ ὁρῶν τοῦ χωρίου χαλεποῦ ὄντος τοὺς τριηράρχους καὶ κυβερνήτας, εἴ που καὶ δοκοίη δυνατὸν εἶναι σχεῖν, ἀποκνοῦντας καὶ φυλασσομένους τῶν νεῶν μὴ ξυντρίψωσιν, ἐβόα λέγων ὡς οὐκ εἰκὸς εἴη ξύλων φειδομένους τοὺς πολεμίους ἐν τῇ χώρᾳ περιιδεῖν τεῖχος πεποιημένους, ἀλλὰ τάς τε σφετέρας ναῦς βιαζομένους τὴν ἀπόβασιν καταγνύναι ἐκέλευε, καὶ τοὺς ξυμμάχους μὴ ἀποκνῆσαι ἀντὶ μεγάλων εὐεργεσιῶν τὰς ναῦς τοῖς Λακεδαιμονίοις ἐν τῷ παρόντι ἐπιδοῦναι, ὀκείλαντας δὲ καὶ παντὶ τρόπῳ ἀποβάντας τῶν τε ἀνδρῶν καὶ τοῦ χωρίου κρατῆσαι.

12

καὶ ὁ μὲν τούς τε ἄλλους τοιαῦτα ἐπέσπερχε καὶ τὸν ἑαυτοῦ κυβερνήτην ἀναγκάσας ὀκεῖλαι τὴν ναῦν ἐχώρει ἐπὶ τὴν ἀποβάθραν· καὶ πειρώμενος ἀποβαίνειν ἀνεκόπη ὑπὸ τῶν Ἀθηναίων, καὶ τραυματισθεὶς πολλὰ ἐλιποψύχησέ τε καὶ πεσόντος αὐτοῦ ἐς τὴν παρεξειρεσίαν ἡ ἀσπὶς περιερρύη ἐς τὴν θάλασσαν, καὶ ἐξενεχθείσης αὐτῆς ἐς τὴν γῆν οἱ Ἀθηναῖοι ἀνελόμενοι ὕστερον πρὸς τὸ τροπαῖον ἐχρήσαντο ὃ ἔστησαν τῆς προσβολῆς ταύτης. [2] οἱ δ᾽ ἄλλοι προυθυμοῦντο μέν, ἀδύνατοι δ᾽ ἦσαν ἀποβῆναι τῶν τε χωρίων χαλεπότητι καὶ τῶν Ἀθηναίων μενόντων καὶ οὐδὲν ὑποχωρούντων. [3] ἐς τοῦτό τε περιέστη ἡ τύχη ὥστε Ἀθηναίους μὲν ἐκ γῆς τε καὶ ταύτης Λακωνικῆς ἀμύνεσθαι ἐκείνους ἐπιπλέοντας, Λακεδαιμονίους δὲ ἐκ νεῶν τε καὶ ἐς τὴν ἑαυτῶν πολεμίαν οὖσαν ἐπ᾽ Ἀθηναίους ἀποβαίνειν· ἐπὶ πολὺ γὰρ ἐποίει τῆς δόξης ἐν τῷ τότε τοῖς μὲν ἠπειρώταις μάλιστα εἶναι καὶ τὰ πεζὰ κρατίστοις, τοῖς δὲ θαλασσίοις τε καὶ ταῖς ναυσὶ πλεῖστον προύχειν.

13

ταύτην μὲν οὖν τὴν ἡμέραν καὶ τῆς ὑστεραίας μέρος τι προσβολὰς ποιησάμενοι ἐπέπαυντο· καὶ τῇ τρίτῃ ἐπὶ ξύλα ἐς μηχανὰς παρέπεμψαν τῶν νεῶν τινὰς ἐς Ἀσίνην, ἐλπίζοντες τὸ κατὰ τὸν λιμένα τεῖχος ὕψος μὲν ἔχειν, ἀποβάσεως δὲ μάλιστα οὔσης ἑλεῖν <ἂν> μηχαναῖς. [2] ἐν τούτῳ δὲ αἱ ἐκ τῆς Ζακύνθου νῆες τῶν Ἀθηναίων παραγίγνονται τεσσαράκοντα· προσεβοήθησαν γὰρ τῶν τε φρουρίδων τινὲς αὐτοῖς τῶν ἐκ Ναυπάκτου καὶ Χῖαι τέσσαρες. [3] ὡς δὲ εἶδον τήν τε ἤπειρον ὁπλιτῶν περίπλεων τήν τε νῆσον, ἔν τε τῷ λιμένι οὔσας τὰς ναῦς καὶ οὐκ ἐκπλεούσας, ἀπορήσαντες ὅπῃ καθορμίσωνται, τότε μὲν ἐς Πρωτὴν τὴν νῆσον, ἣ οὐ πολὺ ἀπέχει ἐρῆμος οὖσα, ἔπλευσαν καὶ ηὐλίσαντο, τῇ δ᾽ ὑστεραίᾳ παρασκευασάμενοι ὡς ἐπὶ ναυμαχίαν ἀνήγοντο, ἢν μὲν ἀντεκπλεῖν ἐθέλωσι σφίσιν ἐς τὴν εὐρυχωρίαν, εἰ δὲ μή, ὡς αὐτοὶ ἐπεσπλευσούμενοι. [4] καὶ οἱ μὲν οὔτε ἀντανήγοντο οὔτε ἃ διενοήθησαν, φάρξαι τοὺς ἔσπλους, ἔτυχον ποιήσαντες, ἡσυχάζοντες δ᾽ ἐν τῇ γῇ τάς τε ναῦς ἐπλήρουν καὶ παρεσκευάζοντο, ἢν ἐσπλέῃ τις, ὡς ἐν τῷ λιμένι ὄντι οὐ σμικρῷ ναυμαχήσοντες.

14

οἱ δ᾽ Ἀθηναῖοι γνόντες καθ᾽ ἑκάτερον τὸν ἔσπλουν ὥρμησαν ἐπ᾽ αὐτούς, καὶ τὰς μὲν πλείους καὶ μετεώρους ἤδη τῶν νεῶν καὶ ἀντιπρῴρους προσπεσόντες ἐς φυγὴν κατέστησαν, καὶ ἐπιδιώκοντες ὡς διὰ βραχέος ἔτρωσαν μὲν πολλάς, πέντε δὲ ἔλαβον, καὶ μίαν τούτων αὐτοῖς ἀνδράσιν· ταῖς δὲ λοιπαῖς ἐν τῇ γῇ καταπεφευγυίαις ἐνέβαλλον. αἱ δὲ καὶ πληρούμεναι ἔτι πρὶν ἀνάγεσθαι ἐκόπτοντο· καί τινας καὶ ἀναδούμενοι κενὰς εἷλκον τῶν ἀνδρῶν ἐς φυγὴν ὡρμημένων. [2] ἃ ὁρῶντες οἱ Λακεδαιμόνιοι καὶ περιαλγοῦντες τῷ πάθει, ὅτιπερ αὐτῶν οἱ ἄνδρες ἀπελαμβάνοντο ἐν τῇ νήσῳ, παρεβοήθουν, καὶ ἐπεσβαίνοντες ἐς τὴν θάλασσαν ξὺν τοῖς ὅπλοις ἀνθεῖλκον ἐπιλαμβανόμενοι τῶν νεῶν· καὶ ἐν τούτῳ κεκωλῦσθαι ἐδόκει ἕκαστος ᾧ μή τινι καὶ αὐτὸς ἔργῳ παρῆν. [3] ἐγένετό τε ὁ θόρυβος μέγας καὶ ἀντηλλαγμένου τοῦ ἑκατέρων τρόπου περὶ τὰς ναῦς· οἵ τε γὰρ Λακεδαιμόνιοι ὑπὸ προθυμίας καὶ ἐκπλήξεως ὡς εἰπεῖν ἄλλο οὐδὲν ἢ ἐκ γῆς ἐναυμάχουν, οἵ τε Ἀθηναῖοι κρατοῦντες καὶ βουλόμενοι τῇ παρούσῃ τύχῃ ὡς ἐπὶ πλεῖστον ἐπεξελθεῖν ἀπὸ νεῶν ἐπεζομάχουν. [4] πολύν τε πόνον παρασχόντες ἀλλήλοις καὶ τραυματίσαντες διεκρίθησαν, καὶ οἱ Λακεδαιμόνιοι τὰς κενὰς ναῦς πλὴν τῶν τὸ πρῶτον ληφθεισῶν διέσωσαν. [5] καταστάντες δὲ ἑκάτεροι ἐς τὸ στρατόπεδον οἱ μὲν τροπαῖόν τε ἔστησαν καὶ νεκροὺς ἀπέδοσαν καὶ ναυαγίων ἐκράτησαν, καὶ τὴν νῆσον εὐθὺς περιέπλεον καὶ ἐν φυλακῇ εἶχον ὡς τῶν ἀνδρῶν ἀπειλημμένων· οἱ δ᾽ ἐν τῇ ἠπείρῳ Πελοποννήσιοι καὶ ἀπὸ πάντων ἤδη βεβοηθηκότες ἔμενον κατὰ χώραν ἐπὶ τῇ Πύλῳ.

Chapters 15–20 describe a temporary truce, and the visit of Spartan ambassadors to Athens to ask for a lasting peace.

21

οἱ μὲν οὖν Λακεδαιμόνιοι τοσαῦτα εἶπον, νομίζοντες τοὺς Ἀθηναίους ἐν τῷ πρὶν χρόνῳ σπονδῶν μὲν ἐπιθυμεῖν, σφῶν δὲ ἐναντιουμένων κωλύεσθαι, διδομένης δὲ εἰρήνης ἀσμένους δέξεσθαί τε καὶ τοὺς ἄνδρας ἀποδώσειν. [2] οἱ δὲ τὰς μὲν σπονδάς, ἔχοντες τοὺς ἄνδρας ἐν τῇ νήσῳ, ἤδη σφίσιν ἐνόμιζον ἑτοίμους εἶναι, ὁπόταν βούλωνται ποιεῖσθαι πρὸς αὐτούς, τοῦ δὲ πλέονος ὠρέγοντο. [3] μάλιστα δὲ αὐτοὺς ἐνῆγε Κλέων ὁ Κλεαινέτου, ἀνὴρ δημαγωγὸς κατ᾽ ἐκεῖνον τὸν χρόνον ὢν καὶ τῷ πλήθει πιθανώτατος· καὶ ἔπεισεν ἀποκρίνασθαι ὡς χρὴ τὰ μὲν ὅπλα καὶ σφᾶς αὐτοὺς τοὺς ἐν τῇ νήσῳ παραδόντας πρῶτον κομισθῆναι Ἀθήναζε, ἐλθόντων δὲ ἀποδόντας Λακεδαιμονίους Νίσαιαν καὶ Πηγὰς καὶ Τροιζῆνα καὶ Ἀχαΐαν, ἃ οὐ πολέμῳ ἔλαβον, ἀλλ᾽ ἀπὸ τῆς προτέρας ξυμβάσεως Ἀθηναίων ξυγχωρησάντων κατὰ ξυμφορὰς καὶ ἐν τῷ τότε δεομένων τι μᾶλλον σπονδῶν, κομίσασθαι τοὺς ἄνδρας καὶ σπονδὰς ποιήσασθαι ὁπόσον ἂν δοκῇ χρόνον ἀμφοτέροις.

22

οἱ δὲ πρὸς μὲν τὴν ἀπόκρισιν οὐδὲν ἀντεῖπον, ξυνέδρους δὲ σφίσιν ἐκέλευον ἑλέσθαι οἵτινες λέγοντες καὶ ἀκούοντες περὶ ἑκάστου ξυμβήσονται κατὰ ἡσυχίαν ὅτι ἂν πείθωσιν ἀλλήλους. [2] Κλέων δὲ ἐνταῦθα δὴ πολὺς ἐνέκειτο, λέγων γιγνώσκειν μὲν καὶ πρότερον οὐδὲν ἐν νῷ ἔχοντας δίκαιον αὐτούς, σαφὲς δ᾽ εἶναι καὶ νῦν, οἵτινες τῷ μὲν πλήθει οὐδὲν ἐθέλουσιν εἰπεῖν, ὀλίγοις δὲ ἀνδράσι ξύνεδροι βούλονται γίγνεσθαι· ἀλλὰ εἴ τι ὑγιὲς διανοοῦνται, λέγειν ἐκέλευσεν ἅπασιν. [3] ὁρῶντες δὲ οἱ Λακεδαιμόνιοι οὔτε σφίσιν οἷόν τε ὂν ἐν πλήθει εἰπεῖν, εἴ τι καὶ ὑπὸ τῆς ξυμφορᾶς ἐδόκει αὐτοῖς ξυγχωρεῖν, μὴ ἐς τοὺς ξυμμάχους διαβληθῶσιν εἰπόντες καὶ οὐ τυχόντες, οὔτε τοὺς Ἀθηναίους ἐπὶ μετρίοις ποιήσοντας ἃ προυκαλοῦντο, ἀνεχώρησαν ἐκ τῶν Ἀθηνῶν ἄπρακτοι.

23

ἀφικομένων δὲ αὐτῶν διελέλυντο εὐθὺς αἱ σπονδαὶ αἱ περὶ Πύλον, καὶ τὰς ναῦς οἱ Λακεδαιμόνιοι ἀπῄτουν, καθάπερ ξυνέκειτο· οἱ δ᾽ Ἀθηναῖοι ἐγκλήματα ἔχοντες ἐπιδρομήν τε τῷ τειχίσματι παράσπονδον καὶ ἄλλα οὐκ ἀξιόλογα δοκοῦντα εἶναι οὐκ ἀπεδίδοσαν, ἰσχυριζόμενοι ὅτι δὴ εἴρητο, ἐὰν καὶ ὁτιοῦν παραβαθῇ, λελύσθαι τὰς σπονδάς. οἱ δὲ Λακεδαιμόνιοι ἀντέλεγόν τε καὶ ἀδίκημα ἐπικαλέσαντες τὸ τῶν νεῶν ἀπελθόντες ἐς πόλεμον καθίσταντο.

AS

[2] καὶ τὰ περὶ Πύλον ὑπ᾽ ἀμφοτέρων κατὰ κράτος ἐπολεμεῖτο, Ἀθηναῖοι μὲν δυοῖν νεοῖν ἐναντίαιν αἰεὶ τὴν νῆσον περιπλέοντες τῆς ἡμέρας (τῆς δὲ νυκτὸς καὶ ἅπασαι περιώρμουν, πλὴν τὰ πρὸς τὸ πέλαγος, ὁπότε ἄνεμος εἴη· καὶ ἐκ τῶν Ἀθηνῶν αὐτοῖς εἴκοσι νῆες ἀφίκοντο ἐς τὴν φυλακήν, ὥστε αἱ πᾶσαι ἑβδομήκοντα ἐγένοντο), Πελοποννήσιοι δὲ ἔν τε τῇ ἠπείρῳ στρατοπεδευόμενοι καὶ προσβολὰς ποιούμενοι τῷ τείχει, σκοποῦντες καιρὸν εἴ τις παραπέσοι ὥστε τοὺς ἄνδρας σῶσαι.

Chapters 24 and 25 describe fighting in and near Sicily between allies of Athens and of pro-Spartan Syracuse.

26

ἐν δὲ τῇ Πύλῳ ἔτι ἐπολιόρκουν τοὺς ἐν τῇ νήσῳ Λακεδαιμονίους οἱ Ἀθηναῖοι, καὶ τὸ ἐν τῇ ἠπείρῳ στρατόπεδον τῶν Πελοποννησίων κατὰ χώραν ἔμενεν. [2] ἐπίπονος δ᾽ ἦν τοῖς Ἀθηναίοις ἡ φυλακὴ σίτου τε ἀπορίᾳ καὶ ὕδατος· οὐ γὰρ ἦν κρήνη ὅτι μὴ μία ἐν αὐτῇ τῇ ἀκροπόλει τῆς Πύλου καὶ αὕτη οὐ μεγάλη, ἀλλὰ διαμώμενοι τὸν κάχληκα οἱ πλεῖστοι ἐπὶ τῇ θαλάσσῃ ἔπινον οἷον εἰκὸς ὕδωρ. [3] στενοχωρία τε ἐν ὀλίγῳ στρατοπεδευομένοις ἐγίγνετο, καὶ τῶν νεῶν οὐκ ἐχουσῶν ὅρμον αἱ μὲν σῖτον ἐν τῇ γῇ ᾑροῦντο κατὰ μέρος, αἱ δὲ μετέωροι ὥρμουν. [4] ἀθυμίαν τε πλείστην ὁ χρόνος παρεῖχε παρὰ λόγον ἐπιγιγνόμενος, οὓς ᾤοντο ἡμερῶν ὀλίγων ἐκπολιορκήσειν ἐν νήσῳ τε ἐρήμῃ καὶ ὕδατι ἁλμυρῷ χρωμένους. [5] αἴτιον δὲ ἦν οἱ Λακεδαιμόνιοι προειπόντες ἐς τὴν νῆσον ἐσάγειν σῖτόν τε τὸν βουλόμενον ἀληλεμένον καὶ οἶνον καὶ τυρὸν καὶ εἴ τι ἄλλο βρῶμα, οἷ᾽ ἂν ἐς πολιορκίαν ξυμφέρῃ, τάξαντες ἀργυρίου πολλοῦ καὶ τῶν Εἱλώτων τῷ ἐσαγαγόντι ἐλευθερίαν ὑπισχνούμενοι. [6] καὶ ἐσῆγον ἄλλοι τε παρακινδυνεύοντες καὶ μάλιστα οἱ Εἵλωτες, ἀπαίροντες ἀπὸ τῆς Πελοποννήσου ὁπόθεν τύχοιεν καὶ καταπλέοντες ἔτι νυκτὸς ἐς τὰ πρὸς τὸ πέλαγος τῆς νήσου. [7] μάλιστα δὲ ἐτήρουν ἀνέμῳ καταφέρεσθαι· ῥᾷον γὰρ τὴν φυλακὴν τῶν τριήρων ἐλάνθανον, ὁπότε πνεῦμα ἐκ πόντου εἴη· ἄπορον γὰρ ἐγίγνετο περιορμεῖν, τοῖς δὲ ἀφειδὴς ὁ κατάπλους καθειστήκει· ἐπώκελλον γὰρ τὰ πλοῖα τετιμημένα χρημάτων, καὶ οἱ ὁπλῖται περὶ τὰς κατάρσεις τῆς νήσου ἐφύλασσον. ὅσοι δὲ γαλήνῃ κινδυνεύσειαν, ἡλίσκοντο. [8] ἐσένεον δὲ καὶ κατὰ τὸν λιμένα κολυμβηταὶ ὕφυδροι, καλῳδίῳ ἐν ἀσκοῖς ἐφέλκοντες μήκωνα μεμελιτωμένην καὶ λίνου σπέρμα κεκομμένον· ὧν τὸ πρῶτον λανθανόντων φυλακαὶ ὕστερον ἐγένοντο. [9] παντί τε τρόπῳ ἑκάτεροι ἐτεχνῶντο οἱ μὲν ἐσπέμπειν τὰ σιτία, οἱ δὲ μὴ λανθάνειν σφᾶς.

27

ἐν δὲ ταῖς Ἀθήναις πυνθανόμενοι περὶ τῆς στρατιᾶς ὅτι ταλαιπωρεῖται καὶ σῖτος τοῖς ἐν τῇ νήσῳ ὅτι ἐσπλεῖ, ἠπόρουν καὶ ἐδεδοίκεσαν μὴ σφῶν χειμὼν τὴν φυλακὴν ἐπιλάβοι, ὁρῶντες τῶν τε ἐπιτηδείων τὴν περὶ τὴν Πελοπόννησον κομιδὴν ἀδύνατον ἐσομένην, ἅμα ἐν χωρίῳ ἐρήμῳ καὶ οὐδ᾽ ἐν θέρει οἷοί τε ὄντες ἱκανὰ περιπέμπειν, τόν τε ἔφορμον χωρίων ἀλιμένων ὄντων οὐκ ἐσόμενον, ἀλλ᾽ ἢ σφῶν ἀνέντων τὴν φυλακὴν περιγενήσεσθαι τοὺς ἄνδρας ἢ τοῖς πλοίοις ἃ τὸν σῖτον αὐτοῖς ἦγε χειμῶνα τηρήσαντας ἐκπλεύσεσθαι. [2] πάντων τε ἐφοβοῦντο μάλιστα τοὺς Λακεδαιμονίους, ὅτι ἔχοντάς τι ἰσχυρὸν αὐτοὺς ἐνόμιζον οὐκέτι σφίσιν ἐπικηρυκεύεσθαι· καὶ μετεμέλοντο τὰς σπονδὰς οὐ δεξάμενοι. [3] Κλέων δὲ γνοὺς αὐτῶν τὴν ἐς αὐτὸν ὑποψίαν περὶ τῆς κωλύμης τῆς ξυμβάσεως οὐ τἀληθῆ ἔφη λέγειν τοὺς ἐξαγγέλλοντας. παραινούντων δὲ τῶν ἀφιγμένων, εἰ μὴ σφίσι πιστεύουσι, κατασκόπους τινὰς πέμψαι, ᾑρέθη κατάσκοπος αὐτὸς μετὰ Θεαγένους ὑπὸ Ἀθηναίων. [4] καὶ γνοὺς ὅτι ἀναγκασθήσεται ἢ ταὐτὰ λέγειν οἷς διέβαλλεν ἢ τἀναντία εἰπὼν ψευδὴς φανήσεσθαι, παρῄνει τοῖς Ἀθηναίοις, ὁρῶν αὐτοὺς καὶ ὡρμημένους τι τὸ πλέον τῇ γνώμῃ στρατεύειν, ὡς χρὴ κατασκόπους μὲν μὴ πέμπειν μηδὲ διαμέλλειν καιρὸν παριέντας, εἰ δὲ δοκεῖ αὐτοῖς ἀληθῆ εἶναι τὰ ἀγγελλόμενα, πλεῖν ἐπὶ τοὺς ἄνδρας. [5] καὶ ἐς Νικίαν τὸν Νικηράτου στρατηγὸν ὄντα ἀπεσήμαινεν, ἐχθρὸς ὢν καὶ ἐπιτιμῶν, ῥάδιον εἶναι παρασκευῇ, εἰ ἄνδρες εἶεν οἱ στρατηγοί, πλεύσαντας λαβεῖν τοὺς ἐν τῇ νήσῳ, καὶ αὐτός γ᾽ ἄν, εἰ ἦρχε, ποιῆσαι τοῦτο.

28

ὁ δὲ Νικίας τῶν τε Ἀθηναίων τι ὑποθορυβησάντων ἐς τὸν Κλέωνα, ὅτι οὐ καὶ νῦν πλεῖ, εἰ ῥᾴδιόν γε αὐτῷ φαίνεται, καὶ ἅμα ὁρῶν αὐτὸν ἐπιτιμῶντα, ἐκέλευεν ἥντινα βούλεται δύναμιν λαβόντα τὸ ἐπὶ σφᾶς εἶναι ἐπιχειρεῖν. [2] ὁ δὲ τὸ μὲν πρῶτον οἰόμενος αὐτὸν λόγῳ μόνον ἀφιέναι ἕτοιμος ἦν, γνοὺς δὲ τῷ ὄντι παραδωσείοντα ἀνεχώρει καὶ οὐκ ἔφη αὐτὸς ἀλλ᾽ ἐκεῖνον στρατηγεῖν, δεδιὼς ἤδη καὶ οὐκ ἂν οἰόμενός οἱ αὐτὸν τολμῆσαι ὑποχωρῆσαι. [3] αὖθις δὲ ὁ Νικίας ἐκέλευε καὶ ἐξίστατο τῆς ἐπὶ Πύλῳ ἀρχῆς καὶ μάρτυρας τοὺς Ἀθηναίους ἐποιεῖτο. οἱ δέ, οἷον ὄχλος φιλεῖ ποιεῖν, ὅσῳ μᾶλλον ὁ Κλέων ὑπέφευγε τὸν πλοῦν καὶ ἐξανεχώρει τὰ εἰρημένα, τόσῳ ἐπεκελεύοντο τῷ Νικίᾳ παραδιδόναι τὴν ἀρχὴν καὶ ἐκείνῳ ἐπεβόων πλεῖν. [4] ὥστε οὐκ ἔχων ὅπως τῶν εἰρημένων ἔτι ἐξαπαλλαγῇ, ὑφίσταται τὸν πλοῦν, καὶ παρελθὼν οὔτε φοβεῖσθαι ἔφη Λακεδαιμονίους πλεύσεσθαί τε λαβὼν ἐκ μὲν τῆς πόλεως οὐδένα, Λημνίους δὲ καὶ Ἰμβρίους τοὺς παρόντας καὶ πελταστὰς οἳ ἦσαν ἔκ τε Αἴνου βεβοηθηκότες καὶ ἄλλοθεν τοξότας τετρακοσίους· ταῦτα δὲ ἔχων ἔφη πρὸς τοῖς ἐν Πύλῳ στρατιώταις ἐντὸς ἡμερῶν εἴκοσιν ἢ ἄξειν Λακεδαιμονίους ζῶντας ἢ αὐτοῦ ἀποκτενεῖν. [5] τοῖς δὲ Ἀθηναίοις ἐνέπεσε μέν τι καὶ γέλωτος τῇ κουφολογίᾳ αὐτοῦ, ἀσμένοις δ᾽ ὅμως ἐγίγνετο τοῖς σώφροσι τῶν ἀνθρώπων, λογιζομένοις δυοῖν ἀγαθοῖν τοῦ ἑτέρου τεύξεσθαι, ἢ Κλέωνος ἀπαλλαγήσεσθαι, ὃ μᾶλλον ἤλπιζον, ἢ σφαλεῖσι γνώμης Λακεδαιμονίους σφίσι χειρώσεσθαι.

29

καὶ πάντα διαπραξάμενος ἐν τῇ ἐκκλησίᾳ καὶ ψηφισαμένων Ἀθηναίων αὐτῷ τὸν πλοῦν, τῶν τε ἐν Πύλῳ στρατηγῶν ἕνα προσελόμενος Δημοσθένη, τὴν ἀναγωγὴν διὰ τάχους ἐποιεῖτο. [**2**] τὸν δὲ Δημοσθένη προσέλαβε πυνθανόμενος τὴν ἀπόβασιν αὐτὸν ἐς τὴν νῆσον διανοεῖσθαι. οἱ γὰρ στρατιῶται κακοπαθοῦντες τοῦ χωρίου τῇ ἀπορίᾳ καὶ μᾶλλον πολιορκούμενοι ἢ πολιορκοῦντες ὥρμηντο διακινδυνεῦσαι. καὶ αὐτῷ ἔτι ῥώμην καὶ ἡ νῆσος ἐμπρησθεῖσα παρέσχεν. [**3**] πρότερον μὲν γὰρ οὔσης αὐτῆς ὑλώδους ἐπὶ τὸ πολὺ καὶ ἀτριβοῦς διὰ τὴν αἰεὶ ἐρημίαν ἐφοβεῖτο καὶ πρὸς τῶν πολεμίων τοῦτο ἐνόμιζε μᾶλλον εἶναι· πολλῷ γὰρ ἂν στρατοπέδῳ ἀποβάντι ἐξ ἀφανοῦς χωρίου προσβάλλοντας αὐτοὺς βλάπτειν. σφίσι μὲν γὰρ τὰς ἐκείνων ἁμαρτίας καὶ παρασκευὴν ὑπὸ τῆς ὕλης οὐκ ἂν ὁμοίως δῆλα εἶναι, τοῦ δὲ αὑτῶν στρατοπέδου καταφανῆ ἂν εἶναι πάντα τὰ ἁμαρτήματα, ὥστε προσπίπτειν ἂν αὐτοὺς ἀπροσδοκήτως ᾗ βούλοιντο· ἐπ᾽ ἐκείνοις γὰρ εἶναι ἂν τὴν ἐπιχείρησιν. [**4**] εἰ δ᾽ αὖ ἐς δασὺ χωρίον βιάζοιτο ὁμόσε ἰέναι, τοὺς ἐλάσσους, ἐμπείρους δὲ τῆς χώρας, κρείσσους ἐνόμιζε τῶν πλεόνων ἀπείρων· λανθάνειν τε ἂν τὸ ἑαυτῶν στρατόπεδον πολὺ ὂν διαφθειρόμενον, οὐκ οὔσης τῆς προσόψεως ᾗ χρῆν ἀλλήλοις ἐπιβοηθεῖν.

30

ἀπὸ δὲ τοῦ Αἰτωλικοῦ πάθους, ὃ διὰ τὴν ὕλην μέρος τι ἐγένετο, οὐχ ἥκιστα αὐτὸν ταῦτα ἐσῄει. [**2**] τῶν δὲ στρατιωτῶν ἀναγκασθέντων διὰ τὴν στενοχωρίαν τῆς νήσου τοῖς ἐσχάτοις προσίσχοντας ἀριστοποιεῖσθαι διὰ προφυλακῆς καὶ ἐμπρήσαντός τινος κατὰ μικρὸν τῆς ὕλης ἄκοντος καὶ ἀπὸ τούτου πνεύματος ἐπιγενομένου τὸ πολὺ αὐτῆς ἔλαθε κατακαυθέν. [**3**] οὕτω δὴ τούς τε Λακεδαιμονίους μᾶλλον κατιδὼν πλείους ὄντας, ὑπονοῶν πρότερον ἐλάσσοσι τὸν σῖτον αὐτοῦ ἐσπέμπειν, τήν τε νῆσον εὐαποβατωτέραν οὖσαν, τότε ὡς ἐπ᾽ ἀξιόχρεων τοὺς Ἀθηναίους μᾶλλον σπουδὴν ποιεῖσθαι τὴν ἐπιχείρησιν παρεσκευάζετο, στρατιάν τε μεταπέμπων ἐκ τῶν ἐγγὺς ξυμμάχων καὶ τὰ ἄλλα ἑτοιμάζων.

[**4**] Κλέων δὲ ἐκείνῳ τε προπέμψας ἄγγελον ὡς ἥξων καὶ ἔχων στρατιὰν ἣν ᾐτήσατο, ἀφικνεῖται ἐς Πύλον. καὶ ἅμα γενόμενοι πέμπουσι πρῶτον ἐς τὸ ἐν τῇ ἠπείρῳ στρατόπεδον κήρυκα, προκαλούμενοι, εἰ βούλοιντο, ἄνευ κινδύνου τοὺς ἐν τῇ νήσῳ ἄνδρας σφίσι τά τε ὅπλα καὶ σφᾶς αὐτοὺς κελεύειν παραδοῦναι, ἐφ᾽ ᾧ φυλακῇ τῇ μετρίᾳ τηρήσονται, ἕως ἄν τι περὶ τοῦ πλέονος ξυμβαθῇ.

31

οὐ προσδεξαμένων δὲ αὐτῶν μίαν μὲν ἡμέραν ἐπέσχον, τῇ δ᾽ ὑστεραίᾳ ἀνηγάγοντο μὲν νυκτὸς ἐπ᾽ ὀλίγας ναῦς τοὺς ὁπλίτας πάντας ἐπιβιβάσαντες, πρὸ δὲ τῆς ἕω ὀλίγον ἀπέβαινον τῆς νήσου ἑκατέρωθεν, ἔκ τε τοῦ πελάγους καὶ πρὸς τοῦ λιμένος, ὀκτακόσιοι μάλιστα ὄντες ὁπλῖται, καὶ ἐχώρουν δρόμῳ ἐπὶ τὸ πρῶτον φυλακτήριον τῆς νήσου. [2] ὧδε γὰρ διετετάχατο· ἐν ταύτῃ μὲν τῇ πρώτῃ φυλακῇ ὡς τριάκοντα ἦσαν ὁπλῖται, μέσον δὲ καὶ ὁμαλώτατόν τε καὶ περὶ τὸ ὕδωρ οἱ πλεῖστοι αὐτῶν καὶ Ἐπιτάδας ὁ ἄρχων εἶχε, μέρος δέ τι οὐ πολὺ αὐτὸ τὸ ἔσχατον ἐφύλασσε τῆς νήσου τὸ πρὸς τὴν Πύλον, ὃ ἦν ἔκ τε θαλάσσης ἀπόκρημνον καὶ ἐκ τῆς γῆς ἥκιστα ἐπίμαχον· καὶ γάρ τι καὶ ἔρυμα αὐτόθι ἦν παλαιὸν λίθων λογάδην πεποιημένον, ὃ ἐνόμιζον σφίσιν ὠφέλιμον ἂν εἶναι, εἰ καταλαμβάνοι ἀναχώρησις βιαιοτέρα. οὕτω μὲν τεταγμένοι ἦσαν.

32

οἱ δὲ Ἀθηναῖοι τοὺς μὲν πρώτους φύλακας, οἷς ἐπέδραμον, εὐθὺς διαφθείρουσιν ἔν τε ταῖς εὐναῖς ἔτι καὶ ἀναλαμβάνοντας τὰ ὅπλα, λαθόντες τὴν ἀπόβασιν, οἰομένων αὐτῶν τὰς ναῦς κατὰ τὸ ἔθος ἐς ἔφορμον τῆς νυκτὸς πλεῖν. [2] ἅμα δὲ ἕῳ γιγνομένῃ καὶ ὁ ἄλλος στρατὸς ἀπέβαινεν, ἐκ μὲν νεῶν ἑβδομήκοντα καὶ ὀλίγῳ πλεόνων πάντες πλὴν θαλαμιῶν, ὡς ἕκαστοι ἐσκευασμένοι, τοξόται δὲ ὀκτακόσιοι καὶ πελτασταὶ οὐκ ἐλάσσους τούτων, Μεσσηνίων τε οἱ βεβοηθηκότες καὶ οἱ ἄλλοι ὅσοι περὶ Πύλον κατεῖχον πάντες πλὴν τῶν ἐπὶ τοῦ τείχους φυλάκων. [3] Δημοσθένους δὲ τάξαντος διέστησαν κατὰ διακοσίους τε καὶ πλείους, ἔστι δ᾽ ᾗ ἐλάσσους, τῶν χωρίων τὰ μετεωρότατα λαβόντες, ὅπως ὅτι πλείστη ἀπορία ᾖ τοῖς πολεμίοις πανταχόθεν κεκυκλωμένοις καὶ μὴ ἔχωσι πρὸς ὅτι ἀντιτάξωνται, ἀλλ᾽ ἀμφίβολοι γίγνωνται τῷ πλήθει, εἰ μὲν τοῖς πρόσθεν ἐπίοιεν, ὑπὸ τῶν κατόπιν βαλλόμενοι, εἰ δὲ τοῖς πλαγίοις, ὑπὸ τῶν ἑκατέρωθεν παρατεταγμένων. [4] κατὰ νώτου τε αἰεὶ ἔμελλον αὐτοῖς, ᾗ χωρήσειαν, οἱ πολέμιοι ἔσεσθαι ψιλοὶ καὶ οἱ ἀπορώτατοι, τοξεύμασι καὶ ἀκοντίοις καὶ λίθοις καὶ σφενδόναις ἐκ πολλοῦ ἔχοντες ἀλκήν, οἷς μηδὲ ἐπελθεῖν οἷόν τε ἦν· φεύγοντές τε γὰρ ἐκράτουν καὶ ἀναχωροῦσιν ἐπέκειντο. τοιαύτῃ μὲν γνώμῃ ὁ Δημοσθένης τό τε πρῶτον τὴν ἀπόβασιν ἐπενόει καὶ ἐν τῷ ἔργῳ ἔταξεν·

33

οἱ δὲ περὶ τὸν Ἐπιτάδαν καὶ ὅπερ ἦν πλεῖστον τῶν ἐν τῇ νήσῳ, ὡς εἶδον τό τε πρῶτον φυλακτήριον διεφθαρμένον καὶ στρατὸν σφίσιν ἐπιόντα, ξυνετάξαντο καὶ τοῖς ὁπλίταις τῶν Ἀθηναίων ἐπῇσαν, βουλόμενοι ἐς χεῖρας ἐλθεῖν· ἐξ ἐναντίας γὰρ οὗτοι καθεστήκεσαν, ἐκ πλαγίου δὲ οἱ ψιλοὶ καὶ κατὰ νώτου. [2] τοῖς μὲν οὖν ὁπλίταις οὐκ ἐδυνήθησαν προσμεῖξαι οὐδὲ τῇ σφετέρᾳ ἐμπειρίᾳ χρήσασθαι· οἱ γὰρ ψιλοὶ ἑκατέρωθεν βάλλοντες εἶργον, καὶ ἅμα ἐκεῖνοι οὐκ ἀντεπῇσαν, ἀλλ᾽ ἡσύχαζον· τοὺς δὲ ψιλούς, ᾗ μάλιστα αὐτοῖς ἐπιθέοντες προσκέοιντο, ἔτρεπον, καὶ οἳ ὑποστρέφοντες ἠμύνοντο, ἄνθρωποι κούφως τε ἐσκευασμένοι καὶ προλαμβάνοντες ῥᾳδίως τῆς φυγῆς χωρίων τε χαλεπότητι καὶ ὑπὸ τῆς πρὶν ἐρημίας τραχέων ὄντων, ἐν οἷς οἱ Λακεδαιμόνιοι οὐκ ἐδύναντο διώκειν ὅπλα ἔχοντες.

A
Level

34

χρόνον μὲν οὖν τινὰ ὀλίγον οὕτω πρὸς ἀλλήλους ἠκροβολίσαντο· τῶν δὲ Λακεδαιμονίων οὐκέτι ὀξέως ἐπεκθεῖν ἢ προσπίπτοιεν δυναμένων, γνόντες αὐτοὺς οἱ ψιλοὶ βραδυτέρους ἤδη ὄντας τῷ ἀμύνασθαι, καὶ αὐτοὶ τῇ τε ὄψει τοῦ θαρσεῖν τὸ πλεῖστον εἰληφότες πολλαπλάσιοι φαινόμενοι καὶ ξυνειθισμένοι μᾶλλον μηκέτι δεινοὺς αὐτοὺς ὁμοίως σφίσι φαίνεσθαι, ὅτι οὐκ εὐθὺς ἄξια τῆς προσδοκίας ἐπεπόνθεσαν, ὥσπερ ὅτε πρῶτον ἀπέβαινον τῇ γνώμῃ δεδουλωμένοι ὡς ἐπὶ Λακεδαιμονίους, καταφρονήσαντες καὶ ἐμβοήσαντες ἀθρόοι ὥρμησαν ἐπ᾽ αὐτοὺς καὶ ἔβαλλον λίθοις τε καὶ τοξεύμασι καὶ ἀκοντίοις, ὡς ἕκαστός τι πρόχειρον εἶχεν. [2] γενομένης δὲ τῆς βοῆς ἅμα τῇ ἐπιδρομῇ ἔκπληξίς τε ἐνέπεσεν ἀνθρώποις ἀήθεσι τοιαύτης μάχης καὶ ὁ κονιορτὸς τῆς ὕλης νεωστὶ κεκαυμένης ἐχώρει πολὺς ἄνω, ἄπορόν τε ἦν ἰδεῖν τὸ πρὸ αὑτοῦ ὑπὸ τῶν τοξευμάτων καὶ λίθων ἀπὸ πολλῶν ἀνθρώπων μετὰ τοῦ κονιορτοῦ ἅμα φερομένων. [3] τό τε ἔργον ἐνταῦθα χαλεπὸν τοῖς Λακεδαιμονίοις καθίστατο· οὔτε γὰρ οἱ πῖλοι ἔστεγον τὰ τοξεύματα, δοράτιά τε ἐναπεκέκλαστο βαλλομένων, εἶχόν τε οὐδὲν σφίσιν αὐτοῖς χρήσασθαι ἀποκεκλημένοι μὲν τῇ ὄψει τοῦ προορᾶν, ὑπὸ δὲ τῆς μείζονος βοῆς τῶν πολεμίων τὰ ἐν αὑτοῖς παραγγελλόμενα οὐκ ἐσακούοντες, κινδύνου τε πανταχόθεν περιεστῶτος καὶ οὐκ ἔχοντες ἐλπίδα καθ᾽ ὅτι χρὴ ἀμυνομένους σωθῆναι.

35

τέλος δὲ τραυματιζομένων ἤδη πολλῶν διὰ τὸ αἰεὶ ἐν τῷ αὐτῷ ἀναστρέφεσθαι, ξυγκλήσαντες ἐχώρησαν ἐς τὸ ἔσχατον ἔρυμα τῆς νήσου, ὃ οὐ πολὺ ἀπεῖχε, καὶ τοὺς ἑαυτῶν φύλακας. [2] ὡς δὲ ἐνέδοσαν, ἐνταῦθα ἤδη πολλῷ ἔτι πλέονι βοῇ τεθαρσηκότες οἱ ψιλοὶ ἐπέκειντο, καὶ τῶν Λακεδαιμονίων ὅσοι μὲν ὑποχωροῦντες ἐγκατελαμβάνοντο, ἀπέθνησκον, οἱ δὲ πολλοὶ διαφυγόντες ἐς τὸ ἔρυμα μετὰ τῶν ταύτῃ φυλάκων ἐτάξαντο παρὰ πᾶν ὡς ἀμυνούμενοι ᾗπερ ἦν ἐπίμαχον. [3] καὶ οἱ Ἀθηναῖοι ἐπισπόμενοι περίοδον μὲν αὐτῶν καὶ κύκλωσιν χωρίου ἰσχύϊ οὐκ εἶχον, προσιόντες δὲ ἐξ ἐναντίας ὤσασθαι ἐπειρῶντο. [4] καὶ χρόνον μὲν πολὺν καὶ τῆς ἡμέρας τὸ πλεῖστον ταλαιπωρούμενοι ἀμφότεροι ὑπό τε τῆς μάχης καὶ δίψης καὶ ἡλίου ἀντεῖχον, πειρώμενοι οἱ μὲν ἐξελάσασθαι ἐκ τοῦ μετεώρου, οἱ δὲ μὴ ἐνδοῦναι· ῥᾷον δ᾽ οἱ Λακεδαιμόνιοι ἠμύνοντο ἢ ἐν τῷ πρίν, οὐκ οὔσης σφῶν τῆς κυκλώσεως ἐς τὰ πλάγια.

36

ἐπειδὴ δὲ ἀπέραντον ἦν, προσελθὼν ὁ τῶν Μεσσηνίων στρατηγὸς Κλέωνι καὶ Δημοσθένει ἄλλως ἔφη πονεῖν σφᾶς· εἰ δὲ βούλονται ἑαυτῷ δοῦναι τῶν τοξοτῶν μέρος τι καὶ τῶν ψιλῶν περιιέναι κατὰ νώτου αὐτοῖς ὁδῷ ᾗ ἂν αὐτὸς εὕρῃ, δοκεῖν βιάσεσθαι τὴν ἔφοδον. [2] λαβὼν δὲ ἃ ᾐτήσατο, ἐκ τοῦ ἀφανοῦς ὁρμήσας ὥστε μὴ ἰδεῖν ἐκείνους, κατὰ τὸ αἰεὶ παρεῖκον τοῦ κρημνώδους τῆς

νήσου προσβαίνων, καὶ ᾗ οἱ Λακεδαιμόνιοι χωρίου ἰσχύι πιστεύσαντες οὐκ
ἐφύλασσον, χαλεπῶς τε καὶ μόλις περιελθὼν ἔλαθε, καὶ ἐπὶ τοῦ μετεώρου
ἐξαπίνης ἀναφανεὶς κατὰ νώτου αὐτῶν τοὺς μὲν τῷ ἀδοκήτῳ ἐξέπληξε, τοὺς
δὲ ἃ προσεδέχοντο ἰδόντας πολλῷ μᾶλλον ἐπέρρωσεν. [3] καὶ οἱ Λακεδαιμόνιοι
βαλλόμενοί τε ἀμφοτέρωθεν ἤδη καὶ γιγνόμενοι ἐν τῷ αὐτῷ ξυμπτώματι, ὡς
μικρὸν μεγάλῳ εἰκάσαι, τῷ ἐν Θερμοπύλαις, ἐκεῖνοί τε γὰρ τῇ ἀτραπῷ
περιελθόντων τῶν Περσῶν διεφθάρησαν, οὗτοί τε ἀμφίβολοι ἤδη ὄντες οὐκέτι
ἀντεῖχον, ἀλλὰ πολλοῖς τε ὀλίγοι μαχόμενοι καὶ ἀσθενείᾳ σωμάτων διὰ τὴν
σιτοδείαν ὑπεχώρουν, καὶ οἱ Ἀθηναῖοι ἐκράτουν ἤδη τῶν ἐφόδων.

37
γνοὺς δὲ ὁ Κλέων καὶ ὁ Δημοσθένης [ὅτι], εἰ καὶ ὁποσονοῦν μᾶλλον ἐνδώσουσι,
διαφθαρησομένους αὐτοὺς ὑπὸ τῆς σφετέρας στρατιᾶς, ἔπαυσαν τὴν μάχην
καὶ τοὺς ἑαυτῶν ἀπεῖρξαν, βουλόμενοι ἀγαγεῖν αὐτοὺς Ἀθηναίοις ζῶντας, εἴ
πως τοῦ κηρύγματος ἀκούσαντες ἐπικλασθεῖεν τῇ γνώμῃ τὰ ὅπλα παραδοῦναι
καὶ ἡσσηθεῖεν τοῦ παρόντος δεινοῦ. [2] ἐκήρυξάν τε, εἰ βούλονται, τὰ
ὅπλα παραδοῦναι καὶ σφᾶς αὐτοὺς Ἀθηναίοις ὥστε βουλεῦσαι ὅτι ἂν ἐκείνοις
δοκῇ.

38
οἱ δὲ ἀκούσαντες παρῆκαν τὰς ἀσπίδας οἱ πλεῖστοι καὶ τὰς χεῖρας ἀνέσεισαν,
δηλοῦντες προσίεσθαι τὰ κεκηρυγμένα. μετὰ δὲ ταῦτα γενομένης τῆς
ἀνοκωχῆς ξυνῆλθον ἐς λόγους ὅ τε Κλέων καὶ ὁ Δημοσθένης καὶ ἐκείνων
Στύφων ὁ Φάρακος, τῶν πρότερον ἀρχόντων τοῦ μὲν πρώτου τεθνηκότος
Ἐπιτάδου, τοῦ δὲ μετ᾽ αὐτὸν Ἱππαγρέτου ἐφῃρημένου ἐν τοῖς νεκροῖς ἔτι
ζῶντος κειμένου ὡς τεθνεῶτος, αὐτὸς τρίτος ἐφῃρημένος ἄρχειν κατὰ νόμον,
εἴ τι ἐκεῖνοι πάσχοιεν. [2] ἔλεγε δὲ ὁ Στύφων καὶ οἱ μετ᾽ αὐτοῦ ὅτι βούλονται
διακηρυκεύσασθαι πρὸς τοὺς ἐν τῇ ἠπείρῳ Λακεδαιμονίους ὅτι χρὴ σφᾶς
ποιεῖν. [3] καὶ ἐκείνων μὲν οὐδένα ἀφέντων, αὐτῶν δὲ τῶν Ἀθηναίων
καλούντων ἐκ τῆς ἠπείρου κήρυκας καὶ γενομένων ἐπερωτήσεων δὶς ἢ τρίς, ὁ
τελευταῖος διαπλεύσας αὐτοῖς ἀπὸ τῶν ἐκ τῆς ἠπείρου Λακεδαιμονίων ἀνὴρ
ἀπήγγειλεν ὅτι [οἱ] 'Λακεδαιμόνιοι κελεύουσιν ὑμᾶς αὐτοὺς περὶ ὑμῶν αὐτῶν
βουλεύεσθαι μηδὲν αἰσχρὸν ποιοῦντας'· οἱ δὲ καθ᾽ ἑαυτοὺς βουλευσάμενοι τὰ
ὅπλα παρέδοσαν καὶ σφᾶς αὐτούς. [4] καὶ ταύτην μὲν τὴν ἡμέραν καὶ τὴν
ἐπιοῦσαν νύκτα ἐν φυλακῇ εἶχον αὐτοὺς οἱ Ἀθηναῖοι· τῇ δ᾽ ὑστεραίᾳ οἱ μὲν
Ἀθηναῖοι τροπαῖον στήσαντες ἐν τῇ νήσῳ τἆλλα διεσκευάζοντο ὡς ἐς πλοῦν,
καὶ τοὺς ἄνδρας τοῖς τριηράρχοις διεδίδοσαν ἐς φυλακήν, οἱ δὲ Λακεδαιμόνιοι
κήρυκα πέμψαντες τοὺς νεκροὺς διεκομίσαντο. [5] ἀπέθανον δ᾽ ἐν τῇ νήσῳ
καὶ ζῶντες ἐλήφθησαν τοσοίδε· εἴκοσι μὲν ὁπλῖται διέβησαν καὶ τετρακόσιοι
οἱ πάντες· τούτων ζῶντες ἐκομίσθησαν ὀκτὼ ἀποδέοντες τριακόσιοι, οἱ δὲ

ἄλλοι ἀπέθανον. καὶ Σπαρτιᾶται τούτων ἦσαν τῶν ζώντων περὶ εἴκοσι καὶ ἑκατόν. Ἀθηναίων δὲ οὐ πολλοὶ διεφθάρησαν· ἡ γὰρ μάχη οὐ σταδαία ἦν.

39

χρόνος δὲ ὁ ξύμπας ἐγένετο ὅσον οἱ ἄνδρες [οἱ] ἐν τῇ νήσῳ ἐπολιορκήθησαν, ἀπὸ τῆς ναυμαχίας μέχρι τῆς ἐν τῇ νήσῳ μάχης, ἑβδομήκοντα ἡμέραι καὶ δύο. [2] τούτων περὶ εἴκοσιν ἡμέρας, ἐν αἷς οἱ πρέσβεις περὶ τῶν σπονδῶν ἀπῆσαν, ἐσιτοδοτοῦντο, τὰς δὲ ἄλλας τοῖς ἐσπλέουσι λάθρᾳ διετρέφοντο. καὶ ἦν σῖτός τις ἐν τῇ νήσῳ καὶ ἄλλα βρώματα ἐγκατελήφθη· ὁ γὰρ ἄρχων Ἐπιτάδας ἐνδεεστέρως ἑκάστῳ παρεῖχεν ἢ πρὸς τὴν ἐξουσίαν. [3] οἱ μὲν δὴ Ἀθηναῖοι καὶ οἱ Πελοποννήσιοι ἀνεχώρησαν τῷ στρατῷ ἐκ τῆς Πύλου ἑκάτεροι ἐπ᾽οἴκου, καὶ τοῦ Κλέωνος καίπερ μανιώδης οὖσα ἡ ὑπόσχεσις ἀπέβη· ἐντὸς γὰρ εἴκοσιν ἡμερῶν ἤγαγε τοὺς ἄνδρας, ὥσπερ ὑπέστη.

40

παρὰ γνώμην τε δὴ μάλιστα τῶν κατὰ τὸν πόλεμον τοῦτο τοῖς Ἕλλησιν ἐγένετο· τοὺς γὰρ Λακεδαιμονίους οὔτε λιμῷ οὔτ᾽ ἀνάγκῃ οὐδεμιᾷ ἠξίουν τὰ ὅπλα παραδοῦναι, ἀλλὰ ἔχοντας καὶ μαχομένους ὡς ἐδύναντο ἀποθνήσκειν. [2] ἀπιστοῦντές τε μὴ εἶναι τοὺς παραδόντας τοῖς τεθνεῶσιν ὁμοίους, καί τινος ἐρομένου ποτὲ ὕστερον τῶν Ἀθηναίων ξυμμάχων δι᾽ ἀχθηδόνα ἕνα τῶν ἐκ τῆς νήσου αἰχμαλώτων εἰ οἱ τεθνεῶτες αὐτῶν καλοὶ κἀγαθοί, ἀπεκρίνατο αὐτῷ πολλοῦ ἂν ἄξιον εἶναι τὸν ἄτρακτον, λέγων τὸν οἰστόν, εἰ τοὺς ἀγαθοὺς διεγίγνωσκε, δήλωσιν ποιούμενος ὅτι ὁ ἐντυγχάνων τοῖς τε λίθοις καὶ τοξεύμασι διεφθείρετο.

Commentary Notes

Summary analysis of chapters 1–10

Book 4 starts with material about Sicily, continued from the end of Book 3.

Chapter 1

Events in and near Sicily: Messana defects from Athens, and the Locrians attack Rhegium.

In the spring of 425 BC, ships from Syracuse (the principal Sicilian city, friendly to Sparta) and its close associate Locri (in southern Italy) take Messana (near the north-eastern tip of Sicily), invited by its citizens; Messana revolts from Athens (to which it surrendered in Book 3). The Syracusans have feared the Athenians may use Messana as a base to attack them. Locri attacks its enemy Rhegium (on the toe of Italy opposite Messana, and allied to Athens) to prevent it intervening in Messana.

– Note how the Greek colony cities of Magna Graecia ('Great[er] Greece'), many of them wealthy, take sides in the Peloponnesian War (see Introduction). Ten years later, in 415, Athens will make an ill-fated attempt to conquer Sicily (described in Books 6 and 7). Thucydides constantly updates us about events in different places, maintaining the chronological framework of his narrative. This account of the western part of the Greek world resumes in Chapter 24.

Chapter 2

The Peloponnesians invade Attica. An Athenian fleets sails for Corcyra and Sicily, and a Peloponnesian one for Corcyra.

At about the same time, the Peloponnesians invade Attica (the territory of Athens) led by king Agis of Sparta, son of Archidamus, and ravage the land. The Athenians despatch to Sicily a fleet of forty ships, with the generals Eurymedon and Sophocles. They are instructed to stop en route at Corcyra (modern Corfu, off north-west Greece, allied to Athens), to support the pro-Athenian democrats there against continuing trouble from exiled anti-Athenian oligarchs (supported by Sparta) whom they had fought in the civil war analysed in detail in Book 3. Meanwhile the Peloponnesians send sixty ships to Corcyra to support the exiles. Demosthenes, not currently in office, accompanies the Athenian fleet, having at his own request obtained permission to make use of the ships as they round the Peloponnese.

– The Peloponnesians invaded Attica every year from 431 to 425, except 429. The preparation of the Athenian fleet was mentioned at the end of Book 3. Eurymedon and Sophocles are two of the ten annually elected *strategoi* ('generals', though in charge of both land and sea forces). Demosthenes at this point is probably a general-elect for the year starting summer 425. What Thucydides says about him is tantalizingly open-ended, but (as we shall see) he already has a cunning plan.

Chapter 3

Demosthenes advises the seizing and fortification of Pylos, to which the Athenian fleet has been forced to put in, but the generals refuse.

Learning during their voyage that the Peloponnesian fleet has already reached Corcyra, Eurymedon and Sophocles want to press on there. They object when Demosthenes asks them to put in at Pylos (on the south-west coast of the Peloponnese) and 'take some necessary action', but a storm forces them to do so anyway. Demosthenes urges them to fortify the place, saying this was why he joined the expedition: he points to the plentiful timber and stone, and the natural strength of the unguarded site. Eurymedon and Sophocles are unimpressed, sarcastically saying there are plenty of deserted promontories in the Peloponnese that he can occupy if he wants to waste public money. Demosthenes however is adamant that Pylos has unique advantages, with an adjacent harbour, and once occupied by Messenians (who speak the same dialect as the Spartans, and could do satisfactory damage if based there).

– Messenia, the south-west part of the Peloponnese, had been conquered by Sparta in the eighth and seventh centuries BC. After a rebellion, some Messenians had been settled at Naupactus on the Gulf of Corinth in the 450s, and were allies of Athens. Demosthenes envisages using some of these men: he had been at Naupactus the previous summer, and perhaps got the idea of fortifying Pylos from them. In any case, he has clearly done his homework.

Chapter 4

The bored Athenian troops on impulse start to build a fort.

The commanders are unpersuaded, but the weather remains unfit for sailing. Finally the unoccupied soldiers take matters into their own hands and begin to fortify the place. They work with a will despite lack of tools, fitting suitably-shaped stones together and carrying clay to bind them on their backs, their hands clasped behind them to prevent it slipping off. They hurry to finish work on the most vulnerable points before the Spartans can get there and oppose them, helped by the strong natural defences of the site which in many places has no need of a wall.

– Each trireme routinely carried ten hoplites, and often more as required, but 'soldiers' here presumably includes the oarsmen. The description of their working methods adds to the dramatic effect of this passage. Like much of Thucydides' account of the Pylos campaign, it stresses the element of lucky accident. Perhaps the role of Demosthenes was greater than the historian allows (though it apparently did not extend to the provision of stone-working tools).

Chapter 5

The Spartans are unconcerned by news of what is going on. Demosthenes is left with five ships at Pylos.

In fact the Spartans are celebrating a festival at the time. When they hear what is happening at Pylos they make little of it, thinking that when they do go there, the Athenians will put up no resistance or be easily taken by force. They are also constrained by the fact that their army is still in Attica. The Athenians fortify the mainland side and other vulnerable parts of the site in six days. They then leave Demosthenes with five ships to garrison it, and the rest of the fleet continues its voyage to Corcyra and Sicily.
– The pious Spartans no doubt had a full liturgical calendar, but 'celebrating a festival' becomes something of a standard excuse for inaction after famous examples during the campaigns of Marathon and Thermopylae in the Persian Wars (Herodotus 6.106 and 7.206). It has been observed that 'in Thucydides people who think that something can easily be done usually turn out to be mistaken' (Rhodes 1998).

Chapter 6

Agis on hearing the news marches his army back to Sparta.

When the Peloponnesians in Attica hear about the occupation of Pylos, they set out for home: Agis and his troops (in contrast to the authorities in Sparta) take it seriously and think they may be needed. Also, having invaded earlier than usual – with the corn not yet ripe – they are running short of food; and unusually wintry weather is afflicting the men. For a variety of reasons therefore they withdraw earlier than intended, after just fifteen days in Attica, making this their shortest invasion.
– Thus ends the last annual invasion of Attica: events at Pylos will change decisively this basic strategy of the Archidamian War (see Introduction).

Chapter 7

The Athenians take but fail to hold Eion in Thrace.

The Athenian general Simonides captures Eion in Thrace (in the north-east Aegean). It is hostile to Athens, but he has gathered some Athenian and allied troops from nearby, and the place is betrayed to him. Immediately, however, the Chalcidians and

Bottiaeans rally to the support of Eion, and Simonides is driven out with the loss of many men.

– Thucydides interrupts his main narrative to notice this minor event in its proper chronological place. There were two places called Eion in Thrace: this is not the well-known one at the mouth of the Strymon but another of uncertain location, though its defenders lived on or near the Chalcidice peninsula, so it was probably close by. Thucydides perhaps includes this minor incident to show the weak position of Athens in the area, preparing the ground for his account of Brasidas' campaign in Thrace later in Book 4.

Chapter 8

The Spartans march against Pylos, and summon their fleet from Corcyra. Demosthenes sends for help from the Athenian fleet. The Spartans plan to blockade Pylos, and they occupy the island of Sphacteria.

The Spartiates along with Perioeci who live nearby make for Pylos; the rest of the Spartans, just returned from Attica, follow more slowly. They also send round the Peloponnese for assistance, and recall their sixty ships from Corcyra: these are transported across the isthmus of Leucas (off the west coast of mainland Greece), undetected by the Athenian ships which are currently at Zacynthus (an island off the north-west Peloponnese). Demosthenes sends two ships to Zacynthus to alert Eurymedon's fleet, which sets off at speed for Pylos. Meanwhile the Spartans plan a land and sea attack on the fort, confident of victory as it has been hastily built and is thinly manned. They intend to block the harbour entrances before Athenian reinforcements arrive. The island of Sphacteria – long, uninhabited and wooded – making both entrances narrow, especially the one near Pylos and the fort. The Spartans plan to block them with ships packed close together and facing outwards. Fearing the island may become a base for Athenian operations, they ferry hoplites across to it and station others on the mainland: faced with hostile territory, the Athenians will have nowhere to land (the coast outside the bay being harbourless) and no base from which to support their men at Pylos. The Spartans hope to avoid a sea-battle and to take the place by siege, as it has no store of food. Acting on this plan, they send contingents of hoplites to Sphacteria in rotation; the last to cross – which will be caught there – numbers 420, plus attendant helots: their commander is Epitadas.

– Spartiates were full citizens of Sparta; Perioeci ('dwellers-around') lived in subject communities but ran their own affairs, often serving in the Spartan army. The 420 men would represent about a tenth of it. Helots were state-owned serfs, often used as attendants to hoplites. The fact that the Athenian fleet has got no further than Zacynthus may suggest it was waiting there deliberately, expecting a recall to Pylos (again implying the campaign may have been more fully planned than Thucydides allows). Demosthenes currently has with him at Pylos only the crews of three ships, i.e. about 600 men.

Commentators have been much occupied with the Spartan plan to block both harbour entrances. Beyond reasonable doubt, 'harbour' means the whole Bay of Navarino (attempts to make it refer only to a small inlet adjacent to Pylos create more problems than they solve), and the 'entrances' are the passages north and south of Sphacteria. There are two related problems about the wider southern one: what Thucydides says, and whether the passage is in fact impracticably wide. He describes the channel adjacent to Pylos (the narrower northern one, in fact about 100 m wide) as providing a 'passage of two ships' (i.e. room for two sailing side by side), then says that the one facing the mainland (the wider southern one, in fact about 1,200 m) is 'of eight or nine' – implying 'ships' again, which would clearly be a serious underestimate. Hence it is suggested that Thucydides does not know or has forgotten its real width, or even that he never went to Pylos at all. But this seems very unlikely, given his otherwise excellent knowledge of the topography. A better solution may be to assume that a word has dropped out, and that he actually wrote 'of eight or nine stades'. The stade was a somewhat variable unit of distance, but assuming he thinks of it as about 135 m, this would give an approximately correct result. A channel of 1,200 m could not be totally filled with the available Spartan ships drawn up as described (so there is at least a measure of exaggeration), but probably could still be effectively blocked with them in rather looser formation. All this said, the plan was not in fact carried out and 'we may wonder how reliably Thucydides was informed about this unfulfilled intention' (Rhodes 1998).

Chapter 9

Demosthenes makes impromptu arrangements to meet the Spartan attack.

Seeing the Spartans intending an attack by land and sea, Demosthenes makes his own preparations. He drags his three remaining triremes on shore below the fort and puts a stockade round them. Having nothing better available, he arms their crews with wicker shields taken from two Messenian boats which arrive, also bringing forty hoplites who are pressed into service. He stations most of both his poorly and fully armed men on the strong side of the fort facing the mainland, instructing them to repel any attack by land. Selecting sixty hoplites and a few archers, he goes down to the sea where he expects the enemy to land – a difficult and rocky stretch, but he thinks they will attempt it because the wall is weakest here (the Athenians not having expected to be at a naval disadvantage). He makes a speech to encourage his hoplites.

   – The arrival of these Messenians (from Naupactus) could be coincidental, but it is more likely that Demosthenes had been in communication with them and that they knew of his plan to occupy Pylos. He clearly had not expected the Spartan fleet from Corcyra to arrive before the Athenian one from Zacynthus.

Chapter 10

Demosthenes addresses his troops, encouraging them to offer firm resistance on the shore.

'You have joined me in facing this danger. Don't try to use your intelligence to weigh the odds stacked against us – just engage the enemy, hoping to win as you have before. At a critical point like this, there is no room for calculation and the danger is best met soonest. Actually most factors are in our favour, if we are not panicked by enemy numbers into throwing away our advantages. This is a hard place for a landing, a fact that will favour us if we stand firm. But if we give way, even this difficult ground will be open to their advance, and they will be the more formidable because it will not be easy for them to retreat. Our best chance of beating them is while they are still on their ships. We should not be too fearful of their numbers. The difficulty of landing will mean that only a few can fight at once – it's not like an army of superior size meeting us on land. Their difficulties in fighting from ships will counterbalance our lack of numbers. As Athenians, you have experience of naval landings. You know that an opponent who stands firm, not intimidated by crashing oars or ships bearing down on him, cannot be shifted. So stand firm, fight them here on the shore, and save us and this place.'

– For the use of speeches in Thucydides, see Introduction: they blend reporting and invention in varying proportions. Pre-battle addresses to troops, largely improvised, naturally contain conventional elements. Their practicability has been questioned, but Demosthenes here has a small audience in a relatively confined space. It has been observed that the enemy do, in fact, subsequently behave as he is here made to predict.

Notes on chapters 11–14

Chapter 11

The Spartans attack Pylos by land and sea. Brasidas shows great energy and courage.

11.1

τοσαῦτα: internal accusative with the following participle – 'so much', i.e. 'in these terms'.

τοῦ . . . παρακελευσαμένου: genitive absolute – 'when Demosthenes had . . .'.

ἐπικαταβάντες: aorist participle of ἐπικαταβαίνω – 'having gone down to face (the enemy)', -κατα- here indicating movement to the coast from a position inland.

ἐτάξαντο: aorist middle of τάσσω – 'they stationed themselves'.

παρ' αὐτὴν τὴν θάλασσαν: literally 'beside the sea itself', i.e. 'right by the sea'.

11.2

ἄραντες: aorist participle of αἴρω, used intransitively (of land and naval forces) in the sense 'get under way, set out, mobilize'.

τῷ . . . κατὰ γῆν στρατῷ: literally 'with the by-land army' (instrumental dative, and sandwiched preposition phrase), i.e. 'with their land army'.

προσέβαλλον: inceptive imperfect – 'they began to attack'. Verbs of attacking take the dative.

τῷ τειχίσματι: the fort built by the Athenians at Pylos, described in 4.2.

τεσσαράκοντα καὶ τρισί: literally 'forty and three' – compound numbers can be expressed either way round with καί, or big then small without. We learned in 8.2 that the Spartans sent sixty ships to Pylos. The rest were probably on the lookout for the Athenian ships.

ἐπέπλει: imperfect of ἐπιπλέω, 'sail/ be on board' as commander.

ὁ Κρατησικλέους: 'the (*understand* son) of Cratesicles' – the usual idiom for a patronymic (father's name, necessary to distinguish people with the same name, Greeks only having one).

Σπαρτιάτης: 'Spartiate' i.e. a Spartan with full citizen rights.

ᾗπερ: adverbial, 'exactly (-περ) where'.

11.3

ἀμφοτέρωθεν . . .: i.e. 'on both sides, on the land side and . . .'.

οἱ δέ . . .: i.e. the Spartans.

κατ' ὀλίγας ναῦς διελόμενοι: 'dividing (their force)' – διελόμενοι is aorist participle of διαιρέομαι (δια- often indicating separation) – 'into groups of a few ships' (κατά used distributively) i.e. 'into small detachments'.

οὐκ ἦν: here for οὐκ ἐξῆν – 'it was not possible'.

προσσχεῖν: aorist infinitive of προσέχω, here used intransitively –'put in, come to land'.

ἀναπαύοντες ἐν τῷ μέρει: literally 'causing them to rest . . .' – i.e. 'relieving them in (their) turn'.

τοὺς ἐπίπλους ἐποιοῦντο: literally 'kept making their sailings-against', i.e. 'mounted constant seaborne attacks'.

AS

προθυμίᾳ ... παρακελευσμῷ: χρώμενοι (literally 'using') goes with both dative nouns, but more natural English would be e.g. 'showing all their determination and giving every encouragement (to one another)' – understand πάντι from πάσῃ.

εἴ πως: with optative 'if somehow they could', 'in the hope of'.

ὠσάμενοι: aorist middle participle of ὠθέω (I push), in the middle 'force back, forcibly dislodge (the occupants)'.

ἕλοιεν: aorist optative of αἱρέω (I take).

11.4

Βρασίδας: this is the fourth time Brasidas (the most talented Spartan military leader of the time) has appeared in Thucydides' narrative. The rapid introduction here suits the context.

ὁρῶν: introducing indirect statement with accusative and participle, the regular construction after a verb of perception.

εἴ που καὶ δοκοίη δυνατόν: optative for past event of indefinite frequency – 'if at any point it actually did (καὶ) seem possible'.

σχεῖν: like προσσχεῖν at 11.3.

φυλασσομένους τῶν νεῶν μὴ ξυντρίψωσιν: literally 'being anxious about the ships in case they should smash them to pieces', μή with the subjunctive here hovering between negative purpose clause and construction after verb of fearing.

ἐβόα λέγων: near-tautology for emphasis – 'he shouted out and said'.

ὡς οὐκ εἰκὸς εἴη: 'that it was not reasonable' – ὡς (an alternative to the more common ὅτι) with an optative verb keeping the tense (here present) of the original speech is the usual construction for an indirect statement introduced by a verb of saying in historic sequence (i.e. taking place in the past); οὐκ εἰκός is an example of litotes (deliberate understatement), here sarcastic.

ξύλων φειδόμενους: 'sparing the timber(s)', a term often used of wooden ships, especially where their expendability is being stressed.

τοὺς πολεμίους ἐν τῇ χώρᾳ: juxtaposition emphasizes the shocking fact.

περιιδεῖν ... πεποιημένους: infinitive after εἰκός, the verb περιοράω (literally 'look round' in apparent unconcern) meaning 'overlook', 'be indifferent to'; the perfect middle participle πεποιημένους (having made for themselves) further stresses what the enemy should not be allowed to get away with.

βιαζομένους ... καταγνύναι: literally 'to break ... in forcing the landing', but verb and participle perhaps better reversed in English – 'to force the landing at the cost of breaking ...'.

τοὺς ξυμμάχους: Thucydides listed the allies who provided ships for the Spartans at 2.9.3 – Corinth, Megara, Sicyon, Pellene, Elis, Ambracia and Leucas (the first five in the Peloponnese and the last two in north-west Greece). Sparta itself was not a strong naval power at the start of the war, though efforts were soon made to rectify this.

ἀντὶ μεγάλων εὐεργεσιῶν: 'in return for their great benefits' – Sparta claimed to be the liberator of Greece (against Athenian imperial ambition), but it is not clear exactly what her allies did gain: 'presumably they were supposed to be grateful for the protection of the Spartan military machine, or for having Sparta prop up their oligarchic governments' (Hornblower 1996).

AS

τὰς ναῦς . . . ἐν τῷ παρόντι ἐπιδοῦναι: 'to make a present of their ships . . . in the present (critical) situation' – ἐπιδίδωμι and the associated noun ἐπίδοσις are especially used of free, voluntary gifts.

ὀκείλαντας: aorist particple of ὀκέλλω (I run [a ship] aground).

παντὶ τρόπῳ: as often, the singular of πᾶς here means 'any possible', 'any and every'.

Chapter 12

Brasidas is wounded and faints. The Athenians recover his shield and later use it for their victory trophy. The Spartans are unable to land because the terrain is difficult and the Athenians stand firm. Thucydides notes the ironies in Athenians defending Spartan land against a Spartan seaborne attack.

12.1

τοιαῦτα ἐπέσπερχε: 'kept spurring on in such terms' – the verb is found in Homer and tragedy, but nowhere else in prose, contributing to the portrayal of Brasidas as heroic (see Introduction); τοιαῦτα is another internal accusative (compare τοσαῦτα at 11.1).

τὸν ἑαυτοῦ κυβερνήτην ἀναγκάσας: matching his action to his words, Brasidas sets an example to the allies by making the steersman of his own ship run it aground.

ἀποβάθραν: 'landing ladder, gangway' – enabling a man to face the shore while descending from a ship.

ἀνεκόπη: aorist passive of ἀνακόπτω, 'was beaten back'.

τραυματισθεὶς πολλά: literally 'having been wounded (with respect to) many things' – accusative of respect, or internal accusative, i.e. 'having suffered many wounds'.

ἐλιποψύχησέ: 'he fainted', literally 'his soul (temporarily) left him' – a Homeric expression and idea.

παρεξειρεσίαν: 'outrigger', a structure built out from a trireme's side to accommodate the rowlocks of the uppermost row of oarsmen. This passage implies that Brasidas could fall into it without falling further, whereas his shield fell right through into the sea. The whole description (with a rare degree of detail about a trireme in action) was useful to the builders of the replica trireme *Olympias* in the 1980s.

περιερρύη: aorist passive of περιρρέω, used in active sense – 'slipped off (from around his arm)'. The shield had two handles, with the left arm passed through one and the left hand grasping the other.

ἐξενεχθείσης: aorist passive participle of ἐκφέρω (I carry out) – here from sea to land, so 'washed ashore'.

ἀνελόμενοι: aorist participle of ἀναιρέομαι (I pick up).

πρός: here 'for (the purpose of)'.

τροπαῖον: a 'trophy' in the original Greek sense, from τρέπω 'I turn (something)', was a (usually temporary) monument set up to claim a victory, marking the spot where the enemy was made to turn, i.e. routed. It typically consisted of a post fixed in the ground adorned with captured enemy armour and weapons, and a placard giving details. The American excavators of the Agora in Athens found a bronze shield (now displayed in the museum there) with a pierced inscription indicating that it was dedicated 'from the Spartans at Pylos' – it may possibly have formed part of the trophy on the battlefield before being taken back to Athens. By mentioning the trophy, Thucydides lets us know in advance the outcome of the battle.

ἔστησαν: transitive aorist of ἵστημι, 'they set up'.

12.2

προυθυμοῦντο: i.e. προ-εθυμοῦντο (unlike ἀπο-, προ- as a prefix retains the omicron, which with the augment produces the contraction -ου-): 'were determined', 'kept making a determined effort'.

χαλεπότητι καὶ ... ὑποχωρούντων: a dative of cause coupled with a causal genitive absolute.

12.3

ἐς τοῦτό τε περιέστη ἡ τύχη ὥστε: result clause, literally 'and fortune turned round to this point/extent, that ...', i.e. 'such was the turn of fortune that ...'; περιέστη is intransitive aorist of περιίστημι. Thus begins an elaborate sentence describing the paradoxical changes. By this means Thucydides underlines how the Pylos campaign broke the deadlock of the first few years of the war.

ἐκ γῆς καὶ ταύτης Λακωνικῆς: literally 'from land, and this Spartan' i.e. 'from land, and Spartan land at that'. The first paradox is that the Athenians, a sea power, are here fighting not only from land, but from land that belongs to the enemy.

ἀμύνεσθαι ἐκείνους ἐπιπλέοντας: correspondingly, 'they (the Athenians) were trying to resist those men (the Spartans) who were sailing against them' – the Spartans too are out of their usual comfort zone; the present infinitive ἀμύνεσθαι follows ὥστε in the result clause, but is translated like imperfect indicative (here 'were trying to ...').

ἐς τὴν ἑαυτῶν πολεμίαν οὖσαν: understand γῆν – the Spartans were trying to disembark on land which was their own but currently in enemy hands, and to oppose the Athenians there; the juxtaposition ἑαυτῶν πολεμίαν underlines the paradox.

ἐπὶ πολὺ γὰρ ἐποίει τῆς δόξης ...: in the rest of this long sentence, Thucydides explains the usual reputation of each side that makes the present events so surprising. The overall meaning is clear enough, but the grammar of this first bit is tricky. Literally something like 'it was making to a great extent of their reputation (for one side to be X, the other Y)' – i.e. 'it formed a great part of their respective reputations (that one side was X, the other Y)'.

ἐν τῷ τότε: understand χρόνῳ.

τοῖς μέν: i.e. the Spartans.

ἠπειρώταις ... καὶ τὰ πεζὰ κρατίστοις: 'landsmen ... and strongest in respect of their land-forces', i.e. enjoying military supremacy on land.

τοῖς δέ: i.e. the Athenians.

AS

Chapter 13

The Spartans attack Pylos for two days without success. They then break off and send for timber to construct siege-equipment, hoping to take the wall facing the harbour. The Athenian fleet arrives from Zacynthus and camps overnight at Prote. Next morning it launches a surprise attack on the Spartans.

13.1

ἡμέραν ... μέρος τι ... τῇ τρίτῃ: two accusatives for time how long contrasted with a dative for time when; τι is intensive, 'for a good part'.

ἐπέπαυντο: pluperfect, following aorist participle ποιησάμενοι – 'after making ... they had (now) stopped', suggesting abrupt cessation and preparing us for a new move on the part of the Spartans. (An alternative explanation is that, because the perfect πέπαυμαι can be used like a present, the pluperfect here has the sense as an imperfect, but this is perhaps less appropriate in the context.)

ἐπὶ ξύλα ἐς μηχανάς: 'to fetch timber for/to make machines' – ἐπί implies that a supply of timber was known to be in readiness, and ἐς (as often) suggests purpose. The 'machines' would be scaling-ladders (which could be constructed quickly), battering-rams and perhaps siege-towers (the wall was high) – but not catapults, which had not yet been invented (their first recorded use is in 399 BC).

παρέπεμψαν: παρα- suggests 'along (the coast)'.

Ἀσίνην: Asine is modern Korone, just round the tip of the western prong of the Peloponnese, facing eastwards into the Messenian Gulf (and not to be confused with the Mycenaean site of the same name near modern Tolon, or a third one in Laconia).

ἐλπίζοντες ...: the participle is used in two slightly different senses – 'thinking the wall ... to possess height (i.e. to be of considerable height), but (nonetheless) expecting to take it by means of ...'.

κατά: 'by' or 'facing'.

ἀποβάσεως ... οὔσης: genitive absolute – 'since a landing was most feasible (at this point)' – with the verb 'to be' again used for 'be possible' (compare οὐκ ἦν at 11.3).

13.2

ἐν τούτῳ: standard expression for 'meanwhile' (understanding τῷ χρόνῳ, but its emphatic position here is perhaps better caught by a translation such as 'it was at this point that ...'); the following δέ is postponed because the composite ἐν τούτῳ counts as one word.

ἐκ τῆς Ζακύνθου: Zacynthus is the most southerly of the Ionian Islands, off the west coast of Greece. It remained loyal to Athens throughout the war, and provided an important naval station en route to southern Italy and Sicily.

παραγίγνονται: historic present for vividness and emphasis.

τεσσαράκοντα: 'forty in number' – emphatic last word: these ships are going to make a difference. But the number (for which the Oxford text follows good manuscripts of Thucydides) is almost certainly wrong, and should be emended to πεντήκοντα (fifty): there were forty ships originally, on their way to Sicily (2.2), five were left with Demosthenes at Pylos (5.2), of which two were later sent on

AS

to join the others (8.3) – so thirty-seven; and we are about to be told that four from Chios and an unspecified number from Naxos had now joined them. Decisive corroboration comes from the fact that later (23.2), when twenty more triremes from Athens are added, the grand total is seventy. Numbers in manuscripts (often written using letters of the alphabet followed by an inverted comma as numerals, e.g. μ'= 40, ν'= 50) are particularly liable to corruption in the process of transmission.

προσεβοήθησαν: 'reinforced', with dative.

φρουρίδων: 'guard-ships' or 'patrol-ships' – from φρουρέω (I keep watch).

Ναυπάκτου: Naupactus is on the north shore of the Corinthian Gulf, facing the Peloponnese. An Athenian squadron was regularly based in this outpost.

Χῖαι: the large island of Chios, off the coast of modern Turkey, had special status among member states of the Athenian Empire. Only it, and Methymna on Lesbos, by this date continued to provide ships as tribute, others having switched to contributing money (which enabled Athens to exercise tighter control).

13.3

ὡς: temporal 'when'.

τε … τε … τε: 'both … and … and', the first two joining ἤπειρον and νῆσον, the third attaching the participle clause.

περίπλεων: 'very full of', 'packed with' (περι- intensifies), with genitive.

ἐκπλεούσας: 'making no move to sail out' – note that -εω verbs whose stem is a single syllable remain uncontracted except where epsilon is followed by another epsilon (producing ει).

ὅπη καθορμίσωνται: 'where they could come to anchor' – deliberative subjunctive.

τότε: 'at that time', implying 'for the time being' (i.e. in the current absence of any better option).

Πρωτήν: Prote is a small island close to the coast about nine miles north-west of Pylos.

ὡς ἐπὶ ναυμαχίαν: 'with a view to fighting a sea-battle'.

ἀνήγοντο: 'they put out to sea' – rather unexpectedly, ἀνα- commonly implies 'to sea' (and κατα- 'to land').

ἤν: (= ἐάν) 'in case', with subjunctive (the construction for the protasis of a future open condition).

ἀντεκπλεῖν: 'sail out (of harbour) against', with dative.

εὐρυχωρίαν: '(wide) open space', in this case 'open water'.

εἰ δὲ μή: the usual way of saying 'but if not', 'otherwise', even when an ἐάν/ ἤν clause has preceded.

ὡς αὐτοὶ ἐπεσπλευσούμενοι: 'with the intention of sailing into (the harbour) themselves to confront (them)' – ὡς with future participle expressing purpose (the future of πλέω and its compounds can be πλεύσομαι or πλευσέομαι).

13.4

οὔτε ἃ διενοήθησαν, φάρξαι τοὺς ἔσπλους, ἔτυχον ποιήσαντες: 'nor had they actually done (*literally* nor did they happen to have done) what they intended, (namely) to block the entrances' – φάρξαι (aorist infinitive of φράσσω) defines the implied antecedent of ἃ (those things which). This may have been because the

Spartans thought the Athenians had gone away completely, not just to nearby Prote. But, although blocking harbours with lines of ships placed tightly together was a frequent device, the Spartan plan referred to in 8.7 may be just a conjecture by Thucydides: see summary analysis of Chapter 8, on his apparent underestimate of the difficulty of blocking the southern entrance.

ὄντι οὐ σμικρῷ: the participle in this position is emphatic – 'which was in indeed not a small one' – another example of litotes, as this is in fact one of the largest natural harbours in Europe.

Chapter 14

The Athenians win a victory over the Peloponnesian fleet, but Spartan troops prevent the Athenians dragging off their beached triremes. The Spartan garrison on Sphacteria is cut off.

14.1
γνόντες: supply an object – 'realizing this'.

τὰς μὲν πλείους: answered by αἱ δὲ ... πληρούμεναι; πλείους is a common contracted form, actually of the nominative πλείονες, but used also for the accusative πλείονας as here.

μετεώρους: 'at sea', 'away from land' (though in the context here, still in the harbour) – two-termination adjective (no separate feminine), because it is a compound.

ἀντιπρῴρους: '(with prows) facing them', and therefore prepared to meet a charge – another two-termination compound.

κατέστησαν: transitive aorist of καθίστημι, 'I put into a certain state', here 'put' or 'turn' to flight.

ἐπιδιώκοντες: often used of hot pursuit, ἐπι- giving emphasis.

ὡς διὰ βραχέος: literally 'as across a short distance', probably implying 'as they naturally could given the short distance (between them and the enemy)', though it could alternatively mean 'as best they could, given the short distance (between the Spartans and the shore)'.

αὐτοῖς ἀνδράσιν: a common idiom, literally 'with the men themselves', i.e. 'men and all', 'complete with crew'.

ταῖς δὲ λοιπαῖς: i.e. those of the μετέωροι that had not been damaged or captured.

καταπεφευγυίαις: perfect participle, indicating that they had completed their flight to the shore.

ἐνέβαλλον: 'they rammed' with the beaks (ἔμβολοι) of their ships.

αἱ δὲ καὶ πληρούμεναι ἔτι: i.e. even before their crews were all on board. Given the following intervention of the Spartan land-forces, the ships mentioned here must have been stationed at or near the Spartan camp (probably close to the modern Gialova): see Map 2.

ἀναδούμενοι ... εἷλκον: the present participle (of ἀναδέομαι, literally 'I tie to myself') implies that the fastening of ropes and towing went on simultaneously, one ship being made fast while another was towed; note the form of the augment in the imperfect εἷλκον (like εἶχον from ἔχω, instead of the more usual eta).

ὡρμημένων: perfect passive participle – 'after the men had been put to flight'.

AS

14.2

ἅ: connecting relative, equivalent to ταῦτα δέ.

περιαλγοῦντες: 'greatly distressed' – the prefix περι- is intensive.

ὅτιπερ: 'because in fact'.

αὐτῶν: emphatic position – 'it was their own men who . . .'.

ἀπελαμβάνοντο: imperfect – 'were in the process of (*or* in danger of) being cut off'.

παρεβοήθουν: 'came to the rescue', the prefix παρα- conveying the notion of active personal support.

ἐπεσβαίνοντες: ἐπ(ι)- implies 'to meet the enemy'.

ξὺν τοῖς ὅπλοις: 'in full armour' – ξύν (= σύν) is often used of what you wear or carry.

ἀνθεῖλκον: 'tried to drag them back' to the safety of the shore.

ἐν τούτῳ . . . κεκωλῦσθαι: perfect infinitive passive – 'each man thought (things) had been hindered (*or* brought to a halt) at this point . . .'.

ᾧ μὴ . . . παρῆν: literally 'at which he himself as well was not present in deed', i.e. 'wherever he was not personally part of the action'.

14.3

τε: connective.

ἀντηλλαγμένου: perfect participle passive of ἀνταλλάσσω (I exchange) – 'the method (of fighting) having in actual fact (καί) been interchanged', i.e. 'the tactics typical of the respective sides in connection with the ships actually being reversed'. Thus Thucydides introduces another paradoxical variation on the recurrent equation of Spartans and land-fighting, Athenians and sea-fighting.

τε . . . τε: giving both sides of the picture – translate e.g. 'the Spartans . . ., whilst the Athenians . . .'.

ὑπὸ προθυμίας καὶ ἐκπλήξεως: i.e. driven by determination to repulse the invading force and by their state of shock what had happened.

ὡς εἰπεῖν: 'so to speak' – a common idiom to soften or justify an excessively bold statement, implying 'it was virtually the case that . . .'.

οὐδὲν ἄλλο ἢ ἐκ γῆς ἐναυμάχουν: 'were doing nothing other than fighting a naval battle from the land'.

ὡς ἐπὶ πλεῖστον: 'to the greatest extent possible' (ὡς with superlative, as in the common expression ὡς τάχιστα 'as quickly as possible').

ἐπεξελθεῖν: literally 'go out in pursuit of', i.e. 'follow up' (with the dative).

ἀπὸ νεῶν ἐπεζομάχουν: 'were fighting an infantry battle from the ships', balancing ἐκ γῆς ἐναυμάχουν. The paradox in this case has been that each side was operating on its favoured element, but using fighting methods characteristic of the other.

14.4

τε: summing up – 'and so'.

τραυματίσαντες: 'having inflicted (numerous) casualties', understanding πολλά from the preceding πολύν.

διεκρίθησαν: 'they separated' – aorist passive in active sense.

ληφθεισῶν: aorist passive participle of λαμβάνω, presumably referring to the ships mentioned in 14.1.

AS

14.5

καταστάντες: intransitive aorist participle of καθίστημι – 'having settled themselves down' now that operations had been suspended. We were earlier told (8.8) that it would be difficult for the Athenians to find a base from which to operate, but Thucydides has not said what sort of camp they actually established, nor where it was – some commentators draw attention to this as a loose end in his unrevised narrative.

οἱ μέν . . .: i.e. the Athenians.

τροπαῖον . . . ἔστησαν: see notes on 12.1.

ἀπέδοσαν: 'gave back as was due', 'duly handed over' – giving back the corpses of the enemy dead was the expected norm in ancient warfare.

ἐκράτησαν: aorist – 'got control of', with the genitive.

περιέπλεον: imperfect – 'proceeded to sail round'. Thus begins the Athenian patrol of Sphacteria.

ὡς: with participle – 'since', 'on the grounds that'.

ἀπειλημμένων: perfect passive participle of ἀπολαμβάνω.

οἱ δ' ἐν τῇ ἠπείρῳ Πελοποννήσιοι: the δέ clause (compare οἱ μέν above) becomes more explicit, to distinguish the main body of the Peloponnesians on the mainland from the few cut off on the island.

ἀπὸ πάντων: 'from every quarter'.

βεβοηθηκότες: perfect participle – 'having arrived in support'. These are the allies summoned in 8.2, four days previously; they would have arrived after the attack on Demosthenes.

κατὰ χώραν: a common expression for 'in position'.

ἐπὶ τῇ Πύλῳ: ἐπὶ implies 'over against', with a sense of menace.

AS

Summary analysis of chapters 15–20

Chapter 15

The Spartan authorities are alarmed. They come to Pylos and quickly make a truce.

When news of what has happened in Pylos reaches Sparta, it is regarded as a major disaster. The Spartans decide that the authorities should go down to the camp, see for themselves, and decide what to do. Having duly seen the impossibility of rescuing their men, and wanting to prevent them dying of starvation or being captured by force of numbers, the authorities decide to try for a truce with the Athenian generals at Pylos, meanwhile sending envoys to Athens to discuss a settlement and to try to get the men back as quickly as possible.

– 'The authorities' (τὰ τέλη, a term regularly used of Sparta) probably refers to the five *ephors* ('overseers'), annually elected chief magistrates, perhaps accompanied by at least some members of the *gerousia* ('council of elders'), made up of the two kings (Sparta had parallel royal families) and twenty-eight elected men over sixty. It has been suggested that, because the Spartans have not, in fact, been overwhelmingly defeated, their behaviour here suggests there was a body of opinion already looking for an opportunity to end the war.

Conversely it is observed that the soldiers on the island probably represented at least a tenth of the Spartan army, and that manpower was beginning to be a source of anxiety (it became a major problem in the following years).

Chapter 16

Thucydides lists the terms of the truce. A Spartan embassy is sent to Athens.

The Athenian generals accept this proposal and a truce is made: the Spartans will bring to Pylos and hand over the ships in which they have fought and all other warships in Laconia; they will not take up arms against the fortification by land or sea. The Athenians will allow the Spartans on the mainland to send to the men on the island kneaded grain, barley-flour, wine and meat, in fixed quantities for each man (half-measures for an attendant): the Athenians will oversee this, and no boat will sail in secretly. The Athenians will keep watch on the island but not land on it; and they will not take up arms against the Peloponnesian force by land or sea. If either side breaks the agreement, the truce will be at an end. The truce will last until the Spartan envoys return from Athens: the Athenians will take and bring them back in a trireme. When they return and the truce ends, the Athenians will return the ships in the same state as they received them. So the truce is made; about sixty ships are handed over; the envoys are dispatched, and on arriving in Athens speak as follows (i.e. in Chapter 17).

– The wording of the truce has every appearance of authenticity. The agreement to hand over all warships in Laconia (rather than just those at Pylos) is perhaps more than might have been expected. The food allowances seem quite generous.

Chapter 17

The Spartan ambassadors begin their speech. They ask for an end to the war consistent with Athenian interests and Spartan dignity in misfortune.

'Athenians, the Spartans have sent us to negotiate for our men on the island, hoping for an outcome both advantageous to you and honourable for us in our unfortunate situation. If we speak at some length, we are not going against our usual custom. We Spartans don't use many words when a few will do, but we do use more when it is necessary to explain considerations conducive to a desired result. Don't take what we say as aggressive, or a lecture, but as a reminder of good policy to people who know about it already. You have the opportunity to make good use of your present success, and to avoid the common error of those unused to handling good fortune – one unexpected success makes them reach out in hope of more. Those who have experienced reversals in both directions are least confident in their successes – and that applies both to your city and to us.'

– The Spartans were famous for their pithy ('laconic') utterance, but this will indeed be quite a long speech. The tone is reasonable. The warning about the dangers of hubristic excess is appropriate on the lips of religious Spartans.

Chapter 18

The envoys attribute Sparta's current troubles to errors of judgement, not loss of power, and urge the Athenians to use their success prudently and moderately.

'Bear this in mind in looking at our present misfortunes. We who have the greatest reputation among the Greeks have now come to you asking for what we previously thought we had power to grant to others. This is not because of a loss of military strength (nor indeed a gain making us over-confident) but because of an error of judgement, which anyone can make. So do not let the present power of your city make you think fortune will always be with you. Wise men assume an uncertain future, and recognize that war follows wherever their fortunes lead. Such men are least likely to stumble because of success, and most likely to come to an agreement in a time of good fortune. That, Athenians, is what you should do with us, so that – if we can't persuade you and you then fail – you will not afterwards be thought to have obtained your present success by luck, when you could leave to posterity a reputation for strength and intelligence.'

– The Spartan envoys here emphasize the mutability of fortune (a prominent theme in Herodotus, tragic drama and Greek literature generally): the usually dominant Spartans themselves are now asking for an end to the war, and urge the Athenians to agree to it because they cannot assume their own present success will continue.

Chapter 19

The envoys offer peace and alliance, pointing out that a lasting settlement must arise through generosity, not through harsh terms which provoke a desire for revenge.

'The Spartans invite you to a treaty to end the war. They offer peace, alliance and good relations. In return they ask for their men on the island. It is better for both sides to avoid the dangers of them forcing an escape or being blockaded into submission. Lasting settlements of major enmities are best achieved not when one side uses his advantage to enforce restrictive oaths and unequal terms but when he makes a generous and reasonable settlement. The other party is then inclined not to resist, but to repay generosity, honour-bound to abide by the terms agreed. Such are the settlements men reserve for their more serious enemies. And it is human nature to make counter-concessions to those who give way willingly, but to carry on taking risks in defiance of one's better judgement against those who are excessively arrogant.'

– It is notable that the Spartans under pressure leave out of account the allies with whom they embarked upon the war. They mention a forced escape from the island, yet they are negotiating precisely because they consider this impossible. The high-sounding appeal to reasonableness in fact exposes the Spartans' weak point: they have nothing specific to offer in exchange for the return of their men.

Chapter 20

The Spartan envoys conclude their speech by saying Athens will gain credit by making a lasting peace, and no Greek power will be able to challenge the combined strength of Athens and Sparta.

'Now is the time for reconciliation, in both of our interests, before something irremediable comes between us and creates undying enmity. While matters are undecided, and you can gain reputation and our friendship, let us be reconciled. Let us choose peace instead of war, and give the other Greeks a respite from their misfortunes. They have been caught up in a war without knowing which side started it. If you exercise your power to end it, you will have their gratitude. You will become friends of the Spartans at their invitation, and you will be granting it as a favour. And think of the advantages: if we and you speak as one, the rest of Greece will be weaker and will give us the greatest honour.'

– The reference to 'something irremediable' euphemistically expresses the fear that the Spartans on Sphacteria may be killed. Formally the war was begun by the Peloponnesians, through the Theban attack on Plataea and the first invasion of Attica (described in Book 2), but before that each side had accused the other of breaking the Thirty Years' Peace of 446 BC (see Introduction).

Notes on chapters 21–23

Chapter 21

Spartan confidence that the Athenians would welcome peace is found to be misplaced. Swayed by Cleon, they refuse Sparta's offer of peace and alliance, and instead 'reach out for more'.

21.1

τοσαῦτα: literally 'so many things' or 'all these things' – here perhaps pointedly used to underline the length at which the Spartans have just spoken.

ἐν τῷ πρὶν χρόνῳ: in 430 BC, after the plague and the second invasion of Attica, the Athenians were keen to come to terms and sent envoys to Sparta, but their overtures were rejected (2.59.2).

ἐπιθυμεῖν . . . κωλύεσθαι: present infinitives here standing for imperfect tenses in the original thought ('the Athenians desired . . . but were prevented'). English needs pluperfects here: 'had desired . . . but had been prevented'.

σφῶν . . . ἐναντιουμένων . . ., διδομένης . . . εἰρήνης: genitive absolutes, the second with conditional force – 'when they themselves opposed it . . . but if peace were offered'.

21.2

οἱ δέ: i.e. the Athenians.

ἔχοντες: causal, 'since they held' – this crucial advantage puts the Athenians in a very strong position.

ἤδη: 'at once'.

ἑτοίμους: 'ready (to make it)', agreeing with 'the Spartans' (supplied); but it has been suggested that this manuscript reading is incorrect and Thucydides may actually have written ἑτοίμας (agreeing with σπονδάς and meaning 'available').

ὁπόταν βούλωνται: 'whenever they wanted' – indefinite clause in primary sequence (here referring to the future).

τοῦ δὲ πλέονος ὠρέγοντο: 'they were reaching out for more' – a recurrent theme in Thucydides' presentation of imperialist Athens, foreshadowing much that is to come (ὀρέγομαι takes the genitive, like other verbs expressing the notion of grasping). In this context the judgement is 'too sweeping and severe' (Hornblower 1996) because – as we shall see – opinions in Athens were in fact sharply divided (a fragment of the lost historian Philochorus seems to indicate that one vote had to be taken three times).

21.3

μάλιστα: emphatic first word, leading into description of the central actor in this drama.

ἐνῆγε: imperfect of ἐνάγω – 'was egging them on'.

Κλέων ὁ Κλεαινέτου: 'Cleon son of Cleaenetus' (see note on 11.2 for use of the patronymic).

This sentence introduces Cleon as if for the first time, though in fact he played an important role in Book 3 (see Introduction) and was introduced in similar terms

AS

there (3.36.6) – but this is probably a deliberate dramatic device (rather than, as some commentators have thought, a sign of incomplete revision by Thucydides of drafts written in the 'wrong' order).

ἀνὴρ δημαγωγός: 'a man who was a people-leader' – δημαγωγός, in origin a neutral descriptive word, came to be applied specifically to a group of politicians active in Athens after the death of Pericles (see 2.65.10), and in a derogatory sense ('rabble-rouser', like its modern derivative 'demagogue'). It is used only here by Thucydides, and it is hard to tell how negative it is – though the historian is certainly not a fan of Cleon (see Introduction).

κατ' ἐκεῖνον τὸν χρόνον: 'at that time' – Cleon took a dominant role in Athenian politics from about 429 until his death in 422 BC, but Thucydides may intend a more specific reference to his recovery of popularity after being on the losing side in the debate over the rebellion of Mytilene in 428, described in Book 3 (see Introduction).

τῷ πλήθει πιθανώτατος: 'most influential with the crowd' – a characteristic which (at least in the eyes of conservative critics) gave rise to the charge of rabble-rousing.

χρή: present tense of the original declaration, as usual in indirect statement introduced by ὅτι/ὡς.

ἐλθόντων: understand 'the men on the island' again as subject of the genitive absolute.

Νίσαιαν καὶ Πηγὰς καὶ Τροιζῆνα καὶ Ἀχαίαν: all these places had been surrendered by Athens to Sparta under the Thirty Years Peace of 446 BC, as described at 1.115.1 (see Introduction). Nisaea and Pegae were respectively the eastern and western ports of Megara, the city state between Athens and Corinth (so this is effectively a demand for the whole of Megara); Troezen and Achaea are in the northern Peloponnese. (The language of surrender and restoration is not strictly applicable to Achaea, an independent state: in this case what was sought was presumably just the renewal of an earlier alliance.) Cleon's demands are meant to sound excessive. Lists typically insert καί between each item and the next, or not at all.

ἀπὸ τῆς προτέρας ξυμβάσεως: 'as a result of the previous settlement', i.e. the Thirty Years Peace.

κατὰ ξυμφοράς: literally 'in line with disasters', i.e. 'in a time of setbacks' – Athens had lost Boeotia (an important region of central Greece) after the battle of Coronea in 447 BC; Euboea (the big island north of Attica) and Megara had soon afterwards revolted, and a Peloponnesian army invaded Attica (1.113–14).

τι μᾶλλον: τι is intensive – 'somewhat more', i.e. 'considerably more' (probably implying 'than the Spartans did').

ὁπόσον ἂν δοκῇ χρόνον: another indefinite clause in primary sequence.

Chapter 22

Cleon attacks a Spartan proposal to confer in private with Athenian commissioners. Negotiations are broken off and the Spartan envoys return home.

22.1

οἱ δέ: i.e. the Spartans.

ξυνέδρους: literally 'people sitting with/together' to discuss an issue, i.e. 'men to confer', 'commissioners' for carrying on negotiations.

σφίσιν: dative after ξυν-, 'to confer with themselves'.

ἐκέλευον: as often with this verb, the object (here 'the Athenians') has to be supplied.

ἑλέσθαι: aorist middle infinitive of αἱρέω – 'to appoint'.

οἵτινες ... ξυμβήσονται: relative pronoun ὅστις with future indicative (here of ξυμβαίνω) to express purpose – 'who ... could make an agreement'.

κατὰ ἡσυχίαν: 'at leisure', implying also 'in a calm atmosphere', i.e. away from the clamour of a crowded gathering.

ὅτι ἂν πείθωσιν ἀλλήλους: another indefinite clause – literally 'as to whatever (neuter of ὅστις) they might persuade each other (to agree)', i.e. 'on whatever terms ...'.

22.2

ἐνταῦθα δή: 'then indeed', 'at this point' (δή as usual giving emphasis) – Cleon chose this particular moment to intervene directly.

πολὺς ἐνέκειτο: πολύς is predicative – 'pressed on vigorously', a metaphor from troops pressing upon a retreating enemy

λέγων γιγνώσκειν ...: 'saying that he knew' – λέγω here followed by an infinitive (present representing imperfect 'I knew' in the original direct speech) instead of the more usual ὅτι clause; γιγνώσκειν as a verb of perception introduces another indirect statement using the participle construction (ἔχοντας ... αὐτούς).

καὶ νῦν: balancing the preceding καὶ πρότερον – 'even before ... and now'.

οἵτινες: here with a causal sense – 'because they were people who ...'.

τῷ μὲν πλήθει: i.e. the democratic Assembly, open to all adult male Athenian citizens – Cleon's own natural sphere.

ὀλίγοις δὲ ἀνδράσι: this in contrast is made to sound like an oligarchic conspiracy, a conference behind closed doors – Cleon plays on the democratic sympathies of his audience.

ὑγιές: literally 'healthy', i.e. 'sound' or 'honest'.

22.3

ὁρῶντες: introducing (within a long and complex sentence) two participles making negative indirect statements, οὔτε ... οἷόν τε ὄν and οὔτε ... ποιήσοντας.

οὔτε ... οἷόν τε ὄν: here logically 'impracticable' rather than 'impossible'.

εἴ τι ... ξυγχωρεῖν: 'even if it did appear advisable to them to make some concession in the face of the disaster'.

μή: with subjunctive, 'for fear that'.

διαβληθῶσιν: aorist passive of διαβάλλω – 'they might get a bad reputation'.

ἐς: here 'with' or 'among'.

εἰπόντες καὶ οὐ τυχόντες: 'for having made proposals and failed' (literally 'not hit the mark').

ἐπὶ μετρίοις: 'on (the) moderate terms'.

ἄπρακτοι: emphatic last word – 'without achieving anything'.

AS

Chapter 23

At Pylos the truce ends and war resumes. The Athenians refuse to return the Peloponnesian ships, and they reinforce the blockade of Sphacteria.

23.1

ἀφικομένων δὲ αὐτῶν: i.e. when the Spartan envoys arrived home from Athens, after an absence of about twenty days.

διελέλυντο: pluperfect passive, but translate 'was terminated' – according to the terms of the truce in 16.2, it was automatically at an end with the return of the envoys.

ξυνέκειτο: impersonal – 'it had been agreed' (the present of ξύγκειμαι is translated as a perfect tense, so the imperfect as a pluperfect).

ἐγκλήματα ἔχοντες: 'having as grounds of complaint (against them)' – the following accusatives (ἐπιδρομήν … and ἄλλα …) are in apposition to ἐγκλήματα.

ἐπιδρομήν: literally 'running-against' i.e. 'raid on' (with dative, as taken by the underlying verb ἐπιτρέχω).

παράσπονδον: 'in breach of the truce' – another two-termination compound adjective.

οὐκ ἀξιόλογα δοκοῦντα εἶναι: 'which did not seem worth mentioning' – in the judgement of the Spartans, and perhaps also that of Thucydides, who is critical of Athenian policy under Cleon's leadership.

οὐκ ἀπεδίδοσαν: imperfect matching the preceding ἀπῄτουν – 'would not …' (i.e. in response to repeated demands).

δή: 'actually', 'of course' – the point was beyond dispute.

εἴρητο: pluperfect passive – 'it had been stated'.

ἐάν …: future open condition, retained from what was said at the time.

ὁτιοῦν: nominative, with καί reinforcing – 'any (condition) whatever'.

παραβαθῇ: aorist passive subjunctive of παραβαίνω.

ἀδίκημα … νεῶν: 'having protested against their retention of the ships (*literally* the affair of the ships) as an act of injustice'.

καθίσταντο: 'applied themselves'.

23.2

τὰ περὶ Πύλον … ἐπολεμεῖτο: 'the war at Pylos was carried on' (neuter plural subject, singular verb).

κατὰ κράτος: 'with all their might'.

Ἀθηναῖοι μὲν … Πελοποννήσιοι δέ: this long sentence has two nominative participle clauses in loose apposition (rather than the expected genitive absolutes), as though 'both sides' had been the subject at the start.

δυοῖν νεοῖν ἐναντίαιν: duals, and instrumental dative – 'with two ships (cruising) in opposite directions'. These would not, in fact, have been enough for an effective blockade – the Athenians must either have had other ships stationed near likely escape-routes, or have been absolutely confident that the Spartans had decided to make the best of a bad job.

αἰεί: 'constantly', 'permanently'.

τῆς ἡμέρας . . . τῆς δὲ νυκτός: genitives for time within which.

καὶ ἅπασαι: 'all without exception'.

περιώρμουν: 'anchored around' the island, forming a cordon.

τὰ πρὸς τὸ πέλαγος: accusative of respect – 'on the side facing the open sea'.

ὁπότε ἄνεμος εἴη: 'when there was a wind' – optative for indefinite clause in historic sequence.

αὐτοῖς: 'for them', 'to assist them'.

ἐς: 'for the purposes of'.

ἑβδομήκοντα: see note on 13.2 on the total number of ships.

σκοποῦντες καιρὸν εἴ τις παραπέσοι: literally 'looking for an opportunity if any should arise', i.e. 'looking to see if any opportunity should arise' – as often, the subject of an indirect question is expressed in advance as the object of the introductory verb, like the biblical 'I know thee who thou art' (Mark 1: 24).

ὥστε τοὺς ἄνδρας σῶσαι: 'to save the men' – strictly the construction for a likely result, with the infinitive explaining καιρὸν, but in effect equivalent to a purpose clause.

Summary analysis of chapters 24 and 25

Chapter 24

Events in and near Sicily. The Syracusans reinforce their fleet at Messana. They and the Locrians prepare to attack the Athenians by sea at Rhegium, to gain control of the strait between the two cities.

Meanwhile in Sicily the Syracusans and their allies bring the rest of the ships they have been preparing to join the ones on guard at Messana. The main instigators are the Locrians, who have invaded the territory of Rhegium. They want a naval engagement, seeing the Athenians have few ships there, and having heard that most of the fleet destined for Sicily is occupied in the blockade of Sphacteria. They are confident of blockading and subduing Rhegium. They will then be in a strong position, as the Athenians will be unable to lie off Rhegium and command the narrow strait between it and Messana. This strait is the so-called Charybdis, through which Odysseus is said to have sailed. Its narrowness and the currents caused by inflowing waters from two great seas explain its dangerous reputation.

– Thucydides interrupts the account of the Pylos campaign to update us on events in Sicily, resuming from Chapter 1 (see summary analysis). He refers to 'Sicily', though city states in south-west Italy are also involved. The Locrian invasion of Rhegium mentioned here is a second one (i.e. subsequent to that described in Chapter 1). The reference to the Athenian fleet being occupied in the blockade of Sphacteria illustrates how the two threads of narrative are intertwined. Thucydides makes several references to Homer, broadly accepting the historicity of the events described in the epics. His purpose here may be to enliven a slightly dull chapter.

Chapter 25

Inconclusive fighting by land and sea between Athenians, Naxians, Rhegians, Sicels and Leontines on one side, and Syracusans, Locrians and Messanans on the other.

In this space the Syracusans and their allies are forced to fight a battle to defend a boat attempting the crossing, and put out against a smaller force of Athenian and Rhegian ships. They are defeated by the Athenians and retreat with the loss of one ship. Later the Locrians withdraw from Rhegian territory. The Syracusan and allied ships gather at Peloris in the territory of Messana, and are joined by their infantry. The Athenians and Rhegians sail up and attack the empty ships; they themselves lose one. Afterwards the Syracusans embark and sail towards Messana. The Athenians move to attack, but the Syracusans attack first and lose another ship. The victorious Syracusans reach Messana.

With news arriving that Camarina (on the south coast of Sicily) is being betrayed to the Syracusans by Archias and his party, the Athenians sail there.

Meanwhile the Messanans launch a land and sea campaign against nearby Naxos. They force the Naxians inside and ravage the land, later approaching also with ships up the river Acesines. Large numbers of Sicels arrive to help resist the Messanans;

the Naxians take heart, make a sudden sally and rout the Naxians, killing over a thousand. The survivors struggle to return home.

The people of Leontini (north of Syracuse) with the Athenians and other allies begin a campaign against Messana, thinking it crippled. The Athenians plan to invade the harbour while land-forces move against the city. But the Messanans and a contingent of Locrians make a sudden sally, rout most of them, and kill a good number. Seeing this, the Athenians land from their ships to support the Leontines; they catch the Messanans and chase them back into the city. They set up a trophy and withdraw to Rhegium. Subsequently the Greeks in Sicily campaign against each other by land without Athenian involvement.

– As in Chapter 1, the Sicilian cities in these incidents fight according to their Athenian or Peloponnesian allegiance. The people of Leontini had invited the Athenians to Sicily in the first place. The Athenian forces from Pylos will finally arrive in Sicily and join in campaigning (Chapter 48), though major involvement lies further ahead, with the Sicilian Expedition described in Books 6–7.

Notes on chapters 26–28

Chapter 26

At Pylos, the blockading Athenians face various difficulties. The Spartans on Sphacteria are able to hold out because helots risk their lives to bring them food.

26.1

ἐν δὲ τῇ Πύλῳ ἔτι . . .: 'In Pylos still . . .' – resuming the story after the preceding chapters dealing with events in Sicily and southern Italy.

κατὰ χώραν: 'in position', as at 14.5.

26.2

ἐπίπονος: 'burdensome' – another two-termination compound adjective.

ἀπορίᾳ: 'through shortage' – causal dative.

ὅτι μή: a common way of saying 'except' when a negative has preceded.

καὶ αὕτη οὐ μεγάλη: 'and this not a big one', i.e. 'and only a small one at that'.

διαμώμενοι τὸν κάχληκα: 'scraping away the shingle'.

ἐπὶ τῇ θαλάσσῃ: 'by the sea'.

οἷον εἰκός: literally 'of the sort likely', i.e. 'of the sort you would expect to find there', so close to the salty sea.

26.3

στενοχωρία . . .: literally 'there was proving to be a narrowness of space for them encamped in a small area', i.e. 'they found themselves cramped for space, as they were . . .'.

τῶν νεῶν . . . ὅρμον: genitive absolute with causal sense.

αἱ μέν . . .: 'some . . .' – grammatically 'ships', but (by a common idiom) actually meaning their crews.

ᾑροῦντο: the middle of αἱρέω here in the sense 'take (for oneself)' – 'took their . . .'.

μετέωροι: 'out at sea', as in 14.1.

26.4

ὁ χρόνος . . . ἐπιγιγνόμενος: i.e. 'the fact that the time (taken up with these operations) was running on'.

παρὰ λόγον: 'contrary to expectation'.

οὕς: relative (without antecedent) in causal sense, equivalent to ἐπεὶ . . . αὐτούς, referring to the Spartans on the island.

ἡμερῶν ὀλίγων: 'within a few days'.

ἐκπολιορκήσειν: future infinitive – 'take by siege', 'blockade successfully'. The prefix ἐκ- often means 'through to a successful conclusion', comparable to 'work out (a problem)' in English.

ἐν νήσῳ: understand ὄντας.

ἁλμυρῷ: 'salty', 'brackish'.

AS

26.5

αἴτιον δὲ ἦν οἱ Λακεδαιμόνιοι προειπόντες: literally 'the reason was the Spartans having given notice' i.e. 'the reason for this was the fact that the Spartans had given notice' (that X should/could do Y).

τὸν βουλόμενον: literally 'the person wishing', the article used generically for 'anybody who wished to'.

ἀληλεμένον: perfect passive participle of ἀλέω, with σῖτον -'ground corn', 'milled grain'.

εἴ τι ἄλλο βρῶμα: literally 'if (there was) any other food', i.e. 'any other item of food'.

οἷ' ἂν ἐς πολιορκίαν ξυμφέρῃ: another indefinite clause – 'of a sort useful for a siege'.

τάξαντες ἀργυρίου πολλοῦ: genitive of price – 'assessing (the service) at a large sum of money', i.e. 'fixing a high price' for successful completion.

τῶν Εἱλώτων τῷ ἐσαγαγόντι: 'to any of the helots who took it in' (for the participle phrase, compare τὸν βουλόμενον above). Helots – literally 'captives' (compare εἷλον) – were the state-owned serfs of Sparta, descended from the original inhabitants of the southern Peloponnese. The Spartans used them on a large scale in the army, especially in and after the Peloponnesian War.

ἐλευθερίαν ὑπισχνούμενοι: 'promising freedom'. As we are about to learn that some did succeed, presumably (if the Spartans kept their promise) they were subsequently freed. It is not known how commonly this was done.

26.6

ἐσῆγον ἄλλοι ... καὶ μάλιστα ...: literally 'others did bring it in, running risks, and especially the helots', i.e. 'people did run risks and get the food in, the helots above all' (Greek typically says 'others and especially X' – putting the emphasized item at the end – where we would say 'X and others').

ἀπαίροντες: intransitive – 'setting out'.

ὁπόθεν τύχοιεν: another indefinite clause with optative in historic sequence, literally 'from wherever they happened (to do so)', i.e. 'from wherever they were in the Peloponnese'.

καταπλέοντες: 'sailing in', 'sailing to land'.

ἔτι νυκτός: 'while it was still night'.

τὰ πρὸς τὸ πέλαγος τῆς νήσου: 'the seaward side of the island'.

26.7

ἐτήρουν ... καταφέρεσθαι: 'they kept a lookout (so as) to be carried to shore'.

ῥᾷον: comparative adverb – 'more easily'.

ὁπότε ... εἴη: again an indefinite clause with optative in historic sequence.

ἐγίγνετο: imperfect (like the preceding ἐλάνθανον) for repeated action, in line with the optative for indefinite frequency.

τοῖς δὲ ... καθειστήκει: literally 'whereas for *them* (i.e. the helots and other Spartan volunteers) the sailing-to-shore had become unsparing' i.e. 'whereas *they* had established the practice of running ashore without regard for the consequences'; καθειστήκει is intransitive pluperfect of καθίστημι.

ἐπώκελλον ... χρημάτων: 'for they were running ashore their boats, which had been valued at a price', i.e. '... had had a value put on them', so their owners

AS

could claim compensation; τετιμημένα is perfect passive participle of τιμάω, here in the sense 'I value'.

κατάρσεις: 'landing-places'.

ἐφύλασσον: 'were on guard', i.e. to recover supplies from wrecked vessels if necessary.

ὅσοι: 'all those who', with an indefinite optative.

γαλήνῃ: equivalent to a dative for time when – 'in (periods of) calm weather'.

26.8

ἐσένεον: 'swam in'.

κατὰ τὸν λιμένα: 'by way of the harbour' – divers would use the most direct route, i.e. from the sandbar by the cove across the channel to the island's northeast tip (see Map 2).

ὕφυδροι: predicatively, telling us where they operated – 'under water'.

καλῳδίῳ: 'by a cord' – diminutive of κάλως (rope).

ἐν ἀσκοῖς: 'in skins', i.e. leather bags.

ἐφέλκοντες: 'dragging behind them'.

μήκωνα μεμελιτωμένην: 'poppy-seed mixed with honey'.

λίνου σπέρμα κεκομμένον: 'pounded linseed' (literally 'seed of flax', a plant producing edible oil).

ὧν: connecting relative, equivalent to τούτων δέ.

ἐγένοντο: here equivalent in meaning to a passive – 'were put in place'.

26.9

τε: summing up – 'and so'.

οἱ μέν . . . οἱ δέ: i.e. 'the Athenians . . . the Spartans . . .'.

μὴ λανθάνειν: a subject has to be supplied, either τὰ σιτία ἐσπεμπόμενα or ἐκείνους (the senders) – 'so that the food being sent in (*or* they) should not escape their (i.e. the Athenians' own) notice'.

Chapter 27

The Athenians begin to regret not making peace with the Spartans. They blame Cleon, who attempts to discredit the messengers from Pylos and is appointed to go and see for himself, whereupon he advocates a fresh expedition. He criticizes the general Nicias for not attacking and capturing the Spartans on Sphacteria.

27.1

πυνθανόμενοι: 'when they (i.e. the Athenians, inferred from ἐν ταῖς Ἀθήναις) learned'.

περὶ τῆς στρατίας, ὅτι ταλαιπωρεῖται: 'about the army, that it was suffering hardship', i.e. simply 'that the army was suffering hardship' – an indirect statement version of the sentence-pattern we saw in 23.2 with an indirect question, where we are told in advance about the subject. The effect here is to emphasize the verb.

καὶ σῖτος . . . ὅτι ἐσπλεῖ: in the second part of the indirect statement, ὅτι is postponed (from its usual place before the subject) to balance the previous clause, and again emphasize the verb; ἐσπλεῖ (literally 'is sailing in', keeping the present tense of the original speech) here means 'was being brought in'.

ἐδεδοίκεσαν: because δέδοικα (I fear) is a perfect used as a present, this pluperfect form is equivalent to an imperfect – 'they were afraid', followed by μή and the optative (the usual construction with a verb of fearing in the past).

σφῶν χειμὼν τὴν φυλακὴν ἐπιλάβοι: 'winter might overtake their blockade' – the reflexive possessive pronoun is put first for emphasis.

ὁρῶντες: 'seeing that . . .' – followed (in a very long sentence) by two accusative participles (ἐσομένην and ἐσόμενον) then two infinitives (περιγενήσεσθαι and ἐκπλεύσεσθαι), all in indirect statement.

ἅμα . . . περιπέμπειν: a parenthesis within the long indirect statement – the nominative participle in οἷοί τε ὄντες agrees with the main subject (the supplied οἱ Ἀθηναῖοι); the words ἐν χωρίῳ ἐρήμῳ are left up in the air, though the meaning is clear – logically we need to supply something like ὄντων ἐκείνων ('with the men being . . .').

ἔφορμον: 'blockade'.

χωρίων: plural – 'region'.

οὐκ ἐσόμενον: 'would not be practicable'.

ἀλλ': 'but on the contrary' introducing a switch from participles to infinitives, perhaps just for variety.

σφῶν ἀνέντων τὴν φυλακήν: genitive absolute, literally 'with them having given up the blockade' – but describing a hypothetical situation, so 'if they gave the blockade' or 'they would have to give up the blockade and . . .'.

τοῖς πλοίοις: 'using the boats (which . . .)' – instrumental dative.

ἦγε: 'were bringing' – singular because neuter plural subject.

χειμῶνα: this time meaning 'stormy weather'.

27.2

τε: connective.

πάντων . . . τοὺς Λακεδαιμονίους: although τοὺς Λακεδαιμονίους is grammatically the object of ἐφοβοῦντο, the meaning is really 'what they most of all feared about the Spartans was that . . .'.

ἔχοντας . . . ἐπικηρυκεύεσθαι: the emphasis is on the participle – 'they thought that it was because they had strong grounds for confidence (*literally* something strong) that they were no longer making overtures (*literally* sending heralds) to them'.

μετεμέλοντο: 'they regretted'.

27.3

Κλέων δὲ γνούς: 'Cleon, knowing . . .' – Thucydides (unusually but repeatedly) tells us what Cleon was thinking, but this is unlikely to be more than inference from his words and deeds.

κωλύμης: formed from κωλύω, but unique to Thucydides – 'prevention', 'blocking'.

οὐ . . . ἔφη: 'said that . . . not . . .'.

τἀληθῆ: crasis (blending two adjacent vowels into one) of τὰ ἀληθῆ.

τοὺς ἐξαγγέλλοντας: 'those bringing news from (Pylos)'.

AS

ἀφιγμένων: perfect participle of ἀφικνέομαι.

πιστεύουσι: present tense of the original speech retained, but English needs past.

κατασκόπους: '(official) observers', 'inspectors'.

ἡρέθη: 'was chosen' – passive of the middle sense of αἱρέω.

μετὰ Θεαγένους: 'with Theagenes' – some manuscripts and modern texts have 'Theogenes', and if this is right he may be the man mentioned as a swearer to the Peace of Nicias (5.19.2).

27.4

καὶ γνούς: see note on 27.3.

ταὐτά: crasis of τὰ αὐτά – 'the same things (as)', with dative.

οἷς: for τούτοις οὕς, a regular idiom (the relative pronoun is attracted into the case of a genitive or dative antecedent, which is then itself omitted) – 'as those whom' (more natural English than the literal 'these').

τἀναντία εἰπών: crasis of τὰ ἐναντία, and the participle has conditional force – 'if he said the opposite'.

ψευδὴς φανήσεσθαι: 'would be shown to be a liar' – switching from a ὅτι clause to a infinitive, still in indirect statement after γνούς (compare the switch from participles to infinitives in 27.1).

ὁρῶν ... στρατεύειν: 'seeing that they were in fact (καί) considerably more eager in their minds to send an expedition' – ὡρμημένους is perfect passive participle of ὁρμάω, τι (literally 'somewhat') gives understated emphasis, and τὸ πλέον is used instead of the adverb μᾶλλον.

μηδὲ διαμέλλειν καιρὸν παριέντας: 'nor to delay, letting slip a (perfect) opportunity' – παριέντας is present participle of παρίημι.

τὰ ἀγγελλόμενα: present participle made into a noun – 'the reports that were coming in'.

ἐπί: 'to attack' them (rather than just trying to starve them out) or perhaps better 'to fetch' them as deportees to Athens.

27.5

ἐς Νικίαν τὸν Νικηράτου στρατηγὸν ὄντα ἀπεσήμαινεν: the verb ἀπεσήμαινεν (ἀπο- implies 'away from others', focusing on one individual) governs both ἐς and the following indirect statement – 'it was to Nicias son of Niceratus ... that he pointed, saying that ...'. Nicias, here given his patronymic, was mentioned twice in Book 3. He has a significant role here in the debate about Pylos, as Cleon's adversary, and he will play a major part in later events of the war, notably as one of the commanders of the Sicilian Expedition (see Introduction). At this point he – unlike Cleon – is one of the ten annually elected generals.

ἐχθρὸς ὢν καὶ ἐπιτιμῶν: 'being an enemy and (accordingly) finding fault with him'.

παρασκευῇ: 'with a (proper) force'.

εἰ ἄνδρες εἶεν οἱ στρατηγοί: 'if the generals were (real) men' – optative here representing (in indirect speech in historic sequence) the present indicative what was said at the time.

καὶ αὐτός γ' ἄν, εἰ ἦρχε, ποῖησαι τοῦτο: 'and he would certainly do this himself if he held office'.

AS

Chapter 28

Nicias offers his command to Cleon, and the Athenians make him accept it. Asking only for light-armed troops, he promises to take Sphacteria within twenty days.

28.1

τῶν τε Ἀθηναίων θορυβησάντων . . .: genitive absolute, to be followed up with nominative participle ὁρῶν, both relating to Nicias' reaction (hence τε . . . καί) – 'when the Athenians made something of an uproar against Cleon . . . and he saw . . .'.

ὅτι οὐ καὶ νῦν πλεῖ: '(asking) why he was not sailing (there) even now'; ὅτι is probably the neuter of ὅστις ('with respect to what?', i.e. 'why?'), though ὅτι = 'because' would also make sense; πλεῖ keeps the present tense of the original direct question.

εἰ ῥᾴδιόν γε αὐτῷ φαίνεται: 'if it seemed to him so easy' – γε emphasizing ῥᾴδιον.

ἐκέλευεν . . . ἐπιχειρεῖν: indirect command – 'he told him to . . . make the attempt'.

τὸ ἐπὶ σφᾶς εἶναι: 'at least as far as they (i.e. the generals) were concerned' (the gathering might decide differently), an unusual idiom – literally 'with respect to the thing dependent on them', the following infinitive εἶναι apparently redundant but (as comparable examples show) giving a limiting sense ('at least', 'at any rate').

28.2

ὁ δέ: i.e. Cleon – a common idiom (preserving an old use of the article as a pronoun) marking a change of subject, to someone mentioned in the previous sentence in a different case.

λόγῳ μόνον: literally 'in word only', i.e. 'in pretence', 'in theory' (contrasted here with τῷ ὄντι ('really')).

ἕτοιμος ἦν: 'was ready (to go)'.

ἀφιέναι: supply τὴν ἀρχήν as object – and again with παραδωσείοντα below.

γνοὺς δέ . . .: 'but when he realized that . . .', introducing indirect statement with participle.

παραδωσείοντα: 'willing to hand over' – a 'desiderative' (from the Latin for 'desire') formed from παραδίδωμι.

ἀνεχώρει: imperfect – 'he tried to back out'.

οὐκ ἔφη αὐτὸς ἀλλ' ἐκεῖνον στρατηγεῖν: 'he said that it was not he himself but Nicias who was a general' – note the switch from nominative and infinitive (where the subject of the indirect statement is the same as that of the introductory verb) to accusative (referring to someone else).

δεδιώς: 'fearing' – perfect participle of δείδω, with present sense.

καὶ οὐκ ἂν οἰόμενος . . . τολμῆσαι: 'even though he (Cleon) thought that he (Nicias) would not have the nerve' – ἄν goes with τολμῆσαι.

οἱ . . . ὑποχωρῆσαι: οἱ is here a dative reflexive pronoun, equivalent to ἑαυτῷ – 'to give way for him(self)'.

28.3

ἐξίστατο: imperfect – 'was for standing out of the way of', 'offered to resign'.

AS

τῆς ἐπὶ Πύλῳ ἀρχῆς: 'his command (of operations) against Pylos'.

ἐποιεῖτο: 'repeatedly appealed to . . . as . . .' (middle ποιέομαι literally means 'I make for myself').

οἷον ὄχλος φιλεῖ ποιεῖν: literally 'the sort of thing a crowd likes to do', i.e. 'as a crowd tends to do' – a common idiom.

ὅσῳ μᾶλλον . . . τόσῳ: literally 'by as much the more . . . by so much', i.e. 'the more . . . the more'.

ὑπέφευγε: 'tried to duck out of'.

ἐξανεχώρει: 'tried to back out of'.

τὰ εἰρημένα: perfect passive participle of λέγω, made into a noun – 'what had been said (by himself)'.

ἐπεβόων: introducing indirect command – 'kept shouting out at him (i.e. Cleon), telling him . . .'.

28.4

ὥστε: 'so', 'the result was that'.

οὐχ ἔχων ὅπως . . .: literally 'not having how . . .', i.e. 'not having the means to . . .', 'not knowing how to . . .' (then deliberative subjunctive put into indirect speech).

ἐξαπαλλαγῇ: aorist passive with active/middle sense – 'extricate himself from', 'get out of'.

ὑφίσταται: historic present to mark a decisive step.

παρελθών: 'coming forward', i.e. before the Assembly.

οὔτε φοβεῖσθαι ἔφη . . . πλεύσεσθαί τε: 'he said that he was not afraid . . . and would sail'.

οὐδένα: emphatically last – 'not a single man'. Cleon is stressing that he will not make costly demands on the Athenians' own manpower.

Λημνίους . . . καὶ Ἰμβρίους: 'Lemnians and Imbrians', i.e. troops from the islands of Lemnos and Imbros in the north Aegean – both Athenian possessions, though we do not know why their soldiers were conveniently present.

πελταστάς: 'peltasts' – a peltast is a light-armed soldier equipped with a small round shield (πέλτη), as distinct from a heavy-armed hoplite.

ἦσαν . . . βεβοηθηκότες: 'had come in support' – periphrastic pluperfect, formed from perfect participle and auxiliary verb (like the pluperfect of a deponent verb in Latin).

ἐκ . . . Αἴνου: from Aenus, a rich city on the coast of Thrace, north of Imbros and Lemnos, and a tribute-paying member of the Athenian empire.

καὶ ἄλλοθεν: since the preceding τε is inside the relative clause, 'and from elsewhere' probably belongs with it (i.e. still talking about peltasts), in which we must assume the loss of and supply another καί before the next item.

τοξότας τετρακοσίους: '(and) four hundred archers' – from an unspecified source (unless more words have dropped out). Archers from Crete and from Scythia (roughly southern Russia) are mentioned elsewhere by Thucydides.

ταῦτα: neuter plural – 'these forces'.

πρός: with dative – 'in addition to', 'on top of'.

ἄξειν Λακεδαιμονίους ζῶντας: 'he would bring the Spartans (to Athens) alive'.

αὐτοῦ: adverb – 'on the spot'.

28.5

τοῖς δὲ Ἀθηναίοις . . .: literally 'on the Athenians fell a certain amount even of laughter . . .', i.e. 'the Athenians were to an extent actually moved to laughter . . .' – reference to laughter by the austere Thucydides are 'rare, and always unpleasant' (Hornblower 1996). This whole scene has something of the atmosphere of comic drama.

τῇ κουφολογίᾳ αὐτοῦ: 'at his light talking' – it seemed empty or frivolous.

ἀσμένοις δ' ὅμως . . . ἐγίγνετο: literally 'but nonetheless it was turning out for . . . being glad', i.e. 'the situation proved pleasing to . . .'.

τοῖς σώφροσι τῶν ἀνθρώπων: literally 'the prudent (ones) of the men', i.e. 'sensible, sober-minded people' – an approving characterization by Thucydides, combining social, political and intellectual assessment for the opponents of Cleon (doubtless including himself, though the view he attributes to this group is, in fact, highly irresponsible in its implications: see below).

δυοῖν ἀγαθοῖν: neuter duals – 'of two good things'.

τοῦ ἑτέρου τεύξεσθαι: future infinitive of τυγχάνω – 'they would obtain one or the other'.

Κλέωνος ἀπαλλαγήσεσθαι: future passive infinitive – 'they would be rid of Cleon' (even if he were not killed, failure would mean the end of his political career). This makes a good quip, but if 'prudent' people really did feel like this, their disapproval of Cleon must have been strong enough to override any qualms about entrusting a significant numbers of allied troops to a man deemed incompetent.

ἤλπιζον: 'they were expecting' (rather than 'hoping' – the emphasis is on what they thought was the more likely outcome).

σφαλεῖσι γνώμης: aorist passive participle of σφάλλω (still dative after τοῖς σώφροσι, in conditional sense – 'if they were foiled in their expectation').

χειρώσεσθαι: understand τὸν Κλέωνα as subject of the infinitive – 'that Cleon would overpower the Spartans for them' (which would be a good outcome for Athens, even though they would have to put up with him crowing about it).

AS

Notes on chapters 29–40

Chapter 29

Cleon chooses Demosthenes as his partner in command. Thucydides describes the difficulties Demosthenes foresaw in attacking the Spartans on the wooded island (even though his troops greatly outnumbered them), before a fortuitous fire.

29.1

ψηφισαμένων: genitive absolute sandwiched between two nominative participles. The Assembly votes that Cleon should take command and have the forces he asked for in 28.4, but his status is left unclear. Nicias does not resign his generalship for the year (he will exercise it again in Chapter 42), and Cleon is not specifically referred to as στρατηγός in the Pylos campaign, nor is he recorded as in command again during 425/4. The most likely explanation is that the Assembly envisaged an additional and temporary appointment to the board of generals.

προσελόμενος: aorist participle of προσαιρέομαι, 'choose so as to attach to oneself', i.e. 'choose as a colleague'. By this time Demosthenes himself (see Chapter 3) will have taken office as a general for 425/4.

τὴν ἀναγωγὴν διὰ τάχους ἐποιεῖτο: 'he set about putting to sea with (all) speed'.

29.2

τὴν ... διανοεῖσθαι: 'had the landing [contemplated by Cleon] in mind himself'. Cleon probably learned this from a message sent by Demosthenes to the Assembly.

κακοπαθοῦντες: 'being in a bad way'.

ἀπορία: 'difficulty' due to the lack of amenities and supplies.

μᾶλλον πολιορκούμενοι ἢ πολιορκοῦντες: 'being blockaded rather than blockading' – as often, Thucydides comments on paradoxical reversal (compare e.g. the reversal of tactics between the two sides, and the 'infantry battle from ships', in 14.3).

ὥρμηντο: pluperfect (as they *had got into* that state), but translate 'were eager', 'were more than willing'.

διακινδυνεῦσαι: literally 'run risks right through', i.e. 'risk everything' in a determined attempt to break the deadlock.

αὐτῷ: referring to Demosthenes (whose men have just been mentioned), not Cleon.

ἔτι: closely with ῥώμην, 'had given him even greater grounds for confidence'.

ἡ νῆσος ἐμπρησθεῖσα: 'the fact that the island had caught fire'.

29.3

πρότερον ... ἐφοβεῖτο: natural English is 'previously he *had been* afraid (to attempt a landing)'.

οὔσης ... ἀτριβοῦς: genitive absolute with participle prominently placed – 'given the fact that the island was ...'.

ἐπὶ τὸ πολύ: 'for the most part' – a very common expression.

πρός: with genitive – 'to the advantage of'.

τοῦτο: 'this fact', i.e. that the island was wooded and pathless.

πολλῷ ... ἂν ... βλάπτειν: the particle ἄν is a 'postpositive' (i.e. cannot come first word) but gravitates towards the start of the sentence even though associated with the closing infinitive βλάπτειν, to describe a potential situation – 'because a large force could land and they [the enemy] could [he thought] by attacking it from a hidden position cause damage [to the Athenians]': i.e. a large force (such as he had at his disposal), incapable of concealment, could suffer casualties at the hands of a numerically inferior but well-hidden foe taking advantage of the terrain.

παρασκευήν: combines the notions of 'preparation' and 'force/resources'.

ὑπό: with genitive – 'because of'.

δῆλα: neuter plural after two feminine nouns denoting things.

καταφανῆ: 'easily seen' (κατα- gives emphasis).

ὥστε προσπίπτειν ἂν αὐτούς: result clause in potential form, 'with the result that they could fall upon them ...'.

ᾗ βούλοιντο: is adverbial ᾗ with optative for an indefinite clause in historic sequence – 'wherever they wished'.

ἐπ' ἐκείνοις: ἐπί with dative – 'in their power', i.e. 'up to them'.

τὴν ἐπιχείρησιν: 'the (making of the) attempt', i.e. 'the initiative'.

29.4

εἰ δ' αὖ ... ἰέναι: 'if on the other hand he were to force his way into thickly wooded ground (so as) to come to meet (the enemy)', i.e. in hand-to-hand fighting – βιάζοιτο is middle optative.

ἐλάσσους ... κρείσσους: 'the smaller number ... superior to ...' – masculine accusative plural comparatives, alternative forms of ἐλάσσονας and κρείσσονας.

τῶν πλεόνων: 'his larger number' – genitive after κρείσσους.

λανθάνειν: closely with the participle, literally 'would escape notice being destroyed', i.e. 'would be destroyed before they realized it'.

τε: 'and so'.

πολὺ ὄν: 'large though it was'.

οὐκ οὔσης τῆς προσόψεως: there being no chance of seeing'.

ᾗ χρῆν: 'where they had to' – augmentless imperfect of χρή.

Chapter 30

When the fire has burned most of the wood off the island, Demosthenes has a better view of the enemy and can plan his attack. Cleon arrives with his force, and a herald is sent to ask the Spartans to surrender.

30.1

Αἰτωλικοῦ πάθους: 'the disaster in Aetolia' (see Map 1). Demosthenes had unsuccessfully invaded this region of west-central Greece in summer 426 (described at 3.94–8). His forces were routed by the Aetolians, and about 120 Athenian hoplites killed. Many of the defeated Athenians became trapped in a wood, which the Aetolians set fire to. Thucydides generally plays down

**A
Level**

Demosthenes' good planning in the Pylos campaign, but here gives him credit for learning from experience. (Some commentators have speculated that the fire on Sphacteria too was started deliberately, on Demosthenes' orders, but Thucydides does not say or imply this.)

μέρος τι: 'to some (considerable) extent'.

οὐχ ἥκιστα: 'not least', with ἀπό 'as a result of'.

ἐσήει: imperfect of ἐσιέναι, literally 'came into (his head)' i.e. 'occurred to him'.

30.2

τῆς νήσου τοῖς ἐσχάτοις: 'the extremities of the island', probably the extreme north-west corner (see Map 2) – it has been observed that the prevailing north-west wind would have been exactly what was required to spread the fire over the whole island.

προσίσχοντας: with dative, 'putting in at' – accusative, as if 'it was necessary that they should . . .' (with accusative and infinitive) had preceded.

ἀριστοποιεῖσθαι: 'to take their midday meal'.

διὰ προφυλακῆς: 'with an advance guard'.

κατὰ μικρὸν τῆς ὕλης: 'a small part of the wood' – prepositional phrase (literally 'to a small extent of') serving as object.

ἀπὸ τούτου: 'following on from this'.

ἐπιγενομένου: 'having (suddenly) arisen'.

τὸ πολὺ αὐτῆς: 'the greater part of it'.

ἔλαθε κατακαυθέν: 'was burned down before anyone realized what was happening'.

30.3

μᾶλλον κατιδών: 'perceiving better (than he had been able to do before)' – followed (as a verb of perception) by participles ὄντας and οὖσαν.

ὑπονοῶν πρότερον: present participle, but a past tense is needed in English – 'having previously suspected'.

ἐλάσσοσι: 'for fewer men' – dative plural of ἐλάσσων.

αὐτοῦ: if the manuscript reading (followed by the Oxford text) is right, this adverbial form (normally 'there') must be being used like αὐτόσε, 'to there'; and Demosthenes must be the subject of ἐσπέμπειν, meaning 'he was allowing to be sent in'. But an easy correction to αὐτοὺς would produce simpler and better sense – 'they (the Spartans) were sending in'.

εὐαποβατωτέραν: 'easier to land on'.

τότε: in contrast with πρότερον.

ὡς . . . ποιεῖσθαι: 'as for a thing of sufficient importance for the Athenians to make more of an effort'.

ἐκ τῶν ἐγγὺς ξυμμάχων: 'from the allies nearby', i.e. Zacynthus and Naupactus (see Map 1).

30.4

ὡς ἥξων: literally 'as being about to come', i.e. 'to say that he was coming'.

ἀφικνεῖται . . . πέμπουσι: historic presents for vividness.

ἅμα γενόμενοι: 'having come together', i.e. 'having conferred'.

A
Level

κήρυκα: heralds (under the protection of the god Hermes, and carrying a staff as identification) were almost universally respected as inviolable, so could safely visit an enemy. They were able to deliver messages and replies, but not negotiate.

στρατόπεδον: i.e. the Spartan camp referred to at 14.1.

ἐφ' ᾧ: with future indicative, 'on condition that they would be kept under guard' – the middle form τηρήσονται here serves as future passive.

φυλακῇ τῇ μετρίᾳ: literally 'custody of the moderate sort', i.e. mildly enforced.

ἕως ἄν: 'until', with aorist subjunctive.

τι περὶ τοῦ πλέονος ξυμβαθῇ: 'some agreement was reached about the larger matter', i.e. that of a general peace.

Chapter 31

When the Spartans reject the proposal to avoid a fight, the Athenians embark by night and land on Sphacteria just before dawn. They attack the first of three positions occupied by the Spartans.

31.1

δέ: because οὐ προσδεξαμένων forms a close-knit unit, δέ is relegated to third position.

μίαν ... ἡμέραν, τῇ ... ὑστεραίᾳ, νυκτός: three different cases in a row – accusative for time how long, dative for time when, and genitive for time within which (νυκτός refers to the early hours of the following day).

ἀπέβαινον: imperfect – 'they started landing'.

πρὸς τοῦ λιμένος: 'from the side facing the harbour' (see Map 2).

ὀκτακόσιοι μάλιστα: 'about 800'.

φυλακτήριον: 'guardpost'.

ὧδε ... διετετάχατο: 'they [i.e. the Spartans] had been posted as follows' – pluperfect, third person plural, using the ending -ατο instead of the usual -ντο (which would be unpronounceable on a stem ending in a consonant).

31.2

τῇ πρώτῃ: i.e. first from the south end of the island.

ὡς τριάκοντα: 'about thirty' (ὡς is an alternative to μάλιστα to express an approximate number).

μέσον ... ὕδωρ: 'the centre, which was also the most level area and lay around the water (-supply)' – i.e. the spring of brackish water referred to at 26.4.

αὐτὸ τὸ ἔσχατον: 'the very extremity', i.e. the northern end.

ἀπόκρημνον: 'sheer', 'precipitous'.

ἐπίμαχον: 'open to attack'.

καὶ γάρ τι καὶ ... ἦν: 'for in fact there was also ...', i.e. in addition the natural strength of the place.

ἔρυμα ... πεποιημένον: 'an ancient strongpoint made of stones roughly laid' – λογάδην (connected with λέγω in the sense 'I pick') implies approximately suitable stones selected without being cut to fit.

A Level

εἰ ... βιαιοτέρα: literally 'if too forced a retreat were to overtake them', i.e. 'in case they were suddenly forced to retreat under extreme pressure'.

τεταγμένοι ἦσαν: periphrastic form of the pluperfect passive, made from perfect passive participle with auxiliary verb (like Latin *instructi erant*).

Chapter 32

The Spartan advance post is overrun, and the main body of the Athenians lands. Thucydides describes Demosthenes' plan to avoid close combat and, using light-armed troops, to attack the Spartans from all sides with missiles.

32.1

διαφθείρουσιν: historic present for vividness.

ἔν τε ταῖς εὐναῖς ἔτι: 'while they were still in their beds' – supply ὄντας or ἐνόντας.

καὶ ἀναλαμβάνοντας: literally 'and ...', but English needs 'or in the act of taking up'.

λαθόντες τὴν ἀπόβασιν: 'having landed without being detected' – literally 'having escaped notice with regard to the landing' (accusative of respect).

οἰομένων αὐτῶν: genitive absolute.

ἐς ἔφορμον τῆς νυκτός: 'to their anchorage (*or* to maintain their blockade) for the night'.

32.2

ἅμα ... γιγνομένῃ: present participle, 'as day began to dawn'.

ὁ ἄλλος στρατός: 'the rest of the army' (a fairly common idiom with ἄλλος – not here 'the other army').

ἀπέβαινεν: imperfect – 'started to land'. This would be along the centre of the island, on each side.

νεῶν ἑβδομήκοντα καὶ ὀλίγῳ πλεόνων: literally 'seventy ships and more by a little', i.e. 'rather more than seventy ships'.

θαλαμιῶν: rowers on the lowest bench of a trireme. The landing-places were cramped, and these men (54 out of a normal crew of 170) would be required to clear emptied triremes out of the way to allow others to put in.

ὡς ἕκαστοι ἐσκευασμένοι: 'each equipped in his own way' – perfect passive participle.

πελτασταί: see note on 28.4.

ἐλάσσους: here nominative plural, alternative form ἐλάσσονες.

τούτων: genitive of comparison.

βεβοηθηκότες: perfect participle.

ὅσοι: 'all those who'.

κατεῖχον: intransitive – 'were stationed'.

32.3

διέστησαν: intransitive aorist of διίστημι, literally 'stood apart', i.e. 'were divided'.

κατά: with accusative, distributively – 'into groups of'.

καὶ πλείους: 'or more' (see note on 32.1).

ἔστι δ' ἧ ἐλάσσους: 'or sometimes fewer' (literally 'and there is where fewer').

A Level

τῶν χωρίων τὰ μετεωρότατα: literally 'the highest of the positions', i.e. 'the highest points of the terrain'. The enemy contingent being surrounded is the main force with Epitadas, as is made clear at 33.1.

ὅπως ... ἢ ... ἔχωσι ... γίγνωνται: series of purpose clauses with subjunctive verbs.

ὅτι πλείστη: 'the greatest possible' (like the use of ὡς with a superlative).

κεκυκλωμένοις: perfect passive participle.

μὴ ἔχωσι πρὸς ὅτι ἀντιτάξωνται: literally 'might not have against what they should take up position', i.e. 'might not know at what to direct their attack'.

ἀμφίβολοι: 'exposed to fire on both sides'.

τῷ πλήθει: causal dative – 'because of the superior number (of the enemy)'.

εἰ ... ἐπίοιεν: 'if they were to attack' – optative of ἐπιέναι.

τοῖς πλαγίοις: 'those on the flank'.

τῶν ἑκατέρωθεν παρατεταγμένων: 'those stationed on one side or the other'.

32.4

κατὰ νώτου: 'in the rear' – a recurrent expression.

ἔμελλον ... ἔσεσθαι: 'were sure to be'.

ᾗ χωρήσειαν: indefinite clause with optative in historic sequence – 'in whatever direction they advanced'.

ψιλοὶ ... ἀπορώτατοι: 'the lightly armed troops (that is) – and the ones hardest to deal with'.

ἐκ πολλοῦ: 'from a great distance', 'at long range'.

ἔχοντες ἀλκήν: 'having strength', i.e. 'being able to fight effectively'.

οἷς ... ἦν: this clause amplifies οἱ ἀπορώτατοι. The relative pronoun has causal force, and μηδέ (rather than οὐδέ) hints at a general application – 'because they were men to whom it was (invariably) impossible even to get near (enough to attack)'.

φεύγοντες ... ἐκράτουν: 'if they were fleeing they had the upper hand' – i.e. in speed, because they were unencumbered.

ἀναχωροῦσιν ἐπέκειντο: 'and if they (i.e. the Spartans) withdrew they pressed the attack' – ἀναχωροῦσιν is dative plural participle.

γνώμη: 'plan', 'intention'.

ἐν τῷ ἔργῳ ἔταξεν: 'he arranged his forces in the actual engagement'.

Chapter 33

The main Spartan force under Epitadas advances but is outmanoeuvred by Demosthenes' tactics.

33.1

οἱ ... περὶ τὸν Ἐπιτάδαν: 'the men under the command of Epitadas' (literally 'around' – but the Greek idiom means 'including him'). Much of the following description is 'focalized' through (i.e. seen through the eyes of) the defending Spartans, and 'may well depend on information obtained by Thucydides from questioning the Spartan prisoners in Athens' (Rhodes 1998).

A Level

καὶ ὅπερ ἦν πλεῖστον: i.e. 'who in fact formed the main force' – καί introduces additional information about them.

ὡς: temporal – 'when'.

εἶδον: with two participles – 'that X had been . . . and that Y was . . .'.

διεφθαρμένον: perfect passive participle.

ἐς χεῖρας ἐλθεῖν: 'to engage hand-to-hand', i.e. at close quarters.

ἐξ ἐναντίας: literally 'from directly opposite', i.e. 'in front'.

καθειστήκεσαν: 'were stationed' – pluperfect of καθίστημι.

ἐκ πλαγίου: 'on the flank'.

33.2

τῇ σφετέρᾳ: 'their own', i.e. 'their distinctive'.

ἐκεῖνοι: i.e. the Athenian hoplites.

ἡσύχαζον: 'remained in position'.

ᾗ . . . προσκέοιντο: 'wherever they ran at them and pressed them hardest' – optative for indefinite clause in historic sequence.

καὶ οἵ: the pronoun (with accent, usually relative 'who') is here a demonstrative, like οὗτοι: 'and *they*'.

ὑποστρέφοντες ἠμύνοντο: 'wheeled round and resisted'.

προλαμβάνοντες . . . τῆς φυγῆς: 'getting the advantage in flight'.

χωρίων τε . . . ὄντων: causal dative 'because of the difficulty of the terrain' followed by genitive absolute 'and with it being rough . . .', using χωρίων in both constructions.

ὅπλα: implying as usual 'heavy arms'.

Chapter 34

As the Spartans begin to tire, the Athenians become more confident, losing their fear of the enemy. The Spartans, deafened by noise and blinded by dust, are unable either to defend themselves or to attack.

34.1

χρόνον . . . ὀλίγον: accusative for time how long.

ἠκροβολίσαντο: 'they skirmished', i.e. fought at long range – a description of the battle overall (not what the Spartans were doing).

τῶν . . . δυναμένων: genitive absolute.

ὀξέως: 'sharply', i.e. 'rapidly'.

ἐπεκθεῖν: 'dash out to attack'.

ᾗ προσπίπτοιεν: 'where they (i.e. the Athenian ψιλοί) attacked' – another indefinite clause in historic sequence.

τῷ ἀμύνασθαι: articular infinitive, dative with βραδυτέρους.

τοῦ θαρσεῖν: another articular infinitive, genitive with τὸ πλεῖστον.

εἰληφότες: 'having acquired' – perfect participle of λαμβάνω.

πολλαπλάσιοι φαινόμενοι: amplifying τῇ ὄψει – 'since they clearly were many times more numerous'.

ξυνειθισμένοι μᾶλλον . . .: 'having become more accustomed' (perfect passive participle), then (literally) 'to them (i.e. the Spartans) no longer appearing

A Level

formidable to them in the same way ...' – i.e. 'having got more accustomed to them, so that they no longer appeared ...'. The immediate experience of the Athenian troops here anticipates the larger importance of the Pylos campaign in dispelling the mystique of Sparta.

ὁμοίως ... ὥσπερ ὅτε: co-ordinated – 'in the same way ... as when'.

ὅτι ... ἐπεπόνθεσαν: pluperfect of πάσχω – 'because they had not immediately experienced things corresponding to their expectation' (ἄξιος with genitive, literally 'worth as much as').

τῇ γνώμῃ δεδουλωμένοι ...: perfect passive participle, literally 'enslaved in spirit as against the Spartans', i.e. at the thought that they were going to fight them – a bold metaphor (Thucydides perhaps exaggerates the men's pessimism to heighten the sense of reversal to come).

καταφρονήσαντες ... ἐμβοήσαντες: aorist participles – 'despising them and raising a shout at them'.

ἀθρόοι: 'altogether' or 'in a body' – can be taken with both ἐμβοήσαντες and ὥρμησαν.

ἔβαλλον: note the switch to imperfect – 'they set about pelting them'.

ὡς ... εἶχεν: 'as each had something to hand', i.e. with whatever weapon each individual had.

34.2

γενομένης ... ἐπιδρομῇ: i.e. the sudden charge and the accompanying yelling filled them with alarm.

τοιαύτης μάχης: 'this kind of fighting'.

κονιορτός: 'cloud of dust'.

κεκαυμένης: perfect passive participle.

ἐχώρει πολὺς ἄνω: 'was rising up in a dense mass' – πολύς is predicative, telling us something new.

τὸ πρὸ αὑτοῦ: i.e. what was in front of you.

ὑπό: 'because of'.

ἀπὸ ... φερομένων: 'being hurled from the hands of ...'. Thucydides rounds off a vivid description before talking about the consequences.

34.3

τε ... ἐνταῦθα: 'thus at this point'.

χαλεπὸν ... καθίστατο: 'started to get difficult'. The Spartans were now engaged in an uphill struggle for survival.

οὔτε ... τοξεύματα: 'the felt caps did not keep off the arrows'.

δοράτια τε ἐναπεκέκλαστο: 'and the spears remained broken off in (their armour/ bodies)' – pluperfect passive third person singular with neuter plural subject.

βαλλομένων: 'as they were hit' – genitive absolute, understanding αὐτῶν.

εἶχόν ... χρήσασθαι: literally 'they were not able (ἔχω with infinitive) to deal with themselves at all', i.e. 'they did not know what to do with themselves'.

ἀποκεκλημένοι ... τοῦ προορᾶν: literally 'being shut off in respect of their sight from seeing in front of them' – perfect passive participle with (redundant) dative of respect and articular infinitive, i.e. their view was blocked and they could not see ahead.

**A
Level**

ὑπό: here again 'because of'.

τὰ . . . παραγγελλόμενα: 'the words of command being given in their own ranks'.

περιεστῶτος: 'encompassing them' – perfect participle (intransitive) of περιίστημι.

οὐκ ἔχοντες . . . ἐλπίδα καθ᾽ ὅτι . . .: with ἔχοντες we return to personal agreement after interruption by a genitive absolute – literally 'not having a hope according to what (way) it was necessary (by) defending themselves to be saved', i.e. they had no hope of being saved because they had no way of defending themselves in order to achieve it.

Chapter 35

After sustaining many wounds, the main Spartan force withdraws from the centre of the island to their third position at the northern end. The ground there favours defence and prevents encirclement. In a protracted struggle both sides suffer from heat and thirst.

35.1

διὰ τὸ . . . ἀναστρέφεσθαι: articular infinitive – 'because they were constantly moving backwards and forwards in the same place' (i.e. the comparatively flat central part of the island).

ξυγκλήσαντες: '(the Spartans) closed their ranks and . . .' – so that each man would have his exposed side protected by his comrade on the right.

τὸ . . . νήσου: i.e. the fort at the northern end (modern Mt Elias), referred to at 31.2.

ὃ οὐ πολὺ ἀπεῖχε: 'which was not far away' – in fact about a mile from the centre of the island, but the withdrawal involved a steep ascent in the face of enemy troops on higher ground.

35.2

ὡς . . . ἐνέδοσαν: 'once they had given way' – temporal ὡς and intransitive aorist of ἐνδίδωμι.

ἐνταῦθα ἤδη: 'there and then' – nearly synonymous adverbs emphasizing the immediate response.

πολλῷ . . . βοῇ: literally 'with much still more shouting', i.e. 'with louder shouting than ever'.

τεθαρσηκότες: perfect participle of θαρσέω.

ἐγκατελαμβάνοντο: 'were caught in (the retreat)'.

παρὰ πᾶν . . . ᾗπερ ἦν ἐπίμαχον: 'to resist at every point where it was open to attack' – ὡς with future participle expressing purpose.

35.3

ἐπισπόμενοι: aorist participle of ἐφέπομαι.

περίοδον . . . εἶχον: 'had no means of getting round and encircling them'.

χωρίου ἰσχύι: 'because of the strength of the position' – dative of cause.

προσιόντες . . . ἐξ ἐναντίας: 'attacking head-on'.

A Level

35.4

χρόνον . . . πλεῖστον: accusatives of time how long.

καί: 'in fact', 'indeed'.

ταλαιπωρούμενοι: 'despite suffering hardship' (i.e. understand καίπερ).

ὑπό: 'because of', with three genitives – δίψης as they were now away from the spring in the middle of the island.

ἐξελάσασθαι: aorist middle infinitive of ἐξελαύνω.

ῥᾷον . . . ἢ ἐν τῷ πρίν: understand χρόνῳ – 'more easily than before'.

οὐκ οὔσης . . . πλάγια: 'as it was impossible to encircle them on the flanks'.

Chapter 36

The Messenian commander leads a party by a hidden route and takes the Spartans by surprise from the rear, attacking and forcing them to give way.

36.1

ἀπέραντον ἦν: 'there was no end to it' (i.e. the engagement – subject omitted).

ὁ . . . στρατηγός: a much later source (Pausanias, writing a guide to Greece in the second century AD) gives his name as Comon.

ἄλλως: with πονεῖν – 'in vain' (literally 'otherwise [than would achieve anything]').

σφᾶς: i.e. the whole assault-force.

εἰ . . . βούλονται: 'if they wanted' (present tense retained from the original direct speech 'if you want').

περιιέναι: 'so as to go round' – explanatory infinitive.

ὁδῷ ἧ ἂν . . . εὕρῃ: for ἣν ἄν (relative attracted into the case of the antecedent) – 'by whatever route he himself could find' (indefinite clause with subjunctive in primary sequence). 'The fact that the Messenians had been at Naupactus for about thirty years, and Thucydides' language, both suggest that he did not already know a route' (Rhodes 1998).

δοκεῖν βιάσασθαι τὴν ἔφοδον: '(he said) he thought he could force the approach' – infinitive δοκεῖν after ἔφη.

36.2

ἃ ᾐτήσατο: antecedent ταῦτα omitted, as often.

ἐκ τοῦ ἀφανοῦς: 'from a point out of sight'.

ὥστε . . . ἐκείνους: equivalent to a purpose clause – 'so that they wouldn't see him'. It is true that the motive in starting out from an ἀφανές position was to keep the enemy in the dark; equally, the latter were completely thrown by the sudden arrival, a point foreshadowed here.

κατὰ . . . προσβαίνων: literally 'approaching by what at each point offered a foothold on the precipitous part of the island', i.e. 'and made his way as opportunity offered at each point along the cliffs of the island' (Rhodes 1998).

χαλεπῶς τε καὶ μόλις: 'with difficulty . . . just about . . .'.

περιελθὼν ἔλαβε: 'he made his way round undetected'.

ἐξαπίνης ἀναφανείς: 'suddenly coming into view'.

τοὺς μέν . . . τοὺς δέ: i.e. 'the Spartans . . . the Athenians'.

A Level

τῷ ἀδοκήτῳ: dative of τὸ ἀδόκητον – 'by the unexpectedness (of this manoeuvre)'.

ἐπέρρωσεν: aorist of ἐπιρρώνυμι.

36.3

γιγνόμενοι . . . ξυμπτώματι . . . τῷ ἐν Θερμοπύλαις: 'being in the same desperate position . . . as at Thermopylae'. When the Persians led by Xerxes invaded Greece in 480 BC, a much smaller Greek army tried to hold the pass at Thermopylae (literally 'Hot Gates', from high-temperature springs nearby) which gave access from Thessaly into central Greece. They were successful until a Persian detachment, guided by a man with local knowledge, found a route through the hills and descended in their rear. At this point most of the Greeks retreated, but the Spartan king Leonidas with 300 Spartans and some others remained and fought to the death. It was this act above all (described in Herodotus Book 7) which gave the Spartans their reputation for bravery, so that the other Greeks expected them never to surrender.

ὡς . . . εἰκάσαι: 'to compare small with great' (infinitive used as in ὡς εἰπεῖν at 14.3) – an early example of what became a common topos (recurrent expression), most famously Virgil's *si parva licet componere magnis* (*Georgics* 4.176), though Thucydides' modesty here sits illogically with his general view of the relative importance of the Persian and Peloponnesian wars (see Introduction).

ἐκεῖνοί τε γὰρ . . .: the sentence now moves in a different direction, developing the comparison between Sphacteria and Thermopylae (ἐκεῖνοι are the Spartans there), but leaving the main clause (begun at καὶ οἱ Λακεδαιμόνιοι) without a finite verb.

τῇ ἀτραπῷ: 'the path' known to everyone – Herodotus 7.175 uses the same word, making it likely that Thucydides alludes not only to the event but to his predecessor's account of it.

οὗτοι: i.e. the Spartans on Sphacteria.

ἀμφίβολοι: 'exposed on both sides'.

μαχόμενοι . . . ἀσθενείᾳ: causal participle followed by causal dative.

σιτοδείαν: 'lack of food'.

ὑπεχώρουν . . . ἐκράτουν: inceptive imperfects – 'began to . . .'. The Sphacteria narrative diverges from the Thermopylae parallel as the Spartans here withdraw rather than fighting to the death.

Chapter 37

Cleon and Demosthenes halt the Athenian attack and call on the Spartans to surrender.

37.1

γνούς: 'realizing' – singular in agreement with the nearer subject. As at 27.3, Thucydides makes a confident statement about Cleon's thought processes – though in this case Demosthenes (who he may subsequently have talked to) is also involved.

[ὅτι]: this word (in the manuscripts, but missing in a papyrus from Oxyrynchus) is redundant and probably an early error (by a copyist expecting an indirect statement with a 'that' clause, instead of the participle version which in fact follows).

A Level

εἰ ... ἐνδώσουσι: 'if the Spartans gave way even the slightest bit further' – a future open condition often uses εἰ with future indicative (rather than ἐάν with subjunctive) where dire consequences are in question.

βουλόμενοι ... ζῶντας: 'wanting to take the men to the Athenians alive' – this was the first option in Cleon's promise at 28.4, and the more attractive one because having live prisoners gave the Athenians an obvious way of threatening the Spartans.

εἴ πως ...: picking up from ἀπεῖρξαν, 'in the hope that ...'.

τοῦ κηρύγματος ἀκούσαντες: 'when they heard the proclamation (offering terms)'.

ἐπικλασθεῖεν ... δεινοῦ: 'they might be (so) broken in their determination (as to) hand over their weapons and yield to the danger confronting them' – τὸ δεινόν often means 'danger' or 'threat'.

37.2

τε: 'and so'.

εἰ βούλονται: as at 36.1.

ὥστε βουλεῦσαι: here for ἐφ'ᾧ – 'on condition that they should decide'.

ὅτι ἐκείνοις δοκῇ: indefinite clause with subjunctive in primary sequence, describing an unconditional surrender – ὅτι is neuter of ὅστις, and ἐκείνοις refers to the Athenians back in Athens, who are remote from the present speakers.

Chapter 38

After consulting their forces on the mainland, the Spartans surrender. Thucydides gives the numbers lost in combat and taken prisoner. Athenian losses are small as there has been no fighting at close quarters.

38.1

παρῆκαν: 'lowered' – aorist of παρίημι.

ἀνέσεισαν: 'waved'.

δηλοῦντες προσίεσθαι: 'showing that they accepted' – present middle infinitive of προσίημι.

γενομένης τῆς ἀνοκωχῆς: genitive absolute – 'when the armistice came into force'.

ξυνῆλθον ἐς λόγους: 'came together for discussions'.

ἐκείνων: i.e. representing the other side.

Στύφων ὁ Φάρακος: 'Styphon son of Pharax' (patroymic, as at 11.2). Here and in the following lines Thucydides shows impressively detailed knowledge of the Spartan commanders and their order of seniority.

τεθνηκότος: perfect participle of θνήσκω – the following τεθνεῶτος is an alternative form.

ἐφῃρημένου: perfect participle of middle ἐφαιρέομαι – 'chosen as successor'.

ἔτι ζῶντος: understand καίπερ – 'although he was still alive' (presumably implying this was discovered subsequently).

ὡς: 'as if'.

αὐτός: i.e. Styphon.

**A
Level**

κατὰ νόμον: 'in accordance with (Spartan) law'.

εἴ ... πάσχοιεν: literally 'in case they should suffer anything' – a common euphemism for 'die' or 'be killed' (like English 'in case anything should happen to them').

38.2

ἔλεγε: the imperfect suggests that the point was put more than once.

βούλονται ... χρή: present tenses retained from the original direct speech.

διακηρυκεύσασθαι πρός: 'communicate by herald with' (see note on 30.4).

ὅτι ... ποιεῖν: '(about) what they ought to do'.

38.3

ἐκείνων ... ἀφέντων: aorist participle of ἀφίημι – 'they (i.e. Cleon and Demosthenes) allowed none of them to go' (since they might not return, and the Athenians did not want to lose any of their captives).

αὐτῶν ... κήρυκας: 'but the Athenians themselves invited heralds from the mainland'.

γενομένων ... τρίς: 'after two or three enquiries had been made'.

ὁ ... ἀνήρ: note the exceptional length of the sandwiched description, with five separate elements.

ὅτι: quite often used like this (strictly redundant, and not translated) to preface a direct quotation.

Λακεδαιμόνιοι ... βουλεύεσθαι: 'The Spartans order you to decide yourselves about yourselves' (Rhodes 1998) – a stark statement that the men are on their own.

μηδὲν αἰσχρὸν ποιοῦντας: implying a condition (hence the negative μηδέν, rather than οὐδέν) – 'provided that you do nothing dishonourable'.

καθ' ἑαυτούς: equivalent to ἐν ἑαυτοῖς – 'among themselves'.

38.4

ἡμέραν ... νύκτα ... ὑστεραίᾳ: two accusatives for time how long followed by dative for time when.

τροπαῖον στήσαντες: as in 14.5.

τἄλλα διεσκευάζοντο ὡς ἐς πλοῦν ...: crasis of τὰ ἄλλα, and the prefix δια- (creating an unusual compound) perhaps suggests 'various' – 'were making the various other preparations for setting sail'.

διεκομίσαντο: causative middle – 'had them brought across'.

38.5

ἐλήφθησαν: aorist passive of λαμβάνω.

τοσοίδε: 'the following numbers'. Thucydides begins a round-up of the casualties and captives.

διέβησαν: this was described at 8.9.

οἱ πάντες: 'altogether'.

ἐκομίσθησαν: i.e. to Athens.

A Level

ὀκτὼ ἀποδέοντες τριακόσιοι: literally '300 lacking 8' (indeclinable ὀκτώ
representing a genitive), i.e. 292.

Σπαρτιᾶται: see note on 11.2.

σταδαία: literally 'of a standing type', i.e. 'fought at close quarters'.

Chapter 39

*Thucydides describes the length of the blockade. Both sides withdraw their main
forces. Cleon returns to Athens with the Spartan prisoners, his promise fulfilled.*

39.1

ὅσον: marking duration – 'for which'. We do not have exact dates, but a plausible
reconstruction assumes the Athenians left Athens in early May (of 425 BC), with
the naval battle in late May, the Assembly giving command to Cleon in late July,
the fighting on Sphacteria about a week into August, and Cleon's return to Athens
about five days later.

39.2

ἀπῆσαν: 'were (going) away' – emendation to ἀπῆσαν (from ἀπεῖναι) would give
simpler sense.

ἐσιτοδοτοῦντο: 'they were supplied with provisions'.

τοῖς ... διετρέφοντο: 'they were sustained by what was shipped in secretly'.

ἦν: prominently placed – 'there was in fact'.

ἐγκατελήφθη: 'were found there' (singular with neuter plural subject).

ἐνδεεστέρως ... ἢ πρὸς τὴν ἐξουσίαν: literally 'more sparingly than in relation
to comparison his resources', i.e. 'more sparingly than he could have done'
(presumably keeping some in reserve in case conditions got even worse).

39.3

οἱ ... Ἀθηναῖοι: i.e. those who came with Cleon – we learn later that a garrison was
left at Pylos (41.2), and that the original fleet moved with Eurymedon and
Sophocles continued to Corcyra and Sicily (46–7).

μὲν δή: 'then', marking the conclusion of an episode.

ἀπέβη: 'was fulfilled'.

ἐντὸς ... ὑπέστη: see 28.4 – ὑπέστη is intransitive aorist of ὑφίστημι ('as he had
undertaken'). Several references in Aristophanes' comedy *Knights*, produced in
January 424, indicate that Cleon took most of the credit for the Athenian success
at Pylos, being rewarded with the right to dine in the town hall (like victorious
Olympic athletes) and with a front seat in the theatre; the play also suggests that
Demosthenes was (understandably) resentful of this.

Chapter 40

*Thucydides describes the amazement in Greece at the Spartan surrender, and recounts
an anecdote about clever arrows.*

**A
Level**

40.1

παρὰ γνώμην ... ἐγένετο: 'of the events in the war this was indeed the most contrary to expectation for the Greeks', i.e. 'none was more unexpected'. A typical Thucydidean superlative (his *Guinness Book of Records* mode), rounding off an account full of paradox and reversal. Because the Sicilian disaster of 413 (described in Book 7) will be equally or even more unexpected, it is likely that 'the war' here refers to the Archidamian War of 431–21, and thus that this passage was written before Thucydides came to see the whole conflict from 431–404 as a unity: see Introduction.

τοὺς ... Λακεδαιμονίους: i.e. those at Sphacteria, not Spartans generally.

ἠξίουν: 'thought it likely'.

ὡς ἐδύναντο: 'as best they could'.

40.2

ἀπιστοῦντές τε ...: in the Oxford text (following most manuscripts), this nominative participle is left hanging; the construction then changes, as a genitive absolute (τινος ἐρομένου) is introduced, with a finite verb (ἀπεκρίνατο) following on directly from that. Possibly something has dropped out, but the sense is clear. Emending to ἀπιστούντων (to produce another genitive absolute) would solve the problem – at any rate the sentence should be translated as if that were what Thucydides had written.

μὴ εἶναι ... ὁμοίους: 'not believing that those who had surrendered were of the same kind as those who had been killed' – μή simply strengthens the element of negation in the participle.

τινος ... ὕστερον: this digressive anecdote, with pointed question and answer, is more in the style of Herodotus (compare e.g. the stories about Themistocles' banter in the run-up to the Battle of Salamis in Book 8) than the usually austere Thucydides. It is notable that the question is asked by an Athenian ally (rather than an actual Athenian) – perhaps an ally from the Peloponnese (familiar with the traditions of the Spartan elite), or from Ionia (keen to challenge Dorian claims to courage).

ἕνα ... αἰχμαλώτων: presumably while they were being held in Athens.

δι' ἀχθηδόνα: 'to cause annoyance'.

εἰ ... αὐτῶν: emphatic – 'whether *the dead* among them' (were X, as the survivors clearly were not).

καλοὶ κἀγαθοί: literally 'fine and good', a frequent term of commendation for upper-class men, used in various contexts and apparently in various city states – 'noble and brave' or 'true, honourable men' might be an appropriate translation here (note that 'brave' is a standard meaning of ἀγαθός in Homer).

ἀπεκρίνατο ... οἰστόν: 'he replied that the spindle – meaning the arrow – would be worth a lot ...'. The anonymous prisoner is stung into a sharp reply: Spartans had the reputation of being taciturn, but capable of devastating one-liners, of which collections were made. 'Spindle' (literally a stick onto which thread is wound as it is spun) is used as a metaphor for 'arrow' in tragedy (both were often made of reed), but the word has two further resonances here. Archery (operating at a distance) was commonly viewed as a womanish or cowardly activity (this is clearly seen in the *Iliad*), and we are surely also meant to think of the three Fates (goddesses of destiny), conventionally represented as spinners.

εἰ . . . διεγίγνωσκε: 'if it could distinguish the brave men'.

δήλωσιν ποιούμενος: 'making the point that . . .'.

ὁ . . . διεφθείρετο: article with participle used generically (rather than of a specific individual): 'whoever got in the way of stones and arrows was destroyed by them', i.e. in this type of combat it was pure chance (τύχη, the root of ἐντυγχάνω) who got killed.

**A
Level**

Vocabulary

While there is no Defined Vocabulary List for A Level, words in the OCR Defined Vocabulary List for AS are marked with * so that students can quickly see the vocabulary with which they should be particularly familiar.

*ἀγαθός -ή -όν	good, brave
*ἀγγέλλω	I announce
*ἄγγελος -ου, ὁ	messenger
*ἄγω, fut. ἄξω, aor. ἤγαγον	I lead, I bring
ἀδίκημα -ατος, τό	wrongdoing, injustice
ἀδόκητον -ου, τό	the unexpected (sight)
ἀδύνατος -ον	unable, impossible
ἀήθης -ες	unused to (+ gen.)
Ἀθήναζε	to Athens
*Ἀθῆναι -ῶν, αἱ	Athens
*Ἀθηναῖοι -ων, οἱ	Athenians
ἀθρόος -α -ον	all together, in a body
ἀθυμία -ας, ἡ	despondency
*αἰεί (= ἀεί)	always, constantly, at each point
Αἶνος -ου, ἡ	Aenus
*αἱρέω, aor. εἷλον, aor. pass. ᾑρέθην	I take, I capture, mid. I take for myself, I choose, I appoint
*αἴρω, aor. ἦρα	I raise, intr. I set out
*αἰσχρός -ά -όν	shameful
*αἰτέω, aor. ᾔτησα	I ask for (act. or mid.)
αἴτιον -ου, τό	cause, reason
*αἴτιος -α -ον	responsible
Αἰτωλικός -ή -όν	Aetolian, in Aetolia
*αἰχμάλωτος -ου, ὁ	prisoner (of war)
ἀκόντιον -ου, τό	javelin
*ἀκούω, aor. ἤκουσα	I hear (+ acc. or gen.)
ἀκροβολίζομαι, aor. ἠκροβολισάμην	I skirmish, I fight at long range
ἀκρόπολις -εως, ἡ	citadel, fortified hill-top
*ἄκων -ουσα -ον (ἀκοντ-)	unwilling, unintentionally
ἀλέω, pf. pass. ἀλήλεμαι	I grind
*ἀληθής -ές	true
ἀλίμενος -ον	without a harbour
ἀλίσκομαι	I am caught
ἀλκή -ῆς, ἡ	strength
*ἀλλά	but
ἀλλήλους -ας -α	each other
ἄλλοθεν	from elsewhere
*ἄλλος -η -ο	other, the rest of
ἄλλως	in vain
ἁλμυρός -όν	brackish, salty
*ἅμα	at the same time (as + dat.), together
ἁμάρτημα -ατος, τό	mistake
ἁμαρτία -ας, ἡ	mistake
*ἀμύνομαι	I defend myself (against), I resist
ἀμφίβολος -ον	exposed to fire on both sides
*ἀμφότεροι -αι -α	both
ἀμφοτέρωθεν	from/on both sides
*ἄν	(makes potential, e.g. would, -ever)
*ἀναγκάζω, aor. ἠνάγκασα, aor. pass. ἠναγκάσθην, fut. pass. ἀναγκασθήσομαι	I force, I compel
*ἀνάγκη -ης, ἡ	necessity, compulsion
*ἀνάγομαι, aor. ἀνηγαγόμην	I put out to sea
ἀναγωγή -ῆς, ἡ	putting out to sea, departure
ἀναδέομαι	I attach ropes to, I take in tow
ἀναιρέω, aor. ἀνεῖλον	I take up, I pick up (act. or mid.)
ἀνακόπτω, aor. pass. ἀνεκόπην	I beat back
ἀναλαμβάνω	I take up

ἀναπαύω — I cause to rest, I relieve

ἀνασείω, aor. ἀνέσεισα — I wave

ἀναστρέφω — I turn (something) round, mid. I move backwards and forwards, I wheel round

ἀναφαίνομαι, aor. pass. pple ἀναφανείς — I appear

*ἀναχωρέω, aor. ἀνεχώρησα — I retreat, I withdraw, I back out

ἀναχώρησις -εως, ἡ — retreat

*ἄνεμος -ου, ὁ — wind

*ἄνευ — without (+ gen.)

*ἀνήρ ἀνδρός, ὁ — man

ἀνθέλκω — I drag back

*ἄνθρωπος -ου, ὁ — man, human being

ἀνίημι, aor. pple ἀνείς — I give up, I relax

ἀνοκωκή -ῆς, ἡ — armistice, ceasefire

ἀνταλλάσσω, pf. pass. ἀντήλλαγμαι — I change, I exchange

ἀντανάγομαι — I put out to sea against

ἀντεκπλέω — I sail out against (+ dat.)

ἀντέπειμι — I advance to meet

ἀντέχω — I hold out, I endure

*ἀντί — in return for, instead of (+ gen.)

ἀντιλέγω — I speak against, I object

ἀντίπρωρος -ον — with the prow facing

ἀντιτάσσω, aor. ἀντιέταξα — I draw up against, mid. I take up position against, I face in battle

ἄνω — up, upwards

ἀξιόλογος -ον — worth mention

*ἄξιος -α -ον — worth, worthy of, corresponding to (+ gen.)

ἀξιόχρεως -ων — worthy, important, considerable

*ἀξιόω — I require, I demand, I expect, I think it likely

ἀπαγγέλλω, aor. ἀπήγγειλα — I report, I bring a message

ἀπαίρω — I set out, I start (from)

ἀπαιτέω — I demand back

ἀπαλλάσσω, aor. pass. ἀπηλλάγην, fut. pass. ἀπαλλαγήσομαι — I release, I remove; pass. I get rid (of, + gen.)

*ἅπας ἅπασα ἅπαν (ἁπαντ-) — all

ἄπειμι (εἰμί I am) — I am away

ἄπειμι (εἶμι I go) — I go away

ἀπείργω, aor. ἀπείρξα — I keep (someone) back

ἄπειρος -ον — inexperienced, unused to

ἀπέραντος -ον — endless

ἀπέρχομαι — I go away

*ἀπέχω — I am away, I am distant

ἀπιστέω — I disbelieve, I am doubtful

*ἀπό — from (+ gen.)

ἀποβάθρα -ας, ἡ — landing ladder, gangway

ἀποβαίνω, aor. ἀπέβην — I land, I disembark, I am unfulfilled

ἀπόβασις -εως, ἡ — landing

ἀποδέω — I lack (+ gen.)

ἀποδίδωμι, fut. ἀποδώσω, aor. ἀπέδωκα (3 pl ἀπέδοσαν) pple ἀποδούς (ἀποδοντ-) — I give back, I give what is due

*ἀποθνήσκω, aor. ἀπέθανον — I die, I am killed

ἀποκλήω, pf. pass. ἀποκέκλημαι — I shut off, I prevent

ἀποκνέω, aor. ἀπέκνησα — I hesitate (to + inf.), I hold back (from + inf.)

ἀπόκρημνος -ον — steep, sheer

*ἀποκρίνομαι, aor. ἀπεκρινάμην — I answer

ἀπόκρισις -εως, ἡ — answer, reply

*ἀποκτείνω — I kill

ἀπολαμβάνω, pf. pass. ἀπείλημμαι — I cut off

*ἀπορέω, aor. ἠπόρησα — I am uncertain, I am at a loss

*ἀπορία -ας, ἡ — lack, shortage, difficulty

ἄπορος -ον — difficult, hard to deal with

ἀποσημαίνω — I point, I signal, I allude

ἄπρακτος -ον — without success, without achieving anything

*ἀπροσδόκητος -ον — unexpected

*ἀργύριον -ου, τό — money, silver

ἀριστοποιέομαι — I have a (midday) meal

ἀρχή -ῆς, ἡ — command, beginning

*ἄρχω — I am in command, I hold office

*ἄρχων -οντος, ὁ — commander, magistrate

ἀσθένεια -ας, ἡ — weakness

Ἀσίνη -ης, ἡ — Asine

ἀσκός -οῦ, ὁ — skin, bag

*ἄσμενος -η -ον — glad, pleased

*ἀσπίς -ίδος, ἡ — shield

ἄτρακτος -ου, ὁ — spindle, arrow

ἀτραπός -οῦ, ἡ — path, track
ἀτριβής -ές — pathless, untrodden
*αὖ — again, on the other hand
*αὖθις — again
αὐλίζομαι, aor. ηὐλισάμην — I camp for the night
αὐτόθι — there, on the spot
*αὐτός -ή -ό — self, (not nom.) him, her, it, (with article) the same
αὐτοῦ — there, on the spot
ἀφανής -ές — unseen, hidden
ἀφειδής -ές — without sparing, regardless of cost
ἀφίημι, aor. pple ἀφείς — I give up, I let go
*ἀφικνέομαι, aor. ἀφικόμην, pf. ἀφῖγμαι — I arrive
Ἀχαία -ας, ἡ — Achaea
ἀχθηδών -όνος, ἡ — annoyance, provocation

*βάλλω, aor. ἔβαλον — I throw, I strike, I pelt, I fire at
βιάζω, aor. ἐβίασα — I force, I force my way, I drive to retreat, I overpower (act. or mid.)
βίαιος -α -ον — forced, violent
*βλάπτω — I harm, I damage, I inflict loss on
*βοάω — I shout
*βοή -ῆς, ἡ — shout
*βοηθέω, pf. βεβοήθηκα — I go to help, I come in support, (with ἐπί) I march against
*βουλεύω, aor. ἐβούλευσα — I consider, I resolve, I decide (act. or mid.)
*βούλομαι — I want, I wish
*βραδύς -εῖα -ύ — slow
Βρασίδας -ου, ὁ — Brasidas
βραχύς -εῖα -ύ — short, brief
βρῶμα -ατος, τό — food

γαλήνη -ης, ἡ — calm weather
*γάρ — for
γέλως -ωτος, ὁ — laughter
*γῆ γῆς, ἡ — earth, land
*γίγνομαι, aor. ἐγενόμην — I become, I happen
*γιγνώσκω, aor. ἔγνων pple γνούς (γνοντ-) — I learn, I observe, aor. I know

*γνώμη -ης, ἡ — mind, judgement, opinion, expectation, determination
δασύς -εῖα -ύ — thickly wooded, overgrown
*δέ — and, but
δέδοικα (pf. as pres.), plpf. as past ἐδεδοίκη — I fear
δείδω, pf. pple δεδιώς — I fear, I am afraid
*δεινός -ή -όν — terrible, formidable, clever
*δέομαι — I ask for, I need (+ gen.)
*δέχομαι — I receive, I accept
*δή — indeed, of course
*δῆλος -η -ον — clear, visible
*δηλόω — I show
δήλωσις -εως, ἡ — point, meaning, explanation
δημαγωγός -οῦ, ὁ — leader of the people
Δημοσθένης -ους, ὁ — Demosthenes
*διά — (+ acc.) because of, on account of, with, to cause; (+ gen.) through, by means of, with
*διαβαίνω, aor. διέβην — I go through, I cross
διαβάλλω, aor. pass. διεβλήθην — I slander, I malign, pass. I get a bad reputation
διαγιγνώσκω — I distinguish
διαδίδωμι — I distribute
διαιρέω, aor. διεῖλον — I divide
διακηρυκεύομαι — I communicate by herald, I send a messenger
διακινδυνεύω — I risk everything, I fight to the end
διακομίζω, aor. διεκόμισα — I bring, I carry across, I recover (something) (act. or mid.)
διακόσιοι -αι -α — 200
διακρίνω, aor. pass. διεκρίθην — I separate
διαλύω, plpf. pass. διελελύμην — I terminate
διαμάω — I scrape through
διαμέλλω — I delay
διανοέομαι, aor. διενοήθην — I intend, I have in mind
διαπλέω, aor. διέπλευσα — I sail through, I sail across
διαπράσσω — I carry through, I accomplish (act. or mid.)

διασκευάζομαι — I make preparations

διασῴζω, aor. διέσωσα — I save

διατάσσω, plpf. pass. διετετάγμην — I post, I arrange

διατρέφω — I sustain throughout

διαφεύγω, aor. διέφυγον — I escape

*διαφθείρω, pf. pass. διέφθαρμαι, fut. pass. διαφθαρήσομαι — I destroy, I kill

*δίδωμι, aor. ἔδωκα inf. δοῦναι — I give

διίστημι, intr. aor. διέστην — I separate, (intr. and pass.) I am divided

*δίκαιος -α -ον — just, honest

*διότι — because

δίς — twice

δίψα -ης, ἡ — thirst

*διώκω — I pursue

*δοκέω — I seem, I seem good, I think, δοκεῖ μοι I decide

*δόξα -ης, ἡ — reputation, opinion

δοράτιον -ου, τό — spear

*δουλόω, pf. pass. δεδούλωμαι — I enslave, I subdue

*δρόμος -ου, ὁ — run

*δύναμαι, aor. ἐδυνήθην — I am able

*δύναμις -εως, ἡ — power, force

*δυνατός -ή -όν — possible

*δύο δυοῖν — two

*ἐάν — if (+ subj.)

*ἑαυτόν -ήν -ό — himself, herself, itself (refl., no nom.)

*ἑβδομήκοντα — seventy

*ἐγγύς — near (+ gen. or as adv.)

ἐγκαταλαμβάνω — I capture in, I find in

ἔγκειμαι — I attack, I press on

ἔγκλημα -ατος, τό — objection, ground of complaint

*ἐθέλω — I am willing

ἔθος -ους, τό — custom

*εἰ — if

εἰκάζω, aor. ἤκασα — I compare, I conjecture

*εἰκός -ότος, τό — (what is) reasonable, appropriate, likely, expected

*εἴκοσι(ν) — twenty

Εἴλως -ωτος, ὁ — Helot

*εἰμί impf. ἦν — I am, (impers. 3rd singular) it is possible

εἴργω — I hinder, I prevent, I bar the way

*εἰρήνη -ης, ἡ — peace

*εἰς μία ἕν — one

*ἐκ, ἐξ — out of, from (+ gen.)

*ἕκαστος -η -ον — each

*ἑκάτερος -α -ον — each of two

ἑκατέρωθεν — from/on each side

*ἑκατόν — 100

*ἐκεῖνος -η -ο — that

*ἐκκλησία -ας, ἡ — assembly

ἐκπλέω, fut. ἐκπλεύσομαι — I sail out

ἔκπληξις -εως, ἡ — alarm, panic

ἐκπλήσσω, aor. ἐξέπληξα — I alarm, I cause consternation to

ἐκπολιορκέω — I take by siege, I blockade successfully

ἐκφέρω, aor. pass. ἐξηνέχθην — I carry out, I carry ashore

ἐλάσσων -ον — less, worse, pl. fewer

*ἐλευθερία -ας, ἡ — freedom

*ἕλκω — I drag

*Ἕλληνες -ων, οἱ — Greeks

*ἐλπίζω — I hope, I think, I expect

ἐλπίς -ίδος, ἡ — hope

ἐμβάλλω, aor. ἐνέβαλον — I attack, I ram (+ dat.)

ἐμβοάω, aor. ἐνεβόησα — I shout, I raise a shout

ἐμπειρία -ας, ἡ — experience, skill

ἔμπειρος -ον — experienced in, familiar with (+ gen.)

ἐμπίπρημι, aor. pass. ἐνεπρήσθην — I burn, I set light to

ἐμπίπτω, aor. ἐνέπεσον — I fall upon, I attack (+ dat.)

*ἐν — in, at, among (+ dat.), ἐν τούτῳ meanwhile, ἐν φυλακῇ under guard

ἐνάγω — I urge on, I egg on, I influence

ἐναντιόομαι — I oppose

*ἐνάντιος -α -ον — opposite, ἐξ ἐναντίας from the front, head-on

ἐναποκλάω, plpf. pass. ἐναπεκεκλάσμην — I break off in

ἐνδεεστέρως — more sparingly

ἐνδίδωμι, fut. ἐνδώσω, aor. ἐνέδωκα inf. ἐνδοῦναι — I give in, I make concessions

*ἐνταῦθα — here, then

ἐντός — within (+ gen.)

*ἐντυγχάνω — I get in the way of (+ dat.)

ἐξαγγέλλω — I bring a report

ἐξαναχωρέω — I withdraw from, I back out of

ἐξαπαλλάσσω, aor. pass. ἐξαπηλλάγην — I rid (someone) of, I extricate

ἐξαπίνης — suddenly

ἐξελαύνω, aor. ἐξήλασα — I drive out (act. or mid.)

ἐξίστημι, impf. mid. ἐξιστάμην — I put out, I drive out, mid. I stand aside, I withdraw

ἐξουσία -ας, ἡ — power, resources, possibility

*ἐπειδή — when, since

ἔπειμι — I go against, I attack (+ dat.), I follow

ἐπεκθέω — I charge out against

ἐπεξέρχομαι, aor. ἐπεξῆλθον — I go in pursuit of, I follow up (+ dat.)

ἐπέρχομαι, aor. ἐπῆλθον — I come upon, I get near to

ἐπερώτησις -εως, ἡ — question, enquiry

ἐπεσβαίνω — I enter (to meet the enemy)

ἐπεσπλέω, fut. ἐπεσπλευσέομαι — I sail in to confront

ἐπέχω, aor. ἐπέσχον — I check, I wait

*ἐπί — (+ acc.) to, onto, to fetch, for, against, (+ gen.) on, to, (+ dat.) at, by, against, in the hands/ power of, on condition of

ἐπιβιβάζω, aor. ἐπεβίβασα — I put on board

ἐπιβοάω — I shout out

ἐπιβοηθέω — I attack, I go to support (+ dat.)

ἐπιγίγνομαι — I come on, I arise, I follow, (of time) I run on

ἐπιδίδωμι — I give, I make a present of

ἐπιδιώκω — I pursue

ἐπιδρομή -ῆς, ἡ — attack, raid

ἐπιθέω — I charge, I attack, I run at (+ dat.)

ἐπιθυμέω — I desire (+ gen.)

ἐπικαλέω — I call on, I appeal to, I protest against

ἐπικαταβαίνω — I go down to face (the enemy)

ἐπίκειμαι — I attack, I press on (+ dat.)

ἐπικελεύομαι — I urge (+ dat.)

ἐπικηρυκεύομαι — I make overtures

ἐπικλάω, aor. pass. ἐπεκλάσθην — I bend, I break, pass. I am broken (in spirit)

ἐπιλαμβάνω, aor. ἐπέλαβον — I come upon, I overtake (+ acc.), mid. I lay hold of (+ gen.)

ἐπίμαχος -ον — open to attack

ἐπινοέω — I plan

ἐπιπλέω — I am on board, I sail against (+ dat.)

ἐπιπλοῦς -οῦ, ὁ — attack

ἐπίπονος -ον — burdensome, troublesome

ἐπιρρώννυμι, aor. ἐπέρρωσα — I encourage, I give new strength to

ἐπισπέρχω — I urge on, I spur on

ἐπισπόμενος -η -ον — following, having followed (aor. mid. pple of ἐφέπω)

Ἐπιτάδας -ου, ὁ — Epitadas

*ἐπιτήδεια -ων, τά — provisions, supplies

ἐπιτιμάω — I blame, I criticize

ἐπιτρέχω, aor. ἐπέδραμον — I charge, I attack (+ dat.)

ἐπιχειρέω — I try, I make an attempt

ἐπιχείρησις -εως, ἡ — attempt, initiative

ἐποκέλλω — I run (something) ashore

*ἔργον -ου, τό — work, deed, action

ἐρημία -ας, ἡ — deserted/uninhabited state

*ἐρῆμος -ον — deserted, uninhabited

ἔρομαι — I ask

ἔρυμα -ατος, τό — fort

ἐς (=εἰς) — to, into, among, for the purpose of (+ acc.)

ἐσάγω — I bring to, I transport

ἐσακούω — I hear

ἔσειμι — I go into, I occur to

ἐσνέω — I swim to/into

ἐσπέμπω — I send to, I send in

ἐσπλέω — I sail into, I am shipped into

ἐσπλοῦς -οῦ, ὁ — sailing in , entrance

*ἔσχατος -η -ον — furthest, (at the) edge/ extremity

*ἕτερος -α -ον — other, another

*ἔτι — still, further, any longer

ἑτοιμάζω — I make ready

*ἕτοιμος -η -ον — ready, easily available

εὐαπόβατος -ον — easy to land on

εὐεργεσία -ας, ἡ | favour, benefit
*εὐθύς | immediately
εὐνή -ῆς, ἡ | bed
*εὑρίσκω, aor. ηὗρον | I find
εὐρυχωρία -ας, ἡ | open space, open sea
εφ' ᾧ | on the condition that
ἐφαιρέομαι, pf. ἐφῄρημαι | I am chosen in addition/ succession
ἐφέλκω | I drag behind
ἐφέπω | I pursue (act. or mid.)
ἔφοδος -ου, ἡ | attack, march (against), approach
ἔφορμος -ου, ὁ | anchorage, blockade
*ἐχθός -οῦ, ὁ | (personal) enemy
*ἔχω, aor. ἔσχον | I have, I have the means/ ability, (aor. sometimes) I put in
*ἕως | until
ἕως -ω, ἡ | dawn

Ζάκυνθος -ου, ἡ | Zacynthus
*ζάω | I live, I am alive

*ἤ | or, than
ἤ | where
*ἤ . . . ἤ | either . . . or
*ἤδη | now, already, at once
*ἥκιστα | least
*ἥκω | I have come
*ἥλιος -ου, ὁ | sun
*ἡμέρα -ας, ἡ | day
ἤν (= ἐάν) | if, in case
*ἤπειρος -ου, ἡ | mainland
ἠπειρώτης -ου, ὁ | landsman
ᾗπερ | where
ἡσσάομαι, aor. ἡσσήθην | I am inferior (to), I am beaten (by), I yield to (+ gen.)
*ἡσυχάζω | I am inactive, I stay still
ἡσυχία -ας, ἡ | leisure

θαλαμιός -οῦ, ὁ | rower on the lowest bench
*θάλασσα -ης, ἡ | sea
θαλάσσιος -α -ον | of the sea, sea-based, nautical
*θαρσέω, aor. ἐθάρσησα, pf. τεθάρσηκα | I am/become confident
Θεαγένης -ους, ὁ | Theagenes
Θερμοπύλαι -ῶν, αἱ | Thermopylae
*θέρος -ους, τό | summer

θνήσκω, pf. τέθνηκα pple τεθνηκώς or τεθνεώς | I die, I am killed
θόρυβος -ου, ὁ | confusion, uproar
Θρασυμηλίδας -ου, ὁ | Thrasymelidas

*ἰέναι | to go
*ἱκανός -ή -ό | enough, sufficient
Ἴμβριοι -ων, οἱ | Imbrians
Ἱππαγρέτας -ου, ὁ | Hippagretas
*ἵστημι, trans. aor. ἔστησα | I set up
ἰσχυρίζομαι | I maintain, I emphasize
*ἰσχυρός -ά -όν | strong
ἰσχύς -ύος, ἡ | strength, power

καθάπερ | as
*καθίστημι, trans. aor. κατέστησα, intr. aor. κατέστην, aor. mid. καθιστάμην, intr. plpf. καθειστήκη | I put (into a certain state), I establish, I appoint, intr. I settle, I come to be, I am stationed, mid. I come to be, I apply myself (to)
καθοράω, aor. κατεῖδον | I see, I observe
καθορμίζω, aor. καθώρμισα | I bring to anchor, mid. I put in
*καί | and, also, even
*καίπερ | although, despite (+ pple)
*καιρός -οῦ, ὁ | opportunity, chance
καίω, pf. pass. κέκαυμαι | I burn
κακοπαθέω | I suffer hardship, I am in a bad way
*καλέω | I call, I invite
*καλός -ή -όν | fine, beautiful
καλῴδιον -ου, τό | small rope, cord
κάταρσις -εως, ἡ | landing-place
*κατά | (+ acc.) by, at, in, among, according to, in line with, to the extent of, into groups of, (+ gen.) down from
κατάγνυμι, inf. καταγνύναι | I break
κατακαίω, aor. pass. κατεκαύθην | I burn down
καταλαμβάνω, aor. κατέλαβον | I seize, I come upon, I overtake
καταπλέω | I sail to land
κατάπλους -ου, ὁ | sailing to shore
κάταρσις -εως, ἡ | landing-place

κατάσκοπος -ου, ὁ	observer, inspector	*κωλύω, pf. pass. κεκώλυμαι	I hinder, I prevent, I bring to a halt
καταφανής -ές	easily seen		
καταφέρω	I carry ashore	λάθρᾳ	secretly
καταφεύγω, pf. καταπέφευγα	I flee for refuge	*Λακεδαιμόνιοι -ων, οἱ	Spartans
*καταφρονέω, aor. κατεφρόνησα	I despise	Λακωνικός -ή -όν	Laconian
		*λαμβάνω, aor. ἔλαβον, pf. εἴληφα, aor. pass. ἐλήφθην	I take, I capture
κατέχω	I gain control of, I check, I am stationed		
κατόπιν	behind	*λανθάνω, aor. ἔλαθον	I escape (the) notice (of), I am unobserved
κάχληξ -ηκος, ὁ	shingle		
*κεῖμαι	I lie, I am placed	*λέγω, aor. εἶπον, pf. pass. εἴρημαι, plpf. pass. εἰρήμην	I say, I speak, I mean
*κελεύω, aor. ἐκέλευσα	I order, I urge, I advise		
		Λήμνιοι -ων, οἱ	Lemnians
*κενός -ή -όν	empty, not manned	*λίθος -ου, ὁ	stone
κήρυγμα -ατος, τό	proposal, proclamation	*λιμήν -ένος, ὁ	harbour
		λιμός -οῦ, ὁ	hunger, famine
*κῆρυξ -υκος, ὁ	herald, envoy	λίνον -ου, τό	flax (a plant); λίνου σπέρμα linseed
*κηρύσσω, aor. ἐκήρυξα, pf. pass. κεκήρυγμαι	I invite, I proclaim, I propose		
		λιποψυχέω, aor. ἐλιποψύχησα	I faint
*κινδυνεύω	I am in danger, I run a risk	λογάδην	as picked up, roughly laid
*κίνδυνος -ου, ὁ	danger, risk	λογίζομαι	I reflect, I reckon
Κλεαίνετος -ου, ὁ	Cleaenetus	*λόγος -ου, ὁ	word, reckoning, expectation, proposal
Κλέων -ωνος, ὁ	Cleon		
κολυμβητής -οῦ, ὁ	diver	*λοιπός -ή -όν	left, remaining, rest
κομιδή -ῆς, ἡ	conveyance	*λύω, pf. pass. λέλυμαι	I dissolve, I terminate
*κομίζω, aor. mid. ἐκομισάμην, aor. pass. ἐκομίσθην	I bring, I convey, mid. I recover		
		*μάλιστα	especially, most, (with num.) about
κονιορτός -οῦ, ὁ	cloud of dust		
*κόπτω, pf. pass. κέκκομαι	I strike, I disable, I grind	*μᾶλλον	more, rather
		μανιώδης -ες	seeming like madness
κουφολογία -ας, ἡ	light talking	μάρτυς -υρος, ὁ	witness
κοῦφος -η -ον	light	*μάχη -ης, ἡ	fight, fighting, battle
*κρατέω, aor. ἐκράτησα	I win, I overcome, I have the upper hand, I gain control of (+ gen.)	*μάχομαι	I fight
		*μέγας -άλη -α	big, great
		*μείζων -ον	bigger, greater
		μελιτόω, pf. pass. μεμελίτωμαι	I mix with honey
Κρατησικλῆς -έους, ὁ	Cratesicles		
κράτιστος -η -ον	strongest, best	*μέλλω	I am about to, I intend, I delay, I am sure to
*κράτος -ους, τό	power, strength, κατὰ κράτος with all one's might		
		*μέν ... δέ	on the one hand ... on the other
κρείσσων -ον	better (than), superior (to) (+ gen.)	*μένω	I remain, I stay, I stand my ground
κρημνώδης -ες	precipitous		
κρήνη -ης, ἡ	spring	*μέρος -ους, τό	part, turn
*κυβερνήτης -ου, ὁ	helmsman, steersman	*μέσος -η -ον	middle (of)
κυκλόω, pf. pass. κεκύκλωμαι	I encircle	Μεσσήνιος -α -ον	Messenian
		μετά	(+ acc.) after, (+ gen.) with
κύκλωσις -εως, ἡ	encircling	μεταμέλομαι	I repent, I regret
κωλύμη -ης, ἡ	hindrance, prevention	*μεταπέμπω	I send for (act. or mid.)

μετέωρον -ου, τό — high ground

μετέωρος -ον — high; out at sea, away from land

μέτριος -α -ον — moderate, medium, mildly enforced

*μέχρι — until (+ gen. or as conj.)

*μή — not; (+ vb. of fearing) that, lest

*μηδέ — not even

*μηκέτι — no longer

μήκων -ωνος, ἡ — poppy, poppy-seed

*μηχανή -ῆς, ἡ — machine, engine of war

*μία — one (f)

*μικρός -ά -όν — small, little

*μόλις — hardly, with difficulty, just about

ναυάγιον -ου, τό — shipwreck

ναύαρχος -ου, ὁ — commander

*ναυμαχέω — I fight a sea-battle

*ναυμαχία -ας, ἡ — sea-battle, naval battle

Ναύπακτος -ου, ἡ — Naupactus

*ναῦς νεώς, ἡ — ship

*νεκρός -οῦ, ὁ — dead body

νεωστί — recently

*νῆσος -ου, ἡ — island

Νικήρατος -ου, ὁ — Niceratus

Νικίας -ου, ὁ — Nicias

Νίσαια -ας, ἡ — Nisaea

*νομίζω — I think

*νόμος -ου, ὁ — law, custom

*νοῦς νοῦ, ὁ — mind

*νῦν — now

*νύξ νυκτός, ἡ — night

νῶτον -ου, τό — back, rear, κατὰ νώτου in the rear

ξύγκειμαι — I am agreed, (impers. 3rd singular) it has been agreed

ξυγκλήω, aor. ξυνέκλησα — I close up, I close ranks

ξυγχωρέω, aor. ξυνεχώρησα — I agree, I make concessions

ξύλον -ου, τό — wood, timber (esp. of/for ships)

ξυμβαίνω, fut. ξυμβήσομαι — I happen, I come together, I make an agreement

ξύμβασις -εως, ἡ — treaty, agreement

*ξύμμαχος -ου, ὁ — ally

ξύμπας -πασα -παν (ξυμπαντ-) — whole

ξύμπτωμα -ατος, τό — desperate position, predicament

ξυμφέρω — I am convenient, I am useful

*ξυμφορά -ᾶς, ἡ — disaster

*ξύν (= σύν) — with (+ dat.)

ξύνεδρος -ου, ὁ — delegate, man to confer with (+ dat.)

ξυνεθίζω, pf. mid. ξυνείθισμαι — I accustom, mid. I become accustomed

ξυνέρχομαι, aor. ξυνῆλθον — I meet

ξυντάσσω, aor. ξυνέταξα — I draw up, mid. I form up

ξυντρίβω, aor. ξυνέτριψα — I shatter, I smash to pieces

ὁ δέ — but he (changing subject)

*ὁ ἡ τό — the, ὁ δέ but he (changing subject), οἱ μέν . . . οἱ δέ some . . . others, one side . . . the other

οἱ — to him (dat. of refl. pron. ἕ)

*ὁδός -οῦ, ἡ — road, route

*οἶκος -ου, ὁ — house, home

*οἶνος -ου, ὁ — wine

οἴομαι — I think

*οἷός τ᾽ εἰμι — I am able, n it is possible

οἷος -α -ον — such as, of the sort which

οἰστός -οῦ, ὁ — arrow

ὀκέλλω, aor. ὤκειλα — I run (a ship) aground

*ὀκτακόσιοι -αι -α — 800

*ὀκτώ — eight

*ὀλίγος -η -ον — small, small amount, pl. few

ὁμαλός -ή -όν — level

*ὅμοιος -α -ον — like, equal (to + dat.)

ὁμοίως — in the same way

ὁμόσε — to the same place, to meet, to close quarters

*ὀξύς -εῖα -ύ — sharp, quick

ὅπη — where

*ὅπλα -ων, τά — arms, weapons

*ὁπλίτης -ου, ὁ — hoplite (heavily armed foot-soldier)

ὁπόθεν — from where

ὁποσονοῦν — however much, however little

ὁπόσος -η -ον — how great, as great as, as much as

ὁπόταν — whenever (+ subj.)

ὁπότε	when	*παραινέω	I advise (+ dat.)
*ὅπως	how, as, in order that	παρακελεύομαι, aor.	I encourage, I advise
*ὁράω, aor. εἶδον	I see	παρεκελευσάμην	
ὀρέγομαι	I desire, I reach out for (+ gen.)	παρακελευσμός -οῦ, ὁ	encouragement
		παρακινδυνεύω	I run risks, I make a rash venture
ὁρμάω, aor. ὥρμησα, pf. mid. ὥρμημαι, plpf. mid. ὡρμήμην	I set in motion, I set off, I make (an attack); mid. I start, I rush, I am eager	παραπέμπω	I send along (the coast)
		παραπίπτω, aor. παρέπεσον	I occur, I arise, I present myself
ὁρμέω	I anchor	παραπλέω	I sail along the coast
ὅρμος -ου, ὁ	anchorage	*παρασκευάζω, aor. παρεσκεύασα	I prepare, mid. I prepare myself, I get ready (for)
*ὅς ἥ ὅ	who, which		
ὅσος -η -ον	as great as, pl. as many as, all those who	παρασκευή -ῆς, ἡ	preparation, armament, force
*ὅστις ἥτις ὅτι	who, which, whoever, whatever	παράσπονδος -ον	contrary to agreement, in breach of truce
ὁστισοῦν ὁτιοῦν	whoever, whatever, n as adv. at all, in any respect	παρατάσσω, pf. pass. παρατέταγμαι	I draw up, I station
		παρείκω	I yield, I give a footing
ὅσῳ ... τόσῳ	the more ... the more	*πάρειμι, impf. παρῆν	I am present, ἐν τῷ παρόντι in the present situation
*ὅτε	when		
*ὅτι	that, because, (+ sup.) as ... as possible	παρεξειρεσία -ας, ἡ	outrigger (attached to side of trireme)
ὅτι μή	except		
ὅτιπερ	because in fact	παρέρχομαι, aor. παρῆλθον	I come forward
*οὐ, οὐκ, οὐχ	not		
*οὐδέ	and not, not even	*παρέχω, aor. παρέσχον	I provide, I cause, I inflict
*οὐδείς -εμία -έν	no-one, nothing, no, (n as adv.) not at all	παρίημι, aor. παρῆκα	I let pass, I lower
*οὐκέτι	no longer	παρακινδυνεύω	I dare recklessly
*οὖν	therefore	*πᾶς πᾶσα πᾶν (παντ-)	all, every, any possible
*οὔτε ... οὔτε	neither ... nor		
*οὗτος αὕτη τοῦτο	this	*πάσχω, aor. ἔπαθον, plpf. ἐπεπόνθη	I suffer, I am treated, I fare
*οὕτω	thus, so, in this way		
ὄχλος -ου, ὁ	crowd	*παύω, aor. ἔπαυσα, plpf. mid. ἐπεπαύμην	I stop, I cause to cease, mid. I cease
ὄψις -εως, ἡ	sight		
πάθος -ους, τό	suffering, calamity, disaster	πεζομαχέω	I fight a land battle
		*πεζός -ή -όν	on foot, on land
*παλαιός -ά -όν	old, ancient	*πείθω, aor. ἔπεισα	I persuade
πανταχόθεν	from/on all sides	*πειράομαι	I try, I assault
*παρά	(+ acc.) along, beside, contrary to	πέλαγος -ους, τό	sea, open sea
		Πελοποννήσιοι -ων, οἱ	Peloponnesians
παραβαίνω, aor. pass. παρεβάθην	I transgress, I break (e.g. a law)		
		Πελοπόννησος -ου, ἡ	Peloponnese
παραβοηθέω	I reinforce, I arrive in support, I come to the rescue of (+ dat.)	*πελταστής -οῦ, ὁ	light-armed soldier
		πέμπω, aor. ἔπεμψα	I send
παραγγέλλω	I give a command	*πέντε	five
παραγίγνομαι	I am near, I arrive	*πεντήκοντα	fifty
*παραδίδωμι, aor. παρέδωκα inf. παραδοῦναι pple παραδούς (παραδοντ-)	I surrender, I hand over, I give up	*περί	(+ acc.) about, around, with, under the command of, (+ gen.) about, concerning
παραδωσείω	I am willing to give up	περιαλγέω	I am greatly distressed

περιγίγνομαι, fut. περιγενήσομαι — I survive, I prevail, I escape

περίειμι (εἰμί I am) — I am left, I survive

περίειμι (εἶμι I go) — I go round

περιέρχομαι, aor. περιῆλθον — I go round

περιίστημι, intr. aor. περιέστην, intr. pf. pple περιεστώς — I set round, intr. I stand round, I turn round, I encompass

περίοδος -ου, ἡ — way round, surrounding

περιοράω, aor. περιεῖδον — I overlook, I allow

περιορμέω — I anchor round

περιπέμπω — I send round

περιπλέω — I sail round

περίπλεως -ων — very full (of, + gen.)

περιρρέω, aor. pass. with act sense περιερρύην — I slip off (from around)

Πέρσαι -ῶν, οἱ — Persians

Πηγαί -ῶν, αἱ — Pegae

πιθανός -ή -όν — persuasive, influential

πῖλος -ου, ὁ — felt cap

*πίνω — I drink

*πίπτω, aor. ἔπεσον — I fall

*πιστεύω — I believe, I trust in (+ dat.)

πλάγιος -α -ον — sideways, on the side

*πλείονες -ων — more, (+ art.) the majority

*πλεῖστος -η -ον — most (n often as adv.)

*πλέω, fut. πλεύσομαι, aor. ἔπλευσα — I sail

*πλέων -ον — more

*πλῆθος -ους, τό — number, crowd

*πλήν — except (+ gen. or as adv.)

*πληρόω — I fill, I man (a ship)

*πλοῖον -ου, τό — boat

*πλοῦς -οῦ, ὁ — voyage

πνεῦμα -ατος, τό — breeze, wind

*ποιέω, aor. ἐποίησα, pf. mid. πεποίημαι — I make, I do (act. or mid.)

*πολεμέω — I make war, I fight

πολεμίοι -ων, οἱ — enemy

*πολέμιος -α -ον — hostile, of the enemy, in enemy hands, at war with

*πόλεμος -ου, ὁ — war

*πολιορκέω, aor. pass. ἐπολιορκήθην — I besiege, I blockade

πολιορκία -ας, ἡ — siege, blockade

*πόλις -εως, ἡ — city, state

πολλαπλάσιος -α -ον — many times as much/many

*πολύς πολλή πολύ — much (also n as adv.), great, pl. many, οἱ πολλοί the majority, ἐκ πολλοῦ at long range

*πονέω — I labour, I struggle

*πόνος -ου, ὁ — labour, trouble, harm, distress

πόντος -ου, ὁ — open sea

*ποτε — at some time, once, ever

*που — somewhere, anywhere

*πρέσβεις -ων, οἱ — envoys, ambassadors

*πρίν — before (+ inf.), until

*πρό — before, in front of (+ gen.)

*προθυμέομαι — I am eager, I am determined

*προθυμία -ας, ἡ — eagerness, energy, determination

προκαλέομαι, impf. προυκαλούμην — I invite, I propose

προλαμβάνω — I get the advantage (in, + gen.)

προλέγω, aor. προεῖπον — I make a proclamation, I give notice, I invite

προοράω — I see in front

προπέμπω — I send ahead

*πρός — (+ acc.) to, towards, facing, for the purpose of, in relation to, with, (+ gen.) on the side facing, in favour of, to the advantage of, (+ dat.) in addition to

προσαιρέομαι, aor. προσειλόμην — I choose in addition, I choose as a colleague

προσβαίνω — I approach

*προσβάλλω, aor. προσέβαλον — I attack (+ dat.)

προσβοηθέω — I reinforce (+ dat.)

προσβολή -ῆς, ἡ — attack, base of operations

προσδέχομαι — I expect, I accept

προσδοκία — expectation

πρόσειμι — I approach, I attack (+ dat.)

προσέρχομαι, aor. προσῆλθον — I approach (+ dat.)

προσέχω, aor. προσέσχον — I put in, I come to land

*πρόσθεν — in front (of, + gen. or as adv.)

προσίημι — I send in, mid. I accept

προσίσχω — I come to land, I put in

πρόσκειμαι — I press hard on, I pursue (+ dat.)

προσλαμβάνω, aor. προσέλαβον — I take/gain in addition, I take as a colleague, I get a start/advantage

προσμίγνυμι, aor. προσέμειξα — I approach, I engage with (+ dat.)

πρόσοψις -εως, ἡ — sight, power of seeing, chance of seeing

προσπίπτω, aor. προσέπεσον — I fall upon, I attack (+ dat.)

*πρότερον — before, previously

πρότερος -α -ον — former

προύχω (προέχω) — I am superior, I excel

προφυλακή -ῆς, ἡ — advance guard, outpost

πρόχειρος -ον — ready to hand

Πρωτή -ῆς, ἡ — Prote

*πρῶτον — first

Πύλος -ου, ἡ — Pylos

*πυνθάνομαι — I learn (of)

*πως — somehow

*ῥᾴδιος -α -ον — easy

ῥώμη -ης, ἡ — strength, power, confidence

*σαφής -ές — clear

σίτιον -ου, τό — food

σιτοδεία -ας, ἡ — lack of food

σιτοδοτέω — I supply with provisions

*σῖτος -ου, ὁ — corn, food

σκευάζω, pf. pass. ἐσκεύασμαι — I equip

*σκοπέω — I look for, I watch for, I consider

σμικρός -ά -όν — small

Σπαρτιάτης -ου, ὁ — Spartiate

σπέρμα -ατος, τό — seed

*σπονδαί -ῶν, αἱ — truce, treaty

σπουδή -ῆς, ἡ — energy, effort, enthusiasm

σταδαῖος -α -ον — of a standing type, hand-to-hand, at close quarters

στέγω — I keep off/out, I protect against

στενοχωρία -ας, ἡ — lack of room, cramped conditions

*στρατεύω — I march, I send an expedition

*στρατηγέω — I am a general

*στρατηγός -οῦ, ὁ — general, commander

*στρατιά -ᾶς, ἡ — army

*στρατιώτης -ου, ὁ — soldier

*στρατοπεδεύομαι — I camp

*στρατόπεδον -ου, τό — camp, naval station, army, force

*στρατός -οῦ, ὁ — army

Στύφων -ωνος, ὁ — Styphon

σφάλλω, aor. pass. ἐσφάλην — I cause to fail, pass. I am mistaken, I suffer a calamity, I am foiled

*σφᾶς, dat. σφίσι — them, themselves (often reinforced as σφᾶς αὐτούς)

σφενδόνη -ης, ἡ — sling

*σφέτερος -α -ον — their, their own

*σῴζω, aor. ἔσωσα, aor. pass. ἐσώθην — I save

σῶμα -ατος, τό — body, person

*σώφρων -ον — sensible, prudent

ταλαιπωρέω — I am distressed, I suffer hardship act. or mid.

*τάσσω, aor. ἔταξα, pf. pass. τέταγμαι — I draw up, I arrange, I assess (+ gen. of price), mid. I station myself, I form up

ταὐτά — crasis of τὰ αὐτά

ταύτῃ — at this point, there

τάχος -ους, τό — speed

τε … καί — both … and

*τε … τε — both … and

*τείχισμα -ατος, τό — fort

*τεῖχος -ους, τό — wall, fort

τελευταῖος -α -ον — last, final

τέλος — at last, finally

*τεσσαράκοντα — forty

*τέσσαρες -α — four

*τετρακόσιοι -αι -α — 400

τεχνάομαι — I contrive, I devise means

τηρέω, aor. ἐτήρησα, fut. pass. τηρήσομαι — I watch, I wait for, I look for an opportunity, I keep under guard

*τιμάω, pf. pass. τιτίμημαι — I honour, I value

*τις, τι (τιν-) — some, someone, something

τιτρώσκω, aor. ἔτρωσα — I wound, I damage

*τοιοῦτος -αύτη -οῦτο — such, of such a sort

*τολμάω, aor. ἐτόλμησα — I dare, I have the nerve

*τόξευμα -ατος, τό — arrow

*τοξότης -ου, ὁ — archer

*τοσοῦτος -αύτη -οῦτο — so great, pl. so many

*τότε — then

*τραυματίζω, aor. ἐτραυμάτισα, aor. pass. ἐτραυματίσθην — I wound

τραχύς -εῖα -ύ — rough, rugged

*τρεῖς τρία — three

*τρέπω — I turn (something), I rout

*τριάκοντα — thirty

*τριακόσιοι -αι -α — 300

τριηραρχέω — I command a trireme

τριήραρχος -ου, ὁ — commander of a trireme

*τριήρης -ους, ὁ — trireme (warship with three banks of oars)

*τρίς — three times

*τρίτος -η -ον — third

Τροιζήν -ῆνος, ἡ — Troezen

*τροπαῖον -ου, τό — trophy

*τρόπος -ου, ὁ — method, custom, style

*τυγχάνω, fut. τεύξομαι, aor. ἔτυχον — I hit the mark, I happen to (+ pple), I obtain (+ gen.)

τυρός -οῦ, ὁ — cheese

*τύχη -ης, ἡ — fortune, chance

ὑγιής -ές — healthy, honest, sound

*ὕδωρ -ατος, τό — water

*ὕλη -ης, ἡ — wood, forest

ὑλώδης -ες — wooded

*ὑπισχνέομαι — I promise

*ὑπό — (+ gen.) by, in the light of, because of

ὑποθορυβέω — I make an uproar

ὑπονοέω — I suspect

ὑποστρέφω — I turn round, I wheel round

ὑπόσχεσις -εως, ἡ — promise

ὑποφεύγω — I shrink from, I duck out of

ὑποχωρέω — I retreat, I withdraw, I give way

ὑποψία -ας, ἡ — suspicion

*ὑστεραία -ας, ἡ — the next day

*ὕστερον — later

ὑφίστημι, intr. aor. ὑπέστην — I place under, intr./mid. I undertake

ὕφυδρος -ον — under water

ὕψος -ους, τό — height

*φαίνομαι, fut. φανήσομαι — I appear

φανερός -ά -όν — clear, conspicuous

Φάραξ -ακος, ὁ — Pharax

φείδομαι — I spare (+ gen.)

φέρω — I carry, pass. sometimes I am hurled

*φεύγω — I flee, I run away

*φημί, past ἔφην — I say

*φιλέω — I like, I love, (+ inf.) I tend to, I usually do

*φοβέομαι — I fear

φράσσω, aor. ἔφαρξα — I block

φρουρίς -ίδος, ἡ — guard-ship

*φυγή -ῆς, ἡ — flight, escape

φυλακή -ῆς, ἡ — guard, custody, guard-post, blockade

φυλακτήριον -ου, τό — fort, outpost

*φύλαξ -ακος, ὁ — guard

*φυλάσσω — I guard, I keep watch (over), mid. I am anxious about (+ gen.)

*χαλεπός -ή -όν — difficult, dangerous

χαλεπότης -ητος, ἡ — difficulty

χαλεπῶς — with difficulty

*χειμών -ῶνος, ὁ — storm, stormy weather, winter

*χείρ χειρός, ἡ — hand, arm

χειρόομαι, fut. χειρώσομαι — I overpower, I capture

Χῖος -α -ον — Chian, of Chios

*χράομαι, aor. ἐχρησάμην — I use, I deal with (+ dat.)

*χρή, impf. χρῆν — it is necessary

*χρήματα -ων, τά — money

*χρόνος -ου, ὁ — time

*χώρα -ας, ἡ — country, land, κατὰ χώραν in place, in position

*χωρέω, aor. ἐχώρησα — I go, I advance

*χωρίον -ου, τό — place, position, ground

ψευδής -ές — false, lying

*ψηφίζομαι, aor. ἐψηφισάμην — I vote

ψιλός -ή -όν — light-armed

*ὧδε — so, thus

ὠθέω, aor. ἔωσα — I push, I force my way, mid. I drive back, I dislodge

*ὡς — as, when, that, + fut. pple in order to, + sup. as ... as possible, ὡς εἰπεῖν so to speak

ὥσπερ — just as

*ὥστε — (so) that, so as to, as a result, with the result that, on the condition that

ὠφέλιμος -η -ον — useful, advantageous

Plato, *Apology*

Introduction by Steven Kennedy

Commentary Notes and Vocabulary by
Benedict Gravell

AS: 18a7–24b2

A-level: 35e–end

Introduction

ἀλλ' ἐλεύθεροι
παρρησίᾳ θάλλοντες οἰκοῖεν πόλιν
κλεινῶν Ἀθηνῶν
But let free men,
who abound in free speech, live in the city
of glorious Athens.
EURIPIDES, *HIPPOLYTUS*, 421

Scholars assume (although it's far from certain) that Plato's earliest texts are those which are most closely concerned with the 'historical' Socrates. If this is true, then the *Apology*, a record of Socrates' self-defence in court, is one of the earliest examples that we have of Plato's writing. This would mean that the *Apology* is one of the oldest extant works of Greek philosophy that survives in its entirety, and in this, there is something quite appropriate. Socrates wrote nothing himself, and yet here, in Plato's version, we find a first and vivid portrayal of this unusual man and philosopher who would cast a spell over some of the greatest thinkers of his own time and ours.

Socrates was so influential in his life and in his 'afterlife' that the most prominent philosophical 'schools' of thought that came after him, like the Stoics and Academics, claimed him as their founder. He charmed and baffled his interlocutors with the use of irony (εἰρωνεία) in his philosophical inquiries, and even made use of it in his defence in court (*Apol.* 38a, and see Commentary). To an Athenian, this irony meant deception: Was Socrates pretending to or feigning ignorance in order to bring about confusion in his antagonists (at least that's what his enemies claimed), or was his irony a special mode of communication, in which he is trying to get his own message across, provided his listeners had the ears to hear him? But no one could say for certain whether Socrates spoke in earnest, or whether, in fact, he really did know what he professed he did not. It was this way of speaking that made him notorious – his use of εἰρωνεία was admired and imitated, as well as hated and despised.

Socrates' most important contribution to philosophy was to turn its gaze away from natural and astronomical phenomena to 'man', and above all, himself. He was the first philosopher to direct philosophy to *ethical* ends, as Cicero says, he 'brought it down from heaven and placed it in the cities' (*Tusc.* 5.10) Socrates became less concerned about the science of nature and instead studied 'man', and what it mean to be 'good' and to 'live well'. We find much of this in Plato's *Apology*. In many ways, his defence in court is less addressed to the charges against him as it is a speech to his fellow Athenians to convince them that his lifelong pursuit to search out what is good and right and fine, which was so vexing and unpleasant to them, was in fact the most important things we can do as humans, and it alone could make us 'wise'. Philosophy was not a set of beliefs, but an active process: it was not to be confined to writing but dedicated to speaking. He sought always to question and to inquire into how man should live, and stated that nothing should be beyond or above examination.

Even in Plato's own time, the *Apology*, proved hugely popular as a work of rhetoric and philosophy, and it remains so today. Among classicists, it has traditionally been one of the first texts of Greek to be read in its entirety, both among the schools and the universities. It contains much of historical interest, and shows us glimpses of the Athenian court system and its laws, Athenian politics and prejudices, its religious practices, and daily life in the agora. But most importantly, Plato's *Apology* is so eloquent, and Socrates so passionate and courageous, that they convince us of what Socrates wanted to persuade his own fellow Athenians to believe, that 'an unexamined life is not worth living' (*Apol.* 38a); to examine for themselves the greatest questions, what is justice, what is wisdom, what is good, and how ought we to live so that we may say we have lived well. And it is for this reason that the *Apology* is, at least in my view, one of the best introductions to Western philosophy there is.

Socrates

For a man about whom so much has been written, we know almost nothing about Socrates' early life. We know from the *Apology* (17d) that he was 70 years of age at his trial, and so we can generally fix his birth around 469 BC. From the accusation against him, we learn that his father's name was Sophroniscus, and that his deme (or district) was Alopeke, which is an area that lies just south of the city of Athens. Socrates' father was said to have been a stonemason, and a much later tradition holds that Socrates himself followed the trade for some time. His wife was named Xanthippe, an aristocratic name, which would suggest that Socrates was a man of some wealth or social status, and by her he had three sons, two of which were still small children at the time of his trial (*Apol.* 41e). This much we can sketch out, though only from passing references found here and there in Greek literature. It is not until about 432 BC, at the age of about 35, that we start to get a fuller picture of the kind of man Socrates was.

We know he was ugly. This fact might not carry much weight for us today, but to the Athenians, good looks were believed to be a sign of good character ('souls'). This is a society, after all, which commonly used the phrase καλὸς κἀγαθός to mean aristocracy, 'the beautiful and the good'. We learn that Socrates was a big drinker (Pl. *Symp*. 214a), and a passionate man in whom fierce angry and sexual desire needed to be restrained by wisdom. He was considered (at least according to Xenophon) to be snub-nosed, bug-eyed, thick lipped and had a belly – all of which seems to agree with Alcibiades' famous description of Socrates resembling a satyr, as well as other strange creatures like stingrays (*Meno* 80) and crabs (Xen. *Symp*. 5.5).

He fulfilled his duty as a citizen and served as a hoplite in the Athenian military at Potidaea and Amphipolis on the north Aegean coast, and at Delium in Boeotia (*Apol*. 28e). He was physically hardy, and his courage became legendary during the Athenian rout at Delium in 424 BC. While the Athenian army was in disarray and panicked flight, Socrates simply walked away from the battle, staring down anyone who tried to pursue him (Pl. *Symp*. 220d, and *Laches*, 181b). And again, perhaps more famously, Alcibiades, the wayward and controversial young man, admits in Plato's *Symposium* that he owed his life to Socrates. While he was at Potidaea, many soldiers witnessed Socrates during that cold winter, 'dressed in such a coat as he always wore (i.e. a threadbare one), and he made his way more easily over the ice barefoot than the rest of us did in our shoes'. Nevertheless, this famous image we have of Socrates' ascetic lifestyle, of a poor, threadbare and ragged philosopher, was probably a result of his philosophical position rather than of any real poverty. Despite all appearances, he must have had some wealth in his early years. Simply from the fact that Athenian hoplites were required to provide their own weapons and armour (which were indeed expensive) we can assume that Socrates' circumstances at this time were sufficiently affluent.

But it was this simple dress and scruffy habit of Socrates that became easily recognizable to Athenians. In the dramatic competition of 423 BC, two Greek comic writers, Ameipsias in his lost play *Connus* and Aristophanes' *Clouds*, lampooned Socrates for his meagre attire. Ameipsias claimed that Socrates walked around barefoot in order to 'insult shoemakers' and another comic poet, Eupolis, calls Socrates a loquacious thief who went around begging. But Socrates, for all his professions of simple living, also knew how to dress up when he needed. In Plato's *Symposium* (174a), Socrates attends a banquet of poets and aristocrats; this time, he is bathed and slippered, a rare event perhaps, but from time to time, Socrates could dress himself up in his finery. Nevertheless, by the time that Socrates' trial occurred, the city of Athens had been hearing these jokes about Socrates for about thirty years. In fact, his dress and looks became so recognizable, that Aristophanes coined the phrase, τό Σωκρατεῖν, 'to Socratize' in order to mock the young men of the city who went around unwashed with long hair, carrying sticks and pretending to ascetic lifestyles. His manner of living aroused curiosity in a wide variety of Athenians, from the young and old to the wealthy elite and the poor, and as well as foreigners.

Socrates likely had the standard training in music and gymnastics that all noble Athenian men enjoyed, and in his youth showed some interest in natural philosophy (what we now call 'science'). But he soon abandoned this interest in the physical world and at the end of his life he emphatically denied it (*Apol*. 19c, 23d, 26d). In fact, it is most likely that he only ever had a passing understanding of the physical theories he is accused of peddling. What he did know, he learned through his conversations with educated people in the agora or through the casual reading of books which were readily available to anyone (*Apol*. 26d). Certainly, his philosophical life did not flourish in a vacuum, and he was acquainted with many different philosophers and philosophies. Socrates professed he was influenced by many different people, both men and women, which was unusual for his time.

But what kind of philosophy did he practice? The picture his accusers wish to create is of a man that peddles a strange and subversive philosophy. This may appear unfair in our own eyes, but we must remember that it would not have seemed so to many of the conservative Athenians who were sitting in the jury and in the audience. Scientific speculation threatened the contemporary morality and religious life, and Socrates' tricks of argumentation and irony were considered tools which could be used for the deconstruction of well-established and traditional beliefs. These threats were met by the aristocracy with vicious reprisals, firstly in comedy, and then in his trial.

The comedian Aristophanes' had no compunction in submitting Socrates to ridicule in his play, *Clouds* in 423 BC. In it, poor Strepsiades is awake in bed unable to sleep from the worry of legal actions brought against him from unpaid debts which have been incurred by his horse-loving son, Pheidippides. He stumbles upon a plan to weasel out of these debts by enrolling his son in Socrates' Phrontisterion ('Thinkery') to learn how to make bad arguments appear good, and good arguments appear bad. In this way, they could avoid paying their debt. But when Pheidippides discovers that this 'Thinkery' is really a place for 'useless' intellectuals, he refuses and so Strepsiades goes himself. He learns about recent 'important' discoveries like how to measure the distance a flea jumps, how a gnat makes its buzzing noise, and a new large pair of compasses which can be used to steal cloaks from the local gymnasium. The character Socrates descends to the stage in a basket from the clouds while the chorus ridicules him, 'you walk proudly along the streets, rolling your eyes, and endure barefoot many hardships, all the while gazing up at the clouds'. But Strepsiades makes a poor student, and forces his son Pheidippides to attend the 'Thinkery' instead with threats and blows. When he arrives, two colleagues of Socrates, the 'Right Argument' and the 'Wrong Argument' debate who can give Pheidippides the best education. The 'Right Argument' offers a life of earnest work and discipline, while the 'Wrong Argument' counters instead with a life of ease, obtained with smooth talking and clever words. The 'Wrong Argument' wins, of course, and when Strepsiades returns to fetch his son at the end of his education, he meets with a pale and scruffy intellectual who, nevertheless, can talk his way out of paying his debts. But these newly learned talents quickly turn son against father, when Pheidippides starts to argue the case that it is perfectly fine for a son to beat his father as well as his mother. The play ends with Strepsiades blaming Socrates for his troubles, and leading his slaves to attack the 'Thinkery', a hotbed of corruption.

The play was poorly received by the Athenians and did not win any prizes. Nevertheless, the play had a lasting influence and was notorious in its times, particularly for its rather unfeeling portrayal of the philosopher. It is specifically mentioned by Socrates in the *Apology* as a factor contributing to Socrates' eventual conviction (even though this does not occur until nearly two decades after the performance of the play). To put all this in perspective, we ought to remember that *Clouds* was a comedy designed to elicit laughter, as was Aristophanes' burlesque of Socrates. The comedy did not require the audience to know the details either of Socrates' teachings (or his contemporaries', for that matter). It was not a play written to attack Socrates alone, but also satirize intellectuals in general. However, for the play to be effective, the audience would have needed broadly to have a picture of who Socrates was, and what he was getting up to. It seems very unlikely that Socrates created a 'Thinkery' of his own, or that he even charged for tuition. Plato states clearly that during his trial, Socrates denied any expertise in matters, and did not teach for money. This made him very different from the sophists, or self-professed teachers who amassed great wealth (see 19e, and Commentary). Socrates taught for free any who would listen, and as a result of this lived in poverty. We can be sure that Plato would have not so frequently drawn a distinction between Socrates and the sophists if Socrates had already developed a reputation for being a hawker of expensive education – rather, it's easier for us to believe that Aristophanes, along with the other comedians, exaggerated and distorted him for a good laugh. And in any case, such a difference was likely to be ignored by the average Athenian.

One thing that both his detractors and his lauders can agree upon is the fact that Socrates' was regularly found in the agora speaking to individuals of all sorts. He argued with them and questioned them about their beliefs and their knowledge, and examined them, through his unique way of irony and dialectic (from διελεγχω, 'to test, expose, investigate'), to see if they really knew what they claimed to know. While he was dressed in his ragged cloak and shoeless, he pestered and argued with people on a daily basis and in a very public place about things which most people assumed to be true. We can easily see how Socrates soon developed a reputation as a bizarre and unsettling individual. He spent much of his life left alone to speak and philosophize in the agora, at least until compelling political events in the Greek world would bring him before the sharp eyes of the *polis*. Rumours again started to swirl about this unconventional man's connection with strange religious views, and early in 399 BC, he was tried and condemned to death in his native Athens by a jury of his fellow citizens.

Political background to the trial

When we read the *Apology*, we find that Socrates needs to continually remind the jurors of the powerful bias that had been nurtured against him. He is afraid, and it turns out quite rightly, that it will sway them to condemn him unjustly. We have already seen that some of this prejudice comes from his portrayal on the stage by Aristophanes, but much of this bias also finds its roots in political partisanship.

At the end of the very long Peloponnesian War which began in 431 BC, Athens suffered a humiliating defeat at the hands of its rival Sparta in 404 BC; this defeat led to the temporary extinction of its democracy. The Athenian Assembly elected thirty men, three from each of its ten tribes, to restore Athens to its pre-democratic 'ancestral' constitution. However, this arrangement quickly formed into a fierce oligarchical regime known as the 'Thirty Tyrants'. These elected men, supported by a local garrison of Spartan soldiers, soon consolidated their power in the city. They quickly assumed despotic control of Athens, and continued uncontested in power for nine months. During their rule, nearly 1,500 Athenians were executed and their property confiscated, while thousands of others fled the city. The Athenian democrats, who had been ousted from the city, gathered together their own forces and in 403 BC restored the democracy after a bloody civil war. One of the first acts of the restored democracy was to introduce a treaty of reconciliation which offered amnesty to both sides of the war in an attempt to bring about toleration and order in city. With the help of Sparta, it was made illegal for anyone to charge another for crimes committed during the rule of the Thirty Tyrants. Nevertheless, fierce hostility remained between the two sides, and it was common to accuse political enemies of remaining in Athens during the democrats' exile – as Socrates did.

Little is known of Socrates' political life during this time. We can say that he played his part as an ordinary citizen, but compared to many other Athenians, he appears to have been largely apolitical. He served in the army as expected, and he allowed his name to go forward for selection by lot to serve on the Council, but that seems to be the full extent of his participation. He says himself (*Apol.* 31c, 32b–c, 32e) that he had not taken any active part in public affairs, never spoke in the Assembly, nor had he brought any prosecutions or volunteered for selection for jury service in the law courts. We have only one account of his active involvement in political life, which took place in 406 BC. After an Athenian victory at sea, the naval commanders, capitalizing on their victory, failed to gather up the dead from the sea and were therefore brought to court for negligence of duty. The people's assembly voted in anger that the generals be tried collectively, instead of individually as the law dictated. Socrates was assigned by lot to the committee which prepared the business for the assembly, and was the only one who opposed the proposal, on the grounds that it was against the Athenian constitution. This defiance of the popular will did not endear him, he was shouted at, and was threatened with impeachment and arrest. This was during the democracy. But afterwards, during the political crises and the oligarchy, Socrates remained in Athens when others fled. This alone was sufficient ground for hostile allegations by the restored democrats, even though he showed defiance. The Tyrants tried to involve him in their persecutions, and when asked to arrest a certain Leon of Salamis, he simply refused and went home (*Apol.* 32d). He might well have been put to death for this (as he claims), had the democrats not been victorious in their fight. Interestingly, there is no evidence from any of our sources that Socrates took any part in the overthrow of the Tyrants – certainly, if he did, it is likely that Plato would have mentioned it, particularly in his *Apology*. His motivation to disobey therefore was not from any political affiliation with the democrats, but simply on the grounds of the immorality and illegality of the oligarchs' actions, 'with all my might I would not to do anything unjust or unholy' – bravery, indeed.

Although he remained largely aloof from any involvement in politics, he had many political friends on both sides of the political spectrum. On the one hand, Socrates could boast that he was close friends with Lysias (the famous orator, who apparently wrote a defence speech for Socrates) and Chaerephon, both were active members of the democratic power, though the latter was dead before Socrates' trial and could in no way be an aid. More problematically, Socrates also had close friends in the oligarchic party, and these personal associations with men of 'unsavoury' reputation (as Socrates suggests) would have been the root of bias that caused his case substantial damage. Among the oligarchical faction were Charmides and Critias (relatives of Plato, after whom two of his dialogues are named), and both would later be killed in the later bloody overthrow of the tyranny. Charmides, Plato's uncle, was one of the Thirty Tyrants, and was widely thought to have been one of Socrates' admirers (Xenophon claims in his *Recollections of Socrates,* 3.7.1, that it was, in fact, Socrates who pushed Charmides to enter politics in the first place); Critias, as leader of the Thirty, gained a reputation for violence and stubbornness, which turned his name into a byword for wickedness. Given his association with such men, Socrates appeared to be a private accomplice of the oligarchy, and even worse, a mentor of two of the leading members. The orator Aeschines asserted such quite emphatically when, during his speech *Against Timarchus,* he exclaimed that 'You, Athenians, killed the sophist Socrates because he was seen to have educated Critias, one of the thirty who overthrew the democracy.' One other political association cast further doubt on Socrates' character: Alcibiades. Plato represents him as an associate of Socrates who, after the defeat of Athens, turned traitor. He was also supposed to be involved, along with other Socratic associates, such as Phaedrus and Eryximachus, in a famous religious scandal of 415 BC. On the day before the Athenian fleet was to set sail to Sicily, the ἑρμαῖ (*Hermae*, plinths or stone blocks with the heads of Hermes) were mutilated throughout the city, an event that was considered very ill-omened for the expedition. Although dead several years before the trial, Alcibiades' reputation cast a long shadow, and for many jurors his infamous and wayward political career and close connection to Socrates would have been an awkward obstacle during the trial.

Socrates also propounded philosophical views that in turn would have made this political connections appear even worse. In the *Apology* 21b–22a, we hear that Socrates is convinced that many of the politicians held in public esteem are in fact quite ignorant, and yet these politicians consider themselves wise. Now these views can be as easily applied to oligarchs as they can be to democrats, but it was the democrats who were in power and sat in the jury, and such views would sound oligarchic in the mouth of the defendant. Furthermore, Socrates argues (*Apol.* 24c–25c) that there ought to be expertise in politics, just like in every other discipline and pursuit; surely, only a few people, and not the many, can improve the city? These remarks, although they stem from sound philosophical principals, were contrary to the prevalent opinion of those in power, and thought to be particularly anti-democratic.

With friends and opinions like these, some scholars have wondered why Socrates wasn't brought to trial sooner than he was. The answer to this, in all likelihood, was the fact that Athens was in such turmoil and poverty after its defeat by Sparta that the necessities of life would have been a more important focus than the pursuit of political and personal annoyances as Socrates. It seems that his accusers waited for a more favourable time for their cause before they attempted to summon Socrates before the courts with their allegations. The penalty for frivolous lawsuits in Athens was 1,000 drachmas, an enormous sum levied against those whose prosecution gained less than a fifth of the jury vote. Despite this threat, the accusers went ahead and seemed sufficiently confident that the prejudice against Socrates at this time was abundant enough to carry their case. In the end, they won, and their confidence well placed, although Meletus himself does show surprise at how close the vote was.

The trial

Socrates' three named prosecutors, Meletus, Anytus, and Lycon, are all private individuals. There was no real public prosecutor in Athens as we have them today, and all actions in the interest of the state were brought to court by citizens, although they might themselves be prominent politicians or public officials.

The three accusers seemed to have had little in common with each other. Meletus was a young man from the deme of Pitthos, and Plato describes him having a 'beak' for a nose, long straight hair, and a beard which is ill grown. He was a son of a tragic poet of the same name but was considered to be 'little known'. Anytus, on the other hand, was wealthy and prominent as a politician. He inherited great wealth from his father who owned a tanning factory, and was elected as a general for his tribe. In 409 BC, he unsuccessfully tried to retake Pylos from the Spartans, and suffered prosecution for his failure. He managed to avoid punishment through bribery. In 404 BC, he first gave his support to the Thirty Tyrants, but these later banished him and as a result he switched allegiances and became a general for the democratic faction. When the democracy was restored in 403 BC, he became one of its leading members. It should be noted, however, that during the stormy political weather of this time, changing sides was not that uncommon. Lycon appears (if it is the same man as the one here) as a rather genial man, and Xenophon, in his *Symposium*, paints him as a loving father whose son, Autolycus, was put to death by the Thirty. He was of the same generation as Socrates, and stood at the forefront of the democratic.

What it was that brought these different men together in their prosecution of Socrates we cannot be sure. Socrates himself suggests that each had different reasons for the case (*Apol.* 23e), and we have no reason to doubt him. Nothing at all is said about why Meletus wished to prosecute. From this alone, many scholars have suggested that in actual fact, Meletus was only the nominal author of the prosecution, and that the main driver was Anytus. One has suggested that Meletus was a puppet whose strings were pulled by Anytus. From what can be made of the extant evidence, Anytus was a powerful political figure of the time, and displayed an almost fanatical hostility towards the sophists and intellectuals. He appears in Plato's dialogue, the *Meno*, in which he has a rather unpleasant conversation with Socrates. When Socrates suggests to him (*Meno*, 91c) that young men might go to the so-called sophists for an education, Anytus replies, god forbid it, the sophists were a plague and corrupting influence on young men. However, we should note that the vehemence with which he expresses his hostility towards the intellectuals was not an unusual sentiment, and in reality seems to represent the ordinary Athenian democrat after the restoration of 403 BC, and the prevailing attitude towards any innovation either in education or the religious practices of the state. If such was Anytus' hatred of the sophists, it could easily enough be aimed towards Socrates. And additionally, if there was any political element to the trial, it would more likely come from Anytus than the other two. Of the third one, Lycon, we know little. Socrates says (*Apol.* 24a) that he is acting on behalf of the orators – although it is unclear what this means. At any rate, if he is the same man as represented in Xenophon's *Symposium*, then we are at a loss to explain why such a friendly and amiable man suddenly turned into Socrates' accuser.

These were the accusers in the court. But for a student new to the *Apology*, it is important to note that during his speech, Socrates never makes any mention of a judge. All his remarks are addressed to the jury, and if we simply relied on what Socrates says in the text alone, we might not know whether there was a judge or not. However, in classical Athens, there were nine important public magistrates, or archons (ἄρχων, a ruler, or commander). Six acted as judges, and were known as the Θεσμοθέται, *Thesmothetae*. Of the other three, one was called the ἐπώνυμος ἄρχων, the Eponymous Archon (after whom the year was named); another was the πολέμαρχος, Polemarch, who was the chief of the army, and the final one was the ἄρχων βασιλεύς, or King Archon, who played an important role in Socrates' trial. The role of the King Archon was to perform the religious duties of the original kings of Athens, which included acting as judge over court cases involving religion, such as prosecutions for impiety.

We know from Plato's *Euthyphro* that Socrates was involved in a γραφή, a criminal prosecution in the interest of the state, and gave his defence in the court of the King Archon. We can generally reconstruct the narrative as follows: Meletus, as Socrates' chief accuser, was required by law to summon Socrates to appear at a preliminary hearing (an ἀνάκρισις) before the King Archon. This meant that he needed to compose a document that clearly stated his accusation and demanded that the defendant (in this case Socrates) appear before the magistrate on a specified day. The summons would have to be served to Socrates in person, and most likely in public for all to see. This was because religious life in Athens was bound up in civic responsibility, and therefore any prosecution for impiety would have been largely in the public eye. In fact, during the delivery of the summons, any other citizen could also append their name to the document if they wished to support the prosecution. Afterwards, during the preliminary hearing, the King Archon would then decide if the case was serious enough to warrant a trial. Anytus and Lycon were down to act as advocates (συνήγοροι) for Meletus. This meant that they shared in the preparation and presentation of the case, and were also liable to the penalty of sycophancy (harassment) if their case failed. However, in the end, simply because the King Archon allowed the hearing to proceed, we can assume that there was enough evidence against Socrates to warrant the trial.

On the day of the trial, Meletus' indictment would be read aloud in front of the jury and the public audience who would no doubt be in attendance. Socrates, because he was widely known at the time, likely drew many spectators (*Apol.* 24e). The spectators would have been separated from the jurors by railings. Several friends of Socrates would also be present at his trial, certainly Plato, Crito, Critobulus and Apollodorus (*Apol.* 38b), and there to listen to and support him in the proceedings. Socrates and his accusers sat before the jury. The jury court (δικαστηρία) of Athens was derived from the 'People's Court' (known as the Ἡλιαία) and was located in the civic centre of Athens, the agora. It is hard to say for certain their exact number, but a jury of about five hundred was typical, although some scholars suggest a jury of five hundred and one jurors, to avoid a tie. All we know for certain is that Socrates addressed a sizeable jury.

These jurors, or δικασταί, were men over the age of thirty and ordinary citizens of the city. All had to be property owners, most were probably farmers. Citizens commonly volunteered for the duty, and about 6,000 names were chosen by lot annually to act as jurors, and from this, different groups were then randomly assigned to Athens' wide and perplexing array of courts. Each juror was paid about three ὀβολοί for their day's work, not a particularly large amount. Few able-bodied men volunteered for this job; most of the volunteers would probably be old men who could no longer earn money by other means, and relied on the courts as a sort of old-age pension. The result of this produced a fair representation in the courts of poor citizens, but not of different age groups. It should also be noted that there was no screening of jurors: in fact, in Aristophanes' comedy *The Wasps*, an old man amuses himself by getting on a jury every day, and by voting everyone guilty. This being so, and combined with the fact that the jury has nearly absolute power in the court, we should not wonder that Socrates was concerned about the bias against him.

When it came to the trial itself, Athenian law provided for different criminal procedures, and this is reflected in the structure of the *Apology* itself through Socrates' three speeches. In Athens, every case to be decided by a jury court was either 'non-assessable' or 'assessable': in the former kind (the ἀτίμητος ἀγών), a punishment was already defined by law if a guilty verdict was returned, whether it was the death penalty, banishment or a fixed fine.

However, in Socrates' case, his trial was a known as a τιμητὸς ἀγών, or a legal action that also had an 'assessment' (a τίμησις), i.e. the punishment was not defined in law. This means that if the jury decided that the defendant was guilty, it then had to decide on the punishment which would be meted out. However, this could not be anything they wanted. In their 'assessment', the jury could only side with one of the claims of the two parties, either the plaintiff's (the τίμημα of Meletus was the death penalty), or the defendant's ἀντιτίμησις, or counter-proposal. The jury was restricted to these two options alone – they could not invent a third if neither of the two proposals appealed to them. We see this format clearly in the structure and division of Socrates' first two speeches in the *Apology*: the first one, which runs from 17a–35e, presents his defence, and the second one, from 35e–38b, contains his ἀντιτίμησις. A third speech also follows in which he responds to his sentence.

An equal period of time was given to each of the prosecution and defence to make their case. There was probably a water clock, and each side had until the water ran out to make their case. There was not much in the way of rules in presenting evidence. The prosecution and defence could say pretty much whatever they wanted. In some way, and rather ironically, Socrates, who in a sense was put to death for practicing free speech (παρρησία), had more freedom of speech at his trial than most defendants do. Socrates cross examined Meletus (24c–28a) in the same fashion he used to speak to individuals in the agora (17c). Socrates is doing nothing unusual here, but following a legally recognized form of interrogating an accuser in the middle of a defence. But the expectation was for Socrates to humble himself before his fellow citizens and make an appeal to the jury – however, he instead chose to deliver his speech in a bold manner, and antagonized them.

The whole proceedings took around three hours, and the jurors voted immediately with no time given for further deliberation. The court herald would ask the jurors to vote for their decision by putting their bronze ballot disc in one of two urns, one urn for guilty and another for innocent. The result: in the first vote, the jurors decided Socrates was guilty, although only by a slim majority. Socrates (in a sense) refused to counter-propose a penalty. He proposed that he should be awarded free meals at the prytaneum for his public service, which was an enormous honour usually reserved only for victors at the Olympic games. His request outraged the jury, since many thought he was openly mocking them, but it is hard to say whether Socrates was speaking with sincerity. At any rate, he eventually yielded to his friends' requests and proposed a penalty of a half talent (38b), which amounts to eight years' of wages for a skilled craftsman – not an insignificant fine. However, it was too late, and his initial suggestion had antagonized the jury to an extent that they voted for death, and more voted for his death than had voted for his guilt. There is a tradition that, in marked contrast to the first and narrow vote for his guilt, in the second vote, 360 voted in favour of the prosecution's suggestion of death, compared to 140 for acquittal. These figures are debatable, however (see pp. xx).

After a guilty verdict, the jury was accustomed to hear a plea for mercy. It was common to thrown oneself on the mercy of the court by bringing forward wives and children. Refusing to grovel in such a way, Socrates only briefly mentions his family, and neither Xanthippe nor any of his sons comes forward.

The charge against Socrates

The wording of the accusation against Socrates is recorded in several places, but most fully by Diogenes Laertius, a late biographer of Greek philosophers. He quotes Favorinus (a second-century AD Roman philosopher), who claimed that the record of the Socrates' indictment could still be found in the Athenian Metroon (or state public archive):

> This indictment and affidavit is sworn by Meletus, the son of Meletus of Pitthos, against Socrates, the son of Sophroniscus of Alopeke: Socrates is guilty of refusing to recognise the gods recognised by the state, and of introducing other new divinities. He is also guilty of corrupting the youth. The penalty demanded is death. (2.40, *trans*. R. D. Hicks)

Socrates recounts the charge at 24b in the *Apology*. Σωκράτη φησὶν καὶ θεοὺς οὓς ἡ πόλις νομίζει οὐ νομίζοντα, 'They say that Socrates does not believe in the gods that the city believes in.' Much has been written by scholars in an attempt to figure out what exactly this phrase means. Some have tried to highlight the distinction between οὐ θεοὺς νομίζοντα (not recognizing the gods of the city) and οὐ θεοὺς εἶναι νομίζοντα, i.e. not recognizing that the gods *exist*, the latter phrase which would imply atheism more broadly. And so it has been suggested that we should understand the Greek νομίζειν ('to think, believe, recognize') in the same sense as the Greek noun νόμος ('custom, law, common practice'). If this is true, then we might interpret the charge (as stated by Meletus) to mean that Socrates did not follow the typical Athenian religious practices or perform the standard rituals, i.e. that he was a non-conformist, not that he was a complete atheist. The problem with this interpretation of the Greek is that Socrates himself does not make such a distinction. In fact, he uses the two versions interchangeably (26b–28a) when he is interrogating Meletus; Meletus, in his reply, makes his point perfectly clear at

26c, when he claims that Socrates ὡς τὸ παράπαν οὐ νομίζεις θεούς, that he 'wholly doesn't not believe in the gods' – in this phrase, it would be hard to believe Meletus only suggested Socrates 'neglected the rituals'.

The charge must have meant that Socrates violated the law against impiety. Greek religious sentiment expected that citizens by and large shared similar *intellectual beliefs* about the gods, not just that they performed the *rituals*. In the *Euthyphro*, 12e, Socrates says, 'Try to teach me what part of justice holiness is, that I may tell Meletus not to wrong me anymore or bring suits against me for impiety, since I have now been duly instructed by you about what is, and what is not, pious and holy.' This implies that lawsuits against impiety were over intellectual or philosophical beliefs, not just correct 'performance' of the rituals. And again, when Socrates exclaims at 26d, 'Do you think you are accusing Anaxagoras, my dear Meletus?', he means that he does not want to be confused with a philosopher and atheist who gave naturalistic explanations to astronomical phenomena; but Socrates does indeed profess the existence of the gods in the *Apology* – that is, he is defending himself against what he thinks is an accusation of atheism.

The law against impiety was vague, and the extent to which it was applicable in any given case needed to be determined on an ad hoc basis, first at the preliminary trial before the King Archon, and then brought in front of a jury. It is important to note that at no point does Socrates (or even Plato) attempt to dispute the *legality* of the charge – only that he is innocent under the law.

The second part of the accusation runs thus: ἕτερα δὲ δαιμόνια καινά, 'he believes in other, new divine beings'. This seems, at first glance, to be paradoxical, particularly given that Meletus has just charged Socrates with atheism. However, it should be noted that this second charge does not accuse Socrates of introducing new gods (θεοί), but is a broader and much more vague accusation of introducing new 'divinities' (δαιμόνια). We are not quite sure what Meletus means by this – are these 'gods', or something else? Whatever he means, it is quite clear that whatever Socrates is introducing, they cannot be legitimate gods in the eyes of traditional Athenians. In a polytheistic society, if Socrates was introducing true divinities into the city of Athens, ones perhaps that the Athenians had simply not heard of before, like a Dionysus or an Asclepius, then it would be a good thing for the city to honour such gods. However, if Meletus' charge is to make sense, then we must interpret the charge to mean that these δαιμόνια are not real, i.e. they are false gods, despite what Socrates professes. Plato records roughly the same thing in the *Euthyphro*, 2b, 'Meletus says that I am a poet or maker of gods, and that I invent new gods and deny the existence of old ones; this is the ground of his indictment.' There Socrates – perhaps speaking loosely – uses the phrase ποιητὴν εἶναι θεῶν, 'a maker of gods'. However, Euthyphro, his interlocutor, immediately understands that what Socrates is referring to was his private δαιμόνιον.

Socrates first mentions his *daimonion* here in the *Apology*. He describes it as a 'divine' thing, a certain voice that has been with him since childhood; it never urged him to go ahead with anything, instead it always warned him away from doing anything morally bad. Socrates claimed that this voice was 'the sign of the god' (40b), and it was something that he trusted implicitly. One of the most dramatic examples of Socrates' trust in his *daimonion* occurs in the *Apology* – this voice remained silent on his way to court and after the sentence of death. The only conclusion Socrates could come to was that he would not be wrong to go to his death.

The accusation of Meletus was broad enough to include this personal spiritual voice, as well as encompass the broader prejudices against Socrates as a religious innovator and natural philosopher (i.e. in Aristophanes' *Clouds*). Certainly, the wording used by Meletus was strategic and purposefully vague, chosen so that the jury might be convinced that Socrates intended to replace the old gods with new ones. Real evidence was unneeded, and it would only take insinuation to suggest to the jury that Socrates was a threat.

The final part of the charge against Socrates was that ἀδικεῖν τούς τε νέους διαφθείροντα, 'does wrong by corrupting the youth'. As before, the prosecution attempts to cast its net very wide. In what way was Socrates supposed to have 'corrupted the youth'? Even Socrates is a bit baffled. At 26b he asks for some help to discern what the accusation meant: 'Do I corrupt the youth by teaching them not to believe in the gods the state believes in, but in other new spiritual beings?' – and Meletus agrees, and this third charge is linked to the first two. There is no evidence from classical Athens that there was a law that prohibited 'corrupting the youth', and the treaty of amnesty in 403 BC only allowed prosecutions against those who had violated a particular and written law. However, the charge of 'corrupting the youth' could be brought in under the law proscribing impiety. We must remember that Athenian religious sentiment strongly supported the respect of parents and elders, and Socrates seemed to encourage the youth to abandon the traditional gods and turn against their parents (as his character does in *Clouds*, see above). Therefore, this charge of corruption was a religious matter and Socrates might appear guilty.

Prison and death

In his speech, Socrates had briefly considered and then rejected the punishment of imprisonment (37c), 'What penalty shall I propose? Imprisonment? Why should I live in prison a slave to those who may be in authority?' He could not be persuaded to give up his usual accustomed manner of speaking freely in the marketplace, and would not even consider leaving Athens behind to go into exile. We know from Socrates' speech that the δεσμωτήριον, or imprisonment, was possible.

The prison in Athens had a long hall that led back to a courtyard and contained twelve square rooms. It was located near the law courts, had a floor plan with separate cells with an easily guarded entrance, and also provided for bathing and other daily necessities. During the excavation, they found a small statue of Socrates along with several small bottles, which likely held poison used to execute prisoners. The usual role of the prison in Athens was to hold those who were awaiting their executions, or who were fined or owed the state money and could not pay. In terms of this punishment, the Athenians were generally quite lenient, and often willingly let those sentenced to death flee from the prison into exile. In fact, even convicted murders held in the prison were expected to make an attempt at a jailbreak and escape into exile (*Crit.* 44b). Exile could still be a heavy burden as an individual would need to abandon their property to go to live among strangers. However, with wealthy friends (as Socrates had), it was possible to re-establish oneself and even gain citizenship in a new city.

Within the building itself, prisoners often had freedom of movement (although they might be chained or put in stocks), and they could have visitors. Two of Plato's dialogues, the *Crito* and the *Phaedo*, are set in prison and recount Socrates' conversations with friends as he is waiting to die. The extent that Socrates needed to wait was unusual. In the Athenian justice system, execution normally followed swiftly upon condemnation, but in Socrates' case, it had to be postponed for about a month. On the day before Socrates' trial, the Athenians had garlanded and sent a ship to Delos. During this annual festival, a ship sailed to this sacred island in order to celebrate Theseus' famous victory over the Minotaur, all in honour of the god Apollo. During its journey, Athens, by law, needed to remain ritually clean, and therefore no executions could take place. It was during this period Socrates remained in prison and continued to philosophize and speak with his friends.

Socrates' execution (or better, his suicide) by hemlock has become a famous scene. But in ancient Athens, there was a more painful and humiliating form of execution, *apotumpanismos* in which the prisoner was (likely) fastened to a wooden beam with iron collars around his wrists, ankles and neck. Death was caused either by exposure, or the collar around the prisoner's neck would slowly be tightened until he died of strangulation. But from around the end of the fifth century BC, Athenians were willing to let executions be conducted instead with the use of hemlock so that prisoners could commit suicide in preference to execution – that is, if they could afford to pay for the poison. It should be noted that hemlock was expensive at around twelve drachma for a single dose, simply because it grew only in remote locations such as Asia Minor. Socrates may have suffered worse things had he not had wealthy friends like Crito to purchase the hemlock.

Plato's *Apology*

An apology, or ἀπολογία, is not what we take it to mean today. Socrates does not 'apologize', he neither feels sorrow or remorse for what he has done, nor does he admit any wrongdoing. His 'apology' is supposed to be a defence, but what we have in Plato's *Apology* is something quite different: as one scholar puts it nicely, Socrates' speech was 'more a defiance than a defence'. In Plato's version of events, when the jurors said they would spare Socrates, provided that he would stop bothering citizens with his philosophical enquiries, Socrates replied that he would never do so. He was thoroughly committed to his way of life, and was too principled to be cowed into abandoning it.

In the years that followed Socrates' death, many authors wrote various philosophical or rhetorical works that purported to be either speeches for the prosecution or the defence. In fact, the trial of Socrates became a widely popular subject for Greek authors, so much so that a whole literature emerged. We have records of works by Xenophon, Lysias, Theodectes of Phaselis, Demetrius of Phalerum, Theon of Antioch, Plutarch and Libanius. Polycrates wrote a work entitled *Accusation of Socrates*, although nothing of the original remains. But many of these authors wrote long after the execution of Socrates, in Hellenistic and Roman times.

The only contemporaries of Socrates to write *Apologies* were Plato, Xenophon and Lysias (*c.* 459–380 BC). Unfortunately, we know nothing of the content or form Lysias' *Apology* took. And what Xenophon wrote was largely heard and recorded at second hand and only later put into Socrates' mouth. On the face of it, it seems that there are no authors who can compete with Plato as a first-hand witness of Socrates' trial.

Plato has certainly shaped the form of Socrates' speech and added artful touches, as all orators do after their speech is delivered and prepared for publication. But Plato likely did his best to record the speech from memory which he heard himself, and may have supplemented it with what he heard from others or what he thought it would be necessary for Socrates to say. Plato himself claims to have been present (*Apol.* 34a, 38b), and therefore this version was widely considered more or less to report the real defence of Socrates. When we read it, we find that the work contains little of Plato's own philosophy, and for this reason it has been assumed that what we see in this dialogue is the 'historical' Socrates.

Nevertheless, as many critics have said before, what Plato presents us is an artist's portrayal and not a photograph. Plato's written version contains many artistic flourishes and employs many of the rhetorical techniques which were commonplace in the mouths of the Attic orators. It is this 'finished' quality of the dialogue that has raised some suspicion of inauthenticity particularly when, at the beginning of his speech, Socrates himself denies (*Apol.* 17b) any skill in oratory and says he can only offer them the simple truth. It is, of course, tempting to read all this as Socrates' usual 'ironic' manner. However, there is some evidence in ancient literature to suggest that what Socrates says during his trial could be typical of other orators in the courts. Gorgias, a famous sophist and orator who was contemporary with Socrates, wrote a work named the *Palamedes*, which was a rhetorical exercise in the form of a defence of the mythical figure of Palamedes who was falsely accused by Odysseus of betraying the Greeks during the Trojan War. There are enough parallels between what Palamedes and Socrates say during their defence that these are unlikely to be the result of simply coincidence (in fact, Socrates names Palamedes at *Apol.* 41b as an example of a man who died of an unjust judgement). There may, therefore, be some playful use of the sophists' art during this first and only time that Socrates was a pleader before a court.

The defiance of Socrates is most readily understood from his words to the jurors after the sentence is passed (*Apol.* 38d–e), 'I have been condemned not by lack of arguments, but of boldness, shamelessness, and an unwillingness to tell you those things you like best to hear.' In Plato's version of his trial, Socrates does not defend himself against the specific charges, but focuses rather on his whole life and way of philosophizing. He treats the actual substance of the accusation only briefly at the beginning and spends the majority of his speech considering and defending his manner of living. Socrates felt that the danger he faced came from the prejudices of anonymous men who would not even face him directly in court. He poignantly remarks that when he is trying to justify himself, it's as if he is fighting with shadows, σκιαμαχεῖν (*Apol.* 18d). In part, this was a strategy of the prosecutors: it would be difficult to present sufficient evidence for the charges alone to sway the jury to convict Socrates in court. His prosecutors therefore relied heavily on the widespread suspicion Socrates had aroused through his conversations in the marketplace and his political associations. It was necessary, as Socrates himself says, to overturn this suspicion if he hoped to escape the court. And so this was one of the prime goals of his speech, although we can say that he largely failed in this.

The *Apology* begins with Socrates' examination of his misrepresentation as an intellectual who undermined the city's religion and corrupted its youth. This reputation, he claims, was a result of Aristophanes' popular caricature of him. In the comedy, he was brushed with two falsehoods, firstly, that he was a natural philosopher like Anaxagoras, and secondly that he was a sophist who took money for his teachings (*Apol.* 19a–24b, and see Commentary). What exactly did Meletus claim that he taught? Socrates could not say for sure: the only kind of wisdom he possessed was the knowledge that he knew nothing. In his attempt to explain to the jury what he means by this, Socrates leaves behind any real 'legal' defence, and launches into a touching and delicate portrayal, one of the finest we have, of what philosophy is.

Here we are told one of its most famous stories: Chaerephon asked the Delphic oracle whether anyone was wiser than Socrates, and the renowned answer was that there was not. The oracle's answer puzzled Socrates, for he certainly didn't pretend to any wisdom. So he went around and sought out someone who might be wiser than he. He examined many men who claimed to be experts, either in politics, poetry or other crafts. But whenever he questioned them, he found they, in fact, did not possess that wisdom which they claimed they did. The conclusion that he eventually arrived at was that all men were less wise than him, only because he was at least aware that he did not know anything.

This realization motivated him to set out 'on a divine mission' to reveal this truth to his fellow citizens. It wouldn't be sufficient for Socrates to proclaim this truth – he needed to convince them of it themselves. The form his 'philosophizing' took was an *elenchus* (ἔλεγχος) which was an examination that took the shape of a dialogue with 'questions and answers' (see *Apol.* 21b and Commentary), and was typical of Plato's early texts. The *elenchus* is a negative method of inquiry; it does not actively try to establish what *is* true, only what is *not* true. At the beginning of a Socratic dialogue, someone would make a claim to knowledge of a difficult subject, such as what 'courage' was, or 'piety', or 'virtue', and the inquiry would then be into what that thing *is* Socrates would pretend to ignorance about the subject (his irony), and would begin by asking questions which his interlocutor would answer. Socrates says that he is trying to discover the nature of the thing (as courage, piety, virtue), but usually in practice he only tests and then eliminates other people's definitions of them. By asking questions and waiting for answers, Socrates would lead his interlocutor to agree to a premise or a statement that would be entirely inconsistent or contrary to their initial claim. The dialogue usually ended with embarrassment for Socrates' interlocutor, with both sides admitting confusion (ἀπορία) and uncertainty on the subject.

Socrates claims in the *Apology* that everyone he has examined has failed his test (*Apol.* 21b–23b). He exposed their self-contradictions, and though they might have claimed to know what 'piety' was, or what 'courage' was, when pressed upon and examined, their own definitions unravelled, and they themselves were left perplexed. This 'Socratic *elenchus*' was his own peculiar way, and formed the basis for his wide unpopularity.

But his mission was not something he could abandon, not even to save his life. Ironically, he claimed his mission was a supreme act of piety: it was in obedience to the god that he did it. He professed to show genuine concern for the minds of the Athenians, and for their wellbeing (*Apol.* 30b): 'virtue does not come from money, but rather money comes from virtue, as well as all other things that are good for man.' By forcing the Athenians to look at themselves, renounce any pretence to wisdom, and search out the good, the noble and the just with sincerity, he would help them become better people, and as better people, they would congregate together to make a better city. In doing so, Socrates said he rendered the greatest benefit to the state, and was therefore deserving of reward, not punishment. His 'divine mission' (and his philosophic life was therefore almost a religious practice) was to make Athenians as perfect as possible – what would naturally follow would be a harmonious state.

For Socrates, there is a close connection between self-knowledge (i.e. what do I really know?) and the best state of the soul. This connection underlies the whole of the *Apology*, although it is never fully delineated in a precise way during Socrates' speech. The Socratic theory that knowledge equates to goodness is alluded to, but more fully addressed in other Platonic dialogues. Here it is presented as a rebuttal to Meletus' charge that Socrates does not believe in the gods; how could it be true, if his whole life of philosophy was done to improve everyone and done in accordance with Apollo's wish? The very heart of his own defence is that he has spent his whole life seeking virtue, and encouraging others to do the same. He has even done so to his own personal disadvantage: he followed Apollo's will, and therefore had no time for political responsibilities, earned only the suspicion and ire of his fellow citizens, and left poor. He will never be released from his mission, not even by the threat of death. Even as he defends himself, he must encourage people to abandon any claim to knowledge (*Apol.* 23b), and care more for their souls than for their wealth (*Apol.* 29d). This truth failed to persuade the jurors, and some were no doubt annoyed that they seemed to have been put on trial in place of Socrates. Instead of rebutting the charge of corruption, Socrates boldly claimed to be the greatest benefactor to the state. His guilty verdict was unsurprising.

Socrates rejected any appeal for sympathy, and he made no appeal to the jurors' emotions. In a culture such as Athens where honour was prized so highly, such demonstrations of abject humiliation became a common means to secure an acquittal. But there was none forthcoming. Socrates does not completely forget his family, it is true (a passing reference is there to elicit some compassion), but he is too old to beg shamefully for his life, nor would his reputation allow him to do so. Through this, Socrates would seem to elevate himself above others, and this may have further roused the jury against him.

Death was the penalty, but Socrates still had more to say in a final farewell. There is no evidence to suggest that his final speech would not have been allowed. Some scholars have suggested it would be impossible for a defendant to say anything further at this point, therefore Socrates' final speech is, in fact, a complete invention by Plato. But others have suggested that although it was not part of the formal procedures, many jurors would stay on to listen simply out of curiosity – it was their last opportunity to hear his unique art of speaking.

Socrates gave a valedictory speech, in part addressed to those who voted for his death, and in part to those who voted for his acquittal. He wonders why they were so impatient for his death; at the age of 70, no doubt nature would soon take its course. He appeals to the usual Athenian concern for honour – what will people say, when they have put him to death? They will claim that he was 'wise' (even if he was not), and revile Athens for their foolish decision to put a good man to death. There is startling defiance in this speech, and much that is moving. 'I would rather die while speaking in my manner, than live while speaking in yours.' But attention should also be drawn to the tragic and even 'heroic' nature of the final speech – Socrates implies a connection between him and Achilles, the great Homeric hero: neither in war, nor in law, ought a man use every way to escape death, but face it bravely. And there is also a sinister element to Socrates' final address to his enemies. Prophetic power came at the hour of death, as Patroclus predicts Hector's death at the hands of Achilles; and as Hector predicts Achilles' death at the hands of Paris. Socrates in turn, condemned as he is, ominously claims, 'punishment weightier than what you have inflicted on me will surely come upon you' – history will not be kind to the jurors who condemned him.

To his friends, Socrates offered consolation. His *daimonion* never deterred him from coming to court and so his death must therefore be a good thing: as Socrates claims, it was either utter annihilation of the soul, or its migration to another place. In the case of the former, it would be an end to the struggles and pain of life; and if the latter, then it can only be a blessing. Apollo had released him from the burden of his mission, and it would be 'better for me to die now and be freed from trouble.' Socrates bore no grudge against his accusers, though they must live with the consequences of their decisions. In a most touching scene, Socrates' last request was for the Athenians to teach his sons to value goodness over wealth – a wonderful final touch – that Socrates hoped, even at the end, that the Athenians, his condemners, might come to understand him, and to dedicate themselves to true morality and justice. The court officials then came to lead Socrates away to prison, when he spoke one of the most enduring lines of Western philosophy, 'We now go each our own way; I to die, and you to live: but which is better, only the god knows.'

Further reading

There are many useful and reliable web resources for Plato's *Apology*, and many books written on the subject, some very approachable for students new to the subject. For the more general student, see *Socrates, A Very Short Introduction*, by C.C.W. Taylor, which offers a broad and general introduction to Socrates' life and philosophy. It contains much in the way of cultural and political background that students new to Plato will find helpful.

City of Sokrates by J.W. Roberts (now rather old) is useful for background information of the Athenian history and legal framework, and very approachable. Also, *Law in Classical Athens*, by D.M. MacDowell is good for the student who wishes to understand the complex legal framework which was operating at the time of Socrates' trial; it offers a good introduction to Athens' confusing system of courts and laws but not all of it needs to be read.

W.K.C. Guthrie, *A History of Greek Philosophy*, IV, 'Plato: the man and his dialogues, earlier period' still remains a good textbook in Platonic studies. It will prove useful to the student who has read Plato more widely; nevertheless, there is a good discussion of the *Apology* on pp. 71–92. Similarly, C.D.C. Reeve's *Socrates in the Apology* is an encompassing study of Socrates the philosopher (and his philosophy) within the context of his trial. More recently, there is also *Plato's Euthyphro, Apology, and Crito: Critical Essays*, a collection edited by Rachana Kamtekar, in which Gregory Vlastos' chapter on 'Socratic Piety', and Donald Morrison's chapter 'On the Alleged Historical Reliability of Plato's *Apology*' prove good background reading for students.

Socrates against Athens, by J.A. Colaiaco, is appropriate for new Sixth Form students. There are several chapters contained therein which treat more in-depth of several topics only touched upon by this short introduction. Recommended are Chapter 3, 'Socrates confronts his old accusers' for a good discussion of 'natural philosophy' and 'sophistry'; and Chapter 8, 'Socrates brings the philosophic mission into court', for a sound treatment of several Socratic theses.

Debra Nails' '*The Trial and Death of Socrates*', found in Blackwell's, *A Companion to Socrates*, has a good introduction to the five 'Trial' dialogues of Plato (*Theaetetus*, *Euthyphro*, *Apology*, *Crito* and *Phaedo*). Also worthy of consultation is Christopher Rowe's essay on '*Socrates in Plato's dialogues*'.

Socrates on Trial, by T.C. Brickhouse and N.D. Smith, offers a weighty and scholarly commentary on the *Apology*, parts of which teachers (with some discretion) may wish to offer to students new to Greek philosophy.

Text

Πρῶτον μὲν οὖν δίκαιός εἰμι ἀπολογήσασθαι, ὦ ἄνδρες   18a7
Ἀθηναῖοι, πρὸς τὰ πρῶτά μου ψευδῆ κατηγορημένα καὶ
τοὺς πρώτους κατηγόρους, ἔπειτα δὲ πρὸς τὰ ὕστερον καὶ
τοὺς ὑστέρους. ἐμοῦ γὰρ πολλοὶ κατήγοροι γεγόνασι πρὸς   b
ὑμᾶς καὶ πάλαι πολλὰ ἤδη ἔτη καὶ οὐδὲν ἀληθὲς λέγοντες,
οὓς ἐγὼ μᾶλλον φοβοῦμαι ἢ τοὺς ἀμφὶ Ἄνυτον, καίπερ
ὄντας καὶ τούτους δεινούς· ἀλλ᾽ ἐκεῖνοι δεινότεροι, ὦ
ἄνδρες, οἳ ὑμῶν τοὺς πολλοὺς ἐκ παίδων παραλαμβά-   5
νοντες ἔπειθόν τε καὶ κατηγόρουν ἐμοῦ οὐδὲν
ἀληθές, ὡς ἔστιν τις Σωκράτης σοφὸς ἀνήρ, τά τε μετέωρα

φροντιστὴς καὶ τὰ ὑπὸ γῆς ἅπαντα ἀνεζητηκὼς καὶ τὸν
ἥττω λόγον κρείττω ποιῶν. οὗτοι, ὦ ἄνδρες Ἀθηναῖοι,   c
<οἱ> ταύτην τὴν φήμην κατασκεδάσαντες, οἱ δεινοί εἰσίν
μου κατήγοροι· οἱ γὰρ ἀκούοντες ἡγοῦνται τοὺς ταῦτα
ζητοῦντας οὐδὲ θεοὺς νομίζειν. ἔπειτά εἰσιν οὗτοι οἱ κατήγοροι πολλοὶ καὶ πολὺν χρόνον ἤδη κατηγορηκότες, ἔτι δὲ   5
καὶ ἐν ταύτῃ τῇ ἡλικίᾳ λέγοντες πρὸς ὑμᾶς ἐν ᾗ ἂν μάλιστα
ἐπιστεύσατε, παῖδες ὄντες ἔνιοι ὑμῶν καὶ μειράκια,
ἀτεχνῶς ἐρήμην κατηγοροῦντες ἀπολογουμένου οὐδενός.
ὃ δὲ πάντων ἀλογώτατον, ὅτι οὐδὲ τὰ ὀνόματα οἷόν τε
αὐτῶν εἰδέναι καὶ εἰπεῖν, πλὴν εἴ τις κωμῳδοποιὸς τυγχά-   d
νει ὤν. ὅσοι δὲ φθόνῳ καὶ διαβολῇ χρώμενοι ὑμᾶς ἀνέπειθον, οἱ δὲ καὶ αὐτοὶ πεπεισμένοι ἄλλους πείθοντες, οὗτοι
πάντες ἀπορώτατοί εἰσιν· οὐδὲ γὰρ ἀναβιβάσασθαι οἷόν τ᾽
ἐστὶν αὐτῶν ἐνταυθοῖ οὐδ᾽ ἐλέγξαι οὐδένα, ἀλλ᾽ ἀνάγκη   5
ἀτεχνῶς ὥσπερ σκιαμαχεῖν ἀπολογούμενόν τε καὶ ἐλέγ-
χειν μηδενὸς ἀποκρινομένου. ἀξιώσατε οὖν καὶ ὑμεῖς,
ὥσπερ ἐγὼ λέγω, διττούς μου τοὺς κατηγόρους γεγονέναι, ἑτέρους μὲν τοὺς ἄρτι κατηγορήσαντας, ἑτέρους δὲ
τοὺς πάλαι οὓς ἐγὼ λέγω, καὶ οἰήθητε δεῖν πρὸς ἐκείνους   e
πρῶτόν με ἀπολογήσασθαι· καὶ γὰρ ὑμεῖς ἐκείνων
πρότερον ἠκούσατε κατηγορούντων καὶ πολὺ μᾶλλον ἢ
τῶνδε τῶν ὑστέρων.

Εἶεν· ἀπολογητέον δή, ὦ ἄνδρες Ἀθηναῖοι, καὶ ἐπι-   5
χειρητέον ὑμῶν ἐξελέσθαι τὴν διαβολὴν ἣν ὑμεῖς ἐν πολλῷ   **19a**
χρόνῳ ἔσχετε ταύτην ἐν οὕτως ὀλίγῳ χρόνῳ. βουλοίμην
μὲν οὖν ἂν τοῦτο οὕτως γενέσθαι, εἴ τι ἄμεινον καὶ ὑμῖν καὶ
ἐμοί, καὶ πλέον τί με ποιῆσαι ἀπολογούμενον· οἶμαι δὲ
αὐτὸ χαλεπὸν εἶναι, καὶ οὐ πάνυ με λανθάνει οἷόν ἐστιν.   5
ὅμως τοῦτο μὲν ἴτω ὅπῃ τῷ θεῷ φίλον, τῷ δὲ νόμῳ
πειστέον καὶ ἀπολογητέον.

Ἀναλάβωμεν οὖν ἐξ ἀρχῆς τίς ἡ κατηγορία ἐστὶν ἐξ ἧς ἡ
ἐμὴ διαβολὴ γέγονεν, ᾗ δὴ καὶ πιστεύων Μέλητός με   **b**
ἐγράψατο τὴν γραφὴν ταύτην. εἶεν· τί δὴ λέγοντες διέβαλ-
λον οἱ διαβάλλοντες; ὥσπερ οὖν κατηγόρων τὴν ἀντωμοσίαν δεῖ ἀναγνῶναι αὐτῶν· "Σωκράτης ἀδικεῖ καὶ
περιεργάζεται ζητῶν τά τε ὑπὸ γῆς καὶ οὐράνια καὶ τὸν   5
ἥττω λόγον κρείττω ποιῶν καὶ ἄλλους ταὐτὰ ταῦτα   **c**
διδάσκων." τοιαύτη τίς ἐστιν· ταῦτα γὰρ ἑωρᾶτε καὶ αὐτοὶ
ἐν τῇ Ἀριστοφάνους κωμῳδίᾳ, Σωκράτη τινὰ ἐκεῖ περιφερόμενον, φάσκοντά τε ἀεροβατεῖν καὶ ἄλλην πολλὴν
φλυαρίαν φλυαροῦντα, ὧν ἐγὼ οὐδὲν οὔτε μέγα οὔτε   5
σμικρὸν πέρι ἐπαΐω. καὶ οὐχ ὡς ἀτιμάζων λέγω τὴν
τοιαύτην ἐπιστήμην, εἴ τις περὶ τῶν τοιούτων σοφός
ἐστιν—μή πως ἐγὼ ὑπὸ Μελήτου τοσαύτας δίκας
φεύγοιμι— ἀλλὰ γὰρ ἐμοὶ τούτων, ὦ ἄνδρες Ἀθηναῖοι,
οὐδὲν μέτεστιν. μάρτυρας δὲ αὐτοὺς ὑμῶν τοὺς πολλοὺς   **d**
παρέχομαι, καὶ ἀξιῶ ὑμᾶς ἀλλήλους διδάσκειν τε καὶ
φράζειν, ὅσοι ἐμοῦ πώποτε ἀκηκόατε διαλεγομένου—
πολλοὶ δὲ ὑμῶν οἱ τοιοῦτοί εἰσιν— φράζετε οὖν ἀλλήλοις εἰ
πώποτε ἢ σμικρὸν ἢ μέγα ἤκουσέ τις ὑμῶν ἐμοῦ περὶ τῶν   5
τοιούτων διαλεγομένου, καὶ ἐκ τούτου γνώσεσθε ὅτι
τοιαῦτ᾽ ἐστὶ καὶ τἆλλα περὶ ἐμοῦ ἃ οἱ πολλοὶ λέγουσιν.

Ἀλλὰ γὰρ οὔτε τούτων οὐδέν ἐστιν, οὐδέ γ᾽ εἴ τινος
ἀκηκόατε ὡς ἐγὼ παιδεύειν ἐπιχειρῶ ἀνθρώπους καὶ
χρήματα πράττομαι, οὐδὲ τοῦτο ἀληθές. ἐπεὶ καὶ τοῦτό γέ   **e**
μοι δοκεῖ καλὸν εἶναι, εἴ τις οἷός τ᾽ εἴη παιδεύειν ἀνθρώ-
πους ὥσπερ Γοργίας τε ὁ Λεοντῖνος καὶ Πρόδικος ὁ Κεῖος
καὶ Ἱππίας ὁ Ἠλεῖος. τούτων γὰρ ἕκαστος, ὦ ἄνδρες, οἷός
τ᾽ ἐστὶν ἰὼν εἰς ἑκάστην τῶν πόλεων τοὺς νέους, οἷς ἔξεστι   5
τῶν ἑαυτῶν πολιτῶν προῖκα συνεῖναι ᾧ ἂν βούλωνται,
τούτους πείθουσι τὰς ἐκείνων συνουσίας ἀπολιπόντας   **20a**
σφίσιν συνεῖναι χρήματα διδόντας καὶ χάριν προσειδέναι.

ἐπεὶ καὶ ἄλλος ἀνήρ ἐστι Πάριος ἐνθάδε σοφὸς ὃν ἐγὼ
ᾐσθόμην ἐπιδημοῦντα· ἔτυχον γὰρ προσελθὼν ἀνδρὶ ὃς
τετέλεκε χρήματα σοφισταῖς πλείω ἢ σύμπαντες οἱ ἄλλοι,   5
Καλλίᾳ τῷ Ἱππονίκου· τοῦτον οὖν ἀνηρόμην—ἐστὸν γὰρ
αὐτῷ δύο ὑεῖ— "Ὦ Καλλία," ἦν δ᾽ ἐγώ, "εἰ μέν σου τὼ ὑεῖ
πώλω ἢ μόσχω ἐγενέσθην, εἴχομεν ἂν αὐτοῖν ἐπιστάτην
λαβεῖν καὶ μισθώσασθαι ὃς ἔμελλεν αὐτὼ καλώ τε
κἀγαθὼ ποιήσειν τὴν προσήκουσαν ἀρετήν· ἦν δ᾽ ἂν οὗτος   b
ἢ τῶν ἱππικῶν τις ἢ τῶν γεωργικῶν· νῦν δ᾽ ἐπειδὴ
ἀνθρώπω ἐστόν, τίνα αὐτοῖν ἐν νῷ ἔχεις ἐπιστάτην λαβεῖν;
τίς τῆς τοιαύτης ἀρετῆς, τῆς ἀνθρωπίνης τε καὶ πολιτικῆς,
ἐπιστήμων ἐστίν; οἶμαι γάρ σε ἐσκέφθαι διὰ τὴν τῶν ὑέων   5
κτῆσιν. ἔστιν τις," ἔφην ἐγώ, "ἢ οὔ;" "Πάνυ γε," ἦ δ᾽ ὅς.
"Τίς," ἦν δ᾽ ἐγώ, "καὶ ποδαπός, καὶ πόσου διδάσκει;"
"Εὔηνος," ἔφη, "ὦ Σώκρατες, Πάριος, πέντε μνῶν." καὶ
ἐγὼ τὸν Εὔηνον ἐμακάρισα εἰ ὡς ἀληθῶς ἔχοι ταύτην τὴν
τέχνην καὶ οὕτως ἐμμελῶς διδάσκει. ἐγὼ γοῦν καὶ αὐτὸς   c
ἐκαλλυνόμην τε καὶ ἡβρυνόμην ἂν εἰ ἠπιστάμην ταῦτα·
ἀλλ᾽ οὐ γὰρ ἐπίσταμαι, ὦ ἄνδρες Ἀθηναῖοι.

"Ὑπολάβοι ἂν οὖν τις ὑμῶν ἴσως· "Ἀλλ᾽, ὦ Σώκρατες, τὸ
σὸν τί ἐστι πρᾶγμα; πόθεν αἱ διαβολαί σοι αὗται γεγό-   5
νασιν; οὐ γὰρ δήπου σοῦ γε οὐδὲν τῶν ἄλλων περιττότερον
πραγματευομένου ἔπειτα τοσαύτη φήμη τε καὶ λόγος
γέγονεν, εἰ μή τι ἔπραττες ἀλλοῖον ἢ οἱ πολλοί. λέγε οὖν
ἡμῖν τί ἐστιν, ἵνα μὴ ἡμεῖς περὶ σοῦ αὐτοσχεδιάζωμεν."   d
ταυτί μοι δοκεῖ δίκαια λέγειν ὁ λέγων, κἀγὼ ὑμῖν πειράσομαι ἀποδεῖξαι τί ποτ᾽ ἐστὶν τοῦτο ὃ ἐμοὶ πεποίηκεν τό τε
ὄνομα καὶ τὴν διαβολήν. ἀκούετε δή. καὶ ἴσως μὲν δόξω
τισὶν ὑμῶν παίζειν· εὖ μέντοι ἴστε, πᾶσαν ὑμῖν τὴν   5
ἀλήθειαν ἐρῶ. ἐγὼ γάρ, ὦ ἄνδρες Ἀθηναῖοι, δι᾽ οὐδὲν ἀλλ᾽
ἢ διὰ σοφίαν τινὰ τοῦτο τὸ ὄνομα ἔσχηκα. ποίαν δὴ σοφίαν
ταύτην; ἥπερ ἐστὶν ἴσως ἀνθρωπίνη σοφία. τῷ ὄντι γὰρ
κινδυνεύω ταύτην εἶναι σοφός· οὗτοι δὲ τάχ᾽ ἄν, οὓς ἄρτι
ἔλεγον, μείζω τινὰ ἢ κατ᾽ ἄνθρωπον σοφίαν σοφοὶ εἶεν, ἢ   e
οὐκ ἔχω τί λέγω· οὐ γὰρ δὴ ἔγωγε αὐτὴν ἐπίσταμαι, ἀλλ᾽
ὅστις φησὶ ψεύδεταί τε καὶ ἐπὶ διαβολῇ τῇ ἐμῇ λέγει. καί
μοι, ὦ ἄνδρες Ἀθηναῖοι, μὴ θορυβήσητε, μηδ᾽ ἐὰν δόξω τι
ὑμῖν μέγα λέγειν· οὐ γὰρ ἐμὸν ἐρῶ τὸν λόγον ὃν ἂν λέγω,   5
ἀλλ᾽ εἰς ἀξιόχρεων ὑμῖν τὸν λέγοντα ἀνοίσω. τῆς γὰρ ἐμῆς,
εἰ δή τίς ἐστιν σοφία καὶ οἵα, μάρτυρα ὑμῖν παρέξομαι τὸν
θεὸν τὸν ἐν Δελφοῖς. Χαιρεφῶντα γὰρ ἴστε που. οὗτος ἐμός
τε ἑταῖρος ἦν ἐκ νέου καὶ ὑμῶν τῷ πλήθει ἑταῖρός τε καὶ   **21a**

συνέφυγε τὴν φυγὴν ταύτην καὶ μεθ᾽ ὑμῶν κατῆλθε. καὶ
ἴστε δὴ οἷος ἦν Χαιρεφῶν, ὡς σφοδρὸς ἐφ᾽ ὅτι ὁρμήσειεν.
καὶ δή ποτε καὶ εἰς Δελφοὺς ἐλθὼν ἐτόλμησε τοῦτο
μαντεύσασθαι—καί, ὅπερ λέγω, μὴ θορυβεῖτε, ὦ   5
ἄνδρες—ἤρετο γὰρ δὴ εἴ τις ἐμοῦ εἴη σοφώτερος. ἀνεῖλεν
οὖν ἡ Πυθία μηδένα σοφώτερον εἶναι. καὶ τούτων πέρι ὁ
ἀδελφὸς ὑμῖν αὐτοῦ οὑτοσὶ μαρτυρήσει, ἐπειδὴ ἐκεῖνος
τετελεύτηκεν.

Σκέψασθε δὴ ὧν ἕνεκα ταῦτα λέγω· μέλλω γὰρ ὑμᾶς   b
διδάξειν ὅθεν μοι ἡ διαβολὴ γέγονεν. ταῦτα γὰρ ἐγὼ
ἀκούσας ἐνεθυμούμην οὑτωσί· "Τί ποτε λέγει ὁ θεός, καὶ
τί ποτε αἰνίττεται; ἐγὼ γὰρ δὴ οὔτε μέγα οὔτε σμικρὸν
σύνοιδα ἐμαυτῷ σοφὸς ὤν· τί οὖν ποτε λέγει φάσκων ἐμὲ   5
σοφώτατον εἶναι; οὐ γὰρ δήπου ψεύδεταί γε· οὐ γὰρ θέμις
αὐτῷ." καὶ πολὺν μὲν χρόνον ἠπόρουν τί ποτε λέγει· ἔπειτα
μόγις πάνυ ἐπὶ ζήτησιν αὐτοῦ τοιαύτην τινὰ ἐτραπόμην.
ἦλθον ἐπί τινα τῶν δοκούντων σοφῶν εἶναι, ὡς ἐνταῦθα
εἴπερ που ἐλέγξων τὸ μαντεῖον καὶ ἀποφανῶν τῷ χρησμῷ   c
ὅτι "Οὑτοσὶ ἐμοῦ σοφώτερός ἐστι, σὺ δ᾽ ἐμὲ ἔφησθα."
διασκοπῶν οὖν τοῦτον—ὀνόματι γὰρ οὐδὲν δέομαι λέγειν,
ἦν δέ τις τῶν πολιτικῶν πρὸς ὃν ἐγὼ σκοπῶν τοιοῦτόν τι
ἔπαθον, ὦ ἄνδρες Ἀθηναῖοι—καὶ διαλεγόμενος αὐτῷ,   5
ἔδοξέ μοι οὗτος ὁ ἀνὴρ δοκεῖν μὲν εἶναι σοφὸς ἄλλοις τε
πολλοῖς ἀνθρώποις καὶ μάλιστα ἑαυτῷ, εἶναι δ᾽ οὔ·
κἄπειτα ἐπειρώμην αὐτῷ δεικνύναι ὅτι οἴοιτο μὲν εἶναι
σοφός, εἴη δ᾽ οὔ. ἐντεῦθεν οὖν τούτῳ τε ἀπηχθόμην καὶ   d
πολλοῖς τῶν παρόντων· πρὸς ἐμαυτὸν δ᾽ οὖν ἀπιὼν ἐλογιζόμην ὅτι τούτου μὲν τοῦ ἀνθρώπου ἐγὼ σοφώτερός εἰμι·
κινδυνεύει μὲν γὰρ ἡμῶν οὐδέτερος οὐδὲν καλὸν κἀγαθὸν
εἰδέναι, ἀλλ᾽ οὗτος μὲν οἴεταί τι εἰδέναι οὐκ εἰδώς, ἐγὼ δέ,   5
ὥσπερ οὖν οὐκ οἶδα, οὐδὲ οἴομαι· ἔοικα γοῦν τούτου γε
σμικρῷ τινι αὐτῷ τούτῳ σοφώτερος εἶναι, ὅτι ἃ μὴ οἶδα
οὐδὲ οἴομαι εἰδέναι. ἐντεῦθεν ἐπ᾽ ἄλλον ᾖα τῶν ἐκείνου
δοκούντων σοφωτέρων εἶναι καί μοι ταὐτὰ ταῦτα ἔδοξε,
καὶ ἐνταῦθα κἀκείνῳ καὶ ἄλλοις πολλοῖς ἀπηχθόμην.   e

Μετὰ ταῦτ᾽ οὖν ἤδη ἐφεξῆς ᾖα, αἰσθανόμενος μὲν καὶ
λυπούμενος καὶ δεδιὼς ὅτι ἀπηχθανόμην, ὅμως δὲ ἀνα-
γκαῖον ἐδόκει εἶναι τὸ τοῦ θεοῦ περὶ πλείστου ποιεῖσθαι·
ἰτέον οὖν, σκοποῦντι τὸν χρησμὸν τί λέγει, ἐπὶ ἅπαντας   5
τούς τι δοκοῦντας εἰδέναι. καὶ νὴ τὸν κύνα, ὦ ἄνδρες   22a
Ἀθηναῖοι—δεῖ γὰρ πρὸς ὑμᾶς τἀληθῆ λέγειν—ἦ μὴν ἐγὼ

ἔπαθόν τι τοιοῦτον· οἱ μὲν μάλιστα εὐδοκιμοῦντες ἔδοξάν
μοι ὀλίγου δεῖν τοῦ πλείστου ἐνδεεῖς εἶναι ζητοῦντι κατὰ
τὸν θεόν, ἄλλοι δὲ δοκοῦντες φαυλότεροι ἐπιεικέστεροι   5
εἶναι ἄνδρες πρὸς τὸ φρονίμως ἔχειν. δεῖ δὴ ὑμῖν τὴν ἐμὴν
πλάνην ἐπιδεῖξαι ὥσπερ πόνους τινὰς πονοῦντος ἵνα μοι
καὶ ἀνέλεγκτος ἡ μαντεία γένοιτο. μετὰ γὰρ τοὺς πολι-
τικοὺς ᾖα ἐπὶ τοὺς ποιητὰς τούς τε τῶν τραγῳδιῶν καὶ
τοὺς τῶν διθυράμβων καὶ τοὺς ἄλλους, ὡς ἐνταῦθα ἐπ᾽   b
αὐτοφώρῳ καταληψόμενος ἐμαυτὸν ἀμαθέστερον ἐκείνων
ὄντα. ἀναλαμβάνων οὖν αὐτῶν τὰ ποιήματα ἅ μοι ἐδόκει
μάλιστα πεπραγματεῦσθαι αὐτοῖς, διηρώτων ἂν αὐτοὺς τί
λέγοιεν, ἵν᾽ ἅμα τι καὶ μανθάνοιμι παρ᾽ αὐτῶν. αἰσχύνομαι   5
οὖν ὑμῖν εἰπεῖν, ὦ ἄνδρες, τἀληθῆ· ὅμως δὲ ῥητέον. ὡς
ἔπος γὰρ εἰπεῖν ὀλίγου αὐτῶν ἅπαντες οἱ παρόντες ἂν
βέλτιον ἔλεγον περὶ ὧν αὐτοὶ ἐπεποιήκεσαν. ἔγνων οὖν αὖ
καὶ περὶ τῶν ποιητῶν ἐν ὀλίγῳ τοῦτο, ὅτι οὐ σοφίᾳ ποιοῖεν
ἃ ποιοῖεν, ἀλλὰ φύσει τινὶ καὶ ἐνθουσιάζοντες ὥσπερ οἱ   c
θεομάντεις καὶ οἱ χρησμῳδοί· καὶ γὰρ οὗτοι λέγουσι μὲν
πολλὰ καὶ καλά, ἴσασιν δὲ οὐδὲν ὧν λέγουσι. τοιοῦτόν τί
μοι ἐφάνησαν πάθος καὶ οἱ ποιηταὶ πεπονθότες· καὶ ἅμα
ᾐσθόμην αὐτῶν διὰ τὴν ποίησιν οἰομένων καὶ τἆλλα   5
σοφωτάτων εἶναι ἀνθρώπων ἃ οὐκ ἦσαν. ἀπῇα οὖν καὶ
ἐντεῦθεν τῷ αὐτῷ οἰόμενος περιγεγονέναι ᾧπερ καὶ τῶν
πολιτικῶν.

Τελευτῶν οὖν ἐπὶ τοὺς χειροτέχνας ᾖα· ἐμαυτῷ γὰρ
συνῄδη οὐδὲν ἐπισταμένῳ ὡς ἔπος εἰπεῖν, τούτους δέ γ᾽   d
ᾔδη ὅτι εὑρήσοιμι πολλὰ καὶ καλὰ ἐπισταμένους. καὶ
τούτου μὲν οὐκ ἐψεύσθην, ἀλλ᾽ ἠπίσταντο ἃ ἐγὼ οὐκ
ἠπιστάμην καί μου ταύτῃ σοφώτεροι ἦσαν. ἀλλ᾽, ὦ ἄνδρες
Ἀθηναῖοι, ταὐτόν μοι ἔδοξαν ἔχειν ἁμάρτημα ὅπερ καὶ οἱ   5
ποιηταὶ καὶ οἱ ἀγαθοὶ δημιουργοί—διὰ τὸ τὴν τέχνην
καλῶς ἐξεργάζεσθαι ἕκαστος ἠξίου καὶ τἆλλα τὰ μέγιστα
σοφώτατος εἶναι—καὶ αὐτῶν αὕτη ἡ πλημμέλεια ἐκείνην
τὴν σοφίαν ἀποκρύπτειν· ὥστε με ἐμαυτὸν ἀνερωτᾶν ὑπὲρ   e
τοῦ χρησμοῦ πότερα δεξαίμην ἂν οὕτως ὥσπερ ἔχω ἔχειν,
μήτε τι σοφὸς ὢν τὴν ἐκείνων σοφίαν μήτε ἀμαθὴς τὴν
ἀμαθίαν, ἢ ἀμφότερα ἃ ἐκεῖνοι ἔχουσιν ἔχειν. ἀπεκρινάμην οὖν ἐμαυτῷ καὶ τῷ χρησμῷ ὅτι μοι λυσιτελοῖ ὥσπερ   5
ἔχω ἔχειν.

Ἐκ ταυτησὶ δὴ τῆς ἐξετάσεως, ὦ ἄνδρες Ἀθηναῖοι,
πολλαὶ μὲν ἀπέχθειαί μοι γεγόνασι καὶ οἷαι χαλεπώταται   23a

καὶ βαρύταται, ὥστε πολλὰς διαβολὰς ἀπ᾽ αὐτῶν γεγονέναι, ὄνομα δὲ τοῦτο λέγεσθαι, σοφὸς εἶναι· οἴονται γὰρ
με ἑκάστοτε οἱ παρόντες ταῦτα αὐτὸν εἶναι σοφὸν ἃ ἂν
ἄλλον ἐξελέγξω. τὸ δὲ κινδυνεύει, ὦ ἄνδρες, τῷ ὄντι ὁ θεὸς   5
σοφὸς εἶναι, καὶ ἐν τῷ χρησμῷ τούτῳ τοῦτο λέγειν, ὅτι ἡ
ἀνθρωπίνη σοφία ὀλίγου τινὸς ἀξία ἐστὶν καὶ οὐδενός. καὶ
φαίνεται τοῦτον λέγειν τὸν Σωκράτη, προσκεχρῆσθαι δὲ
τῷ ἐμῷ ὀνόματι, ἐμὲ παράδειγμα ποιούμενος, ὥσπερ ἂν   b
<εἰ> εἴποι ὅτι "Οὗτος ὑμῶν, ὦ ἄνθρωποι, σοφώτατός
ἐστιν, ὅστις ὥσπερ Σωκράτης ἔγνωκεν ὅτι οὐδενὸς ἄξιός
ἐστι τῇ ἀληθείᾳ πρὸς σοφίαν." ταῦτ᾽ οὖν ἐγὼ μὲν ἔτι καὶ
νῦν περιιὼν ζητῶ καὶ ἐρευνῶ κατὰ τὸν θεὸν καὶ τῶν ἀστῶν   5
καὶ ξένων ἄν τινα οἴωμαι σοφὸν εἶναι· καὶ ἐπειδάν μοι μὴ
δοκῇ, τῷ θεῷ βοηθῶν ἐνδείκνυμαι ὅτι οὐκ ἔστι σοφός. καὶ
ὑπὸ ταύτης τῆς ἀσχολίας οὔτε τι τῶν τῆς πόλεως πρᾶξαί
μοι σχολὴ γέγονεν ἄξιον λόγου οὔτε τῶν οἰκείων, ἀλλ᾽ ἐν
πενίᾳ μυρίᾳ εἰμὶ διὰ τὴν τοῦ θεοῦ λατρείαν.   c
Πρὸς δὲ τούτοις οἱ νέοι μοι ἐπακολουθοῦντες, οἷς
μάλιστα σχολή ἐστιν, οἱ τῶν πλουσιωτάτων, αὐτόματοι,
χαίρουσιν ἀκούοντες ἐξεταζομένων τῶν ἀνθρώπων, καὶ
αὐτοὶ πολλάκις ἐμὲ μιμοῦνται, εἶτα ἐπιχειροῦσιν ἄλλους   5
ἐξετάζειν· κἄπειτα οἶμαι εὑρίσκουσι πολλὴν ἀφθονίαν
οἰομένων μὲν εἰδέναι τι ἀνθρώπων, εἰδότων δὲ ὀλίγα ἢ
οὐδέν. ἐντεῦθεν οὖν οἱ ὑπ᾽ αὐτῶν ἐξεταζόμενοι ἐμοὶ ὀργί-
ζονται, ἀλλ᾽ οὐχ αὑτοῖς, καὶ λέγουσιν ὡς Σωκράτης τίς   d
ἐστι μιαρώτατος καὶ διαφθείρει τοὺς νέους· καὶ ἐπειδάν τις
αὐτοὺς ἐρωτᾷ ὅτι ποιῶν καὶ ὅτι διδάσκων, ἔχουσι μὲν
οὐδὲν εἰπεῖν ἀλλ᾽ ἀγνοοῦσιν, ἵνα δὲ μὴ δοκῶσιν ἀπορεῖν, τὰ
κατὰ πάντων τῶν φιλοσοφούντων πρόχειρα ταῦτα λέγου-   5
σιν, ὅτι "τὰ μετέωρα καὶ τὰ ὑπὸ γῆς" καὶ "θεοὺς μὴ νομίζειν" καὶ "τὸν ἥττω λόγον κρείττω ποιεῖν." τὰ γὰρ ἀληθῆ
οἴομαι οὐκ ἂν ἐθέλοιεν λέγειν, ὅτι κατάδηλοι γίγνονται
προσποιούμενοι μὲν εἰδέναι, εἰδότες δὲ οὐδέν. ἅτε οὖν
οἶμαι φιλότιμοι ὄντες καὶ σφοδροὶ καὶ πολλοί, καὶ   e
συντεταμένως καὶ πιθανῶς λέγοντες περὶ ἐμοῦ, ἐμπεπλήκασιν ὑμῶν τὰ ὦτα καὶ πάλαι καὶ σφοδρῶς διαβάλλοντες.
ἐκ τούτων καὶ Μέλητός μοι ἐπέθετο καὶ Ἄνυτος καὶ
Λύκων, Μέλητος μὲν ὑπὲρ τῶν ποιητῶν ἀχθόμενος,   5
Ἄνυτος δὲ ὑπὲρ τῶν δημιουργῶν καὶ τῶν πολιτικῶν,
Λύκων δὲ ὑπὲρ τῶν ῥητόρων· ὥστε, ὅπερ ἀρχόμενος ἐγὼ   24
ἔλεγον, θαυμάζοιμ᾽ ἂν εἰ οἷός τ᾽ εἴην ἐγὼ ὑμῶν ταύτην τὴν
διαβολὴν ἐξελέσθαι ἐν οὕτως ὀλίγῳ χρόνῳ οὕτω πολλὴν
γεγονυῖαν. ταῦτ᾽ ἔστιν ὑμῖν, ὦ ἄνδρες Ἀθηναῖοι, τἀληθῆ,

καὶ ὑμᾶς οὔτε μέγα οὔτε σμικρὸν ἀποκρυψάμενος ἐγὼ   5
λέγω οὐδ᾽ὑποστειλάμενος. καίτοι οἶδα σχεδὸν ὅτι τούτοις
αὐτοῖς ἀπεχθάνομαι, ὃ καὶ τεκμήριον ὅτι ἀληθῆ λέγω καὶ
ὅτι αὕτη ἐστὶν ἡ διαβολὴ ἡ ἐμὴ καὶ τὰ αἴτια ταῦτά ἐστιν.
καὶ ἐάντε νῦν ἐάντε αὖθις ζητήσητε ταῦτα, οὕτως   b
εὑρήσετε.

*The missing section begins with a cross-examination of Meletus (24b–28a).
Socrates then explains his divine mission in more detail, describing himself as a
gadfly sent to ask difficult questions and challenge orthodoxy (28a–34b), and he
concludes his speech asking the jury to judge him fairly (34b–35d). For more on
these sections, see commentary.*

Τὸ μὲν μὴ ἀγανακτεῖν, ὦ ἄνδρες Ἀθηναῖοι, ἐπὶ τούτῳ   **35e**
τῷ γεγονότι, ὅτι μου κατεψηφίσασθε, ἄλλα τέ μοι πολλὰ   **36a**
συμβάλλεται, καὶ οὐκ ἀνέλπιστόν μοι γέγονεν τὸ γεγονὸς
τοῦτο, ἀλλὰ πολὺ μᾶλλον θαυμάζω ἑκατέρων τῶν ψήφων
τὸν γεγονότα ἀριθμόν. οὐ γὰρ ᾠόμην ἔγωγε οὕτω παρ᾽
ὀλίγον ἔσεσθαι, ἀλλὰ παρὰ πολύ· νῦν δέ, ὡς ἔοικεν, εἰ   5
τριάκοντα μόναι μετέπεσον τῶν ψήφων, ἀπεπεφεύγη ἄν.
Μέλητον μὲν οὖν, ὡς ἐμοὶ δοκῶ, καὶ νῦν ἀποπέφευγα, καὶ
οὐ μόνον ἀποπέφευγα, ἀλλὰ παντὶ δῆλον τοῦτό γε, ὅτι εἰ
μὴ ἀνέβη Ἄνυτος καὶ Λύκων κατηγορήσοντες ἐμοῦ, κἂν
ὦφλε χιλίας δραχμάς, οὐ μεταλαβὼν τὸ πέμπτον μέρος   b
τῶν ψήφων.

Τιμᾶται δ᾽ οὖν μοι ὁ ἀνὴρ θανάτου. εἶεν· ἐγὼ δὲ δὴ τίνος
ὑμῖν ἀντιτιμήσομαι, ὦ ἄνδρες Ἀθηναῖοι; ἢ δῆλον ὅτι τῆς
ἀξίας; τί οὖν; τί ἄξιός εἰμι παθεῖν ἢ ἀποτεῖσαι, ὅτι μαθὼν   5
ἐν τῷ βίῳ οὐχ ἡσυχίαν ἦγον, ἀλλ᾽ ἀμελήσας ὧνπερ οἱ
πολλοί, χρηματισμοῦ τε καὶ οἰκονομίας καὶ στρατηγιῶν
καὶ δημηγοριῶν καὶ τῶν ἄλλων ἀρχῶν καὶ συνωμοσιῶν
καὶ στάσεων τῶν ἐν τῇ πόλει γιγνομένων, ἡγησάμενος
ἐμαυτὸν τῷ ὄντι ἐπιεικέστερον εἶναι ἢ ὥστε εἰς ταῦτ᾽ἰόντα   c
σῴζεσθαι, ἐνταῦθα μὲν οὐκ ᾖα οἷ ἐλθὼν μήτε ὑμῖν μήτε
ἐμαυτῷ ἔμελλον μηδὲν ὄφελος εἶναι, ἐπὶ δὲ τὸ ἰδίᾳ
ἕκαστον ἰὼν εὐεργετεῖν τὴν μεγίστην εὐεργεσίαν, ὡς ἐγὼ
φημι, ἐνταῦθα ᾖα, ἐπιχειρῶν ἕκαστον ὑμῶν πείθειν μὴ   5
πρότερον μήτε τῶν ἑαυτοῦ μηδενὸς ἐπιμελεῖσθαι πρὶν
ἑαυτοῦ ἐπιμεληθείη ὅπως ὡς βέλτιστος καὶ φρονιμώτατος
ἔσοιτο, μήτε τῶν τῆς πόλεως, πρὶν αὐτῆς τῆς πόλεως, τῶν
τε ἄλλων οὕτω κατὰ τὸν αὐτὸν τρόπον ἐπιμελεῖσθαι—τί   d
οὖν εἰμι ἄξιος παθεῖν τοιοῦτος ὤν; ἀγαθόν τι, ὦ ἄνδρες

**A
Level**

Άθηναῖοι, εἰ δεῖ γε κατὰ τὴν ἀξίαν τῇ ἀληθείᾳ τιμᾶσθαι·
καὶ ταῦτά γε ἀγαθὸν τοιοῦτον ὅτι ἂν πρέποι ἐμοί. τί οὖν
πρέπει ἀνδρὶ πένητι εὐεργέτῃ δεομένῳ ἄγειν σχολὴν ἐπὶ τῇ   5
ὑμετέρᾳ παρακελεύσει; οὐκ ἔσθ᾽ ὅτι μᾶλλον, ὦ ἄνδρες
Άθηναῖοι, πρέπει οὕτως ὡς τὸν τοιοῦτον ἄνδρα ἐν πρυτανείῳ σιτεῖσθαι, πολύ γε μᾶλλον ἢ εἴ τις ὑμῶν ἵππῳ ἢ
συνωρίδι ἢ ζεύγει νενίκηκεν Όλυμπίασιν· ὁ μὲν γὰρ ὑμᾶς
ποιεῖ εὐδαίμονας δοκεῖν εἶναι, ἐγὼ δὲ εἶναι, καὶ ὁ μὲν   10
τροφῆς οὐδὲν δεῖται, ἐγὼ δὲ δέομαι. εἰ οὖν δεῖ με κατὰ τὸ   e
δίκαιον τῆς ἀξίας τιμᾶσθαι, τούτου τιμῶμαι, ἐν πρυτανείῳ   37a
σιτήσεως.

Ίσως οὖν ὑμῖν καὶ ταυτὶ λέγων παραπλησίως δοκῶ
λέγειν ὥσπερ περὶ τοῦ οἴκτου καὶ τῆς ἀντιβολήσεως,
ἀπαυθαδιζόμενος· τὸ δὲ οὐκ ἔστιν, ὦ ἄνδρες Άθηναῖοι,   5
τοιοῦτον ἀλλὰ τοιόνδε μᾶλλον. πέπεισμαι ἐγὼ ἑκὼν εἶναι
μηδένα ἀδικεῖν ἀνθρώπων, ἀλλὰ ὑμᾶς τοῦτο οὐ πείθω·
ὀλίγον γὰρ χρόνον ἀλλήλοις διειλέγμεθα. ἐπεί, ὡς
ἐγῷμαι, εἰ ἦν ὑμῖν νόμος, ὥσπερ καὶ ἄλλοις ἀνθρώποις,
περὶ θανάτου μὴ μίαν ἡμέραν μόνον κρίνειν ἀλλὰ πολλάς,   10
ἐπείσθητε ἄν· νῦν δ᾽ οὐ ῥᾴδιον ἐν χρόνῳ ὀλίγῳ μεγάλας   b
διαβολὰς ἀπολύεσθαι. πεπεισμένος δὴ ἐγὼ μηδένα ἀδι-
κεῖν πολλοῦ δέω ἐμαυτόν γε ἀδικήσειν καὶ κατ᾽ ἐμαυτοῦ
ἐρεῖν αὐτὸς ὡς ἄξιός εἰμί του κακοῦ καὶ τιμήσεσθαι τοιού-
του τινὸς ἐμαυτῷ. τί δείσας; ἢ μὴ πάθω τοῦτο οὗ Μέλητός   5
μοι τιμᾶται, ὅ φημι οὐκ εἰδέναι οὔτ᾽ εἰ ἀγαθὸν οὔτ᾽ εἰ
κακόν ἐστιν; ἀντὶ τούτου δὴ ἕλωμαι ὧν εὖ οἶδά τι κακῶν
ὄντων, τούτου τιμησάμενος; πότερον δεσμοῦ; καὶ τί με δεῖ
ζῆν ἐν δεσμωτηρίῳ, δουλεύοντα τῇ ἀεὶ καθισταμένῃ ἀρχῇ,   c
τοῖς ἕνδεκα; ἀλλὰ χρημάτων καὶ δεδέσθαι ἕως ἂν ἐκτείσω;
ἀλλὰ ταὐτόν μοί ἐστιν ὅπερ νυνδὴ ἔλεγον· οὐ γὰρ ἔστι μοι
χρήματα ὁπόθεν ἐκτείσω. ἀλλὰ δὴ φυγῆς τιμήσωμαι;
ἴσως γὰρ ἄν μοι τούτου τιμήσαιτε. πολλὴ μεντἄν με φιλο-   5
ψυχία ἔχοι, ὦ ἄνδρες Άθηναῖοι, εἰ οὕτως ἀλόγιστός εἰμι
ὥστε μὴ δύνασθαι λογίζεσθαι ὅτι ὑμεῖς μὲν ὄντες πολῖταί
μου οὐχ οἷοί τε ἐγένεσθε ἐνεγκεῖν τὰς ἐμὰς διατριβὰς καὶ
τοὺς λόγους, ἀλλ᾽ ὑμῖν βαρύτεραι γεγόνασιν καὶ ἐπι-   d
φθονώτεραι, ὥστε ζητεῖτε αὐτῶν νυνὶ ἀπαλλαγῆναι· ἄλλοι
δὲ ἄρα αὐτὰς οἴσουσι ῥᾳδίως; πολλοῦ γε δεῖ, ὦ ἄνδρες
Άθηναῖοι. καλὸς οὖν ἄν μοι ὁ βίος εἴη ἐξελθόντι τηλικῷδε
ἀνθρώπῳ ἄλλην ἐξ ἄλλης πόλεως ἀμειβομένῳ καὶ ἐξε-   5
λαυνομένῳ ζῆν. εὖ γὰρ οἶδ᾽ ὅτι ὅποι ἂν ἔλθω, λέγοντος
ἐμοῦ ἀκροάσονται οἱ νέοι ὥσπερ ἐνθάδε· κἂν μὲν τούτους

ἀπελαύνω, οὗτοί με αὐτοὶ ἐξελῶσι πείθοντες τοὺς πρεσβυ-
τέρους· ἐὰν δὲ μὴ ἀπελαύνω, οἱ τούτων πατέρες δὲ καὶ   e
οἰκεῖοι δι᾽ αὐτοὺς τούτους.

Ἴσως οὖν ἄν τις εἴποι· "Σιγῶν δὲ καὶ ἡσυχίαν ἄγων, ὦ
Σώκρατες, οὐχ οἷός τ᾽ ἔσῃ ἡμῖν ἐξελθὼν ζῆν;" τουτὶ δή ἐστι
πάντων χαλεπώτατον πεῖσαί τινας ὑμῶν. ἐάντε γὰρ λέγω   5
ὅτι τῷ θεῷ ἀπειθεῖν τοῦτ᾽ ἐστὶν καὶ διὰ τοῦτ᾽ ἀδύνατον
ἡσυχίαν ἄγειν, οὐ πείσεσθέ μοι ὡς εἰρωνευομένῳ· ἐάντ᾽ αὖ   38a
λέγω ὅτι καὶ τυγχάνει μέγιστον ἀγαθὸν ὂν ἀνθρώπῳ
τοῦτο, ἑκάστης ἡμέρας περὶ ἀρετῆς τοὺς λόγους ποιεῖσθαι
καὶ τῶν ἄλλων περὶ ὧν ὑμεῖς ἐμοῦ ἀκούετε διαλεγομένου
καὶ ἐμαυτὸν καὶ ἄλλους ἐξετάζοντος, ὁ δὲ ἀνεξέταστος   5
βίος οὐ βιωτὸς ἀνθρώπῳ, ταῦτα δ᾽ ἔτι ἧττον πείσεσθέ μοι
λέγοντι. τὰ δὲ ἔχει μὲν οὕτως, ὡς ἐγώ φημι, ὦ ἄνδρες,
πείθειν δὲ οὐ ῥᾴδιον. καὶ ἐγὼ ἅμα οὐκ εἴθισμαι ἐμαυτὸν
ἀξιοῦν κακοῦ οὐδενός. εἰ μὲν γὰρ ἦν μοι χρήματα, ἐτιμη-   b
σάμην ἂν χρημάτων ὅσα ἔμελλον ἐκτείσειν· οὐδὲν γὰρ ἂν
ἐβλάβην· νῦν δὲ οὐ γὰρ ἔστιν, εἰ μὴ ἄρα ὅσον ἂν ἐγὼ
δυναίμην ἐκτεῖσαι, τοσούτου βούλεσθέ μοι τιμῆσαι. ἴσως
δ᾽ ἂν δυναίμην ἐκτεῖσαι ὑμῖν που μνᾶν ἀργυρίου· τοσούτου   5
Πλάτων δὲ ὅδε, ὦ ἄνδρες Ἀθηναῖοι, καὶ Κρίτων καὶ Κριτόβουλος καὶ Ἀπολλόδωρος κελεύουσί με τριάκοντα μνῶν
τιμήσασθαι, αὐτοὶ δ᾽ ἐγγυᾶσθαι· τιμῶμαι οὖν τοσούτου,
ἐγγυηταὶ δὲ ὑμῖν ἔσονται τοῦ ἀργυρίου οὗτοι ἀξιόχρεῳ.   10

Οὐ πολλοῦ γ᾽ ἕνεκα χρόνου, ὦ ἄνδρες Ἀθηναῖοι, ὄνομα   c
ἕξετε καὶ αἰτίαν ὑπὸ τῶν βουλομένων τὴν πόλιν λοιδορεῖν
ὡς Σωκράτη ἀπεκτόνατε, ἄνδρα σοφόν—φήσουσι γὰρ δὴ
με σοφὸν εἶναι, εἰ καὶ μή εἰμι, οἱ βουλόμενοι ὑμῖν ὀνειδί-
ζειν· εἰ γοῦν περιεμείνατε ὀλίγον χρόνον, ἀπὸ τοῦ αὐτομά-   5
του ἂν ὑμῖν τοῦτο ἐγένετο. ὁρᾶτε γὰρ δὴ τὴν ἡλικίαν ὅτι
πόρρω ἤδη ἐστὶ τοῦ βίου, θανάτου δὲ ἐγγύς. λέγω δὲ τοῦτο
οὐ πρὸς πάντας ὑμᾶς, ἀλλὰ πρὸς τοὺς ἐμοῦ καταψηφι-   d
σαμένους θάνατον. λέγω δὲ καὶ τόδε πρὸς τοὺς αὐτοὺς
τούτους. ἴσως με οἴεσθε, ὦ ἄνδρες, ἀπορίᾳ λόγων ἑαλωκέναι τοιούτων οἷς ἂν ὑμᾶς ἔπεισα, εἰ ᾤμην δεῖν ἅπαντα ποιεῖν καὶ λέγειν ὥστε ἀποφυγεῖν τὴν δίκην. πολλοῦ γε δεῖ.   5
ἀλλ᾽ ἀπορίᾳ μὲν ἑάλωκα, οὐ μέντοι λόγων, ἀλλὰ τόλμης
καὶ ἀναισχυντίας καὶ τοῦ μὴ ἐθέλειν λέγειν πρὸς ὑμᾶς τοιαῦτα οἷ᾽ ἂν ὑμῖν μὲν ἥδιστα ἦν ἀκούειν—θρηνοῦντός τέ μου
καὶ ὀδυρομένου καὶ ἄλλα ποιοῦντος καὶ λέγοντος πολλὰ
καὶ ἀνάξια ἐμοῦ, ὡς ἐγώ φημι, οἷα δὴ καὶ εἴθισθε ὑμεῖς   e

**A
Level**

τῶν ἄλλων ἀκούειν. ἀλλ᾽ οὔτε τότε ᾠήθην δεῖν ἕνεκα τοῦ
κινδύνου πρᾶξαι οὐδὲν ἀνελεύθερον, οὔτε νῦν μοι μεταμέλει οὕτως ἀπολογησαμένῳ, ἀλλὰ πολὺ μᾶλλον αἱροῦμαι
ὧδε ἀπολογησάμενος τεθνάναι ἢ ἐκείνως ζῆν. οὔτε γὰρ ἐν   5
δίκῃ οὔτ᾽ ἐν πολέμῳ οὔτ᾽ ἐμὲ οὔτ᾽ ἄλλον οὐδένα δεῖ τοῦτο
μηχανᾶσθαι, ὅπως ἀποφεύξεται πᾶν ποιῶν θάνατον. καὶ   **39a**
γὰρ ἐν ταῖς μάχαις πολλάκις δῆλον γίγνεται ὅτι τό γε
ἀποθανεῖν ἄν τις ἐκφύγοι καὶ ὅπλα ἀφεὶς καὶ ἐφ᾽ ἱκετείαν
τραπόμενος τῶν διωκόντων· καὶ ἄλλαι μηχαναὶ πολλαί
εἰσιν ἐν ἑκάστοις τοῖς κινδύνοις ὥστε διαφεύγειν θάνατον,   5
ἐάν τις τολμᾷ πᾶν ποιεῖν καὶ λέγειν. ἀλλὰ μὴ οὐ τοῦτ᾽ ᾖ
χαλεπόν, ὦ ἄνδρες, θάνατον ἐκφυγεῖν, ἀλλὰ πολὺ χαλεπώτερον πονηρίαν· θᾶττον γὰρ θανάτου θεῖ. καὶ νῦν ἐγὼ   **b**
μὲν ἅτε βραδὺς ὢν καὶ πρεσβύτης ὑπὸ τοῦ βραδυτέρου
ἑάλων, οἱ δ᾽ ἐμοὶ κατήγοροι ἅτε δεινοὶ καὶ ὀξεῖς ὄντες ὑπὸ
τοῦ θάττονος, τῆς κακίας. καὶ νῦν ἐγὼ μὲν ἄπειμι ὑφ᾽ ὑμῶν
θανάτου δίκην ὀφλών, οὗτοι δ᾽ ὑπὸ τῆς ἀληθείας ὠφληκό-   5
τες μοχθηρίαν καὶ ἀδικίαν. καὶ ἐγώ τε τῷ τιμήματι
ἐμμένω καὶ οὗτοι. ταῦτα μέν που ἴσως οὕτως καὶ ἔδει
σχεῖν, καὶ οἶμαι αὐτὰ μετρίως ἔχειν.
Τὸ δὲ δὴ μετὰ τοῦτο ἐπιθυμῶ ὑμῖν χρησμῳδῆσαι, ὦ   **c**
καταψηφισάμενοί μου· καὶ γάρ εἰμι ἤδη ἐνταῦθα ἐν ᾧ
μάλιστα ἄνθρωποι χρησμῳδοῦσιν, ὅταν μέλλωσιν ἀποθανεῖσθαι. φημὶ γάρ, ὦ ἄνδρες οἳ ἐμὲ ἀπεκτόνατε, τιμωρίαν
ὑμῖν ἥξειν εὐθὺς μετὰ τὸν ἐμὸν θάνατον πολὺ χαλεπωτέραν   5
νὴ Δία ἢ οἵαν ἐμὲ ἀπεκτόνατε· νῦν γὰρ τοῦτο εἴργασθε
οἰόμενοι μὲν ἀπαλλάξεσθαι τοῦ διδόναι ἔλεγχον τοῦ βίου,
τὸ δὲ ὑμῖν πολὺ ἐναντίον ἀποβήσεται, ὡς ἐγώ φημι.
πλείους ἔσονται ὑμᾶς οἱ ἐλέγχοντες, οὓς νῦν ἐγὼ κατεῖχον,   **d**
ὑμεῖς δὲ οὐκ ᾐσθάνεσθε· καὶ χαλεπώτεροι ἔσονται ὅσῳ
νεώτεροί εἰσιν, καὶ ὑμεῖς μᾶλλον ἀγανακτήσετε. εἰ γὰρ
οἴεσθε ἀποκτείνοντες ἀνθρώπους ἐπισχήσειν τοῦ ὀνειδίζειν
τινὰ ὑμῖν ὅτι οὐκ ὀρθῶς ζῆτε, οὐ καλῶς διανοεῖσθε· οὐ γὰρ   5
ἔσθ᾽ αὕτη ἡ ἀπαλλαγὴ οὔτε πάνυ δυνατὴ οὔτε καλή, ἀλλ᾽
ἐκείνη καὶ καλλίστη καὶ ῥᾴστη, μὴ τοὺς ἄλλους κολούειν
ἀλλ᾽ ἑαυτὸν παρασκευάζειν ὅπως ἔσται ὡς βέλτιστος.
ταῦτα μὲν οὖν ὑμῖν τοῖς καταψηφισαμένοις μαντευσάμενος
ἀπαλλάττομαι.   **10**

Τοῖς δὲ ἀποψηφισαμένοις ἡδέως ἂν διαλεχθείην ὑπὲρ   **e**
τοῦ γεγονότος τουτουῒ πράγματος, ἐν ᾧ οἱ ἄρχοντες
ἀσχολίαν ἄγουσι καὶ οὔπω ἔρχομαι οἷ ἐλθόντα με δεῖ
τεθνάναι. ἀλλά μοι, ὦ ἄνδρες, παραμείνατε τοσοῦτον
χρόνον· οὐδὲν γὰρ κωλύει διαμυθολογῆσαι πρὸς ἀλλήλους   5

ἕως ἔξεστιν. ὑμῖν γὰρ ὡς φίλοις οὖσιν ἐπιδεῖξαι ἐθέλω τὸ   40a
νυνί μοι συμβεβηκὸς τί ποτε νοεῖ. ἐμοὶ γάρ, ὦ ἄνδρες
δικασταί—ὑμᾶς γὰρ δικαστὰς καλῶν ὀρθῶς ἂν καλοίην—
θαυμάσιόν τι γέγονεν. ἡ γὰρ εἰωθυῖά μοι μαντικὴ ἡ τοῦ
δαιμονίου ἐν μὲν τῷ πρόσθεν χρόνῳ παντὶ πάνυ πυκνὴ ἀεὶ   5
ἦν καὶ πάνυ ἐπὶ σμικροῖς ἐναντιουμένη, εἴ τι μέλλοιμι μὴ
ὀρθῶς πράξειν. νυνὶ δὲ συμβέβηκέ μοι ἅπερ ὁρᾶτε καὶ
αὐτοί, ταυτὶ ἅ γε δὴ οἰηθείη ἄν τις καὶ νομίζεται ἔσχατα
κακῶν εἶναι· ἐμοὶ δὲ οὔτε ἐξιόντι ἕωθεν οἴκοθεν ἠναντιώθη   b
τὸ τοῦ θεοῦ σημεῖον, οὔτε ἡνίκα ἀνέβαινον ἐνταυθοῖ ἐπὶ τὸ
δικαστήριον, οὔτε ἐν τῷ λόγῳ οὐδαμοῦ μέλλοντί τι ἐρεῖν.
καίτοι ἐν ἄλλοις λόγοις πολλαχοῦ δή με ἐπέσχε λέγοντα
μεταξύ· νῦν δὲ οὐδαμοῦ περὶ ταύτην τὴν πρᾶξιν οὔτ᾽ ἐν   5
ἔργῳ οὐδενὶ οὔτ᾽ ἐν λόγῳ ἠναντίωταί μοι. τί οὖν αἴτιον
εἶναι ὑπολαμβάνω; ἐγὼ ὑμῖν ἐρῶ· κινδυνεύει γάρ μοι τὸ
συμβεβηκὸς τοῦτο ἀγαθὸν γεγονέναι, καὶ οὐκ ἔσθ᾽ ὅπως
ἡμεῖς ὀρθῶς ὑπολαμβάνομεν, ὅσοι οἰόμεθα κακὸν εἶναι τὸ   c
τεθνάναι. μέγα μοι τεκμήριον τούτου γέγονεν· οὐ γὰρ ἔσθ᾽
ὅπως οὐκ ἠναντιώθη ἄν μοι τὸ εἰωθὸς σημεῖον, εἰ μή τι
ἔμελλον ἐγὼ ἀγαθὸν πράξειν.

Ἐννοήσωμεν δὲ καὶ τῇδε ὡς πολλὴ ἐλπίς ἐστιν ἀγαθὸν   5
αὐτὸ εἶναι. δυοῖν γὰρ θάτερόν ἐστι τὸ τεθνάναι· ἢ γὰρ οἷον
μηδὲν εἶναι μηδὲ αἴσθησιν μηδεμίαν μηδενὸς ἔχειν τὸν
τεθνεῶτα, ἢ κατὰ τὰ λεγόμενα μεταβολή τις τυγχάνει
οὖσα καὶ μετοίκησις τῇ ψυχῇ τοῦ τόπου τοῦ ἐνθένδε εἰς
ἄλλον τόπον. καὶ εἴτε δὴ μηδεμία αἴσθησίς ἐστιν, ἀλλ᾽ οἷον   10
ὕπνος, ἐπειδάν τις καθεύδων μηδ᾽ ὄναρ μηδὲν ὁρᾷ, θαυμά-   d
σιον κέρδος ἂν εἴη ὁ θάνατος· ἐγὼ γὰρ ἂν οἶμαι, εἴ τινα
ἐκλεξάμενον δέοι ταύτην τὴν νύκτα ἐν ᾗ οὕτω κατέδαρθεν
ὥστε μηδὲ ὄναρ ἰδεῖν, καὶ τὰς ἄλλας νύκτας τε καὶ ἡμέρας
τὰς τοῦ βίου τοῦ ἑαυτοῦ ἀντιπαραθέντα ταύτῃ τῇ νυκτὶ   5
δέοι σκεψάμενον εἰπεῖν πόσας ἄμεινον καὶ ἥδιον ἡμέρας
καὶ νύκτας ταύτης τῆς νυκτὸς βεβίωκεν ἐν τῷ ἑαυτοῦ βίῳ,
οἶμαι ἂν μὴ ὅτι ἰδιώτην τινά, ἀλλὰ τὸν μέγαν βασιλέα
εὐαριθμήτους ἂν εὑρεῖν αὐτὸν ταύτας πρὸς τὰς ἄλλας   e
ἡμέρας καὶ νύκτας· εἰ οὖν τοιοῦτον ὁ θάνατός ἐστιν, κέρδος
ἔγωγε λέγω· καὶ γὰρ οὐδὲν πλείων ὁ πᾶς χρόνος φαίνεται
οὕτω δὴ εἶναι ἢ μία νύξ. εἰ δ᾽ αὖ οἷον ἀποδημῆσαί ἐστιν ὁ
θάνατος ἐνθένδε εἰς ἄλλον τόπον, καὶ ἀληθῆ ἐστιν τὰ λεγό-   5
μενα, ὡς ἄρα ἐκεῖ εἰσιν ἅπαντες οἱ τεθνεῶτες, τί μεῖζον
ἀγαθὸν τούτου εἴη ἄν, ὦ ἄνδρες δικασταί; εἰ γάρ τις ἀφι-
κόμενος εἰς Ἅιδου, ἀπαλλαγεὶς τουτωνὶ τῶν φασκόντων   41a
δικαστῶν εἶναι, εὑρήσει τοὺς ὡς ἀληθῶς δικαστάς, οἵπερ

καὶ λέγονται ἐκεῖ δικάζειν, Μίνως τε καὶ Ῥαδάμανθυς καὶ
Αἰακὸς καὶ Τριπτόλεμος καὶ ἄλλοι ὅσοι τῶν ἡμιθέων
δίκαιοι ἐγένοντο ἐν τῷ ἑαυτῶν βίῳ, ἆρα φαύλη ἂν εἴη ἡ   5
ἀποδημία; ἢ αὖ Ὀρφεῖ συγγενέσθαι καὶ Μουσαίῳ καὶ
Ἡσιόδῳ καὶ Ὁμήρῳ ἐπὶ πόσῳ ἄν τις δέξαιτ᾽ ἂν ὑμῶν; ἐγὼ
μὲν γὰρ πολλάκις ἐθέλω τεθνάναι εἰ ταῦτ᾽ ἔστιν ἀληθῆ.
ἐπεὶ ἔμοιγε καὶ αὐτῷ θαυμαστὴ ἂν εἴη ἡ διατριβὴ αὐτόθι,   b
ὁπότε ἐντύχοιμι Παλαμήδει καὶ Αἴαντι τῷ Τελαμῶνος καὶ
εἴ τις ἄλλος τῶν παλαιῶν διὰ κρίσιν ἄδικον τέθνηκεν, ἀντιπαραβάλλοντι τὰ ἐμαυτοῦ πάθη πρὸς τὰ ἐκείνων—ὡς ἐγὼ
οἶμαι, οὐκ ἂν ἀηδὲς εἴη—καὶ δὴ τὸ μέγιστον, τοὺς ἐκεῖ   5
ἐξετάζοντα καὶ ἐρευνῶντα ὥσπερ τοὺς ἐνταῦθα διάγειν, τίς
αὐτῶν σοφός ἐστιν καὶ τίς οἴεται μέν, ἔστιν δ᾽ οὔ. ἐπὶ πόσῳ
δ᾽ ἄν τις, ὦ ἄνδρες δικασταί, δέξαιτο ἐξετάσαι τὸν ἐπὶ
Τροίαν ἀγαγόντα τὴν πολλὴν στρατιὰν ἢ Ὀδυσσέα ἢ   c
Σίσυφον ἢ ἄλλους μυρίους ἄν τις εἴποι καὶ ἄνδρας καὶ
γυναῖκας, οἷς ἐκεῖ διαλέγεσθαι ἐκεῖ καὶ συνεῖναι καὶ ἐξετάζειν
ἀμήχανον ἂν εἴη εὐδαιμονίας; πάντως οὐ δήπου τούτου γε
ἕνεκα οἱ ἐκεῖ ἀποκτείνουσι· τά τε γὰρ ἄλλα εὐδαιμονέ-   5
στεροί εἰσιν οἱ ἐκεῖ τῶν ἐνθάδε, καὶ ἤδη τὸν λοιπὸν χρόνον
ἀθάνατοί εἰσιν, εἴπερ γε τὰ λεγόμενα ἀληθῆ ἐστιν.

Ἀλλὰ καὶ ὑμᾶς χρή, ὦ ἄνδρες δικασταί, εὐέλπιδας εἶναι
πρὸς τὸν θάνατον, καὶ ἕν τι τοῦτο διανοεῖσθαι ἀληθές, ὅτι
οὐκ ἔστιν ἀνδρὶ ἀγαθῷ κακὸν οὐδὲν οὔτε ζῶντι οὔτε   d
τελευτήσαντι, οὐδὲ ἀμελεῖται ὑπὸ θεῶν τὰ τούτου πρά-
γματα· οὐδὲ τὰ ἐμὰ νῦν ἀπὸ τοῦ αὐτομάτου γέγονεν, ἀλλά
μοι δῆλόν ἐστι τοῦτο, ὅτι ἤδη τεθνάναι καὶ ἀπηλλάχθαι
πραγμάτων βέλτιον ἦν μοι. διὰ τοῦτο καὶ ἐμὲ οὐδαμοῦ   5
ἀπέτρεψεν τὸ σημεῖον, καὶ ἔγωγε τοῖς καταψηφισαμένοις
μου καὶ τοῖς κατηγόροις οὐ πάνυ χαλεπαίνω. καίτοι οὐ
ταύτῃ τῇ διανοίᾳ κατεψηφίζοντό μου καὶ κατηγόρουν, ἀλλ᾽
οἰόμενοι βλάπτειν· τοῦτο αὐτοῖς ἄξιον μέμφεσθαι. τοσόνδε   e
μέντοι αὐτῶν δέομαι· τοὺς ὑεῖς μου, ἐπειδὰν ἡβήσωσι,
τιμωρήσασθε, ὦ ἄνδρες, ταὐτὰ ταῦτα λυποῦντες ἅπερ ἐγὼ
ὑμᾶς ἐλύπουν, ἐὰν ὑμῖν δοκῶσιν ἢ χρημάτων ἢ ἄλλου του
πρότερον ἐπιμελεῖσθαι ἢ ἀρετῆς, καὶ ἐὰν δοκῶσί τι εἶναι   5
μηδὲν ὄντες, ὀνειδίζετε αὐτοῖς ὥσπερ ἐγὼ ὑμῖν, ὅτι οὐκ
ἐπιμελοῦνται ὧν δεῖ, καὶ οἴονταί τι εἶναι ὄντες οὐδενὸς
ἄξιοι. καὶ ἐὰν ταῦτα ποιῆτε, δίκαια πεπονθὼς ἐγὼ ἔσομαι   42a
ὑφ᾽ ὑμῶν αὐτός τε καὶ οἱ ὑεῖς. ἀλλὰ γὰρ ἤδη ὥρα ἀπιέναι,
ἐμοὶ μὲν ἀποθανουμένῳ, ὑμῖν δὲ βιωσομένοις· ὁπότεροι δὲ
ἡμῶν ἔρχονται ἐπὶ ἄμεινον πρᾶγμα, ἄδηλον παντὶ πλὴν ἢ
τῷ θεῷ.   5

Commentary Notes

The Apology is divided into three separate speeches.

- 17a–35e: Socrates defends himself against the charge of impiety.
- 35e–38b: Socrates is found guilty and proposes a counter-penalty to death.
- 38c–42a: The jury votes for death, and Socrates responds to the sentence.

The first speech

17a–18a – Opening address

Socrates begins his speech with a forceful and sarcastic jibe, claiming that he almost forgot himself due to the persuasiveness of his accusers' speeches, even though they have hardly spoken a word of truth. The tone of this opening statement immediately confronts us with a compelling character, and raises questions which remain present throughout the speech. Is Socrates staunch and unyielding in the face of a hostile jury, or does he seal his own fate by being foolishly provocative and arrogant? There is no straightforward answer to this, and each reader will form their own interpretation of Socrates as they study the text.

Socrates continues to explain that his accusers' most shameful lie was their claim that the jury should be on their guard against his clever and eloquent language. Socrates instead declares that he will speak in an unembellished fashion, but that he will at least speak the truth. He ends the introduction by asking his audience to judge him on the content of his argument, rather than its presentation.

18a7–19a7 – Prothesis: Statement of the case

Socrates now explains how he will structure his defence. He divides his accusers into two groups: those who have been denouncing him for a long time, and those who are accusing him in the current case. He explains that the past accusers are more dangerous, both as they are anonymous and cannot be opposed in person, and as their views are so entrenched.

18a7

δίκαιός εἰμι ἀπολογήσασθαι: δίκαιος εἰμί + infinitive = 'I have a right to . . .'.

ἀπολογήσασθαι: aorist infinitive. It is used here to refer to a one-off occasion, where the present infinitive would imply repeated or continuous action. This is a distinction known as the 'aspect' of a verb, and one which often has important implications on meaning (see for example notes 18d7 and 20e4). Translate merely as 'to speak in my defence'.

ὦ ἄνδρες Ἀθηναῖοι: Socrates here addresses the jury as 'men of Athens', rather than with the more usual title, ἄνδρες δικασταί (men of the jury). Compare with 40a2 (and see note 40a3), where he claims that he should rightly address those who voted for his acquittal as ἄνδρες δικασταί. For more on the make-up of the jury, see Introduction ('The trial').

18a8

μου ... κατηγορημένα: the accent shows that this must be the perfect passive participle of κατηγορέω, the perfect tense stressing the ongoing nature of these accusations. Verbs of accusation with the prefix κατά- take an accusative of the crime and genitive of the person accused, hence μου here = 'against me' (as at 18b1).

18a9

τὰ ὕστερον: supply κατηγορημένα from before: 'things (accused) later'.

τοὺς ὑστέρους: supply κατηγόρους.

18b1

ἐμοῦ γὰρ πολλοὶ κατήγοροι γεγόνασι: 'For many accusers have risen up against me.' γεγόνασι is the perfect of γίγνομαι.

18b2

καὶ πάλαι: as often καί here is used adverbially ('even', 'also') to emphasize the next word, rather than as a conjunction ('and'). The second καί in the line means 'and'.

πολλὰ ἤδη ἔτη: 'for many years now' (accusative of time how long). An example of tautology after καὶ πάλαι, to stress for how long these accusers have been around. This adds into Socrates' argument that the past accusers are more dangerous than those of the present. ἔτη is accusative plural of ἔτος, which goes like the neuter word γένος. See *Oxford Grammar of Classical Greek* p. 31.

18b3

τοὺς ἀμφὶ Ἄνυτον: 'Anytus and his followers', literally 'the ones around Anytus', with a disdainful tone here. In 23e Socrates lists his accusers as Meletus, Anytus and Lycon, and at 19b he names Meletus as the one who has actually brought the formal charge against him. Anytus, a wealthy political leader, is mentioned here either as he was the most influential of the three, or because Socrates has chosen not to name Meletus out of contempt. For more on the accusers, see Introduction ('The trial').

18b4

καὶ τούτους: 'these men also' – adverbial καί (see note 18b2).

δεινούς: (here) 'fearful' or 'dangerous'. There is no obvious English equivalent for the word δεινός, which can mean 'fearful', as well as 'skilled' or 'clever'. This suggests a certain suspicion of intelligence, which can be used to persuade, influence and deceive people. Note that at 17b (in the opening statement) Socrates says that his current accusers have warned the jury to be on guard because he is δεινὸς λέγειν ('clever at speaking'), a charge Socrates denies because his focus is the truth, rather than persuasion.

ἐκεῖνοι δεινότεροι: supply εἰσί.

Socrates now explains that the past accusers are more dangerous than the current ones, citing the following reasons:

- There are more of them (18c5).
- They have been making accusations for such a long time (18c5 and see 18b2).
- They convinced many when they were young and impressionable (18c6–7).
- When they spread their lies, there is no one present to argue against them (18c8).
- They are anonymous so cannot be refuted (18c9–18d1).
- People have different motives for spreading the lies: some nurture a personal hatred for him, while some have been convinced and spread the slander in earnest (18d2–4).
- They are not present to be examined now (18d4–7).
- People have heard the old claims far more often (18e2–4).

The large number of reasons serves to show just what a difficult task Socrates has to change established public opinion, but it also makes the current accusers appear less powerful.

18b5

οἵ: the accent shows that this is the relative pronoun ('who, which') rather than the definite article οἱ.

τοὺς πολλούς: with the article, meaning 'the many', 'the majority'.

ἐκ παίδων: 'from childhood'.

παραλαμβάνοντες: here παραλαμβάνω means 'get control of'.

18b6

ἔπειθόν τε καὶ κατηγόρουν: the imperfects here stress the continuous nature of the actions to highlight the idea that the past accusers are more dangerous. For κατηγόρεω see note 18a8.

18b7

ὡς: introduces an indirect statement reporting the accusers' words: '(saying) that . . .'.

ἔστιν: the present indicative of εἰμί (except εἶ) retains its accent when it denotes existence, so should be translated here as 'there is'.

τις Σωκράτης: 'some man named Socrates', used contemptuously.

σοφὸς ἀνήρ: in apposition: 'Socrates, a wise man'. The word σοφὸς is used critically here, the accuser being suspicious of Socrates' overly intelligent, questioning nature. For more on σοφός see note 22a5.

τά . . . μετέωρα φροντιστὴς: 'a deep thinker about astronomical phenomena'. τά μετέωρα are literally 'things raised off the ground' and is most likely to be an accusative of respect (meaning 'with respect to . . .' or 'when it comes to . . .'). This was a common misrepresentation of Socrates: the word μετέωρα is used of Socrates' philosophy at line 228 of Aristophanes' *Clouds* (for more on *Clouds* see note 18d1).

18b8

ἀνεζητηκὼς: perfect participle from ἀναζητέω. The prefix ἀνα- here, as often, makes the meaning of the verb more intense. Verbs beginning with more than one consonant (including double consonants ζ, ξ and ψ) reduplicate by adding epsilon. As it is not a temporal augment, it is retained in the participle. The implicit criticism here is of Socrates' impiety. These sorts of naturalistic beliefs were considered irreligious as the celestial bodies were normally considered divine. See also 26b, when Meletus accuses Socrates of believing that the sun is just a stone, and the moon made of earth.

τὸν ἥττω λόγον κρείττω ποιῶν: 'making the worse argument better'. ἥττω and κρείττω are contracted forms of the ending -ονα, from the comparatives of κακός and ἀγαθός respectively. See *Oxford Grammar of Classical Greek* p. 36. Aristophanes' *Clouds* lines 882–884 provides an example of this allegation against Socrates, followed by a comic debate (ἀγών) between the personifications of good and bad argument (889ff). The same accusation was often levelled against the sophists (see note 19e3).

18c2

<οἱ>: not present in manuscripts of the text, but deemed necessary for meaning.

κατασκεδάσαντες: aorist participle from κατασκεδάννυμι, 'scatter'. The metaphor emphasizes the extent to which the slander has been dispersed throughout the city.

18c3

ἀκούοντες: supply 'this slander' or 'what they say'.

18c4

οὐδὲ: like καί (note 18b2), οὐδέ can be used as a conjunction ('and not') or adverbially ('not even' or 'also . . . not'), as here.

οὐδὲ θεοὺς νομίζειν: 'also do not believe in the gods', one of the three formal charges made against Socrates. The word νομίζειν, however, is problematic (see also Introduction – 'The charge against Socrates'). Some commentators cite connection to the word νόμος ('custom', 'common practice'), and take νομίζω to mean that Socrates was charged with not following established religious practice, translating the phrase as 'do not even acknowledge the gods'. Others take it to mean 'believe in', maintaining that the charge was one of atheism. As evidence for this, they refer to Socrates interchangeably adding the word εἶναι to the phrase, which means unequivocally 'do not believe that the gods exist' (e.g. at 26c and 27b). The focus of Socrates' argument also seems to be against this charge (27b–28a) and Xenophon apparently understood it to mean 'believe in' (see *Memorabilia* 1.1.5). In this context too, this meaning makes sense given that natural science was seen to challenge belief in the gods (see note 18b8). Yet the close connection between practice and belief in ancient religion means that the two meanings are not completely incompatible, and the implications of both should be recognized.

ἔπειτά: 'besides', introducing the next reason for fearing the accusers.

εἰσιν: due to the lack of accent, this should not be translated as 'there are' (see note 18b7).

18c5

ἔτι δὲ καὶ: 'and moreover', giving the final reason for his fear. Together the particles δὲ καὶ emphasize the idea that this is yet another reason added to the list.

18c6

ἐν ᾗ ἂν μάλιστα ἐπιστεύσατε: '(the age) at which you especially might have believed'. The particle ἄν is primarily used:

- With a **past tense indicative**: (1) in open conditionals (20b1); (2) for repeated actions in the past (22b4); (3) to express past potentiality or likelihood (as here).

- With the **optative**: (1) in remote conditionals; (2) potential optative meaning 'may', 'might', 'would', 'could' (20c4).

- With the **subjunctive**: in the indefinite construction (19e5).

18c7

παῖδες ὄντες ἔνιοι ὑμῶν: note the word order here (literally '*children* being some of you'). The emphatic placement of παῖδες stresses the impressionability of the audience, helping to explain why these accusers were so dangerous, and helps persuade the jury to question the beliefs which they gained at this suggestible age.

18c8

ἐρήμην κατηγοροῦντες: 'making accusations in a case which was uncontested'. An ἐρήμη δίκη (literally 'solitary case') was the term for an undefended lawsuit, but the word δίκη was frequently omitted.

ἀπολογουμένου οὐδενός: 'since no one was speaking in defence'.

18c9

ὃ ... ὅτι ...: '(the thing) which (is) most absurd of all (is) that ...'. ἐστί must be supplied twice, and the accent shows that ὃ is the relative pronoun rather than the article.

οἷόν τε: supply ἐστί – 'it is possible'.

AS

18d1

κωμῳδοποιὸς τυγχάνει ὤν: when τυγχάνω means 'to happen to . . .', it is followed by a participle. The κωμῳδοποιὸς being referred to is Aristophanes (mentioned openly at 19c3), whose comedy *Clouds,* produced in 423 BC, presented a caricature of Socrates and his philosophy (see also Introduction – 'Socrates'). By alluding to, but not actually naming him (a rhetorical device known as antonomasia), Socrates is being somewhat provocative. Xenophon, in his *Apology* (chapters 1–2) uses the word μεγαληγορία (literally 'big talk') to describe the passive-aggressive, haughty nature of Socrates' speech.

18d2

φθόνῳ καὶ διαβολῇ χρώμενοι: Socrates claims that these men are vilifying him out of personal hatred. φθόνος means 'ill-will', especially 'envy' of another person's good fortune, while διαβολή is an important word in the *Apology,* meaning 'slander', 'prejudice' and 'enmity'.

18d3

οἱ δὲ καὶ αὐτοὶ: 'and others also themselves'. οἱ δὲ when clearly opposed to a larger group is often used without a corresponding οἱ μέν. Socrates is suggesting that the past accusers are made up of different groups with different motives. While the first group mentioned nurtured a personal hatred for Socrates, the second group are convinced of the slander and spread it in good faith.

ἀνέπειθον: for the prefix ἀνα- here see note 18b8.

18d4

ἀπορώτατοί: 'very hard to deal with'. The related verb ἀπορέω means 'be at a loss', 'be puzzled'.

ἀναβιβάσασθαι: literally 'to cause to go up' (causal form of ἀναβαίνω, 'to go up'), but here 'to bring up to the bar' as a witness.

18d5

αὐτῶν: take with οὐδένα.

ἐνταυθοῖ: 'to here', i.e. up in front of the jury where Socrates was.

οὐδ' . . . οὐδένα: translate as a single negative. A negative followed by a compound negative (οὐδείς, οὔποτε etc.) is strengthened.

ἀνάγκη . . . σκιαμαχεῖν ἀπολογούμενόν: 'it is necessary for me, making a defence speech, to fight against shadows'. Supply ἐστί, and ἀνάγκη is followed by the accusative and infinitive construction; the accusative με, agreeing with ἀπολογούμενόν, is implied.

18d6

ὥσπερ: 'as it were', softening the force of the powerful metaphor σκιαμαχεῖν ('fight against shadows'). The metaphor emphasizes Socrates' lack of power in the face of the anonymous, long-standing accusers.

τε καὶ: despite position, joining the two infinitives.

AS

18d7

ἀξιώσατε: 'deem it correct that', 'suppose that'. The tense of imperatives is always by aspect; the aorist here suggests that Socrates is asking the jury to agree temporarily to his distinction for argument's sake.

18d9

ἑτέρους μὲν τοὺς … ἑτέρους δὲ τοὺς …: 'the ones who … and the others who …'. ἕτερος is used in the plural to refer to two different groups, rather than two individuals.

18e1

οἰήθητε: passive deponent aorist imperative (for tense, see note 18d7). See *Oxford Grammar of Classical Greek* p. 60, note 3.

18e2

ἐκείνων … ἠκούσατε: ἀκούω takes the accusative of thing heard, but genitive of person from whom something is heard.

18e3

πολὺ μᾶλλον: 'far more', referring to the intensity of their accusations rather than merely frequency. The accusative πολὺ is being used adverbially, to express measure of difference with a comparative.

18e5

ἀπολογητέον … καὶ ἐπιχειρητέον: 'a defence must be made … and I must try …'. Forms ending in -τέος, -α, -ον are verbal adjectives used to express necessity, equivalent to Latin gerundives. See *Oxford Grammar of Classical Greek* p. 193–4. Here they are used impersonally (subject 'it') and ἐστί should be supplied. Literally: 'it is needing to be spoken in defence … and attempted …'.

19a1

ὑμῶν ἐξελέσθαι: 'to remove from you'. ὑμῶν is a genitive of separation and ἐξελέσθαι is the aorist middle infinitive of ἐξαιρέω (aorist by aspect).

ἐν πολλῷ χρόνῳ ἔσχετε: 'you have acquired over a long time'. The aorist of verbs whose presents denote a state, generally expresses the entrance into the state or the beginning of action (ingressive aorist). Thus the aorist of ἔχω often means to 'obtain' or 'acquire'.

19a2

ταύτην: agreeing with τὴν διαβολὴν in line before, and delayed for emphasis.

ἐν οὕτως ὀλίγῳ χρόνῳ: 'in so short a time'. Note the repetition to emphasize the lack of time: speeches in Athenian courts of law were timed by water-clocks (κλεψύδραι).

βουλοίμην … ἂν …: 'I would like', a potential optative (see note 18c6) followed by the accusative and infinitive construction. The tone is softer than βούλομαι alone.

AS

19a3

οὕτως: 'in this way', i.e. that I would remove the prejudice against me from you.

τι ἄμεινον: 'it is at all better' (supply ἐστί). ἄμεινον is an irregular comparative from ἀγαθός, while τι is used adverbially here to mean 'somewhat' or 'at all' (literally 'with respect to a bit').

19a4

πλέον τί με ποιῆσαι: a second accusative and infinitive after βουλοίμην ... ἄν. πλέον is the neuter comparative of πολύς. The phrase literally means 'for me to do something more', but may be rendered as 'for me to be successful'.

19a5

οὐ πάνυ με λανθάνει οἷόν ἐστιν: 'it doesn't at all escape my notice what sort of thing it is', or 'I am not in any way oblivious of its nature'.

19a6

ἴτω: 'let it go' or 'let it turn out', third person imperative of εἶμι (I will go). In the indicative εἶμι has future meaning, but in all other forms (participle, imperative, infinitive, subjunctive, etc.) it has present meaning and is used instead of equivalent forms of ἔρχομαι. See *Oxford Grammar of Classical Greek* p. 94.

φίλον: supply ἐστί.

τῷ θεῷ: not a particular god, the article is being used generically to refer to the entire category of θεοί.

τῷ δὲ νόμῳ πειστέον: 'it must be obeyed to the law' = 'the law must be obeyed' (ἐστί supplied). On the verbal adjective, see note 18e5.

19a8–24b2 – Defence proper: Against the long-standing accusations

Socrates chooses first to defend himself against the traditional charges against him, which he says have led to his current prosecution. He claims that he is not an expert in natural science and then also denies that he is a paid teacher of wisdom (a *sophist*). He continues to explain how he first gained the reputation for these things.

19a8

Ἀναλάβωμεν: 'Let us take up' or 'examine' – an exhortative subjunctive (aorist due to aspect) introducing the indirect question τίς ... ἐστὶν.

ἡ ἐμὴ διαβολὴ: 'the slander against me'. ἐμὴ here functions as an objective genitive equivalent to ἐμοῦ (as at 18a8).

19b1

ᾗ: dative with πιστεύων.

καὶ: adverbial usage.

Μέλητός με ἐγράψατο τὴν γραφὴν ταύτην: 'Meletus brought this indictment against me'. ἐγράψατο takes two accusatives here: τὴν γραφὴν is a cognate

AS

accusative, one from the same root as the verb (e.g. 'I dreamed a dream'), and με denotes the person affected. There was no state prosecution service, so a private citizen would have to bring a charge against a suspect. There were two types of charge: a γραφή was an accusation relating to a crime against the state of Athens, while a δίκη was for a private matter.

19b3

ὥσπερ οὖν κατηγόρων τὴν ἀντωμοσίαν δεῖ ἀναγνῶναι αὐτῶν: 'And so it is necessary to read their affidavit as if (they were formal) accusers'. An ἀντωμοσία is an 'affidavit', the formal accusation made by a prosecutor under oath, and the comparison introduced by ὥσπερ has been truncated. Socrates' past critics never formally accused him in court, so he here reconstructs what their affidavit would have been so that he can refute it.

19b4

ἀναγνῶναι: aorist infinitive from ἀναγιγνώσκω (tense by aspect).

19c1

ταὐτὰ ταῦτα: 'these same things' – the breathing mark on the third letter of ταὐτὰ (properly called a *coronis* here) shows that it is crasis for τὰ αὐτὰ.

19c2

διδάσκων: this characterizes Socrates as a sophist (see note 19e3).

τοιαύτη τίς ἐστιν: 'it is something like that', referring to the imaginary affidavit. τίς here is the indefinite pronoun (someone, something), and has an accent because it is followed by the enclitic ἐστιν. Enclitics are words which attach themselves to the preceding word and often (as here) throw their accent back onto it.

ἑωρᾶτε: the imperfect of ὁράω is ἑώρων (alpha-contracted).

καὶ αὐτοὶ: 'even you yourselves', adverbial καὶ.

19c3

Ἀριστοφάνους: genitive singular. As at 18d1, Socrates is referring to Aristophanes' play *Clouds*. For declension of Ἀριστοφάνης see *Oxford Grammar of Classical Greek* p. 31.

Σωκράτη τινὰ ἐκεῖ περιφερόμενον . . .: this defines the ταῦτα in the previous line. The 'being carried about' refers to Socrates' entry in a hovering basket at line 218 of *Clouds*. Σωκράτη is accusative and declines like Ἀριστοφάνης above.

19c4

φάσκοντά τε ἀεροβατεῖν: 'saying that he was walking on air'. In the infinitive construction, if the subject of the indirect statement is the same as the subject as the main verb, it is usually not expressed. Aristophanes' Socrates uses the word ἀεροβατέω at line 225 of *Clouds*. In Aristophanes it is used to refer to his suspension in the hovering basket, but also implies that Socrates is not engaging with the real world (compare the English metaphor: 'head in the clouds').

AS

19c5

φλυαρίαν φλυαροῦντα: 'speaking nonsense' (cognate accusative: see note 19b1). The word φλυαρέω means 'talk nonsense' or 'play the fool', and the emphatic repetition of words from the same root allows a stronger rejection of the ridiculous caricature portrayed in Aristophanes.

19c6

πέρι: take with ὧν in previous line. When περί comes after the word it governs, the accent moves onto the first syllable (anastrophe). This is common with other two-syllable words in verse, but happens in prose only with περί.

οὐχ ὡς ἀτιμάζων λέγω τὴν τοιαύτην ἐπιστήμην: ὡς with the present participle means 'because', and the ἐπιστήμην referred to is natural science.

19c8

μή πως ἐγὼ ὑπὸ Μελήτου τοσαύτας δίκας φεύγοιμι: 'may I not at all be prosecuted by Meletus on such great charges'. The lack of accent on πως shows it is the enclitic ('by any means', 'at all') and the optative φεύγοιμι expresses a wish for the future. With an aside, Socrates is wryly suggesting that he has to defend himself against everything (even belittling natural science) in case Meletus adds it to his attack.

19c9

ἀλλὰ γὰρ: 'but in fact' – ἀλλὰ marks a contrast and γὰρ introduces explanation.

ἐμοὶ τούτων . . . οὐδὲν μέτεστιν: 'I have nothing to do with these things'. Literally: 'there is not a share of these things to me'. οὐδὲν is an adverbial accusative ('not at all') – see notes on πολὺ and τι (18e3 and 19a3 respectively). In the *Phaedo* (96ff), Socrates says that as a young man he had been interested in investigating natural phenomena. However, he later turned to more fundamental human questions, such as what it means to be good, and how people should live their lives (see also Introduction).

19d1

μάρτυρας . . . λέγουσιν: this is a particularly long and complex sentence, so requires careful attention to the grammar of each clause (see individual notes below). Socrates is saying that he can provide the jury themselves as witnesses because they have heard him talking in the past, so know that he is not interested in natural science.

μάρτυρας: 'as witnesses' (that he knows little about natural science).

τοὺς πολλοὺς: see note 18b5.

παρέχομαι: παρέχω is the normal word used for supplying witnesses or evidence in a case. The middle here expresses self-interest, its most common usage.

19d2

ἀξιῶ . . . φράζειν: an indirect command.

ὅσοι . . . διαλεγομένου: 'all of you who . . .'. A relative clause describing ὑμᾶς and ὑμῶν.

πολλοὶ . . . εἰσιν: a parenthetical expression which interrupts the grammar of the sentence.

AS

19d3

ἀκηκόατε: for ἀκούω (here perfect tense) with the genitive, see note 18e2.

19d4

φράζετε: after breaking off earlier in the line (πολλοὶ ... εἰσιν) Socrates now resumes his train of thought. However, the sentence which began as an indirect command (ἀξιῶ ... φράζειν) is now resumed with the stronger imperative (φράζετε). This grammatical change of tack is known as anacolouthon, and it gives the speech a more natural flavour.

19d5

ἢ σμικρὸν ἢ μέγα: 'either a little or a lot' – two adverbial accusatives.

19d6

γνώσεσθε ὅτι: the future of γιγνώσκω is the deponent middle γνώσομαι. Indirect statements dependent on γιγνώσκω and other verbs of perception usually take the participle construction, but may be followed by the ὅτι construction to express certain knowledge of a fact. Socrates is sure that the falsity of all the slanders will become clear to the jurors.

19d7

καὶ τἆλλα: 'the other things also' (subject of ἐστί). τἆλλα is crasis of τὰ ἄλλα, and the subject of ἐστί.

19d8

οὐδέν ἐστιν: supply ἀληθές. As οὐδέν is a compound negative it does not cancel out the οὔτε before (see note 18d5).

οὐδέ γ': 'nor even', emphatic after οὔτε. Now Socrates has refuted the idea that he is knowledgeable about natural science, he moves onto defending himself against the claim that he teaches the youth as the sophists do.

τινος ἀκηκόατε ὡς ...: 'you have heard from anyone that ...'. See notes on 19d3 and 18b7.

19e1

χρήματα πράττομαι: 'I am obtaining money for myself', 'I am making money'. This is an allegation made particularly against the sophists.

οὐδὲ τοῦτο ἀληθές: supply ἐστί – 'that is not true either'. οὐδὲ is repeated from before to emphasize Socrates' conviction.

ἐπεὶ: here means 'although' (or shorthand for 'I don't mean to sound harsh, since ...').

εἴ τις οἷός τ' εἴη: 'if anyone should to be able to ...'. The mix of the optative (εἴη) and the present indicative (δοκεῖ) in this conditional is unusual.

19e3

Γοργίας ... Ἤλεῖος: these were three famous sophists, and contemporaries of Socrates. The sophists were travelling speakers and teachers of a variety of subjects including rhetoric and philosophy. Plato is largely critical of them (see, for example, the dialogue *Sophist*), focusing on the exorbitant prices which some charged for their services, and claiming that they were concerned with persuasion and deception rather than truth-seeking (the domain of philosophers). In reality the picture is more nuanced: they were a hugely diverse group; not all charged excessive prices; and they were without doubt integral to the development of Greek thought and philosophy.

Gorgias was from Leontini (a city in Sicily) and particularly known for his rhetorical ability and his belief in the supreme power of oratory. Extant works such as the *Encomium of Helen* reveal his clever techniques of argumentation to further a weak position, revelling in the power of language. Plato's dialogue *Gorgias* involves Socrates interrogating him to expose the flaws of such sophistic rhetoric.

Prodicus of Ceos (an island in the Cyclades) seems to have been particularly interested in linguistics: at Plato *Cratylus* 384b Socrates wishes he had been able to afford to attend his lectures on grammar. He also wrote a (lost) work called *Horai*, concerning Heracles' choice of Virtue over Vice, so was clearly concerned with ethics too. Plato mentions him a number of times, giving him particularly favourable treatment.

Hippias of Elis (a city on the Peloponnese) appears in the Platonic dialogues *Hippias Minor* and *Hippias Major*. He appears to have been a polymath, interested in rhetoric and philosophy, but also astronomy, poetry, music, maths and art. In the dialogues however, he is often presented as arrogant, and only possessing superficial knowledge of these areas.

19e4

τούτων . . . προσειδέναι: another particularly complex sentence. Socrates describes how the sophists travel to cities and persuade the youth, who are able to spend time with anyone else for free, to associate with them instead at a price.

οἷός τ'ἐστὶν: we expect an infinitive after this, but the clause οἷς . . . βούλωνται disrupts the syntax, and we get the verb πείθουσι instead (another anacolouthon, see note 19d4). πείθουσι is able to be plural because ἕκαστος implies multiple subjects. When translating the phrase, it is easiest just to translate πείθουσι as the expected infinitive ('each of these men is able to persuade').

19e5

ἰὼν: participle of εἶμι (to go). For εἶμι see note 19a6.

οἷς ἔξεστι . . .: 'for whom it is possible', a relative clause describing the youths.

τῶν ἑαυτῶν πολιτῶν ... ᾧ ἂν βούλωνται: 'with whoever of their fellow citizens they want'. The subjunctive with ἂν makes the clause indefinite (-ever), and the genitive πολιτῶν is partitive. Despite being able to associate with others for free, the youth still go over to the sophists. The words ἑαυτῶν ('their own', or 'fellow') and πολιτῶν stress that the sophists are outsiders, and chimes with Plato's usual negative presentation of the sophists (see note 19e3).

20a1

τούτους: take with τοὺς νέους. Delayed by the parenthesis (οἷς . . . βούλωνται).

τὰς ἐκείνων συνουσίας: 'the company of those men' (i.e. the ones who they used to associate with for free).

20a2

σφίσιν συνεῖναι: 'to associate with them (instead)'. σφίσιν is the dative plural of σφεῖς, the indirect reflexive pronoun, which is used to refer back to the subject of the main clause when in indirect speech.

χάριν προσειδέναι: 'to be grateful as well' (literally 'to acknowledge a sense of favour too'). προσειδέναι is the infinitive of πρόσοιδα. The prefix πρός often means 'in addition'.

20a3

ἐπεὶ: 'for'. Like at 19e1, this is shorthand, for 'I am saying this since . . .'. Socrates can make these comments about famous sophists because even the small-time sophist in the following story does these things.

καὶ ἄλλος ἀνήρ ἐστι Πάριος ἐνθάδε σοφός: literally 'also another man is, from Paros, here, a wise one'. The order of the words gives the anecdote a colloquial tone. Paros is an island in the Cyclades.

20a4

ἔτυχον γὰρ προσελθὼν: for τυγχάνω see note 18d1. The word here emphasizes the fortuitous nature of the meeting.

20a5

πλείω: contracted form of πλείονα, agreeing with χρήματα. See note 18b8.

σύμπαντες: 'all together' or 'all in one body'. Despite Callias' wealth (see note 20a6), the idea that he has paid more to sophists than everyone else together is a huge exaggeration. This, coupled with the delaying of Callias' name, is humorous and playful.

20a6

Καλλίᾳ τῷ Ἱππονίκου: Καλλίᾳ is dative singular with ἀνδρὶ, and the genitive Ἱππονίκου means 'son of Hipponicus'. Callias was an Athenian political figure, famous for his huge wealth and profligacy.

ἐστὸν γὰρ αὐτῷ δύο ὑεῖ: 'he has two sons' (literally 'there are two sons to him'). ἐστὸν and ὑεῖ are dual forms, used to refer to two things, and rare in Attic Greek. ἐστὸν is present indicative third person dual of εἰμί, and ὑεῖ is the nominative dual of ὑός.

20a7

τὼ ὑεῖ πώλω ἢ μόσχω: τώ is the nominative dual article. πώλω and μόσχω are also nominative duals.

Καλλία: vocative. The direct speech also adds to the colloquial tone of the anecdote.

ἦν δ᾽ ἐγώ: 'I said'. ἦν is imperfect first person singular of ἠμί, a defective verb (only some forms of the verb exist).

20a8

ἐγενέσθην: 'had been born' or simply 'were'. Aorist indicative middle third person dual of γίγνομαι. The aorist indicative is used here as part of a past unfulfilled conditional (if x had happened, y would have happened). This is generally followed by the aorist indicative with ἄν in the main clause, but the imperfect εἴχομεν with ἄν here expresses an unreal state in the present.

εἴχομεν ἄν αὐτοῖν ἐπιστάτην λαβεῖν: 'we would be able to get a trainer for the two of them'. With the infinitive, ἔχω means 'to be able to' and αὐτοῖν is dative dual of αὐτός.

λαβεῖν καὶ μισθώσασθαι: aorist infinitives due to aspect.

20a9

ὅς ἔμελλεν . . . ποιήσειν: 'to make'. This is equivalent to the relative pronoun with a future tense verb (μέλλω here meaning 'to be going to'), a construction used to express purpose.

αὐτὼ καλώ τε κἀγαθὼ: dual accusatives. καλὸς κἀγαθός is a common phrase, literally meaning 'fine and good' (κἀγαθός is crasis of καὶ ἀγαθός). The phrase has a moral dimension ('excellent', 'perfect'), and is often applied to the aristocracy ('well-bred', 'admirable'). Its application to the hypothetical foal or calf sons therefore strikes a note of absurd humour here.

20b1

τὴν προσήκουσαν ἀρετήν: 'in the excellence which befits them' – i.e. skills which make foals or calves successful foals or calves (an acc. of respect – see note 18b7).

ἦν δ' ἄν οὗτος ἢ τῶν ἱππικῶν τις ἢ τῶν γεωργικῶν: 'and he would either be a horseman or a farmer', literally 'one of those related to horses or those related to agriculture'. ἦν . . . ἄν continues the main clause of the conditional.

20b2

ἀνθρώπω ἐστόν: duals again (for ἐστόν see note 20a6).

20b3

αὐτοῖν: dative dual of αὐτός.

νῷ: dative singular of νοῦς. ἐν νῷ ἔχω means 'to have in mind' or 'to intend'.

20b4

πολιτικῆς: either 'befitting a citizen' or 'political'. This and ἀνθρωπίνης explain τοιαύτης.

20b5

ἐσκέφθαι: perfect middle infinitive of σκέπτομαι. Note that the ἐ- is equivalent to reduplication, rather than being a temporal augment, and is therefore retained in the infinitive (see note 18b8).

20b6

ἔφην: first person imperfect of φημί.

Πάνυ γε: 'yes indeed' or 'certainly'.

ἦ δ' ὅς: 'he said'. ἦ is third person imperfect indicative of ἠμί (see note 20a7). ὅς is the relative pronoun, used here as a personal pronoun (he, she, it). This use is common in Homer, but only remains in a few phrases in Attic Greek.

20b7

Τίς ... καὶ ποδαπός: supply ἐστί twice.

πόσου: 'for how much', a genitive of price.

20b8

πέντε μνῶν: 'for five minae' (also genitive of price). A mina was worth 100 drachmae, and one drachma is often said to be around the daily wage of a skilled worker. A large amount, especially given that Evenus would presumably have had multiple students.

εἰ ὡς ἀληθῶς ἔχοι: 'if he really had ...'. Verbs in subordinate clauses within indirect speech (often called 'suboblique') may become optative in Greek. Here ἔχοι is optative because indirect speech is implied in the word μακαρίζω ('say that someone is happy'). This shift to the optative implies that Socrates is not convinced of the idea. ὡς ἀληθῶς is an idiomatic phrase for 'really', 'in truth'.

20c1

ἐμμελῶς: 'at a moderate price'. Given the high fee mentioned before, Socrates is being ironic. Humour is also derived from the implication that if he really did have this skill, it would be very expensive indeed.

20c2

ἐκαλλυνόμην τε καὶ ἡβρυνόμην ἄν: for the two imperfects with ἄν in the main clause of an unfulfilled conditional see note 20a8. The word καλλύνω means to 'beautify' and its middle means to 'pride oneself in something' or 'be proud'. ἁβρύνω means to 'treat delicately', and in the middle to 'live delicately' and therefore to 'give oneself airs', or 'be conceited'. Both words therefore have negative connotations; the underlying message is that they do not possess this knowledge at all.

ἠπιστάμην: 'I understood'. The present of ἐπίσταμαι is conjugated like a perfect middle/passive, while pluperfect middle/passive forms are used for the imperfect (likewise δύναμαι, μέμνημαι and κεῖμαι).

20c3

ἀλλ᾽ οὐ γὰρ: see note 19c9.

20c4

Ὑπολάβοι ἄν: 'might reply' – potential optative (aorist by aspect) with ἄν. ὑπολαμβάνω means to 'take up' and therefore 'to take up what has been said' or 'reply'. Socrates transitions to the next phase of his defence, by anticipating the question of why such a view of him ever developed in the first place.

τὸ σὸν τί ἐστι πρᾶγμα;: 'what is *your* business/occupation?'. The interrogative τίς, τί is usually the first word in a question, but here τὸ σὸν has been moved into an emphatic position, putting the focus of the question fully on Socrates himself, who has until now been explaining what he is not (natural scientist or sophist).

20c6

οὐ γὰρ δήπου: 'for surely it is not the case that . . .', expecting a negative answer.

σοῦ γε . . . πραγματευομένου: 'when *you* were engaging in' – genitive absolute. Note the repetition of the second person pronoun, and its position near the beginning of the sentence. The particle γε also gives extra emphasis to σοῦ, stressing yet again the strength of the accusation. Particles like this are a key feature of the Greek language but can be difficult to translate. They add important shades of meaning which English would often express by stressing certain words in pronunciation, or by changes in pitch and tempo.

οὐδὲν τῶν ἄλλων περιττότερον: 'nothing stranger than the others'. τῶν ἄλλων is a genitive of comparison.

20c8

τι . . . ἀλλοῖον ἤ: 'something different from'. Like a comparative, ἀλλοῖος can be followed by ἤ, or a genitive (see note 20c6). Socrates anticipates the question of why the slander has arisen about him, if he has acted like everyone else.

τί ἐστιν: indirect question.

20d1

αὐτοσχεδιάζωμεν: 'judge hastily', subjunctive due to the purpose clause. αὐτοσχεδιάζω means to 'improvise' and therefore to 'act/speak thoughtlessly'.

20d2

ταυτί: emphatic form of ταῦτα. In Attic Greek the suffix -ι can be added to all demonstratives for emphasis, e.g. οὑτοσί, αὑτή, τουτί and ὁδί, ἡδί, τοδί. If the final letter is α, ε or ο, they are dropped. As the question is fair, Socrates will answer it.

δίκαια: for δίκαιος see note 18a7.

κἀγώ: crasis of καί and ἐγώ.

πειράσομαι ἀποδεῖξαι: ἀποδεῖξαι is the aorist infinitive (by aspect) of ἀποδείκνυμι. Note also that alpha in the contracted verb πειράομαι does not lengthen when σ is added to the stem, as one might expect.

20d3

τί ποτ᾽ ἐστὶν τοῦτο: indirect question introduced by ἀποδεῖξαι: 'whatever it is . . .' or 'what in the world it is . . .'. ποτε here is the enclitic indefinite (ever), rather than the interrogative πότε (note the accent) meaning 'when?'. This indefiniteness suggests the difficulty of assessing this question, and therefore how deep seated the feeling is.

ὃ . . . πεποίηκεν: relative clause. The accent shows that ὅ is the relative pronoun rather than the article (see also note 18b5). The perfect πεποίηκεν shows that this reputation, created in the past, continues into the present.

20d4

ὄνομα: 'name' and therefore 'fame' or 'reputation'.

ἀκούετε δή: 'so listen'. The emphatic particle δή (often 'indeed') with the imperative suggests that the command follows on from what has been said before.

μὲν ... μέντοι ...: note that μέν anticipates some sort of contrast to come, and often does not need translation. While the contrasting idea is often introduced by δέ ('but'), this is not compulsory, and here it is marked by the stronger word μέντοι ('however').

20d5

ἴστε: 'be assured' – imperative of οἶδα. See *Oxford Grammar of Classical Greek* p. 95.

παίζειν: 'to be joking'. παίζω literally means 'to play like a child' (παῖς) and therefore to 'play around' and 'joke'. The word thus has a judgemental tone here.

20d6

ἐρῶ: contracted (ε-ω) future of λέγω.

δι᾽ οὐδὲν ἀλλ᾽ ἢ διὰ σοφίαν τινά: 'because of nothing except/other than some sort of wisdom ...'. The indefinite τινά softens Socrates claim to possess wisdom, and also prepares us for the explanation to come.

20d7

ἔσχηκα: 'I have obtained'. Perfect of ἔχω (see note 19a1).

ποίαν δὴ σοφίαν ταύτην;: 'just what sort of wisdom is this?'. The accusative is used to pick up σοφίαν earlier in the line.

20d8

ἥπερ ...: 'the very sort which ...'. The suffix -περ emphasizes the relative.

ἀνθρωπίνη σοφία: 'human wisdom' or 'wisdom attainable by man'. Socrates does not claim to have the sort of certainty which only gods can reach.

τῷ ὄντι: 'in reality', 'really'. The neuter participle of εἰμί is being used as a dative of respect (literally, 'with respect to what actually is').

20d9

κινδυνεύω: literally 'to run the risk of', but with the infinitive meaning 'to be likely to'.

ταύτην: 'in this (type of wisdom – i.e. human)'; accusative of respect.

οὗτοι ... οὓς ἄρτι ἔλεγον: 'these men ... about whom I was just speaking' (i.e. the sophists). λέγω with the accusative can mean 'speak about/of x'.

τάχ᾽ ἄν: 'perhaps', followed by the potential optative εἶεν (from εἰμί). The tone is ironic; Socrates does not really believe the sophists possess superhuman knowledge.

20e1

μείζω τινά: 'in some wisdom greater ...'. μείζω is an accusative of respect of the irregular comparative of μέγας (for the ending see note 18b8), agreeing with σοφίαν.

κατ᾽ ἄνθρωπον σοφίαν: 'knowledge in accordance with a human', or simply 'human knowledge'.

ἢ οὐκ ἔχω τί λέγω: 'or I don't know what to call it', literally 'I don't have (in mind) what I should say'. τί λέγω is an indirect question, with a subjunctive verb to represent an original deliberative question ('what should I say?'). The tone is again ironic, and implies that the sophists do not really possess knowledge at all.

20e2
ἔγωγε: 'I at least'.

20e3
φησὶ: 'says (that I do)'. φημί means to 'assert' or 'affirm' an opinion.

ἐπὶ διαβολῇ τῇ ἐμῇ: 'for the purpose of slandering me'. The position of τῇ ἐμῇ after the noun serves to add further explanation ('for slandering, I mean that against me'). For ἐμῇ see note 19a8.

20e4
μοι: 'for my sake' or even 'please'. This dative of interest (or ethic dative) makes the request a personal matter between Socrates and the jury.

μὴ θορυβήσητε: 'don't make a noise/interrupt'. μή + aorist subjunctive is used for prohibitions relating to one instance, while μή + imperative is used for general prohibitions (a distinction of aspect). The jury, previously quiet, have started to call out at Socrates' apparent profession of superior knowledge.

μηδ' ἐὰν δόξω: 'not even if I seem'. ἐάν is used with the subjunctive (here δόξω, aorist by aspect) for open conditionals relating to the future.

τι . . . μέγα λέγειν: 'to be saying something big', or 'to be boasting'.

20e5
οὐ γὰρ ἐμὸν ἐρῶ τὸν λόγον ὃν ἂν λέγω: this is a complicated phrase. Attention should be paid to the placement of ἐμὸν in the predicate position (not directly after the article) rather than in the attributive position (directly after the article). A predicate adjective is used to make an assertion, rather than simply to describe something, therefore it means not 'my account', but something closer to 'the account is mine'. ὃν ἂν λέγω is an example of the indefinite construction ('what<u>ever</u> I say'), which uses ἄν + subjunctive when the main verb refers to the present or future (primary sequence) and the optative without ἄν when the main verb is past tense (historic sequence). The whole phrase thus means 'for not mine is the account which I will say, whichever (account) I am going to say', or in more natural English: 'for whatever account I am going to give is not mine'.

20e6
εἰς ἀξιόχρεων ὑμῖν τὸν λέγοντα ἀνοίσω: 'I will refer the account to a speaker who is worthy of your attention.' ἀξιόχρεων is in the predicate position, and is accusative masculine singular (Attic declension; see *Oxford Grammar of Classical Greek* p. 27). ἀξιόχρεως means simply 'worthy of a thing', and its meaning here comes from the context. ἀνοίσω is future of ἀναφέρω, and λόγον (account) should be supplied as its object.

τῆς γὰρ ἐμῆς: supply σοφίας from the next clause. Socrates modestly avoids using the word.

20e7

εἰ δή τίς ἐστιν σοφία καὶ οἵα: 'whether in fact it is some sort of wisdom and what type it is'. εἰ is here introducing an indirect question rather than a conditional, again illustrative of Socrates' modesty. The indefinite τίς has an accent here because it is followed by the enclitic ἐστιν, not because it is the interrogative (who, which).

παρέξομαι: see 19d1.

20e8

τὸν θεὸν τὸν ἐν Δελφοῖς: 'the god in Delphi', i.e. Apollo. The Delphic Oracle, or the Pythia, was the mouthpiece of Apollo in his guise as the god of prophecy. People would visit the sanctuary at Delphi to consult her on a range of matters, and she would utter the words of the god after being worked up into a trance, perhaps under the influence of naturally occurring hallucinogenic gases. αἱ Δελφοί is plural, like many Greek place names (e.g. αἱ Ἀθῆναι).

20e9

Χαιρεφῶντα: Chaerephon was a friend and follower of Socrates named in Xenophon, Plato and Aristophanes.

ἴστε: second person plural of οἶδα (here and at 21a2), rather than the imperative as at 20d5.

που: 'I suppose'.

οὗτος ἐμός τε ἑταῖρος ἦν: the lack of the article means that the subject is οὗτος, and ἐμός ... ἑταῖρος is predicate. ἑταῖρος here means 'friend' or 'companion', but later in the line means 'political adherent', two meanings best captured by the English 'comrade'. This repetition in different senses, coupled with emphatic τε ... καί, emphasizes Chaerephon's reliability as a source, as he is faithful to both Socrates and the jury.

21a1

ἐκ νέου: 'from childhood'. Compare with ἐκ παίδων at 18b5.

ὑμῶν τῷ πλήθει ἑταῖρος: 'a comrade of your democratic party'. πλῆθος is literally 'the multitude' or 'a crowd', but here has a political sense equivalent to the δῆμος (the people, the democracy).

τε καί: shows that the dative τῷ πλήθει goes both with ἑταῖρός and with συνέφυγε (+ dative = go into exile with x).

21a2

συνέφυγε τὴν φυγὴν ταύτην: 'went into the recent exile together with you'. After Athens' defeat at the hands of Sparta in the Peloponnesian War (431–404 BC), the Spartan admiral Lysander set up a puppet government in Athens called the Thirty Tyrants (see also Introduction – ' Political background to the trial'). Property was confiscated and many Athenian democrats were executed or exiled. This was shortlived: democracy was restored in 403 BC and the exiles returned to the city. Although these events happened five years before Socrates' trial, ταύτην expresses how clear the memory still was (translate as 'recent'). Note also the cognate accusative (see note 19b1).

AS

κατῆλθε: κατέρχομαι is the usual word for returning from exile, while φεύγω means to go into exile (as above).

21a3

ὡς σφοδρὸς: 'how intense he was'. ἦν should be supplied in this indirect question. σφοδρός implies excess, violence or impetuousness.

ἐφ᾽ὅτι ὁρμήσειεν: 'in whatever he was eager to do'. ὁρμήσειεν is third person aorist optative (the alternative form ὁρμῆσαι is less common in Attic), used for the indefinite construction in historic sequence (see note 20e5), and aorist by aspect.

21a4

καὶ δή ... καὶ: 'and in particular', to introduce the main point.

ποτε: 'once', 'on one occasion'. Like τίς and τις, the lack of article shows this is the indefinite rather than the interrogative ('when?').

21a5

μαντεύσασθαι: 'to ask the oracle' (aorist by aspect).

Terminology can be difficult here. The Greek word μάντις has a particularly wide range of reference: it may be someone who communicates the words of the god in an altered state of consciousness (usually with a fixed abode, like the oracle at Delphi), or more generally a religious specialist and interpreter of dreams, omens and portents. μαντεῖον, on the other hand, refers to the oracular response, or the seat of the oracle. The word χρησμός also refers to the oracular saying, and the verb χρησμῳδέω is often used of delivering the message. The English can also be problematic. The word 'oracle' can refer to the divine message itself, the seat of the oracle, or the person who receives/gives the message. The words 'prophet/ prophecy' imply that the message relates to the future, which is not necessarily true of an oracle (like the one reported here). There is also considerable overlap with the words 'seer', 'diviner', and 'soothsayer'. In translation, it is most important to be consistent.

ὅπερ λέγω: 'the very thing which I was saying' or 'as I was saying'. Socrates is referring to his previous request for them to be quiet at 20e4.

μὴ θορυβεῖτε: 'don't keep interrupting' or 'stop interrupting'. Compare this with the use of the aorist subjunctive at 20e4.

21a6

εἴ τις ἐμοῦ εἴη σοφώτερος: 'if anyone was wiser than me'. The optative (εἴη) may replace an indicative in indirect speech in historic sequence. ἐμοῦ is genitive of comparison.

ἀνεῖλεν: 'replied', aorist of ἀναιρέω, the usual word for the response of an oracle.

21a7

ἡ Πυθία: for the Pythia, see note on 20e8. The name comes from Apollo's slaying of the serpent Python who used to guard the sanctuary at Delphi.

μηδένα: μή is used in indirect statements rather than the expected οὐ to mark an emphatic declaration, and therefore often of oracular responses.

τούτων πέρι: see 19c6.

AS

21a8

ἀδελφὸς . . . αὐτοῦ: 'his brother'. Chaerephon's brother was called Chaerecrates.

οὑτοσί: 'this man here', see note 20d2.

Socrates now says that he was confused by the claim of the oracle that there was none wiser than him, so he set out to investigate it by trying to find someone wiser. He visited politicians, poets and craftsmen, who all thought that they knew something, but under questioning were exposed as not having any real knowledge. Socrates thus realizes that it is his appreciation of the limits of his own knowledge (and human knowledge in general) which makes him wise. In addition, by embarrassing those reputed to be wise, he incurred their hostility. He claims that this is why the long-standing slander against him first arose.

21b1

Σκέψασθε δὴ: 'so consider'. Σκέψασθε is a second person plural middle imperative, aorist by aspect. For δή with the imperative see note 20d4.

ὧν ἕνεκα: 'why', literally 'on account of what things'. ἕνεκα usually comes after the word it governs (a postposition).

μέλλω . . . διδάξειν: 'I am going to teach'. With this meaning μέλλω takes the future infinitive.

21b3

ἐνεθυμούμην: 'I reflected on it'. ἐνθυμέομαι literally means to 'put something in the θυμός', or 'lay it to heart'. The θυμός was deemed to be the basis of life, feeling and thought. Socrates thus considers these words deeply.

οὑτωσί: see 20d2.

Τί ποτε . . . τί ποτε: the repetition and the indefinite ποτε (see note 20d3) convey Socrates' confusion and his modest refusal to believe that he possesses superior wisdom.

λέγει: 'means'. As well as simply meaning 'to say' λέγω can refer to what someone wishes to say, or 'means' (also in 21b5 and 7).

21b4

τί . . . αἰνίττεται: 'what riddle is he posing'. The verb αἰνίσσομαι is cognate with the noun αἴνιγμα, a 'riddle' or 'dark saying' (whence the English *enigma)*. The ambiguity of the Pythia's prophecies was widely recognized and is a common trope in Greek literature.

21b5

σύνοιδα ἐμαυτῷ: 'I am conscious of', literally 'I know with myself'.

21b6

οὐ γὰρ δήπου ψεύδεταί γε: 'for of course he is not actually lying'. Although he is reluctant to accept that he is so wise, Socrates understands that the error must be in his interpretation of the oracle, rather than its veracity.

οὐ γὰρ θέμις αὐτῷ: 'for that is not right for him'. θέμις means 'that which is laid down or established' by custom or the gods (rather than by statute) and therefore what is 'lawful' or 'right'. The belief that the gods cannot lie or deceive is a particularly Platonic sentiment, and one which is not backed up by traditional Greek myth.

21b7

μὲν … ἔπειτα: μὲν here is not answered by δέ, but ἔπειτα makes the contrast clear.

ἠπόρουν τί ποτε λέγει: 'I was at a loss as to what in the world he meant'. An indirect question, the indicative λέγει being retained for vividness (unlike 21a6, where the optative is used).

21b8

μόγις πάνυ: 'with great reluctance'. Socrates again shows modesty in not wishing to investigate his own wisdom.

ζήτησιν αὐτοῦ τοιαύτην τινὰ: 'a sort of investigation of him, as follows'. A ζήτησις is an inquiry, especially of a philosophic nature. τινὰ again softens the tone, further expressing modesty.

ἐτραπόμην: 'I turned myself', aorist middle of τρέπω.

21b9

τινα τῶν δοκούντων σοφῶν εἶναι: 'one of those reputed to be wise'.

ὡς … ἐλέγξων: 'in order to refute'. ὡς + future participle to express purpose. The verb ἐλέγχω means to 'cross-examine' or 'test' with the aim of refuting something. This is an important word, as 'elenchus' is the term used in English for Socrates' main method of philosophizing, by which he questions an interlocutor in order to reveal inconsistencies in their position, and illuminate key concepts (see also Introduction – 'Plato's *Apology*').

ἐνταῦθα εἴπερ που: 'there, if indeed anywhere'.

21c1

ἀποφανῶν: 'to show'. Future participle of ἀποφαίνω, continuing the construction explained in note 21b9.

21c2

ὅτι: here introduces a direct quotation, and is best left out of translation.

σὺ δ᾽ ἐμὲ ἔφησθα: 'you said that it was me'. ἔφησθα is second person singular imperfect of φημί, and εἶναι should be supplied. See *Oxford Grammar of Classical Greek* p. 96.

21c3

διασκοπῶν: 'examining carefully'. The prefix δια- here implies that Socrates is considering him from all angles.

ὀνόματι γὰρ οὐδὲν δέομαι λέγειν: 'for not at all do I need to identify him by name'. Socrates explains why he calls him merely τοῦτον ('this man').

21c4

ἦν δέ τις τῶν πολιτικῶν: 'but he was one of the men in public life' or simply, 'but he was a politician'.

AS

πρὸς ὃν ἐγὼ σκοπῶν τοιοῦτόν τι ἔπαθον: 'with regard to whom, while examining him, I experienced the following thing'.

21c6

ἔδοξέ μοι οὗτος ὁ ἀνὴρ: Socrates has broken off to explain that it is not necessary to name the politician concerned. Here he resumes his train of thought, but there is an anacolouthon as the nominative διασκοπῶν (21c3) had suggested that Socrates would be the subject of the main verb; instead the sentence changes tack and οὗτος ὁ ἀνὴρ becomes the subject of ἔδοξέ.

21c7

εἶναι δ᾽ οὔ: 'but not actually to be (wise)', dependent on ἔδοξέ μοι. Socrates here distinguishes how things seem (δοκεῖν) with the reality (εἶναι). For εἶναι see note 18b1.

21c8

κἄπειτα: crasis of καὶ ἔπειτα.

ἐπειρώμην: the imperfect may be used for attempted actions in the past (conative imperfect). Translate simply as 'I tried'.

δεικνύναι: present infinitive of δείκνυμι. See *Oxford Grammar of Classical Greek* p. 90.

οἴοιτο ... εἴη: optative verbs due to the indirect speech in historic sequence.

21d1

ἀπηχθόμην: 'I became hated', aorist of ἀπεχθάνομαι. See note 19a1.

21d2

πρὸς ἐμαυτὸν δ᾽ οὖν ἀπιὼν ἐλογιζόμην: Take πρὸς ἐμαυτὸν with ἐλογιζόμην. ἀπιὼν is a compound of εἶμι (to go), see note 19a6.

21d3

τούτου μὲν τοῦ ἀνθρώπου: 'than this man for a start'. The function of μέν is to prepare us for a future contrast, so here, where there is no corresponding δέ clause, it implicitly suggests that Socrates will go on to compare himself with others too.

21d4

κινδυνεύει: see note 20d9.

οὐδέτερος οὐδὲν: Socrates uses two negatives to emphasize that neither knows anything (they do not 'cancel out', see note 18d5).

καλὸν κἀγαθὸν: 'fine and good', see note 20a9.

21d6

οὐκ εἰδώς: 'although he doesn't know anything'. Participle from οἶδα, used concessively.

ὥσπερ οὖν οὐκ οἶδα, οὐδὲ οἴομαι: 'as in fact I don't know anything, I also don't think I do'. οὖν here is in a subordinate (relative) clause, and therefore does not have its usual connective meaning ('therefore'). Instead it gives the idea of actuality, and should be translated as 'in fact', or 'actually'.

21d7

σμικρῷ τινι: 'a little bit (wiser)', a dative of measure of difference. This could either be viewed as sincerely modest, or ironic.

αὐτῷ τούτῳ: 'in just this respect', explained by the clause introduced by ὅτι (that . . .).

ἃ μὴ οἶδα: 'whatever I don't know'. As at 18d7, μὴ gives the clause indefinite, general force.

21d8

ᾖα: imperfect first person singular of εἶμι (to go). See *Oxford Grammar of Classical Greek* p. 94.

ἐκείνου: 'than him', genitive of comparison with σοφωτέρων, referring to the first person Socrates questioned. After his first experience, Socrates continues his investigation by questioning those reputed to be wiser.

21d9

μοι ταὐτὰ ταῦτα ἔδοξε: 'I formed the same impression', literally 'these things seemed the same'. See note 19c1, and note the singular verb with neuter plural subject.

21e1

κἀκείνῳ: 'to him also'; crasis of καί ἐκείνῳ.

21e2

ἐφεξῆς: 'to one after another'.

αἰσθανόμενος μὲν καὶ λυπούμενος καὶ δεδιὼς ὅτι ἀπηχθανόμην: take the ὅτι clause with αἰσθανόμενος: 'realizing, both distressed and afraid, that I was hated'. δεδιὼς is perfect participle from δείδω, which is only used in the present in the first person. Its perfect tense (either δέδοικα or δέδια) is used in Attic with present meaning.

21e4

τὸ τοῦ θεοῦ: 'the god's business', literally 'the thing of the god'.

περὶ πλείστου ποιεῖσθαι: 'to consider of the highest importance'. The common phrase περὶ πολλοῦ ποιέομαι means 'consider of great importance' or 'value', and πλεῖστος is the irregular superlative of πολύς.

21e5

ἰτέον: 'it was necessary to go'. The verbal adjective, or gerundive, from εἶμι (to go) – see note 18e5. The following dative of agent (σκοποῦντι) expresses by whom this action must be done.

σκοποῦντι τὸν χρησμὸν τί λέγει: 'for someone (me) examining what the oracle meant'. This is a very Greek turn of phrase, in which the subject of the subordinate clause is drawn into the main clause as its object (prolepsis). In

English it might be literally rendered as 'for someone examining the oracle, what it meant'.

22a1

νὴ τὸν κύνα: 'by the dog'. A common exclamation of Socrates, maybe to avoid swearing by one of the gods.

22a2

ἦ μὴν: 'truly indeed', an emphatic combination of particles often found in oaths.
τἀληθῆ: 'the truth', crasis of τὰ ἀληθῆ.

22a4

ὀλίγου δεῖν: 'almost'. This idiom literally means 'to be needful of a little' or 'to lack a little', with the infinitive δεῖν being grammatically unconnected to the rest of the sentence (as the English 'so to speak').
τοῦ πλείστου ἐνδεεῖς: 'lacking the most'. Note the contrast between πλείστου and ὀλίγου, to stress how little self-knowledge the highly regarded politicians actually had.
ζητοῦντι: with μοι earlier in the line.

22a5

φαυλότεροι: 'more common' or 'of less worth'. φαῦλος is mostly pejorative, referring to low social status, inferiority, or incompetency in education.
ἐπιεικέστεροι εἶναι ἄνδρες πρὸς τὸ φρονίμως ἔχειν: 'seemed to be more able men with regard to being sensible', with ἔδοξάν supplied from the previous clause. τὸ . . . ἔχειν is an articular infinitive (neuter article with infinitive), meaning 'the act of x-ing' or simply 'x-ing'. ἔχω with an adverb is equivalent to εἰμί with an adjective (in English, 'things are holding well' = 'things are good').
φρονίμως: the adjective φρονίμος, often translated as 'wise', properly means 'in one's right mind', and thus 'sensible' and 'prudent'. This differs from σοφός, which may mean 'skilled' (in any art or field), 'clever' and 'expert' (often used with a hint of irony). There is of course some common ground between the words, and Plato does not make a point of carefully delineating them. However, the choice of φρονίμος here suggests that the unreputed men are more in possession of themselves because they do not profess knowledge which they do not have, rather than that they are actually actively 'wise', or 'expert'.

22a7

ὥσπερ πόνους τινὰς πονοῦντος: 'as I went through such labours, as it were'. This is probably an allusion to the labours of Heracles, to stress the effort Socrates put into his investigation. ὥσπερ softens the force of this comparison (see note 18d6), and πονοῦντος is genitive as ἐμὴν in the previous line implies a genitive idea. Note also the cognate accusative (see note 19b1).
ἵνα μοι καὶ ἀνέλεγκτος ἡ μαντεία γένοιτο: 'so that the oracle might in fact be irrefutable for me'. The optative γένοιτο, which would normally only occur after a past tense verb in a purpose clause, is used because the participle πονοῦντος is used as an historic present. The use of the word ἀν-έλεγκ-τος (un-refute-able),

AS

from the verb ἐλέγχω (see note 21b9), is important. If Socrates, the master of examining inconsistent arguments, cannot refute this, then it must be true.

22b1

διθυράμβων: a dithyramb was an ecstatic choral hymn to Dionysus.

ὡς ἐνταῦθα ἐπ᾽ αὐτοφώρῳ καταληψόμενος ἐμαυτὸν ἀμαθέστερον ἐκείνων ὄντα: 'so that there I would prove openly that I was more ignorant than them'. καταληψόμενος is the future participle of καταλαμβάνειν (ὡς + future participle for purpose). The phrase ἐπ᾽ αὐτοφώρῳ καταλαμβάνειν means 'to catch in the act', which casts Socrates as an investigator, seeking to condemn himself in the interests of the truth.

22b4

ἅ μοι ἐδόκει μάλιστα πεπραγματεῦσθαι αὐτοῖς: '[the poetry] which seemed to me to have been elaborated by them most of all', i.e. the most elaborate passages. πραγματεύομαι means 'to work at something' or to 'elaborate' a work, here with a passive sense. αὐτοῖς is a dative agent, common with perfect passive verbs.

διηρώτων ἄν: 'I would ask', from the verb διερωτάω. ἄν with the imperfect here suggests repeated past action (see note 18c6).

τί λέγοιεν: indirect question, with optative in historic sequence. For the meaning of the verb, see note 21b3.

22b6

ῥητέον: 'it must be said', verbal adjective from ἐρῶ.

ὡς ἔπος ... εἰπεῖν: 'so to speak', a common infinitive absolute (see note 22a4).

22b7

ὀλίγου ... ἅπαντες οἱ παρόντες: 'almost all those present' (i.e. the jurors). In the phrase ὀλίγου δεῖν (see note 22a4), the word δεῖν may be omitted.

αὐτῶν: 'than them', genitive of comparison.

ἂν βέλτιον ἔλεγον: 'would speak in a better way'. The unexpressed condition with ἄν here would be something like 'if they were asked'. βέλτιον is comparative adverb (equivalent to the comparative neuter singular in form) from ἀγαθός.

22b8

περὶ ὧν αὐτοὶ ἐπεποιήκεσαν: 'about the things which they themselves had composed'. περὶ ὧν is equivalent to περὶ τούτων ἅ. This occurs due to relative attraction, by which an accusative relative pronoun may take on the case of a genitive or dative antecedent (hence ὧν for ἅ). The antecedent (τούτων) has also been omitted here. Also note the (rare) instance of the pluperfect tense.

ἔγνων: root aorist from γιγνώσκω. See *Oxford Grammar of Classical Greek* p. 71.

22b9

ἐν ὀλίγῳ: 'in a short time'. Supply χρόνῳ.

ὅτι οὐ σοφίᾳ ποιοῖεν ἃ ποιοῖεν: 'that they do not compose what they compose with wisdom'. Socrates again uses ὅτι with γιγνώσκω (see note 19d6) to express certainty about the poets' lack of wisdom. The optatives are used because the indirect speech is in historic sequence. Note that σοφία may refer to expertise or skill in any art (see note 22a5).

22c1

φύσει τινὶ: 'by some instinct'. φύσις means 'nature', or 'inborn quality', so Socrates means that the poets do not consciously craft poetry with expertise, but that it flows naturally from them, beyond their true understanding. For Plato this is bad because people might assume that a poet has knowledge of what they write about (e.g. medicine, governance, how to live a virtuous life) and try to learn from them. But if they have no real understanding of these things (and cannot explain them when questioned, as here) they are representing them only by imitation and dangerously misleading their audience. For more on Plato's views on poetry see the *Republic* (especially books 3 and 10).

ἐνθουσιάζοντες: 'being inspired'. The word ἐνθουσιάζω literally means to 'be possessed by a god'. The Latin-derived word 'inspired', which suggests a divine force 'blowing' creativity into a poet, thus works well in translation.

22c3

ἴσασιν: third person plural of οἶδα. See *Oxford Grammar of Classical Greek* p. 95.

πολλὰ καὶ καλά: 'many fine things'. Adjectives of quantity such as πολύς are usually joined to other adjectives with καί in Greek, where English uses no connecting word.

ὧν λέγουσι: omitted antecedent and relative attraction (see note 22b8).

22c4

τοιοῦτόν τί μοι ἐφάνησαν πάθος καὶ οἱ ποιηταὶ πεπονθότες: 'in my opinion the poets too clearly experienced just such a thing'. ἐφάνησαν is aorist passive of φαίνω, and πεπονθότες is perfect participle from πάσχω with the cognate accusative πάθος. Note that φαίνομαι followed by a participle means 'to clearly be x-ing', but followed by an infinitive it means 'to appear to be x-ing' (and not actually be).

καὶ οἱ ποιηταὶ: 'the poets also'.

22c5

ἠσθόμην αὐτῶν ... οἰομένων: 'I noticed that they thought'. Like ἀκούω (see 18e2), αἰσθάνομαι and other verbs of perception may be followed by the genitive.

καὶ τἆλλα: 'also in other things', an accusative of respect. Crasis of τὰ ἄλλα.

22c6

ἃ οὐκ ἦσαν: 'in which they were not wise'. The antecedent of ἃ is τἆλλα, and ἃ is also accusative of respect. σοφοί should be supplied.

22c7

περιγεγονέναι: 'that I was superior (to them)'. The perfect infinitive (of περιγίγνομαι) is used because it is referring to a present state.

τῷ αὐτῷ ... ὥπερ καὶ τῶν πολιτικῶν: 'for the exact same reason for which I was also superior to the politicians'. περιγίγνομαι takes a genitive of person and

AS

dative of thing in which someone is superior. περιγίγνομαι must be resupplied in the relative clause, and the suffix -περ adds emphasis (the *exact* same).

22c9

Τελευτῶν: 'finally'. Literally 'finishing off', but often used adverbially.

ἐμαυτῷ γὰρ συνήδη: 'I was conscious of'. Here and in the next line, ἤδη is first person singular, past tense of οἶδα (see *Oxford Grammar of Classical Greek* p. 95). For συνοῖδα, see note 21b5.

22d1

ὡς ἔπος εἰπεῖν: see note 22b6.

τούτους ... γ': 'these men at least'. τούτους is the object of εὑρήσοιμι, and is emphasized through its placement and the particle γε. This suggests that the craftsmen are Socrates' last chance, and that his enquiry is reaching its conclusion.

22d2

ᾔδη ὅτι εὑρήσοιμι: 'I knew that I would find'. For indirect statements using ὅτι with οἶδα, see 19d6 and 22b9. εὑρήσοιμι is the future optative, a form found only in indirect speech in historic sequence, to represent an original future indicative.

22d3

τούτου μὲν οὐκ ἐψεύσθην: 'I was not cheated of this' or 'I was not mistaken in this'. ψεύδω means 'to cheat someone (accusative) of something (genitive)'.

22d4

ταύτῃ: 'in this way'.

22d5

ταὐτόν: 'the same'. This is an alternative form of the word ταὐτό, which is formed by crasis of τὸ αὐτό. It has been emphasized by promotion and separation from its noun (ἁμάρτημα) in order to show Socrates being frustrated yet again in his search.

ταὐτόν ... ὅπερ καὶ οἱ ποιηταὶ καὶ οἱ ἀγαθοὶ δημιουργοί: καὶ is adverbial both times (so not to be translated as 'both ... and ...'). The delayed δημιουργοί is the subject of the main clause, and ποιηταὶ is the subject of the relative clause introduced by ὅπερ: 'even the good craftsmen seemed to have exactly (-περ) the same failing which the poets also had'.

22d6

διὰ τὸ ... ἐξεργάζεσθαι: articular infinitive (see note 22a5) – 'because of performing'.

22d7

ἠξίου: third person imperfect of ἀξιόω, an omicron-contracted verb. See *Oxford Grammar of Classical Greek* p. 78.

AS

καὶ τἄλλα τὰ μέγιστα: 'also in the other most important matters', accusative of respect. Socrates means the concerns of philosophy, such as ethics and politics.

22d8

ἡ πλημμέλεια: a musical metaphor, meaning 'false note', and therefore any 'fault' or 'error' in judgement. Reuse the verb ἔδοξαν (22d5) in this clause.

22e1

ὥστε με ἐμαυτὸν ἀνερωτᾶν: 'with the result that I asked myself'. The use of the infinitive construction in the result clause shows that this was the natural result of Socrates' investigation.

22e2

πότερα δεξαίμην ἂν οὕτως ὥσπερ ἔχω ἔχειν: 'whether I would prefer to be just as I am'. δεξαίμην is the potential optative with ἄν, and for ἔχω with an adverb see 22a5.

μήτε τι σοφὸς ὢν τὴν ἐκείνων σοφίαν μήτε ...: 'neither being at all wise in their wisdom, nor ...', explaining οὕτως ὥσπερ ἔχω. μή is used here due to the influence of the verb δεξαίμην which would use μή if negatived.

22e4

ἢ ἀμφότερα ἃ ἐκεῖνοι ἔχουσιν ἔχειν: 'or whether (I would prefer) to possess both the things which they have', i.e. their wisdom in some areas, and ignorance in others.

22e5

μοι λυσιτελοῖ: 'it was better for me', an impersonal verb.

23a1

καὶ οἷαι χαλεπώταται καὶ βαρύταται: 'of both the most difficult and most grievous kind'. χαλεπός means 'difficult' and therefore 'difficult to bear' or 'painful', while βαρύς means 'heavy', 'burdensome' or 'grievous'. οἷος strengthens the superlatives.

23a2

ὥστε ... ὄνομα δὲ τοῦτο λέγεσθαι, σοφὸς εἶναι: 'and that I am called this name, wise'. Socrates is the implied subject of λέγεσθαι, and εἶναι is used redundantly with verbs of naming. For the pejorative use of σοφός see note 18b7.

23a4

αὐτὸν: taken with με.

ταῦτα ... ἃ ἂν ἄλλον ἐξελέγξω: 'in whatever things I refute someone else for'. ἐξελέγξω is subjunctive (aorist by aspect) with ἄν in the indefinite construction (see 20e5).

23a5

τὸ δὲ: 'but the fact is', 'whereas'.

τῷ ὄντι: see 20d8.

AS

23a7

ὀλίγου τινὸς ἀξία ἐστὶν καὶ οὐδενός: 'is worth little or nothing'. καὶ here marks the climax of thought, rather than introducing a new idea.

23a8

φαίνεται τοῦτον λέγειν τὸν Σωκράτη: 'he seems to be talking about *this* Socrates' (perhaps even with a gesture towards himself). According to Socrates, the oracle used him as an example to illustrate a point, rather than really meaning that he was the wisest. For φαίνεται with the infinitive see note 22c4.

προσκεχρῆσθαι δὲ τῷ ἐμῷ ὀνόματι: 'and to have used my name as well'. προσκεχρῆσθαι is the perfect infinitive of προσχράομαι, with the perfect used because the prophecy has been said and remains true. For the prefix προσ- see note 20a2.

23b1

ἐμὲ παράδειγμα ποιούμενος: 'as he is making me an example', a causal use of the participle.

ὥσπερ ἂν <εἰ> εἴποι ὅτι: 'as he would (do) if he were saying'. Supply ποιοῖτο after ἂν to complete the conditional. On the brackets see note 18c2, and for ὅτι see note 21c2.

23b3

ἔγνωκεν: 'has come to realize'. The perfect tense of γιγνώσκω suggests that the state of knowledge has been gained from reflection.

23b4

τῇ ἀληθείᾳ: 'in truth', dative of accompanying circumstances, used adverbially.

ταῦτ᾽ οὖν: 'and so therefore'. ταῦτα is accusative of respect.

ἐγὼ μὲν: 'I for one.' μὲν here without a corresponding δέ clause implicitly suggests a comparison with others.

23b5

τὸν θεὸν: it is unclear whether Socrates is still referring to Apollo in particular here. The singular of θεός may be used in Greek to refer to a specific god, or to refer to all the gods collectively.

τῶν ἀστῶν καὶ ξένων: partitive genitives with τινα.

23b6

ἄν: contracted form of ἐάν ('if'), followed by the subjunctive οἴωμαι.

ἐπειδάν μοι μὴ δοκῇ: 'whenever one does not seem (wise) to me'. Indefinite construction in primary sequence, using the subjunctive with ἄν (coalesced with ἐπειδή).

23b8

ὑπὸ: 'because of'.

τι τῶν τῆς πόλεως: 'any of the affairs of the city'.

πρᾶξαί μοι σχολὴ γέγονεν: 'I have had no free time to perform'. σχολή is 'leisure' or 'free time', while ἀσχολίας means 'business' or 'occupation'. Socrates presents himself as virtuous because he spends all available time following his divine calling, the examination of wisdom. This also addresses another common criticism of Socrates: his reluctance to engage actively in Athenian democracy and his lack of conventional patriotism.

23b9
ἄξιον λόγου: 'worthy of a word' or 'worthy of mention'. ἄξιον agrees with τι.

23c1
πενίᾳ μυρίᾳ: Socrates served in the army as a hoplite, a heavily armed soldier who was required to provide his own equipment, so he must have come from a relatively affluent background. His disregard for his own affairs had presumably depleted this wealth.

23c2
Πρὸς δὲ τούτοις: 'in addition to this'.

23c3
οἱ τῶν πλουσιωτάτων: υἱοι should be supplied.
αὐτόματοι: 'of their own accord'. Best taken with ἐπακολουθοῦντες, this is in stark contrast to the sophists who need to persuade the youth to follow them. See particularly 19e–20a.

23c6
οἶμαι: used parenthetically here (as well as at 23d8 and 23e1).
ἀφθονίαν ... ἀνθρώπων: 'plenty of men'. ἀφθονία literally means 'freedom from envy', and through the idea that if someone has enough of something they will not envy it in others, it comes to mean an 'abundance' or 'plenty'.

23d1
αὑτοῖς: 'with themselves'. The rough breathing shows that this is a contraction of ἑαυτοῖς.
τίς ἐστι μιαρώτατος: 'is a most foul man'. τίς is the indefinite, with the accent due to the following enclitic ἐστι. μιαρός is a particularly strong word choice, meaning 'stained with blood', 'polluted' or 'foul'. In the Greek imagining, μίασμα ('pollution') was a dangerously contagious force which needed to be purged in order to preserve a society.

23d2
διαφθείρει: here with a moral sense, 'corrupt', rather than 'destroy'.
ἐπειδάν τις αὐτοὺς ἐρωτᾷ: ἐρωτᾷ is subjunctive in an indefinite construction (see note 23b6).

23d3

ὅτι ποιῶν: 'by doing what (does he corrupt them)' or 'what he does to corrupt them'. The elliptical way of speaking adds to Socrates' colloquial tone.

ἔχουσι μὲν οὐδὲν εἰπεῖν: 'they are able to say nothing'. For ἔχω with the infinitive, see note 20a8.

23d4

ἀπορεῖν: 'to be at a loss' or 'perplexed'. Especially in Plato's earlier writings, Socrates' questioning of his interlocutor (elenchus) often results in an impasse, or a state of ἀπορία ('perplexity', 'uncertainty'), being reached. For Socrates this was beneficial and desirable, as a person realizes how little they understand a topic and becomes instilled with a desire to investigate it. The inability of those being questioned to admit their ἀπορία shows that they have still failed to understand why they are being questioned.

23d5

πρόχειρα: 'at hand', 'ready' or 'standard'. Lacking anything concrete, the accusers resort to the stock criticisms of philosophers in order to charge Socrates.

23d6

"τὰ μετέωρα καὶ τὰ ὑπὸ γῆς" καὶ "θεοὺς μὴ νομίζειν" . . .: '"the phenomena above and below the earth" and "not believing in the gods" . . . .' These accusations were reported before at 18b and 19b. The incomplete quotations here are dismissive of the charges, and fit the colloquial style.

23d7

τὰ γὰρ ἀληθῆ . . . οὐκ ἂν ἐθέλοιεν λέγειν: 'for they would not be willing to say the truth'. ἐθέλοιεν is potential optative.

23d9

ἅτε . . . ὄντες: 'since they are'. ἅτε with the participle denotes a cause which the author presents as fact.

23e1

φιλότιμοι: 'honour-loving' or 'ambitious'. τιμή, often translated as 'honour', means 'a reward given for services' or 'what is due someone'. φιλότιμος is thus generally used pejoratively, for those eager to gain reward (material and non-material) for their actions.

23e2

ἐμπεπλήκασιν ὑμῶν τὰ ὦτα: 'they have filled your ears'. ἐμπεπλήκασιν is perfect tense of ἐμπίπλημι, and ὦτα is from οὖς, ὠτός, τό ('ear').

23e4

ἐκ τούτων: 'among these men'.

μοι ἐπέθετο: aorist middle of ἐπιτίθημι. See *Oxford Grammar of Classical Greek* pp. 80–1.

AS

23e5

Μέλητος ... ῥητόρων: Socrates outlines the personal grudges of his accusers, as based on professional resentment. Meletus was probably the son of a tragic poet also called Meletus (although certainty is difficult), Anytus was a politician and Lycon an orator and politician. Anytus was also angry on behalf of craftsmen, because his wealth was built on leather-making.

24a1

ὅπερ ἀρχόμενος ἐγὼ ἔλεγον: 'as I was saying at the beginning'. ἀρχόμενος here has adverbial force (see also note 22c9).

24a3

ὑμῶν ... ἐξελέσθαι: see note 19a1.

οὕτω πολλὴν γεγονυῖαν: 'when it has become so great'. γεγονυῖαν is feminine accusative perfect participle from γίγομαι.

24a6

ὑποστειλάμενος: 'having withheld'. Aorist middle participle of ὑποστέλλω.

οἶδα σχεδὸν ὅτι ...: 'I know all too well that ...'. An example of litotes, or emphasis through understatement (literally 'I almost know'). ὅτι with οἶδα again expresses certainty (see note 19d6).

τούτοις αὐτοῖς: 'for these very things'.

24a7

ὃ καὶ τεκμήριον ὅτι ...: 'which is also evidence that ...' (supply ἐστί). The antecedent of ὃ is the whole preceding clause.

24b1

ἐάντε ... ἐάντε ...: 'whether ... or ...'. ἐάντε is used instead of εἴτε with subjunctives.

οὕτως εὑρήσετε: 'you will find that it is so' (supply ὄντα).

AS

24b3–28a1 – Defence proper: Against the formal charges being brought by Meletus

Having refuted the long-standing allegations against him, Socrates now defends himself against Meletus, who has formally charged him with corrupting the youth, not believing in the gods, and introducing new divinities. Socrates calls Meletus to the stand for questioning, and concentrates on exposing the inconsistencies in the charges themselves.

Meletus first claims, through Socrates' elicitation, that every other Athenian improves the youth, and Socrates alone corrupts them. Socrates suggests that the absurdity of this proposition proves that Meletus is out for his own ends and does not actually care about the youth himself. Socrates also reasons that people do not intentionally harm those they live with, for fear of suffering harm themselves, so if he is in fact corrupting the youth, it must be unintentional. If this were the case, Meletus should have advised and instructed, rather than indicted, him.

Socrates also uses clever questioning to draw out the inconsistencies in the other two charges (not believing the gods, and introducing new divinities). Meletus first claims that Socrates does not believe in any gods whatsoever. He then also agrees that the 'divinities' which Socrates is said to be introducing are either gods themselves, or the children of gods. Socrates explains that if they are the children of gods, he must by extension believe in the gods themselves, thus exposing the contradictions in the charges.

28a2–34b5 – Digression: Socrates describes his divine mission

Socrates now imagines someone asking if he is ashamed of his way of life, for which he is risking death. He explains that he has been ordered by the gods to examine himself and others, and that it would be shameful to ignore this calling, even under the threat of death.

He also describes how he is a blessing to the city. In the same way that a gadfly disturbs a great and noble horse and prevents it from becoming lazy and falling asleep, Socrates bothers the state through his questions in order to prevent it from becoming idle, careless and complacent.

He repeats earlier arguments, and finally invites any in the court (including Plato himself) to come forward if they feel that they, or their relatives, have been corrupted by him. Socrates uses their silence as evidence that he is speaking the truth.

34b6–35d8 – Epilogue: Concluding remarks

Socrates explains that he will not make an emotional appeal, or bring his children out to evoke sympathy, as he wants to be judged impartially, and according to the law.

The jury now vote and find Socrates guilty. We are told at 36a5–6 that he would have been acquitted if thirty votes had changed, and the jury for a large case like this probably consisted of 500. If a tie meant acquittal, this puts the vote at 280–220, but it is not possible to be certain about this figure.

The second speech

An Athenian trial was either an ἀγὼν ἀτίμητος (with a penalty fixed by law) or an ἀγὼν τίμητος (with no fixed penalty). Since this was the latter, if a defendant was found guilty, the accuser spoke naming a penalty (see also Introduction – 'The trial'). The accused then proposed a counter-penalty and the jury voted on which of the two to award. In an unrecorded speech the accusers called for the death penalty (see 36b3), and here Plato records Socrates' proposal of a counter-penalty.

35e1–38b9 – Counter-penalty

Socrates concludes that because he is guilty only of performing a duty to the state, he really deserves to be honoured by receiving free meals from the state. However, he does not have enough time to convince them of his benefit to them. He therefore explains why imprisonment, a large fine, and exile are not appropriate, as they are all demonstrably damaging, while death could be good or bad. Finally he settles on a small fine, which he will be able to pay with the help of some followers.

This is one of the more problematic speeches when it comes to an assessment of Socrates' character and tone. At times, he is clearly insulting towards Meletus, but this could also be viewed as courage in the face of hostility (see note on the 'Opening address', 17a–18a). Elsewhere, such as his call to be fed in the prytaneum, it is difficult to determine whether Socrates is purposefully provocative, or if he genuinely believes what he is saying.

35e1

Τὸ μὲν μὴ ἀγανακτεῖν: 'not being angry', an articular infinitive, best taken as the object of συμβάλλεται (for more translation help, see note 36a1). Its placement at the start of the speech stresses Socrates' lack of anger.

ἐπὶ τούτῳ τῷ γεγονότι: 'at this result'. The following ὅτι clause explains what Socrates is referring to.

36a1

ἄλλα τέ μοι πολλὰ συμβάλλεται: 'many other things contribute to me not being angry', literally 'contribute not being angry to me'.

36a2

καὶ οὐκ ἀνέλπιστόν μοι γέγονεν τὸ γεγονὸς τοῦτο: 'and especially the fact that this happening has happened not unexpected to me'. An anacolouthon because after τέ ... καὶ ... we expect another subject for συμβάλλεται, but instead there is a new main clause; supply ὅτι to aid translation ('the fact that'). 'ἄλλα τέ ... καὶ ...' means 'both the others ... and ...', and is a common Greek idiom for 'especially'. ἀνέλπιστόν derives from the verb ἐλπίζω, which may mean 'hope' or 'expect' (i.e. not necessarily of something desired).

36a3

ἑκατέρων τῶν ψήφων τὸν γεγονότα ἀριθμόν: 'the resulting number of the votes on each side'. ἑκατέρος, like ἕτερος (see note 18d9), is used in the plural to

A Level

refer to groups rather than individuals. The polyptoton of γίγνομαι in this sentence perhaps suggests Socrates' surprise at the vote.

36a4

οὕτω παρ᾽ ὀλίγον: 'by so little'.

36a6

μετέπεσον: 'had changed sides'. The prefix μετα- often implies a change of condition or state. μεταπίπτω therefore literally means to 'fall differently' (perhaps here of the voting pebbles), or simply 'to undergo a change'.

ἀπεπεφεύγη ἄν: 'I would have got off'. The pluperfect here in an unfulfilled past conditional (where the aorist would be more common) places emphasis on the state which would have resulted if the thirty votes had changed.

36a7

Μέλητον ... καὶ νῦν ἀποπέφευγα: 'I have even now got off from Meletus'. Socrates is saying that if the votes against him were divided by the three prosecutors, he would have received more votes than each alone. The use of humour here backs up the claim that he is not angry, but is also an example of Socrates' glib (and potentially confrontational) tone.

ὡς ἐμοὶ δοκῶ: 'I think', literally: 'so I think to myself'.

36a8

ἀλλὰ παντὶ δῆλον τοῦτό γε: supply ἐστί. τοῦτό is explained by ὅτι ('that').

36a9

εἰ μὴ ἀνέβη Ἄνυτος καὶ Λύκων: 'if Anytus and Lycon had not appeared before the court'. ἀνέβη is singular to agree with the nearer subject, but refers to both men.

κατηγορήσοντες: 'to accuse'. The future participle is here used for purpose.

κἂν ὦφλε χιλίας δραχμάς: 'he would have also owed a thousand drachmas'. ὦφλε is the aorist of ὀφλισκάνω, and κἂν is crasis of καὶ ἄν. A thousand drachma was the fine if a prosecutor failed to receive a fifth of the votes, in order to discourage unwarranted litigation. Socrates is pushing the joke, at Meletus' expense.

τὸ πέμπτον μέρος: 'a fifth', literally 'the fifth part'. If we divide our estimation of the votes against Socrates by the three prosecutors (see note on vote above), we get a figure of 93⅓, less than a fifth of the 500 jurors.

36b3

Τιμᾶται δ᾽ οὖν μοι ὁ ἀνὴρ θανάτου: 'But anyway the man is proposing death as the penalty for me'. τιμάω in the middle, the technical term for 'proposing a penalty for someone', takes a genitive of penalty, and a dative of person. δ᾽ οὖν is used here to resume the speech after the joke.

36b4

ἀντιτιμήσομαι: the technical term for proposing a counter-penalty, also taking a genitive of penalty.

A Level

ἢ δῆλον ὅτι τῆς ἀξίας;: 'Or is it clear that I will propose what I deserve?' Supply ἐστί after δῆλον, and ἀντιτιμήσομαι after ὅτι. ἀξία is a thing's 'worth' or a person's 'due' or 'deserts'.

36b5–d2

τί ἄξιός … τοιοῦτος ὤν: a particularly long sentence. Socrates is asking what punishment is right for someone who has neglected their own interests in order to encourage others to be as good and wise as possible, and to care for the city.

36b5

τί ἄξιός εἰμι παθεῖν ἢ ἀποτεῖσαι: 'what do I deserve to suffer or pay'. ἀποτεῖσαι is aorist infinitive of ἀποτίνω.

ὅτι μαθών: an idiom, meaning 'because', but with a sense of surprise.

36b6

οὐχ ἡσυχίαν ἦγον: 'I was not in the habit of keeping quiet.' Socrates is talking about his questioning of people and their convictions. The imperfect is used as he is referring to customary past action.

ἀμελήσας ὧνπερ οἱ πολλοί: 'not having cared about the very things which the majority do care about'. The antecedent of ὧνπερ has been omitted, and ἐπιμελοῦνται (have a care for) should be supplied. ἀμελέω takes the genitive.

36b7

χρηματισμοῦ … γιγνομένων: this is a list of things (all in the genitive after ἀμελήσας) which Socrates has no regard for, all to do with furthering one's own interests.

36b8

δημηγοριῶν: the word δημηγορία literally means 'speech in the assembly'. However, in Plato it often has the pejorative sense of 'popular oratory' or 'clap-trap'.

συνωμοσιῶν καὶ στάσεων: 'conspiracies and political factions'. A συνωμοσία is a group bound together by an oath, thus a 'conspiracy'. στάσις (literally a 'standing' – ἵστημι) here means a 'political party', particularly one formed for seditious purposes. Conspiracies and factions were common in Athens after the Peloponnesian War and the rule of the Thirty Tyrants (see note 21a2).

36c1

ἡγησάμενος ἐμαυτὸν … εἶναι …: 'having thought that I was …'. The accusative ἐμαυτὸν is particularly emphatic, since we would expect a nominative with the infinitive where the subject is the same as the main verb.

τῷ ὄντι: see note 20d8.

ἐπιεικέστερον … ἢ ὥστε …: 'too honourable to …', literally 'more honourable than as to …'.

A
Level

εἰς ταῦτ'ἰόντα σῴζεσθαι: 'to enter into these things and survive'. Socrates' honesty makes him unsuitable for involvement in state politics or conspiracy.

36c2

ἐνταῦθα μὲν οὐκ ἦα οἷ ἐλθὼν . . .: 'I didn't go there, to where having gone . . .' or 'I refrained from the sort of activities which entering into . . .'. Here, and in the previous line, Socrates uses the verb 'to go' in the sense of entering into activities.

μήτε ὑμῖν μήτε ἐμαυτῷ ἔμελλον μηδὲν ὄφελος εἶναι: 'I was likely to be of no help either to you or myself'. The word μηδὲν strengthens the negative idea rather than cancelling it out (see note 18d5).

36c3

ἐπὶ δὲ τὸ ἰδίᾳ ἕκαστον ἰὼν εὐεργετεῖν τὴν μεγίστην εὐεργεσίαν: 'for the sake of going and doing the greatest service to each man in private'. τὸ . . . εὐεργετεῖν is an articular infinitive with the direct object ἕκαστον, while τὴν . . . εὐεργεσίαν is cognate accusative.

36c4

ὡς ἐγώ φημι: 'as I declare'.

36c5

ἐνταῦθα ἦα: 'I went there' or 'I entered into that'. ἐνταῦθα refers back to the idea in ἐπὶ . . . εὐεργεσίαν. The repetition underlines Socrates' decision to do good to his countrymen.

μὴ πρότερον μήτε τῶν ἑαυτοῦ μηδενὸς ἐπιμελεῖσθαι: 'not to have a concern either about anything of his own affairs'. μηδενὸς is the genitive object of ἐπιμελεῖσθαι, while τῶν is partitive genitive (supply a word such as πραγματῶν). πρότερον ('earlier'), coordinated with πρὶν ('before') later in the line, is best omitted in translation.

36c6

πρὶν ἑαυτοῦ ἐπιμεληθείη: 'before he has a concern for himself'. The passive deponent optative ἐπιμεληθείη is suboblique (see note 20b8) in the indirect command introduced by πείθειν.

36c7

ὅπως . . . ἔσοιτο: 'that he might be'. Verbs of effort, such as ἐπιμελέομαι, take the future indicative with ὅπως. ἔσοιτο is future optative (also suboblique) of εἰμί.

μήτε τῶν τῆς πόλεως, πρὶν αὐτῆς τῆς πόλεως: 'or (to have a concern) for the affairs of the city, before (he has a concern) for the city itself'. Supply ἐπιμελεῖσθαι and ἐπιμεληθείη respectively, as in the preceding clauses. The point is that ethical considerations are more important than economic matters.

36d1

οὕτω κατὰ τὸν αὐτὸν τρόπον: 'like this in the same way', tautological.

A Level

τί οὖν εἰμι ἄξιος παθεῖν: Socrates repeats the question asked at the start of the sentence, encouraging the jury to reconsider in light of what he has just said.

36d2
ἀγαθόν τι: 'something good', in answer to the question posed. For Socrates to suggest that he be rewarded, rather than punished, has often been seen as a defiant provocation. One could also see him as bravely defending justice, supporting what he really believes to be the fair penalty, even if it is unpopular.

36d3
κατὰ τὴν ἀξίαν: 'according to what is deserved'.
τῇ ἀληθείᾳ τιμᾶσθαι: τιμᾶσθαι still used technically (see note 36b3), and for τῇ ἀληθείᾳ see note 23b4.

36d4
καὶ ταῦτά γε: 'and furthermore'.
ἀγαθὸν τοιοῦτον ὅτι ἂν πρέποι ἐμοί: 'such a good thing as whatever would be fitting for me'. τοιοῦτον ὅτι is more indefinite than the usual τοιοῦτον οἷον.

36d5
ἀνδρὶ πένητι εὐεργέτῃ: 'for a poor man, your benefactor'. εὐεργέτης ('benefactor', 'well-doer') was an honorific title which could be conferred by a public vote on someone who had performed a special service to the state, such as an Olympic victor (see 36d8–9). See note 23c1 on Socrates' wealth.
δεομένῳ ἄγειν σχολὴν ἐπὶ τῇ ὑμετέρᾳ παρακελεύσει: 'since he needs to be at leisure for the sake of advising you'. If Socrates had to work to support himself, he would not have time to perform his duty to the state.

36d6
οὐκ ἔσθ᾽ ὅτι μᾶλλον … πρέπει οὕτως ὡς …: 'there is nothing that is more fitting as that …'. After μᾶλλον we would expect ἤ ('than'), but the syntax shifts and there is a consecutive (result) clause after ὡς.

36d7
ἐν πρυτανείῳ σιτεῖσθαι: 'be fed in the prytaneum'. The prytaneum was a sort of City Hall, which housed the hearth of the city, as well as laws and the public archives. εὐεργέται (see note 36d5) were also fed here at the public expense. Socrates is therefore proposing not just that he be honoured instead of put to death, but also that he be supported by the state, so that he can continue doing exactly what he has been convicted for. Still, a judgement on whether this is provocatively ironic, or said in earnest, is not straightforward.
ἵππῳ ἢ συνωρίδι ἢ ζεύγει: 'on a single horse, or with a two-horse chariot, or with a four-horse chariot', three different events at the Olympic games.

36d9
Ὀλυμπίασιν: 'at Olympia', a locative dative.

A Level

36d10

ἐγὼ δὲ εἶναι: 'but I (make you prosperous) in reality'. Supply the bracketed words from the previous clause. As at 21c7, the contrast is between appearance (δοκεῖν) and reality (εἶναι).

ὁ μὲν τροφῆς οὐδὲν δεῖται: 'he does not at all need sustenance'. To enter a horse, or chariot, in the Olympic Games required personal wealth. Socrates says that he deserves meals in the prytaneum both because he is a real benefit to the state, and because he is very poor.

37a3

ταυτί: see note 20d2.

37a4

ὥσπερ περὶ τοῦ οἴκτου καὶ τῆς ἀντιβολήσεως: 'as (when I spoke) about lamentation and entreaty'. Socrates is referring to when, in the Epilogue to his main speech (see note 34b6–35d8), he refuses to resort to emotional appeal. This was a common defence tactic, so for Socrates to reject it might have been seen as critical of others, self-righteous and arrogant. The word αὐθαδιζόμενος is also used at 34d.

37a5

ἀπαυθαδιζόμενος: 'arrogantly'. Socrates is aware of the way his proposal of meals may come across (see note 37a5), and he now proceeds to explain the rationale behind his suggestion.

τὸ δὲ οὐκ ἔστιν … τοιοῦτον ἀλλὰ τοιόνδε μᾶλλον: 'whereas this is not so, but it is rather as follows'. τὸ δὲ is either equivalent to τοῦτο δὲ, or (as at 23a5) means 'whereas'.

37a6

πέπεισμαι: 'I am convinced', literally 'I have persuaded myself'.

ἑκὼν εἶναι μηδένα ἀδικεῖν ἀνθρώπων: 'that I do not intentionally harm any human being'. ἑκὼν εἶναι is an infinitive phrase unconnected to the rest of the syntax (see 22a4) and equivalent to ἑκών alone, while μή is used (rather than οὐ) with verbs expressing belief, to denote strong confidence.

ὑμᾶς τοῦτο οὐ πείθω: 'but I cannot persuade you of this'. πείθω here takes a double accusative.

37a8

ὀλίγον γὰρ χρόνον ἀλλήλοις διειλέγμεθα: διειλέγμεθα is perfect of διαλέγομαι ('we have talked'). The perfect is used because Socrates regards his defence as almost over. See note 19a2 for Socrates' earlier complaint about the lack of time available for his appeal.

37a9

ἐγᾦμαι: crasis of ἐγὼ οἶμαι.

ὥσπερ καὶ ἄλλοις ἀνθρώποις: 'as also other men have', literally 'as also (there is) to other men'. Socrates is probably referring to Sparta (see Thucydides 1.132.5).

A Level

He and other philosophers often voiced admiration for Spartan law (e.g. *Crito* 52e), something which was not popular after 27 years of war.

37a10

περὶ θανάτου μὴ ... κρίνειν: 'not to decide a capital case', or 'not to make a judgement concerning death'. The infinitive is in apposition to the word νόμος, defining it. See also the *Laws* 855c–856a, when Plato asserts that capital cases should be tried over three days.

ἀλλὰ πολλάς: 'but in many days' (supply ἡμέρας).

37b1

νῦν δ': 'but as it is'.

οὐ ῥᾴδιον: supply ἐστί.

37b2

ἀπολύεσθαι: 'to refute', or 'to set oneself free from'.

37b3

πολλοῦ δέω ἐμαυτόν γε ἀδικήσειν: 'I am very unlikely to do harm to *myself*', with πολλοῦ δέω literally meaning 'I am lacking much' or 'I am far from'. The polyptoton of ἐγώ, ἐμαυτόν and ἐμαυτοῦ, the emphatic particle γε, and the word αὐτὸς make Socrates' argument here more forceful. Why would someone who refuses to do harm to others ever harm himself?

37b4

του κακοῦ: 'of any evil' or 'of any punishment'. του is an alternative form of τινος, from the indefinite τις (and not the definite article τοῦ).

τιμήσεσθαι: on the use of this verb, see note 36b3.

37b5

τί δείσας;: 'In fear of what (would I propose something bad for myself)?'.

ἢ μὴ πάθω ...: 'Is it (out of fear) that I will suffer ...'. μὴ πάθω is a fear clause, following on from δείσας in the previous sentence. Socrates presents a potential response to the previous question, but this response is itself posed as a question (introduced by ἢ) to emphasize its falsity. He imagines someone claiming that he would propose a punishment to avoid the worse punishment of death. But if he does not know whether death is good or bad, as he has said before (29a), why would he propose something he knows to be bad?

37b6

ὅ φημι οὐκ εἰδέναι οὔτ' ...: 'which I declare that I do not know either ...'. Again, a compound negative reinforces a previous negative (see note 18d5).

37b7

ἕλωμαι: 'should I choose ...', deliberative subjunctive.

A Level

ὧν εὖ οἶδά τι κακῶν ὄντων: 'one (τι) of the things which I know well to be bad'. An example of both relative attraction and an omitted antecedent (see note 22b8), and equivalent to 'τι τούτων ἃ εὖ οἶδα κακὰ ὄντα'.

37b8

πότερον δεσμοῦ;: 'Should I propose imprisonment?'. δεσμοῦ (literally 'chains') is genitive with an implied τιμήσωμαι. Questions introduced by πότερον provide two alternative propositions ('whether ... or ...?'), and are normally answered by ἤ. The alternative here comes at 37c2, but is introduced by the word ἀλλά to add liveliness.

καὶ τί: 'and yet why'. καὶ here expresses opposition.

37c1

τῇ ἀεὶ καθισταμένῃ ἀρχῇ, τοῖς ἕνδεκα: 'to the authority which is appointed on each occasion, to the Eleven'. 'The Eleven' were annually-elected officials charged with managing the prisons and punishments (in apposition to ἀρχῇ), while ἀεί here means 'on each occasion' or 'from time to time', rather than 'always'. Socrates is implying that it is not worth living if he is subject to the whims of whoever happens to gain influence.

37c2

ἀλλὰ χρημάτων καὶ δεδέσθαι: 'but should I propose a fine and to be imprisoned'. χρημάτων (literally 'money') is genitive due to another implied τιμήσωμαι. τιμήσωμαι also takes as its object the infinitive δεδέσθαι (literally 'to have been bound'). For ἀλλὰ here see note 37b8.

ἕως ἂν ἐκτείσω: 'until I pay it in full'. ἐκτείσω is the aorist subjunctive of ἐκτίνω, used in the indefinite construction with ἄν. In Greek, temporal clauses referring to the future use the indefinite construction because they are conceived of as fundamentally unknowable. Here the prefix ἐκ- implies completion ('in full', 'utterly').

37c3

ταὐτόν μοί ἐστιν ὅπερ ...: 'that for me is just the same as that which ...'. For ταὐτόν, see note 22d5. If Socrates proposed a fine rather than imprisonment, he would not be able to pay it and would end up with life in prison anyway.

37c4

ὁπόθεν ἐκτείσω: 'with which to pay it off'. ἐκτείσω here is future indicative, used with the relative ὁπόθεν (literally, 'from where') to express purpose.

ἀλλὰ δὴ φυγῆς τιμήσωμαι;: 'So, then, should I propose exile?' Again Socrates rejects the previous option, and introduces another choice. The rhetorical technique which involves a speaker both posing and answering their own questions is known as hypophora. Socrates appears to have thought of every alternative, which perhaps supports the idea that his request of meals in the prytaneum was genuine and rational rather than purely confrontational.

τιμήσωμαι: deliberative subjunctive.

A
Level

37c5

ἄν μοι τούτου τιμήσαιτε: 'you would fix this as the penalty for me'. The active of τιμάω is used for the jury's decision, while the middle (as seen before) is used of a speaker's proposal.

πολλὴ μεντἄν ... οἴσουσι ῥᾳδίως;: a long sentence. Socrates explains that his judgement would have to be clouded by an excessive desire to live if he were to propose the penalty of exile. He would have to be foolish not to work out that if his fellow citizens have not been able to bear him, others will not be able to put up with him either. He goes on to say how difficult a life of being passed from city to city would be at his age, so again we are faced with a punishment which is known to be bad (exile) compared with a punishment which may be good or bad (death).

πολλὴ μεντἄν με φιλοψυχία ἔχοι: 'However a great love of life would possess me'. μεντἄν is crasis of μέντοι and ἄν.

37c7

ὑμεῖς μὲν ὄντες πολῖταί μου: 'you, although you are my fellow citizens'. The participle here has concessive force. μὲν looks forward to δέ in 37d3.

37c8

οὐχ οἷοί τε ἐγένεσθε ἐνεγκεῖν: 'became unable to bear'. ἐνεγκεῖν is the aorist infinitive of φέρω.

τὰς ἐμὰς διατριβὰς: either 'my way of life' or 'my conversations'.

37d1

ἀλλ' ὑμῖν βαρύτεραι γεγόνασιν καὶ ἐπιφθονώτεραι: 'but that they have become too burdensome and odious to you'. Standalone comparatives may mean 'too' or 'rather'. ἐπίφθονος is 'liable to envy', 'jealousy-provoking' or 'odious'. For βαρύς see note 23a1.

37d2

ζητεῖτε αὐτῶν νυνὶ ἀπαλλαγῆναι: 'you seek right now to be released from them'. νυνὶ is νῦν with deictic -ι (see note 20d2), while ἀπαλλαγῆναι is aorist passive infinitive of ἀπαλλάσσω, 'to escape from', followed by a genitive of separation.

ἄλλοι δὲ ἄρα αὐτὰς οἴσουσι ῥᾳδίως;: 'but that others will, in fact, bear them easily?'. οἴσουσι is the future of φέρω. This is an anacolouthon because we expect another clause corresponding to ὑμεῖς μὲν ... (see 37c7), but instead Socrates asks a rhetorical question. This, and the particle ἄρα, emphasizes how inaccurate this method of reasoning would be.

37d3

πολλοῦ γε δεῖ: 'Far from it!', literally 'it lacks much indeed'.

37d4

καλὸς: ironic. For more on the current argument, see 37c5.

**A
Level**

37d5

ἄλλην ἐξ ἄλλης πόλεως ἀμειβομένῳ: 'passing from one city to another'. ἀμείβω literally means to 'exchange', and from the idea of exchanging places, comes the sense of movement to a place (in the accusative). πόλιν is implied with ἄλλην.

τηλικῷδε: 'at such an age'. At 17d Socrates says that he is seventy years old.

37d6

ζῆν: present infinitive of ζάω.

οἶδ' ὅτι ὅποι ἂν ἔλθω: 'I know that wherever I go'. For οἶδ' ὅτι, see note 19d6. ἂν ἔλθω is the indefinite construction.

λέγοντος ἐμοῦ ἀκροάσονται: like ἀκούω, ἀκροάομαι takes a genitive of person.

κἂν: crasis of καί ἐάν

37d8

ἐξελῶσι: future of ἐξελαύνω.

37e1

οἱ τούτων πατέρες δὲ: 'then the fathers of these men'. δὲ is used here to indicate the main clause (apodosis) of the conditional.

37e2

δι' αὐτοὺς τούτους: 'will drive me out for the sake of these men themselves' (i.e. their sons and relatives). Supply με ἐξελῶσι from the previous clause.

37e4

ἡμῖν ἐξελθὼν ζῆν: 'to live in exile away from us', literally 'to live having gone away for our sake'. ἡμῖν is dative of interest as at 20e4.

37a6

τῷ θεῷ ἀπειθεῖν τοῦτ' ἐστὶν: 'this is to disobey the god'. As it is Socrates' god-given duty to question people and their views, to go into exile and remain in silence is not possible.

ἀδύνατον: supply ἐστί.

38a1

ὡς εἰρωνευομένῳ: 'on the grounds that I am being devious'. εἰρωνεύομαι is a complex word, and one with a particular connection to Socrates. Liddell, Scott and Jones list εἰρωνεία as 'ignorance purposely affected to provoke or confound an antagonist' (equivalent to English 'Socratic irony'), and an εἴρων as 'one who says less than he thinks'. The related English word 'irony', however, refers to saying something contrary to what is meant to be understood (see also Introduction). The Greek word thus often (but not always) implies purposeful deception, while the related English word 'irony' involves a speaker's intention that their audience will comprehend the irony. Especially here, where the word is used in the mouths of Socrates' detractors, the idea of 'being devious' or 'disingenuous' is the primary meaning.

A Level

38a3

τοῦτο, ἑκάστης ἡμέρας περὶ ἀρετῆς τοὺς λόγους ποιεῖσθαι: 'this, to speak about virtue every day', literally 'this, in each day about virtue to produce words'. ποιεῖσθαι is in apposition to τοῦτο, and ἑκάστης ἡμέρας is genitive of time within which. ἀρετή is 'excellence'; in Homer this means heroic and martial 'valour', but in Plato and the philosophers denotes 'moral virtue'.

38a4

τῶν ἄλλων: also goverened by περὶ in 38a3.

38a5

ὁ δὲ ἀνεξέταστος βίος οὐ βιωτὸς ἀνθρώπῳ: 'and that the unexamined life is not worth living for a human being', continuing the indirect statement introduced by λέγω ὅτι at 38a2. ἀνεξέταστος implies both personal examination and examination by others. The word ἀνθρώπῳ reminds us of Socrates' assertion that wisdom involves accepting the limits of human knowledge (see note 20d8).

38a6

ταῦτα δ': 'then in these things'. As at 37e1, the δέ here marks the apodosis of the conditional started in 38a1.

38a7

τὰ δὲ ἔχει μὲν οὕτως: 'but these things are so'. τὰ δὲ is equivalent to ταῦτα δὲ (as at 37a5), and for ἔχω with an adverb see 22a5.

38a8

οὐ ῥᾴδιον: supply ἐστί.

οὐκ εἴθισμαι: 'I am not accustomed'. εἴθισμαι is perfect of ἐθίζω ('become accustomed') to denote a present state.

ἐμαυτὸν ἀξιοῦν κακοῦ οὐδενός: ἀξιοῦν is present infinitive of ἀξιόω (see *Oxford Grammar of Classical Greek* p. 78), which here means to 'think someone (accusative) worthy of something (genitive)'.

38b1

εἰ μὲν γὰρ . . .: '(I say this) for if . . .'. γὰρ does not explain the previous statement, but the reason for saying it.

38b2

ὅσα ἔμελλον ἐκτείσειν: 'as much as I was likely (to be able) to pay off'.

οὐδὲν γὰρ ἂν ἐβλάβην: 'for in no way would I have been harmed'. ἐβλάβην is the aorist passive of βλάπτω.

38b3

νῦν δὲ οὐ γὰρ ἔστιν: supply μοι χρήματα. For νῦν δὲ see note 37b1.

εἰ μὴ ἄρα . . . βούλεσθέ: 'unless in fact you want'

ὅσον . . . τοσούτου . . . μοι τιμῆσαι: 'to fix as my penalty the amount which . . .'. τοσούτου is the antecedent of ὅσον. For τιμῆσαι see note 37c5.

**A
Level**

38b5

μνᾶν: on the value of a mina, see note 20b8. Xenophon estimates the value of Socrates' assets at five minae (*Oeconomicus* 2.3).

38b7

Πλάτων ὅδε: 'Plato here', probably accompanied by a gesture.

Κρίτων ... Ἀπολλόδωρος: three other followers of Socrates, who were all (according to the *Phaedo*, 59b) also present at his death.

　　Crito is the most famous of the three. In the *Apology*, at 33d, Socrates describes him as being the same age and from the same deme as him (Alopece), and he appears to have amassed great wealth through agriculture. Socrates even addresses his final words to him in the *Phaedo* (118a). He is also Socrates' primary interlocutor in both Plato's *Euthydemus*, which concerns the methods of argument employed by sophists, and in *Crito*, where he tries to convince Socrates to escape from prison before his execution.

　　Critobulus was one of Crito's sons, and features less in extant literature than his father. In Xenophon's *Memorabilia (*1.3.8–10) Socrates chastises him for giving in to sensual passion by kissing Alcibiades' son.

　　Apollodorus (of Phaleron, one of Athens' ports) is depicted as being particularly emotional at Socrates' death (see *Phaedo*, 59b and 117d). He is also the main narrator of Plato's *Symposium*, where he is presented as having come late to philosophy (173a), and as fanatically obsessive about Socrates (173d).

38b9

ἐγγυᾶσθαι: 'say that they guarantee its payment'. ἐγγυάω means to 'make a pledge', and in the middle to 'give a guarantee', while an ἐγγυητής (38b10) is a guarantor. In English supply a verb of saying, implied by the word κελεύουσί.

οὗτοι ἀξιόχρεῳ: 'these trustworthy men'. ἀξιόχρεῳ is masculine nominative plural, see note 20e6.

The jury's second vote supports the penalty of death, but a precise result is more difficult to identify.

A vote breakdown of 360–140 is often quoted, using the third century AD biographer Diogenes Laertius as evidence (*Lives and Opinions of Eminent Philosophers* 2.42). The possibility that more jurors voted for the death penalty than had initially found him guilty has been explained as a reaction to the mocking tone of Socrates' counter-penalty speech, and the insignificance of his suggested penalty.

However, critics have recently queried the reliability of Diogenes' account, especially given that it was written five centuries after the trial, and have called into question the idea that the margin of votes increased at all. They claim that, even if Socrates' tone is taken as provocative, to vote for his death after acquitting him would be an inexplicable overreaction. Moreover, in his closing speech, Plato's Socrates addresses all those who acquitted him and praises their skills as jurors (40a3); this may suggest that there were no jurors who both acquitted him and voted for his death.

A Level

The third speech

38c1–42a5 – Closing address

Before Socrates is led off, he first addresses the jurors who have condemned him, repeating the idea that he has defended himself without demeaning himself, while they have succumbed to immorality. He also predicts that, contrary to their expectation, by killing him they will be scrutinized and examined more closely and more severely. Next he addresses his friends and explains that his death must be a good thing, because the 'divine voice' did not oppose him. He then considers the nature of death, before requesting that his sons are reproached if they behave in a way which goes against what Socrates has advocated.

This speech contains the same complexity of interpretation which we have witnessed throughout the *Apology*. The tone in the first address might be seen as openly threatening, but could just be indicative of the firmness of Socrates' beliefs. Equally, the calmness and magnanimity with which he appears to welcome his punishment, might also be seen as unconcerned and defiant.

38c1

Οὐ πολλοῦ γ᾽ ἕνεκα χρόνου: 'Not for the sake of much time'. Socrates means that it is not worth them suffering dishonour for killing him when, as an old man, he would die soon anyway.

ὄνομα ἕξετε καὶ αἰτίαν: 'you will gain a reputation and be accused'. The phrase αἰτίαν ἔχειν means 'to be accused' (literally 'have blame'), and is the usual passive of αἰτιάομαι (hence the following ὑπό).

38c3

ὡς Σωκράτη ἀπεκτόνατε: 'on the grounds that you have killed Socrates'. ὡς introduces an indirect statement, quoting the words of the city's detractors, while ἀπεκτόνατε is the perfect of ἀποκτείνω.

38c5

ἀπὸ τοῦ αὐτομάτου: 'naturally' or 'by chance'. Socrates is referring to his death.

38c6

ὁρᾶτε γὰρ δὴ τὴν ἡλικίαν ὅτι πόρρω ἤδη ἐστὶ τοῦ βίου, θανάτου δὲ ἐγγύς. 'For indeed you see that my age is now far on in life, and near death'. This is an example of prolepsis (see note 21e5), which focuses attention on Socrates' age, while τοῦ βίου is a genitive of time within which. Note also the chiastic order, juxtaposing βίου and θανάτου to emphasize how close to death Socrates is.

38d1

τοὺς ἐμοῦ καταψηφισαμένους θάνατον: 'those who condemned me to death'. καταψηφίζομαι ('vote against', 'condemn') takes a genitive of person, and accusative of penalty (or crime).

A Level

38d2

καὶ τόδε: 'the following also'. While τόδε looks forward, τοῦτο (38c7) refers back.

38d3

με . . . ἑαλωκέναι: 'that I have been convicted'. ἑαλωκέναι is the perfect infinitive of ἁλίσκομαι.

ἀπορίᾳ λόγων . . . τοιούτων οἷς . . .: 'due to a lack of the sort of words by which
    . . .'.

38d5

ὥστε ἀποφυγεῖν τὴν δίκην: 'to be acquitted' (literally 'to escape from the case').
    The result clause here is used to express an intended result, and therefore has a
    sense of purpose.

πολλοῦ γε δεῖ: see note 37d3.

38d6

τόλμης καὶ ἀναισχυντίας: 'of audacity and shamelessness'. τόλμη may mean
    'courage', but also can be used pejoratively to mean 'over-boldness' or 'audacity',
    while ἀναισχυντία is a tolerance for doing or saying shameful things. Socrates is
    not willing to lower himself in order to satisfy and persuade the jury.

38d7

τοῦ μὴ ἐθέλειν: 'of willingness', an articular infinitive. As it is dependent on ἀπορίᾳ,
    which has a negative meaning, μὴ here is redundant (as with verbs of preventing,
    hindering and denying).

38d8

οἳ ἂν ὑμῖν μὲν ἥδιστα ἦν ἀκούειν: 'which would have been most pleasing for
    you to hear'. ἥδιστα is the superlative adjective of ἡδύς, and the infinitive ἀκούειν
    defines its meaning (epexegetic infinitive).

θρηνοῦντός τέ μου καὶ ὀδυρομένου: 'me both lamenting and wailing', genitives
    dependent on ἀκούειν. For this idea see note 37a4.

38d9

πολλὰ καὶ ἀνάξια ἐμοῦ: 'many things unworthy of myself'. ἐμοῦ here is equivalent
    to ἐμαυτοῦ, and for καὶ here see note 22c3.

38e2

τῶν ἄλλων ἀκούειν: 'to hear from others' or 'to hear others saying'.

οὔτε τότε ᾠήθην: 'neither at that time did I think'. τότε refers back to Socrates'
    defence speech. ᾠήθην is passive deponent aorist of οἴομαι.

38e3

οὐδὲν ἀνελεύθερον: 'anything unsuitable for a free man'. For οὐδὲν see note 18d5.

μοι μεταμέλει οὕτως ἀπολογησαμένῳ: 'am I sorry for having made such a
    defence'. The impersonal verb μεταμέλει takes the dative (literally 'it is a cause
    of regret to me').

**A
Level**

38e5

τεθνάναι: perfect infinitive of θνῄσκω, placing emphasis on the state of being dead.
ἐκείνως: 'in that way', as defined at 38d8–e2.
ἐν δίκῃ: 'in a lawsuit'.

38e6

τοῦτο μηχανᾶσθαι, ὅπως ἀποφεύξεται πᾶν ποιῶν θάνατον: 'to devise this,
that he will escape death by any method', literally 'doing everything'. φεύγω has
a middle deponent future, and for the construction with ὅπως see note 36c7. The
word μηχανάομαι means to 'contrive' or 'devise' by art or cunning, frequently in
a bad sense.

39a3

ἄν τις ἐκφύγοι: 'someone might escape', implying likelihood.
ὅπλα ἀφείς: 'by throwing away his weapons'. ἀφείς is the aorist participle of
ἀφίημι.
ἐφ' ἱκετείαν τραπόμενος: 'by turning to supplication'. For the idea of begging for
mercy, see note 37a4. Socrates is comparing undignified conduct and debasement
of principles in court, to cowardice in battle.

39a5

ὥστε διαφεύγειν θάνατον: 'to escape from death', see note 38d5.

39a6

μὴ οὐ τοῦτ' ᾖ χαλεπόν: 'I suspect that this is not difficult'. μὴ (negative μὴ οὐ)
with the subjunctive (here ᾖ, from εἰμί) may be used to express a degree of doubt.
Its use here is ironic, because Socrates is in no doubt that death is easier to evade
than evil.

39a7

χαλεπώτερον πονηρίαν: 'it is more difficult to escape wickedness', supply
ἐστί and ἐκφυγεῖν. πονηρία here has a moral sense, denoting the opposite of
virtue.
θᾶττον γὰρ θανάτου θεῖ: 'for it runs faster than death'. θᾶττον is the comparative
adverb of ταχύς, and θανάτου is genitive of comparison. Note the alliteration,
and the personification of πονηρία to emphasize its threat.

39b2

ἅτε βραδὺς ὢν καὶ πρεσβύτης: 'because I am slow and old'. For ἅτε, see
note 23d9.

39b3

ἑάλων: 'I was captured'. Root aorist of ἁλίσκομαι, see *Oxford Grammar of
Classical Greek* p. 71.
δεινοὶ καὶ ὀξεῖς: 'swift'. ὀξύς means 'sharp', 'quick-witted' or just 'fast', contrasted
with βραδύς. For δεινός see note 18b4.

**A
Level**

39b4

τῆς κακίας: 'wickedness', in apposition to τοῦ θάττονος. Literally 'badness', but like πονηρία used in the moral sense of 'wickedness' or 'vice'. The constant use of different words to refer to this concept (see μοχθηρίαν and ἀδικίαν at 39b5) makes it seem more elusive and thus more dangerous.

ἄπειμι: εἶμι (to go) rather than εἰμί (to be).

ὑφ᾽ ὑμῶν θανάτου δίκην ὀφλών: 'having been condemned to death by you'. ὀφλών is the aorist participle of ὀφλισκάνω, literally 'to owe'. δίκην ὀφλισκάνω means 'to lose a case', and it may be accompanied by a genitive of penalty (or crime).

39b5

οὗτοι δ᾽ ὑπὸ τῆς ἀληθείας ὠφληκότες μοχθηρίαν καὶ ἀδικίαν: 'but these men are condemned for depravity and wrongdoing by the truth'. ὠφληκότες is the perfect participle of ὀφλισκάνω, to emphasize that it is the state they are already in. While ὀφλισκάνω can (see note 39b4) take a genitive of penalty or crime, both may also stand in the accusative. It is therefore ambiguous whether they are condemned 'for' their vice (crime), or 'to' perpetual vice (penalty), although shades of both meaning may be intended.

39b6

καὶ ἐγώ τε τῷ τιμήματι ἐμμένω καὶ οὗτοι: 'And I am abiding by my penalty, and they by theirs.' Supply τῷ τιμήματι and ἐμμένουσι after οὗτοι. It is not wholly clear what their penalty is, but we may suppose that Socrates is referring to an intrinsic punishment, or some damage to the ψυχή, the part of us 'which is improved by right and destroyed by wrong' (see *Crito* 47d).

39b7

ταῦτα . . . οὕτως καὶ ἔδει σχεῖν: 'these things actually had to turn out in this way'. For ἔχω here and in the next line, see note 22a5. The aorist of ἔχω is used in this line to denote entrance into this condition, hence to 'turn out' (see note 19a1). Socrates presents it as expected and natural that he should be convicted, but also 'reasonable' ('μετρίως') that those who convicted him should suffer the consequences (see note 39b5) of their wrongdoing.

39c1

Τὸ δὲ . . . μετὰ τοῦτο: 'And now', literally 'with respect to the (thing) after this'.

39c2

ἐνταῦθα ἐν ᾧ: 'at that time when', literally 'there, in which (time)'.

39c3

ὅταν μέλλωσιν ἀποθανεῖσθαι: 'whenever they are about to die'. ἀποθανεῖσθαι is the future infinitive of ἀποθνήσκω. The idea that men acquire prophetic power at the moment of death was a common ancient belief. See, for example, *Iliad* 22.358–60 where Hector prophesies that Achilles will be killed by Paris at the Scaean Gate, and *Iliad* 16.851–4, where Patroclus predicts Hector's death.

**A
Level**

39c5

πολὺ χαλεπωτέραν ... ἢ οἵαν ἐμὲ ἀπεκτόνατε: 'more difficult to bear than the punishment of death which you have given me', literally 'than the sort you have killed me with'. Socrates sounds particularly resentful as he predicts their punishment here.

39c6

εἴργασθε: perfect of ἐργάζομαι.

39c7

ἀπαλλάξεσθαι τοῦ διδόναι ἔλεγχον: 'that you would escape giving an account' or 'granting a cross-examination'. For the sense of ἔλεγχον see note 21b.

39c8

τὸ δὲ ὑμῖν πολὺ ἐναντίον ἀποβήσεται: 'whereas for you by far the opposite will result'. ἀποβήσεται is the deponent future of ἀποβαίνω, while for τὸ δὲ see 23a5.

39d1

πλείους: contracted form of πλείονες. See *Oxford Grammar of Classical Greek* p. 36.

νῦν ἐγὼ κατεῖχον: 'just now I had been restraining'. νῦν may refer to the immediate past. Socrates claims that he has actually been protecting his accusers from excessive scrutinization.

39d2

ὅσῳ: 'in so far as', 'by the extent to which'.

39d4

ἐπισχήσειν τοῦ ὀνειδίζειν τινὰ: 'you will prevent anyone from reproaching'. ἐπισχήσειν is the future infinitive of ἐπέχω, 'to hold someone (accusative) back from something (genitive)'.

39d5

ὀρθῶς: 'correctly'. ὀρθός means 'straight' or 'upright', and thus 'right' or 'correct'.

39d6

αὕτη ἡ ἀπαλλαγὴ: 'this escape', i.e. from giving an account of one's life.

39d7

ἐκείνη: supply ἡ ἀπαλλαγὴ. This is explained by μὴ ... βέλτιστος.

καλλίστη καὶ ῥᾴστη: irregular superlatives of καλός and ῥᾴδιος.

κολούειν: 'to put down'. The word literally means to 'cut short', but is used metaphorically of cutting something down to size.

39d8

A
Level

ὅπως ἔσται ὡς βέλτιστος: 'to be as good as possible'. For ὅπως see note 36c7. βέλτιστος is used as the superlative of ἀγαθός, particularly with reference to virtue (the alternative ἄριστος is normally used of ability).

39d10

ἀπαλλάττομαι: 'I have finished with' (literally 'I depart from'), taken with the participle μαντευσάμενος.

39e1

ἡδέως ἂν διαλεχθείην: 'I would like to speak with', literally 'I would gladly speak with'. διαλεχθείην is a passive deponent potential optative, and aorist by aspect.

ὑπὲρ: 'concerning'. It could also mean 'on behalf of', as Socrates goes on to say that death must not be a bad thing.

39e2

ἐν ᾧ: 'while', 'during (the time) which'.

οἱ ἄρχοντες: probably referring to the Eleven (see note 37c1).

39c3

ἀσχολίαν ἄγουσι: 'are busy', literally 'are carrying out business'.

ἔρχομαι οἷ: 'I have not yet gone to the place where', i.e. to the Eleven, to be taken away.

τοσοῦτον χρόνον: 'for so long a time', i.e. until they are ready to take me.

40a1

ἕως ἔξεστιν: 'for as long as it is possible'. ἕως here means 'while' rather than 'until'.

τὸ νυνί μοι συμβεβηκὸς τί ποτε νοεῖ: 'what in the world the thing which has just now happened to me means'. An example of prolepsis (see note 21e5), while συμβεβηκὸς is the perfect participle of συμβαίνω.

40a3

ὑμᾶς γὰρ δικαστὰς καλῶν ὀρθῶς ἂν καλοίην: καλῶν is the participle of καλέω. The point is that those who found him guilty are not judges as they have not voted in accordance with justice. See also note 18a7 and the note on the jury's vote on the penalty.

40a4

ἡ γὰρ εἰωθυῖά μοι μαντικὴ ἡ τοῦ δαιμονίου: 'For the prophetic (voice) of the divinity which I have become accustomed to'. εἰωθυῖά is the perfect participle of the verb ἔθω. This is a vague concept which Socrates referred to earlier (31d) as a 'sort of voice which comes, and when it comes it always turns me away from something I am intending to do, but never urges me on'. ἡ μαντική, however, may also mean 'the prophetic faculty', rather than an actual 'voice'. The word δαιμόνιον is also incredibly difficult to pin down. A δαιμόνιον is something

A Level

related to a δαίμων, which may mean: divine power itself (while θεός is the god in person); simply a god or goddess (equivalent to θεός); Fate or Fortune; a minor deity or spirit intermediate between gods and men. Thus, Socrates may here be saying that he actually is under the protection of a particular spirit, or could be referring to some sort of transcendental, enlightened thought, or even just to his own 'voice of reason' (see also Introduction – 'The charge against Socrates').

40a5

ἐν μὲν τῷ πρόσθεν χρόνῳ παντὶ: 'all the time in the past'.

πυκνὴ: 'unremitting'. Its most basic meaning is 'close' or 'crowded', and thus 'frequent' or 'continuous'.

40a6

πάνυ ἐπὶ σμικροῖς: 'on very small matters'. πάνυ is placed before the preposition for emphasis.

40a7

καὶ αὐτοί: καὶ is adverbial here, and αὐτοί agrees with the subject of ὁρᾶτε.

40a8

ἅ γε δὴ οἰηθείη ἄν τις καὶ νομίζεται: 'which undoubtedly someone might think and are generally believed'. ἅ is the object of οἰηθείη, and the subject of νομίζεται. The potential optative is used for what is likely, and the indicative for what is actually the case. This, and the emphatic particles, stress the universality of the idea that death is the worst evil.

40b2

τὸ τοῦ θεοῦ σημεῖον: 'the god's sign'. See above, note 40a4. Xenophon also says that a divinity 'gave signs' (σημαίνειν *Memorabilia* 1.1.2) to Socrates.

ἀνέβαινον ἐνταυθοῖ ἐπὶ τὸ δικαστήριον: 'I came up here before the court'. For ἀναβαίνω in this sense, see note 18d4.

40b3

οὐδαμοῦ: 'in any place', 'at any point', a compound negative, so strengthening οὔτε.

40b6

ἠναντίωται: perfect of ἐναντιόομαι.

40b7

ὑπολαμβάνω: 'I suppose' (here and at 40c1).

40b8

οὐκ ἔσθ᾽ ὅπως: 'it is impossible that', literally 'there is not how'.

40c1

τὸ τεθνάναι: 'being dead', see note 38e5.

A
Level

40c5

Ἐννοήσωμεν δὲ καὶ τῇδε: 'Let us consider also in this way'. Ἐννοήσωμεν is an exhortative subjunctive.

ὡς πολλὴ ἐλπίς ἐστιν ἀγαθὸν αὐτὸ εἶναι: 'how great is the reason to believe that it (i.e. death) is good'. ἐλπίς is a 'hope' or 'expectation', but may also mean 'a reason to expect *or* believe'.

40c6

δυοῖν θάτερόν: 'one of two things'. θάτερόν is crasis for τό ἕτερον, and δυοῖν is genitive (see *Oxford Grammar of Classical Greek* p. 54).

ἢ γὰρ . . .: 'For it is either . . .'.

οἷον μηδὲν εἶναι μηδὲ αἴσθησιν μηδεμίαν μηδενὸς ἔχειν τὸν τεθνεῶτα: 'such that the dead man is nothing and has no perception of anything'. The accusative τὸν τεθνεῶτα is the subject of the infinitives. Notice the piling up of negatives (see note 18d5) to stress the total nothingness of death.

40c8

κατὰ τὰ λεγόμενα: 'according to what is said', i.e. widespread opinion.

μεταβολή τις τυγχάνει οὖσα: 'it happens to be a sort of change'.

40c9

μετοίκησις . . . τοῦ τόπου τοῦ ἐνθένδε: 'migration from this place here'. μετοίκησις is literally a 'change of abode', here followed by the genitive of place from which.

τῇ ψυχῇ: 'for the soul'. See note 39b6. Plato's theory of the soul, and its division into three parts (see particularly the *Republic*), had not yet been fully developed at this stage in his writing.

40c10

καὶ εἴτε . . . μία νύξ: a particularly long sentence. Socrates now expands on the first of the two options. If death is complete nothingness, Socrates argues that it would be a good thing, as anyone who was asked to compare a dreamless night's sleep with other days and nights would choose the dreamless night as better and more pleasant. The word εἴτε ('if') looks forward to εἰ δ᾽ αὖ at 40e4, where he develops the idea of the transmigration of the soul.

40d2

ἂν οἶμαι: 'I think'. The indicative is only used with ἄν in the past tenses, so cannot here go with the present οἶμαι. Instead, it prepares us for ἂν εὑρεῖν at 40e1 seven lines later. The repetition of ἄν, and of οἶμαι ἄν at 40d8, signposts the indefinite flavour of the whole sentence.

εἴ τινα ἐκλεξάμενον δέοι ταύτην τὴν νύκτα: 'if it were necessary for anyone to pick out that night'. δέοι is properly followed by the infinitive εἰπεῖν (40d6), but in translation it is easiest to translate each of the participles here as infinitives.

40d3

οὕτω κατέδαρθεν: 'he slept so deeply'. κατέδαρθεν is the aorist of καταδαρθάνω, and the prefix κατα- strenghtens the notion of the verb (hence 'sleep deeply').

**A
Level**

40d4

τὰς ἄλλας νύκτας τε καὶ ἡμέρας τὰς τοῦ βίου τοῦ ἑαυτοῦ ἀντιπαραθέντα ταύτῃ τῇ νυκτὶ: 'to compare both the other nights and the other days of his life with that night'. ἀντιπαραθέντα is the aorist participle of ἀντιπαρατίθημι (translate as infinitive, see note 40d2), literally 'to place something beside and opposite', and thus 'to compare x (accusative) with y (dative)'.

40d6

δέοι σκεψάμενον εἰπεῖν: 'to give it consideration and to say'. δέοι is here repeated redundantly (see 40d3).

πόσας ἄμεινον καὶ ἥδιον ἡμέρας καὶ νύκτας ταύτης τῆς νυκτὸς βεβίωκεν: 'for how many days and nights he has lived better and more pleasantly than that night'. The accusatives πόσας ... ἡμέρας καὶ νύκτας express time how long, ἄμεινον and ἥδιον are comparative adverbs, and ταύτης τῆς νυκτὸς is a genitive of comparison.

40d8

μὴ ὅτι ... ἀλλὰ: 'that not only ... but ...'. Literally, 'not (to say) that ... but ...'.

ἰδιώτην: 'a private person', 'a normal person'.

τὸν μέγαν βασιλέα ... αὐτὸν: 'the great king himself', i.e. the king of Persia, known for being incredibly rich and happy. If even he would choose unconscious sleep as superior to his normal life, then the state of nothingness must be a good thing.

40e1

ἂν εὑρεῖν: 'would find'. εὑρεῖν is an infinitive in indirect speech after οἶμαι, to represent the optative of a remote future conditional in direct speech.

εὐαριθμήτους ... ταύτας πρὸς τὰς ἄλλας ἡμέρας καὶ νύκτας: 'that they were few in comparison with the other days and nights'. εὐαρίθμητος literally means 'easily countable', and therefore 'few'.

40e2

τοιοῦτον: 'such a thing', i.e. nothingness.

40e3

οὐδὲν πλείων: 'no more'.

ὁ πᾶς χρόνος: 'the whole of time'. πᾶς comes between the article and the noun when it denotes totality.

φαίνεται ... εἶναι: see note 22c4.

40e4

οὕτω δὴ: 'in this case'.

εἰ δ᾽ αὖ οἷον ἀποδημῆσαί ἐστιν ὁ θάνατος: 'But if on the other hand, death is like going away'. ἀποδημέω is the term for 'leaving the city' or 'going abroad'. Socrates now considers whether death is a good thing if it involves the transmigration of the soul.

**A
Level**

40e6

ὡς ἄρα: 'namely that', with ἄρα suggesting scepticism. With this, and the words τὰ λεγόμενα (40c8, and 40e5), Socrates implies that he prefers the idea that death is nothingness.

40e7

τούτου: genitive of comparison after μεῖζον (irregular comparative of μέγας).

41a1

εἰς Ἅιδου: 'to the house of Hades'. Like English, Greek may use the genitive alone, with a word like 'house' or 'dwelling' implied (e.g. 'I'm going to James' tomorrow').

ἀπαλλαγεὶς τουτωνὶ τῶν φασκόντων δικαστῶν εἶναι: 'having escaped from these men here who claim to be judges'.

41a2

τοὺς ὡς ἀληθῶς δικαστάς: 'the real judges'.

41a3

Μίνως τε καὶ Ῥαδάμανθυς καὶ Αἰακὸς καὶ Τριπτόλεμος: attracted into the case of the relative οἵπερ, when the accusative would be expected after δικαστάς.

Minos and Rhadamanthus were brothers, and the sons of Zeus and Europa. In life Minos was king of Crete, most famous for building the labyrinth to house the Minotaur, while Rhadamanthus was king over the islands of the Aegean. After death both became judges in the Underworld. Aeacus was also a child of Zeus and a mythological king of Aegina before he became a judge in Hades. In the *Gorgias* (523e), Rhadamanthus tries the souls from Asia, Aeacus tries those from Europe, and Minos gets the final decision if there is doubt. Triptolemus is usually described as the son of a king of Eleusis. He is connected to Demeter and the Eleusinian Mysteries, and was said to have brought the plough and agriculture to man. This is the only place in which he is named as one of the judges of the Underworld.

41a6

Ὀρφεῖ ... καὶ Μουσαίῳ καὶ Ἡσιόδῳ καὶ Ὁμήρῳ: four men associated with music and poetry.

Orpheus and Musaeus were mythical singers. Orpheus' music was said to have power over the natural world, and he is most famous for his failed attempt to rescue his wife Eurydice from the Underworld. Musaeus is connected to Orpheus either as his son, follower or teacher, and is usually associated with mystic hymns and oracular verse.

Hesiod and Homer were the two poets most admired by the Greeks. Homer needs little introduction, while Hesiod, who was roughly a contemporary of Homer, is most famous for the *Theogony*, which describes the origins of the world, and the didactic poem *Works and Days*.

41a7

συγγενέσθαι ... ἐπὶ πόσῳ ἄν τις δέξαιτ' ἂν ὑμῶν: 'how much would any of you give to meet', literally 'for how much would any of you welcome (the chance)

A
Level

to meet'. The repetition of ἄν here emphasizes τις and ὑμῶν, to stress how widespread the desire to meet these men would be.

ἐγὼ μὲν: see note 23b4.

41b1

ἔμοιγε καὶ αὐτῷ: 'for me even myself', or 'for me personally'.

41b2

ὁπότε ἐντύχοιμι: 'whenever I met with'. Optative used in an indefinite construction.

Παλαμήδει καὶ Αἴαντι τῷ Τελαμῶνος: 'Palamedes and Ajax, the son of Telamon'. Socrates mentions two Greek heroes of the Trojan War who met tragic ends owing to unfair judgements against them.

Palamedes was known for getting Odysseus to come to Troy against his wishes. When Palamedes encourages the Greeks to return home, Odysseus hides gold and a forged letter from Priam (king of Troy) in his tent. The Greeks accuse him of being a traitor and put him to death by stoning.

Ajax is an important character in the *Iliad*, known particularly for his strength and bravery. After the battle, Ajax and Odysseus both claim that they deserve to be awarded Achilles' armour. Through persuasiveness and cunning Odysseus wins the debate, and Ajax commits suicide out of shame.

41b3

εἴ τις ἄλλος: 'whoever else . . .', equivalent of 'if there is anyone else who . . .'.

ἀντιπαραβάλλοντι τὰ ἐμαυτοῦ πάθη: 'and compared my experiences', dative agreeing with ἔμοιγε (41b1). πάθος goes like γένος (see note 18b2).

41b5

καὶ δὴ τὸ μέγιστον: 'and indeed the greatest thing would be', supply ἄν εἴη.

41b6

ἐξετάζοντα καὶ ἐρευνῶντα . . . διάγειν: '(for me) to spend my time examining and investigating'. The participles are accusative to agree with the unexpressed subject of διάγειν (με).

ὥσπερ τοὺς ἐνταῦθα: 'as (I do) those here'.

τίς αὐτῶν: '(to find out) which of them'. τίς introduces an indirect question.

41b7

ἐπὶ πόσῳ δ᾽ ἄν τις δέξαιτο ἐξετάσαι: see note 41a7.

41b8

τὸν ἐπὶ Τροίαν ἀγαγόντα τὴν πολλὴν στρατιάν: this refers to Agamemnon, the leader of the Greek expedition to Troy.

41c1

Ὀδυσσέα ἢ Σίσυφον: both known for cunning and dishonesty. Sisyphus was a mythical king of Ephyra (later called Corinth) who was punished for his deceitfulness by being made to roll a boulder up a hill, which fell back down as

A Level

soon as it reached the top, for eternity. For examples of Odysseus' duplicity, see notes on Palamedes and Ajax.

41c2

ἄλλους μυρίους ἄν τις εἴποι: 'countless others who someone might mention', supply οὕς after μυρίους.

41c4

ἀμήχανον ἂν εἴη εὐδαιμονίας: 'it would be an extraordinary amount of happiness'. ἀμήχανος means 'helpless', 'impossible', and 'extraordinary' ('impossible to describe').
δήπου: 'presumably', used ironically.
τούτου γε ἕνεκα: i.e. for conversing with men and examining them.

41c5

τά τε γὰρ ἄλλα . . . καὶ ἤδη . . .: 'For in other respects . . . and furthermore . . .'. τά . . . ἄλλα is accusative of respect and ἤδη here introduces an additional idea.

41c7

εἴπερ γε τὰ λεγόμενα ἀληθῆ ἐστίν: Socrates again reminds us that death may not be like this.

41c9

ἕν τι τοῦτο διανοεῖσθαι ἀληθές, ὅτι: 'to regard one thing, the following, as true, that . . .'.

41d1

οὐκ ἔστιν ἀνδρὶ ἀγαθῷ κακὸν οὐδέν: 'no evil can come to a good man'.

41d3

οὐδὲ τὰ ἐμὰ νῦν ἀπὸ τοῦ αὐτομάτου γέγονεν: 'and my current situation has not come about by chance'. For ἀπὸ τοῦ αὐτομάτου, see note 38c5.

41d5

πραγμάτων: 'from troubles'.

41e1

τοῦτο αὐτοῖς ἄξιον μέμφεσθαι: 'they deserve blame for this', literally 'this is worthy to blame them with' (with ἐστί supplied).
τοσόνδε μέντοι αὐτῶν δέομαι: 'however I ask this much of them'. δέομαι here means 'to ask for something (accusative) from someone (genitive)'.

41e2

ἐπειδὰν ἡβήσωσι: 'when they grow up'. For the construction see note 37c2.

41e3

ταὐτὰ ταῦτα λυποῦντες ἅπερ ἐγὼ ὑμᾶς ἐλύπουν: 'bothering them with these same things with which I used to bother you'. λυπέω takes a double accusative and for ταὐτὰ ταῦτα see note 19c1.

A Level

41e4

του: for τινος (see note 37b4).

41e5

πρότερον . . . ἢ ἀρετῆς: 'before virtue', literally 'sooner . . . than'.

ἐὰν δοκῶσί τι εἶναι μηδὲν ὄντες: 'if they think they are something, when they are nothing'. For μηδὲν here, see note 22e2.

41e7

ὧν δεῖ: 'for what they should', with relative attraction and omitted antecedent.

42a1

ἐὰν ταῦτα ποιῆτε: 'if you do these things'. The present subjunctive is used by aspect, as this refers to ongoing action rather than a one-off event.

πεπονθὼς ἐγὼ ἔσομαι: 'I will have experienced'. The future of εἰμί used with the perfect participle as a periphrastic future perfect.

42a2

ὥρα ἀπιέναι: 'it is time to depart', supply ἐστί.

42a3

ἀποθανουμένῳ . . . βιωσομένοις: future participles to express purpose.

42a4

πλὴν ἢ: 'except'.

**A
Level**

Vocabulary

While there is no Defined Vocabulary List for A Level, words in the OCR Defined Vocabulary List for AS are marked with * so that students can quickly see the vocabulary with which they should be particularly familiar.

ἁβρύνω	treat delicately; mid., put on airs, be conceited	ἀλήθεια, -ας, ἡ	truth
		τῇ ἀληθείᾳ	in truth
*ἀγαθός, -ή, -όν	good, virtuous	*ἀληθής, -ές	true
ἀγανακτέω	be annoyed, angry	ὡς ἀληθῶς	really
*ἀγνοέω	not know	ἁλίσκομαι, aor.	be captured, convicted
*ἄγω, aor. ἤγαγον	lead	ἑάλων, perf.	
*ἀδελφός, -οῦ, ὁ	brother	ἑάλωκα	
ἄδηλος, -ον	unknown	*ἀλλά	but
*ἀδικέω	wrong, act unjustly, do injustice to	ἀλλ᾽ ἤ	except
		ἀλλὰ γὰρ	but in fact
*ἀδικία, -ας, ἡ	injustice, wrongdoing	*ἀλλήλων (no nom.)	each other, one
*ἄδικος, -ον	unjust, unfair		another
ἀδύνατος, -ον	impossible	ἀλλοῖος, -α, -ον	different
*ἀεί	always, at every moment	*ἄλλος, -η, -ον	other
ἀεροβατέω	walk on air	ἀλόγιστος, -ον	irrational, foolish
ἀηδής, -ές	unpleasant	ἄλογος, -ον	absurd
ἀθάνατος, -ον	immortal	*ἅμα	at the same time
*Ἀθηναῖος, -α, -ον	Athenian	ἀμαθής, -ές	ignorant, foolish
Αἰακός, -οῦ, ὁ	Aeacus	ἀμαθία, -ας, ἡ	ignorance, folly
Ἅιδης, -ου, ὁ	Hades	ἁμάρτημα, -ατος, τό	failing, error
αἰνίττομαι	pose riddles	ἀμείβω	exchange; mid., reply,
*αἱρέω, aor. εἷλον	take; mid., choose, prefer		move from (ἐκ +
*αἰσθάνομαι (+ acc. or gen.), aor. ἠσθόμην	notice, perceive		gen.) to (acc.)
		ἀμείνων, -ονος (comp. of ἀγαθός)	better
αἴσθησις, -εως, ἡ	perception	ἀμελέω (+ gen.)	neglect, have no care
*αἰσχύνομαι	feel ashamed		for
*αἰτία, -ας, ἡ	cause	ἀμήχανος, -ον	helpless, impossible,
αἰτίαν ἔχειν	be accused		extraordinary
*αἴτιος, η, ον	responsible	*ἀμφί (+ acc.)	around
*ἀκούω (+ acc. of thing, + gen. of person), perf. ἀκήκοα	hear, listen to	τούς ἀμφὶ Ἄνυτον	Anytus and his followers
		*ἀμφότερος, -α, -ον	both
		*ἄν	(hypothetical/indefinite particle)
ἀκροάομαι (+ acc. of thing, + gen. of person)	listen to	* ἄν (+ past indic. or opt.)	would, could, might
		* ἄν (+ subj.)	(indefinite construction)

ἄν (contraction of ἐάν; + subj.) — if

*ἀναβαίνω, aor. ἀνέβην — go up, appear before the court

ἀναβιβάζω — cause to go up; mid., call to the stand as a witness

*ἀναγιγνώσκω, aor. ἀνέγνων — to read

ἀναγκαῖος, -α, -ον — necessary

*ἀνάγκη, -ης, ἡ — necessity

ἀναζητέω — investigate

ἀναιρέω, aor. ἀνεῖλον — respond (esp. of an oracle)

ἀναισχυντία, -ας, ἡ — shamelessness

ἀναλαμβάνω, aor. ἀνέλαβον — take up, examine

ἀνάξιος, -α, -ον — unworthy

ἀναπείθω — persuade, mislead

ἀναφέρω, fut. ἀνοίσω — refer

ἀνέλεγκτος, -ον — irrefutable

ἀνελεύθερος, -ον — servile, unsuitable for a free man

ἀνέλπιστος, -ον — unlooked for, unexpected

ἀνεξέταστος, -ον — unexamined, without examination

ἀνερωτάω, aor. ἀνηρόμην — ask, question

ἀνήρ, ἀνδρός, ὁ — man

ἀνθρώπινος, -η, -ον — human, of man, attainable by man

*ἄνθρωπος, -ου, ὁ — human, man

*ἀντί (+ gen.) — instead of

ἀντιβόλησις, -εως, ἡ — entreaty

ἀντιπαραβάλλω — compare

ἀντιπαρατίθημι, aor. part. -παραθείς — compare

ἀντιτιμάομαι — propose as a counter-penalty

ἀντωμοσία, -ας, ἡ — affidavit, sworn accusation

Ἄνυτος, -ου, ὁ — Anytus

ἀξία, -ας, ἡ — worth, due, deserts

*ἄξιός, -α, -ον (+ gen.) — worth, worthy of

ἀξιόχρεως, -ων — trustworthy, worthy of (+ gen.)

*ἀξιόω — deem or think worthy; suppose; (with inf.) expect, ask

ἀπαλλαγή, -ῆς, ἡ — release, escape

ἀπαλλάττω, aor. pass. ἀπηλλάγην — set free from (+ gen.); mid. and pass., be set free from, escape from (+ gen.)

*ἅπας, -ασα, -αν — all

ἀπαυθαδίζομαι — act boldly, act arrogantly

ἀπειθέω (+ dat.) — disobey

ἄπειμι, pres. part. ἀπιών, impf. ἀπῇα — (will) go away

ἀπελαύνω — drive away

ἀπεχθάνομαι, aor. ἀπηχθόμην — be hated

ἀπέχθεια, -ας, ἡ — hatred, enmity

*ἀπό (+ gen.) — from

ἀποβαίνω, fut. ἀποβήσομαι — turn out, result

ἀποδείκνυμι, aor. ἀπέδειξα — show, demonstrate

ἀποδημέω — go abroad, go away

ἀποδημία, -ας, ἡ — going away, migration

*ἀποθνήσκω, fut. ἀποθανοῦμαι — die

*ἀποκρίνομαι — reply

ἀποκρύπτω — hide, conceal; (with double acc.) hide something from someone

*ἀποκτείνω, perf. ἀπέκτονα — kill

ἀπολείπω, aor. ἀπέλιπον — leave behind, abandon

Ἀπολλόδωρος, -ου, ὁ — Apollodorus

ἀπολογέομαι — speak in one's defence, defend oneself, reply

ἀπολύω — set free; mid. refute

*ἀπορέω — be at a loss, perplexed

*ἀπορία, -ας, ἡ — difficulty, lack

ἄπορος, -ον — hard to deal with, difficult

ἀποτίνω, aor. ἀπέτεισα — pay

ἀποτρέπω — deter

ἀποφαίνω, fut. ἀποφανῶ — show, declare

ἀποφεύγω, fut. ἀποφεύξομαι — escape; get off from, be acquitted

ἀποψηφίζομαι — (vote to) acquit

*ἄρα — then, indeed, after all, in fact

*ἆρα — (introduces a question)

*ἀργύριον, -ου, τό — money, silver

*ἀρετή, -ῆς, ἡ — excellence, virtue

*ἀριθμός, -οῦ, ὁ — number

Ἀριστοφάνης, -ους, ὁ — Aristophanes

*ἄρτι — recently

*ἀρχή, ῆς, ἡ — beginning; authority, magistracy, office

*ἄρχομαι — begin

ἄρχων, -οντος, ὁ — magistrate, official

ἀστός, -οῦ, ὁ — citizen

ἀσχολία, -ας, ἡ — occupation, business
ἀσχολίαν ἄγω — be busy
*ἄτε (+ part.) — since, because
ἀτεχνῶς — simply, absolutely
ἀτιμάζω — dishonour, belittle
*αὖ — again, in turn
*αὖθις — again, hereafter
αὐτόθι — there
αὐτόματος, -η, -ον — of one's own accord, spontaneous
ἀπὸ τοῦ αὐτομάτου — naturally, by chance
*αὐτός, -ή, -όν — (adjective) himself, herself, itself, themselves; (pronoun in oblique cases) him, her, it, them
*ὁ αὐτός — the same
αὐτοσχεδιάζω — improvise, act hastily, judge hastily
αὐτοφώρος, -ον — in the act, red-handed
ἐπ' αὐτοφώρῳ καταλαμβάνω — catch in the act, catch openly
ἀφθονία, -ας, ἡ — freedom from envy, plenty, abundance
ἀφίημι, aor. part. ἀφείς — throw away
*ἀφικνέομαι, aor. ἀφικόμην — come, arrive
ἄχθομαι — be grieved, angered
*βαρύς, -εῖα, -ύ — heavy, burdensome, grievous
*βασιλεύς, -έως, ὁ — king
βέλτιστος, -η, -ον (superl. of ἀγαθός) — best
βελτίων, -ονος (comp. of ἀγαθός) — better
*βίος, -ου, ὁ — life
βιόω, fut. βιώσομαι — live
βιωτός, -όν — to be lived, worth living
*βλάπτω, aor. pass. ἐβλάβην — harm
*βοηθέω (+ dat.) — help
*βούλομαι — want
*βραδύς, -εῖα, -ύ — slow
*γάρ — for, that is to say
*γε — (emphasizes preceding word) indeed; at least, at any rate
γεωργικός, ή, όν — agricultural, to do with farming
*γῆ, -ῆς, ἡ — earth, ground
*γίγνομαι, aor. ἐγενόμην, perf. γέγονα — happen, become, turn out, result, be born; perf., have arisen, be

*γιγνώσκω, fut. γνώσομαι, aor. ἔγνων, perf. ἔγνωκα — come to know, realize
Γοργίας, -ου, ὁ — Gorgias
*γοῦν — at all events, at any rate
γραφή, -ῆς, ἡ — indictment
*γράφω — write; mid., indict
*γυνή, γυναικός, ἡ — woman
δαιμονίον, -ου, τό — divinity
*δὲ — and, but
* μὲν ... δὲ ... — on the one hand ... on the other hand ...; often best to omit μέν and translate δέ as 'but'
*δεῖ (+ acc. + inf.) — it is necessary
δείδω, perf. δέδια — fear (perfect frequently used for present)
*δείκνυμι — show
*δεινός, -ή, -όν — fearful, dangerous; skilful, clever
Δελφοί, -ῶν, οἱ — Delphi
*δέομαι — ask for something (acc.) from someone (gen.); (+ gen.) need
*δεσμός, -οῦ, ὁ — chains
δεσμωτήριον, -ου, τό — prison
*δέχομαι — receive, choose, prefer
δέω, aor. ἐδέησα (+ gen.) — lack, need
δέω, aor. ἔδησα, perf. pass. infin. δεδέσθαι — bind, imprison
*δή — (emphatic particle) indeed, in truth, then, so, accordingly
*δῆλος, -η, -ον — clear
δημηγορία, -ας, ἡ — speech in the assembly; popular oratory, clap-trap
δημιουργός, -οῦ, ὁ — craftsman, workman
*δήπου — of course, indeed, presumably, I suppose
οὐ γὰρ δήπου ... — for surely it is not the case that ...
Δία — see Ζεύς
*διά (+ acc.) — because of, for the sake of
διαβάλλω — slander, defame
διαβολή, -ῆς, ἡ — slander, prejudice, enmity

διάγω	spend one's time	ἐθίζω, perf. εἴθισμαι	become accustomed
διαλέγομαι (+ dat.), aor. διελέχθην, perf.		ἔθω, perf. εἴωθα	become accustomed
		*εἰ	if
*διειλεγμαι	converse with, talk to	εἰ μή	if . . . not, unless, expect
διαμυθολογέω	converse, talk	εἴπερ	if indeed
διανοέομαι	think, reason, think of, regard	εἰδέναι	infinitive of οἶδα
		εἶδον	aorist of ὁράω
διανοία, -ας, ἡ	intention	εἶεν	well then
διασκοπέω	examine, consider well	εἶλον	aorist of αἱρέω
διατριβή, -ῆς, ἡ	way of life, conversation, spending of time	*εἰμί, fut. ἔσομαι, impf. ἦν	be
		τῷ ὄντι	really, in truth
διαφεύγω	escape	*εἶμι, impf. ᾖα, pres. part. ἰών	(will) go, come
*διαφθείρω	destroy, corrupt		
*διδάσκω	teach, inform	εἶπον	aorist of λέγω
*δίδωμι, pres. part. διδούς	give	εἰρωνεύομαι	be ironic, be devious
		*εἰς (+ acc.)	to, into
διερωτάω	ask	*εἷς, μία, ἕν	one
διθύραμβος, -ου, ὁ	dithyramb	*εἶτα	then
δικάζω	judge, be a judge	*εἴτε	whether
*δίκαιος, -α, -ον	just, right, fair	* εἴτε . . . εἴτε	whether . . . or
δίκαιός εἰμι (+ infinitive)	have a right to	εἴωθα	perfect of ἐθω
		*ἐκ, ἐξ (+ gen.)	from, among
δικαστήριον, -ου, τό	court	*ἕκαστος, -η, -ον	each
δικαστής, -οῦ, ὁ	judge, juror, juryman	ἑκάστοτε	each time, on every occasion
*δίκη, -ης, ἡ	judgement, justice, lawsuit, case, trial, charge		
		*ἑκάτερος, -η, -ον	each (of two)
		*ἐκεῖ	there
δίκας φεύγω	be prosecuted on a charge	*ἐκεῖνος, -η, -ο	that, those
		ἐκείνως	in that way
διττός, -ή, -όν	double, twofold	ἐκλέγω	pick out, select
*διώκω	pursue	ἐκτίνω, fut. ἐκτείσω, aor. ἐξέτεισα	pay in full
*δοκέω	think; seem, be reputed		
*δουλεύω	be a slave, be enslaved	*ἐκφεύγω	escape
δραχμή, -ῆς, ἡ	drachma	*ἑκών, -οῦσα, -όν	willing
*δύναμαι	be able to	ἔλεγχος, -ου, ὁ	test, account
*δυνατός, -ή, -όν	possible	ἐλέγχω	refute, test, question, cross-examine
δύο, δυοῖν	two		
		ἐλπίς, -ίδος, ἡ	hope, expectation, reason to believe
ἑάλων	aorist of ἁλίσκομαι		
*ἐάν (+ subj.)	if	ἐμαυτόν, -ήν	myself
ἐάντε . . . ἐάντε	if . . . or if, whether . . . or	ἐμμελῶς	modestly, cheaply
		ἐμμένω (+ dat.)	abide by
*ἑαυτόν, -ήν, -ό	himself, herself, itself, themselves	*ἐμός, -ή, -όν	my, of me
		ἐμπίπλημι, perf. ἐμπέπληκα	fill, fill up
ἐβλάβην	aorist passive of βλάπτω		
		*ἐν (+ dat.)	in, at, over
ἐγγυάω	give a pledge; mid., give security, give a guarantee	ἐν ᾧ	while
		ἐναντιόομαι, aor. ἠναντιώθην	oppose, stand in one's way
ἐγγυητής, -οῦ, ὁ	guarantor		
*ἐγγύς (+ gen.)	near	*ἐναντίος, -α, -ον	opposite
*ἐγώ, ἐμοῦ	I	ἐνδεής, -ές (+ gen.)	lacking, in need of
*ἔγωγε	I at least	ἐνδείκνυμι	point out; mid., show, indicate
ἐγῷμαι	crasis of ἐγὼ οἶμαι		
*ἐθέλω	be willing	ἕνδεκα	eleven

*ἕνεκα (+ gen.) — on account of, for the sake of

*ἐνθάδε — here

*ἐνθένδε — from here

ἐνθουσιάζω — be possessed by a god, be inspired

ἐνθυμέομαι — consider

*ἔνιοι, -αι, -α — some

*ἐννοέω — consider

*ἐνταῦθα — here; there; to there

ἐνταυθοῖ — to here, to there

*ἐντεῦθεν — from there; thereupon, as a result

*ἐντυγχάνω, ἐνέτυχον (+ dat.) — meet with

ἐξαιρέω, aor. ἐξεῖλον — take away, remove something (acc.) from someone (gen.)

ἐξελαύνω, fut. ἐξελῶ — drive out

ἐξελέγχω — examine, refute, confute

ἐξεργάζομαι — carry out, perform

ἐξέρχομαι, aor. ἐξῆλθον — go out; go into exile

*ἔξεστι (+ dat. + infin.) — it is possible, it is permitted

ἐξετάζω — examine, scrutinize

ἐξέτασις, -εως, ἡ — investigation

ἔοικα — seem, be likely

ἔπαθον — aorist of πάσχω

ἐπαΐω — profess, understand

ἐπακολουθέω (+ dat.) — follow closely

ἐπεθέμην — aorist middle of ἐπιτίθημι

*ἐπεί — since; for; although

*ἐπειδάν (+ subj.) — whenever

*ἐπειδὴ — since; when

*ἔπειτα — then; besides

ἐπέχω, fut. ἐπισχησω — restrain, hold back someone (acc.) from something (gen.)

*ἐπί (+ acc.) — to, towards, onto, for the sake of

*ἐπί (+ dat.) — on, at, for, for the sake of

ἐπιδείκνυμι, aor. ἐπέδειξα — tell, relate, show make clear

ἐπιδημέω — reside in a place, stay in a city

ἐπιεικής, -ές — reasonable, honourable, fitting, able

ἐπιθυμέω — long, desire

ἐπιμελέομαι (+ gen.) — to have a concern for

*ἐπίσταμαι — know, understand; (+ infinitive) know how to

ἐπιστάτης, -ου, ὁ — trainer, overseer

ἐπιστήμη, -ης, ἡ — knowledge, wisdom

ἐπιστήμων (+ gen.) — acquainted with, versed in

ἐπισχήσω — future of ἐπέχω

ἐπιτίθημι — put on, set upon; mid., attack (+ dat.)

ἐπίφθονος, -ον — jealousy-provoking, odious

ἐπιχειρέω — try, attempt

ἔπος, -ους, τό — word

*ἐργάζομαι, perf. εἴργασμαι — do

ἐρευνάω — seek, examine, investigate

ἐρήμη, -ης, ἡ — undefended case

ἐρήμην κατηγοροῦντες — make accusations in a trial without a defence

*ἔρχομαι, fut. εἶμι, aor. ἦλθον — go

ἐρῶ — future of λέγω

*ἐρωτάω, aor. ἠρόμην — ask

ἔσομαι — future of εἰμί

*ἔσχατος, -η, -ον — furthest, uppermost

*ἑταῖρος, -ου, ὁ — companion, comrade

*ἕτερος — one, the other (of two)

*ἔτι — still, besides, moreover

*ἔτος, -ους, τό — year

*εὐ — well

εὐαρίθμητος, -ον — few, easily countable

εὐδαιμονία, -ας, ἡ — happiness

*εὐδαίμων, -ον — happy, prosperous, fortunate

εὐδοκιμέω — be of good repute, be highly esteemed

εὔελπις, -ιδος — hopeful

εὐεργεσία, -ας, ἡ — benefit, service

εὐεργετέω — do good, benefit

εὐεργέτης, -ου, ὁ — benefactor, well-doer

Εὔηνος, -ου, ὁ — Evenus

*εὐθύς — immediately

*εὑρίσκω, fut. εὑρήσω, aor. εὗρον — find

ἐφεξῆς — successively, to one after another

*ἔχω, impf. εἶχον, aor. ἔσχον, perf. ἔσχηκα — have, possess; (aor. and perf.) obtain, get

* ἔχω + adverb — be

ἔχω + infinitive — be able to

ἔωθεν — at dawn

ἑώρων — imperfect of ὁράω

*ἕως — until, while, as long as

*ζάω, infin. ζῆν   live
ζεῦγος, -ους, τό   yoke; four-horse chariot
*Ζεύς, Διός, ὁ   Zeus
   (acc. Δία)
*ζητέω   seek, investigate
ζήτησις, εως, ἡ   investigation

*ἤ   or (sometimes introducing a question)
*ἤ ... ἤ   either ... or
*ἤ   than, from (in a comparison)
ἤ   (emphatic particle) indeed
ἤ   (introduces open question)
ἦ   3sg imperfect of ἠμί
ἦα   imperfect of εἰμι
ἡβάω   grow up, mature
*ἡγέομαι   think
*ἤδη   now, already, furthermore
*ἡδύς, -εῖα, -ύ, comp.   sweet, pleasant, glad
   ἡδίων, superl.
   ἤδιστος
*ἥκω   have come, come
Ἠλεῖος, -α, -ον   of Elis
ἦλθον   aorist of ἔρχομαι
ἡλικία, -ας, ἡ   age
*ἡμεῖς, ἡμῶν   we
*ἡμέρα, -ας, ἡ   day
ἠμί, 1sg impf ἦν, 3sg   say
   impf ἦ
ἡμίθεος, -ου, ὁ   demigod
ἦν   imperfect of εἰμί
ἦν   1sg imperfect of ἠμί
ἤνεγκα   aorist of φέρω
ἡνίκα   when
ἠρόμην   aorist of ἐρωτάω
Ἡσίοδος, -ου, ὁ   Hesiod
ἡσυχία, -ας, ἡ   peace, quiet
   ἡσύχιαν ἄγω   keep quiet
ἥττων, -ονος (comp.   worse, inferior
   of κακός)
   ἧττον   less

*θάνατος, -ου, ὁ   death, the death penalty
θάτερον   crasis of τὸ ἕτερον
θάττων, -ονος (comp.   faster
   of ταχύς)
*θαυμάζω   amazed at
θαυμάσιος, -α, -ον   wonderful
θέμις, -ιδος, ἡ   custom, right
θεόμαντις, -εως, ὁ   seer

*θεός, -οῦ, ὁ   god
θέω   run
θνήσκω, perf.   die; perf., be dead
   τέθνηκα
θορυβέω   make a noise, interrupt
θρηνέω   wail, lament

-ί   (deictic suffix)
ἰδίᾳ   in private, privately
ἰδιώτης, -ου, ὁ   private person, normal person
ἱκετεία, -ας, ἡ   supplication
*ἵνα (+ subj./opt.)   in order that, so that
Ἱππίας, -ου, ὁ   Hippias
ἱππικός, -ή, -όν   of horses
Ἱππόνικος, -ου, ὁ   Hipponicus
*ἵππος, -ου, ὁ   horse
ἴστε   imperative or 2pl οἶδα
*ἴσως   perhaps, probably
ἴτω   3sg imperative of εἰμι
ἰών   participle of εἰμι

κἀγώ   crasis of καὶ ἐγώ
*καθεύδω   sleep
*καθίστημι   establish, appoint
*καί   and; and yet; even, also
*καί ... καί ...   both ... and ...
καὶ δὴ καί   and in particular
καὶ ταῦτά γε   furthermore
*καίπερ   although
*καίτοι   and yet
κακία, -ας, ἡ   badness, wickedness
*κακός, -ή, -όν   bad, evil
Καλλίας, -ου, ὁ   Callias
καλλύνω   beautify; mid., pride oneself in, be proud
*καλός, -ή, -όν,   fine, good
   superl. κάλλιστος
καλὸς κἀγαθός   crasis of καλὸς καὶ ἀγαθός: fine and good, perfect, admirable, well-bred
κἄν   crasis of καὶ ἄν
κἄν   crasis of καὶ ἐάν
κἄπειτα   crasis of καὶ ἔπειτα
*κατά (+ acc.)   according to, in accordance with, in
*κατά (+ gen.)   against; about, concerning
καταδαρθάνω,   sleep heavily
   aor. κατέδαρθον
κατάδηλος, -ον   visible, manifest
καταλαμβάνω, fut.   catch
   καταλήψομαι

κατασκεδάννυμι,   scatter
   αor. κατεσκέδασα

καταψηφίζομαι   vote against, condemn

κατέρχομαι, αor.   return from exile
   κατῆλθον

κατέχω, impf.   hold back, restrain
   κατεῖχον

*κατηγορέω   accuse, allege

κατηγορία, -ας, ἡ   accusation, charge

κατήγορος, -ου, ὁ   accuser

Κεῖος, -α, -ον   of Ceos

*κελεύω   order

κέρδος, -ους, τό   gain, profit

*κινδυνεύω   run the risk of; be likely
   to (+ infin.)

*κινδύνος, -ου, ὁ   danger

κολούω   restrain

κρείττων, -ονος   better, stronger
   (comp. of ἀγαθός)

*κρίνω   judge, decide

κρίσις, -εως, ἡ   decision, judgement

Κριτόβουλος, -ου,   Critobulus
ὁ

Κρίτων, -ονος, ὁ   Crito

κτῆσις, -εως, ἡ   possession, having

κύων, κυνός, ὁ   dog

*κωλύω   prevent

κωμῳδία, -ας, ἡ   comedy

κωμῳδοποιός, -οῦ,   comic poet
ὁ

*λαμβάνω, αor.   take, get
   ἔλαβον

*λανθάνω   escape one's notice

λατρεία, -ας, ἡ   service

λέγω, fut. ἐρῶ, αor.   say, speak, mention, tell,
   εἶπον   speak about (+ acc.)

Λεοντῖνος, -η, -ον   of Leontini

λογίζομαι   work out, reason,
   consider

*λόγος, -ου, ὁ   word, story, talk, speech,
   account, argument

λοιδορέω   criticize, reproach

*λοιπός, -ή, -όν   remaining, rest of

*λυπέω   vex, distress, bother

λυσιτελεῖ (+ dat.)   it is profitable for, it is
   better for

μακαρίζω   consider happy

*μάλιστα (superl. of   especially
   μάλα)

*μᾶλλον (comp. of   more, rather
   μάλα)

*μανθάνω   learn

μαντεία, -ας, ἡ   prophecy

*μαντεῖον, -ου, τό   oracle

μαντεύομαι   prophesy, consult the
   oracle

μαντικός, -ή, -όν   prophetic

μαρτυρέω   give evidence

μάρτυς, -υρος, ὁ   witness

*μάχη, -ης, ἡ   battle

*μέγας, μεγάλη,   big, great
   μέγα, adv. μέγα,
   comp. μείζων,
   superl. μέγιστος

μειράκιον, -ου, τό   young lad, teenager

Μέλητος, -ου, ὁ   Meletus

*μέλλω   be likely to, intend to; (+
   fut. infin.) be going to

μέμφομαι   blame

*μέν   (signals a coming
   contrast)

*μέν ... δὲ ...   on the one hand ... on
   the other hand ...;
   often best to omit
   μέν and translate δέ
   as 'but'

μεντἄν   crasis of μέντοι ἄν

*μέντοι   however

*μέρος, -ους, τό   part

*μετά (+ acc.)   after

*μετά (+ gen.)   with

μεταβολή, -ῆς, ἡ   change

μεταλαμβάνω   receive as a share

μεταμέλει (+ dat.)   it is a cause of regret

μεταξύ   in the midst

μεταπίπτω, αor.   fall differently, change
   μετέπεσον

μέτεστιν   there is a share of
   something (gen.) to
   someone (dat.)

μετέωρος, -α, -ον   in mid-air, high in the air

   τὰ μετεωρα   astronomical phenomena

μετοίκησις, -εως, ἡ   migration

μέτριος, -α, -ον   moderate, fair

*μή   not (see Oxford
   Grammar of Classical
   Greek p205)

μὴ οὐ (+ subjunctive)   I suspect that ... not, I
   rather think that ...
   not (construction
   used to express
   doubt)

*μηδέ   and ... not, but not, not
   even, nor

μηδέ ... μηδέ   neither ... nor

*μηδείς, μηδεμία,   no one, nothing
   μηδέν

μήν   truly

*μήτε   neither

*μήτε ... μήτε — neither ... nor

μηχανάομαι — devise, contrive

μηχανή, -ῆς, ἡ — way, means

μία — see εἷς

μιαρός, -ά, -όν — stained with blood, polluted, foul

*μικρός, -ά, -όν — small, little

μιμέομαι — imitate, copy

Μίνως, -ωος, ὁ — Minos

μισθόω — rent; mid., hire

μνᾶ, -ᾶς, ἡ — mina

μόγις — with difficulty, with reluctance

*μόνος, -η, -ον, adv. μόνον — only, alone

μόσχος, -ου, ὁ — calf

Μουσαῖος, -ου — Musaeus

μοχθηρία, -ας, ἡ — depravity, wickedness

μυρίος, -α, -ον — countless, immense

*νέος, -α, -ον — new, young

ἐκ νέου — from youth

οἱ νέοι — the youth, young men

νή (+ acc.) — by

*νικάω — win, be victorious

νοέω — think, mean

*νομίζω — think, consider, believe

*νόμος, -ου, ὁ — law, custom

*νοῦς, νοῦ — mind

*νῦν — now

νῦν δέ — as it is

νυνδὴ — just now

νυνὶ — right now

*νύξ, νυκτός, ἡ — night

*ξένος, -ου, ὁ — stranger, foreigner, friend

*ὁ, ἡ, τό — (definite article) the

ὁ δέ (without noun) — but he

τὸ δέ — whereas

*ὅδε, ἥδε, τόδε — this, this here, the following

τῇδε — in this way

ὀδύρομαι — lament, bewail

Ὀδυσσεύς, -έως, ὁ — Odysseus

*ὅθεν — from where

*οἵ — to where

*οἶδα — know

οἰκεῖος — belonging to one's family, one's own

οἱ οἰκεῖοι — relatives, family

*οἴκοθεν — from home

οἰκονομία, -ας, ἡ — managing the household

οἶκτος, -ου, ὁ — lamentation

οἴομαι or οἶμαι, aor. ᾠήθην — think, consider

*οἷος, -α, -ον — of what sort, such as, as

οἷον — like

οἷος (+ superl.) — the most ... kind

*οἷός τε + εἰμί or γίγνομαι (+ inf.) — be able

οἴσω — future of φέρω

*ὀλίγος, -η, -ον — few, little

ὀλίγου (δεῖ) — almost

Ὀλυμπία, -ας, ἡ, loc. Ὀλυμπίασι(ν) — Olympia

Ὅμηρος, -ου, ὁ — Homer

*ὅμως — yet, nevertheless

ὄναρ, ὄνειρος, τό — dream

ὀνειδίζω — rebuke, reproach someone (dat.) for something (acc.)

*ὄνομα, -ατος, τό — name, reputation

ὀνόματι — by name, called

ὀξύς, -εῖα, -ύ — sharp, quick

ὅπη — how, in whatever way

*ὅπλα, -ων, τά — weapons, arms

ὁπόθεν — from where

ὅποι — to where

ὁπότερος, -α, -ον — which (of two)

*ὅπως — how, that, in order that, to

οὐκ ἔσθ᾽ ὅπως ... — it is not possible that ...

*ὁράω, impf. ἑώρων, aor. εἶδον — see

*ὀργίζομαι — get angry with (+ dat.)

*ὀρθός, -ή, -όν — upright, correct

ὁρμάω — stir up, rush into, be eager

Ὀρφεύς, -έως, ὁ — Orpheus

*ὅς, ἥ, ὅ — who, which

ὅς, ἥ, ὅ (+ future indicative) — (expresses purpose)

ἦ δ᾽ ὅς — and he said

*ὅσος, -η, -ον — as much as ; plur., all who, as many as

ὅσπερ, ἥπερ, ὅπερ — the very one who, the very thing which

*ὅστις, ἥτις, ὅτι — whoever, whatever

*ὅταν (+ subj.) — whenever

ὅτι — neuter singular of ὅστις

*ὅτι — the fact that, that

*ὅτι — because

ὅτι μαθών — because

*οὐ, οὐκ, οὐχ — not (see Oxford Grammar of Classical Greek p205)

*οὐδαμοῦ — nowhere

*οὐδέ — and ... not, but not, not even, nor

* οὐδέ ... οὐδέ	neither ... nor
*οὐδείς, οὐδεμία, οὐδέν	no one, nothing
οὐδέν	in no way, not at all
οὐδέτερος, -α, -ον	neither
*οὖν	therefore, and so; actually, in fact
οὔπω	not yet
οὐράνιος, -α, -ον	in heaven, of heaven
οὖς, ὠτός, τό	ear
*οὔτε	neither
*οὔτε ... οὔτε	neither ... nor
*οὗτος, αὕτη, τοῦτο	this; he, she, it
ταύτῃ	in this way
*οὕτω, οὕτως	so, like this, in this way, as
οὑτωσί	thus
ὄφελος, τό (only in nom. and acc. sg.)	help, assistance
ὀφλισκάνω, aor. ὤφλον, perf. ὤφληκα	owe, lose a lawsuit
πάθος, -ους, τό	experience, suffering
*παιδεύω	educate, teach
παίζω	play like a child, joke, be joking
*παῖς, παίδος, ὁ	child, boy
ἐκ παίδων	from childhood
*πάλαι	long ago, before
*παλαιός, -ά, -όν	old
πάντως	at any rate
πάνυ	very, great, altogether, at all
πάνυ γε	yes indeed, certainly
*παρά (+ acc.)	by
*παρά (+ gen.)	from
παράδειγμα, -ατος, τό	example
παρακέλευσις, -εως, ἡ	exhorting, advising
παραλαμβάνω	receive, take to oneself, get control of
παραμένω, aor. παρέμεινα	wait with
παραπλησίως	almost
παρασκευάζω	prepare
*πάρειμι	be present
*παρέχω	provide, supply, furnish
Πάριος, -α, -ον	from Paros
*πᾶς, πᾶσα, πᾶν	all, every; the whole
*πάσχω, aor. ἔπαθον, perf. πέπονθα	suffer, experience
*πατήρ, πατρός, ὁ	father

*πείθω	persuade, convince; mid., obey, believe, trust
*πειράομαι	try, attempt
πειστέον	one must obey, be persuaded
πέμπτος, -η, -ον	fifth
τὸ πέμπτον μέρος	a fifth
πένης, -ητος	poor
πενία, -ας, ἡ	poverty
πέντε	five
πέπονθα	perfect of πάσχω
-περ	(emphatic suffix)
*περὶ (+ acc.)	in the case of
*περί (+ gen.)	concerning, about
περὶ πλείστου ποιεῖσθαι	consider of greatest value, importance
περιγίγνομαι, perf. περιγεγονέναι	to be superior to
περίειμι	go around
περιεργάζομαι	waste one's time
περιμένω, aor. περιέμεινα	wait, wait around
περιττός, -ή, -όν	uncommon, strange
περίφερω	carry about
πιθανός, -ή, -όν	persuasive
*πιστεύω	trust, believe
πλάνη, -ης, ἡ	wanderings
Πλάτων, -ωνος, ὁ	Plato
πλεῖστος, -η, -ον (superl. of πολύς)	greatest, most
πλείων, -ον or πλέων, -ον (comp. of πολύς)	more
πλέον τί ποιέω	succeed, be successful
*πλῆθος, -ους, τό	multitude, crowd, people
πλημμέλεια, -ας, ἡ	false note, error
*πλὴν (ἤ)	except
*πλούσιος, -α, -ον	rich
ποδαπός, -ή, -όν	from what country
πόθεν	from where
*ποιέω	make, do, compose; mid., value, produce
ποίημα, -ατος, τό	poem
ποίησις, -εως, ἡ	poetry
ποιητής, -οῦ, ὁ	poet
*ποῖος, -α, -ον	what sort of
*πόλεμος, -ου, ὁ	war
*πόλις, -εως, ἡ	city
*πολίτης, -ου, ὁ	citizen
πολιτικός, -ή, -όν	political, relating to public life, befitting a citizen
ὁ πολιτικός	public man, politician
*πολλάκις	often, many times
πολλαχοῦ	in many places
*πολύς, πολλή, πολύ	much, great; plur., many, a lot of

οἱ πολλοὶ	the majority	πῶλος, -ου, ὁ	foal
πολύ (adv.)	much	πώποτε	ever
*πονέω	toil	*πως	in some way, somehow
πονηρία, -ας, ἡ	wickedness		
*πόνος, -ου, ὁ	toil	Ῥαδάμανθυς, -υος, ὁ	Rhadamanthus
*πόρρω	forwards, far on	*ῥᾴδιος, -α, -ον,	easy
*πόσος, -η, -ον	how much; plur., how many	superl. ῥᾷστος	
		ῥητέον	needing to be said
*ποτε	once, ever	*ῥήτωρ, -ορος, ὁ	orator
*πότερος, -α, -ον	which (of two)		
πότερον or	introduces question	σημεῖον, -ου, τό	sign
πότερα . . . ἤ (direct	containing two	*σιγάω	be silent
question)	alternative	Σίσυφος, -ου, ὁ	Sisyphus
	propositions;	σιτέομαι	eat, be fed
	πότερον often best	σίτησις, -εως, ἡ	feeding, public
	left untranslated		maintenance
πότερον or πότερα	whether . . . or	σκέπτομαι, perf. inf.	consider, examine
. . . ἤ (indirect		ἐσκέφθαι	
question)		σκιαμαχέω	fight with shadows
που	anywhere, somewhere, I	*σκοπέω	look at, examine
	suppose	σμικρός, -ά, -όν	small, little
*πρᾶγμα, -ατος, τό	business, occupation,	*σός, -ή, -όν	your
	thing; plur., affairs,	*σοφία, -ας, ἡ	wisdom, expertise
	troubles	σοφιστής, -οῦ, ὁ	sophist
πραγματεύομαι	work at, be busy,	*σοφός, -ή, -όν	wise, skilled, expert
	elaborate	στάσις, -εως, ἡ	political faction, party
πρᾶξις, -εως, ἡ	affair, matter	στρατηγία, -ας, ἡ	generalship
*πράττω	do, perform; mid.,	*σύ, σοῦ	you
	obtain for oneself	συγγίγνομαι, aor.	meet with
πρέπει (+ dat.)	it is fitting, befits	συνεγενόμην	
πρεσβύτερος, -ου, ὁ	elder	(+ dat.)	
πρεσβύτης, -ου, ὁ	old man	συμβαίνω, perf.	happen
*πρίν	before	συμβέβηκα	
Πρόδικος, -ου, ὁ	Prodicus	συμβάλλω	throw together; mid.,
προῖκα	freely, for free		contribute
*πρός (+ acc.)	against, to, regarding,	σύμπας, σύμπασα,	all together
	with respect to, with,	σύμπαν	
	in comparison with	συμφεύγω (+ dat.)	go into exile with
*πρός (+ dat.)	in addition to	σύνειμι (+ dat.)	associate with
προσέρχομαι, aor.	go to, meet	σύνοιδα (+ dat.)	know together with
προσῆλθον		ἐμαυτῷ σύνοιδα	be conscious of
προσήκω	to be fitting	συνουσία, -ας, ἡ	association, company
πρόσθεν	before, former	συντεταμένως	eagerly, vigorously
πρόσοιδα, infin.	to know, acknowledge in	συνωμοσία, -ας, ἡ	conspiracy, political
προσειδέναι	addition		union
προσποιέω	make in addition; mid.,	συνωρίς, -ίδος, ἡ	two-horse chariot
	pretend	*σφεῖς, σφῶν	(indirect reflexive) them,
προσχράομαι (+ dat.)	use in addition		themselves
*πρότερον	before, formerly, sooner,	σφοδρός, -ά, -όν	intense, violent,
	earlier		impetuous
πρόχειρος, -ον	at hand, convenient	*σχεδόν	nearly, almost
πρυτανεῖον, -ου, τό	prytaneum	σχεῖν	aorist infinitive of
πρῶτος, -η, -ον	first		ἔχω
*πρῶτον (adv.)	first	σχολή, -ῆς, ἡ	leisure, time
Πυθία, -ας, ἡ	Pythia	σῴζω	save; mid., keep safe,
πυκνός, -ή, -όν	frequent, unremitting		prosper, do well

Σωκράτης, Σωκράτους, ὁ (acc. Σωκράτη)	Socrates	*τρόπος, -ου, ὁ	way
		τροφή, -ῆς, ἡ	nourishment, sustenance, support
τἀληθῆ	crasis of τὰ ἀληθῆ	*τυγχάνω (+ part.), aor. ἔτυχον	happen to
τἆλλα	crasis of τὰ ἄλλα		
ταὐτά	crasis of τὰ αὐτά: the same things	*ὑμεῖς, ὑμῶν	you
		*ὑμέτερος, -α, -ον	your, of you
ταυτί	ταῦτα + -ί: these things here	*ὑός, -οῦ or -έος, ὁ (= υἱός)	son
ταὐτόν	crasis of τὸ αὐτόν = τὸ αὐτό: the same thing	*ὑπέρ (+ gen.)	concerning, on behalf of
*τάχ᾽ ἄν (+ opt.)	probably, perhaps	*ὕπνος, -ου, ὁ	sleep
*ταχύς, εῖα, ύ	fast	*ὑπό (+ gen.)	under, by, at the hands of, because of
*τε	and, both	ὑπολαμβάνω	suppose, take up, reply
*τε ... καί ...	both ... and ...	ὑποστέλλω, aor. ὑπέστειλα	draw in; mid., hold back, withhold
τεθνάναι	perfect infinitive of θνήσκω	*ὕστερον	later
τεκμήριον, -ου, τό	evidence	*ὑστέρος, -α, -ον	later
*τελευτάω	finish, die	*φαίνω, aor. pass. ἐφάνην	show; pass., appear
τελευτῶν	finally		
τελέω	complete, fulfil, accomplish	*φαίνομαι (+ infinitive)	appear, seem to
*τέχνη, -ης, ἡ	craft, skill	*φαίνομαι (+ participle)	clearly be doing something (part.)
τηλικόσδε	of such an age	φάσκω	say, claim
*τιμάω	fix a penalty; mid., propose as a penalty	φαῦλος, -η, -ον	bad, insignificant, common
		*φέρω, fut. οἴσω, aor. ἤνεγκα	bear, carry
τίμημα, -ατος, τό	penalty		
*τιμωρέω	punish	*φεύγω	flee
τιμωρία, -ας, ἡ	punishment	φήμη, -ης, ἡ	report, rumour
*τίς	who, what, which	*φημί, fut. φήσω, impf. ἔφην	say, assert, affirm, declare
τί	why		
*τις, τι	a (certain), one, someone, something, some, a sort of	*φθόνος, -ου, ὁ	malice, envy
		*φίλος, -ου, ὁ	friend
		φίλος, -η, -ον	dear, pleasing
τι	somewhat	φιλοσοφέω	be a philosopher, love wisdom
τοιόσδε, -άδε, -όνδε	such as this		
τοιοῦτος, -αύτη, -οῦτο	of such a kind, such, like that, this sort of, as follows	φιλότιμος, -ον	honour-loving, ambitious
		φιλοψυχία, -ας, ἡ	love of life
*τολμάω	dare	φλυαρέω	speak nonsense
τόλμη, -ης, ἡ	audacity	φλυαρία, -ας, ἡ	nonsense
*τόπος, -ου, ὁ	place	*φοβέομαι	fear
τοσόσδε, -ήδε, -όνδε	so much	φράζω	tell, explain
*τοσοῦτος, -αύτη, -οῦτο	so much, so great, such great; plur., so many	φρονίμος, -ον	in one's right mind, sensible, wise
		φροντιστής, -ου, ὁ	deep thinker
*τότε	then	*φυγή, -ῆς, ἡ	exile
τραγῳδία, -ας, ἡ	tragedy	φύσις, -εως, ἡ	nature, instinct
*τρέπω, aor. ἔτρεπον	turn		
τριάκοντα	thirty		
Τριπτόλεμος, -ου, ὁ	Triptolemus	Χαιρεφῶν, -ῶντος, ὁ	Chaerephon

*χαίρω   enjoy
χαλεπαίνω   be angry, be angry with
                                 (+ dat.)
*χαλεπός, -ή, -όν   difficult, painful
χάρις, -ιτος, ή   thanks, gratitude,
                                 favour
χάριν πρόσοιδα   to be grateful in
                                 addition
χειροτέχνης, -ου, ὁ   craftsman
χίλιοι, -αι, -α   a thousand
*χράομαι (+ dat.)   use, experience
*χρή (+ acc. + inf.)   it is necessary
*χρήματα, -ων, τά   money, fine
χρηματισμός, -οῦ, ὁ   making money
χρησμός, -οῦ, ὁ   oracle
χρησμῳδέω   make a prophecy
χρησμῳδός, -ου, ὁ   prophet
*χρόνος, -ου, ὁ   time

ψευδής, ές   untrue, false
τὰ ψευδῆ   lies

*ψεύδομαι, aor. pass.   cheat, lie, deceive; pass.,
  ἐψεύσθην   be mistaken in
                                 something (gen.)
ψῆφος, -ου, ὁ   pebble; vote
ψυχή, -ῆς, ή   soul

*ὦ . . .   o . . . (in address)
*ὧδε   thus, in this way
*ὥρα, -ας, ή   time
*ὡς   as, how, that,
                                 since
*ὡς (+ participle)   because, on the grounds
                                 that
*ὡς (+ future   in order to
  participle)
*ὡς (+ superlative)   as . . . as possible
*ὥσπερ   as, like, as if, as it were
*ὥστε   with the result that, that,
                                 as to, to

ὦτα   see οὖς
ὦφλον   aorist of ὀφλισκάνω

Xenophon, *Memorabilia*

Introduction, Commentary Notes and
Vocabulary by Charlie Paterson

A-level: Book 1: II.12–II.38

Introduction

In the opening chapters of Book 1 of the *Memorabilia*, Xenophon provides a defence of Socrates against the various accusations and criticisms levelled at the philosopher both inside and outside the law courts in the final years of the fifth century BC. This introduction provides students with an outline of the trial of Socrates, the structure of the defence written by Xenophon and the historical context of the trial. There is also a discussion on the genre of the *Memorabilia*, the rhetorical power of Xenophon's writing and a summary of the main features of his literary style. Suggestions for further reading are also provided to help candidates further their studies on Xenophon, Socrates and Athens in the fifth century BC. By no means is this intended to be an exhaustive introduction; however, it aims to provide students with enough understanding of the author and his subject to encourage them to develop their own personal response to this remarkable text.

The trial of Socrates

In May 399, nearly three decades before the publication of the *Memorabilia*, the King Archon, a magistrate in charge of a religious law court, summoned Socrates to stand trial. The main charge presented to the jurors was certainly impiety, a vague term that came with no set punishment in the Athenian constitution. As with all trials in Athens, the charge was brought by private individuals: Meletus, Anytus and Lycon. They appear to have defined impiety in three ways: failure to worship the gods of the city of Athens, invention of new gods and corruption of the youth. The punishment proposed by the prosecutors was the most severe: death. Socrates was also accused of spreading undemocratic ideology and promoting violent oligarchic revolution among the young men of Athens, particularly in training Critias and Alcibiades, the most notorious characters of the period. However, it is unclear if these accusations were or could be explicitly mentioned in court. The trial, as was customary, was completed in a single day; 280 of the 500 randomly selected Athenian men on the jury found Socrates guilty and went on to approve the proposed punishment. A month later, Socrates administered his own death penalty by drinking a poison derived from hemlock.

In response to the trial, Socrates' devoted students and friends, most notably Plato and Xenophon, soon sought to refute the charges levelled at Socrates in the law courts and the negative image of him found in the popular imagination of Athenians.

Both authors wrote an *Apology*, a defence speech retrospectively put into the mouth of Socrates, and Xenophon presented a second defence of Socrates in the opening chapters of his *Memorabilia*. Both authors also sought to preserve the character and teachings of Socrates: Plato in his numerous philosophical dialogues and Xenophon in a number of Socratic texts. Since Socrates lived his life in conversation and never wrote anything down, these have become our main sources for uncovering the character of Socrates and the events of his trial.

The challenge of getting close to the real Socrates and the events of the trial is a complex field of inquiry; we are left to piece his life and death together with sources written by both friends and enemies across a large time span. Temporal and often geographical distance from the events, as well as differing literary purposes, mean the various accounts of the trial that survive can differ greatly. Plato and Xenophon, both proud friends of Socrates, disagree in several ways with each other and with later sources. To exemplify the difficulty of reconstructing the trial, one could look at the differing views of Socrates' role on the day. Plato and Xenophon's retrospective defence speeches suggest that Socrates spoke at the trial, but it was a tradition among later writers that Socrates remained silent throughout the proceedings. Socrates was given the opportunity to speak against the proposed penalty of death and suggest his own; his choice of punishment is another area in which our sources are problematic. Xenophon's Socrates refuses to propose an alternative penalty to death out of fear that it could be seen as a confession of guilt; Plato's Socrates, on the other hand, arrogantly suggests that the state provide him with free meals at the Prytaneum, an honour reserved for public heroes, before suggesting various fines. The character of Socrates became distorted not only as time elapsed but also as creative writers sought to use the man for their own purposes. Xenophon's presentation of Socrates in the *Memorabilia* is one example of the way authors both preserved and manipulated the historical character for their own purposes.

Memorabilia 1.1.1–1.2.62

Xenophon's *Memorabilia*, originally entitled Ἀπομνημονεύματα in Greek and best translated as 'recollections' in English, is a fascinating and unique part of the outburst of Socratic literature in the early fourth century BC. Most likely written after 371, nearly three decades after Socrates' death, it consists of a rich collection of memories of Socrates, which are presented mainly in the form of conversations and anecdotes. The opening section, 1.1–1.2.64, the vast majority of which is set for examination, is a defence of Socrates against the accusations of impiety and corrupting the youth. Xenophon seeks to prove that Socrates' religious practices are entirely pious and regular in comparison to others and that he can only have had a positive impact on the young men who followed his teaching properly. The second and much more substantial part of the text, 1.3–4.8, is a collection of anecdotes and conversations that characterize the philosopher and his teaching of ethics. It is useful to begin by plotting the charges and defence found in the *Memorabilia* and put them into their historical context before moving on to consider the genre and literary merits of the text.

The defence is not put into the mouth of Socrates, unlike in Xenophon's *Apology*, but is spoken by an anonymous first person narrator, whom we might assume to be

Xenophon himself. After showing his amazement that any juror could believe that Socrates deserved execution, the speaker begins by tackling the charges made at Socrates' trials as presented in the defence speeches that both Plato and Xenophon wrote for Socrates after his death: failure to believe in the Athenian gods, the introduction of new gods and corruption of the youth. The speaker first sets out to show that Socrates' *daimonion*, a divine sign that advised him both positively and negatively, is simply a form of divination that he used for help on matters that humans could not know for themselves. Socrates' trust in the advice of the gods is given as clear proof of his piety, along with his dislike of atheist philosophers, his public worship of the gods and his respect for oaths and the laws. From 1.2, the speaker turns to the charge that Socrates corrupted the young of Athens. This accusation is countered with reference to Socrates' self-control and moderation; a man of such virtue could only inspire others to pursue virtue. The speaker states that a man of prudence could only inspire others to use persuasion rather than violence.

At 1.2.9, the speaker introduces an adversary, who extends the charge of corrupting the youth by blaming Socrates for teaching the young men to despise the laws of the city and holding him responsible for the destructive and violent natures of Critias and Alcibiades. At this point, the speaker appears to go beyond the charges made at the trial. These accusations are not tackled in either Plato or Xenophon's defence speeches and many scholars argue that such political charges could not have been aired in court due to an amnesty on political prosecutions. In his language, Xenophon certainly appears to differentiate between ὁ γραψάμενος, the man bringing the official charge of impiety, and ὁ κατήγορος, the accuser who introduces the political accusations, suggesting the second was not one of the official prosecutors. If such charges were not aired in court it is very likely that Xenophon is responding to criticisms made publicly outside of the trial. These charges are preserved as the key reasons for Socrates' death in the writing of Polycrates, a teacher of rhetoric who wrote a retrospective speech for the prosecution of Socrates in the years after the trial, perhaps *c.* 390.

The speaker defends Socrates against these political charges by showing that Critias and Alcibiades only sought Socrates' friendship while he was useful for their own political gains and that their behaviour was actually at its best when they were among Socrates' retinue. This leads to the speaker attacking the false views held by his adversary on Socrates' instruction to young men, demonstrating his own understanding of the philosopher's views on education, wisdom and virtue. The speaker also provides anecdotes and dialogues to show Critias' later dislike of Socrates and Alcibiades' failure to learn anything other than the rhetoric his ambition sought. Moving on from Critias and Alcibiades, the accuser charges Socrates with convincing the younger generation to despise the older generation, to no longer respect paternal authority, and to spurn family and friends in favour of himself. Xenophon argues that Socrates valued knowledge and that only knowledgeable people should be considered of worth; someone of value is thus helpful because of their knowledge and ability to advise others. The accuser then charges Socrates with using immoral passages of poetry to encourage violence and tyrannical beliefs, but Xenophon reinterprets the lines to show Socrates as a man of the people and of use to the state. Such an argument leads him to the conclusion that Socrates deserved to be honoured by the state rather than killed.

The charges of impiety and corruption of the youth

Impiety was a serious crime in Athens as it covered behaviour that threatened the stability of the state. In the polytheistic religion of Athens, the goodwill of the gods was needed for the city to flourish and it was the responsibility of all the citizens, both publicly and privately, to ensure the gods were gratified through ritual. This took the form of sacrifices and prayers to the gods, either thanking them for what had happened or entreating them for future good fortune, a reciprocal process that was at the centre of civic life; the greatest state events were religious festivals in celebration of particular gods. Divination also played a central role; dreams, the flights of birds and cryptic responses from oracles could be interpreted for an insight into future events. This was a method of ensuring that the gods were favourable to human plans and a way to diagnose divine displeasure before it was too late. Inner belief could only be demonstrated through engagement in public rituals and these common elements of religious practice. Thus, although the crime is one that could be taken very seriously in Athens, it is also one that can be convincingly denied with common knowledge of the defendant's adherence to common ritual.

From the *Memorabilia* and other defences, Socrates is found to have been eccentric but not clearly criminal in his religious beliefs and practices. Although he did engage in public ritual, he is frequently depicted as having a *daimonion*, his own personal guiding divine sign, which appears to be a new take on divination. Socrates' philosophy, as preserved by Plato, moves away from some traditional beliefs by putting much focus on human reasoning and introspection. This focus reduced the traditional role of the gods in human lives, but it did not stray far enough from customary views of the gods to cause alarm when he started philosophizing in Athens. Our evidence comes from authors who are certain to have done as much as possible to defend Socrates' reputation and so cannot always be trusted; nonetheless, their defences can only have been credible if they stayed close to the facts. However, Socrates' public image in Athens is not the one of relative normality that Xenophon and others describe and it is this public image that is being tackled in this defence against impiety.

Aristophanes' *Clouds*, a comedy performed at the City Dionysia festival of 423, presents Socrates, one of the main characters in the play, as an atheist whose teachings and beliefs cause great harm to the Athenians. The aim of comedy is to lampoon and satirize, engaging with popular ideas and misconceptions current among the audience. The characterization of Socrates comes as a result of his confusion with the sophists, travelling teachers and lecturers who educated the young men of Athens for a fee. Their interests included philosophy, mathematics and geography, but in a democracy that valued the spoken word, their skills as teachers of rhetoric were the most highly sought after. They could help men to gain influence and sway public opinion but their popularity meant they were often expensive and so their teaching was only received by the wealthy, undermining the principle of equality among democratic citizens. Even though these men were far from belonging to a single school, they were tarred with the same brush as humanist philosophers who did not believe in the gods and conducted crackpot scientific experiments. It is hard to tell how much Socrates really did overlap with the practices and beliefs of some of these travelling professors, but it was certainly important for those writing defences of him to separate him as far as possible from them.

Socrates' connection with the sophists not only connects him with atheism but also with corruption of the youth. The education in rhetoric that the sophists provided was often criticized as producing young men who could twist any argument, undermine the rule of logic in the arenas of democratic debate and thus subvert the basis of the democracy. The new level of education available to the young generation led them to outdo their elders in argument and begin to question traditional ways of thinking, leading to friction between the younger and older generation. In Aristophanes' *Clouds*, Socrates was able to teach anyone how to make the weak argument strong and the strong argument weak. This leads to corruption and violence: Strepsiades, an old farmer, learns rhetoric in order to conquer his creditors, while his son uses rhetoric to justify beating up his own father. The play ends with a strong condemnation of Socrates' teaching as Strepsiades attempts to burn down Socrates' 'Thinking Shop'. The play shows that Socrates was associated with subverting moral norms, corrupting the youth and exacerbating the generational divide.

It is also clear from Plato's *Apology* that Socrates had gained a reputation for annoying Athenians. This is put down to his *elenchus*, often translated in English as 'cross-examining' or 'scrutiny'. It is the process by which Socrates refutes the statements of an interlocutor and gradually leads them to see the ignorance of their opening statement. By this process, Socrates highlighted many weaknesses in common thinking and demonstrated that many men who thought they were wise were not in fact so. Although an effective method of philosophical exploration, it was infuriating to those who felt they knew best. Plato has Socrates describe himself as a gadfly sent to reproach and persuade the people; in other words, he was a nuisance. This supports the satirized presentation of Socrates found in *Clouds*; however, although this raised laughs in 423, in 399 the charges against Socrates were taken very seriously. To understand this development, it is important to look at the politics in Athens at this time and the political charges that Xenophon aims to refute.

The political charges

The political charges made against Socrates can only be understood in the context of the Athenian democracy in the final years of the fifth century BC. The Athenian constitution was radical for its time: all male citizens over a certain age were considered politically equal in that they could all participate in the functioning of the democracy and receive fair judgement before the law. This was far from the rule of aristocratic oligarchs and tyrants that characterized Athenian politics a century earlier. The three main institutions of the democracy, the Assembly, Council and Law Courts, demonstrate the underlying ideology of the system. The Assembly, the main decision-making body of the democracy, met around 40 times each year and any male citizen over the age of 20, an age at which they were mature and involved in matters of the state, could speak on issues and vote by raising their hand. The minimum number of men required to validate the vote was 6,000 and this number was paid to attend, ensuring men from outside the city and those tied to jobs could take a day off and participate. This ensured a large mix of people took part in the political machinations of the state. The Council of 500 men set the agenda for the Assembly and was made up of 50 men chosen by lot from each of the 10 tribes of Athens; the use of allotment, a form of random selection, was a safeguard against corruption. The presidency of the Council passed from tribe to tribe across the year and no man could sit on the Council more than twice in his lifetime, ensuring power constantly changed hands. The Law Courts were also a vital part of the democracy and for each case juries were chosen at random from a group of 6,000 men just before the trial. The juries were often very large in comparison to modern standards; between 200 and 2,000 men were used to protect against bribery and other forms of corruption.

Although it suffered from many weaknesses, this system did succeed in removing much power from aristocrats and encouraging greater participation. It ensured that men from all across the city state could take part in large numbers. Unsurprisingly, there were many critics of this radical system and the democracy suffered from the assaults of internal enemies who sought to topple it and return power to the traditional ruling class. The wealthy in particular were aggrieved as they had not only lost their ancestral positions but were increasingly leant upon by the state to invest in military or social affairs and support a system they did not agree with. As Athens was flooded with money from its empire, charismatic, *nouveau riche* men emerged and started to dominate politics by charming the people and proposing popular motions, further alienating the conservatives. Aristocrats either stood back from politics, driven out by the thought of co-ruling with the lower classes, or sought support from each other in the form of small aristocratic clubs called *hetaireiai*. From 430, the number of these clubs greatly increased as the wealthy sought like-minded companions. These clubs became anti-democratic think tanks and in fact held much power in politics thanks to the support members would provide for each other in the Council and Assembly.

The natural tensions between those who favoured oligarchic forms of government – the rule of the few over the many – and the democrats, groups often stereotyped as the rich and poor, were further exacerbated by turbulent international affairs. The Peloponnesian War, an enormous struggle for influence over mainland Greece fought by the Spartans and their allies against the Athenians and their allies, had a profound effect on the democracy. Military failures were deemed to be failures of the democracy and confirmed the belief held by oligarchs that the general public could not control an empire or lead the Athenians to victory against the Spartans. They began to strongly criticize the masses as innately stupid and overly emotional in their decision-making. They saw them as limited by their need to labour for money and thus believed that they had very short-term vision and lacked experience of rule. The democracy was also criticized for ruling by whim, being easily led by demagogues, and frequently promoting an average man before an expert.

Two crucial moments of failure towards the end of the fifth century BC toppled the democracy. The first was a disastrous expedition to Sicily from 415 to 413, in which hundreds of ships and a large percentage of Athenian manpower were destroyed or killed. The sudden weakness of Athens led to confidence among its enemies and rebellions sprouted across the Aegean. Under such circumstances, the oligarchs saw the opportunity to take control of foreign affairs and in 411 an oligarchic revolution took place under the leadership of a wealthy Athenian politician named Pisander. The *hetaireiai* murdered leading democrats and held influence over both the Council and Assembly. The oligarchs then set out to create their own powerful council of four hundred men, disenfranchising large numbers of the poor by limiting the citizen body to five thousand. A commission was also established to return the laws to those of their ancestors. Although careful to brand this development in the constitution as a reformed democracy, it was clearly a conservative return to ancestral power structures. The list of five thousand was essentially ignored and the oligarchy, known as the Four Hundred, held power. Although democrats soon regained the upper hand with the support of the Athenian fleet, this brief oligarchy was a clear sign that democracy was vulnerable.

The second moment came in 404 when Athens was finally defeated by Sparta and the Peloponnesian War came to an end. Such a humiliating defeat brought with it peace terms that included the restoration of large numbers of oligarch exiles to Athens and led to a Spartan-backed oligarchy of thirty men, often referred to as the Thirty Tyrants. Once again, men were appointed to draw up a new constitution based on the laws of their ancestors, which mainly involved returning powers to the Areopagus, an aristocratic council and law court. The system looked increasingly Spartan, a constitution often greatly admired by oligarchs: a group of five ephors was created, a magisterial position only otherwise used in Sparta. The Thirty also established a garrison of Spartan troops nearby as defence for the oligarchy. The financing of this and the huge reparations due to returning exiles was expensive and led to ruthless attacks on wealthy men, mainly wealthy foreign business men, robbing them of their property, businesses and often their lives. Despite the commitment of the oligarchs to their new constitution, resistance built and a group of exiled democrats led by Thrasybulus eventually toppled the oligarchy and restored democracy in 403. In the same year, as part of a process of rehabilitation and to avoid lengthy lawsuits, an amnesty was introduced. The details of this are disputed among scholars, but it seems that it blocked prosecution for political crimes committed during this period.

Socrates' political beliefs, as can be inferred from Xenophon's defence, were interpreted by his critics as anti-democratic. His view that allotting officials was foolish certainly sounds as much. The various defences of the philosopher do convincingly show that, much like his religious beliefs, he was not easily categorized: his theories are neither democratic nor oligarchic. He believed in the importance of expert knowledge and feared the ignorant man overruling expert judgement. By conversing with craftsmen and artisans, he sought to demonstrate that those who are experts in one area often dangerously presume that they are, therefore, experts in other areas, particularly politics. For Socrates, this fallacy was not just proof that allotment of members of the Council was foolish but also that any political leader was not to be trusted with all decisions unless he was an expert in the necessary field. Despite having concerns about the system, Socrates played a small role in politics and respected the laws of the state: he was one of the presidents of the Assembly when the generals of the battle of Arginusae were accused of incompetence, and voted against the illegal plan to try all the generals at once. Furthermore, under the Thirty, he refused to follow an order to arrest an innocent man and thus showed his dislike of the regime. Nonetheless, if not oligarchic, Socrates' views were controversial and so his peaceful and virtuous nature needed to be emphasized in his defence to ensure his political views could not be associated with the violence of the oligarchic revolutions of the late fifth century BC.

Critias and Alcibiades

After such internal and external threats, much blame was thrown on the new generation of ambitious politicians, who were seen to have perverted ancestral customs and brought disaster on their city. Critias and Alcibiades stand out as examples of this rebellious generation. Given their extended appearance in Xenophon's defence of Socrates, it is important to look in detail at their careers and their reputation among the Athenians.

Alcibiades, son of Cleinias, was an Athenian politician and a talented general. He was born into a wealthy aristocratic family and had leisure in his youth to spend time with Socrates in the streets of Athens. He came from two of the greatest Athenian families: the Salaminioi and the Alcmaeonids. As a result, he was extremely wealthy and lived the stereotypically lavish lifestyle of an aristocrat. We are told, for example, that in 416 he spent a vast fortune entering seven different teams in the chariot race at the Olympic games and won first, second and fourth place. His stay in Olympia was remembered for its lavishness and he even commissioned the tragedian Euripides to write his victory ode. Although he represented his state so well at the games, his extravagance led to rumours that he lacked self-control and had tyrannical ambitions. Such stories about Alcibiades abound: in the 420s he paid a fortune to put on a dramatic festival but then came to blows with one of his rivals. In comedy, he is mocked for his effeminate fashion sense, love of horses, base desires and passion for fighting. He was talented, ambitious and confident, but also reckless and a symbol of the foppish and unscrupulous new generation.

During his youth, he was a devoted follower of Socrates and is frequently depicted as a close friend of the philosopher. Alcibiades appears in many of Plato's dialogues, most notably in the *Symposium*, in a lengthy relationship with the philosopher. When Alcibiades served as a soldier, he even shared a tent with Socrates. There is much to suggest that Socrates was interested in this young man, not necessarily because of lust but for the political talent Alcibiades demonstrated. It was perhaps in Alcibiades that Socrates found a young man whom he might train to become a new type of moral ruler that the Athenian state needed. Alcibiades was certainly ready in terms of status, wealth and charisma for a career in politics and in 446 he was made the ward of the famous politician Pericles, his mother's cousin. In 424 we first find Alcibiades entering public life on a board revising tribute, a form of taxation across the empire, and in 422 he proposed honours for the people of Siphnos for help they gave to the Athenians. However, a lack of self-control in his private life was matched with, if not surpassed by, his ruthless political ambition.

Both his talent and unscrupulous nature became clear after a peace treaty, known as the Peace of Nicias, was signed between Athens and Sparta in 421 under the auspices of the statesman and general of the same name. Disgruntled by the fact he was overlooked for involvement in the negotiations, Alcibiades instantly sought to undermine the treaty by starting to form a union between Athens, Argos and other Peloponnesian states against Sparta. At the same time, he also demonstrated great skill as a general and was involved in capturing the island of Melos. However, his skill as a general was overshadowed by his cruelty as a victor, as he supported the decree to kill all the men and enslave the women and children. Soon, Alcibiades' lack of control and increasingly self-interested approach to politics and warfare became strikingly clear as his popularity in Athens waned. In 415 there was a move to ostracize Alcibiades from the city. Ostracism was a mechanism for voting men into exile for showing tyrannical intentions; it was another safeguard of the democracy. Wily as ever, he feigned support for his rival Nicias to avoid ostracism from the city before going on to attack Nicias in his ardent support for an expedition to Sicily. He was successful in this and set out as a general to prove his worth to the state. However, he was recalled within days to go on trial for the religious crimes of mutilating the *hermai* of Athens, the protective statues found throughout the city, and mocking archaic religious rites known as the Eleusinian Mysteries; charges that were almost certainly politically motivated. He escaped to the Peloponnese and defected to Sparta, where he betrayed his state and advised the enemy on tactics. After losing the trust of the Spartans, Alcibiades fled to Persia, another enemy of Athens, and by making contact with the rebel Athenian fleet at Samos, he hoped to return to Athens as the leader of an oligarchic coup. This plan failed and the coup of the Four Hundred went ahead without him.

Another twist in the story of Alcibiades came when, in a remarkable volte-face, he was elected general by the Athenian fleet, which had swiftly returned to democracy and stood as its own state outside of the oligarchy of the Four Hundred. He led the fleet very successfully but it was only in 407 that he gained the trust of the Athenians and could return to the city free of the charges of sacrilege that had been hanging over him since 415. Nevertheless, he was welcomed with open arms thanks to his naval success and even given a golden crown by the citizens of Athens. However, after a year of limited naval success and a failed attempt to unite Persia and Athens, a serious defeat for the Athenian navy in the battle of Notium in 406 was the opportunity Alcibiades' political opponents had been waiting for and he fled to Thrace. When the war was finally over, he sought exile in Persia but was murdered through the machinations of the Thirty Tyrants and Sparta. Thus ended the life of a man of great talent but excessive ambition and limited morality. Thucydides, the Athenian historian who wrote a history of the Peloponnesian War, shared the blame for the Athenian failure in the war among the Athenian people and Alcibiades, suggesting his influence in these years was remarkable.

Critias was born into a wealthy Athenian family and became an associate of Socrates in his youth. He was a scholarly young man who devoted himself to literature and philosophy, as well as politics. In addition to writing on philosophy and contemporary issues in prose, he composed elegiac poetry and tragedy. He became particularly impressed with the Spartan way of life and published several works on their political system and education, both of which appealed greatly to Athenian oligarchs and critics of democracy. In 415 he was accused of mutilating the *hermai* of Athens, suggesting that he, like Alcibiades, was being attacked for political reasons, but the charges were quickly dropped. It is likely that in 407 he supported the return of Alcibiades to Athens; when Alcibiades went back into exile, Critias thus fell out of favour and went to Thessaly in north-east Greece. What he became involved in during his stay in Thessaly is unclear; however, it is most likely that he was helping to develop an oligarchic government to create a buffer state for the Spartans and thus demonstrating his support for the enemy regime and the Athenian oligarchs.

When Athens was finally defeated in the Peloponnesian War, Critias returned to his home state and became one of the Thirty Tyrants. He, along with his colleague Charicles, led the commission to reconstruct the laws of the early democracy. He also became notorious for his extreme views, as demonstrated when he publicly denounced his own colleague Theramenes, who was opposed to the brutal plan to kill the rich foreign businessmen of Athens. He was central to the creation of a list of 3,000 men who would retain their rights and he thus caused the exclusion, exile or murder of the rest of the male citizenry. As such an extreme supporter of the oligarchy, he fought bravely to defend the constitution he believed was the best but was killed in the fighting of 403.

For Socrates, a man who was frequently confused for a sophist and whose political views could easily be misinterpreted, association with these young men and other oligarchic aristocrats in their youth was more than enough to gain the enmity of the state, despite several years out of the limelight. It is very likely that his connection to such notorious men led to his trial, particularly since two of the prosecutors are likely to have had personal motives: Lycon's son was killed by the Thirty and Anytus was a hero of the democratic revolution against the Thirty. His reputation as an amusing eccentric in the 420s became much more problematic in the years following the violent oligarchic revolutions. It has been convincingly argued that Athens was looking for a scapegoat to take away the pollution of the previous turbulent years and Socrates fitted the bill. If this interpretation is correct, it is no surprise that Xenophon dedicated so much of his defence of Socrates to political charges.

Xenophon

Before turning to a discussion of the text, it is valuable to consider the author. Xenophon was born in around 430 in the deme of Erchia, a rural district about 10 miles to the northeast of Athens. His family was clearly wealthy enough to buy horses, as Xenophon went on to serve on horseback. His later treatises on horsemanship and the duties of a cavalry officer both provide expert advice on these areas and should be taken as evidence of Xenophon's wealth and status in Athens. The area in which Xenophon grew up was mainly agricultural and his family may have owned and worked farming land. In 431, only a year before Xenophon's birth, the Peloponnesian War began. During the early years of the war, often referred to as the Archidamian War, Spartan troops frequently invaded the rural districts of Athens. Life in the countryside around Athens would certainly have been unsettled and many Athenians abandoned their farms and sought safety within the walls of the city. It is very likely that during these years, Xenophon too went to the city and there became a close associate of Socrates. As a wealthy young man, he had the leisure needed to dedicate time to philosophy.

Xenophon was not only influenced by the philosophy he discussed with Socrates but also came to idolize Socrates himself. His deep respect for him is found in the many Socratic works he wrote later in his life. As well as the *Memorabilia*, he wrote an *Apology*, as previously discussed; the *Symposium*, a banquet in which Socrates and his friends discuss love while also having a light-hearted evening of entertainment and hilarity; and the *Oeconomicus*, a set of dialogues in which Socrates is guided by others in the art of estate management. Despite later being absent from Athens when Socrates came to trial, Xenophon probably experienced the finest years of Socrates' philosophical teaching. It is for his time with Socrates and the resulting works of literature, just as much for his historical and didactic writing, that Xenophon was held in high regard in the following years and centuries; Diogenes Laertius considered him to be one of the three great pupils of Socrates.

Xenophon's early years as a cavalry soldier are undocumented, but he may have fought in Ionia in 409, returning to Athens in 407. When the Thirty Tyrants seized control after Athens' defeat in 404, he remained in Athens and demonstrated his oligarchic leanings by fighting in the cavalry against the invading democrats. Although he later criticized the Thirty in his writings, life would have been difficult for Xenophon under the new democracy, even with the protection of the amnesty mentioned above. It may have been for this reason that he accepted a mercenary role in the army of Cyrus the Younger, which in 401 marched to Babylonia and fought a battle in Cunaxa with the aim of overthrowing Cyrus' brother, Artaxerxes II, the then King of Persia. Whatever the reason for his decision to join this expedition, Xenophon's reputation in Athens cannot have been helped by his agreement to fight for a Persian prince who had supported the Spartan general Lysander during the Peloponnesian War.

Cyrus was soon defeated. However, this defeat was the making of Xenophon's military career as he went on to take the leadership of the 10,000 surviving Greek mercenary soldiers, restore discipline and lead them to safety. He proudly recalls his military adventures in his greatest historical work, the *Anabasis*, in which he presents himself as the hero of the narrative. During the following years, Xenophon's allegiance to Athens became even more questionable; despite a desire to go home, he fought for a Thracian named Seuthes and then the Spartans. He hugely admired the Spartan King Agesilaus and later wrote a biography that could more correctly be defined as hagiography, and clearly placed Agesilaus alongside Socrates as a personal hero. During his time as a Spartan mercenary, Xenophon even fought against the Athenians at Coronea in Boeotia. These years provide several clear reasons for why Xenophon was exiled from Athens around this time.

In exile, Xenophon remained loyal to the Spartans who awarded him with the role of Spartan *proxenos*, a form of diplomat, to Olympia, and a house nearby. Here he purchased an estate and enjoyed a life in retirement from military service, engaging in outdoor and literary pursuits. He married and fathered twin sons whom he sent to Sparta for their education. His clear admiration of the Spartan constitution and militaristic education is evident in his *Constitution of the Spartans,* which heartily details the Spartan system. As power and influence shifted among the Greek states of the Peloponnese, Xenophon moved to Corinth; eventually his exile was repealed as relations between Athens and Sparta started to ease as they united against the common threat of Thebes. Sources are unclear on the final years of Xenophon's life, but it is likely that he did return to Athens as his final works have a more Athenian flavour: his *Ways and Means*, a small pamphlet on the Athenian economy, suggests a renewed patriotism. His sons also went to fight for the Athenians, alongside Sparta, in the battle on Mantinea in 362, where one son, Gryllus, was killed.

Thus Xenophon led a fascinating life when the Greek world was at its most turbulent and the Athenian state was undergoing a golden age of intellectual developments. As well as being a skilled and disciplined cavalry soldier and leader, he was a political thinker with conservative and oligarchic tendencies, a philosopher who greatly respected Socrates' teachings, a teacher in his own right who sought to be of use to those who could benefit from his experience, and a prolific writer. The survival and later imitation of his works shows he was considered worth copying and thus an author of skill and influence. In the *Memorabilia*, his love for Socrates shines through alongside his practical nature and desire to instruct.

Xenophon's literary purpose

Xenophon's presentation of Socrates in the *Memorabilia* has often come under attack from scholars for its perceived failings in comparison to Plato's accounts of Socrates; as an historical source on the life and philosophy of Socrates, Plato is deemed to be the more accurate and profound. Xenophon's presentation of the philosopher as a god-fearing man who sought to be useful to others with his practical advice on moral living is considered banal, and there are certainly factual errors and unconvincing interpretations. For example, Xenophon's argument that the Thirty's ban on the teaching of speaking was aimed specifically at Socrates is unconvincing; it was, more likely, an attempt to reduce the dangerous effect of rhetoric in general. Also, Xenophon's claims to be present at events he describes have been proven to be chronologically impossible in his other Socratic works. In addition to concerns over the accuracy of the text, the bi-partite and rambling structure of the *Memorabilia* has received much criticism. The value of the *Memorabilia* has thus been reduced to providing us with evidence of the political accusations made against the philosopher. Classicists have praised Xenophon's Greek as an excellent example of pure Attic prose style; it is simple and elegant. As such, much of the *Memorabilia* has been confined to language tuition and hacked into pieces for unseen translation. However, the demotion of this author's works comes from the mistaken belief that he intended his Socratic works to be read as historical sources.

The *Memorabilia* can be revived with the belief that it was not intended to be a fully historical source. Although it is hard to place within a genre, the *Memorabilia* has many of the hallmarks of Wisdom Literature. This ancient near-eastern genre came to Greece and took the form of collections of proverbs, maxims and anecdotes attributed to a wise person. Greek didactic poetry, collections of poems intended to teach a recipient certain practical skills, as well as Greek and Latin prose works composed of anecdotes, are closely connected to this genre. The purpose of literature of this sort was to educate and so it was frequently copied and learnt as part of the education process. The teachings of the wise men recorded in Wisdom Literature may not embody their entire work or factually represent their life, but certainly were useful to the community for which the text was written. The style of Wisdom Literature was designed to capture the reader and make the teachings both accessible and memorable. The origins of the genre were predominantly oral and the style of writing often attempts to capture the effects of oral instruction. In characterizing Wisdom Literature in this way, it becomes clear that the *Memorabilia* has a place in this genre.

Firstly, the characterization of Socrates as the central wise man of the text is one that puts great emphasis on his usefulness and practical teaching. Socrates is presented as a paragon of virtue for others to imitate. In particular, his self-control is impressive; Xenophon presents a range of examples of his moderation, extolling his control over his body and base desires, which was visible in his meagre lifestyle. The entire focus of the text is on Socrates' work on ethics (the theories of right and wrong conduct) and politics, and there is no mention of the epistemology (the study of knowledge) and ontology (the study of existence) found in Plato. Xenophon's Socrates is interested in human matters for practical ends, such as managing estates or ruling cities. Furthermore, he is presented as making his philosophy understandable and clear by constant use of analogy: slaves, artisans and animals all appear. This makes his philosophy simple to grasp and interesting. Most importantly, Xenophon's Socrates associates the excellence and honour of a man with his usefulness to others and his state. Socrates himself is helpful in this way and the speaker shows him as well disposed to all types of people and focused on making his associates better men. Thus, Socrates is a true friend and expounds a philosophy of cooperation and mutual benefit. This leads the speaker to the conclusion that Socrates deserved praise and honour from the state, not death. Xenophon even raises Socrates' philanthropy to an almost divine level in using the adjective φιλάνθρωπος (1.2.60) to describe him, a word otherwise reserved for the gods in the *Memorabilia*. Thus, Xenophon's Socrates is not a replica of the real man, but a form of him that is most practical as well as admirable.

Many of the key features of the literary style of the *Memorabilia* are also those of Wisdom Literature. Xenophon brings the teachings of Socrates to life for the reader through memorable anecdotes and vivid direct speech; the moral and political teaching of Socrates is put into real-life settings and given the feel of oral instruction. Although the anecdote in which Socrates implicitly criticizes the Thirty Tyrants with his analogy of the herdsman and engages in a form of *elenchus* with Critias is introduced to show the distance between Critias and Socrates, this passage also provides the first vivid example of Socrates' qualities as a teacher, an introduction to his political theory, an example of his method of philosophical enquiry and proof of his self-control. Not only is Socrates defended against the charges brought against him in 399, but he is also presented as a wise teacher. As well as bringing Socrates to life through recollections of him, the style of writing also clearly imitates Socrates' own style. For example, both Socrates and Xenophon regularly employ analogy and quote poetry. Both also value dialogue and the power of *elenchus* to explore ideas and critically unravel assumptions and poor reasoning. The power of the master is demonstrated by the student who imitates him.

The *Memorabilia* also has a clear didactic nature and Xenophon frequently guides his reader through easily accessible analogies to more complex abstract discussion. At 1.2.19, when he turns to the idea that good men can become bad without sustained effort to be good, Xenophon begins with the image of athletes training their bodies, before providing examples from poetry. This then leads to the practice and discipline needed to learn poetry. In doing so, Xenophon employs images that are directly from the Greek schoolroom; all of his readers would have experience of poetry and athletics. Furthermore, the first extract of poetry is taken from the works of Theognis, a didactic poet. From this point, Xenophon turns to alcoholics and lovers, introducing the dangers to self-discipline that are most easily understood and visible in Greek life, before finally discussing the soul and the appetites of the body in more philosophical language. This passage reads like a well-prepared lesson. This carefully structured teaching is not just found in individual passages, but across the text as a whole. The various aspects of Socrates' teaching found in the early defence are repeated throughout the other books of the text but each time with a new level of complexity. This repetition of the theories means that the reader is frequently exposed to the same ideas but gradually develops their understanding. The whole text is not a rambling eulogy of a wise man but a practical textbook on ethics.

Rhetoric

As well as being a small part of a much greater work of Wisdom Literature, the early sections of the *Memorabilia* are a defence of Socrates and, as such, are a showcase of Xenophon's rhetorical skill and persuasive powers. It is hard to separate the rhetorical aims of the defence from the overall aims of the *Memorabilia*, as many of the techniques employed to convince the reader also draw out the character of Socrates and make the text interesting to read, clear and memorable; the *Memorabilia* has been referred to as a rhetorical form of Wisdom Literature. The arguments of the defence are made from fact and multiple rhetorical devices are then used to convey these arguments in a persuasive manner. It is useful to consider some of the ways in which Xenophon does this.

Characterization is a powerful tool and the contrast of the internal characters of the text adds great force to the defence. The speaker creates a strong contrast between Socrates and the sophists; if Socrates fits in with the normal citizens, he cannot be singled out. The sophists are presented from 1.1.11 as impious fools. Socrates is surprised at their failure to see the difference between what humans can know and what is reserved for the gods. They are referred to as mad men with a wide range of conflicting and impious beliefs who hope to take on the divine powers they attempt to rationalize through experiments. The contrast between Socrates and the sophists continues throughout the text. At 1.2.5 we are told that Socrates would expect no payment for his company and he expressed surprise that anyone could accept money for teaching virtue. We are also frequently reminded of his modest lifestyle and thus lack of interest in financial gain; in fact, he spent his money on others (1.2.60). Furthermore, Socrates is not depicted simply as a teacher of rhetoric, but as a paragon of virtue for others to imitate. The powerful contrast that Xenophon creates in characterizing Socrates and the sophists is a convincing attempt to show Socrates' normality and purely positive qualities.

The characterization of Critias and Alcibiades, and the strong contrast made with Socrates is especially effective. Critias and Alcibiades are depicted as unable to control their emotions. They are found engaging in several forms of excessive behaviour: heterosexual and homosexual lust; illegal use of the laws to attack an individual; corrupt use of rhetoric to make weak arguments strong; and the murder of citizens. Socrates' criticism of Critias as lusting after Euthydemus like a pig is paired with the story of Socrates' run-in with Critias and Charicles, in which Socrates uses *elenchus* to reveal Critias as hot-headed and foolish. The paired anecdotes highlight the excessive and unwise nature of Critias in both his private and public life. At 1.2.40, Alcibiades is presented in an *elenchus* with Pericles in which he convinces Pericles that the rule of the majority is based on force, not persuasion. The ironic use of *elenchus* to make a weak argument strong rather than to lead someone to enlightenment highlights Alcibiades' failure to learn from Socrates as well as supporting the argument that he was only interested in rhetorical skill. Furthermore, almost all the adjectives used to described Critias and Alcibiades are superlatives, highlighting their excessive nature. The stark contrast between Socrates and these two young men demonstrates that Socrates did not influence their behaviour.

The way in which Xenophon presents himself is also an important part of his rhetoric. The main way in which he establishes himself as a credible speaker is by the introduction of an opponent. The anonymous accuser not only structures the defence but also helps to lend weight to Xenophon's arguments. By proposing a set of opposing points from 1.2.9 which can be flattened in quick succession, the accuser helps to demonstrate how successful the speaker's argument is; the more the opposition is set up and defeated, the more convincing Xenophon's argument becomes to his audience. As the dialogue between Xenophon and the accuser continues, the number of lines given to the opposition reduces dramatically and from 1.2.27 until 1.2.49 the accuser remains totally silent. This silence adds to the triumphant nature of Xenophon's argument. It is possible to read the interaction between Xenophon and the accuser as two examples of *elenchus* in which Xenophon plays the role of Socrates, pointing out the failings of the prosecution.

As well as being clever and triumphant, Xenophon also presents himself as a very reasonable man in whom his readers can put their trust. He makes clear that he would not defend the behaviour of Critias and Alcibiades, and does not always dispute the opposition argument in its entirety. By giving some ground, Xenophon comes across as calm and fair-minded. Xenophon presents many of his arguments as his own observations. At 1.2.17, the fact he himself has noticed that teachers make themselves clear to their students makes him appear perceptive and also suggests he has confidence, a characteristic of Xenophon throughout the defence. Xenophon also connects with his audience. The use of analogy to athletics and farming, for example, presents Xenophon as a typical Athenian man with honourable interests. His assumption of standard social stereotypes, such as fathers protecting their sons from bad examples, furthers this characterization. Finally, Xenophon presents himself as very close to Socrates and at 1.2.31 states that he had never heard Socrates make a particular claim. Such closeness to Socrates makes him a more credible speaker and encourages the audience to believe in his characterization of the philosopher.

Not only does Xenophon attempt to win over his audience by presenting himself as one of them, but he also attempts to manipulate the character of the audience. Rhetorical questions are a key way for Xenophon to prompt the readers to think for themselves while also guiding them to the answer he desires. If asked who could fail to know something, the readers are lead to give the answer 'no one' and so put their faith in what is said. Xenophon poses a series of rhetorical questions that show surprise at how the prosecutors persuaded the Athenians at the trial to convict Socrates. Such questions help to differentiate the reader of the text from the Athenians at the real trial, establishing that their conclusion should differ from that of the original jury. By showing his own wonder at the original judgement, Xenophon starts to manipulate his own audience to come to a different verdict.

Xenophon writes in clear and elegant Attic prose and avoids anything florid or excessively rhetorical. Nevertheless, he does use a range of rhetorical and stylistic techniques to help convey his argument and to make the character of Socrates and his teachings more memorable for his readers. This list provides a range of devices, in addition to those already discussed above (anecdote, direct and indirect speech, rhetorical questions), which students should be aware of as they read the passages set for examination. This is by no means an exhaustive list and students should remember that employing the technical terms is not as important as identifying the aim and effect of each device. Xenophon intends to convince his audience of Socrates' innocence and educate them at the same time; the content and meaning of the text are central and it is important not to obscure this behind technical terms. Nevertheless, rhetorical and stylistic devices do play an important role in making the text enjoyable to read, memorable and convincing.

- **Repetition** is found in various forms, either on a large scale across the text or within a single sentence, to drive home a point. For example, Xenophon wonders at how the jury believed the charges three times in the text: 'I have often wondered what were the arguments . . .' (1.1.1.); 'it makes me wonder how the Athenians were ever persuaded . . .' (1.1.20); 'how could he then be guilty of the charges?' (1.2.64).

- **Ring structure** is another form of repetition and is used to structure arguments and to allow for contrast. The most striking presentation of Socrates as a paragon of virtue at 1.2.1–1.2.8 is returned to at 1.2.48; the intervening section deals with the outrageous characters of Critias and Alcibiades. To surround these excessive men with the paragon of virtue is effective in drawing out the contrast between them.

- **Polyptoton**, the repetition of a word in different grammatical forms, is another useful form of repetition. For example, note the various forms of πας found at 1.2.14: **πάντων** Ἀθηναίων, βουλομένῳ τε **πάντα** δι᾽ ἑαυτῶν πράττεσθαι καὶ **πάντων** ὀνομαστοτάτῳ γενέσθαι.

- **Tricolons**, three parallel words, phrases or clauses, are used to draw attention to a point or link together ideas. It is common for the size or significance of ideas to ascend across the three parts of the tricolon; Xenophon will often make the third part far more general or expansive that the first two. At 1.2.17, Xenophon gives three forms of teacher: τίς μὲν γὰρ αὐλητής, τίς δὲ κιθαριστής, τίς δὲ ἄλλος διδάσκαλος; at 1.2.37 Socrates responds to Critias' tricolon with one of his own, rhetorical skill pitted against rhetorical skill: τῶν σκυτέων καὶ τῶν τεκτόνων καὶ τῶν χαλκέων . . . τοῦ τε δικαίου καὶ τοῦ ὁσίου καὶ τῶν ἄλλων τῶν τοιούτων.

- **Polysyndeton**, the use of more conjunctions than is necessary, is used to add drama and impact by increasing the speed of the prose and providing rhythm. It can also draw attention to the number of points being made. This technique is often found with tricolons and can be seen in the examples above.

- **Tautology**, the repetition of an idea in different ways, is commonly used to enforce a point and is exemplified in the tricolon of teachers provided above.

- **Vivid vocabulary and imagery** helps to bring the text to life for the reader, making the process of reading it more enjoyable and the content more memorable. For example, Alcibiades is described as being hunted (θηρώμενος) by the noble women of Thessaly at 1.2.24. The forms of words, such as superlative adjectives and diminutive nouns, should also be noted. For example, superlatives add to the initial description of Critias and Alcibiades at 1.2.12: Κριτίας . . . πλεονεκτίστατός τε καὶ βιαιότατος ἐγένετο, Ἀλκιβιάδης . . . ἀκρατέστατός τε καὶ ὑβριστότατος.

- **Balanced sentences** are used to bring clarity and a logical structure to an argument, and abound in Xenophon's writing. Note that the example of superlatives provided above uses balancing sets of two superlatives.

- **Variation** within and between sentences avoids monotony and makes the text more enjoyable for the reader, demonstrating Xenophon's skill as a writer. At 1.2.21 note how 'to forget' is conveyed in different ways through both variation in vocabulary and polyptoton: ἐπιλανθανομένους . . . λήθην ἐγγιγνομένην . . . ἐπιλάθηταί . . . ἐπιλέλησται.

- **Word order** is often manipulated to add emphasis to ideas. Promotion of words within a phrase is common. Note the position of the participles at 1.2.25: καὶ **ὠγκωμένω** μὲν ἐπὶ γένει, **ἐπηρμένω** δ᾽ ἐπὶ πλούτω, **πεφυσημένω** δ᾽ ἐπὶ δυνάμει, **διατεθρυμμένω** δὲ ὑπὸ πολλῶν ἀνθρώπων. Delaying words or phrases can also have effect, such as the sting in the tail of Socrates' criticism of Critias at 1.2.29: καὶ ταῦτα μηδενὸς ἀγαθοῦ.

- **Antithesis**, the juxtaposition of opposing ideas, is frequently found. ὁ δίκαιος ἄδικος and ὁ σώφρων ὑβριστής found at 1.2.19 are both good examples of Xenophon using this form of contrast to highlight the impossibility of the argument proposed by the accuser.

- **Chiasmus**, the use of an ABBA structure of words or phrases, is another stylish form of word order for various effects. At 1.2.15, an ABA word order is created to emphasize the genitive nouns: πότερόν τις αὐτὼ φῆ τοῦ βίου **τοῦ Σωκράτους** ἐπιθυμήσαντε καὶ **τῆς σωφροσύνης**. Such a structure can be found across long passages to help avoid monotony.

- **Irony and humour** can be found within Xenophon's writing and in his characterization of Socrates. Socrates' comparison of Critias with pigs rubbing themselves against stones at 1.2.30 is inherently amusing: ἐπιθυμῶν Εὐθυδήμω προσκνῆσθαι ὥσπερ τὰ ὕδια τοῖς λίθοις. The use of the diminutive form, piglet, is particularly patronizing. The examples of imagery given above also show the wit that can be found in Xenophon's prose.

- **Dual endings** are used throughout the passage set for examination, almost always for Critias and Alcibiades. Although it is a natural grammatical form to use for the two men, such an extended use of the dual (by far the most extensive use in extant Greek literature) is notable and helps to combine the two characters together as a stereotype of bad oligarchic behaviour. As dual endings are not part of the A-level syllabus, a worksheet detailing the key forms can be found on the website accompanying this anthology.

Further reading

This brief bibliography provides primary reading in the form of translations of Xenophon's Socratic works and other Greek literature that will help students to understand the context of the trial and the various written responses to Socrates. There are also some suggestions for accessible secondary reading on Xenophon, Socrates and Athenian history.

Primary reading

Emlyn-Jones, C., 2005. *Plato: Early Socratic Dialogues*. London: Penguin Books.

MacLeod, M.D., 2008. *Xenophon: Apology and Memorabilia Book 1*. Oxford: Aris & Phillips.

Marchant, E.C., and Todd, O.J., 1923. *Xenophon: Memorabilia, Oeconomicus, Symposium, Apology*. London: Harvard University Press.

Sommerstein, A.H., 1982. *Aristophanes: Clouds*. Oxford: Aris & Phillips.

Tarrant, H. and Tredennick, H., 2003. *Plato: The Last Days of Socrates*. London: Penguin Books.

Waterfield, R. (ed.), 1990. *Xenophon: Conversations of Socrates*. London: Penguin Books.

Secondary reading

Brickhouse, T. and Smith, N.D., 2002. *The Trial and Execution of Socrates: Sources and Controversies*. Oxford: Oxford University Press.

Gray, V., 1998. *The Framing of Socrates: The Literary Interpretation of Xenophon's Memorabilia*. Stuttgart: Franz Steiner Verlag.

Guthrie, W.K.C., 1971. *Socrates*. Cambridge: Cambridge University Press.

Guthrie, W.K.C., 1971. *The Sophists*. Cambridge: Cambridge University Press.

Hughes, B., 2010. *The Hemlock Cup: Socrates, Athens and the Search for the Good Life*. London: Vintage.

Rhodes, P.J., 2006. *A History of the Classical Greek World*. Oxford: Blackwell Publishing.

Strauss, L., 1972. *Xenophon's Socrates*. Ithaca: Cornell University Press.

Waterfield, R., 2009. *Why Socrates Died: Dispelling the Myths*. London: Faber and Faber.

Text

[12]

Ἀλλ᾿ ἔφη γε ὁ κατήγορος, Σωκράτει ὁμιλητὰ γενομένω Κριτίας τε καὶ Ἀλκιβιάδης πλεῖστα κακὰ τὴν πόλιν ἐποιησάτην. Κριτίας μὲν γὰρ τῶν ἐν τῇ ὀλιγαρχίᾳ πάντων πλεονεκτίστατός τε καὶ βιαιότατος ἐγένετο, Ἀλκιβιάδης δὲ αὖ τῶν ἐν τῇ δημοκρατίᾳ πάντων ἀκρατέστατός τε καὶ ὑβριστότατος. [13] ἐγὼ δ᾿, εἰ μέν τι κακὸν ἐκείνω τὴν πόλιν ἐποιησάτην, οὐκ ἀπολογήσομαι· τὴν δὲ πρὸς Σωκράτην συνουσίαν αὐτοῖν ὡς ἐγένετο διηγήσομαι. [14] ἐγενέσθην μὲν γὰρ δὴ τὼ ἄνδρε τούτω φύσει φιλοτιμοτάτω πάντων Ἀθηναίων, βουλομένω τε πάντα δι᾿ ἑαυτῶν πράττεσθαι καὶ πάντων ὀνομαστοτάτω γενέσθαι. ᾔδεσαν δὲ Σωκράτην ἀπ᾿ ἐλαχίστων μὲν χρημάτων αὐταρκέστατα ζῶντα, τῶν ἡδονῶν δὲ πασῶν ἐγκρατέστατον ὄντα, τοῖς δὲ διαλεγομένοις αὐτῷ πᾶσι χρώμενον ἐν τοῖς λόγοις ὅπως βούλοιτο. [15] ταῦτα δὲ ὁρῶντε καὶ ὄντε οἵω προείρησθον, πότερόν τις αὐτὼ φῇ τοῦ βίου τοῦ Σωκράτους ἐπιθυμήσαντε καὶ τῆς σωφροσύνης, ἣν ἐκεῖνος εἶχεν, ὀρέξασθαι τῆς ὁμιλίας αὐτοῦ, ἢ νομίσαντε, εἰ ὁμιλησαίτην ἐκείνῳ, γενέσθαι ἂν ἱκανωτάτω λέγειν τε καὶ πράττειν; [16] ἐγὼ μὲν γὰρ ἡγοῦμαι, θεοῦ διδόντος αὐτοῖν ἢ ζῆν ὅλον τὸν βίον ὥσπερ ζῶντα Σωκράτην ἑώρων ἢ τεθνάναι, ἑλέσθαι ἂν μᾶλλον αὐτὼ τεθνάναι. δῆλω δ᾿ ἐγενέσθην ἐξ ὧν ἐπραξάτην· ὡς γὰρ τάχιστα κρείττονε τῶν συγγιγνομένων ἡγησάσθην εἶναι, εὐθὺς ἀποπηδήσαντε Σωκράτους ἐπραττέτην τὰ πολιτικά, ὧνπερ ἕνεκα Σωκράτους ὠρεχθήτην.

[17]

Ἴσως οὖν εἴποι τις ἂν πρὸς ταῦτα ὅτι ἐχρῆν τὸν Σωκράτην μὴ πρότερον τὰ πολιτικὰ διδάσκειν τοὺς συνόντας ἢ σωφρονεῖν. ἐγὼ δὲ πρὸς τοῦτο μὲν οὐκ ἀντιλέγω· πάντας δὲ τοὺς διδάσκοντας ὁρῶ αὐτοὺς δεικνύντας τε τοῖς μανθάνουσιν ᾗπερ αὐτοὶ ποιοῦσιν ἃ διδάσκουσι καὶ τῷ λόγῳ προσβιβάζοντας. οἶδα δὲ καὶ Σωκράτην δεικνύντα τοῖς συνοῦσιν ἑαυτὸν καλὸν κἀγαθὸν ὄντα καὶ διαλεγόμενον κάλλιστα περὶ ἀρετῆς καὶ τῶν ἄλλων ἀνθρωπίνων. [18] οἶδα δὲ κἀκείνω σωφρονοῦντε, ἔστε Σωκράτει συνήστην, οὐ φοβουμένω μὴ ζημιοῖντο ἢ παίοιντο ὑπὸ Σωκράτους, ἀλλ᾿ οἰομένω τότε κράτιστον εἶναι τοῦτο πράττειν.

[19]

Ἴσως οὖν εἴποιεν ἂν πολλοὶ τῶν φασκόντων φιλοσοφεῖν ὅτι οὐκ ἂν ποτε ὁ δίκαιος ἄδικος γένοιτο, οὐδὲ ὁ σώφρων ὑβριστής, οὐδὲ ἄλλο οὐδὲν ὧν μάθησίς ἐστιν ὁ μαθὼν ἀνεπιστήμων ἄν ποτε γένοιτο. ἐγὼ δὲ περὶ τούτων οὐχ οὕτω γιγνώσκω· ὁρῶ γὰρ ὥσπερ τὰ τοῦ σώματος ἔργα τοὺς μὴ τὰ σώματα ἀσκοῦντας οὐ δυναμένους ποιεῖν, οὕτω καὶ τὰ τῆς ψυχῆς ἔργα τοὺς μὴ τὴν ψυχὴν ἀσκοῦντας οὐ δυναμένους· οὔτε γὰρ ἃ δεῖ πράττειν οὔτε ὧν δεῖ ἀπέχεσθαι δύνανται. **[20]** δι᾽ ὃ καὶ τοὺς υἱεῖς οἱ πατέρες, κἂν ὦσι σώφρονες, ὅμως ἀπὸ τῶν πονηρῶν ἀνθρώπων εἴργουσιν, ὡς τὴν μὲν τῶν χρηστῶν ὁμιλίαν ἄσκησιν οὖσαν τῆς ἀρετῆς, τὴν δὲ τῶν πονηρῶν κατάλυσιν. μαρτυρεῖ δὲ καὶ τῶν ποιητῶν ὅ τε λέγων·

Ἐσθλῶν μὲν γὰρ ἄπ᾽ ἐσθλὰ διδάξεαι· ἢν δὲ κακοῖσι
    συμμίσγῃς, ἀπολεῖς καὶ τὸν ἐόντα νόον,

καὶ ὁ λέγων·

Αὐτὰρ ἀνὴρ ἀγαθὸς τοτὲ μὲν κακός, ἄλλοτε δ᾽ ἐσθλός.

[21]

κἀγὼ δὲ μαρτυρῶ τούτοις· ὁρῶ γὰρ ὥσπερ τῶν ἐν μέτρῳ πεποιημένων ἐπῶν τοὺς μὴ μελετῶντας ἐπιλανθανομένους, οὕτω καὶ τῶν διδασκαλικῶν λόγων τοῖς ἀμελοῦσι λήθην ἐγγιγνομένην. ὅταν δὲ τῶν νουθετικῶν λόγων ἐπιλάθηταί τις, ἐπιλέλησται καὶ ὧν ἡ ψυχὴ πάσχουσα τῆς σωφροσύνης ἐπεθύμει· τούτων δ᾽ ἐπιλαθόμενον οὐδὲν θαυμαστὸν καὶ τῆς σωφροσύνης ἐπιλαθέσθαι. **[22]** ὁρῶ δὲ καὶ τοὺς εἰς φιλοποσίαν προαχθέντας καὶ τοὺς εἰς ἔρωτας ἐγκυλισθέντας ἧττον δυναμένους τῶν τε δεόντων ἐπιμελεῖσθαι καὶ τῶν μὴ δεόντων ἀπέχεσθαι. πολλοὶ γὰρ καὶ χρημάτων δυνάμενοι φείδεσθαι, πρὶν ἐρᾶν, ἐρασθέντες οὐκέτι δύνανται· καὶ τὰ χρήματα καταναλώσαντες, ὧν πρόσθεν ἀπείχοντο κερδῶν, αἰσχρὰ νομίζοντες εἶναι, τούτων οὐκ ἀπέχονται. **[23]** πῶς οὖν οὐκ ἐνδέχεται σωφρονήσαντα πρόσθεν αὖθις μὴ σωφρονεῖν καὶ δίκαια δυνηθέντα πράττειν αὖθις ἀδυνατεῖν; πάντα μὲν οὖν ἔμοιγε δοκεῖ τὰ καλὰ καὶ τἀγαθὰ ἀσκητὰ εἶναι, οὐχ ἥκιστα δὲ σωφροσύνη. ἐν γὰρ τῷ αὐτῷ σώματι συμπεφυτευμέναι τῇ ψυχῇ αἱ ἡδοναὶ πείθουσιν αὐτὴν μὴ σωφρονεῖν, ἀλλὰ τὴν ταχίστην ἑαυταῖς τε καὶ τῷ σώματι χαρίζεσθαι.

[24]

Καὶ Κριτίας δὴ καὶ Ἀλκιβιάδης, ἕως μὲν Σωκράτει συνήστην, ἐδυνάσθην ἐκείνῳ χρωμένω συμμάχῳ τῶν μὴ καλῶν ἐπιθυμιῶν κρατεῖν· ἐκείνου δ᾽ ἀπαλλαγέντε, Κριτίας μὲν φυγὼν εἰς Θετταλίαν ἐκεῖ συνῆν ἀνθρώποις ἀνομίᾳ μᾶλλον ἢ δικαιοσύνῃ χρωμένοις, Ἀλκιβιάδης δ᾽ αὖ διὰ μὲν κάλλος ὑπὸ πολλῶν καὶ σεμνῶν γυναικῶν θηρώμενος, διὰ δύναμιν δὲ τὴν ἐν τῇ πόλει καὶ τοῖς συμμάχοις ὑπὸ πολλῶν καὶ δυνατῶν [κολακεύειν] ἀνθρώπων διαθρυπτόμενος, ὑπὸ δὲ τοῦ δήμου τιμώμενος καὶ ῥᾳδίως πρωτεύων, ὥσπερ οἱ τῶν γυμνικῶν ἀγώνων ἀθληταὶ ῥᾳδίως πρωτεύοντες ἀμελοῦσι τῆς ἀσκήσεως, οὕτω κἀκεῖνος ἠμέλησεν αὑτοῦ. [25] τοιούτων δὲ συμβάντων αὐτοῖν, καὶ ὠγκωμένω μὲν ἐπὶ γένει, ἐπηρμένω δ᾽ ἐπὶ πλούτω, πεφυσημένω δ᾽ ἐπὶ δυνάμει, διατεθρυμμένω δὲ ὑπὸ πολλῶν ἀνθρώπων, ἐπὶ δὲ πᾶσι τούτοις διεφθαρμένω καὶ πολὺν χρόνον ἀπὸ Σωκράτους γεγονότε, τί θαυμαστὸν εἰ ὑπερηφάνω ἐγενέσθην; [26] εἶτα, εἰ μέν τι ἐπλημμελησάτην, τούτου Σωκράτην ὁ κατήγορος αἰτιᾶται; ὅτι δὲ νέω ὄντε αὐτώ, ἡνίκα καὶ ἀγνωμονεστάτω καὶ ἀκρατεστάτω εἰκὸς εἶναι, Σωκράτης παρέσχε σώφρονε, οὐδενὸς ἐπαίνου δοκεῖ τῷ κατηγόρω ἄξιος εἶναι; οὐ μὴν τά γε ἄλλα οὕτω κρίνεται. [27] τίς μὲν γὰρ αὐλητής, τίς δὲ κιθαριστής, τίς δὲ ἄλλος διδάσκαλος ἱκανοὺς ποιήσας τοὺς μαθητάς, ἐὰν πρὸς ἄλλους ἐλθόντες χείρους φανῶσιν, αἰτίαν ἔχει τούτου; τίς δὲ πατήρ, ἐὰν ὁ παῖς αὐτοῦ συνδιατρίβων τω σωφρονῇ, ὕστερον δὲ ἄλλω τω συγγενόμενος πονηρὸς γένηται, τὸν πρόσθεν αἰτιᾶται, ἀλλ᾽ οὐχ ὅσω ἂν παρὰ τῷ ὑστέρω χείρων φαίνηται, τοσούτω μᾶλλον ἐπαινεῖ τὸν πρότερον; ἀλλ᾽ οἵ γε πατέρες αὐτοὶ συνόντες τοῖς υἱέσι, τῶν παίδων πλημμελούντων, οὐκ αἰτίαν ἔχουσιν, ἐὰν αὐτοὶ σωφρονῶσιν. [28] οὕτω δὲ καὶ Σωκράτην δίκαιον ἦν κρίνειν· εἰ μὲν αὐτὸς ἐποίει τι φαῦλον, εἰκότως ἂν ἐδόκει πονηρὸς εἶναι· εἰ δ᾽ αὐτὸς σωφρονῶν διετέλει, πῶς ἂν δικαίως τῆς οὐκ ἐνούσης αὐτῷ κακίας αἰτίαν ἔχοι;

[29]

Ἀλλ᾽ εἰ καὶ μηδὲν αὐτὸς πονηρὸν ποιῶν ἐκείνους φαῦλα πράττοντας ὁρῶν ἐπῄνει, δικαίως ἂν ἐπιτιμῷτο. Κριτίαν μὲν τοίνυν αἰσθανόμενος ἐρῶντα Εὐθυδήμου καὶ πειρῶντα χρῆσθαι, καθάπερ οἱ πρὸς τἀφροδίσια τῶν σωμάτων ἀπολαύοντες, ἀπέτρεπε φάσκων ἀνελεύθερόν τε εἶναι καὶ οὐ πρέπον ἀνδρὶ καλῷ κἀγαθῷ τὸν ἐρώμενον, ᾧ βούλεται πολλοῦ ἄξιος φαίνεσθαι, προσαιτεῖν ὥσπερ τοὺς πτωχοὺς ἱκετεύοντα καὶ δεόμενον προσδοῦναι, καὶ ταῦτα μηδενὸς ἀγαθοῦ. [30] τοῦ δὲ Κριτίου τοῖς τοιούτοις οὐχ ὑπακούοντος οὐδὲ ἀποτρεπομένου, λέγεται τὸν Σωκράτην ἄλλων τε πολλῶν παρόντων καὶ τοῦ Εὐθυδήμου εἰπεῖν ὅτι ὑικὸν αὐτῷ δοκοίη πάσχειν ὁ Κριτίας, ἐπιθυμῶν Εὐθυδήμω προσκνῆσθαι ὥσπερ τὰ ὕδια τοῖς λίθοις. [31] ἐξ ὧν δὴ καὶ ἐμίσει τὸν Σωκράτην ὁ Κριτίας, ὥστε καὶ ὅτε τῶν τριάκοντα ὢν νομοθέτης μετὰ Χαρικλέους ἐγένετο, ἀπεμνημόνευσεν αὐτῷ καὶ ἐν τοῖς νόμοις ἔγραψε λόγων τέχνην μὴ διδάσκειν, ἐπηρεάζων ἐκείνω καὶ οὐκ ἔχων ὅπῃ ἐπιλάβοιτο, ἀλλὰ τὸ κοινῇ τοῖς φιλοσόφοις ὑπὸ τῶν πολλῶν ἐπιτιμώμενον ἐπιφέρων αὐτῷ καὶ διαβάλλων πρὸς τοὺς πολλούς· οὐδὲ γὰρ ἔγωγε οὔτ᾽ αὐτὸς τοῦτο πώποτε Σωκράτους ἤκουσα οὔτ᾽ ἄλλου του φάσκοντος ἀκηκοέναι ᾐσθόμην. [32] ἐδήλωσε δέ· ἐπεὶ γὰρ οἱ τριάκοντα πολλοὺς μὲν τῶν πολιτῶν καὶ οὐ τοὺς χειρίστους ἀπέκτεινον, πολλοὺς δὲ προετρέποντο ἀδικεῖν, εἶπέ που ὁ Σωκράτης ὅτι θαυμαστὸν οἱ δοκοίη εἶναι, εἴ τις γενόμενος βοῶν ἀγέλης νομεὺς καὶ τὰς βοῦς ἐλάττους τε καὶ χείρους ποιῶν μὴ ὁμολογοίη κακὸς βουκόλος εἶναι, ἔτι δὲ θαυμαστότερον, εἴ τις προστάτης γενόμενος πόλεως καὶ ποιῶν τοὺς πολίτας ἐλάττους τε καὶ χείρους μὴ αἰσχύνεται μηδ᾽ οἴεται κακὸς εἶναι προστάτης τῆς πόλεως. [33] ἀπαγγελθέντος δὲ αὐτοῖς τούτου, καλέσαντες ὅ τε Κριτίας καὶ ὁ Χαρικλῆς τὸν Σωκράτην τόν τε νόμον ἐδεικνύτην αὐτῷ καὶ τοῖς νέοις ἀπειπέτην μὴ διαλέγεσθαι. ὁ δὲ Σωκράτης ἐπήρετο αὐτὼ εἰ ἐξείη πυνθάνεσθαι, εἴ τι ἀγνοοῖτο τῶν προαγορευομένων. τὼ δ᾽ ἐφάτην. [34] Ἐγὼ τοίνυν, ἔφη, παρεσκεύασμαι μὲν πείθεσθαι τοῖς νόμοις· ὅπως δὲ μὴ δι᾽ ἄγνοιαν λάθω τι παρανομήσας, τοῦτο βούλομαι σαφῶς μαθεῖν παρ᾽ ὑμῶν, πότερον τὴν τῶν λόγων τέχνην σὺν τοῖς ὀρθῶς λεγομένοις εἶναι νομίζοντες ἢ σὺν τοῖς μὴ ὀρθῶς ἀπέχεσθαι κελεύετε αὐτῆς. εἰ μὲν γὰρ σὺν τοῖς ὀρθῶς, δῆλον ὅτι ἀφεκτέον <ἂν> εἴη τοῦ ὀρθῶς λέγειν· εἰ δὲ σὺν τοῖς μὴ ὀρθῶς, δῆλον ὅτι πειρατέον ὀρθῶς λέγειν. [35] καὶ ὁ Χαρικλῆς ὀργισθεὶς αὐτῷ, Ἐπειδή, ἔφη, ὦ Σώκρατες, ἀγνοεῖς, τάδε σοι εὐμαθέστερα ὄντα προαγορεύομεν, τοῖς νέοις ὅλως μὴ διαλέγεσθαι. καὶ ὁ Σωκράτης, Ἵνα τοίνυν, ἔφη, μὴ ἀμφίβολον ἦ [ὡς ἄλλο τι ποιῶ ἢ τὰ προηγορευμένα], ὁρίσατέ μοι μέχρι πόσων ἐτῶν δεῖ νομίζειν νέους εἶναι τοὺς ἀνθρώπους. καὶ ὁ Χαρικλῆς, Ὅσουπερ, εἶπε, χρόνου βουλεύειν οὐκ ἔξεστιν, ὡς οὔπω φρονίμοις οὖσι· μηδὲ σὺ διαλέγου νεωτέροις τριάκοντα ἐτῶν. [36] Μηδ᾽ ἐάν τι ὠνῶμαι, ἔφη, ἦν πωλῇ νεώτερος τριάκοντα ἐτῶν, ἔρωμαι ὁπόσου πωλεῖ; Ναὶ τά γε τοιαῦτα, ἔφη ὁ Χαρικλῆς· ἀλλά τοι σύγε, ὦ Σώκρατες, εἴωθας εἰδὼς πῶς ἔχει τὰ πλεῖστα ἐρωτᾶν· ταῦτα οὖν μὴ ἐρώτα. Μηδ᾽ ἀποκρίνωμαι οὖν, ἔφη, ἄν τίς με ἐρωτᾷ νέος, ἐὰν εἰδῶ, οἷον ποῦ οἰκεῖ Χαρικλῆς ἢ ποῦ ἐστι Κριτίας; Ναὶ τά γε τοιαῦτα, ἔφη ὁ Χαρικλῆς. [37] ὁ δὲ Κριτίας, Ἀλλὰ τῶνδέ τοί σε ἀπέχεσθαι, ἔφη, δεήσει, ὦ Σώκρατες, τῶν σκυτέων καὶ τῶν τεκτόνων καὶ τῶν χαλκέων· καὶ γὰρ οἶμαι αὐτοὺς ἤδη κατατετρῖφθαι διαθρυλουμένους ὑπὸ σοῦ. Οὐκοῦν, ἔφη ὁ Σωκράτης, καὶ τῶν ἑπομένων τούτοις, τοῦ τε δικαίου καὶ τοῦ ὁσίου καὶ τῶν ἄλλων τῶν τοιούτων; Ναὶ μὰ Δί᾽, ἔφη ὁ Χαρικλῆς· καὶ τῶν βουκόλων γε· εἰ δὲ μή, φυλάττου ὅπως μὴ καὶ σὺ ἐλάττους τὰς βοῦς ποιήσῃς. [38] ἔνθα καὶ δῆλον ἐγένετο ὅτι ἀπαγγελθέντος αὐτοῖς τοῦ περὶ τῶν βοῶν λόγου ὠργίζοντο τῷ Σωκράτει.

Οἵα μὲν οὖν ἡ συνουσία ἐγεγόνει Κριτίᾳ πρὸς Σωκράτην καὶ ὡς εἶχον πρὸς ἀλλήλους, εἴρηται.

Commentary Notes

In Chapter 2 of Book 1, Xenophon refutes the charge that Socrates was a bad influence on the young men of Athens. He presents us with an accuser who turns to Socrates' arguments against using allotment in the democracy, which he claims have made the young men violently turn against their constitution, and points to Critias and Alcibiades, both of whom have committed great injustices against Athens, as examples of the dangerous effect Socrates has on his young companions. Xenophon's main argument is clear from the start: a man who practises excellence and self-control like Socrates can only have the positive effect of making others in their presence more virtuous and that those who are wise avoid violent behaviour and prefer persuasion to show others what they think is the right course.

Section 12

γε: throws emphasis onto the verb but this is difficult to convey in English other than in tone.

ὁ κατήγορος: 'the accuser' – this man, who has just charged Socrates with encouraging his companions to despise the laws of Athens and thus inciting violence among them, is unnamed in the text. At this point Xenophon has already dealt with the charges made by Meletus, Anytus and Lycon, based on what is found in the defence speeches retrospectively written for Socrates by Plato and Xenophon, and moves to other accusations. It is likely that Xenophon is responding to charges posed by Polycrates. (See the Introduction, '*Memorabilia* 1.1.1-1.2.62', for further detail.)

ὁμιλητὰ γενομένω ... ἐποιησάτην: dual endings are used throughout this text for the double act of Critias and Alcibiades; in the plural these words would be ὁμιληταὶ γενόμενοι ... ἐποίησαν. The website accompanying this text provides a detailed resource on the dual form. The participle γενομένω could be temporal or causal: 'after they became ...' or 'since they became ...'.

πλεῖστα κακὰ τὴν πόλιν ἐποιησάτην: ποιέω + acc. + acc. is translated 'to do X to Y'.

Κριτίας: see the Introduction, 'Critias and Alcibiades', for further detail.

ἐν τῇ ὀλιγαρχίᾳ: the oligarchy refers to the Thirty Tyrants, a pro-Spartan oligarchic government of thirty men that took power in Athens in 404 BC after the Athenians lost to Sparta in the Peloponnesian War. (See the Introduction, 'The political charges', for further detail.)

πλεονεκτίστατός τε καὶ βιαιότατος ... ἀκρατέστατός τε καὶ ὑβριστότατος: both Critias and Alcibiades are described by pairs of superlatives. These are all morally loaded terms that demonstrate their total lack of self-control. One can only wonder what the virtuous and moderate Socrates just described in sections 1–4 can have to do with such violent and excessive behaviour.

Ἀλκιβιάδης: see the Introduction, 'Critias and Alcibiades', for further detail.

δὲ αὖ: 'on the other hand'

ἐν τῇ δημοκρατίᾳ: this most likely refers to the Athenian democracy in the decade leading up to the failed Sicilian Expedition of 415–413 BC, during which Alcibiades was immoderate in both his pursuit of power and his private life. Note how Critias and Alcibiades between themselves cover a large range of vices across both constitutional periods of Athens' recent political history. (See the Introduction, 'The political charges', for further detail.)

Section 13

οὐκ ἀπολογήσομαι: Xenophon makes it clear from the start that he is not going to defend Critias and Alcibiades, only Socrates' influence on them. It is interesting to note that Xenophon had much in common with both these men. (See the Introduction, 'Critias and Alcibiades' and 'Xenophon', for further detail.)

ἐκείνω ... ἐποιησάτην: dual forms, ἐκείνω is nominative.

τὴν δὲ πρὸς Σωκράτην συνουσίαν αὐτοῖν ὡς ἐγένετο διηγήσομαι: an example of prolepsis, where the subject of the indirect question (the friendship) is taken out of the indirect question and made the object of the main verb (I shall explain) for greater emphasis. An English translation can also retain the emphasis found in the Greek: 'as to their association with Socrates, I will explain how it came about'.

αὐτοῖν: dual genitive or dative plural form for possession.

Section 14

ἐγενέσθην ... τὼ ἄνδρε τούτω ... φιλοτιμοτάτω ... βουλομένω ... ὀνομαστοτάτω: dual forms, the noun, pronoun and adjectives are all nominative.

μὲν γὰρ δὴ: this cluster of particles implies how obvious or well-known this is, so a good translation would be 'of course'. The μὲν balances with ᾔδεσαν δὲ at the beginning of the next sentence, contrasting the success and influence they had already achieved with the skills they knew Socrates possessed but which they had not yet mastered.

φύσει: 'by nature' – Xenophon makes it clear that these characteristics cannot be linked to Socrates.

φιλοτιμοτάτω ... ὀνομαστοτάτω ... ἐγκρατέστατον: Xenophon continues to use plenty of superlatives. The first two refer to Critias and Alcibiades and again highlight their excessive nature. The third is very much contrasting in meaning and describes Socrates.

πάντα δι᾽ ἑαυτῶν πράττεσθαι: 'to have everything done through them' – i.e. to be in complete control. Such a wish is deeply undemocratic.

ᾔδεσαν δὲ ... ζῶντα ... ὄντα ... χρώμενον: this indirect statement following a verb of knowing is formed by three separate participle clauses with similar structures. The particles μὲν ... δὲ ... δὲ connect the clauses. Note how Xenophon changes from dual verbs to plural verbs with no effect on the meaning.

χρώμενον: 'treating' – the basic sense of the verb is 'to use' or 'to treat like an object'.

ἐν τοῖς λόγοις: 'in arguments'.

ὅπως βούλοιτο: the optative is used here to create an indefinite clause within indirect statement, best translated 'however he wanted'.

Section 15

ταῦτα δὲ ὁρῶντε καὶ ὄντε ... αὐτὼ: the dual accusative participles ὁρῶντε and ὄντε agree with αὐτὼ, which is the accusative of the following indirect statement. They are best translated as causal, 'since they saw this ...'.

οἵω προείρησθον: both forms are dual and although the verb is perfect passive, it is best translated in the perfect first person active as 'the sort of men I have just described'.

πότερόν τις αὐτὼ φῇ ... ἤ: Xenophon wonders who would give the unlikely argument of the accuser rather than his more convincing analysis of the situation. φῇ is a deliberative subjunctive and the main verb for two indirect statements, which are formed by the accusative αὐτὼ and the infinitive ὀρέξασθαι. The accusative and infinitive need to be repeated after ἤ for the second indirect statement. Accusative participles on either side of the πότερόν ... ἤ structure should be translated as causal clauses and thus give the overall structure of the question as 'would anyone say that they did X because ... rather than that they did X because ...'. αὐτὼ refers to Critias and Alcibiades.

τοῦ βίου τοῦ Σωκράτους ἐπιθυμήσαντε καὶ τῆς σωφροσύνης: 'since they longed for ...' – the participle ἐπιθυμήσαντε is in the accusative dual form and is best translated as a causal clause, as shown above.

νομίσαντε: 'since they thought that ...' – another dual accusative participle, which is best translated as a causal clause, as shown above.

εἰ ὁμιλησαίτην ... γενέσθαι ἄν: ὁμιλησαίτην is in the dual optative form. The construction is a future remote condition in indirect statement, best translated 'if they were to keep his company, they would become ...'.

ἱκανωτάτω: this is the dual accusative form. When followed by an infinitive, ἱκανός means 'skilled at'.

λέγειν τε καὶ πράττειν: i.e. they wanted the influence that Socrates' persuasive debating skills had to offer and which would allow them to succeed in politics, not his meagre lifestyle of self-control. Such rhetorical skill was vital if a man wanted to hold any power over the men in the Council or Assembly.

Section 16

ἡγοῦμαι: the main verb introduces an indirect statement. Xenophon makes it as obvious as possible that Critias and Alcibiades were only interested in the skills Socrates could provide with this hyperbolic description of them preferring death to a lifetime of Socratic self-control.

θεοῦ διδόντος: 'if god had given them the choice' – the genitive absolute is a hidden protasis (if-clause) of a past closed or unfulfilled condition. The god is presumably Zeus, but this is purely a rhetorical device and should not be scrutinized for any signs it may give of the piety of the author.

αὐτοῖν: dative dual form.

ἑλέσθαι ἄν: the apodosis (then-clause) of a past closed or unfulfilled condition: 'that they would have chosen'. This is in indirect statement, so what would usually be the aorist indicative is an aorist infinitive.

αὐτώ: accusative dual form.

δῆλω δ᾽ ἐγενέσθην … ἐπραξάτην: Xenophon provides evidence to back up his claim. 'this was made clear by their behaviour' is a more idiomatic translation of 'they became obvious from the things they did'. Note the dual forms of the adjective and both verbs.

ἐξ ὧν: understand ἐξ ὧν ἅ – as is common in Greek, the antecedent (what the relative pronoun refers back to) and the relative pronoun have been telescoped into one.

ὡς … τάχιστα: 'as soon as'.

κρείττονε … ἡγησάσθην … ἀποπηδήσαντε … ἐπραττέτην … ὠρεχθήτην: note the dual forms.

τῶν συγγιγνομένων: the participle should be translated as a noun and it is a genitive of comparison: 'than their companions'.

ἐπραττέτην τὰ πολιτικά: 'took to politics'. Note the use of the imperfect tense here, which can be inceptive, i.e. 'they began to …'.

Section 17

εἴποι τις ἄν: a potential optative, best translated 'someone might say'. Xenophon introduces a possible counter-argument, whether Socrates should have allowed Critias and Alcibiades to gain these political skills without first ensuring they had developed the necessary self-restraint. He then goes on to tackle this point. Such internal opposition is an important part of Xenophon's rhetoric. (See the Introduction, 'Rhetoric', for further detail.)

πρότερον … ἤ: translate both words together at the point ἤ comes in the text.

τοὺς συνόντας: 'his followers'.

σωφρονεῖν: this infinitive contrasts with τὰ πολιτικά, both following the infinitive διδάσκειν. The basic meaning of the verb is 'to be of sound mind' and Xenophon, based on the teaching of Socrates, would define the concept as wisdom required for self-control and moderation, particularly concerning pleasures of the flesh.

οὐκ ἀντιλέγω: Xenophon presents himself as a fair and controlled debater, allowing his hypothetical interlocutor some ground. He is comparable to Socrates in the dialogues of both Xenophon and Plato. However, he only agrees that self-control should be taught before political skills, he does not agree that Socrates failed in this respect.

τοὺς διδάσκοντας ὁρῶ ... δεικνύντας ... προσβιβάζοντας: the main verb here is followed by two supplementary participles in agreement with τοὺς διδάσκοντας, which could be translated as participles to show Xenophon physically sees this ('I see teachers showing . . .') or as an indirect statement that implies Xenophon perceives this ('I understand that teachers show . . .'). The second is more likely here.

τοὺς διδάσκοντας ... τοῖς μανθάνουσιν: translate the participles as nouns: 'teachers . . . to their pupils'.

ἃ διδάσκουσι: read ταῦτα ἃ for ἃ, the antecedent and the relative pronoun have telescoped into one.

τῷ λόγῳ: 'by argument'

προσβιβάζοντας: understand an accusative object, such as τοὺς μανθάνοντας.

οἶδα ... δεικνύντα: an indirect statement formed with a participle follows this verb of knowing. Xenophon moves from a verb of perceiving to one of knowing and promotes the verb to the beginning of the sentence for emphasis.

καλὸν κἀγαθὸν: a common formulation, originally used in Athens for a gentleman or an aristocratic man of high status and nobility with the implication that these qualities came from birth. However, its meaning was developed by Socrates and used by Xenophon to refer more specifically to the moral qualities of an excellent man such as Socrates. The term encompasses self-control, courage, wisdom, piety, morality and generosity of spirit.

διαλεγόμενον κάλλιστα: κάλλιστα is a superlative adverb.

περὶ ἀρετῆς καὶ τῶν ἄλλων ἀνθρωπίνων: 'about virtue and the other human concerns' – virtue, according to Socrates, allowed the human soul to excel and practicing virtue was the route to achieving genuine happiness. Originally only denoting excellence in a skill as displayed through competition or war, it became a moral concept for Socrates and Xenophon, concerned with the principles of right and wrong behaviour, and included justice, piety, wisdom, courage and self-control. Xenophon is both specific and general here to imply that Socrates gave the full moral education that his opponent was asking about.

Section 18

οἶδα κἀκείνω ... σωφρονοῦντε: another indirect statement formed with a participle after a verb of knowing. κἀκείνω and σωφρονοῦντε are in the accusative dual form. κἀκείνω is crasis of καὶ ἐκείνω and the καὶ is best translated here as 'also'. The second sentence begins with οἶδα to show Xenophon's certainty that Critias and Alcibiades did receive an education in self-restraint from Socrates as they demonstrated this in their behaviour as long as they were his companions.

συνήστην: dual verb form.

οὐ φοβουμένῳ ... ἀλλ᾽ οἰομένῳ: two dual accusative participles, best translated as causal clauses, 'not because ... but because ...'.

μὴ ζημιοῖντο ἢ παίοιντο: the optatives are used here in a fearing clause in the historic sequence. Xenophon can confirm that their self-control was genuine because Socrates did not beat his pupils or create an atmosphere of fear, but taught only by example and with the power of persuasion so that genuine behaviour was developed.

οἰομένῳ τότε κράτιστον εἶναι: the participle οἰομένῳ is the introductory verb for an accusative and infinitive indirect statement.

Section 19

εἴποιεν ἄν ... ὅτι: a potential optative, best translated as 'might say', which leads into an indirect statement. Another counter-argument is introduced which questions whether men who gain knowledge can then become ignorant in the future.

τῶν φασκόντων φιλοσοφεῖν: 'those who style themselves as philosophers' – φάσκω often implies an allegation rather than a truthful assertion. This is a clear dig at the sophists. Their interpretation of virtue differed from Socrates' and had a greater focus on teaching the skills of persuasion and influence over others without implying the introspection and constant practice that Socrates' moral definition of the term expounded. There was a popular belief that these expensive teachers dealt in duplicity and trained their students in deceptive reasoning and immorality rather than the lifestyle of virtue that improves the soul and leads to happiness. (See the Introduction, 'The charges of impiety and corruption of the youth', for further detail.)

ἄν ... γένοιτο ... ἄν ... γένοιτο: the potential optative after a negative is best translated 'could become'. Xenophon frequently uses tricolons that lead from the specific to the general.

ἄλλο οὐδὲν: 'with regard to nothing else'.

ὧν μάθησίς ἐστιν: the antecedent of the relative pronoun is missing here but the meaning is clear: 'where learning is possible' or 'which can be learnt'. Use of a noun where a verb is possible is unusual in Greek and so draws attention to the philosophical concept.

ὁ μαθών: 'a knowledgeable man' or more literally 'he who has already learnt it'.

γιγνώσκω: 'I have a view' is the best translation in this context.

ὁρῶ: the main verb of perceiving introduces two balancing indirect statements formed using accusatives and participles. Xenophon provides his own contrasting view that constant training is needed to retain knowledge and to ensure the proper working of the soul, something he compares to the constant training the body requires. Xenophon frequently uses analogies to visible examples of the concept he discusses in order to clarify abstract ideas; Socrates, as depicted by Plato and Xenophon frequently did the same. The many analogies that Xenophon uses come from elementary education in Athens: physical work in the gymnasium, learning to play musical instruments, and learning to recite great works of poetry.

τὰ τοῦ σώματος ... οὐ δυναμένους ποιεῖν: in this first indirect statement, the main participle is δυναμένους and the accusative subject is τοὺς μὴ ...

ἀσκοῦντας ('those who don't train'). μὴ is found here instead of οὐ to give a generic sense as Xenophon is referring to no one in particular, but the sort of person who does not train their body.

τὰ τῆς ψυχῆς ... οὐ δυναμένους: the structure of the second indirect statement mirrors the first, but ποιεῖν needs to be supplied from the first.

ἃ δεῖ πράττειν οὔτε ὧν δεῖ ἀπέχεσθαι δύνανται: for the two relative clauses, the antecedent of the relative pronoun needs to be supplied (e.g. '... *those things* which they must do ...') and each infinitive should be translated after both the main verb δύνανται and δεῖ in the relative clause.

Section 20

δι' ὅ: 'for which reason'

κἂν ... ὅμως: 'even if ... nevertheless' – crasis of καὶ ἐάν introduces the protasis of a conditional in which the apodosis is true in all cases regardless of the condition, i.e. parents always keep their children away from bad company, whether the children are already good or bad.

ὡς τὴν ... ὁμιλίαν ... οὖσαν: an accusative absolute, normally only used instead of a genitive absolute with impersonal verbs, can be used with any verb after ὡς: 'since the company ...'. However, this is very rare.

τὴν δὲ τῶν πονηρῶν κατάλυσιν: this mirrors the structure of the previous phrase, but ὁμιλίαν and οὖσαν τῆς ἀρετῆς need to be repeated from before.

μαρτυρεῖ δὲ καὶ τῶν ποιητῶν ὅ τε λέγων: 'the poet who says the following attests to this'.

Ἐσθλῶν ... νόον: an untangled version of the poetic word order of the opening phrase is διδάξεαι ἐσθλὰ ἀπ' ἐσθλῶν. Xenophon provides a quotation from Theognis, a moralistic elegiac poet from Megara who wrote poetry loaded with advice on how to live a good life. The quotation is one couplet, which is made up of a hexameter followed by a pentameter line. There are only three examples of Xenophon himself quoting poetry in the *Memorabilia*. Plato's Socrates does often use extracts of poetry to support points of moral philosophy.

διδάξεαι: 'you will be taught' – the poetry uses the Ionic dialect of Greek.

ἢν ... συμμίσγῃς: the protasis of an open future conditional, with ἢν for ἐάν in the Ionic dialect, 'if you mix with'.

τὸν ἐόντα νόον: 'even the wits you already have'.

Αὐτὰρ ... ἐσθλός: the verb 'to be' should be understood here. Xenophon provides a second quotation from poetry to support his point that a man's behaviour is changeable depending on the company a man keeps. This time, a single hexameter line is supplied. The author of this quotation is unknown.

τοτὲ ... ἄλλοτε: 'at times ... at other times'.

Section 21

ὁρῶ γὰρ ὥσπερ ... οὕτω καί: the main verb of perceiving introduces two balancing indirect statements formed using accusatives and participles. Just as in

Section 19, Xenophon supports his assertion with a comparison from real life, the theme of which is apt given he has just quoted some poetry.

τῶν ἐν μέτρῳ πεποιημένων ἐπῶν: 'works written in metre'. This is the genitive object of ἐπιλανθανομένους.

τοὺς μὴ μελετῶντας: as in Section 19, μὴ is found here instead of οὐ to give a generic sense as he refers to the sort of person who does not practise writing poetry.

τοῖς ἀμελοῦσι λήθην ἐγγιγνομένην: this unusual formulation for forgetting contrasts with the earlier use of ἐπιλανθανομένους and so avoids tedious repetition. The use of the noun λήθην must be emphatic.

ὅταν ... ἐπιλάθηταί τις: ἀν + subjunctive is used for the indefinite construction, so translate ὅταν as 'whenever'.

ὦν: understand τούτων ἅ, as the relative has been attracted into the genitive and then the antecedent has been omitted. The ἅ should be translated as the object of πάσχουσα.

οὐδὲν θαυμαστὸν: supply ἐστί to give the main verb for an indirect statement that uses the accusative and infinitive construction. The participle ἐπιλαθόμενον is the accusative of the indirect statement ('that he having already forgotten') and ἐπιλαθέσθαι is the infinitive. Both forms of ἐπιλανθάνομαι have genitive objects: τούτων goes with ἐπιλαθόμενον and τῆς σωφροσύνης with ἐπιλαθέσθαι.

Section 22

ὁρῶ ... ἧττον δυναμένους: ὁρῶ introduces an indirect statement made up of two accusatives, which are participles with the article, and the main participle δυναμένους. The meaning is clearly that these men were less able than they were before they fell into bad habits that took their attention away from what they have been taught. Xenophon provides further observations that serve to prove his point that when advice or lessons are neglected, men become forgetful of them. Here, a slippery-slope argument implies that a love affair or drinking are the first step for men to move further and further into bad behaviour and away from a virtuous life.

τῶν τε δεόντων ἐπιμελεῖσθαι καὶ τῶν μὴ δεόντων ἀπέχεσθαι: the infinitives ἐπιμελεῖσθαι and ἀπέχεσθαι follow δυναμένους and both infinitives take genitive objects. τῶν δεόντων = 'what is right'. μὴ is found here instead of οὐ to give a generic sense: 'whatever is not right'.

πρὶν ἐρᾶν: πρίν + infinitive = before.

ὦν πρόσθεν ἀπείχοντο κερδῶν ... τούτων οὐκ ἀπέχονται: κερδῶν goes with τούτων and is the antecedent of ὦν πρόσθεν ἀπείχοντο even though in the Greek it has been drawn into the relative clause.

αἰσχρὰ: can refer to physical features as 'ugly' but also morality as 'shameful'.

νομίζοντες: the participle should be translated as causal, 'since they thought that . . . .'.

Section 23

πῶς οὖν οὐκ ἐνδέχεται ... ἀδυνατεῖν: ἐνδέχεται is followed by two accusative and infinitive indirect statements: σωφρονήσαντα ... σωφρονεῖν and δυνηθέντα ... ἀδυνατεῖν. Following evidence from poetry, fathers and sons, teachers and students, drinkers, and lovers, Xenophon concludes his refutation with a rhetorical question that highlights the ridiculous nature of the counter-argument proposed in Section 19.

πάντα: agrees with τὰ καλὰ καὶ τἀγαθὰ and has been promoted for emphasis.

ἔμοιγε: an emphatic form of ἐμοί: 'to me, at least'.

τὰ καλὰ καὶ τἀγαθὰ: 'splendid and good qualities' – see note on Section 17.

οὐχ ἥκιστα: an emphatic form of litotes, which emphasizes the positive by using the negative. It is best translated into English as 'most of all'.

αἱ ἡδοναὶ πείθουσιν αὐτὴν μὴ σωφρονεῖν: μὴ σωφρονεῖν is an indirect command following πείθουσιν. Xenophon personifies the passions that live within the body and depicts them as persuading the soul to give in to pleasures of the flesh. This enforces the point that constant practise is required for virtue, as the pleasures are always within the body trying to take control. Note that Xenophon has used real life examples up until this point to help make this more abstract discussion clearer for his reader.

τὴν ταχίστην: 'as quickly as possible'.

ἑαυταῖς: refers back to αἱ ἡδοναὶ and is the dative object of χαρίζομαι.

Section 24

Καὶ Κριτίας δὴ καὶ Ἀλκιβιάδης: Xenophon returns from the more abstract discussion to the main point from Section 18: Socrates' influence on Critias and Alcibiades. δὴ marks this return to the main narrative.

συνήστην, ἐδυνάσθην ἐκείνῳ χρωμένω ... ἀπαλλαγέντε ...: as Xenophon returns to Critias and Alcibiades, dual endings return.

συμμάχῳ: 'as an ally' – the military origin of this word casts them as men waging war on their passions with Socrates as a fellow soldier.

ἐκείνου: refers to Socrates.

φυγὼν εἰς Θετταλίαν: 'went into exile in Thessaly' – the chronology of events is twisted for a rhetorical purpose; it is very unlikely that Critias stopped associating with Socrates and was instantly sent into exile. The reality is far more complicated and Critias' behaviour must have been problematic long before his exile. (See the Introduction, 'Critias and Alcibiades', for further detail.)

ἀνομία ... χρωμένοις: Thessalian aristocrats were often stereotyped as arrogant and the *penestai*, a class of labourers comparable to the helots of Sparta, were depicted as lawless and eager for revolution. Here, the Thessalians create a real example of the bad people that fathers were keeping their sons away from in Section 20.

δ' αὖ: see note in Section 12.

κάλλος ... θηρώμενος: an almost comic scene of Alcibiades being pursued by noble women because of his good looks. θηρώμενος is a word from the world of hunting. With many influential women rather ignobly throwing themselves at Alcibiades, Xenophon sets a scene in which it is very difficult to remain moderate and avoid the pleasures of the flesh.

διὰ δύναμιν: Alcibiades was an influential politician and among those who became known as demagogues, charismatic leaders who held great power over the people of Athens.

ἀνθρώπων: this word could cover both men and women and can be used contemptuously in place of the more respectful ἀνδρῶν.

[κολακεύειν]: the square brackets highlight that this word should be deleted from the text. It is likely that during the transmission of the text this was an explanatory gloss. A scribe copying the text is likely to have included the gloss in the main text by mistake.

ὑπὸ δὲ τοῦ δήμου: 'by the common people' – Xenophon is consistent in using δῆμος to refer to the lowest classes of society.

ὥσπερ ... ἀθληταὶ: Xenophon compares the effect of easily standing out as the best man among such an immoderate group with an athlete who easily wins. Xenophon returns to a popular pastime and well-known commonplace to make his argument clear and accessible to his readers.

κἀκεῖνος: this refers back to Alcibiades.

Section 25

τοιούτων δὲ συμβάντων αὐτοῖν: a genitive absolute followed by αὐτοῖν, a dual form of the dative.

ὠγκωμένω ... πηρμένω ... πεφυσημένω ... διατεθρυμμένω: note that all of these participle forms are nominative dual. This is a remarkable list of ways in which these men were naturally immoderate and so far more likely to fall into bad ways when separated from Socrates. Xenophon employs a wide range of descriptive and metaphorical vocabulary. ὀγκόμαι and ἐπαίρομαι are medical terms for swelling like a tumour, physically depicting the idea of their swelling ego and lack of control over themselves. φυσάομαι is similarly used to describe swelling from disease as well at the ballooning of bellows. διαθρύπτω has a basic meaning of break into pieces. As he reaches the climax of this argument, Xenophon's prose reaches a new rhetorical level.

ἐπὶ δὲ πᾶσι τούτοις: 'and in addition to all of this'.

διεφθαρμένω ... γεγονότε: διαφθείρω means 'to destroy utterly' which comes to mean corrupt. Again, the vocabulary is evocative and greatly supports Xenophon's aim to create an image of outside influences having a huge effect on these men. Both participles are nominative dual forms.

πολὺν χρόνον: accusative of time.

τί θαυμαστὸν: understand ἐστί here.

εἰ ... ἐγενέσθην;: εἰ is used to show cause after verbs of emotion and best translated 'that they became ...'. Note that dual endings are used here.

Section 26

εἶτα: expresses contempt or sarcasm when used in a question. This is best translated by tone of voice, but 'I suppose' is also effective.

ἐπλημμελησάτην: a word often used for a musician making a wrong note as well as for causing offence. This might anticipate the analogy of music teachers in Section 27. Note the dual ending here.

τούτου ... αἰτιᾶται: αἰτιάομαι is followed by the accusative of the accused and the genitive of the charge.

ὅτι δὲ ... ἄξιος εἶναι: this rhetorical question has a complicated structure. Start by translating δοκεῖ τῷ κατηγόρῳ ἄξιος εἶναι and note that δοκεῖ is not being used impersonally, but Socrates is the nominative. ἄξιος thus agrees with Socrates in the nominative and is followed by the genitive οὐδενὸς ἐπαίνου. After this, return to the beginning of the question and continue translating with ὅτι as 'for the fact that'.

ἡνίκα ... εἰκὸς εἶναι: ἐστί should be understood with εἰκὸς to then introduce an accusative and infinitive indirect statement: 'at the age when it was likely that'. ἀγνωμονεστάτω and ἀκρατεστάτω are in the accusative dual form.

σώφρονε: a dual accusative form.

οὐ μὴν: οὐ μὴν is a very strong negative, best translated as 'absolutely not'.

τά γε ἄλλα: 'other cases at least' – note that neuter plural nominatives often take a singular verb form.

Section 27

τίς ... διδάσκαλος: Xenophon turns to another analogy and a more common teacher-pupil relationship by which his point can be more easily understood by his audience. Music was an important part of both the religious and secular life of Athenians. Note how Xenophon uses a tricolon that goes from specific to general to show the absolute nature of his point.

ἐὰν ... χείρους φανῶσιν: ἐὰν is used with φανῶσιν, the aorist subjunctive of φαίνομαι, to create a general condition, which is not to be confused with a simple future open conditional. χείρους is in the nominative plural form, an alternative form of χείρονες.

αἰτίαν ἔχει τούτου: 'is blamed for this'.

ἐὰν ὁ παῖς αὐτοῦ συνδιατρίβων τῳ ... πονηρὸς γένηται: see note above on the use of ἐὰν and the subjunctive. Note the balance between τῳ and ἄλλῳ: 'with one teacher ... with another'.

τὸν πρόσθεν: 'the former'.

ἀλλ' οὐχ: this introduces a question which requires the answer yes, 'is it not rather the case that'.

ὅσῳ ... χείρων ... τοσούτῳ μᾶλλον: 'the worse ... the more ...' – technically this is a use of the dative of measure of difference (by as much as ... by so much ...).

ἂν ... φαίνηται: understand 'the son' as the nominative. ἂν + subjunctive here is an example of the indefinite construction in a relative clause, which is best translated as a normal present tense.

ἐπαινεῖ: supply 'the father' as the nominative.

τῶν παίδων πλημμελούντων: perhaps best translated as a temporal clause using 'when'.

ἐὰν αὐτοὶ σωφρονῶσιν: 'provided that …' – ἐὰν + subjunctive is used again for a general condition for which the conclusion is true at any time.

Section 28

οὕτω … κρίνειν: Xenophon now links his discussion of the effect sensible company can have on young men to Socrates.

εἰ … ἐποίει … ἂν ἐδόκει: a present closed condition (if X were happening, Y would be happening) formed using the imperfect indicative with ἂν in the apodosis.

πονηρός: 'wicked' – a word often used with a moral sense.

σωφρονῶν διετέλει: διετέλει takes a supplementary participle. It is best to translate σωφρονῶν as if it is the main verb and translate διετέλει as the adverb 'consistently'.

οὐκ ἐνούσης αὐτῷ κακίας: 'for the fault he did not have'. ἐνούσης … κακίας follows αἰτίαν ἔχοι as the genitive of the blame.

εἰ … διετέλει: another protasis of a present closed condition (if X were happening).

πῶς ἂν + optative = 'how possibly could …'

Section 29

εἰ … ἐπήνει … ἂν ἐπιτιμῷτο: the protasis is a present closed conditional and the apodosis is a potential optative: 'if he were to praise … he might be censured'. Xenophon continues to depict himself as controlled in argument as he comes up with a possible way in which Socrates could fairly be criticized before going on to disprove it with a story of Socrates censuring Critias' lack of self-control in pursuing a young male lover. Such pairings were not uncommon in the Greek world, when young men pursued boys on the threshold of manhood.

ποιῶν: the participle is best translated as a concessive clause with 'although'.

φαῦλα πράττοντας: 'acting meanly'.

ὁρῶν: unlike ποιῶν above, this participle is best translated as a temporal clause with 'when'.

τοίνυν: 'well'.

Κριτίαν … αἰσθανόμενος ἐρῶντα … καὶ πειρῶντα χρῆσθαι: αἰσθανόμενος introduces an indirect statement using the accusative and participle construction: Κριτίαν is the accusative and ἐρῶντα and πειρῶντα are the participles.

Εὐθυδήμου: Euthydemus, son of Diocles, is described in more detail at a later point in the *Memorabilia* (4.2.1ff) as a very handsome young man who prides himself on his wisdom and rhetorical skill. He became one of Socrates' followers.

ἀπέτρεπε: an example of the conative imperfect, which expresses an attempted action in the past: 'he attempted to deter'.

φάσκων: 'by saying' – this then introduces an indirect statement using an accusative and infinitive construction.

ἀνελεύθερόν: 'undignified' or 'not worthy of a free man'.

καλῷ κἀγαθῷ: see note on Section 17.

τὸν ἐρώμενον: a term often used to refer to the younger, passive male in a pederastic relationship. In both poetry and prose it usually refers to a beautiful young man.

ᾧ βούλεται πολλοῦ ἄξιος φαίνεσθαι: the relative pronoun ᾧ is in the dative following φαίνεσθαι. πολλοῦ should be translated 'very' and so the meaning is the same as the superlative of ἄξιος.

προσαιτεῖν: the compound form of the verb implies quite forceful begging.

ὥσπερ τοὺς πτωχοὺς: understand ὥσπερ οἱ πτωχοὶ προσαιτοῦσι. In this comparative clause, the verb has been omitted and the subject is attracted into the case of the other member of the comparison, in this case the accusative Critias.

προσδοῦναι, καὶ ταῦτα μηδενὸς ἀγαθοῦ: προσδοῦναι is translated 'to give more'. καὶ ταῦτα is used to make a final addition to the sentence and emphasize the point being made: 'and what's more'. μηδενὸς ἀγαθοῦ is a partitive genitive: 'something which is of no good' or 'something which has no value'.

Section 30

τοῦ ... ἀποτρεπομένου: a genitive absolute, best translated as a temporal clause with 'when'.

τοῦ δὲ Κριτίου ... τὸν Σωκράτην: Xenophon returns to using the article before proper nouns, which he has not done earlier in the passage. The effect of this is to draw a clear contrast between the two main characters of this section.

τοῖς τοιούτοις: refers back to Socrates' words in Section 29.

λέγεται: 'it is said' – the impersonal form introduces an indirect statement using the accusative and infinitive construction.

ἄλλων ... Εὐθυδήμου: a genitive absolute, best translated as a temporal clause with 'when'. The circumstances of Socrates' words are important, as they show that there were witnesses to this to support Xenophon's claim that Socrates did not praise bad behaviour.

εἰπεῖν ὅτι ... δοκοίη: the infinitive of the first indirect statement leads into a second indirect statement using the ὅτι construction. δοκοίη is in the optative as it is in the historic sequence after the past tense of εἰπεῖν. Note that ὁ Κριτίας is the subject of δοκοίη.

αὐτῷ: 'to him' – i.e. Socrates.

ὑϊκὸν ... πάσχειν: 'to have the nature of a pig'. The pig, famously fat and lazy, was an excellent animal for demonstrating how one could become a slave to one's bodily needs.

Εὐθυδήμῳ προσκνῆσθαι ὥσπερ τὰ ὕδια τοῖς λίθοις: Socrates compares Critias' wish to sleep with Euthydemus to pigs rubbing themselves against stones. He casts Critias as an animal simply trying to scratch an itch, which is not an act of the heart and soul, but a basic need of the flesh. ὕδια is the diminutive form: 'piglet'. However, the diminutive is used to show condescension rather than age.

Section 31

ἐξ ὧν: 'because of this'

ὥστε ... ἔγραψε: a result clause.

τῶν τριάκοντα: 'the Thirty Tyrants' – see notes on the oligarchy in Section 12 and 'The political charges' in the Introduction. When the thirty men were chosen to run the government, their main task was to write new laws and return Athens to the constitution of their forefathers. These new laws led to the creation of a new assembly, the abolition of popular juries and the gradual removal of any democratic opposition. Critias, with his extremist oligarchic leanings, was at the forefront of these developments.

Χαρικλέους: Charicles was one of the Thirty Tyrants and was known to have worked alongside Critias as one of the more extremist oligarchs.

λόγων τέχνην: 'the art of speaking'

μὴ διδάσκειν: μὴ + infinitive follows ἐν τοῖς νόμοις ἔγραψε as a common construction after verbs of preventing or forbidding: 'he wrote a law forbidding . . .'.

οὐκ ἔχων ὅπη ἐπιλάβοιτο: 'with no way to attack him' – the optative here represents the indirect form of what was originally a deliberative subjunctive in direct speech.

τὸ κοινῇ τοῖς φιλοσόφοις ... ἐπιτιμώμενον: the article and participle create a noun, 'the charge commonly brought against philosophers'. This charge against sophists is perhaps best seen in Aristophanes' *Clouds* in which the playwright mocked the sophists and depicted Socrates as their leader, as was a popular view at the time. Despite being quite different from the sophists, Socrates was tarred with the same brush and here Xenophon suggests Critias is one source of this common misconception. (See the Introduction, 'The charges of impiety and corruption of the youth', for further detail.)

διαβάλλων: understand αὐτόν as the accusative object.

οὐδὲ ... οὔτ' ... οὔτ': the later negatives confirm the former, which in practice means οὐδὲ is translated as 'but'.

τοῦτο ... Σωκράτους ἤκουσα: ἀκούω + accusative of thing heard and genitive of the person from whom it is heard. The same applies to αἰσθάνομαι.

ἀκηκοέναι: understand τοῦτο as the accusative of what was heard.

Section 32

ἐδήλωσε δέ: δηλόω is used impersonally: 'and it became clear that this was the case'. The following story of Socrates comparing statesmen to cattle and the resulting reprimand from Critias and Charicles are the proof that Critias wrote the law with Socrates in mind. The connection of this law to Socrates alone is very likely untrue and simply used here for rhetorical force. Another way to translate the impersonal verb would be 'the events that followed made this clear'.

οὐ τοὺς χειρίστους ἀπέκτεινον: 'were killing the most noble men' – a good example of litotes emphasizing the nobility of the men being killed. The Thirty

Tyrants removed their democratic opponents and many noble citizens to secure their hold on power. Scholars estimate that up to 1,500 people were killed during their reign of terror.

εἶπέ που: the που shows that Xenophon is not sure of exactly what Socrates said but only the idea he conveyed, 'he said, I think'. εἶπέ introduces an indirect statement using the ὅτι construction.

οἱ δοκοίη: this is best translated 'he thought'. οἱ is a dative reflexive pronoun and δοκοίη is optative because the indirect statement is in the historic sequence.

εἴ . . . μὴ ὁμολογοίη: 'that he doesn't admit that . . .' – εἰ is best translated 'that', as seen in Section 25. The optative shows that this is a hypothetical case and not a reality.

μὴ αἰσχύνεται μηδ᾽ οἴεται: notice that Xenophon changes from using optative verbs to indicatives to mark the change from a hypothetical case to the actual reality of the statesmen he lives under.

Section 33

ἀπαγγελθέντος δὲ αὐτοῖς τούτου: genitive absolute, τούτου refers back to the cattle analogy and αὐτοῖς to Critias and Charicles.

τόν τε νόμον ἐδεικνύτην: the law is the ban on the teaching of the art of speaking. Note that Xenophon returns to a dual verb form, this time for Critias and Charicles, not Critias and Alcibiades.

μὴ διαλέγεσθαι: μή and the infinitive follow verbs of forbidding.

αὐτὼ: dual accusative form.

εἰ ἐξείη πυνθάνεσθαι, εἴ τι ἀγνοοῖτο: an indirect question in the historic sequence can use the optative form of the verb.

τῶν προαγορευομένων: translate the participle as a noun: 'of the published laws'.

Section 34

τὼ δ᾽ ἐφάτην: 'and they said yes' – note the dual verb ending.

ἔφη: Xenophon turns from indirect to direct speech, allowing the reader to feel as if they are present at the following conversation. The change from indirect to direct speech highlights that what follows is an important part of Xenophon's argument. Note that there are no speech marks in Greek and the verb of speaking is often placed within the direct speech; it is important to be clear what is being said and what is part of Xenophon's own narrative.

παρεσκεύασμαι: the perfect tense can often be translated as the present when it denotes a past action that has led to a present state: 'I am ready'.

ὅπως δὲ μὴ + subjunctive creates a negative purpose clause.

λάθω τι παρανομήσας: understand the accusative reflexive pronoun ἐμαυτόν here and translate with the dependent participle as the main verb and λανθάνω ἐμαυτόν as 'without realizing' (literally this would read 'escape the notice of myself in breaking the law'): 'break the law without realizing'.

τὴν τῶν λόγων τέχνην: Socrates refers to the law as it was described in Section 31 rather than the idea of being banned from talking to boys, which was mentioned in Section 33.

μαθεῖν ... πότερον ... ἢ ... κελεύετε αὐτῆς: a complicated sentence that needs to be broken down carefully. μαθεῖν introduces the indirect question ἀπέχεσθαι κελεύετε αὐτῆς, which should be repeated after both πότερον and then ἢ. The structure of σὺν τοῖς ὀρθῶς λεγομένοις εἶναι νομίζοντες found after πότερον is mainly repeated after the ἢ but λεγομένοις εἶναι νομίζοντες is omitted and needs to be understood for a clear translation.

σὺν τοῖς ὀρθῶς λεγομένοις: 'with correct speaking' – i.e. good reasoning and logic. When μη is used, it becomes 'with bad speaking'.

ἀπέχεσθαι κελεύετε αὐτῆς: supply an accusative object for κελεύετε such as ἐμέ. αὐτῆς refers to the τέχνη, the art of speaking.

τοῖς ὀρθῶς ... τοῖς μὴ ὀρθῶς: understand λεγομένοις εἶναι νομίζοντες from previous sentence.

δῆλον ὅτι: understand ἐστί here. ὅτι introduces an indirect statement.

ἀφεκτέον <ἂν> εἴη: an impersonal neuter gerundive of ἀπέχομαι implying obligation: 'one would need to avoid'. The optative and ἂν here can be considered either a potential optative or the apodosis of a future remote condition. The brackets around ἂν show that it is missing in the manuscripts and has been added to the text by an editor to make good sense of the optative.

τοῦ ὀρθῶς λέγειν: a genitive articular infinitive, otherwise known as a gerund, where the article turns the infinitive into a verbal noun: 'from correct speaking'.

πειρατέον ὀρθῶς λέγειν: another impersonal gerundive which implies obligation and requires ἂν εἴη from the earlier phrase.

Section 35

τάδε σοι εὐμαθέστερα ὄντα: τάδε is an internal accusative of προαγορεύομεν, so comes to mean 'orders' or 'instructions': 'instructions that are easier for you to understand'.

τοῖς νέοις ὅλως μὴ διαλέγεσθαι: a negative indirect command. The story clearly depicts Critias and Charicles as men with total arbitrary power.

Ἵνα ... ἀμφίβολον ἦ: a purpose clause.

[ὡς ἄλλο τι ποιῶ ἢ τὰ προηγορευμένα]: an indirect question best introduced with 'as to how'. The textual critic Cobet decided to delete this section, as it seems ill fitting in this dialogue and could easily have been a note on the text, which has accidentally been copied into the prose. See the discussion on textual criticism in the notes on Section 24.

ὁρίσατέ: a sharp imperative shows the increasing tension in this dialogue.

μέχρι πόσων ἐτῶν: 'up to what age'

Ὅσουπερ ... χρόνου: a genitive of time: 'for as long as'.

βουλεύειν: 'to be a councillor': the Council was a key body in the democratic state, which prepared business for the assembly of the people and oversaw the day to day running of the state across many areas of administration. By the time of Socrates, it consisted of 500 men chosen by lot who held the post for one year.

Only men who were Athenian citizens and at least 30 years of age could serve on the Council.

ὡς οὔπω φρονίμοις οὖσι: ὡς + participle is best translated as a causal clause with 'because'. The adjective and participle are in the dative to agree with the dative that is implied with ἔξεστιν, 'it is not possible for them'.

μηδὲ σὺ διαλέγου: the force of the imperative is strengthened by the inclusion of σύ, which can be conveyed in English by phrasing the command as 'you must not . . .'. The command is a much clearer repetition of what he has just said, surely to really drive home the meaning of the ban to Socrates and perhaps showing further signs of frustration.

τριάκοντα ἐτῶν: genitive of comparison, 'than thirty years old'.

Section 36

Μηδ' ἐάν τι ὠνῶμαι: a general condition with the conative present tense which implies the subject is trying to achieve something: 'not even if I am trying to buy something'.

ἢν πωλῇ νεώτερος τριάκοντα ἐτῶν: Socrates avoids repetition of ἐάν by using a variant form ἤν. Understand ἀνήρ as the nominative of the verb and that νεώτερος agrees with it: 'if a man younger than thirty years old is selling'. It may be best to move away from the Greek slightly by using a noun for πωλῇ: 'if the seller is younger than 30 years old'.

ἔρωμαι: a deliberative subjunctive conveys Socrates' uncertainty.

ὁπόσου πωλεῖ: 'how much he is selling it for' – ὁπόσου is a genitive of price and an accusative object αὐτό should be understood, referring back to the τι at the start of the sentence.

τά γε τοιαῦτα: an accusative of respect: 'in cases like this at least'.

σύγε: the emphatic pronoun makes this a more forceful and insulting response.

εἰδὼς πῶς ἔχει: 'already knowing the answer' – ἔχω takes on the meaning of 'to be' when accompanied by an adverb and so πῶς ἔχει means 'how the situation is'. This would have been a common criticism made by those who found the Socratic method patronizing and frustrating.

τὰ πλεῖστα: 'the majority of your questions' – an internal accusative taking its meaning from the verb ἐρωτᾶν.

ταῦτα οὖν μὴ ἐρώτα: Charicles' annoyance with Socrates is made quite clear in this imperative.

ἄν τίς με ἐρωτᾷ νέος, ἐὰν εἰδῶ: understand ἐάν for ἄν as Socrates provides two more general conditions and ploughs on despite Charicles' order to stop these sorts of questions.

οἷον: 'for example'.

Section 37

ὁ δὲ Κριτίας: Critias interrupts at this point, as surely Socrates hoped he would do, infuriated by Socrates' questioning and sets out specific topics he must avoid.

τῶνδέ: 'the following'.

τῶν σκυτέων καὶ τῶν τεκτόνων καὶ τῶν χαλκέων: Socrates is frequently depicted as using examples of skilled craftsmen like cobblers, carpenters and blacksmiths in his philosophical dialogues. Charicles is annoyed by the frequent use of these examples.

οἶμαι αὐτοὺς ἤδη κατατετρῖφθαι: an indirect statement using the accusative and infinitive construction follows οἶμαι.

διαθρυλουμένους: 'from being incessantly talked about' – the participle agrees with the accusative of the indirect statement.

καὶ τῶν ἑπομένων τούτοις: 'the subjects which follow on from these' – understand με ἀπέχεσθαι δεήσει, based on the earlier sentence, to make sense of the genitive here. The fast pace of their dialogue is reflected in the way the speakers share constructions.

τοῦ τε δικαίου καὶ τοῦ ὁσίου: these topics are known to have been favourites of Socrates thanks to the surviving dialogues written by Plato. The tricolon used here goes from the specific to the general, implying that all-important philosophical discussions can come from such normal and hackneyed examples.

μὰ Δί᾽: 'good heavens' – an exclamation showing complete frustration at the situation. The more colloquial 'for God's sake' might be more appropriate.

καὶ τῶν βουκόλων γε: the scene has perfect ring structure as it starts and ends with the herdsman and a corrupted version of Socrates' original analogy for poor statesmen. Xenophon thus continues to emphasize the point that Socrates at no point allowed immoderate behaviour to be praised or left unquestioned.

εἰ δὲ μή: a verb needs to be understood to complete this short and threatening protasis: 'if you don't (stop talking about these topics)'.

ὅπως μὴ καὶ σὺ ἐλάττους τὰς βοῦς ποιήσῃς: ὅπως μὴ + aorist subjunctive is often found after verbs of caution, 'make sure you don't . . .'. This is a very thinly veiled threat to Socrates that if he continues to discuss these topics with men under thirty years old then he will cause his own death and in that way reduce the 'herd' of Athens.

Section 38

τοῦ . . . λόγου: 'the story'

Οἷα . . . καὶ ὡς . . . εἴρηται: start with the main verb at the end, which introduces the two indirect questions that make up the rest of the sentence.

Κριτίᾳ: dative of possession.

ἐγεγόνει: pluperfect tense.

ὡς εἶχον πρὸς ἀλλήλους: as in Section 36, ἔχω can take on the meaning of 'to be' when used with an adverb, so literally it translates as 'how they were towards each other' but more idiomatic translations can be found.

Vocabulary

While there is no Defined Vocabulary List for A Level, words in the OCR Defined Vocabulary List for AS are marked with * so that students can quickly see the vocabulary with which they should be particularly familiar.

*ἀγαθός -ή -όν	good, noble
ἀγέλη -ης, f.	herd
*ἀγνοέω	to not understand
ἄγνοια -ας, f	ignorance
ἀγνώμων -ον	reckless
*ἀγών -ῶνος, m	contest
*ἀδικέω	to do wrong
*ἄδικος -η -ον	unjust
ἀδυνατέω	to be unable
Ἀθηναῖος -α -ον	Athenian
ἀθλητής -οῦ, m	athlete
*αἱρέομαι, aor. εἱλομην	to choose
*αἰσθάνομαι	(+ acc. + gen.) to hear X from Y, to learn
*αἰσχρός -ά -όν	shameful, disgraceful
*αἰσχύνομαι	to be ashamed
*αἰτία -ας, f.	blame
*αἰτιάομαι	to charge, to accuse
*ἀκούω, perf. ἀκήκοα	(+ acc. + gen.) to hear X from Y
ἀκρατής -ές	intemperate, without self-control, licentious
Ἀλκιβιάδης -ου, m	Alcibiades
*ἀλλά	but
*ἀλλήλους, ἀλλήλας, ἄλληλα	each other, one another
*ἄλλος -η -ο	other, another
ἄλλοτε	at another time
ἀμελέω	(+ gen.) to neglect
ἀμφίβολος -ον	doubtful, ambiguous
*ἄν	particle used in indefinite construction
ἀνελεύθερος -ον	servile, mean
ἀνεπιστήμων -ονος	ignorant
*ἀνήρ, ἀνδρός, m	man

ἀνθρώπινος -η -ον	concerning the affairs of men
*ἄνθρωπος -ου, m	man, person
ἀνομία -ας, f	lawlessness
ἀντιλέγω	to deny, to contradict
*ἄξιος -α -ον	(+ gen.) worthy of
ἀπαγγέλλω, aor. pass. ἀπηγγέλθην	to report
ἀπαλλάσσομαι, aor. ἀπηλλάγην	to depart from, to be free from
ἀπεῖπον	(+ μή + inf.) to forbid
ἀπέχομαι	(+ gen.) to abstain from
*ἀπό	(+ gen.) from
*ἀποκρίνομαι	to answer, to reply
*ἀποκτείνω, aor. ἀπέκτεινα	to kill
ἀπολαύω	to enjoy
*ἀπόλλυμι, fut. ἀπολέω	to lose
*ἀπολογέομαι	to defend, to excuse
ἀπομνημονεύω	(+ dat.) to bear a grudge against
ἀποπηδάω	(+ gen.) to turn away from
ἀποτρέπω	to deter, to prevent
*ἀρετή -ῆς, f	goodness, excellence
ἀσκέω	to exercise, to train
ἄσκησις -εως, f	training
ἀσκητός -ή -όν	gained by practice
*αὖ	in turn, again
*αὖθις	again
αὐλητής -οῦ, m	flute-teacher
αὐτάρ	but
αὐτάρκης -ες	independent

*αὐτός -ή -ό	himself, herself, itself (following definite article) the same (not in nom.) him, her, it	*δίδωμι	to give
		*διηγέομαι	to set out in detail, to explain
Ἀφροδίσια -ων, n. pl	sexual pleasures	*δίκαιος -α -ον	just, fitting
		*δικαιοσύνη -ης, f	justice
βίαιος -α -ον	violent	*δοκεῖ	it seems
*βίος -ου, m	life	*δύναμαι, aor. ἐδυνήθην	to be able
βουκόλος -ου, m	herdsman		
*βουλεύω	to sit in the Council	*δύναμις -εως, f.	influence, power
*βούλομαι	to want, to wish	*δυνατός -ή -όν	powerful
βοῦς, βοός, f.	(pl) cattle		
		*ἐάν (or ἤν)	if
		*ἑαυτόν -ήν -ό	himself, herself, itself
*γάρ	for	ἐγγίγνομαι	(+ dat.) to appear in
*γε	at least, at any rate	ἐγκρατής -ές	(+ gen.) in control of
*γένος -ους, n.	birth, family	ἐγκυλίνδομαι, aor. pass. part. ἐγκυλισθείς	to be wrapped up in
*γίγνομαι, fut. γενήσομαι, aor. ἐγενόμην	to become, to happen, to be		
		*ἐγώ	I
*γιγνώσκω	think	*εἰ	if
*γράφω, aor. ἔγραψα	to write down, to propose	*εἰκός ἐστί(ν)	it is likely, it is probable
		εἰκότως	fairly, reasonably
γυμνικός -ή -όν	gymnastic	*εἰμί, imp. ἦ(ν)	to be
*γυνή, γυναικός, f	woman	εἴργω	to keep X away from
		*εἰς	(+ acc.) into
*δέ	and, but	εἶτα	and then, and so, (in a question) I suppose
*δεῖ, fut. δεήσει	it is necessary		
*δείκνυμι	to show		
*δέομαι	to beg	εἴωθα	to be accustomed to
δέον -οντος, n	correct behaviour, what is right	*ἐκ / ἐξ	(+ gen.) from, out of
		*ἐκεῖ	there
*δή	in truth, indeed, then	*ἐκεῖνος -η -ο	that, (pl) those
*δῆλος -η -ον	evident, obvious	*ἐλάττων -ον	fewer, smaller
*δηλόω	to make clear, to explain	*ἐλάχιστος -η -ον	smallest, least
δημοκρατία -ας, f	democracy	*ἐν	(+ dat.) in
*δῆμος -ου, m	the people	ἐνδέχεται	it is possible
*διά	(+ acc.) because of (+ gen.) by	ἔνειμι	to be in
		*ἕνεκα	(+ gen.) for the sake of, because of
διαβάλλω	to attack a man's character, to slander	*ἔνθα	then
διαθρυλέομαι	to be mentioned incessantly, to be hackneyed	*ἔξεστι	it is possible, it is allowed
διαθρύπτω	to pamper, to spoil, to enervate	*ἐπαινέω, imp. ἐπήνεον	to praise
		ἔπαινος -ου, m	praise
*διαλέγομαι, aor. διελεξάμην, aor. pass. διελέχθην	to converse, to discuss, to argue	ἐπαίρομαι	to be elated, to swell
		*ἐπεί	when
		*ἐπειδή	when, since
διατελέω	(+ participle) to X consistently	ἐπέρομαι	to ask
		ἐπηρεάζω	(+ dat.) to act insultingly towards
*διαφθείρω, perf. διέφθαρκα	to corrupt	*ἐπί	(+ dat.) in addition to
διδασκαλικός -ή -όν	instructive, of teachers	ἐπιθυμέω	(+ gen.) to long for, to wish for
διδάσκαλος -ου, m	teacher		
*διδάσκω, aor. ἐδίδαξα	to teach	ἐπιθυμία -ας, f	passion
		ἐπιλαμβάνω	to attack

*ἐπιλανθάνομαι, aor. ἐπελαθόμην, perf. ἐπιλέλησμαι — (+ gen.) to forget

ἐπιμελέομαι — (+ gen.) to care about

ἐπιτιμάω — to censure, to criticize

ἐπιφέρω — to bring as a charge against

*ἕπομαι — (+ dat.) to follow, to be connected to

ἔπος -εος, n. — word

ἔραμαι, aor. ἠράσθην — to fall in love

ἐράω — (+ gen.) to love

*ἔργον -ου, n. — task, function

ἔρομαι — to ask

*ἔρχομαι, aor. ἦλθον — to go

ἐρῶ, perf. pass. εἴρημαι — to mention

ἔρως -ωτος, m. — love affair

*ἐρωτάω — to ask

ἐσθλός -ή -όν — good

ἔστε — while

*ἔτι — still

*ἔτος -εος, n. — year

Εὐθύδημος -ου, m. — Euthydemus

*εὐθύς — immediately

εὐμαθής -ές — easy to understand, intelligible

*ἔχω, aor. ἔσχον — to have, (+ adverb) to be

*ἕως — while

*ζάω — to live

ζημιόω — to fine

*ἤ — or, then

*ἤ . . . ἤ . . . — either . . . or . . .

*ἡγέομαι — to believe, to think

*ἤδη — already

ἡδονή -ης — pleasure, delight, passion

*ἥκιστα — least

*ἤν (or ἐάν) — if

ἡνίκα — at that time when

ἥπερ — in what way, how

ἧττον — less

θαυμαστός -ή -όν — surprising

*θεός -οῦ, m — god

Θετταλία -ας, f. — Thessaly

θηράω — to hunt

θνήσκω, aor. ἔθανον, perf. τέθνηκα — to die

*ἱκανός -ή -όν — (+ infinitive) skilled at

ἱκετεύω — to beg, to supplicate

*ἵνα — so that, in order that

*ἴσως — equally

καθάπερ — just as

*καί — and, even, also

κακία -ας, f. — evil

*κακός -ή -όν — bad, evil

*καλέω — to summon

κάλλος -εος, n. — beauty

*καλός -ή -όν — moral, virtuous, fine, beautiful

κατάλυσις -εως, f — end, dissolution

καταναλίσκω — to use up, to spend

κατατρίβω, perf. κατατέτριφα — to wear out

κατήγορος -ου, m — accuser, prosecutor

*κελεύω — to order

κέρδος -εος, n. — (pl) profits, gains

κιθαριστής -οῦ, m. — lyre-teacher

κοινῇ — commonly, publicly

*κρατέω — (+ gen.) to conquer

κράτιστος -η -ον — best, most excellent

κρείττων -ον — stronger, superior

*κρίνω — to judge

Κριτίας -ου, m. — Critias

*λανθάνω — (+ participle) to do X without realizing

*λέγω, aor. εἶπον, perf. εἴρηκα — to speak, to say

λήθη -ης, f. — forgetfulness, oblivion

*λίθος -ου, m. — stone

*λόγος -ου, m — word, (pl) conversation

μὰ Δία — by Zeus, good heavens, for god's sake

μάθησις -εως, f — learning

μαθητής -οῦ, m — pupil, student

*μᾶλλον — rather

*μανθάνω, aor. ἔμαθον — to learn

μαρτυρέω — (+ dat.) to bear witness to, to attest to

μελετάω — (+ gen.) to practise, to repeat

*μέν . . . δέ . . . — on the one hand . . . on the other . . .

*μετά — (+ gen.) with

μέτρον -ου, n — metre

*μέχρι — (+ gen.) up to

*μή — not

μηδέ — not even

μηδείς, μηδεμία, μηδέν — no one, nothing

*μήν — indeed, however

*μισέω — to hate

*ναί — yes

*νέος -α -ον — young

νομεύς -έως, m	herdsman	*οὔτε ... οὔτε ...	neither ... nor ...
*νομίζω, aor. ἐνόμισα	to think, to consider	*οὗτος, αὕτη, τοῦτο	this, (pl) these
νομοθέτης -ου, m	legislator	*οὕτω(ς)	in this way, thus
*νόμος -ου, m	law		
νουθετικός -ή -όν	of advice	*παῖς, παιδός, m	son
*νοῦς νοῦ, m	wits	παίω	to strike, to hit
		*παρά	(+ gen.) from
ὀγκόμαι	to be swollen, to be puffed up		(+ dat.) with
		παρανομέω	to break the law
*οἶδα, plup. ᾔδη	to know	παρασκευάζομαι, perf.	to be ready, to be prepared
*οἰκέω	to live	παρεσκεύασμαι	
οἴομαι	to think	*πάρειμι	to be present
οἷον	such as, for example	*παρέχω, aor. παρέσχον	to make
*οἷος -α -ον	such, of the kind which		
		*πᾶς, πᾶσα, πᾶν	all, the whole
ὀλιγαρχία -ας, f	oligarchy	*πάσχω	to experience
ὅλος -η -ον	whole, entire	*πατήρ -τρός, m	father
ὅλως	altogether, at all	*πείθομαι	(+ dat.) to obey
ὁμιλέω	(+ dat.) to be in the company of	*πείθω	to persuade
		*πειράω	to try
ὁμιλητής -οῦ, m	follower, companion	*περί	(+ gen.) about
ὁμιλία -ας, f	company	πλεῖστοι -αι -α	very many, most
*ὁμολογέω	to agree, to admit	πλεονέκτης -ου, m	a greedy man, (as adjective) greedy
*ὅμως	nevertheless		
ὀνομαστός -ή -όν	famous, notorious	πλημμελέω	to make a false note; to offend
ὅπη	by which		
ὁπόσος -η -ον	how much	πλοῦτος -ου, m	wealth
*ὅπως	so that, in order to, just as, however	*ποιέω, aor. ἐποίησα	to make, to do
		ποιητής -οῦ, m	poet
*ὁράω, aor. εἶδον	to see	*πόλις -εως, f	city (often used to refer to Athens)
*ὀργίζομαι, aor. pass. ὠργίσθην	to grow angry		
		*πολίτης -ου, m	citizen
ὀρέγομαι, aor. ὠρεξάμην	(+ gen.) to reach after, to yearn for	πολιτικά -ῶν, n. pl	politics, government
		*πολύς, πολλή, πολύ	much, many
*ὀρθῶς	rightly, justly		
ὁρίζω	to fix a limit	πονηρός -ά -όν	bad
*ὅς, ἥ, ὅ	who, which	*πόσος -η -ον	how many
ὅσιος -α -ον	sacred, pious, religious	*ποτε	ever
*ὅσος -η -ον	as much as	*πότερον ... ἤ ...	rather ... than ... / ... rather than ...
ὅσοσπερ, ὅσηπερ, ὅσονπερ	as much as		
ὅσπερ, ἥπερ, ὅπερ	the very man who, the very thing which	*που	I suppose
		*ποῦ	where?
*ὅταν	whenever	*πράττω, aor. ἔπραξα, perf. πέπραχα, aor. pass. ἐπράχθην	to achieve, to accomplish
*ὅτε	when		
*ὅτι	that		
*οὐ (οὐκ, οὐχ)	not		
*οὐδέ	and not	πρέπον ἐστί(ν)	(+ dat.) it is fitting for, it is appropriate for
*οὐδείς, οὐδεμία, οὐδέν	no one, nothing		
*οὐκέτι	no longer	*πρίν	(+ infinitive) before
*οὐκοῦν	therefore	προαγορεύω	to order publicly
*οὖν	so, then	προάγω, aor. pass. προήχθην	to induce
οὔπω	not yet		

προερέω, aor.   to say beforehand
   προεῖπον, perf.
   προείρηκα
*πρός   (+ acc.) with, in response to, towards, in the presence of
προσαιτέω   to pursue like a beggar
προσβιβάζω   to persuade, to bring over
προσδίδωμι, aor. inf.   to do a favour, (+ gen.) to grant
   προσδοῦναι
*πρόσθεν   previously
προσκνάομαι   to rub oneself against
προστάτης -ου, m   statesman, civic leader
*πρότερον... ἤ...   before
πρότερος -α -ον   former, earlier
προτρέπομαι   to urge on, to encourage
πρωτεύω   to hold first place
πτωχός -οῦ, m   beggar
*πυνθάνομαι   to ask questions, to inquire
πωλέω   to sell
πώποτε   ever
*πῶς   how

*ῥᾳδίως   easily

*σαφῶς   clearly
σεμνός -ή -όν   respectable
σκυτεύς -έως, m   cobbler
σύ   you (sg.)
συγγίγνομαι, aor.   to associate with, to be a comrade
   συνεγενόμην
συμβαίνω   to happen
*σύμμαχος -ου, m   ally, helper
συμμίγνυμι   to mingle with
συμφυτεύομαι   (+ dat.) to be implanted alongside
*σύν   (+ dat.) to be associated with
συνδιατρίβω   (+ dat.) to spend time with, to be a pupil of
σύνειμι, imp. συνῆν   to follow, to associate with
συνουσία -ας, f   association, company, connection
Σωκράτης -ους, m   Socrates
*σῶμα -ατος, n   body
σωφρονέω   to be prudent, to have self-control
σωφροσύνη -ης, f   moderation, self-control, wisdom
*σώφρων -ονος   prudent

*τάχιστος η ον   fastest, quickest
*τε   and
*τε... καί...   both... and...
τέκτων -ονος, m   carpenter
*τέχνη -ης, f.   art, skill
*τιμάω   to honour
*τίς τίς τί   who?, which?
*τις, τις, τι   someone, something
*τοι   in truth, indeed
τοίνυν   well then, therefore
*τοιοῦτος -αύτη -οῦτο   such
τοσοῦτος -αύτη -οῦτο   so much
τοτέ   at times
*τότε   then, at that time
τριάκοντα   30, (with definite article) the Thirty

ὑβριστής -ές   wanton, outrageous
ὕβριστος -η -ον   insolent, outrageous
ὕδιον -ου, n   pig
ὑικὸν πάσχειν   to have the nature of a pig
*υἱός -οῦ, m   son
*ὑμεῖς   you (pl)
ὑπακούω   to listen to, to pay attention to
ὑπερήφανος -ον   arrogant, overbearing
*ὑπό   (+ gen.) by
*ὕστερον   later, afterwards
*ὕστερος -α -ον   latter

*φαίνομαι, aor. ἐφάνην   to appear to be, to seem
φάσκω   to say, to allege
φαῦλος -η -ον   base, bad
φείδομαι   (+ gen.) to be careful with, to use sparingly
*φεύγω   to go into exile
*φημί, aor. ἔφην   to say, to say yes
φιλοποσία -ας, f   alcoholism
φιλοσοφέω   to be a philosopher
φιλόσοφος -ου, m   philosopher
φιλότιμος -ον   ambitious
*φοβέομαι   to be frightened
φρόνιμος -η -ον   prudent, sensible
φυλάττομαι   to be on one's guard, to take care
φυσάομαι   to be puffed up
φύσις -εως, f   nature, character
χαλκεύς -έως, m   blacksmith
χαρίζομαι   (+ dat.) to gratify

Χαρικλῆς -έους, m	Charicles (one of the Thirty Tyrants)	χρηστός -ή -όν	honest, good
		*χρόνος -ου, m	time
χείριστος -η -ον	worst		
χείρων -ον	worse, less skilful	ψυχή -ης, f	soul
*χράομαι	(+ dat.) to make use of, enjoy	ὠνέομαι	to buy
		*ὡς	how, as, since
*χρή, imp. (ἐ)χρῆν	(+ acc. + inf.) it is necessary	*ὡς τάχιστα	as soon as
		*ὥσπερ	just as
*χρῆμα -ατος, n	(pl) money, property, belongings	*ὥστε	with the result that

Homer, *Odyssey*

Introduction by Frederica Daniele

AS: Book 10: 144–399

Commentary Notes and Vocabulary by
Claire Webster

A-level: Book 9: 231–460

Commentary Notes and Vocabulary by
Rob Colborn

Introduction

Epic poetry, Homer and the oral tradition

What is epic poetry?

A starting point in trying to define epic poetry will be to consider how the Greeks might have answered the same question: for the Greeks, an epic poem was a long composition whose subject matter were stories and adventures of the gods and/or heroes. In addition, and perhaps even more importantly, the metre in which epic poetry was composed was a strong defining factor. Both Plato (*Laws* 958e) and Aristotle (*Politics* 1459b32) speak of a 'heroic metre' (ἡρωικός στίχος), by which they mean the dactylic hexameter (see page 274); all surviving Greek epics, including the *Iliad* and the *Odyssey*, are composed in this metre, as is all Roman poetry which defines itself as epic. Finally, as is the case with other genres of Greek poetry, so too was epic poetry defined by its performance context. Both evidence from the Homeric poems themselves and external, later accounts suggest that epic poetry was performed in houses and palaces after dinner, sung or chanted by a professional bard, *aoidos*, to the accompaniment of music played on a lyre. Two *aoidoi* in the *Odyssey*, Phemius and Demodochus, perform what seem to be epic songs in just such circumstances, in Books 1 and 8 respectively, to the sound of their *phorminx* or *kitharis*. Later, public performances of epic poetry by singers called *rhapsodes* (possibly from the Greek *rhabdos*, a staff used by the performers to beat their rhythm; or, more likely, from *rhaptō*, to stitch, pointing to the singer's art of 'stitching songs') seem to have become prevalent in Greek towns and cities, including at civic festivities and events such as the Panathenaic Games in Athens.

Epic poetry is not, however, an exclusively Greek genre. Indeed, almost every stable civilization from the third millennium BC to the present day has its own tradition and form of epic poetry, though the way it is defined – as to its subject matter, metre and performance context – varies from civilization to civilization and especially over time, from antiquity to the present day. You will be familiar with epic poems written later than the Homeric poems, such as Virgil's *Aeneid* or Milton's *Paradise Lost*, each of which in its own way looks back to the Greek epics. Conversely, the Sumerian *Epic of Gilgamesh* (first written down in the eighteenth century BC) is a good example of how different epic traditions may have developed in parallel, though scholars do not exclude mutual influence between Greek and Near Eastern epics or even a common cultural ancestry.

Greek epic: the Homeric poems and the Epic Cycle

The earliest Greek epic poems which survive in full are the *Iliad* and the *Odyssey*, traditionally attributed to a poet named Homer. The *Iliad* narrates the events of the tenth year of the Trojan War. The poem opens with the Greek army fraught with internal strife between their leader Agamemnon and the greatest warrior, the hero Achilles. The quarrel between the two leaders and the wrath of Achilles cause the Trojans, led by prince Hector, to temporarily regain the upper hand, before Achilles is forced to return to the battlefield to avenge the death of his friend Patroclus. Achilles, in turn, kills Hector, thus dashing the hopes of Trojan victory and survival. The *Odyssey* is the story of the return (*nostos*) of the Greek hero Odysseus from Troy to his homeland Ithaca, and of the adventures and vicissitudes of his journey. Odysseus, who appears in the *Iliad* as one of the Greek leaders, is famed for his military prowess and as well as for his cunning intellect. The *Odyssey* is a showcase for both, as Odysseus makes his way through his magical and dangerous adventures and toils to his final destination.

These poems are two of the most widely read works of world literature and the source of inspiration for countless other works of literature, drama, visual and other arts. Already in ancient times the *Iliad* and the *Odyssey* were viewed as the fountainhead of Greek literature – not only later epic poetry but also tragedy, comedy, history, rhetorical writings, lyric poetry and later the ancient novel. Furthermore, Homer and his works were used as go-to guides of wisdom and morality, in a manner almost comparable to religious texts such as the Bible or the Koran.

The *Iliad* and the *Odyssey* were not, however, composed in a vacuum. A number of other Greek epic poems, collectively referred to as the Epic Cycle, survive only in fragmentary form or in summaries compiled by ancient scholars. Some of these told tales of the Trojan War, while others focused on other heroes, including stories about Oedipus and his dynasty (*Oedipodeia, Thebaid*), Herakles (*Heracleia*) and Theseus (*Theseis*).

The poems of the Epic Cycle were probably composed later than the *Iliad* and *Odyssey*, and ancient readers and critics such as Aristotle and the Roman poet Horace deemed them inferior to the 'original' Homeric poems. However, it is hard for modern readers to judge the relative merits of the two, given the fragmentary nature of what has survived. We can nevertheless learn from their existence that epic poetry was a flourishing tradition not limited to the *Iliad* and the *Odyssey*, and that numerous stories, including alternative versions of the stories told in the two Homeric poems, circulated simultaneously, some of which were eventually given a written form.

Who was Homer?

Any published edition of the *Iliad* and the *Odyssey*, including this Anthology, cites their author as Homer. This attribution dates back to antiquity, yet there is no historical certainty as to whether an individual called Homer ever actually existed or whether it was he who composed the *Iliad*, the *Odyssey*, both or neither.

Ancient sources provide us with no reliable dates for Homer's birth or death, and disputes were ongoing about his origins, with many a Greek town claiming to have been the birthplace of the greatest of all poets, among them the island of Chios. The lack of evidence around Homer's circumstances has added to the aura of both authority and mystery surrounding his figure, from antiquity to this day.

As well as the question of the identity of Homer himself, Greek and Roman scholars also discussed the composition of his poems: Longinus, probably writing in the first century AD, thought that the *Odyssey* was composed by Homer in his old age, whereas the *Iliad*, with its martial theme, was the product of the youthful poet (*On the Sublime* ch. 12).

Much later, in the seventeenth century, doubts began to be cast not only about Homer's existence, but also as to whether he or any other individual author could have composed (in the traditional sense of 'written down') poems of such length and elaborate nature, and whose language, style and metre bore the markers of what scholars now call 'oral composition'.

How were the poems composed? The 'Homeric question'

The composition of the Homeric poems has been a matter of contention for centuries, and to this day there is no fully conclusive agreement among scholars on the issue. It is important for us to gain an understanding of what is known as the 'Homeric question' inasmuch as it has bearings on our reading of the poems, including the passages from the *Odyssey* contained in this Anthology. Indeed, whereas we nowadays read the *Iliad* and the *Odyssey* printed on a page, whether real or virtual, those same stories were originally performed orally for audiences to listen to, as were many other epic poems and songs of which only rare fragments survive in written form. Most scholars believe that epic poetry was not only performed, but actually composed, orally. However, disagreement still remains as to what role we should attribute to whoever eventually wrote the poems down: did they just record what was routinely being sung at the time or, as some would argue, did they have a major role in organizing and perhaps modifying the inherited material of oral epic poetry so as to compose the *Iliad* and the *Odyssey* as we read them today?

According to the theory of 'oral composition', the poems which for the last 2,500 or so years have been known as the *Iliad* and *Odyssey* were not the invention of an author (or authors) who composed them by writing them down and creating their plots, characters and themes on the basis of his own imagination. Rather, the poems took shape by being performed by *aoidoi* (bards) who would improvise by drawing on traditional themes and stories and using a shared epic language, style and metre. This theory therefore rejects the very idea of single authorship, and sees the *Iliad* and *Odyssey* as the product of a long tradition, whereby one *aoidos* would add to, and modify, poems performed by his colleagues and predecessors. Indeed, we must not imagine that the poems were from the start fixed in the form – length, structure, order – in which we know (and read) them today, but that they were being varied from one performance to the next by *aoidoi* who were both working with, and contributing to, the inherited epic tradition.

The nature of the language of the Homeric poems, with its use of formulae (i.e. stock phrases and scenes which are repeated identically or almost identically throughout the poems, see page 276), was taken as a crucial indication that the poems were composed orally, and the formulae would have aided *aoidoi* in their composition and memorization. Key figures for the development of the study of 'oral composition' were Milman Parry and Albert Lord, who observed and analysed in particular the tradition of South Slavic heroic epic in the early twentieth century, where formulaic language was used by bards to aid performance and composition. Parry and Lord hypothesized that Greek epic could have originated in a similar way.

Most Homeric scholars would now agree that the *Iliad* and *Odyssey* as we now have them are a product of the oral tradition, inasmuch as their themes, language, metre are not the invention of a single author, but were developed over time through performance. But how, from the fluid form of composition-in-performance, did 'our' *Iliad* and *Odyssey* become 'finished products'? And how, when and by whom were they recorded? Indeed, even if performance and composition of the material of the Homeric poems were two parallel processes, the sheer length of the *Iliad* and *Odyssey* as we now read them (15,693 and 12,110 lines respectively) suggests that they must at some point have been written down, or composed with the aid of writing.

Evidence for how and when the poems reached their canonical written form is scarce. Hypotheses abound, but we will never conclusively know whether the *Iliad* and *Odyssey* were recorded in writing by an oral poet, an *aoidos*, 'Homer' or perhaps two individual poets, who dictated their poem to a scribe or who themselves had learned to write; or if the recording happened later still, by hand of a poet or poets working in the tradition of the *rhapsodes* (Greek sources refer to the poems being recorded by order of the Athenian tyrant Peisistratus in the sixth century BC). Those who favour the former hypothesis suggest that the writing down would have happened at some point towards the end of the eighth or beginning of the seventh century BC, a period at which we know that writing was becoming more widespread in the Greek world. We need not assume that the poems were written down all at once; indeed, writing is likely to have gradually become both a memory and composition aid for performers. The latter hypothesis, on the other hand, is favoured by many inasmuch as it presupposes an external stimulus leading to the poems being recorded in written form.

Those who find fault with the theory of 'oral composition' and with the poems having simply been 'recorded' in writing argue that, in doing away with an author (of both or either poems), it fails to explain the unity of each poem's structure, as well as the cross-references within and between them, and the subtleties and nuances in the treatment of themes, characterization and language, which are what continue to make these two poems a source of wonder and delight for readers today. Recently, highly regarded scholar M.L. West has argued strongly for the *Odyssey* having been composed no earlier than 650 BC, and by attributing its composition in writing to a single 'master poet' (different from and later than the 'master poet' of the *Iliad*) he is likely to keep the Homeric question open, drawing it back towards the debate about the role of the author ('Homer' or whoever they may have been).

The Homeric poems in their social/historical context

Dates and historicity

The mystery surrounding the composition of the Homeric poems means that, unlike with other Greek texts which you will read and have read, we cannot say with certainty when they were composed – initially orally, in performance – nor when they reached written form. Furthermore, readers have always wondered about the historicity of the world (events, locations, culture, society) described in the poems and, over the centuries, attempts have been made at verifying it, by comparing evidence from the poems themselves to archaeological finds, including written documents from Greece and the Near East, historical evidence and the study of the language used.

Evidence for the poems: history, archaeology and linguistics

Was there ever a city of Troy, which a Greek army besieged? Did Achilles and Agamemnon, Hector and Priam, Odysseus and his wife Penelope, actually exist? Is there any evidence for the fall of Troy, or for the voyage of Odysseus? Readers throughout the ages have been fascinated by the idea of finding historical evidence for the Trojan War, but there is no conclusive proof that this event ever took place.

Excavations at the Turkish site of Hisarlik on the Dardanelles, which began with the work of German archaeologist Heinrich Schliemann in the second half of the nineteenth century, have unearthed the remains of a town built and rebuilt many times, with the earliest layer dating back to 3000–2550 BC. Schliemann and his successors have suggested that one of these layers was the Troy of the *Iliad*, but it is unlikely that proof for their hypotheses will ever be found. Further excavations on the Greek mainland, in the towns of Mycenae and Tiryns among others, have revealed remains including buildings, tombs and a wealth of burial goods (among which the famous Mask of Agamemnon) associated with the Mycenaean civilization which developed in Greece from the sixteenth to the late eleventh century BC, and which Schliemann associated with the Achaeans (Greeks) of the Homeric poems. Though neither are proof for the events of the *Iliad* and *Odyssey*, these discoveries help us locate them in a historical bracket of references, albeit one which the later *aoidoi* and *rhapsodes* themselves will in all likelihood have idealized and gradually mythologized.

Historians have pointed out that there are obvious discrepancies between the archaeological finds of the Mycenaean civilization and the world of the poems; some would caution us in attempting to find historical proof for what must be the product of a later age looking back with the inevitable distortion of time to an earlier, 'heroic' age; for others, this world is wholly fictional. Nowadays, most scholars tend to view the world described in the poems as containing a heterogeneous mix of elements from different ages, all the way down to the eighth or seventh centuries BC.

The mention of certain specific objects in the poems has nevertheless been used to try to date them by using the dates of comparable archaeological finds: an example is shields decorated with Gorgon heads, mentioned in the *Iliad*, the earliest example of which is dated to 680 BC. However, such comparisons too can be controversial: the fact that the majority of armour and weaponry in the poems is made of bronze rather than iron has been used to suggest that the poems date back to the Bronze Age (whose end is posited around the end of the second millennium BC), whereas scenes such as the iron tempering in a simile in Book 9 of the *Odyssey* (9.391–3) have been used either to disprove this or to prove that the poems contain multiple layers of material.

Although some of these hypotheses are valid and persuasive, they are still not conclusive, and further archaeological evidence may still emerge to disprove them. Overall, just as the narrative material of the poems developed over time and through successive performances, so did the stories gather elements from different periods. The more ancient elements – from weapons to customs – as they faded into the past, became less familiar and idealized by later *aoidoi* as the baggage of the mythic, heroic world. Indeed, the combination of elements both familiar (i.e. more recent) and unfamiliar was what made these poems epic for eighth or early seventh century BC audiences, and subsequent audiences too.

This is also backed by evidence drawn from the language in which the Homeric poems are written, which has been studied alongside the archaeological evidence. Linguistic studies would posit the composition date (i.e. the date of their latest development, when they reached written form) no earlier than the second half of the eighth century BC, with the *Iliad* being at least one decade earlier than the *Odyssey* (for M.L. West, later still). This is corroborated by the evidence that writing in the new Greek alphabet developed in the late ninth century BC, with the earliest known Greek inscription being dated to 770–750 BC. Thus Homeric language, just like archaeological evidence, offers evidence of how the poems developed over time: indeed, they contains relics of various linguistic phases, including rare words and phrases resembling Mycenaean Greek and which the traditional nature of epic poetry preserved, like fossils, for later audiences.

Homeric society

So what are the features of the 'Homeric world', and 'Homeric society', insofar as we can gather from the poems themselves? Although you will be focusing on the *Odyssey*, references will here be made to the *Iliad* as well. It is important to bear in mind that neither poem presents a consistent picture; furthermore, the two poems display different facets of 'Homeric society', the society at war in the *Iliad* and the society at peace in the *Odyssey*. The former demonstrates politics and the heroic code, the latter offers more evidence for economy and society.

Basic political structures: kings and assemblies

The *Iliad* and the *Odyssey* portray a society ruled by kings (*anax*, pl. *anaktes*) of self-contained polities (Mycenae, Pylos, Ithaca etc.). In the *Iliad*, each king is described as commanding men from his local area, although Agamemnon appears to be the de facto commander-in-chief for all the forces. In the *Odyssey*, kings are responsible for their kingdom and all those that reside in it. Loyalty to one's leader and responsibility of the leader for his people are key values in both poems.

Popular assemblies feature in both poems, although decision-making appears to be in the hands of the most prominent leaders, if not a single individual.

The heroic code

Power and authority are inherited, but the Homeric leader is expected to justify his position through his words and his deeds. In the *Iliad*, this means risking your life in the forefront of the fighting and taking on the enemy's best warriors, even if you are terrified of doing so. In the *Odyssey*, Odysseus displays his heroic credentials in a much wider range of activities – from athletics and hunting to diplomacy and negotiation in many different forms.

The leader who does this gains the respect of his peers, the obedience of his subjects and, most importantly, *geras* (property, prize) and *kleos* (glory, renown), a system of values which scholars refer to as the 'heroic code'. The greatest fear of the Homeric hero is to bring *aidōs* (shame) upon himself and his people, which negates *kleos*, and is measured by the reactions and opinions of others to the words and deeds of the individual.

Class system

The poems offer relatively little as evidence of the life of the Homeric 'common man'. The main narrative of the *Iliad* is almost entirely focused on the warriors and heroes of the Trojan War, who naturally spend most of their time fighting and dying, although we do get glimpses of 'normal' life in the similes that populate the poem, as well as in the images on the Shield of Achilles.

The *Odyssey* shows a more varied human landscape, with shepherds and swineherds and household servants featuring alongside the royal family of Odysseus, Penelope and Telemachus and the Suitors.

The economy: agriculture, husbandry and trade

As far as we can tell, it is a world based on a rural economy, with herding of goats and sheep being prominent, and the main source of income of Odysseus' household. Agriculture is also mentioned in both poems, with cultivations of grain and fruit trees as well as the typical Mediterranean cultures of vines and olive trees referenced, though perhaps occupying a secondary role on Ithaca in the *Odyssey*. Neither poem, however, offers us a detailed view of how the economy worked; what is clear is that Odysseus is rich because his land produces a wealth of material goods – enough food and wine to feed all the Suitors and keep his household going in his absence.

The 'Homeric world' of course also knows seafaring, and both poems offer evidence for the practice of raiding and trading by sea. The mention, especially in the *Odyssey,* of encounters with Phoenicians and Egyptians is evidence for a scale of navigation and trade which stretched to well beyond the Greek-speaking world.

Women, family and guest-friendship

This was a society which placed great value on the family and on the integrity of family ties, including marriage, as evidenced by the *Odyssey* in particular. A household such as Odysseus' includes servants, herders and agricultural workers, all of whom are bound by loyalty to their master and his family. Loyalty and friendship between male characters, of similar or differing age, are strong values in both poems.

Women feature more prominently in the *Odyssey*, where we encounter numerous female characters, both human and superhuman. The former are seen as subordinate to the males (fathers, husbands, even grown-up sons) yet are active members of their households, sitting at banquets with the men when they are not busied by tasks such as weaving and spinning.

Guests (*xenoi*), suppliants and strangers are protected categories, to whom hospitality and kindness is due. Hospitality (*xenia*) will be one of the main themes of the *Odyssey* (on the rules of *xenia* see page 271), but also recurs in the *Iliad*: guest-friendship is a special relationship which binds together a *xenos* and his host long after their first encounter, governing their mutual behaviour, and can be inherited across generations (an example in Book 6 of the *Iliad* is the encounter on the battlefield of the Trojan Glaucus and the Greek Diomedes, whose imminent duel is replaced by an exchange of gifts when they discover that they are *xenoi* due to the *xenia* of their fathers).

Gods and goddesses

Above all, the gods regulate the behaviour of mortals. In both poems they receive prayers and sacrifices, and in turn take a keen interest and even participate in human events. Anyone who fails to give the gods their due or follow their instructions can expect to be punished; retribution is also due for anyone committing *hybris*, i.e. behaving with excessive arrogance, insolence or self-confidence beyond the limits set by the gods.

In the *Odyssey*, Zeus is the protector of *xenoi* and the guarantor of justice, rewarding just mortals and seeing to it that wrongdoers are punished, as well as being the arbitrator between rival gods; it is he who ensures that *moira* (fate) can finally run its course.

The *Odyssey* – story, characters, structure, themes

The *Odyssey* tells the story of the homecoming (*nostos*) of Odysseus after the end of the Trojan War. Like other Greek heroes who feature more briefly in the poem (e.g. Agamemnon, Menelaus, Nestor), Odysseus sets sail from Troy with his fleet, but his homeward journey lasts ten years.

During his *nostos* journey, Odysseus pines for his homeland, his family and his wife Penelope, who is waiting faithfully at home on Ithaca, fending off the advances of the Suitors. When Odysseus finally returns to Ithaca after years spent at sea, jostled by encounters with witches, man-eating giants, nymphs, sirens and even a visit to the Underworld, he is alone, for he has lost all his comrades in the course of his adventures. On Ithaca more danger lies in wait, as Odysseus, in disguise, makes his way to regain control of his *oikos* and power over his realm.

Structure, summary, narrators

The events of the poem are not, however, told in such a linear, chronological order; on the contrary, the story doubles back on itself, with a shift in narrators from the poet to Odysseus himself. Books 1–4 (the so-called Telemachy) follow Odysseus' son Telemachus in his quest to find his father; in Book 5 we meet Odysseus for the first time in the poem, as he prepares to depart from the island of the nymph Calypso where he has been forced to remain for seven years; soon enough, however, he is caught up in a storm stirred up by angry Poseidon and only just manages to escape the god's wrath and land on the island of Scheria. Books 6–8 tell of Odysseus' encounter with its inhabitants, the Phaeacians, who welcome him to their palace and eventually persuade him to reveal his identity and narrate his adventures. Books 9–12 (the Wanderings or *Apologoi*) are a distinctive section of the poem also inasmuch as they are narrated in first person by Odysseus to the audience of the Phaeacians. In an extended flashback, Odysseus here recounts all his adventures and encounters since departing from Troy up to this point:

- Book 9: Cicones; Lotus Eaters; Cyclops (including Passage 1, lines 231–460)
- Book 10: Aeolus; Laestrygonians; Circe (including Passage 2 lines 144–399)
- Book 11: Underworld (*Nekyia*)
- Book 12: Circe (again); Sirens; Scylla, Charybdis; Thrinacia; storm, arrival on Calypso's island (Ogygia).

In Book 13, the third-person narrative resumes and the Phaeacians, as promised, set Odysseus aboard one of their magic ships and transport him to the shores of his beloved Ithaca. Books 14–21 see Odysseus in disguise introduce himself to various members of his household, from Eumaeus the loyal swineherd to his son Telemachus, in his quest to gain access to his palace. While still in disguise, he witnesses the misdemeanours of the Suitors first-hand, meanwhile gaining the confidence of his wife, who believes he is a beggar. In Book 22 he finally takes revenge, with the help of his son and servants, killing all the Suitors as well as any disloyal members of his household; only in Book 23 does he reveal his true identity to Penelope. Book 24, whose authenticity has been disputed since antiquity, sees Odysseus reunited with his elderly father Laertes and regain control of affairs in his *oikos* and on Ithaca as a whole.

Themes and characters

The poem thus tells what is a well-known story, full of danger, magic and deceit, which has inspired works as varied as Virgil's *Aeneid*, Dante's *Divine Comedy*, Joyce's *Ulysses* and the Coen brothers' *O Brother where art thou?* In respect of its high concentration of magical, folk-tale elements, especially in the Wanderings, the *Odyssey* differs from the *Iliad*, its setting being not the heroic context of war but, during Books 9–12, the Otherworld. Such magical elements, characters and settings, though largely absent from the *Iliad*, are, however, a key component of many other Greek myths (think of the stories of Hercules or Orpheus), whereas the journey theme has an obvious parallel in the myth of Jason and the Argonauts. Thus the *Odyssey* shares many of its features with the broader realm of Greek mythology.

The focus of the *Odyssey* is on its protagonist, as is made clear not only by the poem's title but also by its proem or introduction:

ἄνδρα μοι ἔννεπε, μοῦσα, πολύτροπον, ὃς μάλα πολλὰ
πλάγχθη, ἐπεὶ Τροίης ἱερὸν πτολίεθρον ἔπερσεν:
πολλῶν δ' ἀνθρώπων ἴδεν ἄστεα καὶ νόον ἔγνω,
πολλὰ δ' ὅ γ' ἐν πόντῳ πάθεν ἄλγεα ὃν κατὰ θυμόν,
ἀρνύμενος ἥν τε ψυχὴν καὶ νόστον ἑταίρων. (1.1–5)

Tell me, Muse, of the man of many resources who wandered a great deal after he had sacked the sacred citadel of Troy: he saw the cities of many men, and learned their minds, and suffered many sorrows in his heart on the sea as he sought to win his own life and the homecoming of his companions.

The proem draws the audience's attention to the key themes of the poem. First is Odysseus' characterization as the *polytropos* hero, literally 'multiform', 'of many ways', 'resources' or 'wiles'. Odysseus' shrewdness, cleverness, curiosity and dexterity (he is the famed author of the ruse of the Trojan horse, which is recounted by Helen in Book 4, lines 265–89) are indeed on show throughout the poem. In the course of the *Odyssey* and the passages you will read, Odysseus learns, through experience and even through tragic mishaps, how to make use of these skills to his advantage, and to adapt them to the various situations and antagonists with which he is faced. Being *polytropos* allows him to learn to keep out of danger, and this will eventually set him apart from his comrades who succumb to exhaustion, hunger and greed on Thrinacia, where they are destroyed by Zeus for slaughtering and eating the cattle of Helios in Book 12.

Two verbs in the proem, πλάγχθη (*he wandered*) and πάθεν (*he suffered*), point jointly to Odysseus' forced condition in the course of his journey. Suffering, grief and loss are key themes in the poem, from the ongoing pain of Odysseus and his men as they pine for their homeland, to the grief which they undergo as their comrades are lost to the jaws of the Cyclops, the spears of the Laestrygonians, and other perils encountered as they wander across the deep. *Nostos* is the overarching theme of the poem: it refers to the homecoming itself, but also to the journey and process through which the homecoming is achieved; it is a quest and, in the case of Odysseus and his companions, the object of quest are both νόστος and ψυχή (life, survival), the latter as prerequisite of the former. Odysseus' otherworldly adventures can thus be described as an obstacle course in the way of his *nostos*. In Book 9, Odysseus and his chosen comrades risk being trapped and eaten alive in the cave of the Cyclops, depriving them of *nostos*. In other cases the obstacle is more insidious, as it involves *nostos* being temporarily forgotten, its memory suspended, as when in Book 9 three of Odysseus' companions taste the food of the Lotus Eaters, which causes anyone who eats it to forget their *nostos* (9.94–7); or in Book 10, when the goddess-sorceress Circe bewitches Odysseus' men by feeding them a potion which causes them to forget their homeland (10.235–6). Odysseus, who later intervenes to free his companions from Circe's spell, does not succumb to it himself, but later, more subtly, is in danger of forgetting his *nostos* during his year-long stay on Circe's island, so much so that it will be up to his companions to remind him of his homeland and the need to set sail (10.472–4), for the *nostos* to be fulfilled.

Although Odysseus actually reaches Ithaca already in Book 13, his *nostos* is and remains the goal of the entire poem, and as such it is sanctioned by the gods. After the proem, the narrative proper opens *in medias res*, with a banquet in the halls of the gods in which Athena reminds her father Zeus of the fate of Odysseus, who at the time is stranded on Calypso's island, pining for Ithaca; a similar scene occurs at the start of Book 5. The real obstacle in the way of Odysseus' *nostos,* however, is not Calypso but Poseidon, god of the sea and father of Polyphemus, whom Odysseus has wounded and wronged (Book 9), and who opposes Odysseus' *nostos.* Zeus' response (1.76–7) marks the decision that Poseidon will eventually have to yield from his hostility to Odysseus. This sets in motion the action of the poem and the last stage of the *nostos*, from Calypso's island home to Ithaca via the Phacacians.

The gods and religion in the *Odyssey*

Athena, Zeus and Poseidon are the three main gods in the poem. Athena, as Odysseus' protector and at times accomplice, shares the *polytropos* hero's ability to use *metis*, a term which refers to plans and devices and the cunning and skill to craft them. She communicates with Odysseus at key turning points in the poem, such as when in Book 13 goddess and hero agree on a plan of action in order for him to regain the upper hand in his *oikos*. Athena also plays a part in the slaughter of the Suitors in Book 22, first in disguise and then in a glorious *theophany* (divine appearance), raising her *aegis* (shield) to terrify the Suitors. She also favours Odysseus indirectly, by moving other characters – via dreams, portents and apparitions – in such a way as to enable him to overcome obstacles. It is Athena, for example, who sends Telemachus to Pylos in search of his father in Book 1; it is she who ensures Odysseus is welcomed in the land of the Phaeacians in Book 6; and it is she who, at the start of Book 21, suggests to Penelope that she should establish the archery contest which will set in motion Odysseus' revenge against the Suitors. Athena, finally, is present at the very end of the Odyssey, sanctioning the peace on Ithaca in the closing lines of Book 24.

Poseidon, Odysseus' antagonist, is a less prominent character in the poem, but unlike Athena he does feature in the passages in this Anthology, and his presence and power are a guiding motor in delaying the hero's *nostos* until the end of the Wanderings. Poseidon's hostility is explained by Zeus in the scene in Book 1, who refers to Odysseus' encounter with Poseidon's son the Cyclops which the hero himself recounts in Book 9. As a result of Polyphemus' prayer to his father, Odysseus is exposed to the wrath of Poseidon who, acting against the will of the other gods, attempts to destroy him in a purpose-made storm in Book 5 (see page 263). Ultimately, however, Poseidon yields to the will of Zeus, and all but disappears from the poem as from Book 13, leaving Odysseus to face his mortal antagonists instead.

In the two divine assembly scenes (Books 1 and 5), Zeus in effect acts as arbitrator between Athena and Poseidon, and his role overall is that of supreme adjudicator between men and between gods. By sanctioning Athena's support of Odysseus throughout the poem, he in turn indirectly sanctions the hero's victory over the Suitors and, by extension, the accomplishment of his *nostos* according to *moira*. In his support of Odysseus, Zeus does not interfere when other gods have cause to exact punishment for offences against their interests, chiefly Poseidon. However, it is Zeus himself who in Book 12, by destroying the companions near Thrinacia on behalf of the wronged sun-god Helios, fulfils Polyphemus' prophecy-prayer (9.528–34) and brings Odysseus, bereft of his fleet, closer to the end of his *nostos*.

Other gods and superhuman beings intervene in the poem, generally in minor roles as helpers or guides. Sometimes their intervention is assumed by the narrator: in Book 9 Odysseus describes how, after landing on an uninhabited island, nymphs drive wild beasts into the men's nets and adds that '*a god*' provides them with food (9.154–5). Similarly, on Circe's island, Odysseus says that '*some god*' (10.157) sends a stag into his path as he is out hunting in search of food for his distraught comrades. Elsewhere, divine interventions are reported with full narrative authority: we are told that Hermes the messenger is employed by the gods to communicate with Calypso in Book 5 to order the release of Odysseus and the furthering of his *nostos*; and Hermes makes another important appearance in Book 10 where he instructs Odysseus (who is here recounting the event in first person) on how to behave in Circe's presence and gives him the magic plant *moly* as a remedy against her spells.

In the *Odyssey*, justice (*dike*) is in the hands of Zeus, who is called upon by those wronged to seek retribution. Zeus, as well as other gods, is the recipient of prayers and sacrifices; sacrifices (which involve burning the bones or other parts of an animal which is being prepared for a meal, e.g. 9.231 and 9.553) are a necessary means whereby mortals communicate with the gods. Offering a sacrifice is a gift to the gods who will be prompted to reciprocate with support or protection, as Athena reminds Zeus in Book 1, spurring him on to intervene in Odysseus' favour (1.60–2). When sacrifices are not accepted, this is taken as a sinister sign of divine disfavour (though this is rarely made clear, and is often an interpretation by one of the mortals, as in the case of Odysseus' retrospective comment on the Book 9 sacrifice at 9.551–5).

Zeus himself provides an excellent explanation of how human actions relate to divine designs when, in the assembly scene in Book 1, he complains that mortals '*say that evils come from us and instead by themselves too they suffer beyond what is ordained though their own folly* (ἀτασθαλίῃσιν)' (1.33–4). This is what is known as double determination: the actions of mortals, both good and bad, are determined both by their own will and by the intervention or decision of the gods and, ultimately, *moira*. This is often seen when a god or goddess is said to restrain someone about to make a rash decision, or conversely to give strength, courage, or other powers and skills to a mortal. We find an example of the latter when the poet says that Odysseus, battered by the waves of the storm caused by Poseidon, would have perished '*had grey-eyed Athena not given him wisdom*' (5.437). The way this is phrased suggests that the goddess somehow giving (δῶκε) the hero ἐπιφροσύνην. It is important to realize that the fact that Odysseus' wisdom is god-given does not deprive him of the responsibility or merit for his own actions. In this scene, Athena herself does not actually appear; so for some readers, this is simply a poetic rendering of the fact that Odysseus, at the height of danger, took heart, so that with a final, massive effort he was able to reach the shore. Nevertheless, it is telling that Athena is mentioned, suggesting at the very least that Odysseus, finding himself in dire straits, was mindful (or supernaturally reminded!) of his divine protector. In a sense, the two share responsibility for Odysseus' survival; a wise hero such as Odysseus is 'predisposed' to have his wisdom 'boosted' by Athena; with a lesser hero, it would not have worked.

You will encounter a similar scene in the set text, when Odysseus, in the Cyclops' cave, says that he was reflecting on '*how I might seek revenge and Athena might give me the glory*' (δοίη δέ μοι εὖχος Ἀθήνη, 9.316–17). By expressing it thus, Odysseus seems to be admitting that he requires Athena's permission to act and, consequently, reap the glory from his success; but once this permission is granted, the glory would be his, and all the greater precisely inasmuch as it is god-sanctioned. Similarly, the fact that Odysseus receives advice about Circe from Hermes in Book 10, rather than depriving him of the full share of responsibility for his success, only confirms that the gods are on his side.

For actions to be 'doubly determined' there is no need for a god to be explicitly mentioned, as all events ultimately fall under the jurisdiction of *moira*. In the same episode in Book 9, it is Odysseus alone who decides to pursue his innate curiosity, as well as his desire for booty and guest-gifts, and so decides to remain in the Cyclops' cave, ignoring the advice of his more risk-averse companions (9.219–30). Thus he is responsible for exposing himself and his comrades to death and danger and, ultimately, for causing Polyphemus to utter the prayer which will determine the circumstances of his own *nostos*. However, as Polyphemus himself reveals, Odysseus' arrival and his blinding of the Cyclops had been foretold by a seer (9.511–2), so must be part of divine design too, a design within which Odysseus' decisions and actions, as well as their ultimate consequences, are thus 'doubly determined'.

Books 9 and 10

Odysseus' encounters with the Cyclops and with Circe are the first two large-scale encounters of the Wanderings. Although attempts were made since antiquity to identify their locations, neither episode can be situated on a map: indeed, Odysseus' departure from the land of the Cicones (Ismarus, in Thrace (northern Greece), 9.40) at the start of Book 9 marks his departure from the 'real' mappable world and his entrance into the magical Otherworld in which the Wanderings are set. The islands of the Cyclops and Circe's island Aeaea (10.135) both belong to a supernatural dimension, both geographically and humanly. Not only are their landscapes unfamiliar and otherworldly but so too, importantly, are the appearance, habits, manners and powers of their inhabitants. Odysseus, faced with novel experiences, both terrifying and enchanting, appears initially to be out of his depth. In these two episodes, the audience watches him learn how to behave in an environment in which the normal rules of human (and heroic) behaviour either do not apply or are misunderstood – discoveries made at his and his men's expense.

The characters: Odysseus, Polyphemus and Circe

In the Cyclops episode in Book 9, Odysseus leaves the majority of his men on the uninhabited island where they first land and sails with his ship and crew to the land of the Cyclops. He and twelve selected comrades enter the cave of the Cyclops, and become trapped inside when the owner returns from the pastures with his flock of sheep. In a mix of curiosity and boldness, Odysseus has resisted his men's request that they leave the cave, and must now find a stratagem to preserve their *nostos* and *psychē*. A few men fall victim to the Cyclops' cannibalism at dinner time, building up terror in the men's morale. Overnight, Odysseus devises his plan: the next evening the Cyclops is drugged with strong wine and, when he reels over in drunken sleep, the men led by Odysseus blind him with a sizzling-hot stake. When the Cyclops, fearful lest the men should steal his precious flock, sits himself in the doorway of his cave in an attempt to stop them, they steal themselves away tied to and hidden under the shaggy bellies of the rams who are being let out to graze, thus gaining their booty and freedom in one go. It is, however, a narrow escape, and although Odysseus' immediate reaction is to boast of his victory in the face of the defeated Cyclops, causing further danger to his men both in the short and long term, by the time they reach the island of Circe, he has clearly begun to learn from his mistakes.

When the men land on the island of Aeaea in Book 10, Odysseus has lost a chance of easy *nostos* offered by the wind-god Aeolus through the βουλὴ ... κακὴ (*evil counsel*, 10.46) of his comrades, and has subsequently lost all but one ship and crew to the cannibalistic Laestrygonians. Odysseus now makes it his mission to find food for his surviving, grief-stricken comrades, and hunts and kills a superhumanly huge stag, a first sign of the magic of the place. He behaves with greater caution in exploring the island, at all times taking responsibility for his comrades' well-being. When half of his surviving crew is bewitched by Circe and turned into swine, Odysseus takes it upon himself to attempt to rescue them. On his way to the house of Circe, Odysseus is stopped by Hermes, whose instructions as to how to behave in the presence of the goddess are, literally, a godsend. Indeed, when Circe's potion fails to work its magic on Odysseus, the sorceress-goddess realizes he is no regular passer-by. After being recognized by Circe as Odysseus and lying with her, the hero insists on his comrades being freed and returned to their human form, before indulging in Circe's hospitality with all his comrades for an entire year.

Both antagonists have elements of ambiguity which make their potential danger not immediately obvious. Circe combines her divine charm and beauty with her deadly powers. Her epithet καλλιπλοκάμοιο (*pretty-curls* 10.220), the beauty of her voice (ὀπὶ καλῇ 10.221), the divine beauty of her fine weaving (10.223) conjure up an aura of enchantment, and Odysseus' companions are unsure whether she is ἢ θεὸς ἠὲ γυνή (*a goddess or a woman*, 10.228). Only Eurylochus doesn't follow her indoors, fearing a δόλον (*trick*, 10.232) and is proved right when the goddess mixes their food with φάρμακα λύγρ', ἵνα πάγχυ λαθοίατο πατρίδος αἴης (*deadly drugs, so that they would forget their fatherland entirely*, 10.236) and turns them into swine.

With the Cyclops, to whose superhuman size Odysseus repeatedly refers, the danger becomes clear pretty quickly. The initial impression that he might be an innocuous, if gigantic, dairy farmer is soon shattered when he bluntly declares that he will spare neither Odysseus nor his comrades (9.277–8) and, when merry with Odysseus' wine, he offers the hero what he ironically describes as a guest-gift, ξεινήιον (9.370), namely the concession that he will be eaten last.

Consequently, Odysseus' response to his two antagonists must be somewhat different in nature: whereas in the cave he uses his own resources to put the giant out of action by blinding him and outwits him with the name-trick, which effectively prevents him from obtaining help from the Cyclopes, his own sword and cleverness do not suffice to put a powerful goddess like Circe out of action, hence Hermes' intervention. Circe's hostility, however, ceases as soon as she realizes who she is confronted with, and when the men, their metamorphosis reversed, weep in a mix of sorrow and joy, she too appears capable of genuine human compassion (θεὰ δ' ἐλέαιρε καὶ αὐτή, *and the goddess herself was moved too*, 10.399). The narrator does, moreover, offer us a glimpse of a milder, almost humane Cyclops, attentive to his flock and, in his poignant address to his favourite ram, capable of affection and desirous of empathy (ἦ σύ γ' ἄνακτος / ὀφθαλμὸν ποθέεις; *are you perhaps weeping for your master's eye?* 9.452–3).

First person narrative

When reading these episodes, it is important that we are constantly aware of the narrative point of view: our narrator is Odysseus who, with the benefit of hindsight, recounts his adventures to his hosts and saviours the Phaeacians. The disparity between what the audience knows vis-à-vis the characters is deployed by the internal narrator for effect, creating suspense but also, through a careful use of anticipation and foreshadowing, allowing us to understand the meaning and role of a given episode in the Wanderings, and in Odysseus' *nostos* as a whole. Similarly, we need not be confused by the disparity between what Odysseus the protagonist knows versus what, as narrator, he can reveal *post factum*. This affects not only his presentation of the episodes and characters, his ordering of the narrative and the emphasis given to certain items, elements, moments, but also, crucially, the self-presentation of Odysseus and of his relationship with his comrades.

Instances in which the narrator names or alludes to the Cyclops or Circe prior to the moment in the story when he has found out who they, respectively, are, serve as references for the audience but also trigger our expectations about how the hero Odysseus will fare in his encounter with them. For instance, when the men land ashore and catch sight of the cave in Book 9, Odysseus tells us it belonged to ἀνὴρ ... πελώριος (a *monstrous man*), who was unlike '*grain-eating men*' but comparable in his size and isolation to a '*wooded peak*, (9.187–92). Similarly in Book 10, when Odysseus catches sight of smoke on the island, he declares that it was Κίρκης ἐν μεγάροισι (*in Circe's house*, 10.150); later his men find δώματα Κίρκης (*Circe's house*, 10.210) well before they could possibly have known whose house it was.

Odysseus introduces both episodes by describing their inhabitants and the landscape, preparing the audience for the dangers ahead and allowing them to visualize the episodes, located in their otherworldly settings (such descriptions on arrival are a feature of the *xenia* type-scene, on which see page 277). In Book 9, both the uninhabited island where the men first land and the land of the Cyclopes are supernaturally rich in vegetation and wildlife, a sort of paradise-on-earth which recalls the Golden Age of Greek myth in which men lived in harmony with nature and ignorance of farming. The beauty of the natural landscape and wealth of resources stand in contrast with the dangers they conceal. Odysseus introduces the

Cyclopes as ὑπερφιάλων ἀθεμίστων (*arrogant and lawless*, 9.106), adding that 'they have neither assemblies for council nor social norms (θέμιστες), *but they inhabit the peaks of mountains inside hollow caves, each exercising his authority over children and wives, nor do they care about each other*' (9.112–5). When Odysseus and a group of men cross the stretch of sea to visit the land of the Cyclopes, they cannot know what lies in wait for them; Odysseus says only that they have noticed smoke and heard voices and the bleating of livestock (9.166–7), and justifies the mission to his men by saying that they are going to find out 'what sort of men these are, whether arrogant (ὑβρισταί) and savage (ἄγριοι) and unjust (οὐδὲ δίκαιοι) or hospitable (φιλόξεινοι) and whether their mind is pious (νόος ... θεουδής)' (175–6). This triggers the audience's foreknowledge of the nature of the Cyclopes as described a few lines above, which in contrast to the men's ignorance only increases the suspense as the episode builds up.

When in Book 10 the men arrive on a seemingly uninhabited land where the only sign of human presence is smoke rising from the thick of the forest (10.149–50), similar expectations are set up for the audience. Furthermore, here too Odysseus prefaces the description of the episode with an introduction to the island's inhabitant (10.135–139). The description of Circe as δεινὴ θεός ..., / αὐτοκασιγνήτη ὀλοόφρονος Αἰήταο (*dread goddess, sister of baleful Aietes*, 10.136–7) does not bode well and, as we read of the men's tears at the loss of their comrades (10.142–3), devoured not only by the Cyclops but also in the intervening episode of the Laestrygonians, we fear for what awaits them. Herein, then, lies the mastery of the narrator: for whereas the Cyclops reveals himself to be as dangerous as expected and more baneful still in the long term, Circe, though initially presented as an antagonist whose magic powers are superior to Odysseus' wiles, later becomes a helper, who entertains the men in her home and offers guidance about their voyage ahead.

Another of Odysseus-as-narrator's many wiles is the way in which he draws the audience's attention to key items in the story, which will later be revealed as highly significant for the development of events. One such example is what seems at first to be an exceedingly long digression about the wine Odysseus takes with him into the Cyclops' cave, a gift of the priest Maron (9.196 ff.). The wine itself is described in detail, as being sweet and unmixed, kept secret by Maron and his wife, suggesting it is a special wine indeed; Odysseus rounds off this description by saying that he took with him a flask of this wine as '*my strong spirit had thought that we would be meeting a man clothed in great strength, a savage* (ἄγριον), *knowing neither justice nor rules*' (οὔτε δίκας εὖ εἰδότα οὔτε θέμιστας, 9.213–5). Only in retrospect does this decision make full sense, when Odysseus retells what use this wine was put to – not, as we may have anticipated, as a gift, but as an inebriating offering. The double effect of having anticipated a mention of the wine is that the audience is not surprised to see Odysseus suddenly produce a flask of this potent drink when trapped in the cave, and at the same time Odysseus' presents himself in the best light as a prudent and forward-thinking leader. The foreshadowing adds an extra twist to our reading of Odysseus' offer of wine to the Cyclops: what was originally a gift from Maron becomes a fake guest-gift, an *offering* (λοιβὴν 9.349) from Odysseus, one used to the detriment of the Cyclops who in turn has failed to show Odysseus and his men the faintest hint of guest-welcome (*xenia*).

Similar cases of foreshadowing contained in our episodes include the attention paid to the huge rock used by the Cyclops as a door (θυϱεὸν μέγαν . . . ὄβϱιμον, *great, ponderous door* 9.240–1; λίθον ὄβϱιμον, *ponderous rock* 9.305; θυϱεὸν μέγαν 313 = 340), an insurmountable obstacle blocking the men's escape; and to the fact that the rams, usually left outdoors overnight, are exceptionally brought indoors on the night of the blinding (Odysseus comments that the Cyclops did so ἤ τι ὀϊσάμενος, ἢ καὶ θεὸς ὣς ἐκέλευσεν, *either having something in mind, or because a god ordered him thus* 9.339), a fact which will allow the men to escape undetected by the Cyclops. Similarly, in Book 10 great emphasis is placed on the huge sword which Odysseus takes with him, first on his hunting expedition (φάσγανον ὀξὺ *sharp sword* 10.145) and then on his quest to rescue his comrades (ξίφος ἀϱγυϱόηλον . . . μέγα χάλκεον, *silver studded great bronze sword*, 10.261); he will use this sword not, as on the Trojan battlefield, in a heroic duel against an adversary but, following Hermes' instructions, to threaten Circe (ξίφος ὀξὺ 294 cf. 321–2 ἄοϱ ὀξὺ).

Hospitality and prophecy

Xenia is one of the most important themes in the *Odyssey*, and plays a crucial role in the Wanderings, with interesting facets in our two episodes. *Xenia*, translated both as 'hospitality' and 'guest-friendship', describes the rules that govern the relationship between hosts and a strangers (*xenoi*) on the arrival of the latter at the home or land of the former, a relationship which subsequently develops into a permanent bond called guest-friendship. The rules of *xenia*, as depicted in the Homeric poems as well as in later Greek authors, are strict; in the *Odyssey*, adherence to such rules is a marker of civilization. It is customary that the guest is received, fed, entertained and, in the case of an overnight stay, bathed and given a bed; conversations between host and guest play an important role, as does the giving of guest-gifts by the host. The guest is not immediately asked who he is and where he is from, as *xenia* is a sacred duty owed to any stranger notwithstanding his or her identity (for details on *xenia* type-scenes see page 277).

It is as a *xenos* that Odysseus is recounting both episodes to the Phaeacians, on whose land he is stranded having lost his raft, clothes and all possessions to the waves. The Phaeacians are seemingly impeccable hosts, who at the end of the Wanderings in Book 12 will complete their role by providing Odysseus with conveyance back to Ithaca. Neither Cyclops nor Circe, however, behave like standard hosts. Indeed, the Cyclops is presented as the anti-*xenos* par excellence, culminating in the scene in which he devours his guests instead of offering them food, whereas Circe turns her would-be guests into swine, before she herself turns from foe into friend and offers the men year-long, quasi-divine *xenia*. On Aeaea, the men are lured into Circe's trap when they approach her house to find out, according to their mission, how they might leave the island whose location is wholly unknown to them (10.190–3); on the other hand, Odysseus' quest for *xenia* in the land of the Cyclopes is declared as an end in itself, motivated by curiosity rather than need (lines 9.175–6). He plays on this motif in his first exchange with the Cyclops in his cave (9.268 ff.), dangerously testing the giant when he declares that he and his men are suppliants and *xenoi* and hoping for hospitality (εἴ τι πόροις ξεινήιον ἠὲ καὶ ἄλλως / δοίης δωτίνην, ἥ τε ξείνων θέμις ἐστίν, *in case you may give us hospitality or even some sort of gift, as is the custom of xenoi* 9.267–8), naming Zeus ξείνιος as their protector. Too soon will he realize that he does so to little avail, as the Cyclops declares that he cares nothing for the gods and will destroy the men. In the closing scene of the episode, emboldened by having escaped from the blinded Cyclops' jaws, Odysseus tells him that Zeus and the gods have punished him for devouring his ξείνους . . . σῷ ἐνὶ οἴκῳ (*guests in your house*, 9.478), yet he will find that Zeus is not able to uphold this, as Odysseus' actions and words will cause the wrath and punishment of Poseidon.

Prophecies play an important role in the two episodes. Towards the end of both episodes it is revealed that Cyclops and Circe had been forewarned about Odysseus' arrival. At line 9.506 ff. we find out that Polyphemus, who had been tricked into thinking that the visitor's name was Nobody (Οὖτις), had been told by a soothsayer that 'an Odysseus' would blind him; when the truth of the situation becomes clear to him, the Cyclops teases Odysseus back for his righteousness about *xenia*, promising him *gifts* (ξείνια, 9.517) and *conveyance* (πομπήν 9.518) by hand of his father Poseidon, a darkly ironic promise which Odysseus' further angry swearing turns into the prophetic prayer to Poseidon himself (see page 266). It may seem implausible to us that Polyphemus doesn't immediately make the link between what has happened to him and the prophecy according to which he would lose his sight '*at the hands of Odysseus*' (9.512); so late a revelation points to the gullibility of the Cyclops and, at the same time, highlights the cleverness of Odysseus, whose name-trick has kept the giant in the dark all along. In Book 10, by contrast, Circe is quick to make the connection: stunned by the realization that her φάρμακα (*potions*) have not worked on Odysseus and terrified by his attack, she begins to ask him who he is (10.325–9) only to answer her own question by revealing that she had been told of his arrival from Troy by Hermes (ἦ σύ γ' Ὀδυσσεύς ἐσσι πολύτροπος . . . *Indeed you are Odysseus of many resources*, . . . 10.330). In both episodes, the prophecies remind the audience that Odysseus' adventures are in fact 'doubly determined', confirming the narrator's claim, in each case, that *some god* (τις θεὸς 9.142 = 10.141) guided them both to the land of the Cyclops and to Aeaea.

Language and style

Homeric language

The language in which the Homeric poems are composed is a poetic language, whose elevated tone and solemn expressions match the dignity and importance of the subject matter. It was not, however, a language that anyone would have used in everyday life. Scholarly analysis of Homeric Greek has shown that it is an amalgam of dialects from different areas of Greece and which were prevalent at different times. The predominant component is the Ionic dialect (spoken by the Greeks living on the western coast of modern Turkey and on some Aegean islands), with elements of the Aeolic dialect (used in the northern Greek regions of Thessaly and Boeotia, and on the island of Lesbos). In addition, the poems preserve words from earlier or sometimes foreign traditions, which were already obsolete and hence unintelligible to later Greek audiences (Aristotle, in his *Poetics*, calls them *glossai*). There are words in our text which have been a matter of debate since antiquity, such as μῶλυ, the magic plant given to Odysseus as an antidote by Hermes (10.305), and the epithet for Hermes himself, ἀργεϊφόντης, sometimes but not conclusively understood as meaning 'Slayer of Argos' (10.303). In addition, the poems contain words that occur only once in Homer, called *hapax legomenon* ('something said (only) once'), usually taken as a sign of the poet's creativity (an example in our text is μειλίγματα, *tasty morsels*, 10.217; see also notes on 9.385 and 9.387). The heterogeneous nature of Homeric Greek is the linguistic proof of the traditional nature and origin of the poems themselves. Just as their content, as we saw in the first two sections of this Introduction, was elaborated over time through the work and performances of generations of *aoidoi*, so too did the epic language form by accumulation and accretion.

In the passages you will read, you will notice unfamiliar forms and endings of nouns, verbs and other morphological items. These are signs of the mixed origin of the language used, and are in turn expedient for the composition; indeed, forms from different dialects and from different ages coexisting within the language offer the *aoidos* greater flexibility when working within the constraints of the poems' metre (see section on Homeric metre).

The peculiarities listed below are the most common in Homeric Greek; you will find more details of specific, unfamiliar forms in the notes to the set texts. You will notice a tendency of Homeric language to use uncontracted forms (see *diectasis* on page 274), and to use variant forms of words with double or single consonants (even in the protagonist's name: accusative Ὀδυσσῆα 9.503 vs. genitive Ὀδυσῆος 9.511). In words you are familiar with, you will notice vowels changed or lengthened: the most common usages are η for ᾱ; ει for ε; ου for ο.

NOUNS

- First declension nouns present the vowel η where in Classical Greek they would have ᾱ.
- Second declension genitive singular ends in -οιο (the regular -ου is also found).
- Dative plurals have different endings: -ῃσι(ν) is more common than -αις in the first declension, -οισι(ν) as an alternative for -οις in the second and -σι(ν) or in third, where -εσσι(ν) with double σ is also found.
- The ending -φι(ν), originally an instrumental case ending, can be found; it usually stands for the dative, sometimes for the genitive, and more often for the singular than plural.

VERBS

- Augments can be omitted.
- Older endings can be found, such as -μι instead of -ω for the first person singular; -ατο and -αται for -ντο and -νται; -μεναι for the active infinitive ending -ειν; etc.
- -μι verbs take endings you are familiar with from contracted -εω and -οω verbs.

- The verb '*to be*' εἰμί has many different forms, which you will find explained in the notes, including alternatives for the infinitive.

PRONOUNS and ADJECTIVES

- Third plural personal pronoun σφεῖς is used (the dative σφιν or σφίσι is fairly common).
- The article ὁ, ἡ τό is used as a demonstrative pronoun. You will encounter other forms of the article with this function.
- You will find unfamiliar pronouns used. Particularly common is μιν = αὐτόν, αὐτήν, a common alternative to τόν, τήν for the accusative singular pronoun; and οἱ = αὐτῷ (dative singular).
- ὅ, ἥ, τό can also be used as a relative pronoun.
- ὅς, ἥ, ὅν is used as a possessive adjective.

Other peculiarities of the Homeric dialect include:

TMESIS: meaning 'cutting', refers to the fact that prefixes which in Classical Greek are attached to the verb are 'cut' or separated from it and positioned before it or, more rarely, straight after it (e.g. ἐκ δ' ἐγκέφαλος χαμάδις ῥέε, *flowed out*, 9.290, from ἐκρέω). However, it is likely that these prefixes started off as separate, their function closer to that of prepositions, and only later became 'attached' to the verb as we know it in Classical Greek.

DIECTASIS: meaning 'stretching out', is the phenomenon whereby in the Homeric dialect we find two same-timbre vowels (e.g. αα, οω) where in Classical Greek they would be rendered as a contraction (e.g. ὁρόω for Classical ὁράω = ὁρῶ; see e.g. 9.295). Inasmuch as this produces two syllables instead of what in Classical Greek would be one, *diectasis* offers more metrical options. The term *diectasis* is also used for other, regularly uncontracted forms (e.g. see at 9.398) or for forms where an extra vowel is required by the metre (e.g. see at 9.282).

Homeric metre

The Homeric poems are composed in dactylic hexameter, and this verse became the hallmark of epic poetry in Greece and Rome. This metre, which gives the poems their typical rhythm, is supposed to have formed the basis of the musical accompaniment to the poems, and at the same time its cadence would have been a helpful memorization tool for the *aoidoi* who performed them. The regular scheme of the hexameter is formed of the following six (hex-) feet or metrical units:

$$- \cup \cup \mid - \cup \cup \mid - \cup \cup \mid - \cup \cup \mid - \cup \cup \mid - \times$$

Each of the first four feet (dactyls, $\mid - \cup \cup \mid$ = long-short-short) is interchangeable with a spondee $\mid - - \mid$ = long-long. The fifth foot (a dactyl) only rarely can be replaced by a spondee; the sixth and final foot can end in either a long or short syllable, marked ×.

Greek metre is quantitative, which means that it is based on the 'quantity' or length of a syllable. You already know that some vowels are long (η and ω), and others are short (ε and o), whereas others (α, ι and υ) can be either long or short (*anceps*). The length of a syllable takes into account the length of the vowel, but in order to scan the line as a succession of longs and shorts it is necessary to consider how this length is modified by the following consonants. A syllable containing a long vowel or a diphthong will be scanned as long; a syllable ending in a short vowel will be scanned as short, unless the vowel is followed by two or more consonants (the consonants ζ, ξ and φ count as double in themselves), in which case the syllable is long. However, a combination of a consonant + a liquid or nasal consonant (λ, P, λ, μ, ν) can sometimes scan as short.

The regular rhythm and speed of the Homeric line can be modified through the alternation of dactyls and spondees. Furthermore, breaks in the line occur at certain regular points and can add to the expressiveness of the line, with special emphasis when the break corresponds to a break in the meaning. Such a break is called caesura when it occurs within a foot (most common are the 'strong' caesura, after the first syllable of the third foot; and the 'weak' caesura after the second syllable of the third foot, if it is a dactyl) or *diaeresis* when it occurs at the end of a foot (most common is the 'bucolic *diaeresis*', between the fourth and fifth feet). Furthermore, Homeric verse also features enjambements, where the sentence 'runs over' into the following line so as for its grammar or meaning to be complete; enjambements can also be used to add on a word or item, without which the previous line-sentence would have been complete, but which provides a link to a further development of its content.

Elisions and hiatuses are more common in Homeric Greek than in other texts you may have read. An elision occurs when a word is truncated (elided) by its final, short vowel or diphthong when the following word starts with a vowel, and an apostrophe is used to mark this; elisions are commonly used for metrical reasons (see e.g. note on 9.279). Hiatus is the opposite phenomenon, and describes a situation in which two juxtaposed vowels, which we would normally expect to elide, remain separate, both graphically and metrically. When a hiatus occurs in the middle of a word, it is marked in print by two dots above a vowel, like the German Umlaut, e.g. ὄϊς (9.244) (the *omicron* and *iota* here are not a diphthong but two separate vowels in two separate syllables) and similarly ἐϋπλόκαμος (10.144). Linguists argue that the reason for vowels not eliding is that in an earlier phase of the language, the two vowels were actually divided by a consonant, a w-sound letter called digamma (ϝ). As the language evolved, this letter disappeared and was no longer pronounced; however, the two vowels remain separate and the digamma, although it has disappeared, prevents them from eliding, thus affecting how we should scan them metrically (see e.g. note on 9.355, where εἰπέ would have originally been ϝεἰπέ).

Homeric style

A key feature of Homeric verse is the use of *formulae*. These are words, phrases and scenes which are repeated identically or almost identically throughout the poems; their presence in Homeric verse forms the backbone of the original development of the 'oral composition' theory.

Formulae and epithets

You will have noticed that characters are described with the same (or a metrically equivalent) epithet, an adjective or noun used to describe or define a person or thing. Both when the comrades halt before Circe's house and when Odysseus retraces their steps, she is described as 'the goddess of the beautiful locks':

ἔσταν δ' ἐν προθύροισι **θεᾶς καλλιπλοκάμοιο** (10.220)
ἔστην δ' εἰνὶ θύρῃσι **θεᾶς καλλιπλοκάμοιο** (10.310)

The epithet in this case has a descriptive force, and the trait encapsulated in the formula describes not what Odysseus or the comrades can see – we know they have not seen her yet – but what she and goddesses like her are famous for or associated with. Some epithets are exclusive to a specific character. When Circe realizes who her adversary must be, she names him as Ὀδυσσεύς ... **πολύτροπος** (10.330), using the same epithet + name ('naming formula') by which the hero is characterized in the first line of the poem (and in the same metrical position, cf. page 264); the epithet thus carries all the weight of its significance, as well as a nod to the resourcefulness which has allowed Odysseus to overcome her powers.

Most commonly, however, epithets are indeed stock adjectives, utilized in given metrical positions (we might say, as a 'line filler') whether or not their meaning is fully relevant to the scene. This is often the case with gods, whose epithets have been seen as linked to cult titles (e.g. Διὸς **αἰγιόχου**, *of Zeus the Aegis-bearer* 9.275, or Ποσειδάων **ἐνοσίχθων**, *Poseidon the Earth-shaker* 9.283). You will encounter many more such formulas, describing not only characters, but also things and places, from wine to ships and the sea. In the context of oral poetry, the noun-epithet system is a highly efficient one, as evidenced by the fact that, for a given noun or name, there is usually only a single epithet for each metrical pattern.

Formulae and formulaic expressions can occupy half a line, whole lines, or an entire multi-line scene. Formulaic lines are used for things which happen all the time; conversely, the more unusual the thing being narrated or described, the less formulaic the language will be. The beginnings and ends of speeches are often formulaic. A common speech-opening is καί μ' ὀλοφυρόμενος ἔπεα πτερόεντα προσηύδα (*and weeping he spoke winged words*, 10.265), followed by the response line ὡς ἔφατ', αὐτὰρ ἐγώ μιν ἀμειβόμενος προσέειπον (*thus he spoke, and I in turn said in reply*, 270 – see again 10.324 = 265, with ὀλοφυρομένη feminine for Circe, and the reply 336 = 270). A speech will regularly close with the words '*thus I/he/she spoke*', occupying the first three or four syllables: ὡς ἐφάμην 9.287 = 353 = 368; ὡς φάτο 9.281 = ὡς φάτ' 360, cf. ὡς ἔφατ' (notice how these slight variations – use or lack of augment, presence of elisions – allow for different metrical combinations in the rest of the line). You will notice a similar use of formulaic lines or scenes to describe times of day, such as evening and dawn (9.304–5 = 436–7 cf.10.187), for *sententia*-like comments (10.202 = 10.568) and many more. An example of a multi-line scene in our text is 10.368–72, which describes a section of the preparations for the banquet in Circe's house: this sequence is repeated almost identically four times in the *Odyssey*.

Type-scenes

Another feature of Homeric style are repeated scenes or 'type-scenes', scenes which recur throughout the poems and are narrated in a more or less fixed sequence or pattern. In the *Iliad*, the arming of a warrior for battle is a recurrent 'type-scene'. Arrivals are another. If you are reading the Circe episode, you will notice similarities between the companions' arrival at Circe's house and Odysseus', and between Hermes' description of what will happen when Odysseus faces the goddess, and Odysseus' own account of it. Within these scenes, apart from obvious changes in verb person and tense, you will find whole lines or sections repeated or almost repeated (e.g. 10.294–5 cf. 321–2; 299–300 cf.343–4). On the one hand, this shows the expediency of the metrical system, which allows for whole chunks to be reutilized and modified according to need; but the repeated language also has a dramatic force: in the case of Hermes' advice, it shows how the words of a god become reality. As you read these scenes in parallel, you will find yourself looking for more slight variations in what happens and exploring their significance further.

An important category of type-scenes for the Odyssey are *xenia* scenes. The correct customs for receiving of a *xenos* form a set narrative sequence of actions and gestures on the part of the host (see page 271). Each *xenia* scene in the Odyssey is unique, given the different circumstances, location and characters involved, but combines them within the familiar sequence. Books 9 and 10 contain variations of the *xenia* type-scene which are particularly interesting as they are, to a lesser or greater degree, distorted versions of the correct practice of *xenia*. Thus the distortion of the *xenia* type-scene, at a narrative level, reflects the character of the host, with neither the Cyclops nor Circe fully fitting the conventional role of giver of *xenia*.

Odysseus as narrator

Although they belong to a narrative genre, the Homeric poems are rich in direct speech. This is also true of our passages, which belong to the Wanderings and are one long extended speech by Odysseus. As such, the first person narrative itself shares features typical of direct speech elsewhere in the poems, such as the use of introspection: Odysseus' describes his thought and decision-making processes (e.g. 9.299–302, 10.151–155) and often refers to his and his men's feelings, such as fear (e.g. 9.256–7) and sorrow (e.g. 10.201 and 209). Moreover, within Odysseus' narrative, direct speeches by Odysseus and others occur at moments of heightened importance: indeed, it is in the dialogue between Odysseus and Cyclops, and later with Circe, that the hero negotiates his relationship with his antagonists. Similarly, it is through speech that we learn the 'true' feelings of Odysseus' comrades, their reproaches to and trust in their leader. Thus, by letting characters speak for themselves, the narrator gives us a closer glimpse into their personalities, and speech is a key locus of characterization. A character's words can act as a mirror for traits of her character or behaviour: thus the offensive words of the Cyclops, spoken in first person, provoke stronger indignation in the audience than if they had been reported by Odysseus (e.g. Polyphemus' speech at 9.273–80). Furthermore, the use of direct address and emotive language in speeches add to the drama of the scenes.

On the other hand, Odysseus-as-narrator shares many traits with third person narrative sections of the poem, of which the speech-opening and speech-closing formulae are examples. Another is the use of descriptions, whose relative rarity in the poems outside of similes lends importance to when they do occur, often as creators of suspense. In addition to scene-setting descriptions introducing our two episodes (see page 269), a memorable example in Book 10 is Odysseus' description of the preparation of the banquet in Circe's halls (10.348–74). Although it does belong to the *xenia* type-scene (Odysseus the *xenos*, now acknowledged as such, is to be offered food), it is a uniquely lengthy passage rich in detail and supernatural elements (the housemaids are nymphs, 10.350–51), dazzling the audience with the wealth of gold and silver and building up expectations for the banquet to come, only to be cut short by Odysseus' adversative declaration that ἐμῷ δ' οὐχ ἥνδανε θυμῷ (*but it did not please my heart*, 373). Conversely, Odysseus and his men are enthralled when they enter the Cyclops cave (ἐθηεύμεσθα ἕκαστα, *we were amazed at each thing* 9.218), and the detailed description of the owner's dairy-production arrangements (9.218–24) reflects this, just as the subsequent description of the Cyclops' arrival and busy work in the dairy (9.233–49) causes both their amazement and terror (δείσαντες, *afraid* 9.236).

Similes

Finally, a description of Homeric style in the *Odyssey* would be incomplete without a reference to the use of similes themselves. Short similes enrich the narrative with extra imagery, such as when the Cyclops dashes two men to the floor ὥς τε σκύλακας (*like puppies*, 9.289) and devours them ὥς τε λέων ὀρεσίτροφος (*like a mountain lion*, 9.292). Moreover, our passages contain a few notable examples of extended similes, in which elaborate comparisons span two or more lines, and which are a hallmark of Homeric epic style. Readers often focus on similes as containing something of the poet's world; indeed, these include some of the most original imagery and language in the poem (not surprisingly similes contain a high concentration of *hapax legomena*, see examples on page 273). Although the poems contain many similar similes (e.g. warriors in the *Iliad* compared to lions and other wild beasts), only rarely does the same simile occur more than once. The vividness of the descriptive detail brings the scenes alive, allowing for a build-up of suspense, or for a temporary relief or distraction of tension, or even for allusion or exploration of character and emotions.

If you are reading Book 9, you will come across two startling similes for the blinding of the Cyclops: the first, which compares the men turning the blazing pole inside the giant's eye-socket to shipbuilders boring a hole in timber (9.383–8), adds action-packed vividness to the men's work, highlighting the collaboration between Odysseus and his companions; and the second where the eye, as it sizzles and burns, is compared to the tempering of iron in cold water (9.391–4), and the noise of the sizzling eye (σφαραγεῦντο, *the roots 'hissed'* 9.390), compared to the crackle of the iron (μεγάλα ἰάχοντα, *screeching loudly* 392), gives way to the terrifying scream of the Cyclops (σμερδαλέον δὲ μέγ' ᾤμωξεν, *he gave a terrifying loud wail* 9.395) which closes the scene. The imagery taken from the world of craft – shipbuilding and metalworking – offers the audience a real-life counterpart to *polytropos* Odysseus' hard and dangerous work, prolonging the scene and thus building up its tension. Furthermore, the choice of imagery sharpens the contrast between the 'civilized' world of the Greeks, to which Odysseus and his men belong, and the savage Cyclopes.

In Book 10, you will encounter another simile of startling subtlety. When Odysseus' men find Circe's house, the wolves and lions, who are under the goddess' spell, approach them with their tails raised (10.212–5), and are compared to dogs who wag their tails when their master returns after dinner, knowing that he will have some good morsels for them (10.216–7). Whereas the simile suggests that the beasts, like the *fawning* dogs (σαῖνον), were positively inclined towards the men, Odysseus tells us that the men ἔδεισαν, ἐπεὶ ἴδον αἰνὰ πέλωρα (*were fearful, when they saw the dreadful beasts* 219). The men are not aware that these are no ordinary beasts, whereas the audience has learned that they have been bewitched. Thus the simile, in adding an element of strangeness, almost unexpected friendliness, to their behaviour and characterization, allows the audience to build on their foreknowledge in sensing the mystery, as well as danger, which lies ahead, in contrast to the men who are simply terrified.

Further reading

The epic genre, Homeric question, historical context

Dowden, K. (2005), 'The epic tradition in Greece' History' in J.M. Foley (ed.), *A Companion to Ancient Epic*, 188–205, Oxford: Blackwell [for a clear picture of the Greek epic tradition, including Homer and the Cycle].

Martin, R.P. (2005), 'Epic as genre' in J.M. Foley (ed.), *A Companion to Ancient Epic*, 9–19, Oxford: Blackwell [for a discussion of epic as a genre and the position of the Homeric poems within that genre].

Osborne, R. (2005), 'Homer's Society' in J.M. Foley (ed.), *A Companion to Ancient Epic*, 206–19, Oxford: Blackwell [for a more in-depth exploration of the historical context of the poems and reconstruction of 'Homeric society'].

Raaflaub, K. (2005), 'Epic and History' in J.M. Foley (ed.), *A Companion to Ancient Epic*, 55–70, Oxford: Blackwell [for a discussion of the historicity of the poems and historical evidence for them].

Rutherford R. (2013), Chapter 1 'Introduction: Background and Problems' in *Homer, Greece and Rome, New Surveys in the Classics* (41), Cambridge: CUP [for an exhaustive overview of the Homeric question as well as the dating and historic background of the poems].

The *Odyssey* and Books 9 and 10

Heubeck, A. and Hoekstra, A. (1990), *A Commentary on Homer's Odyssey, Volume II, Books IX to XVI*, Oxford: OUP Clarendon Press [an invaluable, detailed tool for readers of Books 9 and 10, detailed notes and an exhaustive introduction].

Rutherford R. (2013), Chapter 3 'The *Odyssey*', in *Homer, Greece and Rome, New Surveys in the Classics* (41), Cambridge: CUP [for a more in-depth introduction to the poem and its themes].

Silk, M. (2004), 'The Odyssey and its explorations' in Fowler, R. (ed.), *The Cambridge Companion to Homer* (31–44), Cambridge: CUP [for an insightful introduction to the human and divine world of the *Odyssey*].

Homeric language, style and metre

Autenrieth, G. (2004), *Homeric Dictionary*, London: Duckworth [a key tool for translators of Homer. You will also find a more detailed list of the peculiarities of the Homeric Dialect in the introduction, pp. xvii–xxi].

Buxton, R. (2004), 'Similes and Other Likenesses' in Fowler, R. (ed.), *The Cambridge Companion to Homer*, 139–55, Cambridge: CUP [for a detailed analysis of Homeric similes and their significance, with examples from both the *Odyssey* and the *Iliad*].

Clarke, M. (2004), 'Formulas, Metre and Type-Scenes' in Fowler, R. (ed.), *The Cambridge Companion to Homer*, 117–38, Cambridge: CUP [for a clear, comprehensive explanation of how formulas work within the Homeric metrical system].

Rutherford R. (2013), 'Poetic Language' (9–11) in 'Introduction: Background and Problems', in *Homer, Greece and Rome, New Surveys in the Classics* (41), Cambridge: CUP [for a brief, clear description of Homeric language, its origins and peculiarities].

Text to *Odyssey* 10: 144–399

ἀλλ' ὅτε δὴ τρίτον ἦμαρ ἐϋπλόκαμος τέλεσ' Ἠώς,
καὶ τότ' ἐγὼν ἐμὸν ἔγχος ἑλὼν καὶ φάσγανον ὀξὺ   145
καρπαλίμως παρὰ νηὸς ἀνήϊον ἐς περιωπήν,
εἴ πως ἔργα ἴδοιμι βροτῶν ἐνοπήν τε πυθοίμην.
ἔστην δὲ σκοπιὴν ἐς παιπαλόεσσαν ἀνελθών,
καί μοι ἐείσατο καπνὸς ἀπὸ χθονὸς εὐρυοδείης
Κίρκης ἐν μεγάροισι, διὰ δρυμὰ πυκνὰ καὶ ὕλην.   150
μερμήριξα δ' ἔπειτα κατὰ φρένα καὶ κατὰ θυμὸν
ἐλθεῖν ἠδὲ πυθέσθαι, ἐπεὶ ἴδον αἴθοπα καπνόν.
ὧδε δέ μοι φρονέοντι δοάσσατο κέρδιον εἶναι,
πρῶτ' ἐλθόντ' ἐπὶ νῆα θοὴν καὶ θῖνα θαλάσσης
δεῖπνον ἑταίροισιν δόμεναι προέμεν τε πυθέσθαι.   155
ἀλλ' ὅτε δὴ σχεδὸν ἦα κιὼν νεὸς ἀμφιελίσσης,
καὶ τότε τίς με θεῶν ὀλοφύρατο μοῦνον ἐόντα,
ὅς ῥά μοι ὑψίκερων ἔλαφον μέγαν εἰς ὁδὸν αὐτὴν
ἧκεν· ὁ μὲν ποταμόνδε κατήϊεν ἐκ νομοῦ ὕλης
πιόμενος· δὴ γάρ μιν ἔχεν μένος ἠελίοιο.   160
τὸν δ' ἐγὼ ἐκβαίνοντα κατ' ἄκνηστιν μέσα νῶτα
πλῆξα· τὸ δ' ἀντικρὺ δόρυ χάλκεον ἐξεπέρησε,
κὰδ δ' ἔπεσ' ἐν κονίῃσι μακών, ἀπὸ δ' ἔπτατο θυμός.
τῷ δ' ἐγὼ ἐμβαίνων δόρυ χάλκεον ἐξ ὠτειλῆς
εἰρυσάμην· τὸ μὲν αὖθι κατακλίνας ἐπὶ γαίῃ   165
εἴασ'· αὐτὰρ ἐγὼ σπασάμην ῥῶπάς τε λύγους τε,
πεῖσμα δ', ὅσον τ' ὄργυιαν, ἐϋστρεφὲς ἀμφοτέρωθεν
πλεξάμενος συνέδησα πόδας δεινοῖο πελώρου,
βῆν δὲ καταλοφάδεια φέρων ἐπὶ νῆα μέλαιναν
ἔγχει ἐρειδόμενος, ἐπεὶ οὔ πως ἦεν ἐπ' ὤμου   170
χειρὶ φέρειν ἑτέρῃ· μάλα γὰρ μέγα θηρίον ἦεν.
κὰδ δ' ἔβαλον προπάροιθε νεός, ἀνέγειρα δ' ἑταίρους
μειλιχίοις ἐπέεσσι παρασταδὸν ἄνδρα ἕκαστον·
"Ὦ φίλοι, οὐ γάρ πω καταδυσόμεθ' ἀχνύμενοί περ,
εἰς Ἀΐδαο δόμους, πρὶν μόρσιμον ἦμαρ ἐπέλθῃ.   175
ἀλλ' ἄγετ', ὄφρ' ἐν νηΐ θοῇ βρῶσίς τε πόσις τε,

μνησόμεθα βρώμης μηδὲ τρυχώμεθα λιμῷ."
    Ὣς ἐφάμην, οἱ δ᾽ ὦκα ἐμοῖς ἐπέεσσι πίθοντο·
ἐκ δὲ καλυψάμενοι παρὰ θῖν᾽ ἁλὸς ἀτρυγέτοιο
θηήσαντ᾽ ἔλαφον· μάλα γὰρ μέγα θηρίον ἦεν.   180
αὐτὰρ ἐπεὶ τάρπησαν ὁρώμενοι ὀφθαλμοῖσι,
χεῖρας νιψάμενοι τεύχοντ᾽ ἐρικυδέα δαῖτα.
ὣς τότε μὲν πρόπαν ἦμαρ ἐς ἠέλιον καταδύντα
ἥμεθα δαινύμενοι κρέα τ᾽ ἄσπετα καὶ μέθυ ἡδύ·
ἦμος δ᾽ ἠέλιος κατέδυ καὶ ἐπὶ κνέφας ἦλθε,   185
δὴ τότε κοιμήθημεν ἐπὶ ῥηγμῖνι θαλάσσης.
ἦμος δ᾽ ἠριγένεια φάνη ῥοδοδάκτυλος Ἠώς,
καὶ τότ᾽ ἐγὼν ἀγορὴν θέμενος μετὰ πᾶσιν ἔειπον·
    "Κέκλυτέ μευ μύθων, κακά περ πάσχοντες ἑταῖροι·
ὦ φίλοι, οὐ γάρ ἴδμεν ὅπη ζόφος οὐδ᾽ ὅπη ἠώς,   190
οὐδ᾽ ὅπη ἠέλιος φαεσίμβροτος εἶσ᾽ ὑπὸ γαῖαν
οὐδ᾽ ὅπη ἀννεῖται· ἀλλὰ φραζώμεθα θᾶσσον
εἴ τις ἔτ᾽ ἔσται μῆτις· ἐγὼ δ᾽ οὔκ οἴομαι εἶναι.
εἶδον γὰρ σκοπιὴν ἐς παιπαλόεσσαν ἀνελθὼν
νῆσον, τὴν πέρι πόντος ἀπείριτος ἐστεφάνωται.   195
αὐτὴ δὲ χθαμαλὴ κεῖται· καπνὸν δ᾽ ἐνὶ μέσσῃ
ἔδρακον ὀφθαλμοῖσι διὰ δρυμὰ πυκνὰ καὶ ὕλην."
    Ὣς ἐφάμην, τοῖσιν δὲ κατεκλάσθη φίλον ἦτορ
μνησαμένοις ἔργων Λαιστρυγόνος Ἀντιφάταο
Κύκλωπός τε βίης μεγαλήτορος, ἀνδροφάγοιο.   200
κλαῖον δὲ λιγέως, θαλερὸν κατὰ δάκρυ χέοντες·
ἀλλ᾽ οὐ γάρ τις πρῆξις ἐγίγνετο μυρομένοισι.
    Αὐτὰρ ἐγὼ δίχα πάντας ἐϋκνήμιδας ἑταίρους
ἠρίθμεον, ἀρχὸν δὲ μετ᾽ ἀμφοτέροισιν ὄπασσα·
τῶν μὲν ἐγὼν ἄρχον, τῶν δ᾽ Εὐρύλοχος θεοειδής.   205
κλήρους δ᾽ ἐν κυνέῃ χαλκήρεϊ πάλλομεν ὦκα·
ἐκ δ᾽ ἔθορε κλῆρος μεγαλήτορος Εὐρυλόχοιο.
βῆ δ᾽ ἰέναι, ἅμα τῷ γε δύω καὶ εἴκοσ᾽ ἑταῖροι
κλαίοντες· κατὰ δ᾽ ἄμμε λίπον γοόωντας ὄπισθεν.
εὗρον δ᾽ ἐν βήσσῃσι τετυγμένα δώματα Κίρκης   210
ξεστοῖσιν λάεσσι, περισκέπτῳ ἐνὶ χώρῳ.
ἀμφὶ δέ μιν λύκοι ἦσαν ὀρέστεροι ἠδὲ λέοντες,
τοὺς αὐτὴ κατέθελξεν, ἐπεὶ κακὰ φάρμακ᾽ ἔδωκεν.
οὐδ᾽ οἵ γ᾽ ὁρμήθησαν ἐπ᾽ ἀνδράσιν, ἀλλ᾽ ἄρα τοί γε
οὐρῇσιν μακρῇσι περισσαίνοντες ἀνέσταν.   215
ὡς δ᾽ ὅτ᾽ ἂν ἀμφὶ ἄνακτα κύνες δαίθεν ἰόντα
σαίνωσ᾽· αἰεὶ γάρ τε φέρει μειλίγματα θυμοῦ·
ὣς τοὺς ἀμφὶ λύκοι κρατερώνυχες ἠδὲ λέοντες
σαῖνον· τοὶ δ᾽ ἔδεισαν, ἐπεὶ ἴδον αἰνὰ πέλωρα.
ἔσταν δ᾽ ἐν προθύροισι θεᾶς καλλιπλοκάμοιο,   220

Κίρκης δ᾽ ἔνδον ἄκουον ἀειδούσης ὀπὶ καλῇ,
ἱστὸν ἐποιχομένης μέγαν ἄμβροτον, οἷα θεάων
λεπτά τε καὶ χαρίεντα καὶ ἀγλαὰ ἔργα πέλονται.
τοῖσι δὲ μύθων ἄρχε Πολίτης, ὄρχαμος ἀνδρῶν,
ὅς μοι κήδιστος ἑτάρων ἦν κεδνότατός τε·   225
  "Ὦ φίλοι, ἔνδον γάρ τις ἐποιχομένη μέγαν ἱστὸν
καλὸν ἀοιδιάει, δάπεδον δ᾽ ἅπαν ἀμφιμέμυκεν,
ἢ θεὸς ἠὲ γυνή· ἀλλὰ φθεγγώμεθα θᾶσσον."
  Ὣς ἄρ᾽ ἐφώνησεν, τοὶ δὲ φθέγγοντο καλεῦντες.
ἡ δ᾽ αἶψ᾽ ἐξελθοῦσα θύρας ὤϊξε φαεινὰς   230
καὶ κάλει· οἱ δ᾽ ἅμα πάντες ἀϊδρείῃσιν ἕποντο·
Εὐρύλοχος δ᾽ ὑπέμεινεν, ὀϊσάμενος δόλον εἶναι.
εἷσεν δ᾽ εἰσαγαγοῦσα κατὰ κλισμούς τε θρόνους τε,
ἐν δέ σφιν τυρόν τε καὶ ἄλφιτα καὶ μέλι χλωρὸν
οἴνῳ Πραμνείῳ ἐκύκα· ἀνέμισγε δὲ σίτῳ   235
φάρμακα λύγρ᾽, ἵνα πάγχυ λαθοίατο πατρίδος αἴης.
αὐτὰρ ἐπεὶ δῶκέν τε καὶ ἔκπιον, αὐτίκ᾽ ἔπειτα
ῥάβδῳ πεπληγυῖα κατὰ συφεοῖσιν ἐέργνυ.
οἱ δὲ συῶν μὲν ἔχον κεφαλὰς φωνήν τε τρίχας τε
καὶ δέμας, αὐτὰρ νοῦς ἦν ἔμπεδος ὡς τὸ πάρος περ.   240
ὣς οἱ μὲν κλαίοντες ἐέρχατο· τοῖσι δὲ Κίρκη
πὰρ ῥ᾽ ἄκυλον βάλανόν τ᾽ ἔβαλεν καρπόν τε κρανείης
ἔδμεναι, οἷα σύες χαμαιευνάδες αἰὲν ἔδουσιν.
  Εὐρύλοχος δ᾽ ἂψ ἦλθε θοὴν ἐπὶ νῆα μέλαιναν,
ἀγγελίην ἑτάρων ἐρέων καὶ ἀδευκέα πότμον.   245
οὐδέ τι ἐκφάσθαι δύνατο ἔπος, ἱέμενός περ,
κῆρ ἄχεϊ μεγάλῳ βεβολημένος· ἐν δέ οἱ ὄσσε
δακρυόφιν πίμπλαντο, γόον δ᾽ ὤϊετο θυμός.
ἀλλ᾽ ὅτε δή μιν πάντες ἀγασσάμεθ᾽ ἐξερέοντες,
καὶ τότε τῶν ἄλλων ἑτάρων κατέλεξεν ὄλεθρον·   250
  "Ἤιομεν, ὡς ἐκέλευες, ἀνὰ δρυμά, φαίδιμ᾽ Ὀδυσσεῦ·
εὕρομεν ἐν βήσσῃσι τετυγμένα δώματα καλὰ
ξεστοῖσιν λάεσσι, περισκέπτῳ ἐνὶ χώρῳ.
ἔνθα δέ τις μέγαν ἱστὸν ἐποιχομένη λίγ᾽ ἄειδεν
ἢ θεὸς ἠὲ γυνή· τοὶ δ᾽ ἐφθέγγοντο καλεῦντες.   255
ἡ δ᾽ αἶψ᾽ ἐξελθοῦσα θύρας ὤϊξε φαεινὰς
καὶ κάλει· οἱ δ᾽ ἅμα πάντες ἀϊδρείῃσιν ἕποντο·
αὐτὰρ ἐγὼν ὑπέμεινα, ὀϊσάμενος δόλον εἶναι.
οἱ δ᾽ ἅμ᾽ ἀϊστώθησαν ἀολλέες, οὐδέ τις αὐτῶν
ἐξεφάνη· δηρὸν δὲ καθήμενος ἐσκοπίαζον."   260
  Ὣς ἔφατ᾽, αὐτὰρ ἐγὼ περὶ μὲν ξίφος ἀργυρόηλον
ὤμοιϊν βαλόμην, μέγα χάλκεον, ἀμφὶ δὲ τόξα·
τὸν δ᾽ ἂψ ἠνώγεα αὐτὴν ὁδὸν ἡγήσασθαι.
αὐτὰρ ὅ γ᾽ ἀμφοτέρῃσι λαβὼν ἐλλίσσετο γούνων

καί μ᾽ ὀλοφυρόμενος ἔπεα πτερόεντα προσηύδα·   265
   "Μή μ᾽ ἄγε κεῖσ᾽ ἀέκοντα, διοτρεφές, ἀλλὰ λίπ᾽ αὐτοῦ.
οἶδα γάρ, ὡς οὔτ᾽ αὐτὸς ἐλεύσεαι οὔτε τιν᾽ ἄλλον
ἄξεις σῶν ἑτάρων· ἀλλὰ ξὺν τοίσδεσι θᾶσσον
φεύγωμεν· ἔτι γάρ κεν ἀλύξαιμεν κακὸν ἦμαρ."
   Ὣς ἔφατ᾽, αὐτὰρ ἐγώ μιν ἀμειβόμενος προσέειπον·   270
"Εὐρύλοχ᾽, ἦ τοι μὲν σὺ μέν᾽ αὐτοῦ τῷδ᾽ ἐνὶ χώρῳ
ἔσθων καὶ πίνων, κοίλῃ παρὰ νηΐ μελαίνῃ·
αὐτὰρ ἐγὼν εἶμι· κρατερὴ δέ μοι ἔπλετ᾽ ἀνάγκη."
   Ὣς εἰπὼν παρὰ νηὸς ἀνήϊον ἠδὲ θαλάσσης.
ἀλλ᾽ ὅτε δὴ ἄρ᾽ ἔμελλον ἰὼν ἱερὰς ἀνὰ βήσσας   275
Κίρκης ἵξεσθαι πολυφαρμάκου ἐς μέγα δῶμα,
ἔνθα μοι Ἑρμείας χρυσόρραπις ἀντεβόλησεν
ἐρχομένῳ πρὸς δῶμα, νεηνίῃ ἀνδρὶ ἐοικώς,
πρῶτον ὑπηνήτῃ, τοῦ περ χαριέστατος ἥβη·
ἔν τ᾽ ἄρα μοι φῦ χειρί, ἔπος τ᾽ ἔφατ᾽ ἔκ τ᾽ ὀνόμαζε·   280
   "Πῇ δὴ αὖτ᾽, ὦ δύστηνε, δι᾽ ἄκριας ἔρχεαι οἶος,
χώρου ἄϊδρις ἐών; ἕταροι δέ τοι οἵδ᾽ ἐνὶ Κίρκης
ἔρχαται, ὥς τε σύες, πυκινοὺς κευθμῶνας ἔχοντες.
ἦ τοὺς λυσόμενος δεῦρ᾽ ἔρχεαι; οὐδέ σέ φημι
αὐτὸν νοστήσειν, μενέεις δὲ σύ γ᾽ ἔνθα περ ἄλλοι.   285
ἀλλ᾽ ἄγε δή σε κακῶν ἐκλύσομαι ἠδὲ σαώσω·
τῆ, τόδε φάρμακον ἐσθλὸν ἔχων ἐς δώματα Κίρκης
ἔρχευ, ὅ κέν τοι κρατὸς ἀλάλκησιν κακὸν ἦμαρ.
πάντα δέ τοι ἐρέω ὀλοφώϊα δήνεα Κίρκης.
τεύξει τοι κυκεῶ, βαλέει δ᾽ ἐν φάρμακα σίτῳ·   290
ἀλλ᾽ οὐδ᾽ ὣς θέλξαι σε δυνήσεται· οὐ γὰρ ἐάσει
φάρμακον ἐσθλόν, ὅ τοι δώσω, ἐρέω δὲ ἕκαστα.
ὁππότε κεν Κίρκη σ᾽ ἐλάσῃ περιμήκεϊ ῥάβδῳ,
δὴ τότε σὺ ξίφος ὀξὺ ἐρυσσάμενος παρὰ μηροῦ
Κίρκῃ ἐπαΐξαι, ὥς τε κτάμεναι μενεαίνων.   295
ἡ δέ σ᾽ ὑποδείσασα κελήσεται εὐνηθῆναι·
ἔνθα σὺ μηκέτ᾽ ἔπειτ᾽ ἀπανήνασθαι θεοῦ εὐνήν,
ὄφρα κέ τοι λύσῃ θ᾽ ἑτάρους αὐτόν τε κομίσσῃ·
ἀλλὰ κέλεσθαί μιν μακάρων μέγαν ὅρκον ὀμόσσαι
μή τί τοι αὐτῷ πῆμα κακὸν βουλευσέμεν ἄλλο,   300
μή σ᾽ ἀπογυμνωθέντα κακὸν καὶ ἀνήνορα θήῃ."
   Ὣς ἄρα φωνήσας πόρε φάρμακον ἀργεϊφόντης
ἐκ γαίης ἐρύσας, καί μοι φύσιν αὐτοῦ ἔδειξε.
ῥίζῃ μὲν μέλαν ἔσκε, γάλακτι δὲ εἴκελον ἄνθος·
μῶλυ δέ μιν καλέουσι θεοί· χαλεπὸν δέ τ᾽ ὀρύσσειν   305
ἀνδράσι γε θνητοῖσι· θεοὶ δέ τε πάντα δύνανται.
   Ἑρμείας μὲν ἔπειτ᾽ ἀπέβη πρὸς μακρὸν Ὄλυμπον
νῆσον ἀν᾽ ὑλήεσσαν, ἐγὼ δ᾽ ἐς δώματα Κίρκης
ἤϊα, πολλὰ δέ μοι κραδίη πόρφυρε κιόντι.

ἔστην δ᾽ εἰνὶ θύρῃσι θεᾶς καλλιπλοκάμοιο·   310
ἔνθα στὰς ἐβόησα, θεὰ δέ μευ ἔκλυεν αὐδῆς.
ἡ δ᾽ αἶψ᾽ ἐξελθοῦσα θύρας ὤϊξε φαεινὰς
καὶ κάλει· αὐτὰρ ἐγὼν ἑπόμην ἀκαχήμενος ἦτορ.
εἷσε δέ μ᾽ εἰσαγαγοῦσα ἐπὶ θρόνου ἀργυροήλου,
καλοῦ δαιδαλέου· ὑπὸ δὲ θρῆνυς ποσὶν ἦεν·   315
τεῦχε δέ μοι κυκεῶ χρυσέῳ δέπᾳ, ὄφρα πίοιμι,
ἐν δέ τε φάρμακον ἧκε, κακὰ φρονέουσ᾽ ἐνὶ θυμῷ.
αὐτὰρ ἐπεὶ δῶκέν τε καὶ ἔκπιον, οὐδέ μ᾽ ἔθελξε,
ῥάβδῳ πεπληγυῖα ἔπος τ᾽ ἔφατ᾽ ἔκ τ᾽ ὀνόμαζεν·
    "Ἔρχεο νῦν συφεόνδε, μετ᾽ ἄλλων λέξο ἑταίρων."   320
ὣς φάτ᾽, ἐγὼ δ᾽ ἄορ ὀξὺ ἐρυσσάμενος παρὰ μηροῦ
Κίρκῃ ἐπήϊξα ὥς τε κτάμεναι μενεαίνων.
ἡ δὲ μέγα ἰάχουσα ὑπέδραμε καὶ λάβε γούνων,
καί μ᾽ ὀλοφυρομένη ἔπεα πτερόεντα προσηύδα·
    "Τίς πόθεν εἰς ἀνδρῶν; πόθι τοι πόλις ἠδὲ τοκῆες;   325
θαῦμά μ᾽ ἔχει ὡς οὔ τι πιὼν τάδε φάρμακ᾽ ἐθέλχθης.
οὐδὲ γὰρ οὐδέ τις ἄλλος ἀνὴρ τάδε φάρμακ᾽ ἀνέτλη,
ὅς κε πίῃ καὶ πρῶτον ἀμείψεται ἕρκος ὀδόντων.
σοὶ δέ τις ἐν στήθεσσιν ἀκήλητος νόος ἐστίν.
ἦ σύ γ᾽ Ὀδυσσεύς ἐσσι πολύτροπος, ὅν τέ μοι αἰεὶ   330
φάσκεν ἐλεύσεσθαι χρυσόρραπις ἀργειφόντης,
ἐκ Τροίης ἀνιόντα θοῇ σὺν νηῒ μελαίνῃ.
ἀλλ᾽ ἄγε δὴ κολεῷ μὲν ἄορ θέο, νῶϊ δ᾽ ἔπειτα
εὐνῆς ἡμετέρης ἐπιβήομεν, ὄφρα μιγέντε
εὐνῇ καὶ φιλότητι πεποίθομεν ἀλλήλοισιν."   335
    Ὣς ἔφατ᾽, αὐτὰρ ἐγώ μιν ἀμειβόμενος προσέειπον·
"ὦ Κίρκη, πῶς γάρ με κέλεαι σοὶ ἤπιον εἶναι,
ἥ μοι σῦς μὲν ἔθηκας ἐνὶ μεγάροισιν ἑταίρους,
αὐτὸν δ᾽ ἐνθάδ᾽ ἔχουσα δολοφρονέουσα κελεύεις
ἐς θάλαμόν τ᾽ ἰέναι καὶ σῆς ἐπιβήμεναι εὐνῆς,   340
ὄφρα με γυμνωθέντα κακὸν καὶ ἀνήνορα θήῃς.
οὐδ᾽ ἂν ἐγώ γ᾽ ἐθέλοιμι τεῆς ἐπιβήμεναι εὐνῆς,
εἰ μή μοι τλαίης γε, θεά, μέγαν ὅρκον ὀμόσσαι
μή τί μοι αὐτῷ πῆμα κακὸν βουλευσέμεν ἄλλο."
    Ὣς ἐφάμην, ἡ δ᾽ αὐτίκ᾽ ἀπόμνυεν ὡς ἐκέλευον.   345
αὐτὰρ ἐπεί ῥ᾽ ὄμοσέν τε τελεύτησέν τε τὸν ὅρκον,
καὶ τότ᾽ ἐγὼ Κίρκης ἐπέβην περικαλλέος εὐνῆς.
    Ἀμφίπολοι δ᾽ ἄρα τῆος ἐνὶ μεγάροισι πένοντο
τέσσαρες, αἵ οἱ δῶμα κάτα δρήστειραι ἔασι.
γίγνονται δ᾽ ἄρα ταί γ᾽ ἔκ τε κρηνέων ἀπό τ᾽ ἀλσέων   350
ἔκ θ᾽ ἱερῶν ποταμῶν, οἵ τ᾽ εἰς ἅλαδε προρέουσι.
τάων ἡ μὲν ἔβαλλε θρόνοις ἔνι ῥήγεα καλά,
πορφύρεα καθύπερθ᾽, ὑπένερθε δὲ λῖθ᾽ ὑπέβαλλεν·
ἡ δ᾽ ἑτέρη προπάροιθε θρόνων ἐτίταινε τραπέζας

ἀργυρέας, ἐπὶ δέ σφι τίθει χρύσεια κάνεια·   355
ἡ δὲ τρίτη κρητῆρι μελίφρονα οἶνον ἐκίρνα
ἡδὺν ἐν ἀργυρέῳ, νέμε δὲ χρύσεια κύπελλα·
ἡ δὲ τετάρτη ὕδωρ ἐφόρει καὶ πῦρ ἀνέκαιε
πολλὸν ὑπὸ τρίποδι μεγάλῳ· ἰαίνετο δ᾽ ὕδωρ.
αὐτὰρ ἐπεὶ δὴ ζέσσεν ὕδωρ ἐνὶ ἤνοπι χαλκῷ,   360
ἔς ῥ᾽ ἀσάμινθον ἕσασα λό᾽ ἐκ τρίποδος μεγάλοιο,
θυμῆρες κεράσασα κατὰ κρατός τε καὶ ὤμων,
ὄφρα μοι ἐκ κάματον θυμοφθόρον εἵλετο γυίων.
αὐτὰρ ἐπεὶ λοῦσέν τε καὶ ἔχρισεν λίπ᾽ ἐλαίῳ,
ἀμφὶ δέ με χλαῖναν καλὴν βάλεν ἠδὲ χιτῶνα,   365
εἷσε δέ μ᾽ εἰσαγαγοῦσα ἐπὶ θρόνου ἀργυροήλου,
καλοῦ δαιδαλέου· ὑπὸ δὲ θρῆνυς ποσὶν ἦεν·
χέρνιβα δ᾽ ἀμφίπολος προχόῳ ἐπέχευε φέρουσα
καλῇ χρυσείῃ, ὑπὲρ ἀργυρέοιο λέβητος,
νίψασθαι· παρὰ δὲ ξεστὴν ἐτάνυσσε τράπεζαν.   370
σῖτον δ᾽ αἰδοίη ταμίη παρέθηκε φέρουσα,
εἴδατα πόλλ᾽ ἐπιθεῖσα, χαριζομένη παρεόντων·
ἐσθέμεναι δ᾽ ἐκέλευεν· ἐμῷ δ᾽ οὐ ἥνδανε θυμῷ,
ἀλλ᾽ ἥμην ἀλλοφρονέων, κακὰ δ᾽ ὄσσετο θυμός.
    Κίρκη δ᾽ ὡς ἐνόησεν ἔμ᾽ ἥμενον οὐδ᾽ ἐπὶ σίτῳ   375
χεῖρας ἰάλλοντα, κρατερὸν δέ με πένθος ἔχοντα,
ἄγχι παρισταμένη ἔπεα πτερόεντα προσηύδα·
    "Τίφθ᾽ οὕτως, Ὀδυσεῦ, κατ᾽ ἄρ᾽ ἕζεαι ἶσος ἀναύδῳ,
θυμὸν ἔδων, βρώμης δ᾽ οὐχ ἅπτεαι οὐδὲ ποτῆτος;
ἦ τινά που δόλον ἄλλον ὀίεαι· οὐδέ τί σε χρὴ   380
δειδίμεν· ἤδη γάρ τοι ἀπώμοσα καρτερὸν ὅρκον."
    Ὣς ἔφατ᾽, αὐτὰρ ἐγώ μιν ἀμειβόμενος προσέειπον·
"ὦ Κίρκη, τίς γάρ κεν ἀνήρ, ὃς ἐναίσιμος εἴη,
πρὶν τλαίη πάσσασθαι ἐδητύος ἠδὲ ποτῆτος,
πρὶν λύσασθ᾽ ἑτάρους καὶ ἐν ὀφθαλμοῖσιν ἰδέσθαι;   385
ἀλλ᾽ εἰ δὴ πρόφρασσα πιεῖν φαγέμεν τε κελεύεις,
λῦσον, ἵν᾽ ὀφθαλμοῖσιν ἴδω ἐρίηρας ἑταίρους."
    Ὣς ἐφάμην, Κίρκη δὲ διὲκ μεγάροιο βεβήκει
ῥάβδον ἔχουσ᾽ ἐν χειρί, θύρας δ᾽ ἀνέῳξε συφειοῦ,
ἐκ δ᾽ ἔλασεν σιάλοισιν ἐοικότας ἐννεώροισιν.   390
οἱ μὲν ἔπειτ᾽ ἔστησαν ἐναντίοι, ἡ δὲ δι᾽ αὐτῶν
ἐρχομένη προσάλειφεν ἑκάστῳ φάρμακον ἄλλο.
τῶν δ᾽ ἐκ μὲν μελέων τρίχες ἔρρεον, ἃς πρὶν ἔφυσε
φάρμακον οὐλόμενον, τό σφιν πόρε πότνια Κίρκη·
ἄνδρες δ᾽ ἂψ ἐγένοντο νεώτεροι ἢ πάρος ἦσαν   395
καὶ πολὺ καλλίονες καὶ μείζονες εἰσοράασθαι.
ἔγνωσαν δ᾽ ἐμὲ κεῖνοι, ἔφυν τ᾽ ἐν χερσὶν ἕκαστος.
πᾶσιν δ᾽ ἱμερόεις ὑπέδυ γόος, ἀμφὶ δὲ δῶμα
σμερδαλέον κονάβιζε· θεὰ δ᾽ ἐλέαιρε καὶ αὐτή.

Commentary Notes

Odyssey 10

140–88

The whole of this passage follows a typical sequence of events for the arrival of Odysseus and his men at a new place on their journey: they beach their ships in a harbour to which Odysseus says a god has guided them, disembark and sleep. When dawn comes, they explore/hunt/feast/sleep. The following dawn usually brings the start of their next adventure . . .

144

τρίτον ἦμαρ: it is now the third day since Odysseus and his men have arrived at Circe's island, Aeaea. They have spent the last two days 'eating out their hearts with weariness and sorrow' after the loss of all their comrades, who were killed and eaten by horrific giant cannibals, the Laestrygonians.

ἐϋπλόκαμος . . . Ἠώς: 'Dawn with her beautiful tresses/lovely hair': Eos is the goddess of the dawn; ἐϋπλόκαμος is an example of a 'Homeric epithet'. These are adjectives used regularly by Homer to describe people and places: ἐϋπλόκαμος is often used of women and goddesses. Some, like this one, are generic, whereas others apply regularly to a particular individual, eg πολύμητις, 'of many wiles', used of Odysseus (see Introduction for further discussion of this topic). Note the diaeresis on ἐϋπλόκαμος indicating that the ἐ and υ are pronounced, and scanned, separately rather than as one syllable.

τέλεσ': aorist of τελέω: the Homeric form of the aorist often does not have an augment. Dawn 'brought the day to fulfilment': i.e. full daylight. The final vowel is elided to fit the metre or to avoid a hiatus (where a word ending in a vowel is followed by another beginning with a vowel). Whereas in Latin verse, you have to work out for yourself where to elide syllables, in Homer the elision is done for you!

145

τότ': τότε. Correlative with ὅτε on the previous line, so does not need to be translated.

ἐγών: this is the Homeric form of ἐγώ, used before a word beginning with a vowel. This whole book is narrated by Odysseus to the Phaeacians, hence the 'I' refers to Odysseus.

ἔγχος ... φάσγανον: Odysseus is armed for his exploration/hunting expedition with the spear (ἔγχος) and sword (φάσγανον) of the Homeric hero. A spear or lance was the preferred weapon in battle; heroes usually carried two.

146

ἀνήϊον: first person singular imperfect tense of ἄνειμι, 'I go up', i.e. go inland from the shore.

νηός = νέως, from νηῦς, the Homeric form of ναῦς.

147

εἴ πως ... ἴδοιμι ... πυθοίμην: 'in the hope that I might see ... or hear'.

ἔργα ... βροτῶν: Literally 'the deeds of mortals', but perhaps best translated 'signs of human activity'. The use of βροτός ('mortal man') is striking because Odysseus is about to encounter not a mortal man, but an immortal woman.

148

ἔστην: first person singular intransitive aorist active of ἵστημι = 'I took my stand'.

παιπαλόεσσαν: 'rugged'.

149

ἐείσατο: third person singular aorist of εἴδομαι, 'I appear': the addition of an extra ε before an ε (as well as before or after an η, as in ἠέλιος, the sun) is known as diectasis, and is common in Homer. (See Introduction).

χθονὸς εὐρυοδείης: the epithet εὐρυόδεια, meaning 'wide-wayed' or 'wide-wandered' is habitually attached to the earth by Homer, and always in this genitive singular phrase. The implication is that humans can, and do, like Odysseus, travel widely across the face of the earth. The Ionic dialect substitutes η for α in the first declension.

150

Κίρκης: with narrative hindsight, Odysseus identifies the source of the smoke for his audience: he and his men only learned later, and to their cost, that it was Circe's home from which he saw the smoke rising.

μεγάροισι: the –οισι(ν) ending is an alternative dative plural ending for -οις in Homer.

δρυμὰ πυκνὰ καὶ ὕλην: an example of the sort of tautology frequently used in Homer, where two words of similar or parallel meaning are used.

151

μερμήριξα: aorist (unaugmented: see note on l.144) of μερμηρίζω, 'I ponder/think over': a characteristic verb for Odysseus with his resourceful mind.

δ' = δέ: as above, the elision is done for you.

κατὰ φρένα καὶ κατὰ θυμόν: the φρήν is literally the diaphragm, but because it includes the part of the body containing the heart and vital organs it comes to mean the seat of the emotions, feelings and intellect, and therefore 'mind' or 'thoughts'. Similarly θυμός can denote the seat of the emotions, life, and the faculty of reason, so has a variety of meanings including heart, soul and life. In English we would probably translate this phrase as 'in my mind and heart'.

152

ἠδὲ: 'and': properly follows ἠμέν, just like μέν and δέ, but is often used by itself, as here, just like καί.

πυθέσθαι: 'to find out more'; the verb must be read intransitively here.

ἐπεί: It is hard to know whether we should translate this as 'when' or 'because': is it merely an expression of time, or does it carry a causal implication?

αἴθοπα: αἴθοψ: this adjective can mean gleaming or sparkling, or fiery-looking. It is appropriately used of smoke when flames or sparks are mingled with it.

153

μοι φρονέοντι: present participle: 'to me as I thought it over'. In Homer, contracted verbs are often left uncontracted.

δοάσσατο: 'it seemed': another unaugmented aorist. This is the Homeric equivalent of the Attic verb ἔδοξε.

κέρδιον: neuter comparative adjective: 'more profitable' i.e. 'better'.

154

πρῶτ᾽ ἐλθόντ᾽: you will be getting used to the automatic elisions by now.

νῆα: accusative of νηῦς, the Homeric form of ναῦς.

θοὴν: from θοός, 'swift': a standard Homeric epithet for ships.

θῖνα: accusative of θίς, a word originally meaning 'a heap', then 'the shore' of the sea, perhaps because the shore is a heap of sand?

155

ἑταίροισιν: see note on μεγάροισι, l.149.

δόμεναι ... προέμεν: Homeric infinitives of δίδωμι and προίημι.

156

ἦα: this is the Homeric form of the first person singular imperfect tense of εἰμί. Taken with the participle κιών, the phrase means something like 'as I went, I was ...'

νεός: an alternative form of the genitive of νηῦς, ship, after σχεδόν. (See note on line 146.)

157

ὀλοφύρατο: the third person singular aorist from ὀλοφύρομαι, to lament, mourn, bewail, commiserate with; the meaning is almost 'took pity on me'.

μοῦνον ἐόντα: 'being alone', agreeing with με: translate as 'in my loneliness' or 'alone as I was'. Note the Homeric forms of these two words: the lengthened syllable in μοῦνον for μόνον and the addition of the ε to the participle of εἰμί.

158

ῥά– = ἄρα: it does not require translating.

ὁδὸν αὐτὴν: the αὐτὴν emphasizes the serendipity of the event: 'into my very path'; we might say 'right at my feet'.

Note the belief prevalent in Homer that nothing happens by chance: the stag has been sent into Odysseus's path by a god, just as a god led them to the harbour where they are currently moored.

159

ὁ: the forms of the definite article in Homer have demonstrative force. As in this example, they are often used as pronouns which refer back to someone/something just mentioned (here, ὁ μὲν refers back to ἔλαφον μέγαν).

ποταμόνδε: 'towards the river', the -δε suffix denotes motion towards, as in Ἀθήναζε (= Ἀθηνᾶς- δε) 'to Athens'.

κατήϊεν: third person singular imperfect tense of κάτειμι.

νομοῦ ὕλης: 'his pasture in the wood'.

160

πιόμενος: future participle to express purpose: 'in order to drink'.

δή: for emphasis; can be translated as 'indeed', or omitted in English.

μιν: the Homeric form of the accusative third person pronoun, used for all genders (i.e. equivalent to αὐτόν, αὐτήν, αὐτο).

ἔχεν: the basic meaning of ἔχω is 'to have' or 'hold', but here it must mean something like 'to guide' or 'steer', a meaning relatively common in Homer.

ἠελίοιο: for the extra ε, see note on line 149; the -οιο ending is the alternative Homeric genitive singular ending for the second declension.

161

τὸν: see note on line 159.

ἐκβαίνοντα: 'as it was coming out', i.e. from the wood.

μέσα νῶτα: 'in the middle of his back'.

162

πλῆξα: unaugmented aorist of πλήσσω.

τὸ: again, see note on line 159. We would expect τὸν here to refer to the deer: the neuter is probably picking up the case from the closest noun, νῶτα.

163

κὰδ: κατά becomes κὰδ before the letter δ.

κονίῃσι: Homeric dative plural of κονία. -ῃσι(ν) or -ῃς are the usual Homeric dative plural forms for the first declension.

μακών: aorist participle of μηκάομαι. The aorist participle gives this the meaning 'It gave a cry and fell . . .', or we might say 'It fell with a cry'.

ἀπὸ δ᾽ ἔπτατο: the ἀπὸ is really a prefix, separated by tmesis from the rest of the verb.

The way in which Homer describes Odysseus's killing of the stag is reminiscent of the descriptions in the *Iliad* of warriors' deaths on the battlefield, and it is worth noting that Homeric heroes were characterized by their ability to kill animals just as much as their ability to kill people.

164

τῷ: masculine dative singular used as dative pronoun (see note on line 159) 'on him' after ἐμβαίνων.

164–5

τῷ δ᾽ ἐγώ ... εἰρυσάμην: again, reminiscent of scenes in the *Iliad* in which one warrior, having killed another, draws his weapon out of his victim, often standing on the chest to help pull it out.

165

τό: the article used as a demonstrative pronoun (see note on line 159), referring back to δόρυ in the previous line.

κατακλίνας: aorist participle of κατακλίνω.

γαίη: dative of γαῖα (= γῆ).

166–8

αὐτὰρ ἐγὼ σπασάμην ... πλεξάμενος: this is typical of the detailed descriptions which Homer gives us of Odysseus making various things (a rope, a raft ...) throughout his journey.

167

ὅσον τ᾽ ὄργυιαν: literally 'as much as a fathom of it', i.e. 'a fathom in length'. An ὄργυια ('fathom') was the measurement from finger-tip to finger-tip of a man's outstretched arms, i.e. about 6 feet. Ancient measurements often necessarily have reference to body parts.

ἐΰστρεφὲς ἀμφοτέρωθεν: 'well-twisted from both ends'.

ἐΰστρεφὲς: for the pronunciation and scansion, see note on ἐϋπλόκαμος in line 144.

168

δεινοῖο: see note on line 160.

πελώρου: from πέλωρον, a 'monster' or 'prodigy', because the stag is supernaturally enormous, being a gift from the gods. The stag is a worthy victim for a hero such as Odysseus.

169

βῆν: first person singular unaugmented aorist of βαίνω.

καταλοφάδεια: adverb meaning 'down over the neck', describing the manner of carrying an animal draped around one's shoulders with the animal's feet tied together and held under one's chin. It is a mark of Odysseus' heroic stature that he is able to carry the prodigious beast like this, though he admits that even he could not manage it merely slung over one shoulder.

170

ἦεν: third person singular Homeric imperfect tense of εἰμί with the meaning 'it was possible'.

171

μάλα γὰρ μέγα θηρίον ἦεν: once again, Odysseus emphasizes the huge size of the stag.

172–3

ἀνέγειρα ... ἕκαστον: a rather charming image of Odysseus, having provided food, gently waking up his men one by one with soothing words after their horrifying ordeal.

ἐπέεσσι: Homeric dative plural of ἔπος. In Homer the dative plural ending of the third declension often has a doubled -σ-.

174–77

Ὦ φίλοι ... λιμῷ: typical of the comforting and inspiring speeches with which Odysseus motivates his men at times of crisis.

174

περ: this particle adds a concessive force to the word to which it is added, as appropriate in context. Here it is taken with ἀχνύμενοί to mean 'despite our grief', 'grieving though we are'.

175

Ἀΐδαο δόμους: the 'House of Hades' is the Underworld. In Greek myth, Hades, brother of Zeus and Poseidon, was allotted the realm beneath the Earth when the universe was divided between the three.

μόρσιμον ἦμαρ: note the belief, strong in the Homeric epics, that everyone and everything has a predestined day of death or destruction which can neither be anticipated nor escaped.

176

ὄφρ': supply ἔστι: 'while there is ...'.

177

μνησόμεθα: aorist subjunctive of μιμνήσκω/μνάομαι (+ genitive) with 'jussive' force: 'let us ...'. In Homer the subjunctive may appear with a short vowel, as here, or a long vowel, as τρυχώμεθα below.

τρυχώμεθα: also a jussive subjunctive.

178

ἐφάμην: first person singular imperfect tense of φημί.

ἐπέεσσι: see note on line 170.

179

ἐκ ... καλυψάμενοι: an example of tmesis (see note on line 163); this is the aorist participle of ἐκκαλύπτω: the men have had their heads covered in what was a recognized sign of grief.

ἀτρυγέτοιο: ἀτρύγετος is a traditional epithet of the sea and is traditionally derived from τρυγάω, to harvest or gather, with privative ἀ, therefore meaning 'barren' or 'harvestless'. This may seem odd to us, thinking of the 'harvest' of fish, but Homeric heroes do not eat fish: they are only ever described as feasting on meat. An alternative derivation has it equal to ἄτρυτος, which means restless or untiring.

180

θηήσαντ᾽: third person plural aorist of θεάομαι.

μάλα γὰρ μέγα θηρίον ἦεν: the size of the deer is again emphasized, using the same phrase as in line 171.

181

τάρπησαν: third person plural aorist passive of τέρπω.

182

νιψάμενοι: aorist participle of νίζω.

183

πρόπαν ἦμαρ: 'all day long'.

185

ἐπὶ . . . ἦλθε: tmesis again.

186

κοιμήθημεν: aorist passive of κοιμάω, to put to sleep, with the meaning 'we rested'.

187

ῥοδοδάκτυλος: at the beginning of our extract, Dawn was described as ἐϋπλόκαμος. Here she is given her frequent epithet 'Rosy-fingered', emblematic of the way in which the sun's rays spread up like fingers from the horizon at daybreak.

188

ἐγὼν: see note on line 145.

ἀγορὴν = ἀγοράν. (See note on line 149).

189

Κέκλυτέ: aorist imperative of κλύω, + genitive of the thing listened to.

μευ: the Homeric form of μου.

190–92

ὅπη . . . οὐδ᾽ ὅπη . . . οὐδ᾽ ὅπη . . . οὐδ᾽ ὅπη: the repetition in these lines gives Odysseus's speech a rather dignified rhetorical quality, at the same time emphasizing that they have no idea at all where they are. These lines are an 'epexegesis', or explanation, of the words ζόφος and ἠώς in line 190, drawing on the belief that the sun drives his chariot beneath the Earth during the night and rises again at dawn.

190

ἴδμεν = ἴσμεν.

193

εἴ τις ἔτ᾽ ἔσται μῆτις: 'in the hope that there will yet be a plan', i.e. in the hope that a plan comes to mind.

ἐγὼ δ’ οὐκ οἴομαι εἶναι: this seems an uncharacteristically gloomy point of view for the πολύμητις Odysseus.

194

σκοπιὴν ἐς παιπαλόεσσαν ἀνελθών: notice the echo of the words of line 148. Such repetition, along with repeated formulas and formulaic phrases, has been advanced as evidence that the Homeric poems derive from an oral tradition, with the stories and poetic diction passed on from generation to generation. (See Introduction for further discussion.)

195

τὴν πέρι πόντος ἀπείριτος ἐστεφάνωται: the verb στεφανόω means to surround in a circle, like a στέφανος, a crown or ring. τὴν is being used as a relative pronoun with πέρι used as a ‘postposition’ (rather than a ‘preposition’), i.e. it means ‘around which . . .’. The Loeb edition translates this rather attractively as ‘about which is set as a crown the boundless deep’.

197

ἔδρακον: aorist of δέρκομαι (first singular).
δρυμὰ πυκνὰ καὶ ὕλην: the same phrase was used in line 150.

198

τοῖσιν: dative of possession.
φίλον: φίλος = dear, but in Homer often something more like simply ‘one’s own’. This must also be singular for plural, given τοῖσιν earlier in the line and μνησαμένοις at the beginning of the next. These lines are relatively common in Homer, with the participle at the beginning of the following line explaining what has led them to despair.

199

Ἀντιφάταο: Ἀντιφάτης is king of the Laestrygonians, with whom Odysseus and his men have had a terrifying encounter at lines 103ff of Book 10, when all their comrades apart from those on Odysseus’ own vessel were eaten by the king and his giant man-eating people. -αο or -εω are the Homeric genitive singular endings for masculine nouns of the first declension.
ἔργων . . . βίης . . .: genitives because verbs of remembering take the genitive.

200

μεγαλήτορος: this seems on the face of it an inappropriate epithet to apply to the Cyclops (unless it is taken to mean ‘great-hearted’ in the sense of ‘proud’ rather than ‘heroic’), but it is a feature of oral poetry that sometimes epithets suit a particular position in the line for metrical reasons, making the actual meaning of the word of secondary importance.

201

κατὰ . . . χέοντες: tmesis.

202

ἀλλ’ οὐ γάρ τις πρῆξις ἐγίγνετο μυρομένοισιν: ‘but in fact no result came to them weeping/as they wept’: we would probably say ‘but weeping didn’t do them any good’. If Homer was making a general proverbial point here (‘It’s no good crying over spilt milk’), the verb would be in the so-called ‘gnomic’ aorist, rather than the imperfect tense, so this is just a remark on the specific circumstances.

203

ἐϋκνήμιδας: ‘well-greaved’, a Homeric epithet for warriors, referring to their leg-armour (greaves), which covered the lower leg rather like bronze shin-pads. It seems unlikely that the men have their greaves on at this point in the story – more likely this is simply used as a standard description, and probably for metrical reasons (see note on line 200 above).

δίχα ... ἠρίθμεον: lit. ‘I counted in two’, i.e. ‘I divided into two groups’.

204

ὄπασσα: first person singular Homeric aorist of ὀπάζω, ‘send with’.

205

τῶν μὲν ... τῶν δ’: translate ‘of one group ... of the other group ...’

Εὐρύλοχος: Eurylochus is the most fully characterized of Odysseus’ comrades and is his second-in-command. He frequently, however, seeks to go against Odysseus’ orders, and tries to persuade the men not to obey. Most significantly, in Book 12 he persuades the men to kill and eat the Cattle of the Sun, which they have been expressly forbidden to do, with terrible consequences.

206

κυνέη: this word literally means ‘dog’s skin’, but refers to a leather soldier’s cap (presumably originally made from dog’s skin). Here it is described as χαλκήρεϊ ‘fitted with bronze’, so means ‘helmet’.

207

ἐκ δ’ ἔθορε κλῆρος: in Homer, lots are drawn by placing tokens in a helmet, but rather than an individual picking out the tokens, the helmet is shaken until one token jumps out.

208

βῆ δ’ ἰέναι: literally ‘he set out to go’, so translate as ‘he went on his way’.

ἅμα τῷ: ‘along with’.

δύω καὶ εἴκοσ’ ἑταῖροι: ‘twenty-two comrades’ are half the remaining crew members, following the loss of others on the way to the Cicones, Cyclops and Laestrygonians.

209

ἄμμε = ἡμᾶς, ‘us’.

κατὰ ... λίπον: tmesis.

κλαίοντες … γοόωντας: 'weeping … groaning': Homer emphasizes the misery and hopelessness of the men by telling us that both those setting out and those remaining behind were distressed.

210

βήσσῃσι: Homeric dative plural of βῆσσα, a 'wooded glen'. See note on κονίῃσι, line 163.

τετυγμένα: perfect passive participle of τεύχω 'make'. Take with ξεστοῖσιν λάεσσι in the next line and translate as 'made from polished stone'.

Κίρκης: once again, Odysseus is anticipating his own narrative by identifying Circe at this point as the owner of the house.

Circe is one of the female characters who play major roles in the *Odyssey*. Others are Penelope, Odysseus' wife, left at home in Ithaca ruling in his place and defending herself from the advances of the worthless suitors while she awaits his return; Calypso, the nymph who keeps Odysseus on her island of Ogygia for seven years and wants to make him her husband, until Hermes is sent to order her to release him; Nausicaa, the daughter of King Alcinous and Queen Arete of the Phaeaecians, who is thinking of her own marriage when she meets Odysseus and poignantly asks him to remember her when he returns home; Athene, Odysseus' steadfast champion among the gods; and Eurycleia, Odysseus' old nurse, who recognizes him despite his beggar's disguise when he returns home at last.

211

λάεσσι: see note on ἐπέεσσι, line 170.

περισκέπτῳ: 'to be seen on all sides': in other words, 'visible from far off'.

212

μιν: 'it' (see note on μιν in line 160); referring to the house.

213

τούς: see note on line 159. Here the article is being used as a relative pronoun, 'which'.

κατέθελξεν: third person singular aorist of the verb καταθέλγω 'I subdue with spells'.

This line at first makes us think that the lions and wolves are simply wild animals bewitched by Circe to tame them, but their subsequent behaviour, as they approach Odysseus' men with their tails wagging, encourages us to realize that they are themselves men who have been transformed into beasts.

214

ὁρμήθησαν: third person plural aorist passive of ὁρμάω meaning 'they rushed'.

ἄρα τοί γε: this combination of particles taken together emphasizes the surprising nature of what is happening. Translate as 'actually'.

215

περισσαίνοντες: present participle of περισσαίνω, literally 'wag the tail around' so 'fawn upon'. The existence of such a verb in Greek shows that even from ancient times the phenomenon of dogs coming up to one wagging their tails was familiar.

216

ὡς δ' ὅτ' ἄν: 'as when . . .', introducing a simile. (See Introduction for discussion of Homeric similes.) Homer is comparing the unfamiliar happenings of his story to things familiar to the listener, and to us. We can immediately imagine the scene described, dogs crowding around their master when he comes home, hoping for treats, as it is something we are still familiar with from our own lives.

217

μειλίγματα θυμοῦ: 'things to appease their temper'. In other words, titbits to soothe them and stop them reacting like guard dogs.

218

ὥς: 'so', picking up the simile and relating it to the current happenings.

τοὺς ἀμφὶ: 'around them': the article used as a demonstrative pronoun (see note on line 159); for the position of ἀμφί, see note on line 195.

κρατερώνυχες: an adjective derived from κρατερός (strong) + ὄνυξ (claw), so meaning 'with strong claws'.

219

τοὶ: The Homeric form of οἱ, used demonstratively: 'they'.

220

καλλιπλοκάμοιο: 'with beautiful locks', 'fair-tressed', another generic Homeric epithet applied to goddesses or women.

222

ἐποιχομένης: Circe is described as 'going up and down in front of' her loom. In ancient times, looms were made by hanging the warp threads vertically, weighted with stones or special loom-weights at the bottom. The weft threads were then woven by walking up and down passing the shuttle between them.

ἱστὸν . . . μέγαν ἄμβροτον: Circe, as a goddess, has a 'great immortal loom', but the task she is performing would have been the regular occupation of ordinary women throughout the ancient world, as we know from references in literature as well as vase paintings.

οἷα: οἷα does not seem to be referring back to anything particular in the sentence: translate as 'such as are the deeds (or 'is the handiwork') of goddesses'.

223

λεπτά τε καὶ χαρίεντα καὶ ἀγλαά: the combination of adjectives emphasizes the superhuman beauty of Circe's weaving.

πέλονται: translate simply as 'are'.

225

κήδιστος ἑτάρων . . . κεδνότατός τε: Odysseus describes Polites here as 'the dearest and trustiest of my comrades', but he is not mentioned by name anywhere else.

227

καλόν: used here adverbially: 'beautifully'.

ἀμφιμέμυκεν: literally 'mooed all around', but here the floor 'echoed all around' with the sound of Circe's singing.

228

ἢ θεὸς ἠὲ γυνή: note how readily the men assume that this could be a goddess just as easily as a woman.

φθεγγώμεθα: this is a first person plural jussive subjunctive: 'let us speak'. See note on line 177.

229

φθέγγοντο καλεῦντες: 'calling they spoke', i.e. 'they called out and spoke'.

231

ἀϊδρείῃσιν: 'in their stupidity' or 'folly'.

233

εἷσεν: transitive: 'she seated them . . .'

234

ἐν δέ: the adverbial usage of ἐν (see the entry for ἐν in Liddell, Scott and Jones, section C). Translate 'and then'.

A drink/mixture similar to the one that Circe is making is mentioned in other places, e.g. in Nestor's tent in Book 11 of the *Iliad*, and is known as '*kykeon*'. Many Greek recipes today still include both cheese and honey.

236

αἴης: genitive of αἶα = γαῖα. See note on line 149. It is genitive because λαθοίατο ('forget') takes genitive of the thing forgotten.

238

ῥάβδῳ: her 'staff' or 'stick'. It is tempting to translate it as 'wand', but that gives the wrong impression of Circe's magic – she does not require a wand to perform her spells.

πεπληγυῖα . . . ἐέργνυ: 'having struck them she shut them up (into pig-sties) '. . .' i.e. 'she struck them and shut them up (into pig-sties) . . .'.

239–40

κεφαλὰς φωνήν τε τρίχας τε/καὶ δέμας: the list emphasizes the complete bodily transformation of the men into pigs, which makes the next clause 'αὐτὰρ νοῦς ἦν ἔμπεδος ὡς τὸ πάρος περ' ('but their mind was unimpaired, just as it had been before') even more shocking for the audience.

242

πάρ . . . ἔβαλεν: tmesis.

ἄκυλον βάλανόν τ' . . . καρπόν τε κρανείης: as well as providing a contrast with the *kykeon* she served them when they first entered her house, the list of suitable foodstuffs (including two different types of acorn) emphasizes the men's complete transformation into pigs.

κρανείης: the 'Cornelian cherry' or dogwood tree, the fruit of which is edible to humans as well as pigs.

243

χαμαιευνάδες: 'wallowing'; 'lying/sleeping on the ground' (from χαμαί + εὐνάζω) further emphasizes the men's degradation.

245

ἐρέων: future participle to express purpose.

246

ἱέμενός: middle participle from ἵημι + περ = 'though he longed to'.

247

κῆρ ... βεβολημένος: 'stricken in his heart': κῆρ is accusative of respect or of the part affected.

247

ἐν δέ: the adverbial usage again, as in line 234 above, but this time translate as 'and further'; 'moreover'.

οἱ = his (= dative of ἕ).

ὄσσε: 'eyes': an example of the dual form, found quite commonly in Homer, but much rarer in later literature. It is used both for things of which there are naturally two, such as eyes or shoulders (see note on line 261 below) and for circumstances in which two people do things as a pair (see note on lines 333 and 334 below).

248

δακρυόφιν: Homeric genitive plural of δάκρυον, 'tear'. We would say 'his eyes filled with tears'.

ὤϊετο: here meaning something like 'intended', 'was set on'.

μιν ... ἀγασσάμεθ᾽ ἐξερέοντες: 'we were amazed questioning him' i.e. 'we questioned him in amazement'.

251

Ἥιομεν: first person plural Homeric imperfect of εἶμι.

ἀνὰ δρυμά: 'through the woods'.

252–3

Note how similar these lines and those following are to the description of the comrades' arrival at Circe's house in lines 210–11 and following, but this time presented through the medium of Eurylochus' direct speech. This is another feature of oral poetry.

259

ἀολλέες: masculine plural of ἀολλής: 'all together'.

261–2

περὶ ... ἀμφὶ ...: both should be taken with ὤμοιιν βαλόμην, 'I slung (my sword/ bow) around/about (my shoulders)'.

ὤμοιιν: another example of the dual, this time of ὦμος, 'shoulder', here in the genitive.

262

μέγα χάλκεον: 'a great one of bronze', referring back to ξίφος in the previous line.

τόξα: plural of τόξον, 'bow', but frequently used for singular.

263

τὸν: 'him', i.e. Eurylochus.

ἠνώγεα: 'I ordered': strictly pluperfect of ἄνωγα, but used as imperfect, since ἄνωγα is itself a perfect tense, but with present meaning.

αὐτὴν ὁδὸν ἡγήσασθαι: 'to go before on the same road' i.e. 'to lead me back by the same route', almost just 'to show me the way'.

264

ἀμφοτέρῃσι: 'with both hands'.

ἀμφοτέρῃσι λαβὼν ἐλλίσσετο γούνων: word order here suggests the translation 'seizing me with both hands, he besought me by my knees', where γούνων is the genitive of the thing by which one prays, rather than the alternative translation, 'seizing me with both hands by the knees, he besought'. (See line 324 for the other usage.) This seems to us a very strange thing to do, but clasping someone about the knees is the standard way in Homer of showing the desperation of one's plea. Thetis clasps Zeus' knees and grasps his beard/chin in the *Iliad* when she is begging him to guide Achilles' fate in the Trojan War. Obviously the beard-grasping element can only be employed if the besought person is seated ...

265

πτερόεντα: 'winged', an epithet commonly applied by Homer to words, which gives a rather lovely image of them fluttering out of a person's mouth.

266

Μή μ᾽ ἄγε ... ἀλλὰ λίπ᾽: the two imperatives in this one line give a sense of Eurylochus' desperation not to return to Circe's house.

267

ἐλεύσεαι: second person singular Homeric future tense of ἔρχομαι. Eurylochus emphasizes what he regards as the futility of returning to Circe's house: he believes that the men who have been turned into pigs are lost, and that if Odysseus follows after them, he will never make it out alive. The two parts of his warning are: οὔτ᾽ αὐτὸς ἐλεύσεαι: you will neither return yourself, and οὔτε τιν᾽ ἄλλον ἄξεις σῶν ἑτάρων: nor will you bring back any other of your comrades.

268

τοίσδεσι: dative plural of ὅδε, 'these men here', with the unusual 'double dative' form, where the second part of the word declines as well as the first.

269

φεύγωμεν: see note on line 177.

ἀλύξαιμεν: first person plural optative from ἀλύσκω, 'we might escape'.

270

μιν ἀμειβόμενος προσέειπον: 'answering I addressed him' so 'I answered him and said'. This is a common formula in Homeric accounts of conversation.

271

ἦ τοι: these particles together give a reassuring force to the beginning of Odysseus' reply, almost 'Don't worry . . .'.

    Odysseus' speech to Eurylochus demonstrates his best qualities as leader – he does not push a terrified man to do something he cannot face, but realizes that it his own duty to face the danger himself for the sake of his lost comrades.

273

κρατερὴ δέ μοι ἔπλετ' ἀνάγκη: literally 'There exists strong compulsion for me', i.e. 'I've got no choice', 'It's my duty to do this'.

274

ἀνήϊον: see note on line 146.

275–6

ἔμελλον . . . ἵξεσθαι: 'I was about to reach'.

ἱερὰς: 'sacred' or 'holy', but perhaps 'mystic' would be a better translation here. This word is applied to a wide variety of things in Homer, not all of which could sensibly be described as actually sacred or holy (e.g. a fish). The idea is of something other-worldly or with supernatural qualities. Here it gives us the idea that the woods through which Odysseus is walking are filled with supernatural possibilities.

276

πολυφαρμάκου: 'knowing many drugs', so 'skilled in enchantments'.

277

Ἑρμείας = Ἑρμῆς.

χρυσόρραπις: 'with a wand of gold', epithet of Hermes, who is always depicted in art as carrying his wand, or caduceus, the symbol of his role as herald or messenger of the gods.

277–8

μοι . . . ἀντεβόλησεν/ἐρχομένῳ: 'met me as I went'.

νεηνίῃ ἀνδρὶ ἐοικώς: 'like a young man': Hermes appears in disguise, as is usually the case when gods appear to mortals in the epic poems.

279

ὑπηνήτῃ: 'just getting a beard'. As the line goes on to explain, in ancient Greek times this was conventionally thought to be the time at which a young man was most attractive.

τοῦ περ χαριεστάτος ἥβη: 'whose youth is at its most graceful'; 'in whom youth is fairest': an unusal instance of the superlative appearing as an adjective of two terminations.

280

ἔν τ᾽ ἄρα μοι φῦ χειρί: 'he grasped my hand tightly' or 'clung fast to my hand'. This formulaic phrase is used to describe warm greetings – the verb literally means to implant something in something else, hence the dative object, and gives a vivid sense of the heartiness of the handshake described! The same formula is used in line 397.

281

The opening of Hermes' address to Odysseus is notable for its directness. Homer shows us that even the bravest and most resourceful hero is an ignorant weakling in the face of the gods.

Πῆ: 'where?' The force is almost 'Where do you think you're going now?'

282

ἐών: present participle of εἰμί. See note on line 157.

ἐνί: add 'house'.

283

πυκινοὺς κευθμῶνας: either 'closely-barred' or 'close-set' sties. In other words, either the sties have strong fences, or there are a lot of them crowded next to each other.

284

λυσόμενος: future participle to express purpose. The middle verb is significant – these are Odysseus' men and he has come to set them free 'for himself' or to 'get them set free'.

285

νοστήσειν: the verb νοστέω means to return, often carrying the idea of having had a lucky escape. It is where we derive our word 'nostalgia', a longing to return.

αὐτὸν ... γ᾽: emphasize that if he goes on without help, even Odysseus will not get home again. The sense is: 'Have you come to rescue your companions? You *yourself* won't even make it home; *even* you will remain where the others are.'

μενέεις: 'you will remain': Homeric future tense of μένω.

286

σαώσω: 'I will save': Homeric future tense of σώζω.

287

τῆ: 'there!': always followed by the imperative in Homer. Here the imperative is ἔρχευ: 'go'.

288

κρατὸς: genitive of κράς ('head') dependent on ἀλάλκῃσιν: 'it will ward off ... from your head'.

289

ἐρέω: verbs of speaking are more commonly followed by an accusative and infinitive construction. Here, however, there is simply a direct object, 'I will describe, tell you about'.

290

κυκεῶ: accusative of κυκεών, the barley potion made by Circe as described earlier.

292

ἕκαστα: 'each and every thing', so 'everything'.

293

ἐλάση: third person singular aorist subjunctive of ἐλαύνω, after ὁππότε κεν (= ὁπόταν): 'when she strikes . . .'.

περιμήκεϊ ῥάβδῳ: as before, there is no implication that the rod or staff itself is magic: exactly these words are used in Book 12 to describe a fishing rod.

294

ἐρυσσάμενος: aorist middle participle from ἐρύω, 'I draw': 'having drawn', so 'draw (your sword) and . . .'.

295

ἐπαΐξαι: infinitive used as imperative of ἐπαΐσσω: 'rush at'. The same is true of κέλεσθαί in line 299.

ὥς . . . μενεαίνων: 'as though intending': ὥς + participle to express the ostensible or feigned reason for doing something.

299

μακάρων: 'the blessed ones' i.e. the gods; genitive of thing by which an oath is sworn.

300–1

κακόν: has two different meanings in these two lines. In 300, Hermes is advising Odysseus to make Circe swear an oath not to πῆμα κακὸν βουλευσέμεν ἄλλο 'plot any new evil to harm you'. In 301, he is warning him how this might happen when he is off his guard in a state of undress 'in case she renders (θήῃ) you (σ᾽) weak (κακόν) and unmanned (ἀνήνορα) when you have been stripped naked (ἀπογυμνωθέντα)'.

θήῃ: aorist subjunctive of τίθημι after μή: 'in case she makes/renders (you)'.

302

ἀργειφόντης: 'the slayer of Argus', an epithet of Hermes deriving from the story in which he lulled the 100-eyed giant Argus to sleep and killed him. Hera took Argus' 100 eyes and set them in the tail of her favourite bird, the peacock.

304

ῥίζῃ: 'at the root'.

ἔσκε: third person singular imperfect of εἰμί. This is the 'iterative' form, which indicates a continuously repeated action.

ῥίζη . . . ἄνθος: the line moves pleasingly from the root to the flower.

305

μῶλυ: 'moly'. People have long wondered whether this mysterious magical herb might be identifiable as a real plant. One theory suggests that it could be a snowdrop: snowdrops contain a substance which counteracts the effects of poisoning from plants such as deadly nightshade or mandrake. The symptoms of such poisoning include amnesia, delusions and hallucinations. If Circe's φάρμακα included deadly nightshade, the snowdrop might indeed have cured the men.

307

μακρὸν: μακρός can refer to both length ('long') and height ('tall'). Here, in reference to Mt Olympus, it means something like 'lofty', 'high', etc.

308

ἀν᾽ = ἀνά: (here) 'through'.

309

ἤϊα: 'I went': Homeric first person singular imperfect of εἶμι.

κραδίη = καρδία, 'heart'.

310

εἰνὶ = ἐν.

311

This is the third time that we are taken through this same sequence of actions. The first time was when Eurylochus' party came across Circe, and the second time was when Eurylochus went back to the ships and described to Odysseus what had happened to the men. In that case, the description was almost identical (as we might expect). This time, however, there are noticeable changes to the narrative, e.g. in lines 231 and 257 the men 'obeyed foolishly', but when Odysseus approached Circe's home in line 313 he 'obeyed troubled at heart'.

313

ἀκαχήμενος ἦτορ: 'troubled at heart': the verb is the participle of ἀχεύω and the noun is accusative of respect as in line 247.

314

εἷσε δέ μ᾽ εἰσαγαγοῦσα: 'she led me in and seated me . . .'.

To one unacquainted with her previous actions, Circe's behaviour here would, on the face of it, seem to accord with the ideal of *xenia*, the ancient social code that dictated that one showed hospitality to strangers first and asked questions later. In the *Odyssey*, adherence or otherwise to this code marks out the civilized from the barbarian (e.g. the Phaeacians versus the Cyclops). (See Introduction for more information on the concept of *xenia*.)

314-15

ἀργυροήλου/καλοῦ δαιδαλέου: the string of adjectives with no conjunctions (asyndeton) focuses our attention on the unusual beauty of the chair.

δαιδαλέου: 'cunningly made': a variant of the word δαίδαλος, which is of course also the name of the most cunning craftsman in myth.

316-17

τεῦχε δέ μοι κυκεῶ ... ἐν δέ τε φάρμακον ἧκε, κακὰ φρονέουσ᾽ ἐνὶ θυμῷ: we are familiar with Circe's methods by now.

319

ἔπος τ᾽ ἔφατ᾽ ἔκ τ᾽ ὀνόμαζεν: 'she spoke and called (me) by name': a formulaic phrase. Here, as elsewhere, followed by a failure to use the name!

320

Ἔρχεο ... λέξο: 'go ... lie down': imperatives of ἔρχομαι and λέγω.

συφεόνδε: 'towards the sty'. See note on line 159.

321

ἄορ: 'sword': the word properly refers to a sword which hung from a belt.

ἐγὼ δ᾽ ... μενεαίνων: compare these lines with Hermes' instructions in lines 294–5.

324

ὑπέδραμε: 'she ran in under': third person singular aorist of ὑποτρέχω. The prefix gives the idea of Circe ducking under Odysseus' outstretched sword and arm.

λάβε γούνων: 'she clasped my knees'. This is a slightly different usage from 264: here the genitive is of the part seized or grasped.

325

Τίς πόθεν: the juxtaposition of these two words, and the repeated questioning in this line, helps to convey Circe's frantic desire to find out the identity of this man, presumably the first not to be bewitched by her potion.

τοκῆες: 'parents': Homeric plural of τοκεύς.

326

θαῦμά μ᾽ ἔχει: Literally 'amazement holds me', i.e. 'I am astonished', 'I am amazed'.

οὔ τι: 'not at all', to be taken with ἐθέλχθης.

327

οὐδὲ ... οὐδέ: the repetition emphasizes the uniqueness of the occurrence.

328

ἕρκος ὀδόντων: 'the fence of the teeth'. This vivid Homeric phrase is used when we would simply say 'lips', but should be translated in full.

329

ἐν στήθεσσιν ... νόος: we would not normally think of the νόος 'mind' as being located in the στήθεσσιν 'breast', but see note on line 151.

330

ἐσσι: 'you are': Homeric second person singular of εἰμί.

πολύτροπος: 'turning many ways', so 'resourceful', 'versatile' or 'wily'. Often applied to Odysseus and a good example of the person-specific rather than generic type of epithet.

331

ἐλεύσεσθαι: future infinitive of ἔρχομαι. Circe now admits that Odysseus' arrival has been prophesied by Hermes.

333

νῶϊ: 'we (two)': the dual form of the personal pronoun.

334

ἐπιβήομεν: jussive subjunctive of ἐπιβαίνω (see note on line 177), which takes a genitive object, hence εὐνῆς ἡμετέρης.

μιγέντε: dual participle of μίγνυμι, here meaning 'to have sex with'. Circe's repeated use of the dual form seems appropriate given that she is suggesting that they should go to bed together, and also seems to seek to isolate the two of them as a pair, ignoring the rest of the men. This is reinforced by Circe's use of the first person plural possessive pronoun in the phrase εὐνῆς ἡμετέρης ('our' rather than 'my' bed).

335

πεποίθομεν ἀλλήλοισιν: 'let us put our trust in one another', an unlikely proposition given the circumstances.

338

ἥ μοι σῦς μὲν ἔθηκας ... ἑταίρους: 'you who have turned my comrades into pigs'.

339

δολοφρονέουσα: 'devising a trick', 'artful-minded': a word derived from a combination of δόλος 'trick' and φρονέω 'think'. As at line 153 the verb is left uncontracted.

341

ὄφρα με γυμνωθέντα κακὸν καὶ ἀνήνορα θήῃς: Odysseus is mindful of Hermes' warning, delivered in line 301.

343

τλαίης: second person singular optative of τλάω 'endure', 'bear', 'submit': here best translated as 'agree'.

345

ἀπόμνυεν: literally 'she swore away from', so 'she swore not to': third person singular imperfect of ἀπόμνυμι.

346

ὄμοσέν τε τελεύτησέν τε τὸν ὅρκον: 'when she had sworn and completed the oath': the tautology here stresses both the solemnity of the oath-taking and the fact that she has definitely sworn it in full.

347

καὶ τότ᾽: almost 'only then . . .'

It is shocking to modern audiences that Penelope is expected to remain faithful to Odysseus for the twenty years that he is away, whereas Odysseus is seemingly free to sleep with whoever he likes. Defenders of Odysseus' position might argue that he has little choice here, or on Calypso's island, and that certainly in the latter case he is described as reluctant to sleep with her every night, and spending every day weeping by the shore of the sea.

348ff.

In these lines Homer gives us a particularly lingering and detailed description of the preparation of Odysseus' bath and supper. These would be a standard set of actions in welcoming a guest, but here they carry added significance because of the contrast between Circe's initial 'welcome' and the return to the expected standards of behaviour that follows: now that Odysseus has deflected Circe's initial attempt to turn him into a pig, she is displaying *xenia* to the full. Circe is the only character in the *Odyssey* who changes from bad to good host in this way.

349

ἔασι = εἰσί.

350

ταί: 'they': feminine plural of the demonstrative pronoun.

350–1

ἔκ τε κρηνέων . . . ποταμῶν: in other words, Circe's serving women are nymphs, semi-divine beings who inhabit the natural world.

351

εἰς ἅλαδε: 'to the sea': εἰς just reinforces the -δε suffix.

352

τάων = τῶν.

ἔνι: a postposition, i.e. going with the word which precedes it (θρόνοις) rather than with the one which follows.

353

καθύπερθ᾽, ὑπένερθε: the juxtaposition of these two words in the middle of the line has a pleasing effect, especially when you remember that the poem was originally heard not read.

λῖθ᾽ = λιτ᾽ (the rough breathing on ὑπέβαλλεν turns the τ into θ). This is the elided form of λιτά, accusative of λίς ('smooth'), used as a noun to mean 'smooth linen cloth'.

354

ἐτίταινε: 'laid out'.

352–8

ἡ μὲν ... ἡ δ᾽ ἑτέρη ... ἡ δὲ τρίτη ... ἡ δὲ τετάρτη: we are told what each nymph does in turn, enhancing the busy atmosphere of the scene.

356

κρητῆρι ... ἐκίρνα: 'mixed in a mixing bowl': Greeks never drank wine undiluted. κρητήρ is the Homeric form of κρατήρ, a '*krater*' or bowl made specifically for the purpose of mixing wine with water, and from which the wine was then ladled out. The fact that her wine is mixed in a *krater* marks Circe out as civilized: drinking undiluted wine was regarded by the Greeks as one of the characteristics of barbarians.

358

ἐφόρει: this is the frequentative form of φορέω, implying that the maid went back and forth repeatedly bringing water for the bath.

ἰαίνετο: 'became hot': middle of ἰαίνω 'I heat'.

361

ἔς ῥ᾽ ἀσάμινθον ἕσασα λό᾽: 'she seated me in a bath-tub and washed me'. λό᾽ is third person singular imperfect tense of λούω.

362

θυμῆρες κεράσασα: 'mixing it to my liking', i.e. mixing the hot and cold water together to the temperature Odysseus wants.

A bath is the standard welcome home for a hero tired and dirty from travel and/or war, and Odysseus enjoys several in the course of the poem.

364

λίπ᾽ ἐλαίῳ: 'richly with olive oil'.

366–7

These lines are the same as 314–15, but the circumstances have changed and the meal to which Odysseus is sitting down is not poisoned.

368–9

χέρνιβα ... ἐπέχευε ... ὑπὲρ ... λέβητος: the water is poured from the jug over the hands of the guest and caught in the basin beneath.

372

χαριζομένη παρεόντων: 'giving freely of her store'.

373

ἐσθέμεναι: 'to eat': infinitive of ἔσθω = ἐσθίω.

374

ἥμην: 'I was sitting': third person singular imperfect of ἧμαι.

ἀλλοφρονέων: 'thinking of other things', 'distracted': the verb is easy to interpret if you think of it in two parts: ἀλλο + φρονέω.

376

ἰάλλοντα: from ἰάλλω, here meaning to 'stretch out' the hands towards food.

378

Τίφθ' = τίπτε (= τί ποτε). Old-fashioned dictionaries translate this as 'Why, pray, . . .?' We could say 'Why, tell me, . . .?'

κατ' . . . ἔζεαι: tmesis.

ἴσος: 'like', + dative.

379

ἅπτεαι: second person singular of ἅπτομαι, 'take hold of': we would probably say 'touch' here. + genitive of the thing taken hold of (βρώμης . . . ποτῆτος).

381

δειδίμεν: Homeric infinitive from δείδω.

Odysseus' behaviour in these lines is an important sign that he actually does care for his men – at least here. His actions elsewhere in the poem show a reckless disregard for his companions, and indeed all of them will perish before he reaches the island of Ithaca.

384

τλαίη: the same verb as at line 343. Here translate as 'could bring himself . . .'.

πάσσασθαι: Homeric infinitive from πατέομαι, to eat or partake of, + genitive.

385

λύσασθ': the middle verb carries the sense 'to get (someone) set free' or 'set free for oneself' as against simply 'to set (someone) free'.

ἐν ὀφθαλμοῖσιν ἰδέσθαι: 'to see before one's own eyes'.

386

πρόφρασσα: Homeric feminine form of πρόφρων, 'gracious(ly)'.

φαγέμεν: aorist (Homeric) infinitive of ἐσθίω.

390

ἐκ . . . ἔλασεν: tmesis; understand 'them' as the object, i.e. Odysseus' men, who are still currently in the form of pigs.

ἐννεώροισιν: 'nine years old'. It is unclear whether there is anything particularly significant about the choice of age here, unless it just means 'fully grown'.

392

προσάλειφεν: 'applied as ointment'. Notice that although the original charm had to be drunk, the antidote is applied externally.

393–4

ἐκ ... ἔρρεον: tmesis; 'fell off'.

ἃς ... τό: both relative pronouns, i.e. 'the hairs *which* the poison *that* Circe had applied earlier had made grow'.

ἔφυσε: intransitive: 'made grow'.

395–6

νεώτεροι ... εἰσοράασθαι: this is most likely a sort of compensation for having to endure being turned into pigs, although perhaps it is simply that, by contrast with their hoggish appearance, they *seem* to be handsomer etc. than they were before.

εἰσοράασθαι: an epexegetic infinitive, i.e. 'they were younger and more handsome *to behold*'.

397

ἔφυν τ᾽ ἐν χερσὶν: see note on line 280.

398

ἱμερόεις: 'passionate', but also carries the sense of something pleasurable – they are partly weeping with relief.

ὑπέδυ: literally 'plunged' (from ὑποδύομαι), but better turned round to mean 'overwhelmed'.

399

σμερδαλέον κονάβιζε: 'resounded terribly'. σμερδαλέον is often used to mean 'grim(ly)' or 'terrifying(ly)' and the whole phrase is used elsewhere of the clash of armour, but that is obviously not quite the meaning here. What is being described is the incredible noise made by twenty-two men weeping passionately all at once.

καὶ: 'even', not 'and'; in Homer, gods and goddesses rarely show any emotion for the suffering of humans, so the fact that 'even' the goddess shows pity to Odysseus' men is important.

Vocabulary

Odyssey 10

While there is no Defined Vocabulary List for A-level, words in the OCR Defined Vocabulary List for AS are marked with * so that students can quickly see the vocabulary with which they should be particularly familiar.

ἄγαμαι, 1st p. aorist ἀγασσάμεθ'	wonder	ἄλσος -εος, τό	grove
		ἀλύσκω, aor. optative ἀλύξαιμεν	flee from, avoid
ἀγγελίη, ἡ	message		
ἄγε, ἄγετε	come on!	ἄλφιτον, τό	barley
ἀγλαός -ή -όν	bright, shining, splendid	ἄμβροτος -ον	immortal
ἀγορή -ῆς, ἡ	assembly	ἀμείβω	in middle, reply; pass
ἄγχι	near	ἄμμε	us
*ἄγω	lead, bring	*ἀμφί	around
ἀδευκής, ές	not sweet, bitter	ἀμφιέλισσα	rowed on both sides
ἀείδω	sing	ἀμφιμυκάομαι	echo
ἀέκων, -ουσα, -ον	unwilling	ἀμφίπολος	handmaid
αἶα, αἴης, ἡ	land	*ἀμφότερος	either/both
Ἄϊδης, gen. Ἀΐδαο	Hades	ἀμφοτέρωθεν	from both ends
αἰδοῖος, -η, -ον	revered	*ἀνάγκη, ἡ	necessity
ἀϊδρείη	ignorance, folly	ἀνακαίω	kindle, light
ἄϊδρις	unknowing, ignorant	ἀναμίσγω	mix in
αἴθοψ	fiery-looking, mixed with flame	ἄναξ, ἄνακτος, ὁ	lord
		ἀνατλῆναι, 3rd s. aor. ἀνέτλη	bear up against, endure
αἰνός	dread, dire, grim		
*αἱρέω, aor. part. ἑλών	take, grasp, seize	ἄναυδος -ον	speechless, dumb
ἀϊστόω	in passive, vanish	ἁνδάνω	please, delight, gratify
αἶψα	quickly, straight away	ἀνδροφάγος -ον	man-eating
ἀκαχήμενος	see ἀχεύω	ἀνεγείρω	wake up, rouse
ἀκήλητος -ον	proof against enchantment	ἄνειμι, imp. ἀνήϊον	go up, go inland
		ἀνήνωρ	unmanly
ἄκνηστις -ιος, ἡ	spine	*ἀνήρ, ἀνδρός, ὁ	man
*ἀκούω	hear	ἄνθος -ους, τό	flower
ἄκρις -ιος, ἡ	mountain peak	ἀνίσταμαι	stand up
ἄκυλος, ὁ	acorn	ἀννεῖται, 3rd s. of ἀνανέομαι	rise up
ἄλαδε	towards the sea		
ἄλαλκε, 3rd s. aor. subj. ἀλάλκησιν	ward off	ἀντιβολέω	meet
		ἀντικρύ	right through
*ἄλλος -η -ο	another	Ἀντιφάτης, gen. Ἀντιφάταο	Antiphates
ἀλλοφρονέω	think of other things		

ἄνωγα (perfect with   command, order
  present sense)
ἀολλής -ές   all together
ἄορ, ἄορος, τό   sword
ἀπαναίνομαι, aor. inf.   refuse, reject
  ἀπανήνασθαι
ἀπείριτος -ον   boundless, immense
ἀποβαίνω, aor.   go away, depart
  ἀπέβην
ἀπογυμνόω   strip bare
ἀπόμνυμι   take an oath away
               from, swear not to
ἀποπέτομαι   fly off
ἅπτομαι   take hold of
ἀργύρεος -α -ον   of silver
ἀργυρόηλος -ον   silver-studded
ἀριθμέω   count
ἀρχός, ὁ   leader
*ἄρχω, imp. ἦρχον   lead
ἀσάμινθος, ἡ   bath-tub
ἄσπετος -ον   unceasing, abundant
ἀτρύγετος -ον   unharvested, barren
αὐδή, ἡ   voice, speech
αὖθι   on the spot, there
αὐτάρ   but
ἀχεύω, part.   grieve, mourn
  ἀκαχήμενος
ἀχνύμενοί, pass. part.   grieve
  of ἀχεύω
ἄχος -εος, τό   pain, distress

*βαίνω, aor βῆν   walk, go
βάλανος, ἡ   acorn
*βάλλω   throw
βῆσσα, ἡ   wooded glen
βίη, ἡ   strength, force
*βοάω, aor. βόησα   shout
βολέω   be stricken
*βουλεύω, fut. inf.   plan, devise
  βουλευσέμεν
βροτός, ὁ   mortal, man
βρώμη, ἡ   food
βρῶσις -εως, ἡ   meat

γάλα, γάλακτος, τό   milk
*γίγνομαι   become
*γιγνώσκω, 3rd p. aor.   recognize
  ἔγνωσαν
γοάω   groan, weep
γόνυ, gen. pl γούνων   knee
γόος, ὁ   weeping, wailing
γυῖον, τό   limb
γυμνόω   strip naked
*γυνή, ἡ   woman

δαιδάλεος -α -ον   cunningly wrought

δαίνυμαι   feast
δαίτη, ἡ   feast, banquet
δαίτηθεν   from a feast
δάκρυον, τό   tear
δάπεδον, τό   floor
δείδω, aor. ἔδεισα   fear
*δείκνυμι, aor. ἔδειξα   show
*δεινός -ή -όν   fearful, mighty
*δεῖπνον, τό   meal
δέμας, τό   body
δέπας -αος, τό   cup, goblet
δέρκομαι, aor. ἔδρακον   see
*δεῦρο   here
δήνεα (only in pl)   counsels, plans, arts
δηρόν   too long
*δίδωμι, inf. δόμεναι   give
διέκ   out through
διοτρεφής -ές   cherished by Zeus
δίχα   in two
δοάσσατο   it seemed
*δόλος, ὁ   trick
δολοφρονέων -ουσα   wily-minded, evilly
  -ον   planning
δόμεναι   see δίδωμι
δόμος, ὁ   house (often in plural)
δόρυ, τό   spear
δρήστειρα, ἡ   working woman
δρυμός, pl δρυμά   copse, thicket
*δύναμαι   be able
δύστηνος -ον   wretched, unhappy,
               unfortunate
δύω   two
δῶμα -ατος, τό   house (often in plural)

*ἐάω, aor. εἴασα   allow
ἔγχος -εος, τό   spear
ἐγών (ἐγώ)   I
ἔδω, inf. ἔδμεναι   eat
ἔειπον   spoke
ἐέργνυ   see ἔργνυμι
ἐέρχατο   see ἔργνυμι
ἔθορε   see θρώσκω
εἶδαρ -ατος, τό   food
εἴδομαι, 3rd s. aor.   appear
  ἐείσατο
εἴκελος, εἴκελος   like
εἴκοσι   twenty
εἰσάγω   lead in
εἰσοράω   look upon, behold
*ἕκαστος -η -ον   each; in n plural,
               everything
ἐκβαίνω   step out of
ἐκκαλύπτω   uncover
ἐκλύω   in middle, get set free
ἐκπεράω, aor.   pass through
  ἐξεπέρησε

ἐκπίνω, aor. ἔκπιον — drink out/off
ἐκφαίνω — in passive, appear
ἔκφημι, inf. ἐκφάσθαι — speak out
ἔλαιον, τό — olive-oil
*ἐλαύνω, aor. ἔλασα — drive, strike
ἔλαφος, ὁ — deer, stag
ἐλεαίρω — take pity on
ἐλεύσεαι — see ἔρχομαι
ἐμβαίνω — step on
ἔμπεδος -ον — firm, unimpaired
ἐμφύω, aor. w. tmesis ἔν . . . φῦ — clasp
*ἐναντίος -α -ον — opposite
ἔνδον — within, inside
*ἔνθα — then, there, where
ἐνί — in
ἐννέωρος — nine years old
ἐνοπή, ἡ — voice, noise
ἐξερέω — ask, inquire
ἐοικώς — seeming like
ἐπαΐσσω, aor. ἐπήϊξα — rush at
ἐπέρχομαι — come upon
ἐπιβαίνω, 1st p. aor. subj. ἐπιβείομεν — go upon
ἐπιτίθημι — lay out, put
ἐπιχέω — pour over
ἐποίχομαι — ply, go up and down in front of
ἕπομαι* — follow
ἔπος -εος, τό — word
ἔργνυμι, 3rd s. imperfect ἐέργνυ, 3rd pl plup. ἐέρχατο — confine, shut up
ἔργον, τό — work, deed
ἐρείδω — (in middle) prop oneself, lean on
ἐρίηρος -ον — faithful, trusty
ἐρικυδής -ές — glorious
ἕρκος -εος, τό — fence
Ἑρμείας, Ἑρμείαο, ὁ — Hermes
ἐρύω, aor. εἴρυσα — drag, draw, pull
*ἔρχομαι, 2nd s. fut. ἐλεύσεαι — come
ἐρῶ, fut. of εἴρω — say, speak, tell
*ἐσθίω, aor. inf. φαγέμεν — eat
ἐσθλός, ἐσθλός — good
ἔσθω, pres. inf. ἐσθέμεναι — eat
*ἑταῖρος, ὁ — comrade, companion
*ἕτερος -α -ον — one (of two)
ἐϋκνήμις — well-greaved, well-equipped with greaves
εὐνάω, aor. inf. pass. εὐνηθῆναι — have sexual intercourse with

εὐνή, ἡ — bed
ἐϋπλόκαμος — fair-tressed, with beautiful locks
εὑρίσκω, aor. εὑρον — find
Εὐρύλοχος, ὁ — Eurylochus
εὐρυόδεια — wide-wayed, wide-wandered
ἐϋστρεφής -ές — well-twisted
ζέω, 3rd s. aor. ζέσσεν — boil
ζόφος, ὁ — darkness
ἥβη, ἡ — youth
*ἡγέομαι — go before, lead the way
ἠδέ, correlative to ἠμέν — and
*ἡδύς, ἡδεῖα, ἡδύ — pleasant, sweet
ἠέλιος, ὁ — sun
ἦεν, imp. of εἰμί — be, be able
ἧμαι — sit
ἦμαρ -ατος, τό — day
ἦμος — when
ἠνοψ -οπος — gleaming
ἤπιος -α -ον — gentle, kind
ἠριγένεια — early-born, child of morning
ἦτορ, τό — heart
Ἠώς, Ἠοῦς, ἡ — Dawn
θάλαμος, ὁ — chamber, bedroom
*θάλασσα, ἡ — sea
θαλερός -ά -όν — thick, frequent
θᾶσσον — rather quickly
θαῦμα -ατος, τό — wonder, astonishment
*θεά, ἡ — goddess
*θεάομαι — gaze at
θέλγω, aor. inf. θέλξαι — enchant, bewitch
θέμενος — see τίθημι
θεοειδής -ές — godlike
*θεός, ὁ — god
θηρίον, τό — wild animal
θίς, θινός, ὁ — seashore
θνητός -ή -όν — mortal
θρῆνυς -υος, ὁ — footstool
θρίξ, τριχός, ἡ — hair
θρόνος, ὁ — chair
θρώσκω — leap, jump
θυμαρής -ές — delightful
θυμός, ὁ — soul, heart, temper
θυμοφθόρος -ον — soul-destroying
ἰαίνω — heat
ἰάλλω — stretch out, reach
ἰάχω — cry, shout
ἴδοιμι, ἴδον — see ὁράω
*ἱερός -ά -όν — divine, sacred

ἵζω, 3rd s. aor. εἷσεν — seat
*ἵημι, middle part. — wish to, desire
  ἱέμενος
ἱκνέομαι, fut. inf. — come
  ἵξεσθαι
ἱμερόεις — pleasurable
*ἴσος -η -ον — like
ἱστός, ὁ — loom

καθύπερθε — over, above
*κακός -ή -όν — bad, evil
*καλέω — call
καλλίονες, pl comp. — finer, more handsome
  of καλός
καλλιπλόκαμος — with beautiful locks
*καλός -ή -όν — fine, beautiful
κάματος, ὁ — toil, trouble
καπνός, ὁ — smoke
καρπαλίμως — swiftly
καρπός, ὁ — fruit
*κατά (in the phrase — in
  κατὰ φρένα καὶ
  κατὰ θυμόν)
καταδύω, fut. — go down, sink
  -δύσομαι
καταθέλγω — subdue by spells
κατακλάω — break, snap
κατακλίνω — lay down
καταλοφάδεια — on the neck
καταχέω — pour out, let flow, shed
κατήϊεν, imp. of — go down
  κάτειμι
κεδνός -ή -όν — trusty
κεῖσε — there
*κελεύω — order
κεράννυμι, aor. part. — mix
  κεράσασα
κερδίων -ον — more profitable, better
κευθμών -ῶνος, ὁ — sty
*κεφαλή, ἡ — head
κήδιστος -η -ον — dearest
κῆρ, τό — heart
Κίρκη, ἡ — Circe
κιρνάω, 3rd s. imp. — mix
  ἐκίρνα
κίω — go
κλαίω, imp. κλαῖον — weep, wail, lament
κλῆρος -ου, ὁ — lot, token used for
  drawing lots
κλισμός, ὁ — couch
κλύω, aor. imperative — listen, hear
  κέκλυτε
κνέφας, τό — darkness
κοῖλος -η -ον — hollow
κοιμάομαι — fall asleep
κολεόν, τό — sheath, scabbard

κομίζω* — take care of
κοναβίζω — resound, ring
κονία, ἡ — dust
κραδίη, ἡ — heart
κράνεια, ἡ — cornelian cherry
κράς, κρατός, ἡ — head
κρατερός -ά -όν — strong, stout, mighty
κρατερῶνυξ — strong-clawed
κρέας, τό — flesh
κρήνη, ἡ — spring, fountain
κρητήρ -ῆρος, ὁ — mixing bowl
κτείνω, aor. inf. — kill
  κτάμεναι
κυκάω — stir
κυκεών -ῶνος, ὁ — potion, posset
Κύκλωψ -ωπος, ὁ — Cyclops
κυνέη, ἡ — helmet
κύπελλον, τό — goblet
κύων, ὁ — dog

λᾶας, dat. pl λάεσσι — stone
Λαιστρυγών — Laestrygonian
λανθάνομαι — forget
λέβης -ητος, ὁ — basin
λείπω, aor. λίπον — leave
λέξο, imperative of — lie down
  λέγω
λεπτός -ή -όν — fine, delicate
λέων -οντος, ὁ — lion
λίγα — loudly, clearly
λιγέως — shrilly, loudly
λιμός -οῦ, ὁ — hunger
λίπα — richly
λίσσομαι — beg, pray
λῖτα (plural) — smooth linen cloths
λούω — wash
λύγος, ἡ — withy, twig
λυγρός -ά -όν — baneful, harmful
λύκος, ὁ — wolf
*λύομαι — get someone set free

μάκαρες, οἱ — the blessed ones, gods
*μακρός -ά -όν — long, tall, high
μεγαλήτωρ -ορος, — great-hearted
  ὁ, ἡ
μέγαρον, τό — large room, in plural
  house, palace
*μέγας, μεγάλη, μέγα — big
μέθυ, τό — wine
μείζονες, pl comp. of — bigger, taller
  μέγας
μείλιγμα -ατος, τό — soothing scrap
μειλίχιος -α -ον — gentle, soothing
μέλας, μέλαινα, — black
  μέλαν
μέλι, τό — honey

μελίφρων -ον	sweet to the mind, delicious	ὄλεθρος, ὁ	ruin, destruction, death
μέλος -εος, τό	limb	ὀλοφύρομαι	lament, wail, take pity on
μενεαίνω	desire earnestly	ὀλοφώιος -ον	deadly, destructive
μένος -εος, τό	force, strength	Ὄλυμπος, ὁ	(Mount) Olympus
μερμηρίζω, aor. μερμήριξα	be anxious, be in doubt	*ὄμνυμι, aor. inf. ὀμόσσαι	swear
*μέσος/μέσσος -η -ον	middle	ὀνομάζω	call by name
μηκάομαι, aor. part. μακών	shriek, bleat, moan	ὀξύς -εῖα -ύ	sharp, keen
μηρός, ὁ	thigh	ὀπάζω, aor. ὄπασσα	send with
μῆτις, ἡ	plan, wisdom, device	ὄπη	in which way, where
μίγνυμι, dual aor. pass. μιγέντε	in passive: have sexual intercourse with	ὄπισθεν*	behind
		ὁππότε	when
μιμνήσκομαι	call to mind, remember	*ὁράω, aor. εἶδον	see
μόρσιμος -ον	appointed by fate, destined	ὄργυια, ἡ	fathom
		ὀρέστερος -α -ον	of the mountains
μοῦνος	alone	*ὅρκος, ὁ	oath
μῦθος, ὁ	word	*ὁρμάω	in passive: rush at
μύρομαι	shed tears, bewail	ὄρχαμος, ὁ	leader, chief
μῶλυ, τό	moly	*ὅσος -η -ον	as great as
		ὄσσε, τώ	the (two) eyes
νεανίης -ου, ὁ	young man	οὐλόμενος -η -ον	accursed
νέμω	deal out, distribute	οὐρή, ἡ	tail
νεώτεροι, pl comp. of νέος	younger	*ὀφθαλμός, ὁ	eye
		ὄφρα	so that, in order that
νῆσος, ἡ	island	ὄψ, ὀπός, ἡ	voice
νηῦς, νηός, ἡ	ship		
νίζω, aor. part. middle νιψάμενοι, aor. inf. mid. νίψασθαι	wash the hands	πάγχυ	wholly, completely
		παιπαλόεις -εσσα -εν	rugged
		πάλλω	shake
νιψάμενοι	see νίζω	*παρά + gen	from beside
νίψασθαι	see νίζω	παρασταδόν	standing beside
νοέω	realize	παρατίθημι	place beside
νομός, ὁ	pasture	*πάρειμι	be present
νοστέω	come home, return	παρίστημι	place beside; in middle, stand beside
νοῦς, contracted form of νόος, ὁ	mind		
		πάρος	formerly, before
νώï (dual)	we	*πάσχω	suffer, endure, experience
νῶτα, τά (plural for singular)	back	πατρίς	of one's fathers
		*πείθομαι	trust
		πεῖσμα -ατος, τό	rope
ξεστός -ή -όν	polished (of stone or metal)	πέλω	come into existence, be
		πέλωρον, τό	prodigy, monster
*ξίφος -εος, τό	sword	πένθος -εος, τό	grief, sorrow
		πένομαι	toil, work
		περικαλλής -ές	very beautiful
*ὅδε, ἥδε, τόδε	this	περιμήκης	very long
*ὁδός, ἡ	road, path, way	περισαίνω	wag the tail around, fawn upon
ὀδούς -όντος, ὁ	tooth		
Ὀδυσσεύς -έως, ὁ	Odysseus	περίσκεπτος -ον	to be seen on all sides, visible from far away
οἴγω, aor. ὤϊξε	open		
*οἶδα	know	περιωπή, ἡ	place commanding a wide view
*οἶνος, ὁ	wine		
οἴομαι	think, suspect	πῆ	which way?
οἶος -η -ον	alone	πῆμα -ατος, τό	misery, calamity

πίθοντο, aor. of πείθομαι	obey	ῥέω	flow, fall, drop off
πίμπλημι	fill	ῥηγμίν -ῖνος, ἡ	shore
*πίνω, fut. πίομαι, aor. opt. πίοιμι	drink	ῥῆγος -εος, τό	rug, blanket
*πίπτω, aor. ἔπεσον	fall	ῥίζα -ης, ἡ	root
πλέκω, aor. ἔπλεξα	twine, make	ῥοδοδάκτυλος -ον	rosy-fingered
πλήσσω, aor. πλῆξα, perf. part. πεπληγυῖα	strike	ῥώψ, ῥωπός, ἡ	brushwood
πόθεν	whence?, where from?	σαίνω	wag the tail
πόθι	where?	σίαλος, ὁ	fat hog
*πόλις, ἡ	city	*σῖτος, ὁ	food
Πολίτης	Polites	σκοπιάζω	keep lookout
πολλόν	very much	σκοπιή, ἡ	rock
*πολύ	much	σμερδαλέος	terrible, fearful
πολύτροπος -ον	versatile, of many wiles	σπάω	pick
πολυφάρμακος -ον	knowing many drugs	στεφανόω	surround
πόντος, ὁ	sea	συνδέω, aor. συνέδησα	bind together
πορφύρεος -η -ον	purple	σῦς, συός, ὁ	pig, hog
πορφύρω	heave, surge, swirl	συφεόνδε	towards the sty
πόσις, ἡ	drink	συφεός, ὁ	pig-sty
ποταμόνδε	towards a river	*σχεδόν	near
*ποταμός, ὁ	river	*σώζω, fut. σαώσω	save, rescue
ποτής -ῆτος, ἡ	drink	ταμίη, ἡ	housekeeper
πότμος, ὁ	fate, destiny, lot	*τελευτάω	bring to pass, accomplish
πότνια, ἡ	lady, mistress, queen	τελέω, aor. τέλεσα	accomplish, fulfil
*πούς, ποδός, ὁ	foot	τέρπω, aor. τάρπην	delight, gladden
Πράμνειος	Pramnian	*τέσσαρες	four
πρῆξις -ιος, ἡ	result	τέταρτος -η -ον	fourth
*πρίν	before	τεύχω, neut. perf. part. τετυγμένα	make, make ready
προέμεν	see προίημι	τῇ	there!
πρόθυρον, τό	door	τῆος	meanwhile
προίημι, inf. προέμεν	send on	*τίθημι	put, place
προπάροιθε	before, in front of	τίπτε	why, tell me?
πρόπας -πασα -παν	with ἦμαρ: all day long	τιταίνω	pull out, lay out
προρέω	flow forth	τίφθ'	see τίπτε
προσαλείφω	rub	τοκεύς -έως, ὁ	parent
προσαυδάω	speak to	*τόξον, τό	bow
προσεῖπον, aor. προσέειπον	speak to	*τότε	then
		τράπεζα -ης, ἡ	table
προφράζω, aor. πρόφρασσα	tell, speak out	τρίπους -ποδος, ὁ	tripod, three-legged cauldron
πρόχοος, ἡ	jug	*τρίτος -η -ον	third
*πρῶτος -η -ον	first	τρίχες/τρίχας	see θρίξ
πτερόεις -εσσα -εν	winged	Τροίη, ἡ	Troy
πυκινός -ή -όν	close, compact, close-packed	τρύχω	wear out
		τυρός, ὁ	cheese
πυκνός -ή -όν	close, thick		
*πυνθάνομαι, aor. πυθόμην	perceive	*ὕδωρ, ὕδατος, τό	water
		*ὕλη, ἡ	forest, woodland
*πῦρ, τό	fire	ὑλήεις -εσσα -εν	wooded
πω	yet	ὑπένερθε	beneath, below
*πως	in any way	ὑπηνήτης -ου, ὁ	one that is just getting a beard
ῥάβδος, ἡ	rod, stick	ὑποδείδω	shrink in fear

ὑποδύομαι	plunge	*χαλεπός -ή -όν	difficult
ὑπομένω	remain behind	χάλκεος -είη -εον	of bronze
ὑποτρέχω, 3rd s. aor.	run in under	χαλκήρης -ες	fitted with bronze
ὑπέδραμε		χαλκός, ὁ	copper (cauldron)
ὑψίκερως	with high antlers	χαμαιεύνης	sleeping on the ground, wallowing
φαγέμεν	see ἐσθίω	χαρίεις, superlative	graceful, beautiful
φαεινός -ή -όν	shining, radiant	χαριεστάτη	
φαεσίμβροτος -ον	bringing light to mortals	χαρίζομαι	show favour or kindness
φαίδιμος -ον	shining, radiant, glorious	*χείρ, χειρός, ἡ	hand
*φαίνομαι	appear	χέρνιψ, ἡ	water for washing hands
φάρμακον, τό	drug		
φάσγανον, τό	sword	χθαμαλός -ή -όν	low-lying
*φέρω	carry	χθών, χθονός, ἡ	earth, land
*φημί, imp. ἐφάμην	speak	χιτών -ῶνος, ὁ	tunic
φθέγγομαι	speak, utter	χλαῖνα -ης, ἡ	cloak
*φίλος, ὁ	friend	χλωρός -ά -όν	yellow
φιλότης -ητος, ἡ	love	χρίω	anoint
φορέω, frequentative of φέρω	carry to and fro	χρύσεος -η -ον	golden
		χρυσόρραπις	with a wand of gold
φράζομαι	think upon	χῶρος, ὁ	place
φρήν, ἡ	midriff, mind		
φρονέω	think, ponder	*ὧδε	thus
φύσις, ἡ	nature	ὦκα	swiftly
φύω	plant, make grow	ὦμος, ὁ	shoulder
*φωνή, ἡ	voice	ὠτειλή, ἡ	wound

Text to *Odyssey* 9: 231–460

ἔνθα δὲ πῦρ κήαντες ἐθύσαμεν ἠδὲ καὶ αὐτοὶ
τυρῶν αἰνύμενοι φάγομεν, μένομέν τέ μιν ἔνδον
ἥμενοι, ἧος ἐπῆλθε νέμων. φέρε δ᾽ ὄβριμον ἄχθος
ὕλης ἀζαλέης, ἵνα οἱ ποτιδόρπιον εἴη,
ἔντοσθεν δ᾽ ἄντροιο βαλὼν ὀρυμαγδὸν ἔθηκεν·   235
ἡμεῖς δὲ δείσαντες ἀπεσσύμεθ᾽ ἐς μυχὸν ἄντρου.
αὐτὰρ ὅ γ᾽ εἰς εὐρὺ σπέος ἤλασε πίονα μῆλα,
πάντα μάλ᾽ ὅσσ᾽ ἤμελγε, τὰ δ᾽ ἄρσενα λεῖπε θύρηφιν,
ἀρνειούς τε τράγους τε, βαθείης ἔκτοθεν αὐλῆς.
αὐτὰρ ἔπειτ᾽ ἐπέθηκε θυρεὸν μέγαν ὑψόσ᾽ ἀείρας,   240
ὄβριμον· οὐκ ἂν τόν γε δύω καὶ εἴκοσ᾽ ἄμαξαι
ἐσθλαὶ τετράκυκλοι ἀπ᾽ οὔδεος ὀχλίσσειαν·
τόσσην ἠλίβατον πέτρην ἐπέθηκε θύρῃσιν.
ἑζόμενος δ᾽ ἤμελγεν ὄϊς καὶ μηκάδας αἶγας,
πάντα κατὰ μοῖραν, καὶ ὑπ᾽ ἔμβρυον ἧκεν ἑκάστῃ.   245
αὐτίκα δ᾽ ἥμισυ μὲν θρέψας λευκοῖο γάλακτος
πλεκτοῖς ἐν ταλάροισιν ἀμησάμενος κατέθηκεν,
ἥμισυ δ᾽ αὖτ᾽ ἔστησεν ἐν ἄγγεσιν, ὄφρα οἱ εἴη
πίνειν αἰνυμένῳ καί οἱ ποτιδόρπιον εἴη.
αὐτὰρ ἐπεὶ δὴ σπεῦσε πονησάμενος τὰ ἃ ἔργα,   250
καὶ τότε πῦρ ἀνέκαιε καὶ εἴσιδεν, εἴρετο δ᾽ ἡμέας·
   "ὦ ξεῖνοι, τίνες ἐστέ; πόθεν πλεῖθ᾽ ὑγρὰ κέλευθα;
ἦ τι κατὰ πρῆξιν ἦ μαψιδίως ἀλάλησθε
οἷά τε ληϊστῆρες, ὑπεὶρ ἅλα, τοί τ᾽ ἀλόωνται
ψυχὰς παρθέμενοι, κακὸν ἀλλοδαποῖσι φέροντες"   255
   ὣς ἔφαθ᾽, ἡμῖν δ᾽ αὖτε κατεκλάσθη φίλον ἦτορ
δεισάντων φθόγγον τε βαρὺν αὐτόν τε πέλωρον.
ἀλλὰ καὶ ὧς μιν ἔπεσσιν ἀμειβόμενος προσέειπον·
   "ἡμεῖς τοι Τροίηθεν ἀποπλαγχθέντες Ἀχαιοὶ
παντοίοις ἀνέμοισιν ὑπὲρ μέγα λαῖτμα θαλάσσης,   260

οἴκαδε ἱέμενοι, ἄλλην ὁδόν, ἄλλα κέλευθα
ἤλθομεν· οὕτω που Ζεὺς ἤθελε μητίσασθαι.
λαοὶ δ' Ἀτρεΐδεω Ἀγαμέμνονος εὐχόμεθ' εἶναι,
τοῦ δὴ νῦν γε μέγιστον ὑπουράνιον κλέος ἐστί·
τόσσην γὰρ διέπερσε πόλιν καὶ ἀπώλεσε λαοὺς   265
πολλούς· ἡμεῖς δ' αὖτε κιχανόμενοι τὰ σὰ γοῦνα
ἱκόμεθ', εἴ τι πόροις ξεινήϊον ἠὲ καὶ ἄλλως
δοίης δωτίνην, ἥ τε ξείνων θέμις ἐστίν.
ἀλλ' αἰδεῖο, φέριστε, θεούς· ἱκέται δέ τοί εἰμεν,
Ζεὺς δ' ἐπιτιμήτωρ ἱκετάων τε ξείνων τε,   270
ξείνιος, ὃς ξείνοισιν ἅμ' αἰδοίοισιν ὀπηδεῖ."
   ὣς ἐφάμην, ὁ δέ μ' αὐτίκ' ἀμείβετο νηλέϊ θυμῷ·
"νήπιός εἰς, ὦ ξεῖν', ἢ τηλόθεν εἰλήλουθας,
ὅς με θεοὺς κέλεαι ἢ δειδίμεν ἢ ἀλέασθαι·
οὐ γὰρ Κύκλωπες Διὸς αἰγιόχου ἀλέγουσιν   275
οὐδὲ θεῶν μακάρων, ἐπεὶ ἦ πολὺ φέρτεροί εἰμεν.
οὐδ' ἂν ἐγὼ Διὸς ἔχθος ἀλευάμενος πεφιδοίμην
οὔτε σεῦ οὔθ' ἑτάρων, εἰ μὴ θυμός με κελεύοι.
ἀλλά μοι εἴφ' ὅπη ἔσχες ἰὼν εὐεργέα νῆα,
ἤ που ἐπ' ἐσχατιῆς, ἢ καὶ σχεδόν, ὄφρα δαείω."   280
   "ὣς φάτο πειράζων, ἐμὲ δ' οὐ λάθεν εἰδότα πολλά,
ἀλλά μιν ἄψορρον προσέφην δολίοις ἐπέεσσι·
   "νέα μέν μοι κατέαξε Ποσειδάων ἐνοσίχθων,
πρὸς πέτρῃσι βαλὼν ὑμῆς ἐπὶ πείρασι γαίης,
ἄκρῃ προσπελάσας· ἄνεμος δ' ἐκ πόντου ἔνεικεν·   285
αὐτὰρ ἐγὼ σὺν τοῖσδε ὑπέκφυγον αἰπὺν ὄλεθρον."
   "ὣς ἐφάμην, ὁ δέ μ' οὐδὲν ἀμείβετο νηλέϊ θυμῷ,
ἀλλ' ὅ γ' ἀναΐξας ἑτάροις ἐπὶ χεῖρας ἴαλλε,
σὺν δὲ δύω μάρψας ὥς τε σκύλακας ποτὶ γαίῃ
κόπτ'· ἐκ δ' ἐγκέφαλος χαμάδις ῥέε, δεῦε δὲ γαῖαν.   290
ἤσθιε δ' ὥς τε λέων ὀρεσίτροφος, οὐδ' ἀπέλειπεν,
ἔγκατά τε σάρκας τε καὶ ὀστέα μυελόεντα.
ἡμεῖς δὲ κλαίοντες ἀνεσχέθομεν Διὶ χεῖρας,
σχέτλια ἔργ' ὁρόωντες· ἀμηχανίη δ' ἔχε θυμόν.   295
αὐτὰρ ἐπεὶ Κύκλωψ μεγάλην ἐμπλήσατο νηδὺν
ἀνδρόμεα κρέ' ἔδων καὶ ἐπ' ἄκρητον γάλα πίνων,
κεῖτ' ἔντοσθ' ἄντροιο τανυσσάμενος διὰ μήλων.
τὸν μὲν ἐγὼ βούλευσα κατὰ μεγαλήτορα θυμὸν
ἆσσον ἰών, ξίφος ὀξὺ ἐρυσσάμενος παρὰ μηροῦ,   300
οὐτάμεναι πρὸς στῆθος, ὅθι φρένες ἧπαρ ἔχουσι,

χεῖρ' ἐπιμασσάμενος· ἕτερος δέ με θυμὸς ἔρυκεν.
αὐτοῦ γάρ κε καὶ ἄμμες ἀπωλόμεθ' αἰπὺν ὄλεθρον·
οὐ γάρ κεν δυνάμεσθα θυράων ὑψηλάων
χερσὶν ἀπώσασθαι λίθον ὄβριμον, ὃν προσέθηκεν.   305
ὣς τότε μὲν στενάχοντες ἐμείναμεν Ἠῶ δῖαν.
    ἦμος δ' ἠριγένεια φάνη ῥοδοδάκτυλος Ἠώς,
καὶ τότε πῦρ ἀνέκαιε καὶ ἤμελγε κλυτὰ μῆλα,
πάντα κατὰ μοῖραν, καὶ ὑπ' ἔμβρυον ἧκεν ἑκάστῃ.
αὐτὰρ ἐπεὶ δὴ σπεῦσε πονησάμενος τὰ ἃ ἔργα,   310
σὺν δ' ὅ γε δὴ αὖτε δύω μάρψας ὁπλίσσατο δεῖπνον.
δειπνήσας δ' ἄντρου ἐξήλασε πίονα μῆλα,
ῥηϊδίως ἀφελὼν θυρεὸν μέγαν· αὐτὰρ ἔπειτα
ἂψ ἐπέθηχ', ὡς εἴ τε φαρέτρῃ πῶμ' ἐπιθείη.
πολλῇ δὲ ῥοίζῳ πρὸς ὄρος τρέπε πίονα μῆλα   315
Κύκλωψ· αὐτὰρ ἐγὼ λιπόμην κακὰ βυσσοδομεύων,
εἴ πως τισαίμην, δοίη δέ μοι εὖχος Ἀθήνη.
    "ἥδε δέ μοι κατὰ θυμὸν ἀρίστη φαίνετο βουλή.
Κύκλωπος γὰρ ἔκειτο μέγα ῥόπαλον παρὰ σηκῷ,
χλωρὸν ἐλαΐνεον· τὸ μὲν ἔκταμεν, ὄφρα φοροίη   320
αὐανθέν. τὸ μὲν ἄμμες ἐΐσκομεν εἰσορόωντες
ὅσσον θ' ἱστὸν νηὸς ἐεικοσόροιο μελαίνης,
φορτίδος εὐρείης, ἥ τ' ἐκπεράᾳ μέγα λαῖτμα·
τόσσον ἔην μῆκος, τόσσον πάχος εἰσοράασθαι.
τοῦ μὲν ὅσον τ' ὄργυιαν ἐγὼν ἀπέκοψα παραστὰς   325
καὶ παρέθηχ' ἑτάροισιν, ἀποξῦναι δ' ἐκέλευσα·
οἱ δ' ὁμαλὸν ποίησαν· ἐγὼ δ' ἐθόωσα παραστὰς
ἄκρον, ἄφαρ δὲ λαβὼν ἐπυράκτεον ἐν πυρὶ κηλέῳ.
καὶ τὸ μὲν εὖ κατέθηκα κατακρύψας ὑπὸ κόπρῳ,
ἥ ῥα κατὰ σπείους κέχυτο μεγάλ' ἤλιθα πολλή·   330
αὐτὰρ τοὺς ἄλλους κλήρῳ πεπαλάσθαι ἄνωγον,
ὅς τις τολμήσειεν ἐμοὶ σὺν μοχλὸν ἀείρας
τρῖψαι ἐν ὀφθαλμῷ, ὅτε τὸν γλυκὺς ὕπνος ἱκάνοι.
οἱ δ' ἔλαχον τοὺς ἄν κε καὶ ἤθελον αὐτὸς ἑλέσθαι,
τέσσαρες, αὐτὰρ ἐγὼ πέμπτος μετὰ τοῖσιν ἐλέγμην.   335
ἑσπέριος δ' ἦλθεν καλλίτριχα μῆλα νομεύων.
αὐτίκα δ' εἰς εὐρὺ σπέος ἤλασε πίονα μῆλα
πάντα μάλ', οὐδέ τι λεῖπε βαθείης ἔκτοθεν αὐλῆς,
ἤ τι ὀϊσάμενος, ἢ καὶ θεὸς ὣς ἐκέλευσεν.
αὐτὰρ ἔπειτ' ἐπέθηκε θυρεὸν μέγαν ὑψόσ' ἀείρας,   340
ἑζόμενος δ' ἤμελγεν ὄϊς καὶ μηκάδας αἶγας,

πάντα κατὰ μοῖραν, καὶ ὑπ' ἔμβρυον ἧκεν ἑκάστῃ.
αὐτὰρ ἐπεὶ δὴ σπεῦσε πονησάμενος τὰ ἃ ἔργα,
σὺν δ' ὅ γε δὴ αὖτε δύω μάρψας ὁπλίσσατο δόρπον.
καὶ τότ' ἐγὼ Κύκλωπα προσηύδων ἄγχι παραστάς,   345
κισσύβιον μετὰ χερσὶν ἔχων μέλανος οἴνοιο·

"Κύκλωψ, τῆ, πίε οἶνον, ἐπεὶ φάγες ἀνδρόμεα κρέα,
ὄφρα ἰδῇς οἷόν τι ποτὸν τόδε νηῦς ἐκεκεύθει
ἡμετέρη. σοὶ δ' αὖ λοιβὴν φέρον, εἴ μ' ἐλεήσας
οἴκαδε πέμψειας· σὺ δὲ μαίνεαι οὐκέτ' ἀνεκτῶς.   350
σχέτλιε, πῶς κέν τίς σε καὶ ὕστερον ἄλλος ἵκοιτο
ἀνθρώπων πολέων, ἐπεὶ οὐ κατὰ μοῖραν ἔρεξας."

"ὣς ἐφάμην, ὁ δὲ δέκτο καὶ ἔκπιεν· ἥσατο δ' αἰνῶς
ἡδὺ ποτὸν πίνων καί μ' ᾔτεε δεύτερον αὖτις·

"δός μοι ἔτι πρόφρων, καί μοι τεὸν οὔνομα εἰπὲ   355
αὐτίκα νῦν, ἵνα τοι δῶ ξείνιον, ᾧ κε σὺ χαίρῃς.
καὶ γὰρ Κυκλώπεσσι φέρει ζείδωρος ἄρουρα
οἶνον ἐρισταφύλον, καί σφιν Διὸς ὄμβρος ἀέξει·
ἀλλὰ τόδ' ἀμβροσίης καὶ νέκταρός ἐστιν ἀπορρώξ.'
"ὣς ἔφατ'· αὐτάρ οἱ αὖτις πόρον αἴθοπα οἶνον.   360
τρὶς μὲν ἔδωκα φέρων, τρὶς δ' ἔκπιεν ἀφραδίῃσιν.
αὐτὰρ ἐπεὶ Κύκλωπα περὶ φρένας ἤλυθεν οἶνος,
καὶ τότε δή μιν ἔπεσσι προσηύδων μειλιχίοισι·

"Κύκλωψ, εἰρωτᾷς μ' ὄνομα κλυτόν, αὐτὰρ ἐγώ τοι
ἐξερέω· σὺ δέ μοι δὸς ξείνιον, ὥς περ ὑπέστης.   365
Οὖτις ἐμοί γ' ὄνομα· Οὖτιν δέ με κικλήσκουσι
μήτηρ ἠδὲ πατὴρ ἠδ' ἄλλοι πάντες ἑταῖροι."

"ὣς ἐφάμην, ὁ δέ μ' αὐτίκ' ἀμείβετο νηλέϊ θυμῷ·
"Οὖτιν ἐγὼ πύματον ἔδομαι μετὰ οἷς ἑτάροισιν,
τοὺς δ' ἄλλους πρόσθεν· τὸ δέ τοι ξεινήϊον ἔσται."   370
ἦ καὶ ἀνακλινθεὶς πέσεν ὕπτιος, αὐτὰρ ἔπειτα
κεῖτ' ἀποδοχμώσας παχὺν αὐχένα, κὰδ δέ μιν ὕπνος
ᾕρει πανδαμάτωρ· φάρυγος δ' ἐξέσσυτο οἶνος
ψωμοί τ' ἀνδρόμεοι· ὁ δ' ἐρεύγετο οἰνοβαρείων.
καὶ τότ' ἐγὼ τὸν μοχλὸν ὑπὸ σποδοῦ ἤλασα πολλῆς,   375
ᾗος θερμαίνοιτο· ἔπεσσί τε πάντας ἑταίρους
θάρσυνον, μή τίς μοι ὑποδείσας ἀναδύη.
ἀλλ' ὅτε δὴ τάχ' ὁ μοχλὸς ἐλάϊνος ἐν πυρὶ μέλλεν
ἅψεσθαι, χλωρός περ ἐών, διεφαίνετο δ' αἰνῶς,
καὶ τότ' ἐγὼν ἄσσον φέρον ἐκ πυρός, ἀμφὶ δ' ἑταῖροι   380
ἵσταντ'· αὐτὰρ θάρσος ἐνέπνευσεν μέγα δαίμων.

οἱ μὲν μοχλὸν ἑλόντες ἐλάϊνον, ὀξὺν ἐπ’ ἄκρῳ,
ὀφθαλμῷ ἐνέρεισαν· ἐγὼ δ’ ἐφύπερθεν ἐρεισθεὶς
δίνεον, ὡς ὅτε τις τρυπᾷ δόρυ νήϊον ἀνὴρ
τρυπάνῳ, οἱ δέ τ’ ἔνερθεν ὑποσσείουσιν ἱμάντι   385
ἁψάμενοι ἑκάτερθε, τὸ δὲ τρέχει ἐμμενὲς αἰεί·
ὣς τοῦ ἐν ὀφθαλμῷ πυριήκεα μοχλὸν ἑλόντες
δινέομεν, τὸν δ’ αἷμα περίρρεε θερμὸν ἐόντα.
πάντα δέ οἱ βλέφαρ’ ἀμφὶ καὶ ὀφρύας εὗσεν ἀϋτμὴ
γλήνης καιομένης· σφαραγεῦντο δέ οἱ πυρὶ ῥίζαι.   390
ὡς δ’ ὅτ’ ἀνὴρ χαλκεὺς πέλεκυν μέγαν ἠὲ σκέπαρνον
εἰν ὕδατι ψυχρῷ βάπτῃ μεγάλα ἰάχοντα
φαρμάσσων· τὸ γὰρ αὖτε σιδήρου γε κράτος ἐστίν·
σμερδαλέον δὲ μέγ’ ᾤμωξεν, περὶ δ’ ἴαχε πέτρη,   395
ἡμεῖς δὲ δείσαντες ἀπεσσύμεθ’· αὐτὰρ ὁ μοχλὸν
ἐξέρυσ’ ὀφθαλμοῖο πεφυρμένον αἵματι πολλῷ.
τὸν μὲν ἔπειτ’ ἔρριψεν ἀπὸ ἕο χερσὶν ἀλύων,
αὐτὰρ ὁ Κύκλωπας μεγάλ’ ἤπυεν, οἵ ῥά μιν ἀμφὶς
ᾤκεον ἐν σπήεσσι δι’ ἄκριας ἠνεμοέσσας.   400
οἱ δὲ βοῆς ἀΐοντες ἐφοίτων ἄλλοθεν ἄλλος,
ἱστάμενοι δ’ εἴροντο περὶ σπέος ὅττι ἑ κήδοι·
    “τίπτε τόσον, Πολύφημ’, ἀρημένος ὧδ’ ἐβόησας
νύκτα δι’ ἀμβροσίην καὶ ἀΰπνους ἄμμε τίθησθα;
ἦ μή τίς σευ μῆλα βροτῶν ἀέκοντος ἐλαύνει;   405
ἦ μή τίς σ’ αὐτὸν κτείνει δόλῳ ἠὲ βίηφιν;”
    τοὺς δ’ αὖτ’ ἐξ ἄντρου προσέφη κρατερὸς Πολύφημος.
“ὦ φίλοι, Οὖτίς με κτείνει δόλῳ οὐδὲ βίηφιν.”
    “οἱ δ’ ἀπαμειβόμενοι ἔπεα πτερόεντ’ ἀγόρευον·
εἰ μὲν δὴ μή τίς σε βιάζεται οἶον ἐόντα,   410
νοῦσόν γ’ οὔ πως ἔστι Διὸς μεγάλου ἀλέασθαι,
ἀλλὰ σύ γ’ εὔχεο πατρὶ Ποσειδάωνι ἄνακτι.”
    ὣς ἄρ’ ἔφαν ἀπιόντες, ἐμὸν δ’ ἐγέλασσε φίλον κῆρ,
ὡς ὄνομ’ ἐξαπάτησεν ἐμὸν καὶ μῆτις ἀμύμων.
Κύκλωψ δὲ στενάχων τε καὶ ὠδίνων ὀδύνῃσι   415
χερσὶ ψηλαφόων, ἀπὸ μὲν λίθον εἷλε θυράων,
αὐτὸς δ’ εἰνὶ θύρῃσι καθέζετο χεῖρε πετάσσας,
εἴ τινά που μετ’ ὄεσσι λάβοι στείχοντα θύραζε·
οὕτω γάρ πού μ’ ἤλπετ’ ἐνὶ φρεσὶ νήπιον εἶναι.
αὐτὰρ ἐγὼ βούλευον, ὅπως ὄχ’ ἄριστα γένοιτο,   420
εἴ τιν’ ἑταίροισιν θανάτου λύσιν ἠδ’ ἐμοὶ αὐτῷ
εὑροίμην· πάντας δὲ δόλους καὶ μῆτιν ὕφαινον,

ὥς τε περὶ ψυχῆς· μέγα γὰρ κακὸν ἐγγύθεν ἦεν.
ἥδε δέ μοι κατὰ θυμὸν ἀρίστη φαίνετο βουλή.
ἄρσενες ὄϊες ἦσαν ἐϋτρεφέες, δασύμαλλοι,   425
καλοί τε μεγάλοι τε, ἰοδνεφὲς εἶρος ἔχοντες·
τοὺς ἀκέων συνέεργον ἐϋστρεφέεσσι λύγοισι,
τῆς ἔπι Κύκλωψ εὗδε πέλωρ, ἀθεμίστια εἰδώς,
σύντρεις αἰνύμενος· ὁ μὲν ἐν μέσῳ ἄνδρα φέρεσκε,
τὼ δ' ἑτέρω ἑκάτερθεν ἴτην σώοντες ἑταίρους.   430
τρεῖς δὲ ἕκαστον φῶτ' ὄϊες φέρον· αὐτὰρ ἐγώ γε,
ἀρνειὸς γὰρ ἔην, μήλων ὄχ' ἄριστος ἁπάντων,
τοῦ κατὰ νῶτα λαβών, λασίην ὑπὸ γαστέρ' ἐλυσθεὶς
κείμην· αὐτὰρ χερσὶν ἀώτου θεσπεσίοιο
νωλεμέως στρεφθεὶς ἐχόμην τετληότι θυμῷ.   435
ὣς τότε μὲν στενάχοντες ἐμείναμεν Ἠῶ δῖαν.
    ἦμος δ' ἠριγένεια φάνη ῥοδοδάκτυλος Ἠώς,
καὶ τότ' ἔπειτα νομόνδ' ἐξέσσυτο ἄρσενα μῆλα,
θήλειαι δ' ἐμέμηκον ἀνήμελκτοι περὶ σηκούς·
οὔθατα γὰρ σφαραγεῦντο. ἄναξ δ' ὀδύνῃσι κακῇσι   440
τειρόμενος πάντων ὀΐων ἐπεμαίετο νῶτα
ὀρθῶν ἑσταότων· τὸ δὲ νήπιος οὐκ ἐνόησεν,
ὥς οἱ ὑπ' εἰροπόκων ὀΐων στέρνοισι δέδεντο.
ὕστατος ἀρνειὸς μήλων ἔστιχε θύραζε
λάχνῳ στεινόμενος καὶ ἐμοὶ πυκινὰ φρονέοντι.   445
τὸν δ' ἐπιμασσάμενος προσέφη κρατερὸς Πολύφημος·
    "Κριὲ πέπον, τί μοι ὧδε διὰ σπέος ἔσσυο μήλων
ὕστατος; οὔ τι πάρος γε λελειμμένος ἔρχεαι οἰῶν,
ἀλλὰ πολὺ πρῶτος νέμεαι τέρεν' ἄνθεα ποίης
μακρὰ βιβάς, πρῶτος δὲ ῥοὰς ποταμῶν ἀφικάνεις,   450
πρῶτος δὲ σταθμόνδε λιλαίεαι ἀπονέεσθαι
ἑσπέριος· νῦν αὖτε πανύστατος. ἦ σὺ ἄνακτος
ὀφθαλμὸν ποθέεις, τὸν ἀνὴρ κακὸς ἐξαλάωσε
σὺν λυγροῖς ἑτάροισι δαμασσάμενος φρένα οἴνῳ,
Οὖτις, ὃν οὔ πώ φημι πεφυγμένον ἔμμεν ὄλεθρον.   455
εἰ δὴ ὁμοφρονέοις ποτιφωνήεις τε γένοιο
εἰπεῖν ὅππῃ κεῖνος ἐμὸν μένος ἠλασκάζει·
τῷ κέ οἱ ἐγκέφαλός γε διὰ σπέος ἄλλυδις ἄλλῃ
θεινομένου ῥαίοιτο πρὸς οὔδεϊ, κὰδ δέ κ' ἐμὸν κῆρ
λωφήσειε κακῶν, τά μοι οὐτιδανὸς πόρεν Οὖτις."   460

Commentary Notes

Odyssey 9

231–3

Odysseus relates how, on reaching the Cyclops' cave, he and his companions help themselves to his cheese while they await his return. This may strike modern readers as an imprudent act of theft, but it is fully in accord with the ancient Greek customs of hospitality, or *xenia* (see Introduction p. 000). *Xenia* is a running theme of the *Odyssey* as a whole and lies at the heart of the Cyclops episode, which is set in motion by Polyphemus' violation of these customs. It is worth remembering, lastly, that Odysseus is relating the episode at the court of the Phaeacians, who have shown themselves to be paragons of *xenia*, so Odysseus may be playing to his audience to a degree.

231

κήαντες: a participle from ἔκηα, the Homeric aorist of καίω 'I kindle, light'.

ἐθύσαμεν: in mentioning the sacrifice, Odysseus sets up a contrast with the godless Polyphemus, who will show no heed to the gods. Presumably the offering is of cheese found in the cave.

ἠδὲ καὶ αὐτοί: 'and we ourselves also'.

232

τυρῶν αἰνύμενοι: αἴνυμαι 'I take' is followed by a partitive genitive. Being a large group, the men require several units of cheese to feed themselves, hence the plural τυρῶν.

φάγομεν, μένομέν τε: respectively an aorist from ἐσθίω and an imperfect from μένω. In both cases the augment is omitted, a common feature of Homeric Greek.

μιν: 'him', an accusative singular third person pronoun (see Introduction, p. 000). The word designates the yet unnamed occupant of the cave, whom the Greeks are yet to meet.

233

ἧος: the Homeric form of ἕως, here meaning 'until'.

νέμων: 'herding his flocks'.

233–5

The Cyclops returns with some dry wood for his fire. Odysseus, as narrator, seizes the opportunity for illustrating the strength of his host: the wood is a 'mighty burden' (ὄβριμον ἄχθος) that makes a huge roar (ὀρυμαγδὸν) when placed down.

234

ἀζαλέης: the Ionic dialect, which forms the basis of Homeric Greek, does not change η to α after ε, ι or ρ as Attic does, but retains the η.

ἵνα οἱ ποτιδόρπιον εἴη: 'so that it would be there for him at supper-time'.

οἱ is a dative third person singular pronoun, 'for him' (see Introduction, p. 000).

ποτιδόρπιον: literally 'for supper', an adjective agreeing here with ἄχθος (233).

235

ἄντροιο: genitive, after ἔντοσθεν. In Homer, the genitive singular of the second declension can end either in -ου (as in Attic) or in -οιο.

ὀρυμαγδὸν: a striking choice of word, most commonly used of the din made by a mass of people (such as forces in battle or men at work) or force of nature (such as the sea or a river). Used here of the noise from just one arm-load of wood falling to the floor, the word hints at the extraordinary strength of the giant.

236

Odysseus runs and hides along with his men. Polyphemus' appearance or manner of arrival has disabused Odysseus of his hope that the giant will offer some *xenia* (9.229) and confirmed their suspicion that he will be a man 'ignorant of laws and customs' (9.215). Odysseus will now appeal to Polyphemus for *xenia* only once their escape is cut off and he has spotted them.

ἐς = Attic εἰς, 'into'. Both forms are used in Homer, depending on the requirements of the metre.

237

αὐτὰρ: although strictly meaning 'but, however', the word is often used to give the next step in a quick succession of events ('and (then)'), with no contrast implied.

ὅ: 'he'. In Homer, what looks like the definite article is usually a pronoun, either a relative or (as here) a demonstrative, depending on context.

γ': in Homer, γε and several other particles (ἄρα, ῥα, δή, τε) often serve only to fill out the metre or (as here) to avoid a hiatus. In such cases they are best left untranslated.

238

πάντα μάλ᾽ ὅσσ᾽ ἤμελγε: 'all those he was in the habit of milking'. μάλα is often used in Homer to intensify πᾶς ('every single one').

ὅσσ᾽ = ὅσ(α). In Homer, ὅσος and τόσος (= Attic τοσοῦτος) can occur with either a single or double -σ-.

ἀρνειούς τε τράγους τε: 'the rams and the goats', explaining τὰ δ᾽ ἄρσενα in the preceding line.

238–9

Odysseus may have told us that the Cyclopes have no regard for laws or each other (9.106–15), but Polyphemus is happy to leave the males of his flocks outside at night, with no fear of their being driven off by thieves. See also on 401–12 for further indication that Odysseus has exaggerated his first description of the Cyclopes.

θύρηφιν: 'outdoors', an adverb but originally a dative of place, formed with the Homeric dative ending -φι(ν) (for the origin of which see on 406).

239

ἔκτοθεν αὐλῆς: 'outside in the courtyard' (adverb, then genitive of place), rather than 'outside the courtyard' (preposition with genitive), which would leave the rams and goats free to roam the island.

βαθείης: usually 'deep' but also 'high', as here. The courtyard presumably has a high fence or wall.

240–3

Polyphemus closes up his cave with an enormous (μέγαν, ὄβριμον, ἠλίβατον) rock. Adding to his picture of the Cyclops' strength, Odysseus tells us that not even twenty-two wagons could shift the rock. The most important consequence, however, is left implicit: the small band of men is now trapped in the cave.

240

θυρεόν: 'door-stone'. We are not told where exactly Polyphemus places the stone, but can assume that as a door-stone, its purpose is to block the entrance to the cave.

ὑψόσ': 'on high'. Polyphemus has no need to raise the stone so high, but the detail gives the audience an early clue as to the immense strength of the giant, who does not even struggle to move it.

ἀείρας: aorist participle of ἀείρω, the Homeric form of αἴρω 'I lift'.

241–2

In the *Iliad*, the Trojan prince Hector throws a stone that two of today's men could barely have lifted onto one wagon. The comparison here is an exaggerated example of the same type. It is not clear how twenty-two wagons could share the burden of a single stone, unless simply dragging it with cables from its point of rest.

τόν: best taken as a personal pronoun 'it', with a new sentence beginning after ὄβριμον.

οὐκ ἂν ... ὀχλίσσειαν: apodosis of a future remote conditional ('they would not (be able to) raise it') with the protasis ('if'-clause) left implicit ('if they were to try'). The use of a future, rather than a past closed, conditional lends vividness and reminds those familiar with the story that, at the time of telling, the rock is still there and in use.

οὔδεος: genitive singular of (τὸ) οὖδας 'ground'. In Attic we might expect a contracted form *οὔδους. Homer, however, very frequently uses uncontracted forms of words with contract vowels or inserts an extra short vowel artificially before a long one, for the sake of the metre. The name for both practices is diectasis: see Introduction p. 000.

ὀχλίσσειαν: third plural aorist optative of ὀχλίζω 'I heave up', with the -σ- doubled for the sake of the metre.

243

τόσσην = Attic τοσαύτην: see on 238.

244–5

These lines recur with minimal variation at 308–9 and identically at 341–2. Repetition is an inevitable feature of any text which, like the Homeric epics, derives from an oral tradition (see Introduction p. 000). However, these and other repetitions will build up an impression of the Cyclops as a creature of habit.

244

ἤμελγεν: imperfect, 'began to milk'.
ὄϊς: an irregular accusative plural.

245

πάντα κατὰ μοῖραν: 'each one in its due turn'. Surprisingly, the masculine πάντα is used, owing perhaps to the use of both ὄϊς and αἴξ as either feminine or masculine. For a contrasting use of the phrase κατὰ μοῖραν ('as is proper'), see on 352.

ὑπ' . . . ἧκεν: 'he placed (a lamb) under (each)', from ὑφίημι 'I place under'. This is an example of tmesis, the separating of a prefix from the rest of a verb by another intervening word. Polyphemus is placing the lambs under the ewes to allow them to suckle.

246

θρέψας: aorist participle of τρέφω, used here in the technical sense 'curdle, thicken'. Polyphemus is presumably using an agent such as fig juice, as the process is clearly a quick one.

247

After gathering up (ἀμησάμενος) the solid curds, Polyphemus places them in woven baskets (πλεκτοῖς ἐν ταλάροισιν), presumably to drain off excess liquid whey.

248–9

ὄφρα οἱ εἴη | πίνειν αἰνυμένῳ: 'so that it would be there for him to take and drink'. In Homer, ὄφρα is often used to introduce a purpose clause.

250

'When he had finished busying about these tasks of his' (Hammond's Duckworth translation (2000)). This is another repeated line (310, 343) adding to the impression of Polyphemus as a creature of habit.

δή: see on 237. In Homer, the particle often comes at the start of a temporal or conditional clause.

σπεῦσε: 'had pressed on with', an augmentless aorist of σπεύδω. The tense brings the implication that he has completed his tasks.

τὰ ἃ ἔργα: 'these tasks of his'. τὰ is a demonstrative, not an article (see on 237). ἃ is a neuter accusative plural of the third person possessive adjective ὅς (also ἕος), a 2-1-2 adjective.

251

The sudden discovery of the Greeks is relayed in a single, heart-stopping line. Odysseus had told us that Polyphemus' wood was to be burnt at supper-time (234). We are left to deduce for ourselves that, as the fire is now lit, the giant's thoughts must be on his next meal.

καὶ τότε: cannot be translated here, but throws a spotlight on what follows as a crucial event.

ἡμέας = Attic ἡμᾶς, with diectasis.

252–5

Polyphemus asks the men who they are and whether they are pirates. The questions, though blunt, are not themselves a mark of poor hospitality: the friendly and welcoming Nestor utters the very same lines to Telemachus at 3.71–4. The difference is that Nestor first offers his guests some refreshment and justifies his enquiry, while the Cyclops merely dives in, a first sign of his scorn for *xenia*.

252

ξεῖνοι = Attic ξένοι, a wonderfully ambiguous term of address, leaving it unclear whether Polyphemus sees them as his guests or merely strangers.

πλεῖθ': more sinister ambiguity, as πλεῖτε could be either a present (suggesting that their travels will continue) or an augmentless imperfect (suggesting they are now over).

253

ἦ: can introduce a closed question (much like ἄρα) or, if repeated, a question with several alternatives.

τι ... ἀλάλησθε: 'have you been off on some wanderings?' The verb is a perfect from ἀλάομαι 'I wander, roam'.

κατὰ πρῆξιν: 'on business'. πρῆξις is the Ionic equivalent of Attic πρᾶξις.

254

οἷά τε: 'just as', a special use of the neuter plural of οἷος.

ὑπεὶρ = ὑπὲρ, with the second syllable artificially lengthened for metrical convenience.

τοί: relative pronoun, nominative masculine plural.

ἀλόωνται: a diectasis from ἀλάομαι 'I wander' (see Introduction, p. 000).

255

παρθέμενοι: aorist middle participle from παρα-τίθημι, with shortening of the prefix (a feature called apocope). The verb, like its English counterpart 'I put at stake', is a metaphor from gambling.

256

ἔφαθ᾽ = ἔφατο. In past tenses, Homeric Greek uses the middle of φημί as well as the active, with identical meaning.

ἡμῖν ... ἦτορ: 'our heart(s)': the pronoun is a possessive dative. ἦτορ must be read as a singular-for-plural noun, as required by δεισάντων in the following line.

κατεκλάσθη: aorist passive of κατακλάω, 'I break, crush', a striking metaphor used elsewhere for the feeling on receipt of bad news. Here, however, the tone and stature of Polyphemus are enough to elicit the response.

257

δεισάντων: aorist participle from δείδω 'I fear'. The word introduces an explanatory genitive absolute ('since we were afraid of'), despite ἡμῖν in the previous line.

φθόγγον τε βαρὺν αὐτόν τε πέλωρον: '(fearing) his deep voice and the monster himself'. This is the first detail Odysseus has offered about the Cyclops' appearance, and it is a vague one. Odysseus' Phaeacian audience are familiar enough already with the Cyclopes, their former neighbours (6.5), so do not need to hear a description. From our perspective as readers, however, the suppression of detail is a powerful narrative tool, leaving the giant's horrifying form entirely to his audience's imagination. It is nonetheless surprising that we are never told that the Cyclops has only one eye, when that detail is so essential to the story.

258–71

In a long reply, Odysseus answers the Cyclops' first question ('Who are you?') very generally, describing in brief their journey from Troy at the behest of Agamemnon, but without revealing his own name or origin. The decision is a fortunate one: As Odysseus will later discover, Polyphemus had received a prophecy that someone with his name would one day come and blind him (9.506–11). Despite his claims of fear (256–7), Odysseus strives to present himself as a brave hero, rather than appeal to his host's pity, as he does with Nausicaa in Book 6. The latter had asked whether his travels were commercial or piratical, and Odysseus' response seems calculated to make the Trojan War sound like little more than an act of piracy. Odysseus ends by asking his host to respect the conventions of *xenia*, out of respect for Zeus, the protector of strangers.

258

ἀλλὰ καὶ ὥς: 'but even so'.

ἔπεσσιν: dative plural of ἔπος. In Homer, the dative plural ending of the third declension often has a doubled -σ-.

259–62

In contrast with the Cyclops' punchy opening questions (252), Odysseus' first sentence, with the main verb delayed to the fourth line, is long-winded and convoluted, capturing the frightened hero's lack of composure. The heavy spondees of the opening line (259) also lend a sense of a nervous speaker still gathering his courage.

259

ἀποπλαγχθέντες: 'having been led off course', aorist passive participle from ἀποπλάζω.

260

παντοίοις ἀνέμοισιν: 'by all manner of winds'. In Homer, the dative plural of the second declension can end either in -οις or in -οισι(ν).

261

οἴκαδε ἱέμενοι: 'longing (to go) home'. ἵεμαι, when used in the sense 'I yearn', is usually followed by a genitive or infinitive but here 'to go' is left implicit.

261–2

ἄλλην ὁδὸν, ἄλλα κέλευθα ... ἤλθομεν: 'we have come by another way, by other routes', a rather euphemistic way of putting that they are lost. Aside from his decision not to share his name, origin and ancestry, Odysseus is trying to impress the Cyclops, presenting himself in the best possible light.

262

Odysseus supposes that he and his men have come to the island by the will of Zeus. This is a clever detail to mention, as it gives Polyphemus all the more reason to offer his guests proper *xenia*, of which Zeus is the patron deity (270). Characters in Homer are generally shown to assume that Zeus has a grand plan for mortals, so Polyphemus is likely to believe the claim.

263

Ἀτρεΐδεω: 'of the son of Atreus'. In Homer, the genitive singular of first declension masculine nouns end in -εω (read as a single syllable) or -αο. Patronymics ('son of X') are commonplace in Homer and tend to be formed with the first declension suffix -ίδης.

264

τοῦ: a relative pronoun (see on 237).

ὑπουράνιον: Odysseus is careful to qualify Agamemnon's glory as the greatest 'under heaven'. He may hope to set an example to Polyphemus by showing due acknowledgement of the gods as the superiors of mortals.

265–6

Again the self-praise is exemplarily free of arrogance. Odysseus is proud to have been part of Agamemnon's force (εὐχόμεθ᾽ εἶναι, 263) but resists using first person verbs in naming the Greeks' achievements at Troy. Perhaps picking up on the violent nature of his host, Odysseus' focus is on the killing he himself has contributed towards.

τόσσην ... πόλιν: for the pronoun see on 238. Odysseus stresses the greatness of the captured city, responding, we might imagine, to an unimpressed reaction from the Cyclops at the naming of the city at 259.

διέπερσε: 'he thoroughly laid waste to', aorist of διαπέρθω. The prefix δια- lends an intensifying force to the verb.

266

κιχανόμενοι: 'on reaching (here)', present middle participle, but with active sense, from κιχάνω.

266–7

τὰ σὰ γοῦνα | ἱκόμεθ': 'we come to your knees as suppliants'. ἱκνέομαι (from which we have the common compound ἀφικνέομαι 'I arrive'), is used in a special sense for the approach of suppliants, or ἱκέται (269: a cognate noun). Supplication, in which a prospective guest grasps the knees of his host in a gesture of submission, marks the beginning of many instances of *xenia* in the *Odyssey*.

267

εἴ ... πόροις: 'in case you may give (us)'. A conditional clause (often with πως 'somehow': compare 10.147) can be used to express the motive for an action. πόροις is an aorist optative from a verb with no attested present.
ξεινήϊον: a token of friendship, given in recognition of *xenia*.

267–8

ἠὲ καὶ ἄλλως | δοίης δωτίνην: 'or even give us a gift of some other sort'. Perhaps again we are to imagine these words as a response to an expression of incomprehension on the face of the unwelcoming Cyclops. This could also account for the following explanation of the custom (ἥ τε ξείνων θέμις ἐστίν).
ἠὲ = ἤ 'or', with diectasis.

268

The run of spondees hint at an understandable hesitation: Odysseus has so far received scant sign of *xenia* from the giant, and must realize that the request of a gift is a bold move.
Δοίης: is a second singular aorist optative active from δίδωμι 'I give'.

269

αἰδεῖο: second singular present imperative from αἰδέομαι 'I show respect towards'. The form combines the common Homeric diectasis of the imperative ending -ου to -εο with a contraction of αἰδε-εο to αἰδεῖο.
φέριστε: 'most excellent fellow', a vocative of an irregular superlative, found elsewhere as φέρτατος. The adjective has a comparative φέρτερος (276) but no positive degree.
δέ: used here instead of the more logical γάρ, which would not scan.
τοὶ = Attic σοί.

270–1

As suppliants and ξεῖνοι, the Greeks are under the protection of 'Zeus *xenios*', the title assigned him as patron of supplication and *xenia*. Note the emphatic placement of each part of this title at the start of the line.

272–80

The Cyclops replies with arrogant scorn for both guest and gods. This show of arrogant scorn towards both begins a sequence of events leading to Polyphemus' blinding, prefiguring tragedy's common narrative pattern of hubris leading to a downfall. Note the run of four lines all beginning with a negative (275–9), underscoring the Cyclops' hostility to Odysseus' suggestion.

272

ἐφάμην: see on 256.

νηλέϊ θυμῷ: 'with a ruthless heart', a so-called dative of accompanying circumstance.

273

ὦ ξεῖν': see on 252. The address is surely designed to mock Odysseus, whose speech has made full rhetorical use of the vocabulary of *xenia*.

εἰλήλουθας: Homeric alternative to ἐλήλυθας, a perfect from ἔρχομαι.

274

A relative clause, but with conditional force ('You're a fool if . . .').

κέλεαι: second person singular of κέλομαι 'I order'. Instead of the second person singular middle ending -η, Homer generally has a diectasis -εαι.

δειδίμεν: active infinitive from δείδω 'I fear'. In Homer the infinitive endings -(ε)μεν and -(ε)μεναι are used alongside those familiar from Attic.

ἀλέασθαι: aorist infinitive from ἀλέομαι 'I avoid', a strange verb for Polyphemus to use, as Odysseus had not told him to 'avoid' the gods. Presumably he means something along the lines of 'to avoid incurring the wrath of the gods', as suggested by the verb's use at 411.

275–6

According to Polyphemus, the Cyclopes give no thought to Zeus or the other gods, whom he deems their inferiors. These words will later be shown to be no more than braggadocio (see on 410–12).

275

Κύκλωπες: it is only at this point that the Greeks learn the name of the race to which the giant belongs. Meaning 'circle-eyed', the name would immediately strike them as appropriate, even though we are never explicitly told that they have only one eye.

αἰγιόχου: 'aegis-bearing' a recurrent epithet of Zeus. In Homer, both Zeus and Athena are said to carry an αἰγίς, the true nature of which is unclear. In some ancient representations it is a shield, in others a piece of clothing made of animal skin. In the *Iliad*, the sight of Athene's aegis spreads terror among men, and accordingly some representations show on it an image of the Gorgon's head.

276

ἐπεὶ ἦ πολὺ φέρτεροί εἰμεν: 'since we are far better, for sure'. In no Greek myth does such arrogance end well for the boaster. ἦ ('certainly') and πολὺ (adverbial, 'by far') drive home the extent of this arrogance.

εἰμεν = Attic ἐσμεν.

277

ἀλευάμενος: aorist participle from ἀλέομαι 'I avoid'.

πεφιδοίμην: aorist optative from φείδομαι 'I shrink from'. In Homer, the aorist stem of this verb (πεφιδ-) includes a reduplication.

278

σεῦ = σοῦ.

ἑτάρων = ἑταίρων. Both forms are used in Homer, depending on the requirements of the metre.

279

ἰών: 'on coming (here)'.

εἴφ' = εἶπε, with elision and assimilation before a rough breathing.

280

που: 'somewhere'.

δαείω: aorist subjunctive from the verb ἐδάην 'I learned', for which there is no attested present. In Homer, when a first person singular active subjunctive is formed on stems ending in -η-, the -η- tends to change to -ει-.

281

πειράζων: 'trying it on'.

εἰδότα πολλά: causal, 'on account of my great wisdom' (literally 'knowing many things'). Odysseus is surely overstating the level of intelligence required in detecting the Cyclops' ruse. He may be trying to restore the good opinion of his audience after the ill-advised decision to visit the Cyclops (against the better judgement of his men), a mistake he places tellingly little emphasis on.

282

ἄψορρον: adverbial, 'in reply'.

ἐπέεσσι: dative plural of ἔπος. The doubling of the ε (by diectasis) is for metrical reasons. On the double σ see on 258.

283–93

Odysseus tries to persuade the Cyclops that he and his men are the sole survivors from a shipwreck on the edge of the island. Whether the Cyclops believes him is left unclear. At any rate, he responds by devouring two of Odysseus' crew, spiting his claim to have 'escaped sheer destruction along with these men' (286).

283

νέα: an alternate accusative singular of ναῦς (compare Attic ναῦν).

μοι: possessive dative.

κατέαξε: aorist from κατάγνυμι, 'I break'.

284

πρὸς ... βαλών: aorist participle with tmesis, from προσβάλλω 'I dash (*accusative*) against (*dative*)'.

ὑμῆς: feminine genitive singular of ὑμός, an epic alternative to ὑμέτερος.

285

ἔνεικεν = Attic ἤνεγκεν, from φέρω.

286

αἰπὺν: 'sheer', high', a widespread but evocative metaphor, 'death being regarded as the plunge from a high precipice' (Liddell, Scott and Jones).

288–91

The horrifying suddenness of the men's murder is conveyed in a rush of verbs and participles. The numerous verbs in tmesis (ἐπὶ . . . ἴαλλε, σὺν . . . μάρψας, ἐκ . . . ῥέε, διὰ . . . ταμών and perhaps also ποτὶ . . . κόπτ᾽) are striking, and capture some of the confusion of the scene.

289–90

The brutality is underscored by the hard alliteration of velar consonants (κ, χ, γ).

289

ὥς τε σκύλακας: 'like puppies', the crucial points of comparison being their helplessness and the fragility of their bodies. The simile casts an unheroic light upon the death of the unnamed men.

τε: in epic often occurs at the beginning of similes, in which cases it need not be translated.

289–90

ποτὶ γαίῃ | κόπτ᾽: 'smashed upon the ground'. The single enjambed syllable is given fitting emphasis. ποτί (= πρός) is originally from the Doric dialect, but became a staple of epic diction.

291

The same line recurs at 311 and 344.

ἐκ . . . ῥέε = ἐξερρεῖ 'flowed out', in tmesis, with diectasis and no augment.

τούς: demonstrative, 'them' (see on 237).

διὰ . . . ταμών: aorist participle of διατέμνω 'I cut in two', an especially appropriate candidate for tmesis.

292

ἤσθιε: imperfect, 'began to eat': the Cyclops takes his time over the meal, and wastes none of the meat (293).

294

ἀνεσχέθομεν: 'we held up', an alternative Homeric aorist from ἀνέχω.

295

σχέτλια ἔργ᾽ ὁρόωντες: 'on seeing his merciless deeds'. For the adjective, see below on 351. ὁρόωντες = ὁρῶντες 'seeing', with diectasis.

ἀμηχανίη δ᾽ ἔχε θυμόν: 'and a sense of helplessness took hold of our heart(s)'.

296–306

After his meal, the Cyclops lies down to sleep among his flocks. In true heroic fashion, Odysseus' first urge is to strike the sleeping giant. He then realizes, however, that they need him to remove the door-stone before they can escape.

296

Κύκλωψ: it is only from the point in the story where Odysseus the character first hears the term Κύκλωψ that Odysseus the narrator starts using it himself. This seems deliberate: Odysseus will do the same with the Cyclops' name, Polyphemus (see on 403). This withholding of information helps his audience, who learn it only at the point at which he did, put themselves in his shoes.

297

κρέ᾽ = κρέα, accusative plural from τὸ κρέας '(piece of) meat'.

ἐπ᾽ . . . πίνων: in tmesis, from ἐπιπίνω 'I drink after eating'.

ἄκρητον γάλα: 'milk unmixed (with water)'. There is evidence that Greeks would drink milk diluted, which would make the Cyclops' behaviour seem even more alien.

299–301

'I planned in my great heart . . . to wound him . . .' The word-order is complicated by the promotion of τὸν (him) and delay of οὐτάμεναι 'to wound' into emphatic positions at the start of lines, and to reflect the sequence of imagined events.

μεγαλήτορα θυμὸν: 'great(-hearted) heart', a recurrent Homeric formula (see Introduction, p. 000). Though usually translated as 'heart', θυμός can denote both the faculty of reason and the seat of the emotions.

οὐτάμεναι: infinitive of οὐτάω 'I wound, strike'. See on 274.

πρὸς: best translated here with 'in'.

ὅθι φρένες ἧπαρ ἔχουσι: 'where the midriff holds liver'. The φρένες, also seen as seat of the emotions and intellect, are the parts of the body directly above the waist.

302

ἕτερος δέ με θυμὸς ἔρυκεν: 'but a second thought held me back'. Odysseus' change of mind is mirrored in the strong pause before this phrase, with the final syllable of ἐπιμασσάμενος lengthened artificially before the caesura.

χεῖρ᾽ ἐπιμασσάμενος: 'after feeling it out with my hand' (χεῖρ᾽ = dative χειρί).

303–5

These lines have the form of a past remote conditional, but with the protasis omitted (see on 241–2). **κε** and **κεν** are commonly used in Homer as equivalents of ἄν.

303

ἄμμες = ἡμεῖς, borrowed into the epic lexicon from the Aeolic dialect.

αὐτοῦ: 'there' (adverb).

αἰπὺν ὄλεθρον: an internal (or cognate) accusative, '(we would have died) a total death'.

304

δυνάμεσθα = ἐδυνάμεθα. The first person plural ending -(ό)μεσθα is commonplace.

305

ἀπώσασθαι: aorist infinitive middle from ἀπωθέω 'I push aside'.

306

The line is a slight, but sinister, variation on a recurrent formula, used as recently as 9.151: 'and then, having fallen asleep (ἀποβρίξαντες), we awaited the holy Dawn' (see Introduction, p. 000). Line 306 recurs, with increased pathos, at 436.

Ἠῶ δῖαν: 'divine Dawn' (accusative).

308–9
See on 244–5.

310
See on 250.

311

The echoes of earlier lines in 308–10 have established a sense of routine in the Cyclops' actions. 311 is also made up of familiar components, borrowing half-lines from 289 and 291, lending a grim sense that eating men is becoming part of that routine. Though we are spared the gory detail of the previous passage, the brevity and matter-of-factness of this second description of death are equally unnerving.

312

δειπνήσας: 'after he had had his meal', as striking a euphemism for the murder as the English phrase.

313

ῥηϊδίως = ῥαδίως, 'easily', a galling detail in light of Odysseus' reflections at 304–5.

314

ἂψ ἐπέθηχ': 'he put it back in place again'. ἐπέθηκε, here elided with assimilation before a rough breathing, is an aorist from ἐπιτίθημι 'I put upon'. The pause after αὐτὰρ ἔπειτα ('but then . . .') at the end of the previous line creates a touch of suspense before this galling detail.

ὡς εἴ τε φαρέτρῃ πῶμ' ἐπιθείη: '(as easily) as if he had put a lid (πῶμα) on a quiver'. The point of comparison is made more obvious in the Greek through the polyptoton of ἐπιτίθημι 'I put upon' (here in the aorist optative), which can be used both of lids and the closing up of doors.

315

πολλῇ δὲ ῥοίζῳ: 'with much whistling', an instrumental dative. The spondaic opening of the line is fitting for the drawn-out sound it describes.

316

κακὰ βυσσοδομεύων: 'brooding dark designs'.

317

εἴ πως: 'in case somehow': see on 267.

τισαίμην: aorist optative middle from τίνω, which in the middle has the special
  sense 'I take vengeance'.

δοίη δέ μοι εὖχος Ἀθηνη: '(and in case) Athena might grant me my prayer'. In
  recounting his adventures to the Phaeacians, this is the first time Odysseus has
  mentioned his divine helper.

318

κατὰ θυμὸν: 'in my mind', with θυμός meant in its capacity as the seat of the
  intellect.

319–28

Odysseus keeps his audience waiting for the details of the plan. It becomes gradually
  clear that Polyphemus' stake will be used to fashion a weapon, and that its target
  is his eye (333). We will discover the finer details (such as the role of the wine)
  only as they unfurl.

319

ῥόπαλον: the word can denote either a walking-stick or, perhaps more likely in the
  Cyclop's case, a club for beating.

παρὰ σηκῷ: the Cyclops has a 'pen' (σηκός) for his flocks inside the cave, as well
  as a 'courtyard' (αὐλή) outside.

320

χλωρὸν: 'green' in the sense of being fresh and not yet dried out. It must therefore
  be hardened by heat before its point is adequately sharp.

321–4

Odysseus and his crew liken the stake in size to a ship's mast. The choice and great
  detail of the comparison, contrived at the moment of seeing the stake
  (εἰσόροωντες), may reflect the captives' longing for the relative safety of the sea.

321

αὐανθέν: 'once it was dried out', aorist passive participle from αὐαίνω 'I dry out,
  wither'.

ἐΐσκομεν: must, given the context, be an augmentless imperfect rather than present.

322

νηὸς: Homeric genitive singular of ναῦς.

324

'Such was its length (and) such (was) its thickness to look upon.' This explanatory
  (or 'epexegetic') use of the infinitive is widespread in Homer.

ἔην = ἦν.

εἰσοράασθαι = εἰσορᾶσθαι, with diectasis. In Homer, the active and middle of ὁράω are used equivalently.

325–8

The hurry and frenzy of the activity is reflected in the strong concentration of verbs and participles in these lines.

325

τοῦ ... ὅσον ... ὄργυιαν: Odysseus cuts off 'a fathom's length of it' (literally 'as much as a fathom of it'). An ὄργυια is the distance spanned by outstretched arms, or about six feet (one fathom).

παραστάς: 'standing beside (it)', aorist intransitive active participle from παρ-ίστημι.

326

ἀποξῦναι: aorist infinitive of ἀπ-οξύνω 'I make sharp', or better here, 'I taper'. Odysseus goes on to say that he sharpened the stake himself (ἐθόωσα ... ἄκρον: 327–8). One manuscript gives ἀποξῦσαι 'to make smooth' (instead of ἀποξῦναι), which may for this reason be preferable.

328

ἐπυράκτεον: 'I hardened it in the fire', an uncontracted imperfect. Weapons finished in this manner were used from prehistoric times.

329–30

Odysseus conceals the sharpened stake in the masses of animal dung spread throughout the cave. This is not being kept for fertilizer (the island of the Cyclopes, Odysseus has said, yields fruit without cultivation: 9.108–11). Rather, it is another mark of the Cyclops' barbarity. Odysseus' disgust is accentuated fittingly by an alliteration of hard velar consonants (κ, χ).

330

σπείους: a genitive singular from σπέος 'cave' found only in the *Odyssey*.

κέχυτο: perfect passive from χέω 'I pour'.

μεγάλ᾽ ἤλιθα πολλή: an almost exclamatory description of the quantity of dung: πολλή is intensified by μεγάλ(α) and ἤλιθα, both adverbs here meaning 'greatly'.

331–5

Odysseus orders the remaining men (of whom there are eight) to cast lots as to who will join him in driving the stake into the Cyclops' eye. The use of the lot is common among Homeric heroes and widespread in the *Iliad*. Some suggest that the use of the lot here is a relic of an earlier stage in the story's development, with the heroes casting lots to find out who will be eaten next.

331

κλήρῳ πεπαλάσθαι: 'cast lots (using the lot)'. The pleonasm is less jarring in Greek than in English and, as with many Homeric pleonasms, it may be better to leave some of the Greek (κλήρῳ here) untranslated. πεπαλάσθαι is an aorist middle infinitive, with reduplication, from πάλλω 'I shake (the lots)'.

332

ὅς τις τολμήσειεν: '(to find out) who would dare', an indirect question. The expression of purpose is left implicit.

ἐμοὶ σὺν: 'with me'. σύν here is postpositional (it follows its noun).

τρῖψαι: aorist infinitive of τρίβω 'I rub'. Here, however, the verb must have the sense 'I drive into', or the like.

333

γλυκὺς ὕπνος: the choice of epithet offers a powerful contrast with the violent image with which the line opens.

334–5

The men chosen by lot are the ones Odysseus would himself have chosen, which would have struck him as a good omen. The sentence has the form of a past remote conditional with the protasis ('if'-clause) left implicit.

334

ἔλαχον: 'they selected by lot', an aorist from λαγχάνω.

335

ἐλέγμην = ἐλεγόμην 'I counted myself', a reflexive middle from λέγω. The first vowel of the ending has been omitted (a phenomenon called syncope).

336–44

closely echo (and in places repeat) the first description of Polyphemus' routine (237–50). As well as adding to the impression of him as a creature of habit, the repetition also casts into relief the differences in his behaviour here.

336

ἑσπέριος: 'in the evening', an adjective where we might expect an adverb.

338–9

Unlike at 238–9, Polyphemus brings in all his sheep, including the males: either he suspects something (τι ὀϊσάμενος) or even (ἦ καὶ) a god has put the thought into his mind (θεὸς ὣς ἐκέλευσεν). It is this decision that will allow the Greeks to escape, and Odysseus begins to suspect that a god was on their side (see also 381).

338

πάντα μάλ᾽: see on 238.

339

θεὸς ὣς ἐκέλευσεν: 'a god has told him (to act) thus'.

342–4

see explanatory notes on 245, 250 and 311 respectively. The near-exact repetition
of 311 confirms our suspicion that meals of two men are becoming part of
the Cyclops' routine. Only six of his companions are now left. We do not
discover whether the two eaten here were among those chosen by lot to blind the
Cyclops.

345

προσηύδων: 'I began to address', imperfect of προσαυδάω.

346

κισσύβιον: some sort of drinking vessel, perhaps made of ivy-wood (κισσός).

347

τῆ: 'Here!', an interjection always followed by an imperative in Homer.

ἐπεὶ φάγες ἀνδρόμεα κρέα: a causal clause. Odysseus presumes the giant would
appreciate something to wash his dinner down with. Feigning goodwill, Odysseus
hides his horror at his comrades' fate, speaking of it with a striking matter-of-
factness.

348

'So you may see what a good drink (literally 'what sort of a drink') this (is that) our
ship had concealed'. Odysseus aptly uses the pluperfect ἐκεκεύθει, sticking to his
story that their ship has been destroyed.

νηῦς = ναῦς (nom.).

349

λοιβὴν: Odysseus calls the drink a 'libation', a type of offering usually reserved for
gods. Presumably, his aim is to flatter Polyphemus, who ranks himself as the gods'
superior (275–8), but to the tale's audiences the irony is clear.

φέρον: an imperfect, where a present or perfect might be expected. The rationale for
the tense is, presumably, that he has paused to address the Cyclops.

349–50

εἴ μ᾿ ἐλεήσας οἴκαδε πέμψειας: '(to see) if . . .': for the idiom, see on 267.

350

μαίνεαι οὐκετ᾿ ἀνεκτῶς: 'your madness is no longer tolerable'. Elsewhere Homer
uses the verb μαίνομαι to express the consequences of excessive drinking, lending
a touch of irony here in light of Odysseus' plan.

351

σχέτλιε: a common word of rebuke in Homer, meaning 'unyielding' or 'merciless'.
Deriving from ἔχω, it accuses the addressee of too stubbornly holding on to a
course of action.

πῶς κέν τίς . . . ἄλλος ἵκοιτο: a direct question with a potential optative, 'How
should anyone else come?' The question takes the form of a conditional with the

protasis ('If you carry on like this') left implicit. The question carries the brave presumption that some of his party will live to tell other men of their treatment at the hands of the Cyclops.

ἵκοιτο: aorist optative from ἱκνέομαι: see on 266–7.

352

πολέων: is the usual genitive plural of πολύς in Homer.

οὐ κατὰ μοῖραν ἔρεξας: 'you have not acted in a proper way'. This is best taken not as a litotes emphasizing the extent of the outrage, but as a tactful understatement, part of Odysseus' attempt to de-escalate the situation. For us, however, the words sound particularly pointed as we recall that the Cyclops in fact likes to behave κατὰ μοῖραν, albeit in a different sense (see 245, 309 and 342).

ἔρεξας: second singular aorist active of ῥέζω, 'I act'.

353

δέκτο: 'he received', an irregular Homeric aorist of δέχομαι.

ἔκπιεν: 'he drank it dry', aorist from the colourful compound ἐκ-πίνω.

ἥσατο: 'he was pleased', an alternative, middle aorist of ἥδομαι.

αἰνῶς: 'terribly'. The word, like the translation offered, has the double sense of 'very much' and 'frighteningly', which is very appropriate in this context.

354

πίνων: in Homer the -ι- of the present stem can be long or short.

355–9

Feigning friendliness, the Cyclops asks Odysseus for his name, promising him a ξείνιον (token of friendship and hospitality: see on 267) in return. His use of the term and mention of the gods show he is pretending to share Odysseus' social and religious values. Really he is setting up a cruel joke for his own amusement, as his ξείνιον is not of a kind to delight its recipient (368–70).

355

δός μοι ἔτι πρόφρων: 'keep it coming, and with good cheer'. πρόφρων introduces a touch of politeness as Polyphemus builds up to his sinister promise of a ξείνιον (356).

δός: second person singular aorist active imperative of δίδωμι.

τεόν: 'your', a Homeric equivalent of Attic σόν.

356

τοι: dative of the second singular pronoun (Attic σοι). In Homer, this pronoun has forms beginning with both τ- and σ-.

δῶ: first singular aorist subjunctive of δίδωμι.

ᾧ κε σὺ χαίρῃς: for κε see on 303–5. The verb is a potential subjunctive ('you may take pleasure in') from χαίρω, which takes a dative.

358

σφιν Διὸς ὄμβρος ἀέξει: 'the rain from Zeus makes (it) grow for them'. The early Greek poets use Ζεύς, the sky-god, as a metonymy for the sky itself: Alcaeus writes, ὕει μὲν ὁ Ζεῦς ('Zeus rains').

σφιν: dative of advantage, of the third plural personal pronoun σφεῖς.

359

'But this (the wine) is a little stream of ambrosia and nectar': these being the food and drink of the gods, this is high praise from Polyphemus, but also somewhat at odds with his earlier disdain for the gods (276–7).

ἀπορρώξ: literally means 'distributary', a stream branching off from a river.

361

ἀφραδίῃσιν: 'in his thoughtlessness', a dative of cause.

362

'But when the wine had made its way around the Cyclops' senses'. The accusative Κύκλοπα here is unexpected.

ἤλυθεν: Homeric aorist of ἔρχομαι.

365

ὥς περ = ὥσπερ.

ὑπέστης: 'you promised', an intransitive active aorist from ὑφίσταμαι, 'I promise'.

366–70:

In a single moment we discover that Odysseus and Polyphemus are both trying to deceive each other: Odysseus claims that his name is 'Nobody', while the Cyclops reveals that his promised ξείνιον is nothing more than to eat Odysseus last of all.

366

Οὖτις ἐμοί γ᾽ ὄνομα: 'Nobody is my name'. The phrasing is well chosen, since to say 'I am Nobody' would sound like an attempt to hide, not divulge, his name.

Οὖτις: is a more convincing pseudonym in Greek than 'Nobody' is in English: note the difference in accent from οὔτις, 'nobody'. Some translators have preferred 'Noman', but 'no man' now sounds too archaic an alternative for 'nobody'.

Οὖτιν: to ensure Polyphemus does not detect the ruse, Odysseus makes a point of also using the accusative. This makes it all the clearer that it is a name and not just the pronoun οὔτις (whose accusative is οὔτινα).

369

There is irony here in the near-homophony of Οὖτιν with οὔτιν᾽ (accusative), as Polyphemus has tasted his last of human flesh.

πύματον ... μετὰ οἷς ἑτάροισιν: 'last among his companions'. πύματον here must be scanned with a heavy final syllable, an irregularity which most often occurs at the caesura, as here. This lends an added weight to the word as the last step in the set-up of Polyphemus' grim joke.

οἷς: 'his': not the relative, but the identical possessive pronoun.

370

Polyphemus triumphantly reveals his surprise in a hard-hitting half-line: this offer to eat Odysseus last is the promised ξείνιον.

371

ἦ: 'he spoke', a third singular aorist that, in Homer, always marks the end of a speech.
ἀνακλινθείς: aorist passive participle with middle meaning, 'having leant back'.

372

ἀποδοχμώσας παχὺν αὐχένα: 'having twisted his thick neck around', so that he is lying on his back (ὕπτιος) with his head to one side. The details serves to explain why the Cyclops does not choke on his own vomit.

372–3

καδ . . . ἤρει: tmesis of καθῆρει, 'began to overpower'. καδ is an apocope of κατὰ (see on 255), occurring frequently in epic before a following δ-.

373

ἐξέσσυτο: 'spewed out', a lively verb used elsewhere of warriors rushing out to fight.

374

ἐρεύγετο: either 'belched' or 'vomited', but perhaps the former here, as it is clear from what comes before that Polyphemus has already vomited.
οἰνοβαρείων: nominative, literally 'heavy with wine'. The cause of the Cyclops' condition is clear enough already, but this colourful adjective at line-end drives home the degree of his drunkenness.

375

τὸν μόχλον: 'the stake mentioned before': τὸν here is not the definite article but a demonstrative (see on 237).
ὑπὸ σποδοῦ . . . πολλῆς: 'under a great pile of ash' (σποδός is feminine). The ash is presumably still very hot from the fire.

376

ἧος: here introduces a purpose clause, 'so that it would get hot'.

377

μή τίς μοι ὑποδείσας ἀναδύη: 'so that I would have none of them shrinking in fear'. μοι here serves only to express Odysseus' interest in the matter (the so-called ethic dative).
ἀναδύη: is an intransitive third singular aorist optative of ἀναδύω 'I shrink from'.

379

ἄψεσθαι: future infinitive, here meaning 'to catch fire', but literally 'take hold of' (as at 386).
περ = καίπερ.
ἐών: present participle of εἰμί with diectasis (see on 251).

380

ἀμφὶ: adverbial, 'round about'.

381

θάρσος ἐνέπνευσεν μέγα δαίμων: 'a god breathed great courage into (us)'. Odysseus is now more confident that they had divine help (contrast 338–9), but does not know from whom. As is the case throughout his travels between Troy and Scheria, home of the Phaeacians, his usual helper Athena is nowhere to be seen.

383

ἐφύπερθεν ἐρεισθείς: 'having put my weight down on it from above', the passive here with a middle meaning. The Cyclops' head is presumably no longer twisted to the side (as at 372) but now faces upwards.

384–6

This is the first of two similes that illustrate the Cyclops' blinding and string out the scene with agonizingly vivid detail. We learn that Odysseus and his men do not merely drive the hot stake into Polyphemus' eye, but spin it as carpenters do when drilling holes in timber.

384

δίνεον: imperfect, 'I began to spin it round', as if it were a drill. Here, and at 388, the enjambement places added weight on this gruesome detail.

τρυπῷ: third singular present optative of τρυπάω, 'I bore'. Though it does not affect the meaning, most editors emend to a subjunctive (τρυπᾷ), the normal mood for similes beginning ὡς ὅτε (compare 391–3).

385

τρυπάνῳ: a type of drill driven by a leather strap (ἱμάς). The word occurs only here in Homer (a so-called hapax legomenon: see Introduction, p. 000).

οἱ δέ: 'and the others', that is, the other workmen.

ὑποσσείουσιν: 'they whirl it around from below', presumably meaning from the bottom end of the drill.

386

αἰεί = ἀεί.

387

πυριήκεα: 'sharpened to a point in the fire', another hapax legomenon (see on 385).

388

τὸν … περίρρεε: 'flowed out around it' (the stake).

389

'The heat singed his entire eyelid and brow all over'. βλέφαρα and ὀφρύας here must be poetic plural-for-singular.

οἱ: possessive dative, 'his'.

390

γλήνης καιομένης: genitive absolute. Again, enjambement is used to highlight a gruesome detail.

σφαραγεῦντο: 'were sputtering', a striking onomatopoeia. The ending -εῦντο is a contraction from -έοντο.

οἱ: another possessive dative, this time of the eyeball.

πυρὶ: dative of place, 'in the fire'.

ῥίζαι: by 'roots' the poet may mean the optic nerve and surrounding tissue at the back of the eyeball. If so, the point is that the stake has been driven right through to the back of the eye-socket.

391–2

The second simile offers an aural detail to complement the visual image of the first: the noise of the heated stake as it enters the eyeball is like that of glowing iron when a smith places it in water.

391

ἠέ = ἤ, 'or'.

σκέπαρνον: an adze, a type of carpenter's cutting tool with a blade at a right angle to the handle.

392

εἰν = ἐν.

μεγάλα: adverbial, 'greatly'. The final vowel is artificially lengthened here.

ἰάχοντα: 'roaring, hissing', a potent choice of verb, used elsewhere of crying in agony (compare its use at 395).

393

The noise from the iron is a mark of its strength. The adversative αὖτε and particle γε bring out the contrast on this point between the event of the simile and that of the narrative: the noise from the eyeball is by no means a show of its strength.

φαρμάσσων: 'as he tempers (literally 'treats') it'.

394

σίζ᾽: 'was sizzling', another fine onomatopoeia.

395

σμερδαλέον: adverbial, 'terribly'.

ᾤμωξεν ... ἴαχε: two more onomatopoeic verbs, expressing respectively Polyphemus' groans and the cave's echoing of his cries.

397

πεφυρμένον: 'made wet', perfect passive participle of φύρω.

398

τὸν: demonstrative, referring to the stake.

ἔρριψεν ἀπὸ ἕο χερσὶν: 'tore it away from him(self) with his hands'. ἕο is a diectasis of οὗ, genitive of the third singular pronoun.

400

δι᾽ ἄκριας ἠνεμοέσσας: 'among the windswept peaks'. In Homer, διά with an accusative is often used to mean 'throughout, through'.

401–12

The other Cyclopes gather outside Polyphemus' cave, but leave when he tells them 'Nobody' has hurt him. Odysseus, as narrator, had described the Cyclopes as generally antisocial and having no care for their neighbours' welfare (9.112–15). Here, however, they respond with evident concern for Polyphemus, who in turn addresses them as his φίλοι (408). This all suggests some exaggeration on Odysseus' part, surely fuelled by his hatred for Polyphemus.

401

ἀΐοντες: ἀΐω with a direct object means 'I hear', but with the genitive means 'I give ear to, heed'.

ἄλλοθεν ἄλλος: 'each (coming from) a different direction', a singular phrase in apposition to the plural subject, as is common in expressions comprising ἄλλος and its cognates.

402

ἱστάμενοι: a present middle participle, so 'coming and standing', rather than 'standing' (aorist intransitive, στάντες).

περὶ σπεός: belongs with the participle and not the main verb. The postponement of the phrase, cutting off the verb from the indirect question, produces a more complex word-order that mirrors the confusion of the scene outside the cave.

ὅττι: a Homeric alternative for the indefinite relative pronoun ὅ τι. Homer uses the indefinite relative, as here, to introduce indirect questions (in Attic we would have expected just τί).

ἑ: accusative of the third singular personal pronoun.

403

The other Cyclopes reveal to Odysseus his captor's name, which, as part of his poor show of *xenia*, he had neglected to share. Aside from Zeus' brief summary of the Cyclops episode in Book 1 (1.68–71), this is the first time Polyphemus is named in the *Odyssey*, a striking and surely deliberate omission. By revealing his name only at the point where he himself discovered it, Odysseus makes it easier for his audience to put themselves in his shoes. (See similarly on 296.)

τίπτε: a shortened Homeric form of τί ποτε 'what?', or (as here) 'why?' (accusative of respect).

τόσον: adverbial, 'so much', 'so loudly'.

ἀρημένος: a participle of uncertain meaning, but always used of people in some sort of plight. It is most often interpreted as 'distressed' or 'worn out'.

404

δι': see on 400.

ἀμβροσίην: 'divine', a conventional Homeric epithet of the night, supposedly because night, as a time of rest, was seen as a gift from the gods.

ἄμμε: accusative, 'us': see on 303.

τίθησθα: Homeric second singular present indicative active of τίθημι.

405–6

ἦ μή τίς: 'surely nobody'. ἦ μή in Homer is equivalent to ἆρα μή 'surely not' in Attic. The poet has carefully formulated the question to trigger the required response from Polyphemus at 408 (see below). However, there is a second pun at work: it sounds very much as if the Cyclopes are asking whether cunning (μῆτις) is causing Polyphemus harm. Odysseus himself will flag up this second pun later (414).

σευ ... ἀέκοντος: genitive absolute, of which the intervening words are not part. σευ is a Homeric genitive singular of σύ.

ἐλαύνει and κτείνει are so-called 'conative' presents, meaning 'is *trying* to drive off' and 'is *trying* to kill'.

406

βίηφιν: Homeric dative singular of βίη 'force', here an instrumental dative. The ending -φι(ν) originally belonged to the instrumental case, which at an earlier stage in the language was merged with the dative and ceased to be a case in its own right.

407

Πολύφημος: see on 403.

408

Οὖτίς: the difference in the accent from οὔτις, 'nobody' had stopped Polyphemus detecting the ruse earlier (see on 366). Now, with the wall of the cave between them and Polyphemus groaning in agony as he speaks, the Cyclopes are bound not to hear any difference, and fall accordingly for Odysseus' trick.

409

ἔπεα πτερόεντ': accusative plural and direct object of ἀγόρευον. The Cyclopes speak 'winged words' in reply. The phrase is very common in Homer and means that the words had the means to 'fly' to the ears of their addressees.

410–12

If there is no intruder wronging him, say the Cyclopes, it must be a sickness (νοῦσος) from Zeus, and Polyphemus should pray to his father Poseidon to intercede. The advice reveals the emptiness of Polyphemus' earlier bragging that Cyclopes need not pay any heed to the gods (273–8).

410

εἰ ... μή τίς σε βιάζεται: the words could be misheard by Polyphemus as 'if cunning (μῆτις) is overpowering you'. This could explain why he does not reply and point out their error: he may not even realize that they have misunderstood his Οὖτις for οὔτις.

σε … οἶον ἐόντα: 'and you are on your own', a participle phrase standing in for another main clause in parataxis. ἐόντα = Attic ὄντα with diectasis.

411

The Cyclopes reasonably assume some sort of sickness has been sent from Zeus, the god whom Homeric characters generally see as presiding over destiny. (Hence the disease cannot be avoided.)

νοῦσόν = Attic νόσον.

οὔ πως ἔστι: 'it is in no way possible'. ἔστι here is used equivalently with ἔξεστι.

Διὸς μεγάλου: '(sent) from great Zeus', a genitive of source. The epithet 'great' drives home the key point that the Cyclopes do, in fact, revere the gods, despite Polyphemus' hubristic boasts (273–8).

412

εὔχεο: second person singular middle imperative active. In Attic, the ending is normally contracted to -ου.

πατρὶ Ποσειδάωνι: meant literally: the Cyclopes are Poseidon's sons. With the blinding of Polyphemus begins that god's enmity towards Odysseus.

413–23

The Cyclopes depart at once, presumably out of fear for their neighbour's disease. Polyphemus rolls back the door-stone, but then stands blocking his captives' escape.

413

ἔφαν: Homeric third person plural, 'they spoke'.

ἐγέλασσε = ἐγέλασε 'laughed', with σ doubled for metrical convenience.

414

μῆτις ἀμύμων: Odysseus seizes the opportunity to make a pun. It is not just his cunning (μῆτις) that has deceived the Cyclopes, but much confusion has also arisen from the use of the phrase μή τις 'nobody': see on 405–6 and 410. Appropriately for the pun, the epithet ἀμύμων 'blameless, excellent' is used elsewhere both of Odysseus' cunning (μῆτις) and of individuals.

415

The groaning of the Cyclops is mirrored in the recurrent ω-sounds.

ὠδίνων ὀδύνῃσι: 'in agony from his pains'. The cognate dative of cause ὀδύνῃσι lends fitting emphasis to his suffering.

416

ψηλαφόων: participle with diectasis from ψηλαφάω 'I grope about for'. The word is a hapax legomenon (it occurs only here in Homer), making it all the more striking a descriptor.

ἀπό ... εἶλε: tmesis.

θύραων: genitive of separation ('from the doorway').

417

εἰνὶ = ἐν.

418

εἴ: see on 267.

χεῖρε: 'his two hands', accusative dual of χείρ.

που: 'I suppose'. Here and in the following line, the particle gives the impression that Odysseus can only imagine what is going through the head of a creature as barbarous and alien as the Cyclops.

μετ᾽ ὄεσσι: with the dative, μετά means 'among'. ὄεσσι is a dative plural of οἶς 'sheep'.

419

ἤλπετ᾽: imperfect from ἔλπομαι, 'I hope, expect'.

ἐνὶ = ἐν.

420

ὅπως: here introduces a purpose clause, in historic sequence.

ὄχ᾽ ἄριστα: adverbial, 'in the best way by far'. The intensifier ὄχ(α) ('by far') is only ever found before ἄριστος.

421

εἴ: 'in case': see on 267.

θανάτου: 'from death', a genitive of separation.

422

πάντας δὲ δόλους ... ὕφαινον: 'I began to contrive (literally, 'weave') all kinds of tricks.' The metaphor of weaving is used in Homer of schemes and stories.

423

ὥς τε περὶ ψυχῆς: 'since it was a matter of life and death' (literally 'as (being) about life').

μέγα ... κακὸν: substantive, 'a great evil'.

424–36

Odysseus conceives and executes a plan for their escape: he and his men strap themselves to the bellies of rams and await the dawn.

424

μοι ... φαίνετο βουλή: the verb is well chosen, leaving it ambiguous whether Odysseus means it transitively ('the plan was shown to me') or intransitively ('the plan appeared to me'). This is consonant with the idea of 'dual motivation' in Homer, whereby many events seem to occur through both divine and human agency at once.

425–6

Odysseus offers a rich description of the Cyclops' rams full of rare and graphic adjectives (ἐϋτρεφέες, δασύμαλλοι, ἰοδνεφές). For the story it is important that they are big and woolly enough each to conceal a man; but the other qualities ascribed to them add to the fantastical impression of the fictional island.

426

καλοί τε μεγάλοι τε: the line opens with three long syllables, the first and third artificially so. While the motivation is metrical, this gives the impression of Odysseus lingering over his description of their beauty.

ἰοδνεφὲς εἶρος ἔχοντες: 'having wool dark as a violet flower' (ἴον). The evocative description suggests that their colour, while not exactly purple, is nonetheless striking.

427–31

Odysseus binds the rams together in threes and conceals a man under the middle ram in each group. The man is supported by the willow bonds (a detail left implicit until 443).

427

ἀκέων: 'quiet, silent', nominative masculine singular (an adjective with participle form).

ἐϋστρεφέεσσι λύγοισιν: 'with finely twisted willow twigs'. The fine twigs of the willow tree twist as they grow.

428

τῆς ἔπι: 'upon which', a feminine dative plural of the Homeric relative pronoun followed by a postpositional ἔπι (note the accent on the first syllable).

εὗδε: 'used to sleep', 'would sleep', an unaugmented imperfect from (καθ)εύδω.

πέλωρ, ἀθεμίστια εἰδώς: 'the monster, expert in lawlessness' (literally 'knowing lawless things'), a pointedly paradoxical description. The detail is somewhat out of place at this precise point, the focus being Odysseus' plan. However, it creates the rather effective sense that the very mention of the Cyclops still makes the storyteller, Odysseus, shudder.

429

σύντρεις αἰνύμενος: 'taking hold of three (rams) together'. The subject is Odysseus, following on from 427.

φέρεσκε: 'would carry', an imperfect from φέρω formed with the iterative suffix -σκ-, whose original purpose was to express that an action was repeated.

430

τὼ δ' ἑτέρω ... ἴτην: dual, 'and the other two went'. ἴτην is the third person dual aorist of εἶμι 'I shall go'.

σώοντες: 'saving', participle with contraction and diectasis from σαόω 'I save', a Homeric equivalent (and cognate) of σῴζω. Note the plural participle agreeing with a dual subject and verb, a sign that the dual number was already a relic at the time of composition.

431–4

Odysseus hides himself beneath the best (and presumably biggest) ram of the
flock. After a first person opening (αὐτὰρ ἐγώ γε) the sentence is interrupted
by a parenthesis with Odysseus' ram as the subject (432, ἀρνειὸς γὰρ
ἔην ...). In 433–4 the subject is once again the narrator. The interruption
gives the sense that Odysseus is distracted briefly by the recollection of
this especially fine ram: a worthy saviour for a hero: whose merits Odysseus is
at pains to express. For clarity's sake, however, it may be best to translate
loosely here: 'But for me there was a ram ... Grabbing hold of it beneath its
back ...'

432

ἀρνειὸς γὰρ ἔην: 'for there was a ram', an existential use of εἰμί.
ὄχ᾽ ἄριστος: see on 420.

433

τοῦ = αὐτοῦ here, with λαβών 'having caught hold of' governing the genitive. It
cannot be a relative pronoun as there would otherwise be no main clause for
αὐτὰρ ἐγώ γε (431) to belong to.
ἐλυσθείς: aorist passive participle, with middle meaning, from ἐλύω 'I curl up'.

434–5

It is only revealed later (463) that Odysseus is, like his men, strapped to the belly of
his ram. However, after saying that he 'lay' (κείμην, 434) under the ram, Odysseus
seems to contradict himself immediately, saying he had to hold on tight with his
hands to the ram's belly. An explanation may come from ancient representations
of the scene, which show him attached to the ram only by cords placed just above
the waist and the knee. Odysseus would then have to hold on tight to support his
upper body.
χερσὶν ἀώτου θεσπεσίοιο ... ἐχόμην: 'I clung to the wondrous fleece with my
hands.' This middle sense of ἔχω ('I hold fast to, cling to') is followed by a genitive,
as often with verbs of taking and grasping.

435

νωλεμέως: 'unceasingly', that is, without letting go. The adverb makes best sense if
taken not with στρεφθείς (as does Autenrieth 2004) but with ἐχόμην.
τετληότι θυμῷ: 'with a daring heart'. τετληότι is properly a perfect participle from
τλάω 'I dare'.
στρεφθείς: another passive participle with middle meaning. One possible sense is
'having turned around', in which case Odysseus has turned himself so he is facing
upwards, allowing him to hold fast to the fleece. Autenrieth alternatively interprets
the participle as 'having twisted myself' tightly up into the wool (whereby
Odysseus can support his weight).

436–7

The lines echo verbatim the description of the previous dawn (306–7). The repetition
brings into relief the changes that have taken place in Polyphemus' household:

whereas on the day before he had milked his ewes with the usual rigour, they are now left unmilked and in pain (439).

437–45

Polyphemus lets out his flocks to pasture. He feels their backs, hoping to discover men among the sheep, but does not catch any.

438

νομόνδ᾽: 'to pasture'.

439

The bleating of the unmilked ewes is matched by the assonance of η.

θήλειαι: 'the females': the noun (ἄρνες 'sheep') is left implicit.

ἐμέμηκον: imperfect, with reduplication, from μηκάομαι 'I bleat'.

440

οὔθατα γὰρ σφαραγεῦντο: 'for their udders were fit to burst' (literally, 'were bursting'), an exaggeration for vivid effect: overly full udders will be palpably uncomfortable for the ewe but are not in danger of causing damage.

ἄναξ: 'their master', a rather pointed word in light of his injury, prompting the reader to wonder whether Polyphemus can sustain himself as a shepherd without his eyesight.

442

ὀρθῶν ἑσταότων: 'as they stood there, upright', agreeing with πάντων οἴων (441). The rams come to a standstill (ἑσταότων) as they reach the entrance of the cave while Polyphemus feels their backs. They remain standing (ὀρθῶν) as they wait, a detail crucial for the welfare of the men.

τό: a demonstrative pronoun best left untranslated, as it merely looks forward to the content of the ὡς-clause (443).

νήπιος: 'foolish', a common Homeric term but especially piquant here in light of the Cyclops' fate: Polyphemus in his hubris had called Odysseus the same thing at 273 for expecting a Cyclops to heed the gods.

443

ὥς = ὅτι here.

οἱ: 'his', a possessive dative of the third person pronoun.

ὑπ᾽: (ὑπό, 'under') governs the dative στέρνοισι here: εἰροπόκων οἴων is a dependent possessive genitive.

δέδεντο: 'they had been tied', an augmentless pluperfect passive from δέω 'I bind'.

444

'The ram was last among the flocks to go to the door.' The sense is obscured by the word-order, with ἀρνειός separating ὕστατος from μήλων.

445

Odysseus makes sure his audience knows in advance the real reason why his ram, though leader of the flock, is so slow to leave the cave: it is labouring under the weight of its wool (λάχνῳ) and of Odysseus as he thinks his cunning thoughts (ἐμοὶ πυκινὰ φρονέοντι). This is a fitting point for Odysseus to boast of his cleverness, but there is also some humour in the image of the hero hanging, no less deep in thought, from the ram's belly.

447–60

Polyphemus addresses his favourite ram in a long speech. Its first part is full of pathos and irony, as the Cyclops wonders whether the ram, usually first out of the cave, is lingering behind in grief for his master's lost eye. Polyphemus' evident fondness for the ram evokes, for the first time, some sympathy towards the giant. This, however, soon evaporates as he describes the gruesome revenge he wishes to exact upon Odysseus (458–60).

447

κριὲ πέπον: 'gentle ram' (vocative). πέπων (literally, 'cooked', hence 'soft, mellow') is a frequent term of endearment in early hexameter poetry and lends an unprecedented humanizing touch to the Cyclops here.

τί μοι ὧδε . . . ἔσσυο: μοι: is a so-called ethic dative, used to express an individual's interest in the events described. Here the ethic dative can be translated with the addition of a clause (following Hammond 2000): 'Why do I find you like this, coming out last?'

448

οὔ τι πάρος: 'never before' (literally, 'in no matter in the past', with τι an accusative of respect).

449–51

The tricolon of clauses beginning (πολὺ) πρῶτος is pathetic, hinting at a longing for the normality of the past. Polyphemus' description of the ram's behaviour is no less touching, offering three pastoral vignettes, idyllic scenes that the giant can no longer see for himself.

λελειμμένος . . . οἰῶν: 'left behind by the sheep'. οἰῶν here is a genitive of separation.

450

μακρὰ βιβάς: 'taking great strides'. The expression, used repeatedly in the *Iliad* for heroes going into combat, hints at the high regard in which Polyphemus holds his favourite ram. βιβάς is a present active participle from a verb not otherwise attested in Homer, but clearly of related sense to βαίνω.

πανύστατος: 'the very last of all'.

452–3

ἦ σὺ ἄνακτος | ὀφθαλμὸν ποθέεις: 'surely you are feeling bad for the loss of your master's eye'. ποθέω, properly 'I feel longing for', also comes to mean 'I miss, regret' of something lost.

ἐξαλάωσε: aorist from ἐξαλαόω 'I blind utterly', the emphatic prefix ἐξ- lending further potency to the striking verb choice.

455

Οὖτις: the pseudonym, delayed to the end of the clause, is placed emphatically at the line-opening.

ὃν οὔ πω φημι πεφυγμένον ἔμμεν: 'who I think has not yet escaped'. The threat is not empty, as the Greeks' escape is still far from complete.

πεφυγμένον ἔμμεν: a periphrastic perfect passive infinitive from φεύγω (ἔμμεν = εἶναι). As elsewhere in Homer, the perfect passive of φεύγω is here active in meaning.

456–7

In a case of pathetic irony, Polyphemus' rejection of society and its customs have left him wishing he had a friend to talk to and help him.

456

εἰ δὴ ὁμοφρονέοις: 'If only you could think as I do', a wish, not the protasis of a conditional. In Greek verse εἰ alone can introduce a wish, and in Homer the present optative can express an unattainable wish, as here.

ποτιφωνήεις ... | εἰπεῖν: 'capable of speaking, to tell me ...'. The use of the infinitive here is unconventional.

457

ὄππη = ὄπῃ 'in which direction', an indirect interrogative.

458–9

Polyphemus fantasizes about spreading his mutilator's brains over the floor of his cave. We are reminded of how he smashed his first victims like puppies (289–90) and are left to wonder how much crueller he would be in his wrath.

458

τῷ: 'in that case', a dative of the demonstrative pronoun used adverbially.

459

θεινομένου: 'being struck down, slain', a possessive genitive after ἐγκέφαλος, despite the possessive dative earlier (οἱ).

ῥαίοιτο πρὸς οὔδεϊ: 'would be smashed upon the ground'. ῥαίοιτο is a present passive optative from ῥαίω 'I break, shatter'. With the dative, πρός means 'next to, upon'.

459–60

κὰδ ... λωφήσειε: tmesis of καταλωφήσειε, 'it would give relief to'. For κὰδ see on 372–3.

460

κακῶν: genitive of separation, '(relief) from the evils'.

οὐτιδανὸς ... Οὖτις: the wordplay of the Greek may best be captured by 'that nobody, Nobody'. It is fitting that Οὖτις should be the last word to leave the Cyclops' mouth before he learns the true identity of his mutilator.

Vocabulary

While there is no Defined Vocabulary List for A-level, words in the OCR Defined Vocabulary List for AS are marked with * so that students can quickly see the vocabulary with which they should be particularly familiar.

*ἀγαθός -ή -όν	good, noble	ἀλλοδαπός -ή -όν	foreign
Ἀγαμέμνων, ὁ	Agamemnon	ἄλλοθεν	from a different direction
ἄγγος, τό	jar		
ἀγορεύω	address, speak to	*ἄλλος -η -ον	other, different, another
ἄγχι	nearby	ἄλλυδις ἄλλη	all over the place; now here, now there
ἀείρω, aor. ἄειρα	raise, lift		
ἀέκων, ἀέκουσα, ἀέκον	unwilling	ἄλλως	otherwise
		*ἅλς, ἁλός, ὁ	sea, salt
ἀζάλεος -η -ον	dry	ἀλύω	be distraught
ἀθεμίστιος -ον	lawless	*ἅμα	together, together with (+ dat.)
Ἀθήνη, ἡ	Athena (goddess and helper of Odysseus)		
		ἄμαξα, ἡ	wagon
αἰγίοχος -η -ον	aegis-bearing (an epithet of Zeus)	ἀμάω, aor. ἤμησα	draw, gather
		ἀμβρόσιος -η -ον	divine
*αἰδέομαι	revere, respect	ἀμείβομαι	reply
αἰδοῖος -η -ον	deserving respect, revered	ἀμέλγω	milk
		ἀμηχανίη, ἡ	helplessness
*αἰεί	always (= ἀεί)	ἄμμες	=ἡμεῖς
*αἷμα, τό	blood	ἀμύμων -ον	excellent, noble, blameless
αἴνυμαι	take		
αἰνῶς	terribly	ἀμφί	round about (at 380, 389)
αἴξ, αἰγός, ὁ/ἡ	goat		
αἰπύς -εῖα -ύ	steep, sheer	ἀμφίς	around (+ acc.)
*αἱρέω, aor. εἷλον	take; (mid.) choose	ἀναδύω	shrink in fear
*αἰτέω	ask	ἀναΐσσω, aor. part. ἀναΐξας	spring forward
ἀΐω	hear		
ἀκέων -ουσα	softly, silently	ἀνακαίω	kindle, burn
ἄκρη, ἡ	headland, cape	ἀνακλίνομαι	lean back
ἄκρητος -ον	unmixed	*ἄναξ, ἄνακτος, ὁ	lord, master
ἄκρις, τό, pl ἄκρια	hill-top, peak	ἀνδρόμεος -η -ον	human
*ἄκρος -η -ον	at the furthest point, end; (as noun) end, tip	ἀνεκτῶς	tolerably
		*ἄνεμος, ὁ	wind
ἀλάομαι, perf. ἀλάλημαι	wander	ἀνέχω, Hom. aor. ἀνεσχέθον	hold up
ἀλέγω	avoid	ἀνήμελκτος -η -ον	unmilked
ἀλέομαι (or ἀλεύομαι)	avoid, shun	*ἀνήρ, ἀνδρός, ὁ	man
*ἀλλά	but	ἄνθος, τό	bloom, flower

ἄνθρωπος, ὁ	man, person, human	βιβάς	striding (pres. act. part. from an unattested cognate of βαίνω)
ἄντρος, ὁ	cave		
ἀνώγον, ἠνώγον	commanded, ordered (impf. with no pres.)	*βίη, ἡ	force (βίηφιν = by force)
ἅπας, ἅπασα, ἅπαν	all, every	βλέφαρον, τό	eyelid
ἄπειμι	depart	*βοάω	shout
*ἀπό	from (+ gen.)	*βοή, ἡ	cry, shout
ἀποδοχμόω	bend sideways	*βουλεύω	plan, deliberate, decide
ἀποκόπτω, aor. ἀπέκοψα	cut off	*βουλή, ἡ	plan, advice
		βυσσοδομεύω	brood over, ponder deeply
ἀπολείπω	leave off, stop		
*ἀπόλλυμι, aor. act. ἀπώλεσα, aor. mid. ἀπωλόμην	destroy, (mid.) die	γαῖα -ης, ἡ	ground; land, country; earth
ἀπονέομαι	return	γάλα, γάλακτος, τό	milk
ἀποξύνω, aor. ἀπώξυνα	sharpen	*γάρ	for
		γαστήρ, -έρος, ἡ	stomach, belly
ἀποπλάζω, aor. pass. ἀπεπλάγχθην	lead off course	*γε	at any rate
		*γελάω, Hom. aor. ἐγέλασσα	laugh
ἀποσ(σ)εύομαι	run away		
*ἅπτομαι	touch; set on fire	*γίγνομαι, aor. ἐγενομην	happen
ἀπωθέω, aor. ἀπῶσα	push aside, drive back		
ἀρημένος -η -ον	distressed, worn out	γλήνη, ἡ	eyeball
ἀρνειός, ὁ	ram	*γλυκύς -εῖα -ύ	sweet
ἄρουρα	earth, ground	γόνυ, τό (Homeric pl γοῦνα)	knee
ἄρσην gen. ἄρσενος	male		
ἆσσον	nearer		
Ἀτρείδης, ὁ	son of Atreus	δαείω	aor. subj. of ἐδάην, 'I learned' (no attested present)
αὖ	again, moreover		
αὐαίνω, aor. ηὕηνα	dry out, wither	δαίμων, ὁ	divine spirit, god
αὐλή, ἡ	courtyard	δαμάζω, aor. ἐδαμά(σ)σα	overcome, subdue
ἄϋπνος -ον	sleepless		
αὐτάρ	but, moreover	δασύμαλλος -ον	thick-fleeced, woolly
αὖτε	again, in turn, on the contrary	*δέ	and, but
		δείδω, aor. ἔδεισα	be afraid
*αὐτίκα	at once, presently	δειπνέω	dine
ἀϋτμή, ἡ	heat, breath	δεῖπνον, τό	meal, supper
*αὐτός -ή -όν	him/her/it/them; him-/her-/itself, themselves; (the) same	*δεύτερος -η -ον	second
		δεύω	make wet
		*δέχομαι, Hom. 3sg. aor. (ἔ)δεκτο	receive
αὐτοῦ	there (adv.)		
αὐχήν -ένος, ὁ	neck	δέω	tie, bind
ἀφαιρέω, aor. ἀφεῖλον	remove, take away	*δή	indeed
ἀφικάνω	arrive at	*διά	throughout, among (+ gen.), among (+ acc.)
ἀφραδίη, ἡ	foolishness		
Ἀχαιός, ὁ	Achaean (i.e. Greek)	διαπέρθω, aor. διέπερσα	destroy utterly, sack
ἄχθος, τό	weight		
ἄψορρον	back, in reply	διαφαίνομαι	glow
ἄωτον, τό	finest wool	*δίδωμι, aor. ἔδωκα	give
		δινέω	spin around
*βαθύς -εῖα -ύ	deep	δῖος -α -ον	heavenly, noble
*βάλλω, aor. ἔβαλον	throw	δόλιος -η -ον	crafty, deceitful
βάπτω	dip	δόλος, ὁ	trick
*βαρύς -εῖα -ύ	deep	δόρπον, τό	evening meal
βιάζω	act with violence, overpower	δόρυ, τό	wood; spear

*δύναμαι	be able	ἐπέρχομαι, aor. ἐπῆλθον	approach
*δύω	two		
δωτίνη, ἡ	gift	*ἐπί	upon (+ gen.); upon, against (+ dat.)
ἐγγύθεν	nearby	ἐπιάλλω	send upon, lay upon
ἔγκατα, τά	entrails	ἐπιμαίομαι, aor. ἐπεμασσάμην	handle, feel, grasp
ἐγκέφαλος, ὁ	brains		
*ἐγώ(ν)	I	ἐπιπίνω	drink after eating
ἔδω	eat up, devour	ἐπιτίθημι, aor. ἐπέθηκα	place upon, put in place
ἐεικόσορος, ὁ	with twenty oars		
ἕζομαι	sit down	ἐπιτιμήτωρ, ὁ	avenger
*ἐθέλω	wish, be willing	*ἔπος, τό	word
*εἰ	if; to see if	*ἔργον, τό	task, job, work
*εἴκοσι	twenty	ἐρείδω, aor. ἤρεισα	press down, lean
*εἶμι, pres. part. ἰών	I shall go	ἐρεύγομαι	belch out, disgorge
εἰν(ί)	= ἐν	ἔρομαι	ask
εἰροπόκος -ον	woolly, fleecy	ἐρύκω	hold back, hinder
εἶρος, τό	wool	ἐρύω, aor. εἴρυσ(σ)α	draw, pull
*εἰς	into (+ acc.)	*ἔρχομαι, aor. ἦλθον or ἤλυθον, Hom. perf. εἰλήλουθα	go, come
εΐσκω	liken, compare		
εἰσοράω, aor. εἴσιδον	see, look at		
*ἐκ	out of (+ gen.)	*ἐρωτάω	ask
*ἕκαστος -η -ον	each	*ἐς	= εἰς
ἑκάτερθεν	on each side	*ἐσθίω, aor. ἔφαγον; fut. ἔδομαι	eat
ἐκλέγω, fut. ἐξερέω	tell, say		
ἐκπεράω	go across	ἐσθλός -ή -όν	good, noble
ἐκρέω	flow out	ἐσχατιή, ἡ	edge, shore
ἐκσεύομαι, 3rd s. aor. ἐξέσσυτο	rush out	*ἕτα(ι)ρος, ὁ	companion, friend
		*ἕτερος -η -ον	other, the other, another
ἐκτέμνω, aor. ἐξέταμον	cut out, hew into shape	*ἔτι	still
ἔκτοθεν	outside	*εὖ	well
ἐλαΐνος -η -ον	of olive wood	εὕδω	sleep
*ἐλαύνω, aor. ἤλασα	drive	εὐεργής -ές	well-made
ἐλεέω	have pity or mercy on	*εὑρίσκω, aor. εὗρον	find
ἔλπομαι	hope, expect	*εὐρύς -εῖα -ύ	broad, wide
ἐλύω, aor. εἴλυσα	curl up, roll up	ἐϋστρεφής -ές	well-twisted
ἔμβρυον, τό	young one	ἐϋτρεφής -ες	well-fed
ἐμμενής -ές	constant	*εὔχομαι	boast, claim; pray
*ἐμός -ή -όν	my	εὖχος, τό	prayer, vow
ἐμπίμπλημι, aor. ἐνέπλησα	fill	εὕω	singe
		ἔχθος, τό	hate, enmity
ἐμπνέω, aor. ἐνέπνευσα	inspire	*ἔχω, aor. ἔσχον	have, hold; keep
*ἐν	in (+ dat.)		
ἔνδον	inside	ζείδωρος -η -ον	life-giving
ἔνερθεν	below	*Ζεύς, Διός ὁ	Zeus
*ἔνθα	then, there		
ἐνοσίχθων, ὁ	earth-shaker (an epithet of Poseidon)	ἤ	introduces a question or strong claim
ἔντοσθεν	inside	*ἤ, ἠε	or
ἐξαλαόω	blind utterly	ἠδέ	and
ἐξαπατάω	deceive	*ἥδομαι, Hom. aor. mid. ἡσάμην	enjoy, take pleasure in
ἐξελαύνω, aor. ἐξήλασα	drive out		
		ἠλασκάζω	flee from, avoid
ἐξερύω	pull out	ἠλίβατος -η -ον	high, steep; deep
*ἐπεί	when, since	ἤλιθα	very much (adv.)
*ἔπειτα	then	ἧμαι	sit

*ἡμεῖς	we	κατακλάω	break, crush
*ἡμέτερος -η -ον	our	κατακρύπτω	hide, conceal
ἥμισυς -εια -υ	half	κατατίθημι, aor.	place down
ἦμος	when	κατέθηκα	
ἠνεμόεις -εσσα -εν	windy	κε, κεν	= ἄν
ἦος	until, while	κεῖμαι	lie (down)
ἧπαρ -ατος, τό	liver	κεῖνος -η -ον	that
ἠπύω	call out, roar	κέλευθον, τό	way, track
ἠριγένειος -α -ον	early-born (an epithet	*κελεύω	order
	of Dawn)	κέλομαι	order
ἦτορ, τό	heart	κεύθω	conceal
Ἠώς, ἡ (acc. Ἠώ)	Dawn (personified)	κήδω	trouble, distress
		κήλεος -ον	burning
*θάλασσα, ἡ	sea	κικλήσκω	call
*θάνατος, ὁ	death	κισσύβιον, τό	drinking-cup
θάρσος, τό	courage	κιχάνω	meet, encounter;
θαρσύνω	encourage, embolden		(at 266) arrive
θείνω	strike down, slay	κλαίω	weep
θέμις, ἡ	custom	κλέος, τό	fame
*θεός, ὁ	god	κλῆρος, ὁ	lot
θερμαίνω	warm, heat	κλυτός -ή -όν	renowned, glorious
θερμός -ή -όν	warm	*κόπτω	strike, cut
θεσπέσιος -η -ον	marvellous, divine	κρατερός -ή -όν	mighty
θήλειος -η -ον	female	κρέας, τό (pl κρέα)	flesh
θοόω	sharpen	κριός, ὁ	ram
θυμός, ὁ	spirit, heart	Κύκλωψ, -ωπις, ὁ	Cyclops
θυρεόν, τό	door-stone		
*θύρη, ἡ	door; θύραζε = towards	λαγχάνω, aor. ἔλαχον	obtain by lot
	the door	λαῖτμα, τό	depth, gulf
θύρηφιν	outside	*λαμβάνω, aor. ἔλαβον	catch
*θύω	sacrifice	λανθάνω, aor. ἔλαθον	escape the notice of
			(+ acc.)
ἰάχω	cry; make a loud sound,	λαός, ὁ	the people, men
	resound	λάσιος -η -ον	shaggy
*ἵημι, aor. ἧκα	send (in mid. at 261,	λάχνος, ὁ	wool
	'yearn')	*λέγω, aor. εἶπον	say, tell, speak; (mid.)
ἱκάνω	come		choose
ἱκέτης, ὁ	suppliant	*λείπω, aor. ἔλιπον	leave
ἱκνέομαι, aor. ἱκόμην	come to	λευκός -ή -όν	white
ἱμάς -άντος, ὁ	leather strap	λέων, ὁ	lion
*ἵνα	in order that	ληϊστήρ, ὁ	robber
ἰοδνεφής -ες	dark as the violet	*λίθος, ὁ	stone
	flower, dark purple	λιλαίομαι	long for, desire
*ἵστημι, aor. ἔστησα	make to stand, put	λύγος, ἡ	willow twig, withy
ἱστός, ὁ	mast	λυγρός -ή -όν	mournful, causing
			misery
κάδ	= κατά	λύσις, ἡ	release, deliverance
καθέζομαι	sit down	*λύω, aor. ἔλυσα	release, set free
*καί	and	λωφάω	rest, recover from
*καίω, Homeric aor.	kindle, set on fire		(+ gen.)
ἔκηα			
*κακός -ή -όν	bad, evil	μαίνομαι	rage, be angry, be
καλλίτριχος -η -ον	with lovely hair		mad
*κατά	according to, in (+ acc.),	μάκαρ, gen. μάκαρος	blessed, happy
	throughout (+ gen.)	μάλα	very, very much
κατάγνυμι, aor.	break, shatter	μαψιδίως	aimlessly, at random
κατέαξα		μεγαλήτωρ, -ορος	great-hearted

*μέγας, μεγάλη, μέγα	great, big	οἷα τε	such as
μειλίχιος -η -ον	honey-sweet	*οἶδα, part. εἰδώς -ότος	know
*μέλας, μέλαινα, μέλαν	black	*οἴκαδε	homewards
*μέλλω	be about to (+ fut. inf.)	*οἰκέω	live, dwell
μένος, τό	force, might	οἰμώζω, aor. ᾤμωξα	wail, lament
*μένω, aor. ἔμεινα	stay, wait for	οἰνοβαρείων	heavy with wine
*μέσος -η -ον	middle	*οἶνος, ὁ	wine
*μετά	with, among (+ dat.)	οἴομαι, aor. ὠϊσάμην	think, suspect
*μή	not	οἶος -η -ον	alone
μηκάομαι, impf. ἐμέμηκον	bleat	ὄϊς, ὁ/ἡ	sheep
μηκάς, -άδος, ἡ	bleating one	ὄλεθρος, ὁ	destruction, death, ruin
μῆκος, τό	length, height	ὁμαλός -ή -όν	even, regular, consistent
μῆλον, τό	flocks (in pl)	ὁμοφρονέω	be of the same mind, share another's thoughts
*μήτηρ, ἡ	mother		
μητίομαι	devise, contrive	*ὄνομα, τό	name
μῆτις, ἡ	cunning, wisdom, skill; plan	ὀξύς, ὀξεῖα, ὀξύ	sharp
		ὅπη	where
μιν	him, her, it	ὀπηδέω	accompany
μοῖρα, ἡ	share, lot, fate (κατὰ μοῖραν = in proper turn)	ὁπλίζω, aor. ὥπλισ(σ)α	prepare
		ὅππη	(to) where
μοχλός, ὁ	bar, stake	ὅπως	so that (at 420)
μυελόεις -εσσα -εν	full of marrow	ὄργυια, ἡ	the length of arms outstretched (about six feet)
μυχός, ὁ	corner		
		ὀρεσίτροφος -η -ον	reared in the mountains
*ναῦς, ἡ	ship	*ὀρθός -ή -όν	upright
νέμω	graze, put to pasture; (mid.) feed, graze	ὄρος, τό	mountain
		ὀρυμαγδός, ὁ	loud noise, din
νηδύς, ἡ	belly	*ὅς ἥ ὅ	who, which
νήϊος -η -ον	for ships	*ὅσ(σ)ος -η -ον	as much as, as great as; (in pl) as many as
νηλεής, ές	pitiless, ruthless		
νήπιος -η -ον	foolish, silly	ὀστέον, τό	bone
νοέω	notice	*ὅτε	when
νομεύω	put to graze	*οὐ	not
νομόνδε	out to pasture	οὖδας, -εος, τό	floor
*νοῦσος, ἡ	disease (= νόσος)	*οὐδέ	and not, nor, not even
*νῦν	now	*οὐδείς, οὐδεμία, οὐδέν	nobody, nothing
*νύξ, νύκτος, ἡ	night		
νωλεμέως	unceasingly, firmly	οὖθαρ, -ατα, τό	udder
νῶτα, τά	back	*οὐκέτι	no longer
		*οὔνομα, τό	name (= ὄνομα)
ξεινήϊον, τό	gift of guest-friendship	οὐτάω	wound, hit
ξείνιος -η -ον	of guest-friendship (an epithet of Zeus)	*οὔτε … οὔτε	neither … nor …
		οὐτιδανός -ή -όν	worthless, of no account
*ξεῖνος, ὁ	stranger, foreigner, guest, host	*οὕτω(ς)	in this way
		*ὀφθαλμός, ὁ	eye
*ξίφος, τό	sword	ὄφρα	in order that
		ὀφρῦς -ύος, ἡ	brow
ὄβριμος -ον	strong, mighty	ὄχα	by far
*ὅδε, ἥδε, τόδε	this	ὀχλίζω, aor. ὤχλισσα	roll
*ὁδός, ἡ	way, road		
ὀδύνη, ἡ	pain	πάλλω, Hom. aor. mid. inf. πεπαλάσθαι	shake (used of lots)
ὅθι	where		
οἱ	for him (dative pronoun)		

πανδαμάτωρ, ὁ — that which overcomes all
παντοῖος -η -ον — of every sort
πανύστατος -η -ον — last of all
*παρά — beside (+ gen.)
παρατίθημι, aor. — place beside; (mid.) put
 παρέθηκα; mid. aor. — at risk, hazard
 παρεθέμην
παρίστημι, intr. aor. — stand beside
 part. παραστάς
πάρος — previously (adv.)
*πᾶς πᾶσα πᾶν — all, every
*πατήρ, ὁ — father
πάχος, τό — thickness
παχύς -εῖα -ύ — thick
πειράζω — attempt, 'try it on'
πεῖραρ, -ατος, τό — limit, end, furthest point
πέλεκυς, ὁ — axe
πέλωρ, ὁ — monster
πέλωρος -η -ον — monstrous, huge
πέμπτος -η -ον — fith
*πέμπω — send
πέπων — gentle; mellow
περ — = καίπερ (at 379)
περιρρέω — flow around
πετάσσω — stretch out
πέτρη, ἡ — rock
*πίνω — drink
*πίπτω, aor. ἔπεσον — fall
πίων gen. πίονος — fat
πλεκτός -ή -όν — woven
*πλέω — sail
*πόθεν — from where?
ποθέω — miss, long for; feel bad about something lost
ποίη, ἡ — grass
*πόλις, ἡ — city
*πολύς πολλή πολύ — much, (in pl) many
*πονέω — work hard, toil
πόντος, ὁ — sea
πόρω — offer, give
Ποσειδάων, ὁ — Poseidon (god of the sea)
*ποταμός, ὁ — river
ποτί — = πρός
ποτιδόρπιος -η -ον — for dinner
ποτιφωνήεις -εσσα — capable of speaking
 -εν
ποτός, ὁ — drink
*που — I suppose; somewhere
πρῆξις, ἡ — trade
*πρός — against, upon (+ dat.), towards, upon, in (+ acc.)
προσαυδάω — address, speak to
προσβάλλω — I dash (acc.) against (dat.)

πρόσθεν — beforehand
προσλέγω, aor. — address, speak to
 προσεῖπον
προσπελάζω, aor. — bring near to
 προσεπέλασα
προστίθημι, aor. — put in place
 προσέθηκα
πρόσφημι — address
πρόφρων — willing
*πρῶτος -η -ον — first
πτερόεις -εσσα -εν — winged (an epithet of words)
πυκινός -η -ον — dense-packed; cunning
πύματος -η -ον — last
*πῦρ, τό — fire
πυρακτέω — harden in the fire
πυριήκης -ες — with a fiery point
πω — ever
πῶμα, τό — lid
*πως — somehow
*πῶς; — how?

ῥα — unemphatic particle, equivalent to ἄρα
ῥαίω — break, shatter
ῥέζω, aor. ἔρεξα — do, make, act
*ῥηϊδίως — easily
ῥίζη, ἡ — root
ῥίπτω, aor. ἔρριψα — throw
ῥοδοδάκτυλος -ον — rosy-fingered (an epithet of Dawn)
ῥοή, ἡ — stream
ῥοῖζος, ἡ — whistling, whizzing noise
ῥόπαλον, τό — club, cudgel
σαόω — save
σάρξ, σάρκος, ἡ — flesh
σεύομαι, aor. ἐσσύμην — rush
σηκός, ὁ — pen, fold
σίδηρος, ὁ — iron
σκέπαρνον, τό — adze
σκύλαξ, -ακος, ὁ — puppy, young of an animal
σμερδαλέος -η -ον — terrible to look upon or hear
*σός σή σόν — your
σπέος, σπεῖος, τό — cave
σπεύδω — hurry
σποδός, ἡ — ash, embers
σταθμός, ὁ — stable, pen
στείνω — burden, weigh down, strain
στείχω — go, walk
στενάχω — groan
στέρνον, τό — chest, breast

στρέφω	twist, turn	ὑποσσείω	whirled around from
συμμάρπτω, aor.	seize, grap together		underneath
συνέμαρψα		ὑπουράνιος -η -ον	under heaven
*σύν	with (+ dat.)	ὕπτιος -η -ον	high
συνέργω	fasten together	ὕστατος -η -ον	last
σύντρεις	three together	*ὕστερος -η -ον	later
σφαραγέομαι	crackle, sputter; burst	ὑφαίνω	weave
*σχεδόν	nearby	ὑφίημι, aor. ὕφηκα	place under (+ dat.)
σχέτλιος -η -ον	merciless, cruel;	ὑφίσταμαι, aor.	agree, undertake
	wretched; unyielding	ὑφέστην	
		ὑψηλός -ή -όν	high
τάλαρος, ὁ	basket	ὑψόσε	aloft, on high
τανύω (aor.	stretch out		
ἐτάνυσ(σ)α)		*φαίνομαι (aor. pass.	appear
τείρω	distress, weaken	ἔφανη)	
τεός -ή -όν	your	φαρέτρη, ἡ	quiver (of arrows)
τέρην -εινα -εν	soft, delicate	φαρμάσσω	treat, temper
τέσσαρες -α	four	φάρυγξ, -υγος, ἡ	throat
τετράκυκλος -η	four-wheeled	φείδομαι, Hom. aor.	avoid, shrink from
-ον		πεφιδόμην	
τηλόθεν	far from	φέριστος -η -ον	best
*τίθημι, aor. ἔθηκα	put, place	φέρτερος -η -ον	better
τίνω, aor. ἔτ(ε)ισα	pay a debt; (mid.) take	*φέρω, Hom. aor.	bring, carry
	vengeance	ἤνεικα	
τίπτε	why	φεύγω, perf. mid. pass.	flee, escape
*τις, τι	someone, something	part. πεφυγμένος	
*τίς, τί	who? what?	*φημί, mid. aor.	say
τοι	well, let me tell you	ἔφαμην	
	(particle)	φθόγγος, ὁ	voice
*τολμάω	dare	*φίλος -η -ον	dear; friend (as noun)
τόσ(σ)ος -η -ον	so great, so much; (in pl)	φοιτάω	roam about
	so many	φορέω	carry habitually, carry
*τότε	then		around
τράγος, ὁ	male goat	φορτίς, -ίδος, ἡ	merchant (ship)
*τρεῖς, τρία	three	φρήν, φρένος, ἡ	midriff; heart,
*τρέπω	turn, direct		mind
*τρέφω, aor. ἔτρεψα	rear; thicken, curdle	φρονέω	think, be minded; be
*τρέχω, aor. ἔδραμον	run		wise
τρίβω, aor. ἔτριψα	rub; drive into (at 332)	φύρω	make wet
τρίς	three times	φῶς, φωτός, ὁ	man
Τροίηθεν	from Troy		
τρύπανον, τό	drill, borer	χαίρω	rejoice, take pleasure in
τρυπάω	bore, pierce	χαλκεύς, ὁ	bronze-smith
τυρός, ὁ	cheese	χαμάδις	on the floor (adv.)
		*χείρ, χειρός, ἡ	hand
ὑγρός -ή -όν	wet	χέω, perf. κέχυκα	pour; spread
*ὕδωρ, ὕδατος, τό	water	χλωρός -ή -όν	green, pale
*ὕλη, ἡ	wood		
ὑμός -ή -όν	your	ψηλαφάω	feel about, grope
ὑπείρ	= ὑπέρ	ψυχή, ἡ	soul, life
ὑπεκφεύγω, aor.	escape	ψωμός, ὁ	morsel, bit
ὑπεξέφυγον			
*ὑπέρ	over (+ acc.)	*ὤ	O (introduces a
ὕπνος, ὁ	sleep		vocative)
*ὑπό	under (+ dat.)	*ὧδε	in this way
ὑποδείδω, aor.	be afraid	ὠδίνω	be in agony
ὑπέδεισα		*ὡς	in this way, so; like; that

Sophocles, *Antigone*

Introduction, Commentary Notes and
Vocabulary by Matthew McCullagh

AS: 1–99, 497–525, 531–581, 891–928

A-level: 162–222, 248–331, 441–496,
998–1032

Introduction

Sophocles' *Antigone* is one of the best-known and influential of Greek plays. It has attracted the attention of philosophers such as Hegel and has inspired adaptations by playwrights such as Brecht and Anouilh. It continues to be widely performed to this day. One of the reasons for the continuing interest in the play is that the conflicts it dramatizes (between men and women, the young and the old, the family and the state) are timeless in their relevance. However, it should not be forgotten that the original play is the product of a culture with a very different outlook to our own, not least in its view of the role of drama. It will be helpful to begin, therefore, with some remarks on the historical context of the play and the conventions of Greek tragedy before looking in more detail at *Antigone* itself.

Historical context

Antigone is one of the highlights of the literature that survives from fifth century BC Athens. Its date is not wholly certain, although it is most likely to have been written around 441. Athens at this point was at the height of its power. Since the end of the Persian Wars earlier in the century, it had become the leading city in Greece, as head of what had begun as an anti-Persian defensive league but had developed into an empire, whose subjects paid an annual revenue to Athens. The legacy of Athenian power can still be seen in buildings such as the Parthenon, which was built during this period.

Since the beginning of the fifth century BC, Athens had been governed by a political system of radical democracy. Each citizen belonged to their own local community (deme). These were divided into ten tribes, formed of equally weighted groups from the city, coast and country areas. Sovereign power lay in the Assembly (*Ekklesia*), open to all Athenian citizens and in which any citizen could speak during meetings. The Assembly met regularly throughout the year and required a quorum of 6,000 for particularly important decisions. In addition to the Assembly, there was an executive Council (*Boule*), on which 500 citizens, selected by lot, served annually; at any given time 50 men sat in full-time session on the Council. Most citizens would thus at some point serve as part of the Athenian government. Political offices were generally decided by lottery, considered fairer than election, although an important exception was the role of general (*strategos*), which remained elective. Ten generals were elected each year, one from each tribe; even here, some democratic accountability remained, as generals were held to account by their men at the end of their year's service. The role of general offered particular scope for men from wealthy families to occupy a position of leadership; the most famous example is Pericles, who was de facto leader of Athens until his death in 429. The legal system was also run along democratic lines, with large juries being selected by lottery from ordinary citizens.

The political background of fifth century BC Athens is fundamental to understanding Greek tragedy. Tragedy was itself an invention of democratic Athens, performed as a communal activity, as will be discussed in more detail below. Despite being set in a mythological past, the plays are full of references to democratic practice (e.g. Aeschylus' *Oresteia* trilogy depicts the development of trial by democratic jury, its finale being set in Athens). Much of the dialogue of tragedy consists of speech making and attempts to persuade other characters or groups, in the case of the chorus. It cannot be a coincidence that the plays were performed before audiences for whom public debate and collective decision making were everyday occurrences.

Athenian tragedy

One of the most distinctive institutions of democratic Athens was the theatre. The Athenian theatre, however, was very different from what a modern audience would recognize. To begin with, our surviving Greek tragedies were performed as part of a religious festival, the City Dionysia, held each spring in honour of Dionysus, god of wine, ecstasy and theatre. The festival began with a grand procession through Athens, in which citizens were arranged according to the ten tribes; they carried bowls of wine, while resident foreigners brought bowls of water, symbolic of their lesser status. The procession ended at the theatre of Dionysus, followed by sacrifice of animals to the god. On the same day, there was a competition between the tribes of choral dances by men and youths, arranged in groups of 50.

The remaining four days of the festival were made up of drama, three dedicated to tragedy and one to comedy. Each of the three days of tragedy contained an entire day of drama written by a single playwright. Tragedians were expected to put on four plays, three tragedies, followed by a satyr play; satyr plays used similar mythological themes to tragedy but featured choruses of satyrs, wild followers of Dionysus, and perhaps had the function of re-establishing the festival mood at the end of the day. We do not know which other plays accompanied *Antigone* (it is often printed together with Sophocles' two Oedipus plays as a trilogy, but the three plays were actually written years apart). From what we know about Sophocles' practice, though, it is likely that it was not part of a connected trilogy, although there may have been thematic links between the plays.

The three tragedians putting on their plays at a festival were competing against each other. They had been selected the previous year by a state official, chosen by lot, and a wealthy citizen (the *choregos*) took on the cost of funding the play. Professional actors were assigned to the playwrights by the state, while the choruses were made up of ordinary citizens. The production of the plays thus combined democratic participation of the masses with an outlet for display by those from wealthy or noble backgrounds. The winning dramatist was voted upon at the end of the competition by a group of citizens chosen by lot. Victory would have brought prestige to both the playwright and his *choregos*.

The theatre of Dionysus was open-air, with the seating area cut into the south side of the hill of the Acropolis looking down upon the performance area below. In the fifth century BC, the spectators would have sat on wooden benches. The size of the audience would have been much larger than that of a modern play (estimates range between 6,000 and 14,000), so we should imagine an atmosphere more like that of a concert or football match than a modern play. It is likely, though not certain, that the audience was all male. The performance area the spectators looked down upon consisted of a circular (or possibly rectangular) area, the orchestra, in which the chorus performed. In the centre of this area was a small altar. Behind the orchestra was a wooden building (skene), with a door in the centre, which in many plays serves as a family house or palace. In *Antigone*, the skene represents Creon's palace, which is also the home of most of the characters in the play. It is disputed whether there was a stage in front of this building upon which the actors performed or whether they performed in the area of the orchestra. If there was a stage, it was probably a small-scale structure. Leading into the orchestra were two entrances (*eisodoi*) from the left and right sides of the theatre.

All parts were played by men and actors performed wearing masks. These would have enabled the audience to recognize characters from a long distance away and may also have had some amplificatory effect. They may have been able to produce particular theatrical effects on occasion; for example, it has been suggested that Antigone and Ismene would have worn identical masks, emphasizing their sisterhood. Given the size and the acoustics of the theatre, it is likely that actors used expansive gestures and performed facing directly towards the audience. Only three speaking actors were used, although there could also be silent extras. In plays that have more than three speaking parts, such as *Antigone*, actors were able to play more than one part by changing masks between scenes.

Greek tragedy also uses a chorus, by this time made up of fifteen men, who, after their initial entry, remained onstage throughout. The chorus is generally a group linked to one of the characters (in *Antigone* the chorus are Theban elders summoned by Creon). The chorus performed songs, written in highly elaborate rhythm and accompanied by music from an *aulos*, a reed instrument with two pipes which sounded something like bagpipes, though not as noisy. They danced as they sang and the effect of the whole must have been breathtaking.

The role of the chorus is hard for modern readers to appreciate. They often present a moderate middle ground between different opinions expressed by the characters, while their songs deal with similar issues to those raised in the spoken sections of the play, but presented from a different perspective. The role of the chorus also shows the importance of democracy in Athenian culture. Characters in tragedy, such as Antigone and Creon, are often presented as trying to persuade the chorus to accept their point of view. The public, collective nature of Athenian society was thus an essential part of its drama.

The typical structure of a Greek tragedy is simple. Plays usually begin with a prologue, featuring one or more of the actors. Sophocles' surviving plays generally start with a dialogue between characters that introduces the action and themes of the play. The chorus then march in with an opening song (*parodos*), after which scenes of spoken dialogue (episodes) alternate with choral songs (*stasima*). The tragedy ends with an exodus, conclusion, with the actors and chorus leaving the performance area.

Other notable conventions of Greek tragedy are its use of time and space. Plays generally take place in real time, or at least over the course of a single day, with some stretching of time allowed during choral songs. For example, in *Antigone*, over the course of the second choral song (first *stasimon*), the Guard has had time to return to his post, catch Antigone burying Polynices, and bring her back to Creon. They also take place in a fixed location (scene changes are very rare); the action of *Antigone* takes place entirely in the area in front of Creon's palace.

These distinctive conventions of Greek tragedy have some interesting links with the contents of the plays. Since tragedy is highly limited in what can be shown onstage, with only a small cast and strict unity of time and place, it tends to focus on moments of fateful decision and the processes that lead up to them, rather than trying to depict all the action of the mythological stories onstage. Events before or after the play or outside what can be shown onstage are reported by characters within the play (e.g. the Chorus sing about the battle between Eteocles and Polynices in their opening song, while the Messenger reports the offstage death of Eurydice).

The use of dramatic space is also interesting. While on one level the performance area of a Greek tragedy was very simple and literalistic, it was also used in a symbolic way that reflected the themes of the play. One important contrast we find in several plays is between the inner space of the stage building and the outer space of the stage/orchestra. As a representation of the home, the stage building is typically associated with the family, women and secrecy. The outer space, by contrast, is the male sphere, associated with public life. In *Antigone*, the palace is presented as the proper place of women: Creon confines Antigone and Ismene within it at 578–80, remarking that women should not be allowed to roam free; and another female character, Eurydice, is strongly associated with the palace, from which she emerges, speaks and then returns to die. The notable exception to this is Antigone, the use of dramatic space thus visually enacting her anomalous status.

The exits from the stage also have a symbolic value: one exit often leads to the outside world and has associations of wildness and nature, while the other leads into the city and is associated with civilization. In *Antigone*, one exit leads outside the city to where Polynices' corpse lies unburied, while the other leads into Thebes. While the other female characters tend to enter and exit the stage via the palace, Antigone repeatedly departs via the exit that leads outside the city, again demonstrating that she does not conform to expected feminine behaviour.

Sophocles

Sophocles was born *c.* 495 and died in 405. He was the most successful tragedian of his day, winning more victories in dramatic competitions than either Aeschylus or Euripides, and had a long career, spanning around 60 years. Although he wrote over 120 plays, only seven survive complete (*Ajax, Antigone, Electra, Oedipus at Colonus, Oedipus Tyrannus, Philoctetes* and *Trachiniae*), together with a substantial fragment of a satyr play (*Ichneutae*) and smaller fragments of other plays.

As well as his career as a playwright, Sophocles seems to have played a significant role in Athenian public life. We know that he came from a wealthy family and held the offices of *Hellenotamias* (public treasurer) in 443/2, of *strategos* in 441, along with Pericles (he is said to have been elected to this position as a result of his successful production of *Antigone*), and *proboulos* (commissioner) during the political crisis of 412 to 411. There is also a story that he was responsible for receiving the image of the god Asclepius into his house, when the deity was introduced into Athens in 420.

Sophocles was responsible for a number of innovations in dramatic practice. He increased the number of actors from two to three, significantly increasing the possibilities open to playwrights, particularly given that individual actors could play multiple parts. He also expanded the chorus from 12 to 15 and is said to have introduced 'scenery painting', although we do not know exactly what this would have looked like.

One of the most distinctive features of Sophocles' plays, in which they are notably different from those of the earlier playwright Aeschylus, is their focus on a single central character, the 'tragic hero'. Sophocles is particularly fond of powerful and uncompromising central characters whose intransigence leads them towards disaster, for example Oedipus in *Oedipus Tyrannus*. *Antigone* is interesting in having a clash between two figures of this kind, Antigone and Creon. Sophoclean tragedy was highly influential on the later development of tragedy, particularly since his *Oedipus Tyrannus* was taken as the model tragedy by the philosopher Aristotle, who in his *Poetics* proposed an account of tragedy as dealing with a hero undergoing a reversal of fortunes (*peripeteia*) as the result of an 'error' (*hamartia*).

The background story

The story of the house of Oedipus was one of the most popular subjects for Greek tragedy and was also told in many other works of ancient literature. Although we tend to think of Greek myths as having a single, definitive version, it is important to remember that the details of ancient myths were fluid and authors had considerable latitude to rework even well-known stories. To give an example, we know from an early vase and a Greek commentary on *Antigone* that in another version of the story, Ismene was killed by Tydeus, one of the Seven against Thebes, who is already dead at the beginning of our play. The evidence of our other sources suggests that Sophocles has been innovative in several respects in retelling the story. One particularly important innovation in *Antigone* is that the story of Polynices' non-burial and its consequences is presented as a conflict within a single family, something not so prominent in other versions.

Nevertheless, we can reconstruct the basic details of the back story that would have been familiar to the original audience of *Antigone*. Many years before the play begins, Oedipus, King of Thebes, had unwittingly married his mother, Jocasta, and killed his father, Laius. Oedipus had children with Jocasta; two sons, Eteocles and Polynices, and two daughters, Antigone and Ismene. Jocasta, upon learning the truth, killed herself, while Oedipus blinded himself in horror and later died, either in exile or after staying at Thebes for several years. He had at some point cursed his two sons, and after his death they ended up quarrelling over his kingdom. Polynices, who had married Argeia, daughter of the Argive king Adrastus, led an army against Thebes to win it for himself. The seven greatest warriors in his army attacked the seven gates of Thebes (the famous Seven against Thebes) and were defeated by the

Theban army. Polynices fought his own brother Eteocles and the two killed each other. A young son of Creon, Megareus, also died either before or during the battle (1303). At this point, the action of *Antigone* begins.

Structure of the play

1–99:   The play opens at dawn the day after the battle. Antigone has called Ismene out of the palace, where they are wards of their uncle Creon, Jocasta's brother, who is now ruler of Thebes. Antigone relates the news that Creon has buried Eteocles, but has decreed that no-one is to bury Polynices' body, on pain of death. She announces her intention to bury Polynices and, after Ismene tries unsuccessfully to dissuade her, goes off to bury him, while Ismene returns to the palace.

100–61:   The chorus, a group of Theban elders, enter the stage, singing a song of victory over the invading Argive army (the *parodos*).

162–331:   Creon enters and reiterates his intention to leave Polynices, whom he regards as a traitor, unburied and prey for dogs and birds. The chorus agree to his decision, but express some reservations. A Guard then enters and announces that someone has attempted to bury the body. Creon reacts furiously, accusing the Guard of corruption and threatening him with death if the culprit is not found.

332–75:   The chorus sing the famous 'Ode to Man' (first *stasimon*), praising the ingenuity of mankind, while pointing out the limitations imposed by death.

376–581:   The Guard reappears, leading in his prisoner, Antigone, who has been caught trying to bury Polynices' body, and describes what happened. Creon dismisses the Guard and interrogates Antigone, who justifies her action as in accordance with the unwritten laws of the gods. Creon resolves to execute her. Creon extends his fury to Ismene, whom he summons from the palace, accusing her of complicity in the plot and threatening to execute her as well. Ismene tries to take joint responsibility for the burial, but is rejected by Antigone. She then tries to dissuade Creon from executing Antigone, without success, and introduces some new information – Antigone is betrothed to Creon's son, Haemon. Even this, however, is not enough to make Creon relent.

582–625:   The chorus sing about the misfortunes of the house of Oedipus, whose latest descendants have been condemned to death (second *stasimon*).

626–780:   Creon's son, Haemon, enters and a dialogue between them follows. Creon begins by setting out the need for obedience within the family; Haemon replies respectfully, but points out that the citizens disapprove of Creon's decree and asks him to reconsider. A bitter clash follows, in which Creon accuses Haemon of valuing Antigone above his duties as a son, while Haemon becomes more critical of his father. Creon finally threatens to kill Antigone in his presence and Haemon storms offstage. The chorus persuade Creon to spare Ismene, but he vows that Antigone will be put to death by being entombed alive.

781–800:   The chorus sing a short song to Eros, whom they say has caused the quarrel that has just taken place (third *stasimon*).

801–82:   Antigone re-enters and engages in a ritual lament (*kommos*) with the chorus.

883–943:   Antigone and Creon meet for the last time. Creon urges the speedy removal of Antigone to her tomb; Antigone responds with a final address to the tomb that is also to be her bridal chamber, justifying her actions on the grounds that a brother is irreplaceable, while a husband and children are not, and lamenting the neglect of the gods. Antigone is then led away to her death.

944–87:   The chorus sing a song (fourth *stasimon*) comparing Antigone to three mythological figures: Danae, unjustly imprisoned by her father; Lycurgus, justly imprisoned by Dionysus; and Cleopatra, imprisoned by Phineus and her children blinded.

988–1114:   The blind prophet Teiresias enters and gives a long speech depicting the displeasure of the gods at the failure to bury Polynices, since sacrifices are failing and the city altars are polluted with carrion. Creon accuses him of conspiring against him, and Teiresias replies angrily, predicting the death of Haemon. Creon anxiously asks the chorus for advice: they urge him to release Antigone and bury Polynices. Creon rushes offstage to undo his actions.

1115–54:   The chorus sing a hymn to Dionysus, praying to him to come and rescue the city (fifth *stasimon*).

1155–1256:   A Messenger arrives and announces Haemon's death. Eurydice, Creon's wife, suddenly emerges from the palace and demands to hear what has happened. The Messenger recounts how Creon first buried Polynices and then went to Antigone's tomb, where he found Haemon lamenting over Antigone's dead body. After reproaching his father, Haemon killed himself. Eurydice rushes back inside the palace.

1257–1353:   Creon returns, bringing with him the body of Haemon. As Creon laments his son's death, the Messenger returns, announcing that Eurydice has killed herself by the family altar. Her body is also brought onstage. The play ends with Creon, a broken man, being led offstage, while the chorus reiterate the importance of piety and moderation.

Antigone and Creon

At the heart of *Antigone* lies the conflict between Antigone and Creon. Much discussion of the play has focused on which, if either of them, should be seen as 'right'. Most modern readers are likely to side with Antigone: contemporary sensibilities are sympathetic to an individual challenging the authority of an oppressive state, as well as a woman opposing an entirely male regime.

Antigone is undoubtedly an admirable figure in several respects. She powerfully argues for the importance of familial ties and is determined to pursue the course that she believes to be right, regardless of the cost. Her fearlessness in the face of death is reminiscent of the Greek male ideal (e.g. 460–4), as is her use of the term κλέος 'glory' (502), a term strongly associated with Homeric heroes and referring to the fame won by accomplishments in the military sphere. Antigone applies it to her achievement in burying her brother, and perhaps she could be viewed as behaving heroically in the only area open to a Greek woman, the home and the family.

However, Antigone is also flawed in many ways and is not an ideal figure to champion the cause of the family. She is presented as utterly negative, her speech being characterized by extensive use of negative forms (e.g. 3–6, 69–70, 450–7), and her treatment of the other characters in the play is cold and harsh, particularly her sister Ismene (e.g. 93–4, 543). She shows inconsistency in her treatment of her own family, since she treats Polynices as a 'friend' (φίλος) throughout the play, regardless of his actions, whereas she threatens to make her living relative, Ismene, as an 'enemy' (ἐχθρός) (86, 93–4). Indeed, she is prepared to set her dead relatives above her living ones, e.g. in her claim that a dead brother is of more importance than a living husband at 904–20, a passage that has so troubled some readers (e.g. Goethe) that they have argued it must be an interpolation. The chorus recognize her harsh character, describing her as 'savage offspring of a savage father' (471).

We should also bear in mind how Antigone would have been perceived by a contemporary audience, probably composed entirely of men. Athenian women were always under the protection of a guardian (κύριος), first their father or other relative and then their husband. Antigone goes against the expected behaviour of a woman in defying the authority of her guardian and king Creon (486–9, 531–3, 658–60). She does not appear to care about her fiancé Haemon (on the assumption that Ismene speak 572 (see note on this line)), and fails in what would have been seen as the key role of a woman: to marry, have children and perpetuate her family line. This theme is made clear in the play in her presentation as a 'bride of Hades' (e.g. 891, 916–8), a perversion of the normal course of a woman's life. As the play goes on, Antigone seems to recognize this and withdraws from several of her earlier opinions, regretting that she will die unmarried and childless (917–18; cf. 813–16, 867, 876). There is also an irony in that, by her determination to honour her own family, she ends up destroying it: not only does she turn against her living kin but by dying she prevents the family line from continuing into the future (e.g. 806 ff.).

Her opponent in the play, Creon, is also a champion of a key area of Athenian life: the city and its values. Although his decree not to bury Polynices may seem barbaric to us, it would not necessarily have been seen as wrong by an Athenian audience. There is evidence that traitors could be refused burial and Plato (*Laws* 909) advocates that a religious trickster should be thrown over the borders of a state unburied. Since Creon treats Polynices as a traitor (e.g. 198–202), the audience may have felt that he had some justification in refusing him burial (the chorus seem divided in their view of it at 211–14).

Even if we have some sympathy with Creon's outlook, though, he is also clearly an unsatisfactory representative of his position. There is inconsistency in his refusal to bury Polynices, when his own position is based on his close kinship with him (174). He is quick to anger (e.g. 280, 726–7) and fixated on his own authority (e.g. 173–4). His obsession with not being bested by a woman makes him seem somewhat ridiculous (e.g. 484, 525, 578–9). As the play goes on, his language becomes increasingly imperious (e.g. 291–2, 473–79), and he crosses over into paranoia, in accusing the Guard of taking bribes, threatening him with death (293–314) and then accusing the blameless Ismene of involvement in the burial of Polynices (489–90). This tyrannical behaviour would not have gone down well with an Athenian audience of democratic citizens. His attitude towards his own family is particularly brutal, as he dismisses the death of his own son's bride in grotesque language (569) and threatens to kill Antigone before Haemon's eyes (760–1). As with Antigone, his obsessive single-mindedness leads to him harming that which he seeks to protect, as he becomes responsible for polluting the city (997 ff., 1015).

Antigone and Creon, then, are representatives of different fundamental principles, Antigone of the values of the family and Creon of those of the state, but are flawed in their refusal to consider anything outside their own narrow compass. Their difference in outlook can be demonstrated by their use of the key term φίλος, which incorporated all those to whom one had ties of friendship. Antigone uses this term only to refer to relatives (e.g. 10, 73, 81, 898–9), while Creon uses it mostly of political friends (e.g. 187, 190). Both are partly correct, but are unable to see the other's point of view. Despite their conflict being the driving force behind the play, the two of them have very little interaction within the play and, where they do, they are speaking at cross purposes (e.g. 450–96).

On this view, *Antigone* can be read as suggesting that both sets of values need to be recognized and that neglect of either leads to disaster. The play itself provides some evidence for this interpretation, for example in the famous choral ode at 332–83 (the Ode to Man). The ode presents an ambiguous view of mankind's achievements, described as δεινός (332–3), both 'clever' and 'terrible', a word which is applied to both Antigone and Creon (96, 323, 408, 690). Towards the end of the ode (368–70), the chorus state that 'when he (i.e. man) applies the laws of the earth and the sworn justice of the gods, he is high in the city', i.e. a combination of the values of the two protagonists is necessary for a city to function successfully.

Other characters

The other characters in the play interact with the two central figures in various ways. Several of them offer a more measured outlook than the uncompromising Antigone and Creon and attempt to reason with them, although in every case their advice is rejected or comes too late. Antigone's sister Ismene contrasts with her as a moderate and reasonable character, who sympathizes with her position, while advocating caution (e.g. 49–68). She refuses to assist her, but demonstrates loyalty to Antigone when she reappears later in the play, siding with her and taking joint responsibility for the burial of Polynices, only to be rejected by her in turn (531–81). However, her contribution is ultimately ineffective; she is not mentioned after line 771 and Antigone refers to herself as the last remaining woman of the royal house (941). The Guard is another prudent character, although he comes across as somewhat comical (223–36), and has some success in reasoning with Creon (315–31). He is promptly dismissed upon discovering Antigone burying Polynices' body (444–5).

Creon's two closest family members, his son and wife, are both casualties of the conflict between him and Antigone. Haemon is an intermediate figure between the prudence of Ismene and the Guard on the one hand and the fervour of Antigone and Creon on the other. He begins as another voice of moderation in the play, showing appropriate respect for his father and arguing that more than one person can have a right opinion (705–7), only for this to turn into anger and frustration, and he ends committing passionate suicide at the tomb of Antigone (1223–5). Eurydice only appears very briefly (1183–91) and has one of the shortest number of lines of a character in Greek tragedy. She can be seen as representative of the destruction of Creon's house and family, with her death taking place significantly by the family altar (1301–5).

Teiresias is a common character in Greek tragedy and a number of plays contain a scene involves him advising a monarch, only to be insulted and dismissed, before then being proved right (Sophocles' *Antigone* and *Oedipus Tyrannus*, Euripides' *Phoenissae* and *Bacchae*). As a spokesman of the gods, he offers a voice of authority in the play, although he too is initially rejected by Creon (1033–45) and accused of seeking κέρδος 'gain' (1047), a word repeated throughout the play (cf. 310, 462, 1032). His advice comes too late to be able to save Antigone and Haemon.

The role of the chorus has been much discussed, as the choral odes in *Antigone* are particularly abstract and hard to interpret. It has even been argued that they should be seen purely as musical interludes, with no relevance to the themes of the play, although this is not a particularly helpful approach. One way of looking at them is as offering more general analyses of the specific examples of human behaviour exhibited by the characters in the play. The four central *stasima* offer various comments on the limitations faced by man. The first *stasimon* (the Ode to Man) dwells on the achievements of man, but also his limitations (e.g. 361–2, 365–6, 368–9). As suggested above, Antigone and Creon are prime examples of human beings who act boldly but run up against these limits. The next *stasimon* (582–630) points out further limitations on man: some families, like the Labdacids, are cursed and Zeus punishes the transgressions and false hopes of man. The third *stasimon* deals with the power of Eros (781–800), which will be responsible for the death of Haemon. The fourth *stasimon* (944–87) offers various mythological parallels to Antigone's position, dealing with the changes in human life and their dependence on the gods. The chorus begin and finish with a *parodos* and fifth *stasimon*, relating more directly to the action. In both, they turn out to be mistaken: the *parodos* is a celebration of victory over the Argives (100–61), but we have already learnt from the prologue that trouble is brewing, while in the final *stasimon* (1115–54) they pray for Dionysus to come and heal the city, but this is undercut immediately afterwards as we hear that Haemon and Antigone are both dead. While the chorus may offer moments of insight during the play, then, they too can be mistaken and are ultimately ineffectual in averting disaster. All the other characters in the play thus fall short in some respect in reconciling the conflicting values of the protagonists.

Language and style

The Greek selections in this book all come from dialogue passages of *Antigone*. The language of tragic dialogue varies between two different modes, longer speeches (rhesis) and exchanges of single lines between different characters (stichomythia), sometimes alternating with exchanges of two lines per character (distichomythia). The choral odes work on different principles: they are constructed of groups of rhythmically corresponding pairs of stanzas called strophe and antistrophe ('turn' and 'counter-turn'), which would have been sung while the chorus danced. As well as spoken dialogue and the full-blown songs of the chorus, we also find recitative, intermediate between the two. A common example of this mode is the ritual lament between characters (*kommos*), used to address feelings of intense emotion (the scene between Antigone and the chorus at 801–82 is a *kommos*).

The two different modes of dialogue are suited to different types of expression. Rhesis allows characters to speak at length, e.g. to give an account of their views or to attempt to persuade their listeners (e.g. Creon at 280–314, Antigone at 891–928). When characters first enter the stage, they begin either with rhesis or swiftly move into it (e.g. Creon's first words are a lengthy rhesis at 162–210, establishing his attitude towards kingship and the key concept of φιλία, as well as reiterating the terms of his decree).

The much more fast-paced stichomythia can be used for swift exchange of information or aggressive interchanges, such as an interrogation (e.g. 508–23). Scenes often make use of both modes, switching from one into the other (e.g. the opening scene between Antigone and Ismene (1–99) moves from rhesis to stichomythia at 39–48 and 78–92, as the sisters begin to clash). Special effects can be gained by suddenly shifting between one mode and the other. The confrontation between Creon and Antigone, for example, begins with stichomythia at 441–9, as Creon interrogates Antigone, only for Creon's third question to prompt a sudden and surprising rhesis from Antigone (450–70), as she launches into her declaration that Creon's laws are not those of Zeus.

A particular variety of rhesis is the 'messenger speech', used to report offstage events to the audience. The standard type of Messenger appears only in one scene, to deliver his message. In *Antigone*, the speech by the Messenger who reports the death of Haemon at 1192–1243 is of this kind. Messenger speeches are often epic in tone, describing violent, dramatic scenes, with distinctive vocabulary and morphology. The speeches of the Guard (249–77) and Teiresias (998–1032) show elements of the messenger speech in their vivid descriptions of offstage activity (e.g. the grotesque description of failed portents and sacrifices at 999–1022).

The language of Greek tragedy is a distinctively poetic variety of Attic Greek that shows the influence of Homeric language, the ultimate source of all later serious poetry in Greek. Various grammatical usages are common which we either do not, or rarely find, in prose:

- Omission of the definite article where it would be required in prose (e.g. 15 Ἀργείων στρατός 'the army of the Argives').

- Alternative (older) dative plural endings in -οισι and -αισι for normal -οις and -αις (e.g. πλεκταῖσιν ἀρτάναισι (54) for prose πλεκταῖς ἀρτάναις).
- Alternative accusative pronoun forms σφε (44, 516) and νιν (491, 577) used instead of the corresponding forms of αὐτός.
- Placement of prepositions after the noun they govern (anastrophe) (e.g. with περί at 193, 283).
- Simple verbs instead of the normal compound forms used in prose (e.g. ὄλλυμι for normal ἀπόλλυμι (59 etc.)).

The language of these selections also shows a wide range of stylistic features that are characteristic of tragedy. In examining such features, it is important to focus on the effect they have, rather than simply listing them. Examples and suggestions about their effect are offered below:

- Item of vocabulary that are not found in prose (e.g. κάρα (1), ἀτωμένη (17), καλχαίνουσ᾽ (20), ἀμπλάκημα (51)), giving the language a feeling of being detached from everyday speech and elevated.
- Conversely, prosaic words can be used for special effect (e.g. Creon's use of μισθαρνοῦντες 'hiring' (302) and λημμάτων (313) 'acquisitions' sounds coarse).
- Periphrasis (i.e. phrases instead of single words), used to elevate the language to a grand tone (e.g. Ἰσμήνης κάρα 'head of Ismene' (1), a Homeric type of expression).
- Accumulation of alpha-private adjectives for emotional effect (e.g. ἄκλαυτον, ἄταφον 'unwept, unburied' (29), ἄλεκτρον, ἀνυμέναιον 'unwedded, without a wedding song' (917)).
- Compound adjectives, which can be readily coined in poetry to add grandeur to the language (e.g. δημόλευστον 'from public stoning' (36)).
- A particularly common type of compound is formed from the stem αὐτο- ('self', 'one's own'), e.g. αὐτοφώρων (51), αὐτουργῷ (52), αὐτοκτονοῦντε (56). Such forms are particularly suitable in *Antigone*, as they highlight the self-destructive, incestuous nature of Oedipus' family.
- Nouns in -μα are particularly characteristic of tragic language, e.g. κιδύνευμα (42) for normal κίνδυνος. When this type of noun is applied to a person, it has a contemptuous tone (e.g. λάλημα 'chatterbox' (320)).
- Metonymy (i.e. expression of one concept via a related one) is a common poetic usage (e.g. Ἥφαιστος (1007) 'fire' is a striking alternative to πῦρ, but the main point is that the gods have abandoned Thebes).
- Contrasting terms are frequently juxtaposed for stylistic effect, either to add emphasis or to stress an opposition between antagonists or viewpoints. Examples can be found throughout these selections (e.g. φίλους ... ἐχθρῶν 'friends ... enemies' (10); οὔθ᾽ ἡδὺς οὔτ᾽ ἀλγεινός 'neither pleasant not painful' (12); δυοῖν ... δύο / μιᾷ 'two ... two ... one' (13–14); θερμήν ... ψυχροῖσι 'hot ... cold' (88)).

- Conversely, forms of the same word (polyptoton) or related forms from the same root (figura etymologica) can be juxtaposed to emphasize the importance of a particular point. For example, in **φίλη** μετ' αὐτοῦ κείσομαι, **φίλου** μέτα 'I shall lie with him, a friend with a friend' (73), the polyptoton of φίλος stresses the mutual relationship between them; in σοὶ δ' εἰ δοκῶ νῦν μῶρα δρῶσα τυγχάνειν / σχεδόν τι μώρῳ μωρίαν ὀφλισκάνω 'If I seem to you now to be happening to act foolishly, perhaps I incur the charge of foolishness in the eyes of a fool' (469–70), the figura etymologica of μώρῳ μωρίαν (as well as the polyptoton of μῶρα . . . μώρῳ) makes Antigone's contempt for Creon abundantly clear.

- A particular type of juxtaposition involves terms that would normally be contradictory to produce a striking effect (oxymoron). Antigone uses this device to portray the perverseness of a situation where what she regards as acts of piety are treated as criminal (ὅσια πανουργήσασ' 'having committed acts of holy crime' (74), τὴν δυσσέβειαν εὐσεβοῦσ' ἐκτησάμην 'through being pious I have gained the charge of impiety' (924)).

- Repetition of vocabulary in general is characteristic of tragic language, allowing important concepts to be echoed continuously; for example, the word φίλος and related forms crop up again and again (e.g. φίλη μὲν . . . προσφιλὴς δὲ . . . φίλη δέ (898–9) 'a friend . . . friendly . . . a friend').

- The previous example illustrates another characteristically rhetorical feature of tragic language, the set of three parallel words or phrases, which typically increase in length towards a climax (ascending tricolon). Antigone's address to the chamber in which she is to be buried (ὦ τύμβος, ὦ νυμφεῖον, ὦ κατασκαφὴς οἴκησις ἀείφρουρος 'O tomb, O bridal chamber, O deep-dug ever-guarded dwelling' (891–2)) begins her final speech in a grand style. The compound adjective ἀείφρουρος is attested only here (*hapax legomenon*), adding further dignity to the expression.

- Word order can also be used for stylistic effect. One common phenomenon in Greek is to place an emphatic word early in a sentence (e.g. in τάφου . . . / τὸν μὲν προτίσας, τὸν δ' ἀτιμάσας ἔχει (21) 'he has honoured one with a tomb and deprived the other one of it, τάφου is placed at the beginning to stress the idea of burial; in Ἐτεοκλέα μέν (23), Eteocles' name is put first as the subject matter of the sentence).

- A related phenomenon is the use of pauses, especially after enjambement, stressing the word at the beginning of the line (e.g. in κεῖνον δ' ἐγὼ / θάψω. 'I **shall bury** him' (72–3), θάψω is strongly emphatic; cf. τὸν γοῦν ἐμόν, καὶ τὸν σόν, ἢν σὺ μὴ θέλῃς / ἀδελφόν· (45–6) 'my **brother** at any rate, and yours, if you are unwilling'.)

- At a wider level, speakers are differentiated by linguistic variety, according to their character and emotional state. For example, the restrained Ismene tends to speak in balanced sentences (e.g. 49–68, with long sentences with structuring words such as ἔπειτα . . . τρίτον and pauses at line end), whereas Antigone's language is characterized by an abundance of negatives (e.g. 4–6, 69–70), lots of questions (e.g. 2–10) and shorter, curt sentences (e.g. 69–77). Creon's language is full of moralizing statements (*gnomai*) (e.g. 175–7, 580–1).

The metre of the play

Greek poetry operates on different principles from English poetry, being based upon patterns of light and heavy syllables (indicated by the symbols ∪ for a light syllable, – for a heavy one and × where either can stand). The metre of all the selections contained in this book is known as iambic trimeters. This is the metre of most of the spoken dialogue in Greek tragedy. Several other metres are used in Greek drama; the choral odes, for example, are written in complex and elaborate metres, with each ode having its own particular metrical pattern.

As the name suggests, iambic trimeters consist of three units based around an iambic pattern (∪ –), with the basic rhythm as follows: ∪ – ∪ – | ∪ – ∪ – | ∪ – ∪ ×. The final syllable of the line can be either light or heavy, as there is a natural pause there. This pattern is often presented as six 'feet', with each unit consisting of two feet, and we will use feet as our units here for ease of presentation. In order to accommodate words of different metrical shapes, quite a lot of variation is permitted in this basic pattern, particularly at the beginning of the line. The different units found are: iamb (∪ –), spondee (– –), tribrach (∪∪∪), dactyl (– ∪∪) and anapaest (∪∪ –). The full set of possibilities is given below:

1	2	3	4	5	6
∪ –	∪ –	∪ –	∪ –	∪ –	∪ ×
– –	– –	– –	– –	– –	
∪∪∪	∪∪∪	∪∪∪	∪∪∪		
– ∪∪	– ∪∪				
∪∪ –					

In addition to these possibilities, an anapaest is permitted in any of the first five feet of the line in order to accommodate proper names that would otherwise not fit (e.g. Ἀντιγόνη (11)). Although the full scheme may look rather complicated, in practice the most common patterns consist of iambs and spondees and the other types of feet are much less common.

Syllables that contain a diphthong (i.e. a pair of vowels pronounced together such as αι, ευ) or a long vowel (i.e. η, ω and the long variants of α, ι, υ) are heavy. Syllables containing a short vowel can also be heavy if they are followed by two or more consonants, although there are some additional details here. A short vowel will form a heavy syllable if it is followed by:

i)   a double consonant (i.e. ζ, ξ or ψ);

ii) any two consonants, unless they are a combination of a plosive (π β φ, τ δ θ, κ γ χ) plus liquid (λ ρ) or nasal (μ ν) in the same word, in which case a preceding short vowel may be either light or heavy (e.g. ἀθλίως (26) scans as – ∪ –, with heavy α before θλ, but ἄκλαυτον (29) scans as ∪ – ∪, with light α before κλ);

iii) γμ, γν, δμ or δν;

iv) any two consonants belonging to different words (e.g. in line 4 οὐδὲν γάρ, the short ε of οὐδέν forms a heavy syllable) or different parts of a compound.

A heavy syllable will be formed in the case of i), ii) and iii) when the short vowel ends a word and the two consonants begin the next word (e.g. in ὅ τι Ζεύς (2), the short ι of ὅ τι is lengthened before Ζ; in κατὰ χθονός (24), the final α of κατά is lengthened before χθ).

Single vowels may be either long or short by nature. As ε and ο are inherently short vowels and η and ω inherently long, there is only uncertainty in the case of α, ι and υ. You can find out the quality of vowels from a good dictionary such as James Morwood's *Pocket Oxford Greek Dictionary* (Oxford University Press, 2002), which marks long vowels with a macron (–).

A short vowel at the end of a word is elided before a vowel at the beginning of the next. In Greek, unlike Latin, such elisions are marked in the text with an apostrophe (e.g. ἆρ᾽ οἶσθ᾽ ὅ τι (2)). A less familiar type of vowel loss is aphaeresis (or prodelision), where a short vowel at the beginning of a word is elided after a preceding long vowel (e.g. μὴ 'μοῦ (83) for μὴ ἐμοῦ. This is also marked with an apostrophe. A word ending with a long vowel is not usually placed before a word beginning with a long vowel to avoid the clash of vowels. When this does happen, the two vowels slur together to produce a single long syllable by a process called synizesis (e.g. μὴ and εἰ- form a single syllable in μὴ εἰδόσιν (33)).

An example of an iambic line with light and heavy syllables and foot divisions indicated would thus run:

```
– – | ∪    – | – || – |    ∪ – | ∪    – | ∪ ×
κήρυγμα θεῖναι τὸν στρατηγὸν ἀρτίως
```

Note that heavy syllables are formed by long vowels, diphthongs and the combinations of short vowel followed by two consonants, e.g. the α in ἀρτίως and the first ο in τὸν στρατηγόν. In the line above, the ‖ symbol marks the caesura, a word-break in the middle of a foot within the line. This is most commonly found after the first syllable of the third foot, but can also occur after the first syllable of the fourth foot. Compare a line with a fourth foot caesura:

```
–    – | ∪  – | ∪ – |  ∪ ‖ –  | –  – | ∪ ×
ὦ κοινὸν αὐτάδελφον Ἰσμήνης κάρα
```

The metrical break at the caesura is often accompanied by a pause in the sense. This can be used to emphasize a contrast still further (e.g. τὸν μὲν προτίσας, ‖ τὸν δ᾽ ἀτιμάσας ἔχει 'he has honoured one and dishonoured the other' (22); μὴ 'μοῦ προτάρβει· ‖ τὸν σὸν ἐξόρθου πότμον (83) 'do not fear for me; set your own destiny straight'). Occasionally, the caesura can be formed by an elision at the end of the third foot (e.g. 44, 57). This 'quasi-caesura' sometimes seems to be used for special effect (e.g. in καίτοι πόθεν κλέος γ᾽ ἂν εὐκλεέστερον 'And yet from where (would I have obtained) more glorious glory?' (502), the important word κλέος is emphasized by the unusual rhythm).

Glossary of technical terms

Technical terms used in the Commentary are indicated there in bold. Definitions can be found below. Many of these terms are also explained and exemplified in the Introduction.

Anaphora	repetition of a word or phrase at the beginning of successive clauses.
Anastrophe	placing of a preposition after the noun it governs.
Aphaeresis	loss of a vowel by elision at the beginning of a word.
Assonance	repetition of vowel sounds within a phrase or sentence.
Caesura	pause midway through a line of verse.
Ethic dative	dative case used to express interest felt by the person indicated.
Figura etymologica	adjacent placing of different words with same etymological derivation for rhetorical effect (cf. polyptoton).
Hapax legomenon	a word attested only once.
Hyperbaton	figure of speech whereby words normally associated are separated.
Hypermetric elision	elision of vowels between lines of verse.
Iambic trimeters	the metrical pattern generally used for spoken passages in tragedy.
Litotes	use of negative expression to affirm a positive point, often with a double negative.
Metonymy	figure of speech whereby a thing or concept is named by the name of something else associated with the thing or concept.
Parodos	entrance song of a chorus in Greek drama.
Polyptoton	adjacent placing of the same word in different forms for rhetorical effect (cf. figura etymologica).
Polysyndeton	use of several conjunctions in close succession.
Proleptic	application of adjective to noun in anticipation of the result of the action it describes.
Rhesis	term for a speech in Greek drama.
Stasimon	song of a tragic chorus that follows their entrance song (*parodos*).
Stichomythia	dialogue in which two characters speak alternate lines of verse.
Synizesis	slurring together of two separate vowel sounds to produce a single syllable.
Tricolon	set of three parallel words, phrases or clauses. Where the parts increase in size, magnitude, intensity or word length, it is known as an ascending tricolon.
Zeugma	figure of speech whereby a single word joins different parts of a sentence.

Further reading

There are several good modern translations of *Antigone*. Robert Fagles' Penguin Classics translation (*The Three Theban Plays*, 1984) is well known and the translation by H.D.F. Kitto has been reissued in the Oxford World's Classics series (*Sophocles: Antigone, Oedipus the King* and *Electra*, 2008). Particularly suitable for students is the volume by David Franklin and John Harrison in the Cambridge Translations from Greek Drama series, containing helpful notes and stimulating questions for discussion (*Sophocles: Antigone*, Cambridge, 2003).

For editions of the whole play in Greek, Sir Richard Jebb's famous edition, with notes and facing translation, is still very valuable (reprinted by Bristol Classical Press, 2004) and the excellent modern edition by M. Griffith (*Sophocles: Antigone*, Cambridge, 1999) contains a detailed introduction to the whole play.

For more general discussion of *Antigone* and Greek drama, see:
Hall, E. (2010) *Greek Tragedy: Suffering under the Sun*, Oxford.
Ormand, K. (ed.), (2012) *A Companion to Sophocles*, Hoboken.
Steiner, G. (1986) *Antigones*, Oxford.
Wiles, D. (2000) *Greek Theatre Performance: An Introduction*, Cambridge.
Winnington-Ingram, R.P. (1980) *Sophocles: An Interpretation*, Cambridge.

For more information on tragic style, see:
Rutherford, R. (2012) *Greek Tragic Style. Form, Language and Interpretation*, Cambridge.
For more information on the scansion of iambic trimeters, see:
West, M.L. (1987) *Introduction to Greek Metre*, Oxford.

Text

ΑΝΤΙΓΟΝΗ

ὦ κοινὸν αὐτάδελφον Ἰσμήνης κάρα,
ἆρ᾿ οἶσθ᾿ ὅ τι Ζεὺς τῶν ἀπ᾿ Οἰδίπου κακῶν —
ἆ, ποῖον οὐχὶ νῷν ἔτι ζώσαιν τελεῖ;
οὐδὲν γὰρ οὔτ᾿ ἀλγεινὸν οὔτ᾿ †ἄτης ἄτερ†
οὔτ᾿ αἰσχρὸν οὔτ᾿ ἄτιμόν ἐσθ᾿, ὁποῖον οὐ   5
τῶν σῶν τε κἀμῶν οὐκ ὄπωπ᾿ ἐγὼ κακῶν.
καὶ νῦν τί τοῦτ᾿ αὖ φασι πανδήμῳ πόλει
κήρυγμα θεῖναι τὸν στρατηγὸν ἀρτίως;
ἔχεις τι κεἰσήκουσας;ἢ σε λανθάνει
πρὸς τοὺς φίλους στείχοντα τῶν ἐχθρῶν κακά;   10

ΙΣΜΗΝΗ

ἐμοὶ μὲν οὐδεὶς μῦθος, Ἀντιγόνη, φίλων
οὔθ᾿ ἡδὺς οὔτ᾿ ἀλγεινὸς ἵκετ᾿ ἐξ ὅτου
δυοῖν ἀδελφοῖν ἐστερήθημεν δύο,
μιᾷ θανόντοιν ἡμέρᾳ διπλῇ χερί·
ἐπεὶ δὲ φροῦδός ἐστιν Ἀργείων στρατὸς   15
ἐν νυκτὶ τῇ νῦν, οὐδὲν οἶδ᾿ ὑπέρτερον,
οὔτ᾿ εὐτυχοῦσα μᾶλλον οὔτ᾿ ἀτωμένη.
Αν.   ἤδη καλῶς, καί σ᾿ ἐκτὸς αὐλείων πυλῶν
τοῦδ᾿ οὕνεκ᾿ ἐξέπεμπον, ὡς μόνη κλύοις.
Ισ.   τί δ᾿ ἔστι; δηλοῖς γάρ τι καλχαίνουσ᾿ ἔπος.   20
Αν.   οὐ γὰρ τάφου νῷν τὼ κασιγνήτω Κρέων
τὸν μὲν προτίσας, τὸν δ᾿ ἀτιμάσας ἔχει;
Ἐτεοκλέα μέν, ὡς λέγουσι, †σὺν δίκῃ
χρησθεὶς† δικαίᾳ καὶ νόμῳ, κατὰ χθονὸς
ἔκρυψε τοῖς ἔνερθεν ἔντιμον νεκροῖς,   25

τὸν δ᾽ ἀθλίως θανόντα Πολυνείκους νέκυν
ἀστοῖσί φασιν ἐκκεκηρῦχθαι τὸ μὴ
τάφῳ καλύψαι μηδὲ κωκῦσαί τινα,
ἐᾶν δ᾽ ἄκλαυτον, ἄταφον, οἰωνοῖς γλυκὺν
θησαυρὸν εἰσορῶσι πρὸς χάριν βορᾶς.   30
τοιαῦτά φασι τὸν ἀγαθὸν Κρέοντα σοὶ
κἀμοί, λέγω γὰρ κἀμέ, κηρύξαντ᾽ ἔχειν,
καὶ δεῦρο νεῖσθαι ταῦτα τοῖσι μὴ εἰδόσιν
σαφῆ προκηρύξοντα, καὶ τὸ πρᾶγμ᾽ ἄγειν
οὐχ ὡς παρ᾽ οὐδέν, ἀλλ᾽ ὃς ἂν τούτων τι δρᾷ,   35
φόνον προκεῖσθαι δημόλευστον ἐν πόλει.
οὕτως ἔχει σοι ταῦτα, καὶ δείξεις τάχα
εἴτ᾽ εὐγενὴς πέφυκας εἴτ᾽ ἐσθλῶν κακή.

Ισ. τί δ᾽, ὦ ταλαῖφρον, εἰ τάδ᾽ ἐν τούτοις, ἐγὼ
     λύουσ᾽ ἂν εἴθ᾽ ἅπτουσα προσθείμην πλέον;   40

Αν. εἰ ξυμπονήσεις καὶ ξυνεργάσῃ σκόπει.

Ισ. ποῖόν τι κινδύνευμα; ποῦ γνώμης ποτ᾽ εἰ;

Αν. εἰ τὸν νεκρὸν ξὺν τῇδε κουφιεῖς χερί.

Ισ. ἦ γὰρ νοεῖς θάπτειν σφ᾽, ἀπόρρητον πόλει;

Αν. τὸν γοῦν ἐμόν, καὶ τὸν σόν, ἢν σὺ μὴ θέλῃς,   45
     ἀδελφόν· οὐ γὰρ δὴ προδοῦσ᾽ ἁλώσομαι.

Ισ. ὦ σχετλία, Κρέοντος ἀντειρηκότος;

Αν. ἀλλ᾽ οὐδὲν αὐτῷ τῶν ἐμῶν μ᾽ εἴργειν μέτα.

Ισ. οἴμοι· φρόνησον, ὦ κασιγνήτη, πατὴρ
     ὡς νῷν ἀπεχθὴς δυσκλεής τ᾽ ἀπώλετο,   50
     πρὸς αὐτοφώρων ἀμπλακημάτων, διπλᾶς
     ὄψεις ἀράξας αὐτὸς αὐτουργῷ χερί·
     ἔπειτα μήτηρ καὶ γυνή, διπλοῦν ἔπος,
     πλεκταῖσιν ἀρτάναισι λωβᾶται βίον·
     τρίτον δ᾽ ἀδελφὼ δύο μίαν καθ᾽ ἡμέραν   55
     αὐτοκτονοῦντε τὼ ταλαιπώρω μόρον
     κοινὸν κατειργάσαντ᾽ ἐπαλλήλοιν χεροῖν.
     νῦν δ᾽ αὖ μόνα δὴ νὼ λελειμμένα σκόπει
     ὅσῳ κάκιστ᾽ ὀλούμεθ᾽, εἰ νόμου βίᾳ
     ψῆφον τυράννων ἢ κράτη παρέξιμεν.   60
     ἀλλ᾽ ἐννοεῖν χρὴ τοῦτο μὲν γυναῖχ᾽ ὅτι
     ἔφυμεν, ὡς πρὸς ἄνδρας οὐ μαχουμένα·
     ἔπειτα δ᾽ οὕνεκ᾽ ἀρχόμεσθ᾽ ἐκ κρεισσόνων
     καὶ ταῦτ᾽ ἀκούειν κἄτι τῶνδ᾽ ἀλγίονα.
     ἐγὼ μὲν οὖν αἰτοῦσα τοὺς ὑπὸ χθονὸς   65

ξύγγνοιαν ἴσχειν, ὡς βιάζομαι τάδε,
τοῖς ἐν τέλει βεβῶσι πείσομαι. τὸ γὰρ
περισσὰ πράσσειν οὐκ ἔχει νοῦν οὐδένα.

Αν.   οὔτ᾽ ἂν κελεύσαιμ᾽ οὔτ᾽ ἄν, εἰ θέλοις ἔτι
πράσσειν, ἐμοῦ γ᾽ ἂν ἡδέως δρῴης μέτα.   70
ἀλλ᾽ ἴσθ᾽ ὁποῖά σοι δοκεῖ, κεῖνον δ᾽ ἐγὼ
θάψω. καλόν μοι τοῦτο ποιούσῃ θανεῖν.
φίλη μετ᾽ αὐτοῦ κείσομαι, φίλου μέτα,
ὅσια πανουργήσασ᾽· ἐπεὶ πλείων χρόνος
ὃν δεῖ μ᾽ ἀρέσκειν τοῖς κάτω τῶν ἐνθάδε.   75
ἐκεῖ γὰρ αἰεὶ κείσομαι· σὺ δ᾽ εἰ δοκεῖ
τὰ τῶν θεῶν ἔντιμ᾽ ἀτιμάσασ᾽ ἔχε.

Ισ.   ἐγὼ μὲν οὐκ ἄτιμα ποιοῦμαι, τὸ δὲ
βίᾳ πολιτῶν δρᾶν ἔφυν ἀμήχανος.

Αν.   σὺ μὲν τάδ᾽ ἂν προὔχοι· ἐγὼ δὲ δὴ τάφον   80
χώσουσ᾽ ἀδελφῷ φιλτάτῳ πορεύσομαι.

Ισ.   οἴμοι, ταλαίνης ὡς ὑπερδέδοικά σου.

Αν.   μὴ 'μοῦ προτάρβει· τὸν σὸν ἐξόρθου πότμον.

Ισ.   ἀλλ᾽ οὖν προμηνύσῃς γε τοῦτο μηδενὶ
τοὔργον, κρυφῇ δὲ κεῦθε, σὺν δ᾽ αὔτως ἐγώ.   85

Αν.   οἴμοι, καταύδα· πολλὸν ἐχθίων ἔσῃ
σιγῶσ᾽, ἐὰν μὴ πᾶσι κηρύξῃς τάδε.

Ισ.   θερμὴν ἐπὶ ψυχροῖσι καρδίαν ἔχεις.

Αν.   ἀλλ᾽ οἶδ᾽ ἀρέσκουσ᾽ οἷς μάλισθ᾽ ἁδεῖν με χρή.

Ισ.   εἰ καὶ δυνήσῃ γ᾽· ἀλλ᾽ ἀμηχάνων ἐρᾷς.   90

Αν.   οὐκοῦν, ὅταν δὴ μὴ σθένω, πεπαύσομαι.

Ισ.   ἀρχὴν δὲ θηρᾶν οὐ πρέπει τἀμήχανα.

Αν.   εἰ ταῦτα λέξεις, ἐχθαρεῖ μὲν ἐξ ἐμοῦ,
ἐχθρὰ δὲ τῷ θανόντι προσκείσῃ δίκῃ.
ἀλλ᾽ ἔα με καὶ τὴν ἐξ ἐμοῦ δυσβουλίαν   95
παθεῖν τὸ δεινὸν τοῦτο· πείσομαι γὰρ οὖν
τοσοῦτον οὐδὲν ὥστε μὴ οὐ καλῶς θανεῖν.

Ισ.   ἀλλ᾽ εἰ δοκεῖ σοι, στεῖχε· τοῦτο δ᾽ ἴσθ᾽, ὅτι
ἄνους μὲν ἔρχῃ, τοῖς φίλοις δ᾽ ὀρθῶς φίλη.

100–61: *The Chorus sing an ode of victory, celebrating the previous day's defeat of the invading Argive army. At the end of it, they announce the arrival of Creon, new King of Thebes.*

AS

ΚΡΕΩΝ

ἄνδρες, τὰ μὲν δὴ πόλεος ἀσφαλῶς θεοὶ
πολλῷ σάλῳ σείσαντες ὤρθωσαν πάλιν·
ὑμᾶς δ᾽ ἐγὼ πομποῖσιν ἐκ πάντων δίχα
ἔστειλ᾽ ἱκέσθαι, τοῦτο μὲν τὰ Λαΐου   165
σέβοντας εἰδὼς εὖ θρόνων ἀεὶ κράτη,
τοῦτ᾽ αὖθις, ἡνίκ᾽ Οἰδίπους ὤρθου πόλιν

·   ·   ·   ·   ·

κἀπεὶ διώλετ᾽, ἀμφὶ τοὺς κείνων ἔτι
παῖδας μένοντας ἐμπέδοις φρονήμασιν.
ὅτ᾽ οὖν ἐκεῖνοι πρὸς διπλῆς μοίρας μίαν   170
καθ᾽ ἡμέραν ὤλοντο παίσαντές τε καὶ
πληγέντες αὐτόχειρι σὺν μιάσματι,
ἐγὼ κράτη δὴ πάντα καὶ θρόνους ἔχω
γένους κατ᾽ ἀγχιστεῖα τῶν ὀλωλότων.
ἀμήχανον δὲ παντὸς ἀνδρὸς ἐκμαθεῖν   175
ψυχήν τε καὶ φρόνημα καὶ γνώμην, πρὶν ἂν
ἀρχαῖς τε καὶ νόμοισιν ἐντριβὴς φανῇ.
ἐμοὶ γὰρ ὅστις πᾶσαν εὐθύνων πόλιν
μὴ τῶν ἀρίστων ἅπτεται βουλευμάτων
ἀλλ᾽ ἐκ φόβου του γλῶσσαν ἐγκλῄσας ἔχει   180
κάκιστος εἶναι νῦν τε καὶ πάλαι δοκεῖ·
καὶ μεῖζον᾽ ὅστις ἀντὶ τῆς αὑτοῦ πάτρας
φίλον νομίζει, τοῦτον οὐδαμοῦ λέγω.
ἐγὼ γάρ, ἴστω Ζεὺς ὁ πάνθ᾽ ὁρῶν ἀεί,
οὔτ᾽ ἂν σιωπήσαιμι τὴν ἄτην ὁρῶν   185
στείχουσαν ἀστοῖς ἀντὶ τῆς σωτηρίας,
οὔτ᾽ ἂν φίλον ποτ᾽ ἄνδρα δυσμενῆ χθονὸς
θείμην ἐμαυτῷ, τοῦτο γιγνώσκων ὅτι
ἥδ᾽ ἐστὶν ἡ σῴζουσα καὶ ταύτης ἔπι
πλέοντες ὀρθῆς τοὺς φίλους ποιούμεθα.   190
τοιοῖσδ᾽ ἐγὼ νόμοισι τήνδ᾽ αὔξω πόλιν,
καὶ νῦν ἀδελφὰ τῶνδε κηρύξας ἔχω
ἀστοῖσι παίδων τῶν ἀπ᾽ Οἰδίπου πέρι·
Ἐτεοκλέα μέν, ὃς πόλεως ὑπερμαχῶν
ὄλωλε τῆσδε, πάντ᾽ ἀριστεύσας δορί,   195
τάφῳ τε κρύψαι καὶ τὰ πάντ᾽ ἀφαγνίσαι
ἃ τοῖς ἀρίστοις ἔρχεται κάτω νεκροῖς·
τὸν δ᾽ αὖ ξύναιμον τοῦδε, Πολυνείκη λέγω,
ὃς γῆν πατρῴαν καὶ θεοὺς τοὺς ἐγγενεῖς
φυγὰς κατελθὼν ἠθέλησε μὲν πυρὶ   200
πρῆσαι κατ᾽ ἄκρας, ἠθέλησε δ᾽ αἵματος
κοινοῦ πάσασθαι, τοὺς δὲ δουλώσας ἄγειν,

τοῦτον πόλει τῇδ᾽ ἐκκεκήρυκται τάφῳ
μήτε κτερίζειν μήτε κωκῦσαί τινα,
ἐᾶν δ᾽ ἄθαπτον καὶ πρὸς οἰωνῶν δέμας   205
καὶ πρὸς κυνῶν ἐδεστὸν αἰκισθέν τ᾽ ἰδεῖν.
τοιόνδ᾽ ἐμὸν φρόνημα, κοὔποτ᾽ ἔκ γ᾽ ἐμοῦ
τιμῇ προέξουσ᾽ οἱ κακοὶ τῶν ἐνδίκων.
ἀλλ᾽ ὅστις εὔνους τῇδε τῇ πόλει, θανὼν
καὶ ζῶν ὁμοίως ἔκ γ᾽ ἐμοῦ τιμήσεται.   210

Χο.   σοὶ ταῦτ᾽ ἀρέσκει, παῖ Μενοικέως, ποεῖν
τὸν τῇδε δύσνουν κὰς τὸν εὐμενῆ πόλει·
νόμῳ δὲ χρῆσθαι παντί, τοῦτ᾽ ἔνεστί σοι
καὶ τῶν θανόντων χὠπόσοι ζῶμεν πέρι.

Κρ.   ὡς ἂν σκοποὶ νῦν ἦτε τῶν εἰρημένων—   215
Χο.   νεωτέρῳ τῳ τοῦτο βαστάζειν πρόθες.
Κρ.   ἀλλ᾽ εἴσ᾽ ἕτοιμοι τοῦ νεκροῦ γ᾽ ἐπίσκοποι.
Χο.   τί δῆτ᾽ ἂν ἄλλ᾽ ἐκ τοῦδ᾽ ἐπεντέλλοις ἔτι;
Κρ.   τὸ μὴ ᾽πιχωρεῖν τοῖς ἀπιστοῦσιν τάδε.
Χο.   οὔκ ἔστιν οὕτω μῶρος ὃς θανεῖν ἐρᾷ.   220
Κρ.   καὶ μὴν ὁ μισθός γ᾽ οὗτος. ἀλλ᾽ ὑπ᾽ ἐλπίδων
ἄνδρας τὸ κέρδος πολλάκις διώλεσεν.

223–47: *A Guard enters and announces that someone has buried Polynices' body, in direct contravention of Creon's orders.*

Κρ.   τί φής; τίς ἀνδρῶν ἦν ὁ τολμήσας τάδε;

ΦΥΛΑΞ

οὐκ οἶδ᾽· ἐκεῖ γὰρ οὔτε του γενῇδος ἦν
πλῆγμ᾽, οὐ δικέλλης ἐκβολή. στύφλος δὲ γῆ   250
καὶ χέρσος, ἀρρὼξ οὐδ᾽ ἐπημαξευμένη
τροχοῖσιν, ἀλλ᾽ ἄσημος οὑργάτης τις ἦν.
ὅπως δ᾽ ὁ πρῶτος ἡμὶν ἡμεροσκόπος
δείκνυσι, πᾶσι θαῦμα δυσχερὲς παρῆν.
ὁ μὲν γὰρ ἠφάνιστο, τυμβήρης μὲν οὔ,   255
λεπτὴ δ᾽ ἄγος φεύγοντος ὡς ἐπῆν κόνις.
σημεῖα δ᾽ οὔτε θηρὸς οὔτε του κυνῶν
ἐλθόντος, οὐ σπάσαντος ἐξεφαίνετο.
λόγοι δ᾽ ἐν ἀλλήλοισιν ἐρρόθουν κακοί,
φύλαξ ἐλέγχων φύλακα, κἂν ἐγίγνετο   260
πληγὴ τελευτῶσ᾽, οὐδ᾽ ὁ κωλύσων παρῆν.
εἷς γάρ τις ἦν ἕκαστος οὑξειργασμένος,
κοὐδεὶς ἐναργής, ἀλλ᾽ ἔφευγε μὴ εἰδέναι.
ἦμεν δ᾽ ἕτοιμοι καὶ μύδρους αἴρειν χεροῖν,
καὶ πῦρ διέρπειν καὶ θεοὺς ὁρκωμοτεῖν,   265

**A
Level**

τὸ μήτε δρᾶσαι μήτε τῳ ξυνειδέναι
τὸ πρᾶγμα βουλεύσαντι μηδ᾽ εἰργασμένῳ.
τέλος δ᾽ ὅτ᾽ οὐδὲν ἦν ἐρευνῶσιν πλέον,
λέγει τις εἷς, ὃ πάντας ἐς πέδον κάρα
νεῦσαι φόβῳ προὔτρεψεν· οὐ γὰρ εἴχομεν   270
οὔτ᾽ ἀντιφωνεῖν οὔθ᾽ ὅπως δρῶντες καλῶς
πράξαιμεν. ἦν δ᾽ ὁ μῦθος ὡς ἀνοιστέον
σοὶ τοὔργον εἴη τοῦτο κοὐχὶ κρυπτέον.
καὶ ταῦτ᾽ ἐνίκα, κἀμὲ τὸν δυσδαίμονα
πάλος καθαιρεῖ τοῦτο τἀγαθὸν λαβεῖν.   275
πάρειμι δ᾽ ἄκων οὐχ ἑκοῦσιν, οἶδ᾽ ὅτι·
στέργει γὰρ οὐδεὶς ἄγγελον κακῶν ἐπῶν.

Χο.   ἄναξ, ἐμοί τοι μή τι καὶ θεήλατον
     τοὔργον τόδ᾽ ἡ ξύννοια βουλεύει πάλαι.

Κρ.   παῦσαι, πρὶν ὀργῆς καί με μεστῶσαι λέγων,   280
     μὴ ᾽φευρεθῇς ἄνους τε καὶ γέρων ἅμα.
λέγεις γὰρ οὐκ ἀνεκτὰ δαίμονας λέγων
πρόνοιαν ἴσχειν τοῦδε τοῦ νεκροῦ πέρι.
πότερον ὑπερτιμῶντες ὡς εὐεργέτην
ἔκρυπτον αὐτόν, ὅστις ἀμφικίονας   285
ναοὺς πυρώσων ἦλθε κἀναθήματα
καὶ γῆν ἐκείνων καὶ νόμους διασκεδῶν;
ἢ τοὺς κακοὺς τιμῶντας εἰσορᾷς θεούς;
οὐκ ἔστιν. ἀλλὰ ταῦτα καὶ πάλαι πόλεως
ἄνδρες μόλις φέροντες ἐρρόθουν ἐμοὶ   290
κρυφῇ, κάρα σείοντες, οὐδ᾽ ὑπὸ ζυγῷ
λόφον δικαίως εἶχον, ὡς στέργειν ἐμέ.
ἐκ τῶνδε τούτους ἐξεπίσταμαι καλῶς
παρηγμένους μισθοῖσιν εἰργάσθαι τάδε.
οὐδὲν γὰρ ἀνθρώποισιν οἷον ἄργυρος   295
κακὸν νόμισμ᾽ ἔβλαστε. τοῦτο καὶ πόλεις
πορθεῖ, τόδ᾽ ἄνδρας ἐξανίστησιν δόμων·
τόδ᾽ ἐκδιδάσκει καὶ παραλλάσσει φρένας
χρηστὰς πρὸς αἰσχρὰ πράγμαθ᾽ ἵστασθαι βροτῶν·
πανουργίας δ᾽ ἔδειξεν ἀνθρώποις ἔχειν   300
καὶ παντὸς ἔργου δυσσέβειαν εἰδέναι.
ὅσοι δὲ μισθαρνοῦντες ἤνυσαν τάδε,
χρόνῳ ποτ᾽ ἐξέπραξαν ὡς δοῦναι δίκην.
ἀλλ᾽ εἴπερ ἴσχει Ζεὺς ἔτ᾽ ἐξ ἐμοῦ σέβας,
εὖ τοῦτ᾽ ἐπίστασ᾽, ὅρκιος δέ σοι λέγω,   305
εἰ μὴ τὸν αὐτόχειρα τοῦδε τοῦ τάφου
εὑρόντες ἐκφανεῖτ᾽ ἐς ὀφθαλμοὺς ἐμούς,
οὐχ ὑμῖν Ἅιδης μοῦνος ἀρκέσει, πρὶν ἂν
ζῶντες κρεμαστοὶ τήνδε δηλώσηθ᾽ ὕβριν,

ἵν᾽ εἰδότες τὸ κέρδος ἔνθεν οἰστέον 310
τὸ λοιπὸν ἁρπάζητε, καὶ μάθηθ᾽ ὅτι
οὐκ ἐξ ἅπαντος δεῖ τὸ κερδαίνειν φιλεῖν.
ἐκ τῶν γὰρ αἰσχρῶν λημμάτων τοὺς πλείονας
ἀτωμένους ἴδοις ἂν ἢ σεσωσμένους.

Φυ. εἰπεῖν τι δώσεις, ἢ στραφεὶς οὕτως ἴω; 315
Κρ. οὐκ οἶσθα καὶ νῦν ὡς ἀνιαρῶς λέγεις;
Φυ. ἐν τοῖσιν ὠσὶν ἢ 'πὶ τῇ ψυχῇ δάκνῃ;
Κρ. τί δὲ ῥυθμίζεις τὴν ἐμὴν λύπην ὅπου;
Φυ. ὁ δρῶν σ᾽ ἀνιᾷ τὰς φρένας, τὰ δ᾽ ὦτ᾽ ἐγώ.
Κρ. οἴμ᾽ ὡς λάλημα, δῆλον, ἐκπεφυκὸς εἶ. 320
Φυ. οὔκουν τό γ᾽ ἔργον τοῦτο ποιήσας ποτέ.
Κρ. καὶ ταῦτ᾽ ἐπ᾽ ἀργύρῳ γε τὴν ψυχὴν προδούς.
Φυ. φεῦ·
ἦ δεινόν, ᾧ δοκεῖ γε, καὶ ψευδῆ δοκεῖν.
Κρ. κόμψευέ νυν τὴν δόξαν· εἰ δὲ ταῦτα μὴ
φανεῖτέ μοι τοὺς δρῶντας, ἐξερεῖθ᾽ ὅτι 325
τὰ δειλὰ κέρδη πημονὰς ἐργάζεται.
Φυ. ἀλλ᾽ εὑρεθείη μὲν μάλιστ᾽· ἐὰν δέ τοι
ληφθῇ τε καὶ μή, τοῦτο γὰρ τύχη κρινεῖ,
οὐκ ἔσθ᾽ ὅπως ὄψῃ σὺ δεῦρ᾽ ἐλθόντα με.
καὶ νῦν γὰρ ἐκτὸς ἐλπίδος γνώμης τ᾽ ἐμῆς 330
σωθεὶς ὀφείλω τοῖς θεοῖς πολλὴν χάριν.

332–440: The Guard exits the stage, whereupon the Chorus sing an ode celebrating the ingenuity of man ('Ode to Man'). This ends with the Guard returning to the stage, bringing with him Antigone, whom he and his fellow guards have caught burying Polynices' body.

Κρ. σὲ δή, σὲ τὴν νεύουσαν ἐς πέδον κάρα,
φής, ἢ καταρνῇ μὴ δεδρακέναι τάδε;
Αν. καὶ φημὶ δρᾶσαι κοὐκ ἀπαρνοῦμαι τὸ μή.
Κρ. σὺ μὲν κομίζοις ἂν σεαυτὸν ᾗ θέλεις
ἔξω βαρείας αἰτίας ἐλεύθερον· 445
σὺ δ᾽ εἰπέ μοι μὴ μῆκος, ἀλλὰ συντόμως,
ᾔδησθα κηρυχθέντα μὴ πράσσειν τάδε;
Αν. ᾔδη· τί δ᾽ οὐκ ἔμελλον; ἐμφανῆ γὰρ ἦν.
Κρ. καὶ δῆτ᾽ ἐτόλμας τούσδ᾽ ὑπερβαίνειν νόμους;
Αν. οὐ γάρ τί μοι Ζεὺς ἦν ὁ κηρύξας τάδε, 450
οὐδ᾽ ἡ ξύνοικος τῶν κάτω θεῶν Δίκη
τοιούσδ᾽ ἐν ἀνθρώποισιν ὥρισεν νόμους·
οὐδὲ σθένειν τοσοῦτον ᾠόμην τὰ σὰ
κηρύγμαθ᾽ ὥστ᾽ ἄγραπτα κἀσφαλῆ θεῶν
νόμιμα δύνασθαι θνητά γ᾽ ὄνθ᾽ ὑπερδραμεῖν. 455

**A
Level**

οὐ γάρ τι νῦν γε κἀχθές, ἀλλ᾽ ἀεί ποτε
ζῇ ταῦτα, κοὐδεὶς οἶδεν ἐξ ὅτου ᾿φάνη.
τούτων ἐγὼ οὐκ ἔμελλον, ἀνδρὸς οὐδενὸς
φρόνημα δείσασ᾽, ἐν θεοῖσι τὴν δίκην
δώσειν· θανουμένη γὰρ ἐξῄδη, τί δ᾽ οὔ;   460
κεἰ μὴ σὺ προὐκήρυξας. εἰ δὲ τοῦ χρόνου
πρόσθεν θανοῦμαι, κέρδος αὔτ᾽ ἐγὼ λέγω.
ὅστις γὰρ ἐν πολλοῖσιν ὡς ἐγὼ κακοῖς
ζῇ, πῶς ὅδ᾽ οὐχὶ κατθανὼν κέρδος φέρει;
οὕτως ἔμοιγε τοῦδε τοῦ μόρου τυχεῖν   465
παρ᾽ οὐδὲν ἄλγος· ἀλλ᾽ ἄν, εἰ τὸν ἐξ ἐμῆς
μητρὸς θανόντ᾽ ἄθαπτον <ὄντ᾽> ἠνεσχόμην
κείνοις ἂν ἤλγουν· τοῖσδε δ᾽ οὐκ ἀλγύνομαι.
σοὶ δ᾽ εἰ δοκῶ νῦν μῶρα δρῶσα τυγχάνειν,
σχεδόν τι μώρῳ μωρίαν ὀφλισκάνω.   470

Χο.   δῆλον· τὸ γέννημ᾽ ὠμὸν ἐξ ὠμοῦ πατρὸς
      τῆς παιδός· εἴκειν δ᾽ οὐκ ἐπίσταται κακοῖς.

Κρ.   ἀλλ᾽ ἴσθι τοι τὰ σκλήρ᾽ ἄγαν φρονήματα
      πίπτειν μάλιστα, καὶ τὸν ἐγκρατέστατον
      σίδηρον ὀπτὸν ἐκ πυρὸς περισκελῆ   475
      θραυσθέντα καὶ ῥαγέντα πλεῖστ᾽ ἂν εἰσίδοις.
      σμικρῷ χαλινῷ δ᾽ οἶδα τοὺς θυμουμένους
      ἵππους καταρτυθέντας· οὐ γὰρ ἐκπέλει
      φρονεῖν μέγ᾽ ὅστις δοῦλός ἐστι τῶν πέλας.
      αὕτη δ᾽ ὑβρίζειν μὲν τότ᾽ ἐξηπίστατο,   480
      νόμους ὑπερβαίνουσα τοὺς προκειμένους·
      ὕβρις δ᾽, ἐπεὶ δέδρακεν, ἥδε δευτέρα,
      τούτοις ἐπαυχεῖν καὶ δεδρακυῖαν γελᾶν.
      ἦ νῦν ἐγὼ μὲν οὐκ ἀνήρ, αὕτη δ᾽ ἀνήρ,
      εἰ ταῦτ᾽ ἀνατεὶ τῇδε κείσεται κράτη.   485
      ἀλλ᾽ εἴτ᾽ ἀδελφῆς εἴθ᾽ ὁμαιμονεστέρα
      τοῦ παντὸς ἡμῖν Ζηνὸς ἑρκείου κυρεῖ,
      αὐτή τε χἠ ξύναιμος οὐκ ἀλύξετον
      μόρου κακίστου· καὶ γὰρ οὖν κείνην ἴσον
      ἐπαιτιῶμαι τοῦδε βουλεῦσαι τάφου.   490
      καί νιν καλεῖτ᾽· ἔσω γὰρ εἶδον ἀρτίως
      λυσσῶσαν αὐτὴν οὐδ᾽ ἐπήβολον φρενῶν.
      φιλεῖ δ᾽ ὁ θυμὸς πρόσθεν ᾑρῆσθαι κλοπεὺς
      τῶν μηδὲν ὀρθῶς ἐν σκότῳ τεχνωμένων.
      μισῶ γε μέντοι χὤταν ἐν κακοῖσί τις   495
      ἁλοὺς ἔπειτα τοῦτο καλλύνειν θέλῃ.

Αν.   θέλεις τι μεῖζον ἢ κατακτεῖναί μ᾽ ἑλών;

Κρ.   ἐγὼ μὲν οὐδέν· τοῦτ᾽ ἔχων ἅπαντ᾽ ἔχω.

Αν.   τί δῆτα μέλλεις; ὡς ἐμοὶ τῶν σῶν λόγων

      ἀρεστὸν οὐδέν, μηδ᾽ ἀρεσθείη ποτέ,   500

      οὕτω δὲ καὶ σοὶ τἄμ᾽ ἀφανδάνοντ᾽ ἔφυ.

      καίτοι πόθεν κλέος γ᾽ ἂν εὐκλεέστερον

      κατέσχον ἢ τὸν αὐτάδελφον ἐν τάφῳ

      τιθεῖσα; τούτοις τοῦτο πᾶσιν ἁνδάνειν

      λέγοιμ᾽ ἄν, εἰ μὴ γλῶσσαν ἐγκλῄοι φόβος.   505

      ἀλλ᾽ ἡ τυραννὶς πολλά τ᾽ ἄλλ᾽ εὐδαιμονεῖ

      κἄξεστιν αὐτῇ δρᾶν λέγειν θ᾽ ἃ βούλεται.

Κρ.   σὺ τοῦτο μούνη τῶνδε Καδμείων ὁρᾷς.

Αν.   ὁρῶσι χοὖτοι· σοὶ δ᾽ ὑπίλλουσιν στόμα.

Κρ.   σὺ δ᾽ οὐκ ἐπαιδῇ, τῶνδε χωρὶς εἰ φρονεῖς;   510

Αν.   οὐδὲν γὰρ αἰσχρὸν τοὺς ὁμοσπλάγχνους σέβειν.

Κρ.   οὔκουν ὅμαιμος χὠ καταντίον θανών;

Αν.   ὅμαιμος ἐκ μιᾶς τε καὶ ταὐτοῦ πατρός.

Κρ.   πῶς δῆτ᾽ ἐκείνῳ δυσσεβῆ τιμᾷς χάριν;

Αν.   οὐ μαρτυρήσει ταῦθ᾽ ὁ κατθανὼν νέκυς.   515

Κρ.   εἴ τοί σφε τιμᾷς ἐξ ἴσου τῷ δυσσεβεῖ.

Αν.   οὐ γάρ τι δοῦλος, ἀλλ᾽ ἀδελφὸς ὤλετο.

Κρ.   πορθῶν δὲ τήνδε γῆν· ὁ δ᾽ ἀντιστὰς ὕπερ.

Αν.   ὅμως ὅ γ᾽ Ἅιδης τοὺς νόμους τούτους ποθεῖ.

Κρ.   ἀλλ᾽ οὐχ ὁ χρηστὸς τῷ κακῷ λαχεῖν ἴσος.   520

Αν.   τίς οἶδεν εἰ κάτω ᾽στιν εὐαγῆ τάδε;

Κρ.   οὔτοι ποθ᾽ οὑχθρός, οὐδ᾽ ὅταν θάνῃ, φίλος.

Αν.   οὔτοι συνέχθειν, ἀλλὰ συμφιλεῖν ἔφυν.

Κρ.   κάτω νυν ἐλθοῦσ᾽, εἰ φιλητέον, φίλει

      κείνους· ἐμοῦ δὲ ζῶντος οὐκ ἄρξει γυνή.   525

526–30: The Chorus announce the arrival of Ismene, whose face is drenched with tears.

Κρ.   σὺ δ᾽, ἣ κατ᾽ οἴκους ὡς ἔχιδν᾽ ὑφειμένη

      λήθουσά μ᾽ ἐξέπινες, οὐδ᾽ ἐμάνθανον

      τρέφων δύ᾽ ἄτα κἀπαναστάσεις θρόνων,

      φέρ᾽, εἰπὲ δή μοι, καὶ σὺ τοῦδε τοῦ τάφου

      φήσεις μετασχεῖν, ἢ ᾽ξομῇ τὸ μὴ εἰδέναι;   535

Ισ.   δέδρακα τοὔργον, εἴπερ ἥδ᾽ ὁμορροθεῖ,

      καὶ ξυμμετίσχω καὶ φέρω τῆς αἰτίας.

Αν.   ἀλλ᾽ οὐκ ἐάσει τοῦτό γ᾽ ἡ δίκη σ᾽, ἐπεὶ

      οὔτ᾽ ἠθέλησας οὔτ᾽ ἐγὼ ᾽κοινωσάμην.

Ισ.   ἀλλ᾽ ἐν κακοῖς τοῖς σοῖσιν οὐκ αἰσχύνομαι   540

      ξύμπλουν ἐμαυτὴν τοῦ πάθους ποιουμένη.

Αν.   ὧν τοὔργον Ἅιδης χοἱ κάτω ξυνίστορες·
      λόγοις δ᾽ ἐγὼ φιλοῦσαν οὐ στέργω φίλην.

Ισ.   μήτοι, κασιγνήτη, μ᾽ ἀτιμάσῃς τὸ μὴ οὐ
      θανεῖν τε σὺν σοὶ τὸν θανόντα θ᾽ ἁγνίσαι.   545

Αν.   μή 'μοὶ θάνῃς σὺ κοινά, μηδ᾽ ἃ μὴ 'θιγες
      ποιοῦ σεαυτῆς. ἀρκέσω θνήσκουσ᾽ ἐγώ.

Ισ.   καὶ τίς βίου μοι σοῦ λελειμμένῃ πόθος;

Αν.   Κρέοντ᾽ ἐρώτα· τοῦδε γὰρ σὺ κηδεμών.

Ισ.   τί ταῦτ᾽ ἀνιᾷς μ᾽ οὐδὲν ὠφελουμένη;   550

Αν.   ἀλγοῦσα μὲν δῆτ᾽, εἰ γελῶ γ᾽, ἐν σοὶ γελῶ.

Ισ.   τί δῆτ᾽ ἂν ἀλλὰ νῦν σ᾽ ἔτ᾽ ὠφελοῖμ᾽ ἐγώ;

Αν.   σῶσον σεαυτήν. οὐ φθονῶ σ᾽ ὑπεκφυγεῖν.

Ισ.   οἴμοι τάλαινα, κἀμπλάκω τοῦ σοῦ μόρου;

Αν.   σὺ μὲν γὰρ εἵλου ζῆν, ἐγὼ δὲ κατθανεῖν.   555

Ισ.   ἀλλ᾽ οὐκ ἐπ᾽ ἀρρήτοις γε τοῖς ἐμοῖς λόγοις.

Αν.   καλῶς σὺ μὲν τοῖς, τοῖς δ᾽ ἐγὼ 'δόκουν φρονεῖν.

Ισ.   καὶ μὴν ἴση νῷν ἐστιν ἡ 'ξαμαρτία.

Αν.   θάρσει. σὺ μὲν ζῇς, ἡ δ᾽ ἐμὴ ψυχὴ πάλαι
      τέθνηκεν, ὥστε τοῖς θανοῦσιν ὠφελεῖν.   560

Κρ.   τὼ παῖδε φημὶ τώδε τὴν μὲν ἀρτίως
      ἄνουν πεφάνθαι, τὴν δ᾽ ἀφ᾽ οὗ τὰ πρῶτ᾽ ἔφυ.

Ισ.   οὐ γάρ ποτ᾽, ὦναξ, οὐδ᾽ ὃς ἂν βλάστῃ μένει
      νοῦς τοῖς κακῶς πράσσουσιν, ἀλλ᾽ ἐξίσταται.

Κρ.   σοὶ γοῦν, ὅθ᾽ εἵλου σὺν κακοῖς πράσσειν κακά.   565

Ισ.   τί γὰρ μόνη μοι τῆσδ᾽ ἄτερ βιώσιμον;

Κρ.   ἀλλ᾽ ἥδε μέντοι—μὴ λέγ᾽· οὐ γὰρ ἔστ᾽ ἔτι.

Ισ.   ἀλλὰ κτενεῖς νυμφεῖα τοῦ σαυτοῦ τέκνου;

Κρ.   ἀρώσιμοι γὰρ χἀτέρων εἰσὶν γύαι.

Ισ.   οὐχ ὥς γ᾽ ἐκείνῳ τῇδέ τ᾽ ἦν ἡρμοσμένα.   570

Κρ.   κακὰς ἐγὼ γυναῖκας υἱέσι στυγῶ.

Ισ.   ὦ φίλταθ᾽ Αἷμον, ὥς σ᾽ ἀτιμάζει πατήρ.

Κρ.   ἄγαν γε λυπεῖς καὶ σὺ καὶ τὸ σὸν λέχος.

Χο.   ἦ γὰρ στερήσεις τῇσδε τὸν σαυτοῦ γόνον;

Κρ.   Ἅιδης ὁ παύσων τούσδε τοὺς γάμους ἐμοί.   575

Ισ.   δεδογμέν᾽, ὡς ἔοικε, τήνδε κατθανεῖν.

Κρ.   καὶ σοί γε κἀμοί. μὴ τριβὰς ἔτ᾽, ἀλλά νιν
      κομίζετ᾽ εἴσω, δμῶες· ἐκ δὲ τοῦδε χρὴ
      γυναῖκας εἶναι τάσδε μηδ᾽ ἀνειμένας.
      φεύγουσι γάρ τοι χοἱ θρασεῖς, ὅταν πέλας   580
      ἤδη τὸν Ἅιδην εἰσορῶσι τοῦ βίου.

*582–890: After the next Choral song, in which the Chorus recounts the woes of the
family of Oedipus, Creon's son, Haemon, enters the stage. Haemon at first tries to
reason with his father, but the two become increasingly angry at each other, and*

Creon threatens to kill Antigone before Haemon's eyes. The Chorus sing another ode, on the power of love, followed by a lament between them and Antigone, in which she bewails her fate. Creon enters and orders his guards to confine her alive in an underground chamber, where she is to die.

Αν. ὦ τύμβος, ὦ νυμφεῖον, ὦ κατασκαφὴς
οἴκησις ἀείφρουρος, οἷ πορεύομαι
πρὸς τοὺς ἐμαυτῆς, ὧν ἀριθμὸν ἐν νεκροῖς
πλεῖστον δέδεκται Φερσέφασσ᾽ ὀλωλότων·
ὧν λοισθία 'γὼ καὶ κάκιστα δὴ μακρῷ   895
κάτειμι, πρίν μοι μοῖραν ἐξήκειν βίου.
ἐλθοῦσα μέντοι κάρτ᾽ ἐν ἐλπίσιν τρέφω
φίλη μὲν ἥξειν πατρί, προσφιλὴς δὲ σοί,
μῆτερ, φίλη δὲ σοί, κασίγνητον κάρα.
ἐπεὶ θανόντας αὐτόχειρ ὑμᾶς ἐγὼ   900
ἔλουσα κἀκόσμησα κἀπιτυμβίους
χοὰς ἔδωκα. νῦν δέ Πολύνεικες, τὸ σὸν
δέμας περιστέλλουσα τοιάδ᾽ ἄρνυμαι.
καίτοι σ᾽ ἐγὼ 'τίμησα τοῖς φρονοῦσιν εὖ.
οὐ γάρ ποτ᾽ οὔτ᾽ ἄν εἰ τέκν᾽ ὧν μήτηρ ἔφυν,   905
οὔτ᾽ εἰ πόσις μοι κατθανὼν ἐτήκετο,
βίᾳ πολιτῶν τόνδ᾽ ἄν ᾐρόμην πόνον.
τίνος νόμου δὴ ταῦτα πρὸς χάριν λέγω;
πόσις μὲν ἄν μοι κατθανόντος ἄλλος ἦν,
καὶ παῖς ἀπ᾽ ἄλλου φωτός, εἰ τοῦδ᾽ ἤμπλακον,   910
μητρὸς δ᾽ ἐν Ἅιδου καὶ πατρὸς κεκευθότοιν
οὐκ ἔστ᾽ ἀδελφὸς ὅστις ἄν βλάστοι ποτέ.
τοιῷδε μέντοι σ᾽ ἐκπροτιμήσασ᾽ ἐγὼ
νόμῳ, Κρέοντι ταῦτ᾽ ἔδοξ᾽ ἁμαρτάνειν
καὶ δεινὰ τολμᾶν, ὦ κασίγνητον κάρα.   915
καὶ νῦν ἄγει με διὰ χερῶν οὕτω λαβὼν
ἄλεκτρον, ἀνυμέναιον, οὔτε του γάμου
μέρος λαχοῦσαν οὔτε παιδείου τροφῆς,
ἀλλ᾽ ὧδ᾽ ἐρῆμος πρὸς φίλων ἡ δύσμορος
ζῶσ᾽ ἐς θανόντων ἔρχομαι κατασκαφάς·   920
ποίαν παρεξελθοῦσα δαιμόνων δίκην;
τί χρή με τὴν δύστηνον ἐς θεοὺς ἔτι
βλέπειν; τίν᾽ αὐδᾶν ξυμμάχων; ἐπεί γε δὴ
τὴν δυσσέβειαν εὐσεβοῦσ᾽ ἐκτησάμην.
ἀλλ᾽ εἰ μὲν οὖν τάδ᾽ ἐστὶν ἐν θεοῖς καλά,   925
παθόντες ἄν ξυγγνοῖμεν ἡμαρτηκότες·
εἰ δ᾽ οἵδ᾽ ἁμαρτάνουσι, μὴ πλείω κακὰ
πάθοιεν ἢ καὶ δρῶσιν ἐκδίκως ἐμέ.

AS

929–97: *Antigone is led off to her death, and the Chorus sing an ode comparing her situation to the fate of various mythological figures. Teiresias, a blind old prophet, enters the stage, accompanied by a boy who guides him.*

ΤΕΙΡΕΣΙΑΣ

γνώσῃ, τέχνης σημεῖα τῆς ἐμῆς κλυών.
ἐς γὰρ παλαιὸν θᾶκον ὀρνιθοσκόπον
ἵζων, ἵν᾽ ἦν μοι παντὸς οἰωνοῦ λιμήν,   1000
ἀγνῶτ᾽ ἀκούω φθόγγον ὀρνίθων, κακῷ
κλάζοντας οἴστρῳ καὶ βεβαρβαρωμένῳ·
καὶ σπῶντας ἐν χηλαῖσιν ἀλλήλους φοναῖς
ἔγνων· πτερῶν γὰρ ῥοῖβδος οὐκ ἄσημος ἦν.
εὐθὺς δὲ δείσας ἐμπύρων ἐγευόμην   1005
βωμοῖσι παμφλέκτοισιν· ἐκ δὲ θυμάτων
Ἥφαιστος οὐκ ἔλαμπεν, ἀλλ᾽ ἐπὶ σποδῷ
μυδῶσα κηκὶς μηρίων ἐτήκετο
κἄτυφε κἀνέπτυε, καὶ μετάρσιοι
χολαὶ διεσπείροντο, καὶ καταρρυεῖς   1010
μηροὶ καλυπτῆς ἐξέκειντο πιμελῆς.
τοιαῦτα παιδὸς τοῦδ᾽ ἐμάνθανον πάρα
φθίνοντ᾽ ἀσήμων ὀργίων μαντεύματα.
ἐμοὶ γὰρ οὗτος ἡγεμών, ἄλλοις δ᾽ ἐγώ.
καὶ ταῦτα τῆς σῆς ἐκ φρενὸς νοσεῖ πόλις.   1015
βωμοὶ γὰρ ἡμῖν ἐσχάραι τε παντελεῖς
πλήρεις ὑπ᾽ οἰωνῶν τε καὶ κυνῶν βορᾶς
τοῦ δυσμόρου πεπτῶτος Οἰδίπου γόνου.
κᾆτ᾽ οὐ δέχονται θυστάδας λιτὰς ἔτι
θεοὶ παρ᾽ ἡμῶν οὐδὲ μηρίων φλόγα,   1020
οὐδ᾽ ὄρνις εὐσήμους ἀπορροιβδεῖ βοάς,
ἀνδροφθόρου βεβρῶτες αἵματος λίπος.
ταῦτ᾽ οὖν, τέκνον, φρόνησον. ἀνθρώποισι γὰρ
τοῖς πᾶσι κοινόν ἐστι τοὐξαμαρτάνειν·
ἐπεὶ δ᾽ ἁμάρτῃ, κεῖνος οὐκέτ᾽ ἔστ᾽ ἀνὴρ   1025
ἄβουλος οὐδ᾽ ἄνολβος, ὅστις ἐς κακὸν
πεσὼν ἀκεῖται μηδ᾽ ἀκίνητος πέλει.
αὐθαδία τοι σκαιότητ᾽ ὀφλισκάνει.
ἀλλ᾽ εἶκε τῷ θανόντι, μηδ᾽ ὀλωλότα
κέντει. τίς ἀλκὴ τὸν θανόντ᾽ ἐπικτανεῖν;   1030
εὖ σοι φρονήσας εὖ λέγω· τὸ μανθάνειν δ᾽
ἥδιστον εὖ λέγοντος, εἰ κέρδος λέγοι.

Commentary Notes

1–99: Antigone and Ismene

It is dawn on the day after the battle between the Argives and Thebans and the death of Eteocles and Polynices. Antigone and Ismene enter the stage from the palace. They discuss Creon's decree forbidding burial to Polynices. Antigone intends to defy Creon and bury her brother; Ismene tries unsuccessfully to dissuade her. The two sisters go their separate ways, Antigone out of the city to where Polynices is buried, Ismene back inside the palace.

1–10

Antigone addresses her sister, asking her if she has heard the news about Creon's decree. Her passionate and forceful character is already visible in her opening words. She begins with an elaborate greeting to Ismene, followed by a series of increasingly agitated questions (four in ten lines).

1

ὦ κοινὸν αὐτάδελφον Ἰσμήνης κάρα: (literally 'O common full-sisterly head of Ismene') is a high-flown expression of a kind common in tragedy. The opening line of the play hints at what will be its key theme, since κοινόν and αὐτάδελφον both stress the family bond (αὐτάδελφος is a stronger form of ἀδελφός). As well as the relationship between the two sisters, it may also hint at the bond between Antigone and her brother Polynices (it is used of him at line 503 and 696 and at Aes. *Theb.* 718). Ἰσμήνης κάρα 'head of Ismene' is a common type of tragic periphrasis (cf. 899, 915) and means something like 'my dear Ismene'.

2–4

While the basic sense of these lines is clear ('Zeus has brought down every possible evil upon us'), there are peculiarities in the Greek and there has been much debate about the exact words used by Sophocles.

2–3

The text used in this edition means 'Do you know which one of the evils (that come) from Oedipus Zeus – Ah! What does he not bring to pass for us two while we are still alive?' Antigone breaks off mid-sentence as she is overcome by emotion, using the exclamation ἆ (this is a modern suggestion for the manuscript reading ὁποῖον).

τῶν ἀπ᾽ Οἰδίπου κακῶν: refers to the string of disasters stemming from the girls' father Oedipus.

νῷν ἔτι ζώσαιν: is in the dual, the first of many dual forms in this play, based as it is around relationships between various pairs (Antigone and Ismene, Eteocles and Polynices, Antigone and Polynices, and Antigone and Haemon). It could be either dative ('brings to pass for us') or a genitive absolute ('while we are still alive').

4–6

Antigone expands her previous statement with an impassioned outburst on the woes the sisters have already endured. She stresses the point by the use of litotes ('there is nothing bad that I haven't seen amongst our woes'), a long string of negatives (οὐδέν ... οὔτ᾽ ... οὔτ᾽ ... οὔτ᾽ ... οὔτ᾽ ... οὐ ... οὐκ, where the final οὐκ in line 6 is unnecessary and has been repeated for emphasis) and four adjectives with assonance of a sounds. There is a problem with the text in the second element: the manuscripts read ἄτης ἄτερ 'without ruin', although we would expect a word with the opposite meaning. The correct reading is uncertain, although was presumably another adjective meaning 'bad' (e.g. ἀτήριον).

6

τῶν σῶν τε κἀμῶν: partitive genitive (= 'nothing amongst your misfortunes and mine'). The pairing of σῶν and κἀμῶν again highlights the closeness of the sisters' relationship.

ὄπωπ᾽: poetic perfect of ὁράω.

7–8

The woes of the past have been compounded by a further new indignity. Antigone's anger is emphasized by the pairing τί ... αὖ 'what new thing?'.

7

πανδήμῳ πόλει: 'for the whole citizen body'. The application of the decree to all the citizens is brought out by the repetition of this idea in the adjective and the noun. Note how in tragedy, like other Greek poetry, the definite article can be omitted where it would be needed in prose, and its use is in fact rather sparing.

8

τὸν στρατηγόν: Antigone refers to Creon as 'the general', suggesting that his authority is military only. Unlike the other characters in the play, she never calls him 'king' but usually refers to him as 'Creon'. Her antipathy towards him is already apparent.

9

ἔχεις τι: 'Do you know anything?'

10

φίλους ... ἐχθρῶν: 'friends ... enemies'. Antigone's first speech ends with terms that will be central to the play – who should be seen as a friend and who as an

AS

enemy? For Antigone, Polynices' status as her brother makes him an inalienable φίλος (a Greek word that covers both family and friends), whereas to Creon, his treachery has made him an ἐχθρός. Sophocles' language is often capable of multiple interpretations. Here, the primary sense of Antigone's words is 'misfortunes *due to* our enemies' (i.e. the Argive invaders who accompanied Polynices), but there is a secondary sense of 'misfortunes *that come from* our enemies' (i.e. Creon).

11–17

Ismene's response. Ismene speaks with a more conciliatory tone than Antigone, responding to her impassioned questions with two long, balanced sentences.

11

ἐμοὶ μέν: μέν here does not have a contrasting δέ, but there is an implied contrast ('to me (as opposed to others)').

Ἀντιγόνη: a word of this metrical shape (a choriamb) would not normally be permitted in iambic trimeters, but proper names are treated as an exception.

φίλων: objective genitive 'any report *about* our friends'.

12

ἐξ ὅτου: 'from the time when'.

13–14

The perverseness of the two brothers' mutual slaughter is stressed by some numerical wordplay: polyptoton of δυοῖν . . . δύο 'two', framing the line, with the idea repeated in διπλῆ χερί 'by each other's hands', opposed to μιᾷ 'one' (night).

15

ἐπεί: 'ever since'.

16

ἐν νυκτὶ τῇ νῦν: 'last night'.

16–17

'I know nothing further, whether I am more fortunate or more in distress'. οἶδα has a mixture of constructions here: first the accusative οὐδέν . . . ὑπέρτερον, which is expanded in line 17 by the participles εὐτυχοῦσα and ἀτωμένη. Remember that, after a verb of knowing/perceiving where the subject of the main verb and indirect statement are the same, the nominative case is retained.

18

ἤδη καλῶς: 'I knew it well'. Antigone's response to her sister is rather sharp. Since she already knew the facts about Creon's edict, it is clear she was only questioning her sister to see if she had also acquired the news.

αὐλείων πυλῶν: 'the courtyard gates'. The front door of a Greek house, leading from the courtyard (αὐλή) onto the street, was called the αὐλεῖος θύρα. The use of the plural and of πύλη for θύρα is typically elevated tragic language. In Greek

AS

culture, the house was seen as the proper place of women, and Antigone's needing to call Ismene out of it for a secret conversation shows that something is up. Antigone has symbolically made her first move from the private, feminine space of the house into the public, male space of the stage.

ἐξέπεμπον: imperfect because the meaning is 'this was my reason in summoning you from the house'.

20

δηλοῖς ... καλχαίνουσ': 'you are clearly brooding over some news'. δηλόω plus participle means 'to be clearly doing X'. καλχαίνω is a rare verb, the basic meaning of which is 'to be purple' (derived from the word κάλχη 'purple murex'), but here means something like 'brood', because of its association with the sea. Darkness is often used as a symbol of anxiety in Greek.

21–2

Antigone begins her response to Ismene with another impassioned question.

τάφου: 'of a tomb': strictly a genitive of separation with ἀτιμάσας in 22 (= 'deprived of the honour of a tomb'), although it effectively goes with both participles, suggesting with προτίσας the idea of 'considered worthy of the honour of a tomb'. Note the word order, with τάφου brought to the front of the sentence for emphasis (hyperbaton), as Antigone begins her question with the most important idea.

νῷν: genitive of the dual first person pronoun νώ.

τὼ κασιγνήτω: accusative plural dual, anticipating the accusatives τὸν μέν ... τὸν δέ ('our brothers ... one ... the other'). Strict grammar would lead us to expect the genitive here, but this 'whole and part' construction, where the larger term is in the same case as the more specific, is common in Greek.

22

προτίσας ... ἀτιμάσας ἔχει: the aorist participle plus ἔχω can be used with the meaning of the perfect. Sometimes it seems to be used simply as an alternative to the perfect, but it can also stress the continuing effect of the action, as perhaps is the meaning here. The construction is common in Sophocles.

23–30

Antigone contrasts the very different fates of Eteocles and Polynices, with three lines given to Eteocles but five to the more concerning circumstances of Polynices.

23–4

†σὺν δίκη / χρησθείς† δικαίᾳ καὶ νόμῳ: the daggers here indicate that the text has become corrupted to such an extent that the original reading seems beyond recovery. The basic idea of this line and half seems to be something like 'justly and lawfully'.

25

τοῖς ἔνερθεν ἔντιμον νεκροῖς: 'so that he is honoured in the eyes of the dead below'. ἔντιμον is predicative. The souls of the unburied were thought to be rejected by the dead in Hades.

27

ἀστοῖσι: 'to the citizens'. Creon's decree is directed at the entire citizen body.

ἐκκεκηρῦχθαι: 'it has been decreed'. The ἐκ- prefix shows how widely the proclamation was made.

27–8

τὸ μὴ / . . . καλύψαι μηδὲ κωκῦσαί τινα: 'that no-one should bury or lament him'. The article is frequently added to the infinitive in poetic language.

29

ἄκλαυτον, ἄταφον: the ideas of lamentation and burial are repeated from line 28, with a stress on what Polynices will lack given by the double alpha-privative adjectives. Greek burial rites required the body to be washed by the women of the family, then buried or burnt to the accompaniment of laments, again the role of women.

29–30

οἰωνοῖς γλυκὺν / θησαυρὸν εἰσορῶσι πρὸς χάριν βορᾶς: (literally) 'a sweet store of food for birds looking upon it regarding delight in feeding'. Antigone shows her bitterness with a macabre description of birds feasting upon Polynices' corpse. The sinister idea of the birds' pleasure in eating his flesh is stressed (γλυκύν 'sweet' . . . χάριν 'pleasure'), with the description of his body as a θησαυρός 'storehouse' continuing the idea. The birds are personified almost as human enemies, since victors are often presented as gloating over the corpses of their enemies.

31

τὸν ἀγαθὸν Κρέοντα: 'the good Creon', clearly sarcastic.

31–2

σοὶ / κἀμοί, λέγω γὰρ κἀμέ: 'to you and to me, for I mean me as well'. Antigone shows her indignation that Creon could possibly have included her amongst the recipients of the decree.

32

κηρύξαντ᾽ ἔχειν: 'has announced': accusative and inferior version of the participle plus ἔχω construction (cf. 22 above).

33

τοῖσι μὴ εἰδόσιν: the negative μὴ is used here with the participle because this phrase denotes a type of person ('those who do not know'). μὴ and εἰ- slur together and are treated as a single long syllable (synizesis).

34–5

ἄγειν / οὐχ ὡς παρ᾽ οὐδέν: 'he is not treating the matter as of no importance'.

AS

35

ὃς ἂν τούτων τι δρᾷ . . .: 'whoever does any one of these things, (for him) death by public stoning in the city is prescribed'. The antecedent of the indefinite clause (τούτῳ or similar), which would be expected by strict grammar, is omitted, as often in such constructions.

36

δημόλευστον: 'by public stoning': a rare word, probably coined for this context. Stoning was regarded as a particularly suitable death for traitors.

37–8

Antigone ends with a challenge to Ismene to put her cards on the table.

37

σοι: an 'ethic' dative (= 'that's how things stand for you').

38

πέφυκας: this perfect form is often used in tragedy as a synonym for εἰμί, but has the added idea of 'be by nature'.

38

ἐσθλῶν κακή: 'a worthless (daughter) of normal (parents)', with genitive of origin after πέφυκας.

39–48

As the atmosphere becomes more excited, the sisters shift from extended speeches (rhesis) into rapid exchange of individual lines (stichomythia).

39

ταλαῖφρον: 'wretched', 'poor sister'.
εἰ τάδ' ἐν τούτοις: 'if that's how things are'.

39–40

τί . . . λύουσ' ἂν εἴθ' ἅπτουσα προσθείμην πλέον: 'what more would I contribute either by loosening or tightening?' λύουσ' . . . ἅπτουσα are ontrasting (a 'polar' expression, common in Greek), conveying the idea of 'whatever I do'.

41

Sophocles builds tension by having Antigone ask her sister whether she will co-operate with her (an idea stressed by the two verbal compounds in ξυν-) before actually revealing her plan. We also see Antigone's determination: she has already decided what to do without a lengthy process of deliberation.

42

κίνδευμα: internal accusative after the verbs in 41. It is common in stichomythia for a construction to be continued in subsequent lines. Ismene shows her more fearful nature by introducing the word 'danger'.

AS

ποῦ γνώμης ποτ' εἶ: literally 'where ever in thought are you?, i.e. 'what on earth are you planning?'.

43

κουφιεῖς: '(whether) you will lift' (for burial). Antigone continues the construction of line 41. Lifting the body for burial was the task of men: Antigone is proposing she and Ismene take on what would normally be a task for the community.

44

ἦ γάρ: introduces a surprised question ('Do you really . . .?')

σφ' = σφε. This form is used as an alternative accusative third person pronoun, masculine or feminine, singular or plural.

ἀπόρρητον πόλει: 'a thing forbidden to the city' (neuter accusative in apposition to the previous statement)

This line has a 'quasi-caesura' after σφ'. As well as the much more common third or fourth foot caesuras, the caesura in an iambic line can come after an elision at the end of the third foot.

45–6

Antigone breaks the one-line stichomythic pattern with a double line, where she vehemently asserts her determination to bury Polynices. 'I'll certainly (γοῦν) bury my brother, and yours too, if you don't want to'. (ἤν = ἐάν; θέλω = ἐθέλω).

47

Κρέοντος ἀντειρηκότος: 'when Creon has forbidden it' (genitive absolute).

48

οὐδέν: 'not at all', 'in no way' (adverbial).

αὐτῷ ... μέτα: 'it is his business' (μέτα = μέτεστι; NB the difference of accent from the normal preposition μετά).

τῶν ἐμῶν μ' εἴργειν: 'to keep me from my own' (genitive of separation).

49–68

Ismene responds in measured tones to Antigone, as she tries to dissuade her from burying Polynices, repeatedly urging her to use reason (φρόνησον 49, σκόπει 58, ἐννοεῖν 61, νοῦν 68). She begins by drawing attention to the troubled history of the girls' family, using emotive language (ἀπεχθὴς δυσκλεής τ' 50, λωβᾶται 54, ταλαιπώρω 56) and stressing the self-inflicted or mutually destructive aspect of their misfortunes (αὐτοφώρων 51, αὐτὸς αὐτουργῷ 52, αὐτοκτονοῦντε 56, κοινόν, ἐπαλλήλοιν 57 and repetition of 'two' (διπλᾶς 51, διπλοῦν 53, δύο 55)), as a warning to Antigone not to bring the same type of death upon herself. She then moves on to consider the position of the two sisters, arguing that as women they are unable to oppose the decisions of men, before concluding with a final appeal to moderation (67–8).

50

νῷν: dative of the dual first person pronoun νώ ('for the two of us').

AS

51

πρός ... ἀμπλακημάτων: 'as a result of crimes'.

52

ἀράξας: 'having smashed', a brutal way to describe Oedipus' self-blinding.

53

ἔπειτα: 'then, next', probably of logical, rather than temporal, sequence, if Jocasta is conceived of as dying before Oedipus, as in Sophocles' play *Oedipus Tyrannus*.

54

ἀρτάναισι: 'noose'. Plural for singular is common in poetry.

56–7

The duals αὐτοκτονοῦντε τὼ ταλαιπώρω are followed by the plural verb κατειργάσαντ'.

57

Another 'quasi-caesural' line, with caesura after elided κατειργάσαντ'.

58

μόνα ... λελειμμένα: nominative feminine dual endings.
μόνα δή: 'all alone'. The particle δή emphasizes the preceding word.

59

νόμου βίᾳ: 'in violation of the law'.

60

ψῆφον: here 'decree' rather than 'vote'.
τυράννων: vague use of the plural; clearly referring to Creon.
κράτη: 'powers'.

61

γυναῖχ': elided form of γυναῖκε, nominative dual. Translate after ὅτι; it comes earlier in the sentence for emphasis ('to reflect that we are *women*').

62

ἔφυμεν: this aorist form effectively has present meaning = 'be by nature' (cf. 79).
ὡς ... οὐ μαχουμένα: ὡς: with the participle marks a belief or intentions (= 'that we are not supposed to fight against men').

63

οὕνεκ': 'that'.
ἀρχόμεσθ': first plural -μεσθα for -μεθα is common in poetry.
ἐκ κρεισσόνων: 'by the stronger'. It was traditional Greek belief that women ought to be subservient to men.

64

ἀκούειν: 'to pay attention', 'give heed to'. This is an infinitive expressing a result with ὥστε omitted.

ταῦτ' ... ἀλγίονα: accusatives of respect ('to pay attention both in these things and things still more painful than these').

65

ἐμοὶ μέν: μέν does not have a corresponding δέ, but there is an implied contrast with 'you' or 'others' (as at lines 11 and 78). Ismene is more tactful than the more explicit Antigone, leaving her opposition to her to be inferred.

66

τάδε: accusative of respect ('in these matters').

67

τοῖς ἐν τέλει βεβῶσι: 'those in authority'. Ismene again uses a vague plural to refer to Creon's authority (cf. τυράννων 60).

69–77

Antigone scornfully rejects Ismene's proposals and reaffirms her commitment to burying Polynices. Rather than responding directly to the individual points made by Ismene, she stresses the bonds of φιλία between her and her brother, a counterpoint to Ismene's account of their family history, and the claims due to the gods and the dead, rather than Ismene's stress on the temporary, worldly authority of Creon. She speaks in short, punchy sentences, with repetition of key terms (φίλη ... φίλου 73, κείσομαι 73 ... κείσομαι 75), rather than the longer, end-stopped sentences used by Ismene.

69

Antigone unleashes her anger immediately, beginning with a pair of negatives (οὔτ' ... οὔτ'). Unlike Ismene, she does not address her sister by a title (cf. ὦ κασιγνήτη 49).
ἔτι: 'in the future'.

69–70

ἄν ... ἄν: in long clauses ἄν is frequently repeated, often, as here, after an initial negative and then a later emphatic word.

70

ἐμοῦ ... μέτα: 'with me'. In poetry, most disyllabic prepositions can follow their noun (anastrophe), with shift of accent to the first syllable in this usage (cf. the different usage at 48).

71

ἴσθ': from εἰμί ('be as seems good to you').
ὁποία = τοιαύτη ὁποία, with the antecedent τοιαύτη omitted and ὁποία attracted into the nominative.

AS

72

θάψω: emphasized by the enjambment and pause immediately after.

73

φίλη μετ' αὐτοῦ ... φίλου μέτα: Antigone stresses the bonds of φιλία tying her to Polynices by polyptoton of φίλος, as well as the repetition of μετά (cf. 70 for the anastrophe of φίλου μέτα).

74

ὅσια πανουργήσασ': a striking oxymoron ('having committed a holy crime'). Antigone introduces one of the key themes of the play, the idea that duty to the gods may conflict with human laws.

74–5

ἐπεί ... ἐνθάδε: 'since the time during which I must satisfy those below is longer than (that during which I must satisfy) those here'. οἱ κάτω and οἱ ἐνθάδε are common tragic terms for 'the dead' and 'the living' respectively.

ὅν: accusative of time how long.

τῶν ἐνθάδε: genitive of comparison.

76

ἐκεῖ: 'there' (i.e. the underworld). Another common tragic usage.

σύ: emphatic. Antigone is making a sharp distinction between herself and Ismene.

77

τὰ τῶν θεῶν ἔντιμ': 'the laws honoured by the gods' (literally 'the honoured things of the gods').

ἀτιμήσασ' ἔχε: 'hold in dishonour' (cf. 22). Antigone brings out the impiety of not burying Polynices by repetition of the stem τιμ- 'honour' in ἔντιμ' ἀτιμήσασ' (figura etymologica).

78–99

After lengthier statements of their opposed views, Antigone and Ismene conclude the scene with an exchange of irregular stichomythia. Over the course of this first scene, the two sisters have grown further apart and their unity at the beginning of the scene, brought out, e.g., by extensive use of dual forms, has been replaced by opposition, with repeated use of forms of ἐγώ and σύ to signal the difference between them.

78

ἐγὼ μέν: μέν emphasizes ἐγώ and does not have a corresponding δέ (cf. 65).

ἄτιμα ποιοῦμαι: 'I dishonour' (= ἀτιμάζω).

78–9

τὸ δὲ / ... δρᾶν: accusative of respect ('as for doing it'). It is best translated as a simple infinitive 'to do'.

AS

79

βίᾳ πολιτῶν: 'against the wishes of the citizens' (cf. 59).

80

τάδ' ἂν προὔχοι': 'you may make these excuses'. προὔχοι' = προὔχοιο (< προέχοιο). The second person of the potential optative with ἂν can have the force of a mild command.

δή: emphasizes ἐγώ.

81

χώσουσ': 'to heap up', often used of raising a burial mound.

πορεύσομαι: Antigone prepares to exit the stage via a side-entrance, while Ismene remains on stage and will return to the palace through the main doors. The stage movement mirrors the drama we have just witnessed. The sisters entered together, but are now being physically separated; Ismene returns to the home, while Antigone ventures off into the wilderness outside the city.

83

μὴ 'μοῦ προτάρβει: 'Don't be afraid for *me*! 'μοῦ = emphatic ἐμοῦ, with elision of the first syllable (aphaeresis).

ἐξόρθου: 'straighten out'.

84–7

Ismene, realizing that Antigone is not to be dissuaded from the burial, requests that she at least keep her actions secret. Antigone declares that it should be proclaimed to all.

84

ἀλλ' οὖν . . . γε: 'Well, anyway, at least don't announce this to anyone'. ἀλλ' οὖν is used to signal a more moderate suggestion introduced upon rejection of a first, while γε emphasizes προμηνύσῃς.

85

κρυφῇ . . . κεῦθε: Ismene emphasizes the request for secrecy, repeating the idea in the verb and adverb.

σὺν δ' αὔτως ἐγώ: 'and I will <hide it> likewise as well'. σύν is adverbial here.

86

πολλόν: 'much (more hateful)'. This is an epic form for Attic πολύ.

87

ἐὰν μὴ πᾶσι κηρύξῃς τάδε: Antigone wants Ismene 'to announce this to all', exactly mirroring Creon's decree to the whole citizen body (cf. 7–8, 27).

88

θερμὴν ἐπὶ ψυχροῖσι καρδίαν: 'a hot heart for chilling deeds'. θερμός can mean 'passionate', 'rash' (cf. 'hot-headed'), while ψυχρός suggests

AS

'chilling', 'dreadful'. 'Hot' and 'cold' often have connotations of 'life' and 'death'.

89

ἁδεῖν: aorist infinitive of ἁνδάνω 'please'.

90

εἰ καὶ δυνήσῃ γ': 'Yes (γε), if you actually (καί) can . . .'. εἰ . . . δυνήσῃ is a vivid future condition, common in warnings and threats.

91

ὅταν δή: implies 'when (and only when)'.

πεπαύσομαι: 'I shall be finished' (future perfect).

92

ἀρχήν . . . οὐ: 'not at all' (ἀρχήν here used adverbially).

93–4

εἰ . . . λέξεις, ἐχθαρῇ μὲν . . . / ἐχθρὰ δὲ . . . προσκείσῃ: Antigone uses a vivid future conditional, with a future indicative in the protasis, giving a threatening tone.

ἐχθαρῇ: 'you will be hated' (future middle with passive meaning).

ἐχθρά . . . προσκείσῃ: 'you will incur the hatred of' (literally 'you will be attached as an enemy to . . .'), implying a permanent relationship.

95

ἔα: scans as a monosyllable (synizesis).

95–6

τὴν ἐξ ἐμοῦδυσβουλίαν / . . . τὸ δεῖνον τοῦτο: 'my rashness . . . this awful thing'. Both phrases are somewhat sarcastic, since they refer mockingly to the concerns Ismene has expressed for Antigone.

97

μὴ οὐ: scanned as one syllable (synizesis). μὴ οὐ for μή with infinitive is regular after a negative main verb.

99

As Antigone leaves the stage, Ismene sums up her view of her actions. Antigone is behaving 'crazily' (ἄνους), but 'truly a friend to her own' (τοῖς φίλοις δ' ὀρθῶς φίλη), the reciprocity of the φιλία relationship emphasized by polyptoton of φίλος.

The Chorus, a group of Theban elders, march onto stage (parodos) and sing a song of thanks to the gods of Thebes, celebrating the previous day's victory. It ends with them announcing the entry of Creon, who has assembled them for a meeting.

AS

162–222: Creon and the Chorus

Creon, the new King of Thebes, comes onto the stage. He gives a long speech (rhesis), in which, after thanking the Chorus for their loyalty, he sets out his view of kingship, presenting a very different account of φιλία to the one set out by Antigone in the first scene. For Creon, loyalty to the city takes precedence over family ties. He reiterates his decision to leave Polynices unburied, on the grounds that he is a traitor. The scene ends with a short discussion between Creon and the Chorus, where they agree to ensure his decree is upheld, albeit somewhat reluctantly.

162
δή: strengthens the contrastive force of μέν.
πόλεος: for πόλεως.

164
πομποῖσιν: 'by means of messengers'.
ἐκ πάντων δίχα: 'apart from all (the others)'.

165
ἔστειλ' ἱκέσθαι: 'I summoned you to come forth'.

165–7
τοῦτο μέν . . . / τοῦθ' αὖθις: 'first . . . secondly'.

165–6
τὰ Λαΐου / . . . θρόνων . . . κράτη: 'the powers belonging to Laius's throne'.

167
After this line, we would expect Creon to say something like 'you were also loyal followers to Oedipus', before talking about his death in 168. The text printed here assumes that a line or two has been lost from our manuscripts after 167.

168
κείνων: The plural here is rather vague and could mean 'of Laius and Oedipus' or 'Oedipus and Jocasta'. If something has been lost from the text here, the reference was originally probably clearer.

172
αὐτόχειρι σὺν μιάσματι: 'with pollution caused by striking each other'. αὐτόχειρ is another of the αὐτο- compounds common in this play (cf. note on 49–68), stressing the self-destructive nature of Oedipus' family.

173
δή: emphasizes the phrase κράτη . . . πάντα ('*all* the power').

**A
Level**

174

γένους κατ᾽ ἀγχιστεῖα: 'because of closeness of kinship'. ἀγχιστεῖα is found only here (hapax legomenon).

176

ψυχήν ... φρόνημα ... γνώμην: 'spirit ... thought ... judgement'.

178–9

ὅστις ... /μὴ ... ἅπτεται: 'whoever fails to grasp ...'. μή is used here, since this is the equivalent of an indefinite clause in primary sequence with subjunctive plus ἄν.

180

ἐγκλῄσας ἔχει: 'keeps shut' (for this construction, cf. note on 22).

182

μεῖζον᾽ ... ἀντί: 'more important than' (literally 'greater in preference to').

183

οὐδαμοῦ λέγω: 'I place him nowhere' (literally 'say he is nowhere').

185

ἄτην: This word originally meant something like 'madness', 'delusion', but then came to be applied to the outcome of this ('ruin').

187–8

φίλον ... / θείμην: 'I would regard as a friend'. Note how this contrasts with Antigone's view at line 10.

189

ἥδ᾽ ἐστὶν ἡ σῴζουσα: Feminine, as ναῦς is understood with this phrase ('This is the ship that keeps us safe'). Creon is again using the 'ship of state' metaphor (cf. 162–3).

189–90

ταύτης ἔπι / πλέοντες ὀρθῆς: '(Only) by sailing upon this upright (can we make friends for ourselves)'. ἔπι follows ταύτης by anastrophe (cf. 70).

192–206

Creon gives the terms of his decree, recalling Antigone's words in the first scene at several points (e.g. 203–6; cf. 27–30). We are being encouraged to see a direct contrast between the two of them.

192

ἀδελφά: 'things akin to these'. ἀδελφά here is used as an adjective (neuter plural), meaning 'related to'. This is a common usage, but here obviously has connotations of the more familiar meaning 'brother'.

A Level

192

κηρύξας ἔχω: 'I have announced' (cf. 22).

193

πέρι: anastrophe of the preposition (cf. 70, 189).

196

τὰ πάντ' ἐφαγνίσαι: 'to make all kinds of holy offerings over him'. The ἐπί in ἐφαγνίζειν (found only here) suggests offerings made 'over' the tomb. This would primarily include libations (χοαί), which were thought to penetrate the earth for the dead to drink.

197

τοῖς ἀρίστοις ... νεκροῖς: 'to the noblest dead'. The dative is more widely used after verbs of motion in poetry.

199

γῆν ... θεούς: Strictly speaking, these accusatives should come after ἠθέλησε μέν, but they are emphasized by coming earlier in the sentence.

201

κατ' ἄκρας: 'from top to bottom'.

202

τοὺς δέ: 'the rest (of the Thebans)'.

203

τάφῳ: 'with a tomb'. This properly belongs with κτερίζειν in line 204, but is emphasized by coming earlier.

205

ἐᾶν δ' ἄθαπτον ... δέμας: 'to leave his corpse unburied'.

206

αἰκισθέν τ' ἰδεῖν: 'shameful (literally 'having been disgraced') to see'. ἰδεῖν is an epexegetic infinitive.

207

ἔκ γ' ἐμοῦ: 'in my eyes at least' (cf. 210). γε goes with ἐμοῦ.

208

τιμ ῇ προέξουσ': 'shall surpass in honour'.

210

τιμήσεται: 'shall be honoured'. The future middle is quite often found with passive meaning in tragedy (cf. 93).

A
Level

211

ποεῖν = ποιεῖν. This form can be used where needed to fit the metre.

213

ἔνεστί σοι: 'it is in your power'.

214

καὶ τῶν θανόντων χὠπόσοι ζῶμεν πέρι: 'both concerning the dead and those of us who are alive'. χὠπόσοι = καὶ ὁπόσοι. πέρι goes with τῶν θανόντων, while χὠπόσοι ζῶμεν is an elliptical construction for περὶ ἡμῶν ὁπόσοι ζῶμεν.

215

ὡς ἄν ... ἦτε: 'See to it that you are ...'. In expressions of taking care to do something, the introductory verb ('take care', 'be sure to', etc.) can be omitted. The normal construction is ὅπως μή + future indicative, but a purpose clause is here used with the same meaning (NB primary sequence purpose clauses introduced by ὡς or ὅπως can take an optional ἄν).

216

νεωτέρῳ τῳ: 'on some younger man' (τῳ = τινι).

219

τὸ μὴ 'πιχωρεῖν: The infinitive is used here, since the construction continues from the previous line, so the meaning is '(I command you) not to ...'. τὸ μὴ 'πιχωρεῖν is equivalent to simple μὴ ἐπιχωρεῖν ('πιχωρεῖν = ἐπιχωρεῖν 'side with', with initial elision (aphaeresis)).

τοῖς ἀπιστοῦσιν τάδε: ἀπιστέω: is here equivalent to ἀπειθέω 'disobey'.

220

οὔκ ἔστιν οὕτω μῶρος ὅς: This clause is equivalent to a consecutive clause with ὥστε (= 'There is no-one so foolish as to desire ...'). The construction is more common with ὅστις.

221

καὶ μὴν ὁ μισθός γ': καὶ μήν shows agreement with the previous statement, while γε emphasizes ὁ μισθός ('Yes, indeed, this certainly is the reward ...'). Creon makes the death penalty for burial unambiguous—just as the Guard is about to reveal that the corpse has been buried.

222

κέρδος: Creon is obsessed with 'profit', continually using the language of commerce (cf. 295–9). The contrast with the unworldly Antigone could not be greater.

διώλεσεν: Greek can use the aorist in proverbial statements (the 'gnomic' aorist) where we would use the present. Translate as 'destroys'.

A
Level

248–331: Creon and the Guard

Following Creon's statement of his position, a Guard comes onto the stage. He is rather long-winded, and he has often been seen as a somewhat comic character. His opening words show his nervousness about the news that he will have to report to Creon, and he makes heavy weather of exonerating himself from any blame. Creon is beginning to get irritated when the Guard reveals the shocking news that someone has sprinkled dust on the corpse of Polynices and symbolically buried it – a direct violation of Creon's decree. Creon responds in utter fury, accusing the Guard and his comrades of accepting bribes. The scene ends with the Guard leaving to try to find the culprit.

248
τίς ἀνδρῶν: Note the irony, as Creon assumes the perpetrator must be a man.

249–57
The Guard outlines the discovery of Polynices' burial. He paints a scene of utter mystery, with no visible signs of how the burial was completed. This may be done partly to exonerate the guards from blame, but also suggests that higher powers are at work behind the burial, a point picked up by the Chorus at 278–9. This could be dramatic irony, since the audience know that Antigone is responsible, but perhaps hints at divine anger at Polynices' non-burial, something that will become clear later in the play (cf. 998–1032). The Guard's language is disjointed and full of technical terms (e.g. γενῆδος 249, δικέλλης 250, ἡμεροσκόπος 253), showing his agitation.

249
του = τινος

250
δικέλλης ἐκβολή: 'throwing up of the earth by a mattock' (a kind of hand-tool).

252
ἄσημος οὐργάτης τις ἦν: 'the doer was someone unnoticed' (οὐργάτης = ὁ ἐργάτης). Like Creon, the Guard uses a masculine noun to describe the unknown burier.

253
ἡμίν = ἡμῖν. This alternative form, with a short final ι, is used to provide a short final syllable for metrical reasons.

255
ὁ μέν: 'He' refers to Polynices. He is so much on the characters' minds that it is not necessary to use his name.

256
ἄγος φεύγοντος ὥς: 'as of someone avoiding trying to avoid pollution'. This is a genitive of possession, with τινος understood. When ὡς is placed after its noun

A
Level

like this, it is accented ὥς. Someone walking past an unburied corpse without burying it was thought to incur pollution.

258

του = τινος. This goes with both θηρὸς and κυνῶν ('any beast or any dog (literally of dogs)'); cf. 205–6.

259

λόγοι δ᾽ ἐν ἀλλήλοισιν ἐρρόθουν κακοί: An unusual expression. Rather than the guards being the subject, the confusion is emphasized by the personification of λόγοι, together with the unusual and vivid verb ῥοθέω 'be in uproar'. The Guard is also reluctant to blame any one individual.

260

φύλαξ ἐλέγχων φύλακα: Strictly speaking, this is ungrammatical, as the nominative φύλαξ is not in apposition with λόγοι in 259, but the construction used gives a more spontaneous, conversational feel. The idea of the guards being pitted against one another is emphasized by the polyptoton of φύλαξ . . . φύλακα.

260–1

κἂν ἐγίγνετο / πληγὴ τελευτῶσ᾽: 'And it would finally have come to blows'. κἂν = καὶ ἄν. The participle of τελευτάω can be used adverbially to mean 'finally'. The fact that the dispute quickly turns towards violence is a typical ancient Greek view of lower-class characters.

ὁ κωλύσων: 'Someone to stop it'.

262

ἐναργής: 'clearly guilty' (literally clear).

ἔφευγε: here means something like 'denied', so is followed by μή plus the infinitive (verbs of denying often have a redundant μή before the infinitive). μὴ εἰδ- forms a single syllable (synizesis).

264–5

The Guard stresses his point with hyperbolic imagery and a tricolon listing the lengths to which they were prepared to go to assert their innocence (also with polysyndeton of καί . . . καί . . . καί). If the Guard is a slave, he has reason to fear mistreatment, as slaves' testimony was only admissible under torture.

265

θεοὺς ὀρκωμοτεῖν: 'to swear by the gods'.

τὸ . . . δρᾶσαι = δρᾶσαι

268

οὐδὲν . . . πλέον: 'nothing better'.

ἐρευνῶσιν: understand ἡμῖν ('for us as we were enquiring').

**A
Level**

270

προὔτρεψεν: 'made', 'impelled'.

οὐ ... εἴχομεν: 'we did not know how', followed first by the infinitive ἀντιφωνεῖν, then by the deliberative question ὅπως ... πράξαιμεν.

271–2

οὔθ᾽ ὅπως δρῶντες καλῶς / πράξαιμεν: 'nor how, by doing it, we could fare well.' The guards are unable either to argue against the man's suggestion (ἀντιφωνεῖν) or to see how they could benefit by carrying it out (δρῶντες). ὅπως ... καλῶς / πράξαιμεν is the indirect historic equivalent of πῶς καλῶς πράξωμεν ('how are we to fare well?', a deliberative question).

272–3

ἀνοιστέον / σοί: 'must be reported to you'.

274

ταῦτ᾽ ἐνίκα: 'This view prevailed'.

275

καθαιρεῖ ... λαβεῖν: 'condemns me to get'.

τἀγαθόν: obviously saracastic.

276

ἄκων οὐχ ἑκοῦσιν: 'Unwilling for those who are not willing'. The disagreeability of the task is stressed by the repetition of the same root (figura etymologica).

οἶδ᾽ ὅτι: adverbial in meaning ('no doubt').

278–9

The Chorus suggest that the mysterious burial could be the work of the gods.

278

ἐμοί τοι: 'For myself, to be sure ...' A typically non-committal comment from a tragic chorus.

μή: Supply ἐστί. μή plus indicative is used for a cautious assertion ('that perhaps it is of divine origin ...').

279

ἡ ξύννοια βουλεύει πάλαι: 'My mind has for some time been advising me ...' πάλαι can mean 'time just past' as well as 'long ago'.

280–314

As the Guard had anticipated, Creon reacts with fury to the news. He dismisses the Chorus' suggestion of divine intervention with seething contempt, then blames the faction within the city that he assumes has bribed the guards and finally threatens the guards themselves with torture and death. Although Creon positions himself as the guardian of law and order, his obsession with his own authority

A Level

and some strikingly undemocratic language (e.g. 291–2) do not present him in a favourable light.

280

πρὶν ὀργῆς καί με μεστῶσαι: 'before you actually fill me with anger'. καί goes with μεστῶσαι, a strong word ('stuff full'). ὀργῆς comes early for emphasis: Creon is an easily angered man.

281

''φευρεθῆς = ἐφευρεθῆς (with aphaeresis).

283

τοῦδε τοῦ νεκροῦ πέρι: for περὶ τοῦδε τοῦ νεκροῦ, with anastrophe of περί.

284

ὑπερτιμῶντες: 'honouring exceedingly', a rare compound that brings out Creon's bitter sarcasm.

286–7

πυρώσων ... / ... διασκεδῶν: future participles with purpose meaning.

κἀναθήματα / καὶ γῆν ἐκείνων καὶ νόμους διασκεδῶν: a tricolon of things that Polynices came to 'scatter'. διασκεδῶν governs all three nouns, more obviously νόμους than the others (zeugma). Creon's anger is resulting in somewhat strained language.

289

οὔκ ἔστιν: 'it is not so'.

ταῦτα: object of μόλις φέροντες 'taking these (edicts) badly' (290); it refers to Creon's decree.

καὶ πάλαι: 'even from the start' (cf. 279).

290

ἐρρόθουν ἐμοί: 'were babbling against me'.

291

κάρα σείοντες: 'tossing their heads'. The image is of animals refusing to go beneath the yoke.

292

λόφον: λόφος is normally used of animal necks. Creon's language here is that of a brutal tyrant.

292

ὡς στέργειν ἐμέ: ὡς = ὥστε. στέργειν = 'to be content with'.

293

ἐκ τῶνδε: 'by these men' (ἐκ is here used in the sense of ὑπό).

A
Level

294

εἰργάσθαι: note that the verb of perceiving ἐξεπίσταμαι is here followed by an infinitive.

295–9

Creon laments the corrupting power of money. This is a common theme of Greek literature, but in this context perhaps portrays him as a suspicious tyrant, as well as completely misguided about the real issues at stake.

295

οἷον: 'like'.

296

νόμισμ᾽: There is some wordplay here, as νόμισμα is here used in its original sense 'institution', but normally means 'money'.

296–7

τοῦτο ... / ... τόδ᾽ ... / τόδ᾽: A tricolon of evils caused by money, highlighted by the anaphora of demonstrative pronouns. Creon personifies money as an active, malevolent force.

299

χρηστάς ... αἰσχρά: emphatic juxtaposition.
ἵστασθαι: 'to get involved with'.

300–1

πανουργίας ... / παντὸς ἔργου: πανουργία 'villany' comes from παν + εργ- (i.e. being prepared to do anything), so this is an example of figura etymologica, stressing the effects of money's influence.

301

εἰδέναι: 'to become familiar with'.

302

μισθαρνοῦντες: a rather vulgar word, elsewhere found only in prose, showing Creon's contempt for such people.

303

χρόνῳ ποτ᾽: 'at long last'.
ὡς = ὥστε.

304–12

Creon's speech comes to a climax with an elaborate nine-line sentence, in which he finally addresses the Guard and threatens him and his companions with being sought (cf. 319).

A
Level

304

Ζεύς: Notice how both Creon and Antigone (e.g. 450) appeal to Zeus. Both believe they have the support of the highest god.

306–7

εἰ μὴ ... / ... ἐκφανεῖτ': εἰ + future indicative is here used for a future open conditional. This is common in threats.

306

τὸν αὐτόχειρα: Creon continues to use the masculine singular, assuming that one *man* is responsible.

308

ὑμίν = ὑμῖν (for this alternative form, cf. 253).

308–9

Execution by being first hung up and then left to starve or being beaten to death was considered particularly suitable for traitors.

309

τήνδε δηλώσηθ' ὕβριν: This probably means '(until) you display (the consequences) of this outrage', i.e. allowing themselves to be bribed (Creon is keen on public humiliation of those who have offended him), although some understand it as 'until you reveal (who is responsible) for this outrage'.

310

εἰδότες τὸ κέρδος ἔνθεν οἰστέον: literally 'knowing profit from where it ought to be brought' (understand ἐστί after οἰστέον), i.e. 'knowing where you must get your profit' (i.e. from some source other than taking bribes).

312

τὸ κερδαίνειν: 'profit'.

315–31

The scene finishes with a brief exchange of individual lines between the Guard and Creon (stichomythia). As well as rounding off the scene, there is some notable dramatic irony, e.g. in the continuing reference to the perpetrator as male (319, 325) and the discussion of false belief (323).

315

δώσεις: 'will you allow?'.
οὕτως: 'just like this'.
ἴω: deliberative subjunctive.

317

'πὶ τῇ ψυχῇ: 'in your heart' ('πὶ = ἐπί).

**A
Level**

318

τί δὲ ῥυθμίζεις τὴν ἐμὴν λύπην ὅπου: 'Why are you trying to define the source of my grief?' (literally 'my grief from where it comes' (understand ἐστί after ὅπου)).

319

ὁ δρῶν σ' ἀνιᾷ τὰς φρένας: 'the perpetrator (NB the masculine) annoys your mind' (literally 'annoys you in your mind').

320

ἐκπεφυκὸς εἶ: 'you are naturally' (literally 'you have been born to be').

321

οὔκουν ... γ': 'Well, anyway, I certainly never did this deed'.

322

καὶ ταῦτ' ... γε: 'Yes, you did (γε) and what's more (καὶ ταῦτ)'.

323

ἦ δεινόν, ᾧ δοκεῖ γε, καὶ ψευδῆ δοκεῖν: (literally) 'Indeed it is terrible, to whom something *seems* the case, that it should also seem falsely.' What the Guard means is that Creon is basing his belief on mere appearances, which is bad in itself, but that this belief is also false. Although the Guard is referring to the specific charge of having taken a bribe, his words are full of unconscious irony.

324

κόμψευέ νυν τὴν δόξαν: 'Make clever statements about that "belief" of yours'. Creon dismisses the Guard's statement as mere quibbling. The adjective κομψός (and related verb κομψεύω) means 'clever, ingenious', often with a pejorative sense of 'too clever'.

324–5

εἰ δὲ ... μὴ / φανεῖτε: εἰ + future indicative for a threat again (cf. 306–7).
ταῦτα ... / ... τοὺς δρῶντας: 'Those who do this'. ταῦτα is placed first for emphasis (hyperbaton).

327

εὑρεθείη: 'may he be found' (optative of wish).
μάλιστ': 'preferably'.

329

οὐκ ἔσθ' ὅπως ὄψῃ: 'There is no way you will see . . .'. Rather ironic, given that he returns at line 384!

Following this scene, the Chorus sing a famous ode (the 'Ode to Man'), praising man's ingenuity both in overcoming the constraints of the natural world (e.g. sea

A
Level

travel, farming) and his intellectual achievements (e.g. language, government). The only obstacle they say he cannot overcome is death. The ode begins by describing man as δεινός (both 'clever' and 'terrible'), and much of the language in the ode is ambiguous about whether these achievements should be seen as positive or negative. The ode finishes with praise of those who obey the laws of both the city and the gods and a wish to avoid the reckless. Some points you should consider in reading the ode:

- Who do you think the Chorus are talking about?
- Might our view of the ode change as the plays goes on?

The next scene begins with a dramatic revelation: the Guard returns, leading in Antigone, who has been caught trying to rebury Polynices' body. After listening to the Guard's account, Creon turns his attention to Antigone.

441–96: Creon and Antigone

Creon and Antigone argue about the morality of burying Polynices' corpse. Both stubbornly stick to their positions, and Antigone introduces a new claim, that she is obeying the eternal 'laws of the gods' (454–5). As the scene goes on, both parties become angrier and Creon accuses Ismene too of involvement, threatening to kill her as well.

441
σὲ δή: understand καλῶ. The use of the accusative on its own gives a harsh tone.

νεύουσαν εἰς πέδον κάρα: Antigone has remained silent so far, looking down at the ground. Her separation from Creon is emphasized, as they literally cannot see eye to eye.

καταρνεῖ μὴ δεδρακέναι: verbs of denying often take an extra μή before the following infinitive.

443
τὸ μή: understand δρᾶσαι.

444
σὺ μὲν κομίζοις ἂν σεαυτὸν: 'You may take yourself off'. The optative with ἄν can have the force of a mild command.

445
μῆκος: accusative, with adverbial force ('at great length').

446
ᾔδησθα κηρυχθέντα: 'Did you know it had been announced?'. Creon gives Antigone an opportunity to deny the charge.

447
τί δ᾽ οὐκ ἔμελλον: 'How could I not (know)?' Antigone's defiance is reflected in her three curt sentences *in one line*.

**A
Level**

448

καὶ δῆτ': 'and yet . . .'.

450–70

Antigone justifies her actions in a famous speech, where she draws a contrast between the eternal unwritten laws of the gods and changeable human laws. Her allegiance lies only to the former, setting up a clear contrast with Creon. She goes on to say that she is not afraid to die, as death in her circumstances will be a blessing.

450–5

οὐ . . . οὐδ' . . . οὐδέ: Antigone rejects Creon's authority with a dramatic ascending tricolon of negative clauses, emphasized by the anaphora of negative words, all placed first in their lines. Note how Antigone frequently speaks in negative terms (cf. 4–6).

450

οὐ . . . τί μοι: 'Certainly not in my view . . .'.
Ζεύς: Compare Creon's appeal to Zeus (304).

451

οὐδ' ἡ ξύνοικος τῶν κάτω θεῶν Δίκη: Δίκη ('Justice', 'Right') was personified as a goddess by the Greeks. Here she is presented as an ally of the gods of the underworld.

453

τὰ σά: Emphatically placed at line end and so rather contemptuous.

454–5

ἄγραπτα κἀσφαλῆ θεῶν / νόμιμα . . . θνητά γ' ὄνθ': Note the contrast of unwritten and unfailing divine laws with mortal ones (emphasized by γ').

456

ἀεί ποτε: 'for ever'.

457

ἐξ ὅτου: 'when' (literally 'from which time').
'φάνη = ἐφάνη.

458

ἐγὼ οὐκ: -ω οὐκ slur together to give a single syllable (synizesis).
ἀνδρός: a rather pointed word. Antigone is not just a rebel, but a woman opposing a man.

460

τί δ' οὔ: 'How could I not?'.

461–2

τοῦ χρόνου / πρόσθεν: 'before my time'.

A
Level

462

κέρδος: Compare Antigone's use of this word with Creon's earlier in the play (310).
αὖτ' = αὐτό.

466

παρ' οὐδὲν ἄλγος: literally 'is a pain to no extent', i.e. 'is not at all painful'.

466–8

ἄν . . . / . . .. / . . . ἄν: ἄν is often repeated in long clauses.

466–7

εἰ τὸν ἐξ ἐμῆς / μητρὸς θανόντ᾽ ἄθαπτον <ὄντ'> ἠνεσχόμην: 'If I had endured
   that the son of my own mother, when he had died, should be unburied . . .'.

468

κείνοις: 'by those things'.

469–70

Antigone finishes her speech with undisguised defiance, emphasized by the polyptoton
   of μῶρα . . . /. . . μώρῳ μωρίαν.

470

σχεδόν τι: 'perhaps', with a sarcastic tone.
μώρῳ μωρίαν ὀφλισκάνω: (literally) 'I incur the charge of foolishness in the eyes
   of a fool'.

471

δῆλον: 'It is clear' (understand ἐστί).
ὠμόν . . . ὠμοῦ: striking polyptoton, emphasizing the similarity of father and
   daughter.

473–96

Creon's response. He addresses his speech to the chorus-leader (koryphaios), referring
   to Antigone in the third person throughout, perhaps showing he is too angry to
   talk to her directly. He ignores Antigone's arguments and focuses on how he will
   tame her, with violent imagery of iron shattering and horses being broken in. At
   the end of his speech, he makes even wilder accusations, including Ismene as a
   participant in the plot.

473

πίπτειν: metaphorical of 'thoughts', perhaps with the idea of trees falling in the wind.
μάλιστα . . . ἐγκρατέστατον: Creon's rage is shown by the use of two superlatives
   in one line.

475

σίδηρον ὀπτὸν ἐκ πυρὸς περισκελῆ: 'iron heated by (literally 'from') the fire so
   that it becomes hard'. περισκελῆ is proleptic.

**A
Level**

477

σμικρῷ: emphatic positioning at line beginning.

478

ἐκπέλει: 'it is permitted'.

479

ὅστις δοῦλός ἐστι τῶν πέλας: '(for someone) who is a slave of those around them'. The antecedent (e.g. τούτῳ) has to be understood, as often with this kind of clause. Describing Antigone as a δοῦλος ('slave') makes Creon sound like a tyrant.

480–2

ὑβρίζειν … / … / ὕβρις: ὕβρις is a strong word, implying an aggressive violation of another. The point is stressed by the repetition of different forms from the root (figura etymologica).

483

τούτοις: 'in these things'.

δεδρακυῖαν γελᾶν: 'to laugh in having done it'. Being laughed at by one's enemies was seen as supremely humiliating.

484–5

Creon declares that he is no man if he allows himself to be beaten by a woman. In the highly patriarchal society of ancient Athens, this sort of view would have been typical.

484

ἦ νῦν: 'for sure'.

485

ταῦτ᾽ … κράτη: 'victory in these matters'.

κείσεται: 'will reside'.

486–7

ἀλλ᾽ εἴτ᾽ ἀδελφῆς εἴθ᾽ ὁμαιμονεστέρα / τοῦ παντὸς ἡμῖν Ζηνὸς ἑρκείου κυρεῖ: 'But whether she is (κυρεῖ) my sister's child (literally 'of my sister') or closer in blood than our whole family …'. τοῦ παντὸς … Ζηνὸς ἑρκείου literally means 'the entire Zeus of the courtyard', the deity of the altar in a Greek home, but stands for 'the whole family' by metonymy.

488

οὐκ ἀλύξετον: 'they shall not escape' (third person dual).

489

καὶ γὰρ οὖν: 'For indeed (γὰρ οὖν) I blame her too (καί)'. By attacking the entirely blameless Ismene, Creon has crossed over into the realm of paranoid tyranny. Any sympathy the audience may have had for his position before is rapidly disappearing.

A Level

489–90

ἴσον / ... τοῦδε βουλεῦσαι τάφου: 'of having plotted an equal share in this burial'.

491

νιν = αὐτήν.

493

φιλεῖ: 'tends to', 'has a habit'.

πρόσθεν ἡρῆσθαι κλοπεύς: 'to have been caught out beforehand as a secret thief'.

494

τῶν μηδὲν ὀρθῶς ἐν σκότῳ τεχνωμένων: 'when people are planning no good in the darkness'. With participles, μή and its compounds are used rather than οὐ when a type of person is being referred to.

495

γε μέντοι: 'and yet'.

χὤταν = καὶ ὅταν 'also when'.

497–525: Antigone and Creon

Antigone and Creon finally engage directly in a short exchange, mostly in stichomythia, with one short speech from Antigone. Both put forward their views forcefully (Creon, that Polynices lost his right to burial by his treachery, Antigone, that this right is divinely sanctioned and inalienable), unable to find common ground.

498
ἐγὼ μὲν οὐδέν: 'I want nothing more.'

499
τί δῆτα μέλλεις: 'Then why are you waiting?'.

499–500
τῶν σῶν λόγων / ἀρεστὸν οὐδέν: 'Nothing in your words is pleasing'.
μηδ᾿ ἀρεσθείη ποτέ: 'and may it never be pleasing' (ἀρεσθείη = aorist passive optative of ἀρέσκω, used with middle meaning).

501
σοὶ τἄμ᾿: emphatic opposition (τἄμ᾿ = τὰ ἐμά).

502
This line's caesura is formed by the elision after κλέος γ᾿. The unusual rhythm gives the line a slower movement that highlights the striking phrase κλέος ... εὐκλεέστερον (literally 'more glorious glory' (figura etymologica)). κλέος is typically associated with male heroes winning glory in battle, an option not open to Antigone, who argues that her glory has come from defiance in burying her brother come what may.

504
τιθεῖσα: 'by trying to place' (present participle).
τούτοις: This refers to the Chorus. Antigone is trying to elicit the approval of the Theban community.

506
πολλά ... ἀλλ᾿ εὐδαιμονεῖ: 'is fortunate in many other ways' (accusative of respect).

508–9
ὁρᾷς / ὁρῶσι: 'see things this way'.

511
γάρ: 'No, for . . .'.

512
χὠ κατάντίον θανών: Eteocles.

AS

513

ἐκ μιᾶς: understand μητρός.

514

πῶς δῆτ᾽: 'Then how . . .?'.
τιμᾶς χάριν: 'do you bestow a tribute?'

516

εἴ τοί: 'Yes, if . . .'.
ἐξ ἴσου: 'on a level with'.

518

πορθῶν δὲ τήνδε γῆν· ὁ δ᾽ ἀντιστὰς ὕπερ: 'But (he died) trying to destroy this
    land, while the other (died) making a stand on behalf of (it)'. With ὕπερ,
    understand τῆσδε γῆς. The fast pace of stichomythia means words often need to
    be supplied from the context.

520

ἀλλ᾽ οὐχ ὁ χρηστὸς τῷ κακῷ λαχεῖν ἴσος: 'But the good man is not equal to the
    bad for obtaining (these rites)'.

523

οὔτοι συνέχθειν, ἀλλὰ συμφιλεῖν ἔφυν: 'Nevertheless my nature is (ἔφυν =
    literally 'I am by nature') not to join in hatred but in love'. Antigone summarizes her
    position with a striking line, using two compound verbs συνέχθειν and συμφιλεῖν
    not found elsewhere in classical Greek and presumably coined for this context.

524–5

εἰ φιλητέον, φίλει / κείνους: 'if you need to love, love them'. Creon's contempt is
    emphasized by the polyptoton of forms of φιλέω.

525

γυνή: Emphatically placed at the end of the line. Creon is near-obsessive about not
    giving way to a woman.

Following Creon's words, the Chorus announce the arrival of Ismene from the
palace, her face drenched in tears.

531–81: Ismene, Antigone and Creon

Ismene enters from the palace and a three-way scene ensues between her, Creon and
Antigone, mostly conducted in fast-paced stichomythia. Ismene claims joint
responsibility for the burial of Polynices, a brave – and surprising – show of support
for her sister, only to be harshly rejected by Antigone. A new piece of information is
introduced in this scene: Creon's son, Haemon, is betrothed to Antigone. Creon is not
swayed by this, however, from condemning both sisters to death.

531–2

κατ' οἴκους ὡς ἔχιδν' ὑφειμένη / λήθουσά μ' ἐξέπινες: 'Like a viper lurking (ὑφειμένη) hidden within the house you were drinking (my blood)'. A striking simile, comparing Ismene to a poisonous snake; ὑφειμένη and λήθουσα both suggest secrecy.

533

ἄτα: 'a pair of ruins' (accusative plural dual).

535

'ξομῇ = ἐξομῇ (future of ἐξόμνυμι).

537

ξυμμετίσχω καὶ φέρω τῆς αἰτίας: The prefixes ξυμ- and μετα- apply to both verbs ('I jointly take a share of, and bear, the blame').

539

'κοινωσάμην = ἐκοινωσάμην.

542

ὧν τοὔργον Ἅιδης χοὶ κάτω ξυνίστορες: 'Of whose deed (it was), Hades and those below (are) witnesses'.

543

λόγοις δ' ἐγὼ φιλοῦσαν οὐ στέργω φίλην: 'I have no fondness for a friend who loves (only) in words'. Antigone's insistence on the importance of actively fulfilling the demands of φιλία is brought out by the wordplay φιλοῦσαν . . . φίλην (figura etymologica).

544–5

μήτοι . . . μ' ἀτιμάσῃς τὸ μὴ οὐ / θανεῖν τε σὺν σοὶ τὸν θανόντα θ' ἁγνίσαι: 'Don't consider me unworthy of dying with you and sanctifying the corpse.' μὴ οὐ is usual after a negative prohibition (the additional τό with the infinitive is optional).

546

μὴ 'μοὶ θάνῃς σὺ κοινά: 'Don't you share in my death!'. κοινά has adverbial force.

546–7

μηδ' ἃ μὴ 'θιγες / ποιοῦ σεαυτῆς: 'and don't claim as yours (something) which you laid no hand upon'. 'θιγες = ἔθιγες.

548

σοῦ λελειμμένη: 'abandoned by you'.

551

ἀλγοῦσα μὲν δῆτ', εἰ γελῶ γ', ἐν σοὶ γελῶ: 'Indeed (δῆτ') I do feel pain, if when I mock (i.e. Creon), I mock you (as well).' The Greek text is uncertain here.

AS

552

τί δῆτ᾽: 'In what way, then . . .?'

ἀλλὰ νῦν: 'now at least'.

554

κἀμπλάκω: 'am I really to miss out?' (deliberative subjunctive).

556

ἀλλ᾽ οὐκ ἐπ᾽ ἀρρήτοις γε τοῖς ἐμοῖς λόγοις: 'But (you did not choose to die) without my views being stated' (literally 'on the basis of (ἐπ᾽) my words unspoken').

557

καλῶς σὺ μὲν τοῖς, τοῖς δ᾽ ἐγὼ 'δόκουν φρονεῖν: 'You seemed to be right to some (Creon and his followers), I to others (Polynices and the dead)'. The contrast between the two sisters is highlighted by the chiasmus σὺ μὲν τοῖς, τοῖς δ᾽ ἐγώ.

558

καὶ μὴν: 'and yet'.

'ξαμαρτία = ἐξαμαρτία.

561–2

τὼ παῖδε . . . τώδε τὴν μὲν . . . / . . . τὴν δ᾽: The accusative dual τὼ παῖδε . . . τώδε is specified by the accusative singulars τὴν μὲν . . ./. . . τὴν δ᾽. Translate 'of these two children, one . . . the other' (cf. 21–2).

562

ἀφ᾽ οὗ τὰ πρῶτ᾽ ἔφυ: 'her whole life' (literally 'from when she was first born').

563

γάρ: 'Yes, for . . .'.

563–4

οὐδ᾽ ὃς ἂν βλάστῃ μένει / νοῦς τοῖς κακῶς πράσσουσιν: 'not even their natural good sense (literally 'whatever good sense is born in them') remains for those who fare badly'.

565

σοὶ γοῦν: 'For you, at least, (it did) . . .'.

ὅθ᾽ εἵλου σὺν κακοῖς πράσσειν κακά: 'when you chose to do evil with evildoers'. Creon plays on the phrase κακῶς πράσσω 'fare badly' used by Ismene to say that she has 'done bad things' (κακὰ πράσσειν). The point is highlighted by the polyptoton of κακοῖς . . . κακά.

567

ἀλλ᾽ ἥδε μέντοι – μὴ λέγ᾽· οὐ γὰρ ἔστ᾽ ἔτι: 'But as for her—don't mention her, for she is no longer alive.' Creon begins to talk about Antigone, but then breaks off, dismissing her as effectively dead already.

568

This is the first mention of Haemon or Antigone's betrothal in the play. It would be worth considering why Sophocles has waited until now to reveal this information.

569

ἀρώσιμοι γὰρ χἀτέρων εἰσὶν γύαι: 'Yes, for others also have fields to plough'. The metaphor of males 'sowing their seeds' in female 'furrows' is common in Greek, but Creon's response is nevertheless crude and callous.

570

οὐχ ὥς γ᾽ ἐκείνῳ τῇδέ τ᾽ ἦν ἡρμοσμένα: 'Not as suitable as this one was for him and her' (literally 'not as things were suited . . .').

572–6

There is disagreement amongst editors here about who speaks some of these lines: is 572 spoken by Antigone or Ismene and are 574 and 576 spoken by Ismene or the Chorus? It would be worth considering the difference this makes, particularly in the case of 572.

573

ἄγαν γε λυπεῖς: 'You trouble me only too much . . .' (understand με).
τὸ σὸν λέχος: 'the marriage you speak of'.

574

ἦ γάρ: 'Are you really . . .?'.

575

Ἅιδης: There is some unconscious irony here, as Antigone and Haemon are eventually going to be reunited in death.

576

δεδογμέν᾽ = δέδοκται (understand ἐστί) 'it has been decided'.

577

καὶ σοί γε κἀμοί: 'yes, both by you and by me', i.e. I have made my decision and you are stuck with it.
μὴ τριβὰς ἔτ᾽: 'Don't cause any more delays!' (understand ποιεῖσθε).
νιν = αὐτάς.

578

ἐκ . . . τοῦδε: 'from now on'.

578–9

χρὴ / γυναῖκας εἶναι τάσδε: 'they must be women' (i.e. behave in a manner appropriate to women).

AS

580–1

Creon concludes with a two-line sententious comment that seems particularly callous in the circumstances.

580

τοι: 'you know'.

891–928: Antigone

Antigone gives her last speech of the play before being led off to her death. She begins with an address to her tomb and the family she will meet in the underworld. She then reaffirms the rightness of her decision to bury Polynices, using the argument that a husband or children would be replaceable but that a brother is not, using an argument closely paralleled by a famous passage in Herodotus (3.119) (it is not certain whether the Sophocles or Herodotus passage was written first). Finally, she laments her fate and the gods' apparent lack of concern, as she prepares herself for death.

891–2

ὦ τύμβος, ὦ νυμφεῖον, ὦ κατασκαφὴς / οἴκησις: Antigone begins with an address to the underground chamber where she is to be buried alive. The grim paradox that this place is to be simultaneously tomb, bridal chamber and permanent dwelling is brought out by the use of an ascending tricolon, with anaphora of ὦ.

891

τύμβος: nominative used with the force of a vocative.

894

Φερσέφασσ᾽: Persephone. She is appropriately mentioned here, as a fellow bride of Hades, taken from her family to the underworld.

895

κάκιστα δὴ μακρῷ: 'by far the most sadly'. κάκιστα is adverbial and is emphasized both by δή and μακρῷ.

896

πρίν μοι μοῖραν ἐξήκειν βίου: 'before the term of my life has come'.

897

ἐν ἐλπίσιν τρέφω: 'I am confident' (= ἐλπίζω).

898

φίλη μέν . . . προσφιλὴς δέ . . . / . . . φίλη δέ: Antigone emphasizes the importance of her familial ties with two lines of address to them, containing another ascending tricolon, with anaphora of forms of the keyword φίλος.

AS

900

ὑμᾶς ἐγώ: emphatic juxtaposition. ὑμᾶς includes father, mother and brother(s).

900–2

Burial rites (washing and preparing the corpse, then pouring libations over the tomb) were traditionally performed by the women of the family.

904

σ' ἐγὼ 'τίμησα . . . εὖ: 'I did well to honour you'. 'τίμησα = ἐτίμησα.
τοῖς φρονοῦσιν: 'in the eyes of the wise'.

905–7

ἄν . . . / . . . / . . . ἄν: Repetition of ἄν, as commonly in a long clause.

905–6

τέκν' . . . / . . . πόσις: Both subjects of ἐτήκετο.
ἐτήκετο: 'been mouldering' (literally 'melting'), a vivid image.

907

βίᾳ πολιτῶν: 'in defiance of the citizens' (cf. 79).

908

τίνος νόμου . . . πρὸς χάριν: 'In deference to what law . . .?'.

909

κατθανόντος: '(if my first husband) had died'. Genitive absolute, with a noun for 'husband' to be understood from πόσις.

910

τοῦδ': This refers to the hypothetical first husband.

911

ἐν Ἅιδου: 'in (the house) of Hades', with a dative noun meaning 'house' to be understood. This is a common expression in tragedy.
κεκευθότοιν: 'lying hidden' (genitive dual).

913

ἐκπροτιμήσασ': 'having honoured you especially'. Antigone stresses how greatly she has honoured Polynices with an emphatic compound verb, found only here (hapax legomenon).

916

διὰ χερῶν . . . λαβών: 'having taken hold of me forcibly' (literally by means of hands).

917–8

Antigone stresses her loss of a normal life with a string of negatives (alpha-privative adjectives ἄλεκτρον, ἀνυμέναιον, followed by οὔτε . . . οὔτε). She has a propensity for negative language throughout the play (cf. note on 450–5).

AS

917

του: (= τινος) goes with both γάμου and τροφῆς.

919

ἐρῆμος πρὸς φίλων: 'deserted by my friends'. Antigone has, however, been supported by Ismene and Haemon throughout the play.

920

ζῶσ᾽ ἐς θανόντων: emphatic juxtaposition.

922–3

ἐς θεούς ... βλέπειν: 'to look to the gods (for help)'.

923

ἐπεί γε δή: 'since, to be sure, . . .'.

924

τὴν δυσσέβειαν εὐσεβοῦσ᾽ ἐκτησάμην: 'by being pious I have acquired (the reputation) of impiety'. Antigone highlights the unfairness of being executed for doing what is right with the juxtaposition of δυσσέβειαν εὐσεβοῦσ᾽ (figura etymologica).

926

παθόντες ἂν ξυγγνοῖμεν ἡμαρτηκότες: 'by my suffering I would acknowledge that I have done wrong' (with poetic plural for singular).

927–8

μὴ πλείω κακὰ / πάθοιεν ἢ καὶ δρῶσιν ἐκδίκως ἐμέ: 'may they suffer no worse evils than they are in fact (καί) unjustly doing to me!'.

AS

998–1032: Teiresias

Led in by an attendant, the blind prophet Teiresias, a venerable figure and well known for his insight, has entered the stage. Creon, disturbed by his manner, has asked him what the matter is (988–97). Teiresias replies with a speech full of vivid and dramatic imagery, in which he reveals the gods' displeasure at the non-burial of Polynices, shown by the abnormal behaviour of birds and failed sacrificial offerings. Normal religious practice has come to a standstill, for the city's altars are polluted with carrion from Polynices' corpse. Teiresias concludes that Creon's decision not to bury Polynices is to blame and tries to persuade him to relent.

999

ὀρνιθοσκόπον: Divination from the observation of birds' behaviour was common in the ancient world; it could include their flight, resting positions, sounds and manner of feeding.

999–1002

Note the graphic imagery in these lines.

1000

λιμήν: 'gathering-place'.

1002

κλάζοντας: accusative, although it refers back to ὀρνίθων. The phrase φθόγγον ὀρνίθων is treated as though it were φθεγγομένους ὄρνιθας.

βεβαρβαρωμένῳ: To a seer who can normally understand the significance of bird sounds, it is as though they are speaking an unintelligible foreign language.

1003

ἐν χηλαῖσιν: 'with their claws'.

φοναῖς: 'murderously' (literally 'with carnage').

1004

οὐκ ἄσημος: 'quite clear' (litotes).

1005

ἐμπύρων ἐγευόμην: 'I began to try burnt offerings'. This type of divination involved observing the reaction when sacrificial offerings (thigh bones (μηρία) wrapped in fat, topped with gall bladder (χολή)), were placed on a fire.

1007

Ἥφαιστος: 'Hephaestus' stands for 'fire' by metonymy, but there is an obvious implication of divine displeasure.

A
Level

1007–8

ἐπὶ σποδῷ / μυδῶσα κηκὶς μηρίων ἐτήκετο: 'upon the embers a damp ooze dripped from the thigh bones'. A grotesque description, particularly as the words μυδῶσα and ἐτήκετο could also apply to a putrefying corpse.

1009–11

These lines contain four main verbs, all connected by καί (polysyndeton). The effect is of a rapid stream of actions.

1012

παιδὸς τοῦδ' ... πάρα = παρὰ παιδὸς τοῦδε, with anastrophe of παρά.

1015

ταῦτα ... νοσεῖ: 'suffers this disease' (ταῦτα is an 'internal' accusative).
τῆς σῆς: emphatically placed ('as a result of *your* will').

1017–18

πλήρεις ὑπ᾽ οἰωνῶν τε καὶ κυνῶν βορᾶς / τοῦ δυσμόρου πεπτῶτος Οἰδίπου γόνου: 'filled by birds and dogs with carrion from the ill-fated fallen son of Oedipus'. The terms of Creon's decree (205–6) have come back to haunt him.

1019

κᾆτ᾽ = καὶ εἶτα 'And so'.

1019–22

Several rare words in these lines (θυστάδας, ἀπορροιβδεῖ, ἀνδροφθόρου) add a note of grandeur to the summary of the failed religious ceremonies.

1021

This line lacks a normal caesura, giving it a slow, doom-laden feel.

1022

βεβρῶτες: The plural is unexpected after the singular ὄρνις ... ἀπορροιβδεῖ in the previous line. It may be a construction according to the sense of the passage (a 'constructio ad sensum'), as there would have been more than one bird, but it is possible the Greek text has been corrupted here.

1025

ἐπεὶ δ᾽ ἁμάρτῃ: Supply τις ('Whenever someone makes a mistake ...'). Indefinite clauses with the subjunctive are sometimes found without the usual ἄν in verse.

1028

τοι: 'you know'.

1031

εὖ ... εὖ: Teiresias makes clear his good intentions with repetition of this word.

A Level

μανθάνειν δ': Iambic trimeters do not usually have elision between lines, as they behave as individual units, but occasionally a line-final word ending in a vowel is elided before a vowel at the beginning of the next (hypermetric elision).

1032

εὖ λέγοντος: 'from one who offers good advice'.

εἰ κέρδος λέγοι: 'if he speaks profitably'. The optative λέγοι is used to make the statement as general as possible. Note how Teiresias presents a different view of the word κέρδος 'profit', 'gain', which has occurred a number of times in the play. For him, it is something to be obtained through learning; for Creon, it is the money that has corrupted his guards (cf. 310); while for Antigone, it is the release in death from a life full of troubles (cf. 464). Which interpretation do you think shows the best insight into the events of the play?

A
Level

Vocabulary

While there is no Defined Vocabulary List for A-level, words in the OCR Defined Vocabulary List for AS are marked with * so that students can quickly see the vocabulary with which they should be particularly familiar.

ἀ	ah!	ἀλγέω	feel pain, suffer
ἄβουλος, -ον	ill-advised	ἀλγίων, -ον	more painful
*ἀγαθός, -η, -ον	good	ἄλγος, -ους, n.	pain
*ἄγαν	very much	ἀλγύνω	pain, grieve, distress
*ἄγγελος, -ου, m.	messenger	ἄλεκτρος, -ον	unwedded
ἁγνίζω	purify	ἁλίσκομαι (aor. ἑάλων)	be captured
ἀγνώς, -ῶτος	unknown		
ἄγος, -ους, n.	pollution	ἀλκή, -ῆς, f.	strength
ἄγραπτος, -ον	unwritten	*ἀλλά	but
ἀγχιστεῖα, -ων, n.	closeness	*ἀλλήλους, -ας, -α	each other
*ἄγω	lead	*ἄλλος, -η, -ο	other, another
*ἀδελφή, -ῆς, f.	sister	ἀλύσκω (fut. ἀλύξω)	flee from
*ἀδελφός, -οῦ, m.	brother	*ἅμα	at the same time
Ἅιδης, -ου, m.	Hades	*ἁμαρτάνω (perf. ἡμάρτηκα)	make a mistake
*ἀεί / αἰεί	ever, always		
ἀείφρουρος, -ον	ever-watching	ἀμήχανος, -ον	impossible
ἄθλιος, -α, -ον	wretched	ἀμπλακεῖν (aorist stem only)	miss
ἄθυμος, -ον	fainthearted, spiritless		
αἰκίζω	maltreat	ἀμπλάκημα, -ατος, n.	mistake
*αἷμα, -ατος, n.	blood	*ἀμφί (+ accusative)	about
Αἵμων, -ονος	Haemon	ἀμφικίων, -ον	with pillars all round
*αἱρέω (perf. middle ᾕρημαι)	take; (middle) choose	*ἄν	would, could (indefinite)
		ἀνάθημα, -ατος, n.	offering
*αἴρω	lift; (middle) take on oneself	ἄναξ, ἄνακτος, m.	king, master
		ἀναπτύω	sputter
*αἰσχρός, -ά, -όν	disgraceful, shameful	ἀνατεί	without harm
*αἰσχύνω	shame; (middle) feel ashamed	ἀνδάνω (aor. inf. ἁδεῖν)	please
		ἀνδρόφθορος, -ον	of a slain man
*αἰτέω	ask for	ἀνεκτός, -όν	bearable, sufferable
*αἰτία, -ας, f.	charge, blame	ἀνέχομαι (aor. ἠνεσχόμην)	endure
ἀκέομαι	apply a remedy		
ἀκίνητος, -ον	unmoved, motionless	*ἀνήρ, ἀνδρός, m.	man
ἄκλαυτος, -ον	unlamented	ἀνθίσταμαι (aor. ἀντέστην)	make a stand
*ἀκούω	hear		
ἄκρα, -ας, f.	peak	*ἄνθρωπος, -ου, m.	man, person
*ἄκων, -ουσα, -ον	unwilling	ἀνιάω	grieve, distress
ἀλγεινός, -ή, -όν	painful, grievous		

ἀνιαρός, -ά, -όν			grievous, troublesome
ἀνίημι (perf. midd.			relax; (middle) be
   ἀνεῖμαι)				relaxed, let free
ἀνοιστέος, -α, -ον			must be brought
ἄνολβος, -ον			unlucky
ἄνους, -ουν			without understanding,
                     silly
ἀντερῶ (perf.			speak against
   ἀντείρηκα)
*ἀντί (+ genitive)			instead of
Ἀντιγόνη, -ης, f.			Antigone
ἀντιφωνέω			reply
ἀνυμέναιος, -ον			without the wedding
                     song
ἀνύω				accomplish
ἀπανάστασις, -εως, f.		revolution
ἀπαρνέομαι			deny utterly
*ἅπας, ἅπασα, ἅπαν		all, every
ἀπεχθής, -ές			hateful
ἀπιστέω				disobey
*ἀπό (+ genitive)			from
*ἀπόλλυμαι (aor.			die
   ἀπωλόμην)
ἀπόρρητος, -ον			forbidden
ἀπορροιβδέω			shriek forth
*ἅπτω				fasten; (middle) touch
*ἆρα				(introduces a question)
ἀράσσω (aor. ἤραξα)		smash
Ἀργεῖος, -α, -ον			Argive
ἄργυρος, -ου, m.			silver
ἀρέσκω (aor. pass		please
   ἠρέσθην)
ἀρεστός, -ή, -όν			acceptable, pleasing
*ἀριθμός, -ου, m.			number
*ἄριστος, -η, -ον			best
ἀριστεύω			be best
ἀρκέω (fut. ἀρκέσω)		suffice
ἁρμόζω (perf. midd.			fit together
   ἥρμοσμαι)
ἄρνυμαι				win, gain
ἁρπάζω				snatch away, carry off
ἄρρητος, -ον			unspoken
ἀρρώξ, -ωγος			unbroken
ἀρτάνη, -ης, f.			noose
ἀρτίως				just now, recently
*ἀρχή, -ῆς, f.			rule
ἀρχήν				at first
*ἄρχω				rule
ἀρώσιμος, -ον			fit for ploughing
ἄσημος, -ον			without sign
ἀστός, -ου, m.			citizen
*ἀσφαλής, -ές			safe
ἀτάομαι				suffer, be in distress
ἄταφος, -ον			unburied
ἄτερ (+ genitive)			without
ἄτη, -ης, f.			madness, ruin

ἀτιμάζω				dishonour
ἄτιμος, -ον			dishonoured
*αὖ				in turn, again
αὐδάω				speak
αὐθαδία, -ας, f.			stubbornness
*αὖθις				again
αὔλειος, -α, -ον			belonging to the
                  courtyard
αὔξω				increase
αὐτάδελφος, -ον			belonging to a brother/
                  sister
αὐτοκτονέω			kill one another
*αὑτόν				= ἑαυτόν himself
*αὐτός, -ή, -ό			himself; same; him, her,
                  it, them
αὐτουργός, -όν			self-working
αὐτόφωρος, -ον			self-detected
αὐτόχειρ, -ος			with one's own hand
αὕτως				likewise
ἀφαγνίζω			purify, consecrate
ἀφανδάνω			displease
ἀφανίζω				make vanish

*βαίνω (perf. part.			go, walk
   βεβώς, -ῶτος)
βαρβαρόομαι			become wild
βαρύς, -εῖα, -ύ			heavy, serious
βαστάζω				deal with
*βία, -ας, f.			force
βιάζω				force, compel
βιβρώσκω (perf. part.		eat
   βεβρώς, -ῶτος)
*βίος, -ου, m.			life
βιώσιμος, -ον			to be lived
βλαστάνω (aor.			grow
   ἔβλαστον)
*βλέπω				see, look
*βοή, -ῆς, f.			shout
βορά, -ας, f.			food
βούλευμα, -ατος, n.		resolution, purpose
*βουλεύω			take counsel,
                  deliberate
*βούλομαι			want
βροτός, -οῦ, m.			mortal
*βωμός, -οῦ, m.			altar

γάμος, -ου, m.			wedding
*γάρ				for
*γε				at least, at any rate
*γελάω				laugh
γενηίς, -ίδος, f.			pickaxe, mattock
γέννημα, -ατος, n.		child
*γένος, -ους, n.			race, family
*γέρων, -οντος, m.			old man
γεύομαι				taste
*γῆ, -ῆς, f.			earth

*γίγνομαι	become	*δύναμαι	am able
*γιγνώσκω	find out	δυσβουλία, -ας, f.	bad advice
γλυκύς, -εῖα, -ύ	sweet	δυσδαίμων, -ον	unlucky
*γλῶσσα, -ης, f.	tongue	δυσκλεής, -ές	inglorious
γόνος, -ου, m.	child	δυσμενής, -ές	hostile
*γοῦν	at least, at any rate	δύσμορος, -ον	ill-fated
γύης, -ου, m.	field	δύσνους, -ουν	badly disposed
*γυνή, γυναικός, f.	woman	δυσσέβεια, -ας, f.	impiety, ungodliness
		δυσσεβής, -ές	ungodly, impious
δαίμων, -ονος, m. or f.	god, goddess	δύστηνος, -ον	wretched, unhappy
δάκνω	bite	δυσχερής, -ές	hard to handle
*δέ	and, but		
*δεῖ	it is necessary	*ἐάν	if
δείδω (aor. ἔδεισα)	fear	*ἐάω (fut. ἐάσω)	allow
*δείκνυμι (fut. δείξω, aor. ἔδειξα)	show	ἐγγενής, -ές	native
		ἐγκλήω	shut in
δειλός, -ή, -όν	cowardly	ἐγκρατής, -ές	powerful
*δεινός, -ή, -όν	terrible, strange	*ἐγώ	I
δέμας, n.	body	ἐδεστός, -ή, -όν	eatable
*δεῦρο	to here	*ἐθέλω	be willing, wish
*δεύτερος, -α, -ον	second	*εἰ	if
*δέχομαι (perf. δέδεγμαι)	receive	εἴκω	give way, retire
		*εἰμί	be
*δή	indeed (emphasizes previous word)	*εἶμι	go
		εἴπερ	if really, if indeed
*δῆλος, -η, -ον	clear, certain	εἴργω	keep away
*δηλόω	show	*εἰς, ἐς (+ accusative)	into
δημόλευστος, -ον	publicly stoned	εἰσακούω	listen to
*δῆτα	certainly, of course	εἰσοράω	look upon, behold
*διά (+ genitive)	through, by means of	εἴσω, ἔσω	within
διασκεδάννυμι (fut. διασκεδάω)	scatter about	*εἶτα	then, next
		*εἴτε … εἴτε	whether … or
διασπείρω	scatter	*ἐκ, ἐξ (+ genitive)	from, out of
*δίδωμι (fut. δώσω, aor. ἔδωκα)	give	*ἕκαστος, -η, -ον	each
		ἐκβολή, -ῆς, f.	throwing out
διέρπω	creep	ἐκδιδάσκω	teach thoroughly
*δίκαιος, -α, -ον	just	*ἐκεῖ	there
δίκελλα, -ης, f.	hoe, two-pronged fork	*ἐκεῖνος, -η, -ον	that
		ἔκκειμαι	be left bare of
*δίκη, -ης, f.	justice	ἐκκηρύσσω (perf. midd. ἐκκεκήρυγμαι)	announce publicly
Δίκη, -ης, f.	Justice (personified as goddess)		
		ἐκμανθάνω (aor. ἐξέμαθον)	learn thoroughly
διόλλυμι (aor. act. διώλεσα, midd. διωλόμην)	destroy utterly; (middle) die		
		ἐκπέλει	it is permitted
διπλοῦς, -ῆ, -οῦν	double	ἐκπέμπω	send out
δίχα	apart	ἐκπίνω	drink out
δμώς, -ωός, m.	household slave	ἐκπράσσω	bring about, achieve,
*δοκέω	think, seem	ἐκπροτιμάω	honour above all
δόμος, -ου, m.	house	ἐκτός (+ gen.)	outside
δόξα, -ης, f.	expectation	ἐκφαίνω (fut. ἐκφανέω)	reveal; (middle) appear
δόρυ (dat. δορί), n.	spear		
*δοῦλος, -ου, m.	slave	ἐκφύομαι (perf. ἐκπέφυκα)	be born
*δουλόω	enslave		
*δράω (aor. ἔδρασα, perf. δέδρακα)	do	*ἑκών, -οῦσα, -όν	willing
		ἐλέγχω	accuse

*ἐλεύθερος, -α, -ον	free	ἐρευνάω	seek
*ἐλπίς, -ίδος, f.	hope, expectation	*ἐρῆμος, -ον	deserted, abandoned
*ἐμαυτόν, -ήν	myself	ἑρκεῖος, -α, -ον	belonging to the front court
*ἐμός, -ή, -όν	mine		
ἔμπεδος, -ον	secure	*ἔρχομαι	go
ἔμπυρα, -ων, τά	burnt offerings	*ἐρωτάω	ask (a question)
ἐμφανής, -ές	visible	ἐσχάρα, -ας, f.	altar for burnt offerings
*ἐν (+ dat.)	in	Ἐτεοκλῆς, -οῦς, m.	Eteocles
ἐναργής, -ές	visible, manifest	*ἕτερος, -α, -ον	one, the other
ἔνδικος, -ον	just	*ἔτι	yet, still
ἔνερθε	from beneath	*ἕτοῖμος, -η, -ον	ready
ἔνεστι	is in the power of	*εὖ	well
*ἐνθάδε	here	εὐαγής, -ές	free from pollution, pure
ἔνθεν	from where	*εὐγενής, -ές	noble
*ἐννοέω	consider	εὐδαιμονέω	be fortunate
ἔντιμος, -ον	honoured	εὐεργέτης, -ου, m.	benefactor
ἐντριβής, -ές	proved by testing	εὐθύνω	guide straight
ἐξαμαρτάνω	make a mistake	*εὐθύς	immediately
ἐξαμαρτία, -ας, f.	mistake	εὐκλεής, -ές	famous
ἐξανίστημι	make get up	εὐμενής, -ές	favourable
ἐξεπίσταμαι	know thoroughly	εὔνους, -ουν	well-disposed, friendly
ἐξεργάζομαι	work out, bring to completion,	*εὑρίσκω	find
		εὐσεβέω	be pious
ἐξερέω	will speak out	εὔσημος, -ον	of good signs
*ἔξεστι	it is possible	εὐτυχέω	be fortunate
ἐξήκω	have reached	ἐφευρίσκω	find
ἔξοιδα	know thoroughly	ἐχθαίρω	hate, detest
ἐξόμνυμι (fut. ἐξομέομαι)	swear	ἐχθές	yesterday
		*ἐχθρός, -ά, -όν	enemy, hostile
ἐξορθόω	set upright	ἔχιδνα, -ης, f.	viper
ἔξω (+ genitive)	outside	*ἔχω	have
ἔοικα	seem		
ἐπαιδέομαι	be ashamed	*ζάω	live
ἐπαιτιάομαι	accuse	*Ζεύς, gen. Διός or Ζηνός, m.	Zeus
ἐπάλληλος, -ον	mutual		
ἐπαμαξεύω (perf. midd. ἐπημάξευμαι)	travel over with chariots	*ἤ	or
		ἤ	indeed
ἐπαυχέω	exult in	ἤ	where
*ἐπεί	when, since	*ἡγεμών, -όνος, m.	leader
ἔπειμι	be upon	*ἡδέως	pleasantly
*ἔπειτα	then, next	*ἤδη	already, by this time
ἐπεντέλλω	command besides	*ἡδύς, -εῖα, -ύ	pleasant
ἐπήβολος, -ον	in possession of	*ἥκω	have come, be present
*ἐπί	(+genitive) upon; (+ dative) for, on	*ἡμεῖς	we
		*ἡμέρα, -ας, f.	day
ἐπικτείνω	kill in addition	ἡμεροσκόπος, -ον	watching by day
ἐπίσκοπος, -ου, m.	overseer	*ἤν	if
*ἐπίσταμαι	understand	ἡνίκα	at the time when
ἐπιτύμβιος, -ον	upon a tomb	Ἥφαιστος, -ου, m.	Hephaestus
ἐπιχωρέω	yield, give way		
ἔπος, -ους, n.	word	θᾶκος, -ου, m.	seat
ἐράω	love	*θάπτω	bury
*ἐργάζομαι (perf. εἴργασμαι)	work	*θαρσέω	be confident
		θαῦμα, -ατος, n.	wonder
ἐργάτης, -ου, m.	worker	θεήλατος, -ον	sent by a god
*ἔργον, -ου, n.	work		

θέλω	am willing, want
*θεός, -ου, m. or f.	god
θερμός, -ή, -όν	hot
θήρ, θηρός, m.	beast of prey
θηράω	hunt, chase
θησαυρός, -ου, m.	store, treasure
θιγγάνω (aor. ἔθιγον)	touch, handle
*θνήσκω (fut. θανοῦμαι, aor. ἔθανον, perf. τέθνηκα)	die
θνητός, -ή, -όν	mortal
*θρασύς, -εῖα, -ύ	bold
θραύω	shatter
θρόνος, -ου, m.	throne, power
θῦμα, -ατος, n.	sacrifice
θυμόομαι	be angry
θυστάς, -άδος	sacrificial
ἵζω	sit
ἱκνέομαι (aor. ἱκόμην)	come
*ἵνα	in order to; where
*ἵππος, -ου, m.	horse
Ἰσμήνη, -ης, ἡ	Ismene
*ἴσος, -η, -ον	equal
*ἵστημι	make to stand; (middle) stand
ἴσχω	have
Καδμεῖος, -α, -ον	Cadmean, Theban
καθαιρέω	condemn
*καί	and
*καίτοι	and yet
*κακός, -ή, -όν	bad
*καλέω	call
καλλύνω	beautify
*καλός, -ή, -όν	fair, good
καλυπτός, -ή, -όν	covered
καλύπτω	hide
καλχαίνω	seethe
κάρα, n.	head
καρδία, -ας, f.	heart
κάρτα	very, extremely
κασιγνήτη, -ης, f.	sister
κασίγνητος, -ου, m.	brother
*κατά	(+ accusative) by, according to, throughout; (+ genitive) down from
καταθνήσκω (aor. stem κατθαν-)	die
κατακτείνω	kill
καταντίον	right opposite
καταρνέομαι	deny strongly
καταρρυής, -ές	slipping away
καταρτύω	train, discipline

κατασκαφή, -ῆς, f.	destruction
κατασκαφής, -ές	dug down
καταυδάω	speak out, speak plainly
κάτειμι	go down
κατεργάζομαι	achieve
κατέρχομαι (aor. κατῆλθον)	return from exile
κατέχω	possess, get hold of
κάτω	downwards, below
*κεῖμαι (fut. κείσομαι)	lie
κεῖνος, -η, -ον	that
*κελεύω	order
κεντέω	goad, spur on
κερδαίνω	gain, derive profit
κέρδος, -ους, n.	gain, profit
κεύθω (perf. κέκευθα)	hide; be hidden
κηδεμών, -όνος, m.	protector
κηκίς, -ῖδος, f.	ooze
κήρυγμα, -ατος, n.	proclamation
*κηρύσσω	proclaim
κινδύνευμα, -ατος, n.	danger
κλάζω	screech
κλέος, n.	fame, reputation
κλοπεύς, -έως, m.	thief
κλύω (aor. ἔκλυον)	hear
κοινόομαι	communicate
*κοινός, -ή, -όν	common
*κομίζω	bring, convey
κομψεύω	quibble about
κόνις, -εως, f.	dust
κοσμέω	adorn, arrange
κουφίζω (fut. κουφιέω)	lift up
*κράτος, -ους, n.	strength
κρείσσων, -ον	stronger, mightier
κρεμαστός, -ή, -όν	hung
Κρέων, -οντος, m.	Creon
*κρίνω (fut. κρινέω)	judge
κρυπτέος, -ον	must be hidden
*κρύπτω	hide, cover
κρυφῇ	secretly, in secret
*κτάομαι	get, acquire
κτείνω (fut. κτενέω)	kill
κτερίζω	give funeral rites
κύων, κυνός, m.	dog
κυρέω	be
κωκύω	lament
*κωλύω	hinder, prevent
λαγχάνω (aor. ἔλαχον)	obtain by lot
Λάιος, -ου, m.	Laius (father of Oedipus)
λάλημα, -ατος, n.	chatterbox
*λαμβάνω (aor. ἔλαβον, aor. pass. ἐλήφθην)	take

λάμπω	shine	μίασμα, -ατος, n.	pollution
*λανθάνω	escape one's attention	*μισέω	hate
*λέγω (fut. ἐρέω, perf. midd. εἴρημαι)	say, speak	μισθαρνέω	work for money
		*μισθός, - οῦ, m.	pay, reward
*λείπω (perf. midd. λέλειμμαι)	leave, abandon	μοῖρα, -ας, f.	part
		*μόλις	scarcely, with difficulty
λεπτός, -ή, -όν	fine, light	*μόνος / μοῦνος, -η, -ον	alone, solitary
λέχος, -ους, n.	bed		
λήθω	escape one's attention	μόρος, -ου, m.	fate, destiny
λῆμμα, -ατος, n.	gain	μυδάω	be damp, dripping
*λιμήν, -ένος, m.	harbour, haven	μύδρος, -ου, m.	lump of hot iron
λίπος, -ους, n.	animal fat	*μῦθος, -ου, m.	word, speech
λιτή, -ης, f.	prayer, entreaty	μωρία, -ας, f.	foolishness
*λόγος, -ου, m.	word	*μῶρος, -α, -ον	foolish
*λοιπός, -ή, -όν	remaining		
λοίσθιος, -α, -ον	last	ναός, -ου, m.	temple
λούω	wash	*νεκρός, -οῦ, m.	corpse
λόφος, -ου, m.	back of the neck	νέκυς, -υος, m.	corpse
*λυπέω	annoy, harass	νέομαι	go
*λύπη, -ης, f.	pain, grief	*νέος, -α, -ον	young, new
λυσσάω	rage	νεύω	nod
*λύω	release	*νικάω	conquer
λωβάομαι	mistreat	νιν	him, her, it, them
		νοέω	think
*μακρός, -ά, -όν	long	*νομίζω	think
*μάλιστα	especially	νόμιμα, -ων, n.	laws, usages
*μᾶλλον	more	νόμισμα, -ατος, n.	custom, money
*μανθάνω (aor. ἔμαθον)	learn	*νόμος, -ου, m.	law
		*νοσέω	be sick
μάντευμα, -ατος, n.	oracle	*νοῦς, -οῦ, m.	mind
μαρτυρέω	give evidence	νυμφεῖον, -ου, n.	(singular) bridal chamber; (plural) bride
*μάχομαι (fut. μαχέομαι)	fight		
*μέγας, μεγάλη, μέγα	big	*νῦν	now
*μέλλω	be about to, intend	νυν	now (consequence)
*μέν	on the one hand	*νύξ, νυκτός, f.	night
Μενοικεύς, -έως, m.	Menoeceus (father of Creon)	νώ	we two (dual)
*μέντοι	however	ξυγγιγνώσκω (aor. ξυνέγνων)	forgive
*μένω (fut. μενέω)	stay, wait	ξύγγνοια, -ας, f.	forgiveness
*μέρος, -ους, n.	share, portion	ξύμμαχος, -ον	allied
μεστόω	fill	ξυμμετίσχω	join in sharing
*μετά	(+ accusative) after; (+ genitive) with	ξύμπλους, -ουν	sailing with
		ξυμπονέω	toil with
μετάρσιος, -ον	high in the air	ξύναιμος, -ον	of common blood, kindred
μετέχω (aor. μετέσχον)	have a share in		
*μή	not	ξυνεργάζομαι	work with
*μηδέ	and not, not even	ξυνίστωρ, -ορος	witnessing
*μηδείς, μηδεμία, μηδέν	not one	ξύννοια, -ας, f.	meditation
		ξύνοιδα	share knowledge
μῆκος	at length	ξύνοικος, -ον	dwelling with
μήν	indeed		
μηρία, -ων, n.	thigh-bones	*ὁ, ἡ, τό	the
μηρός, -οῦ, m.	thigh	*ὅδε, ἥδε, τόδε	this
*μήτηρ, μητρός, f.	mother	*οἶδα	know
μήτοι	certainly not		

Οἰδίπους, -ου m.	Oedipus	*οὔτε … οὔτε	neither … nor
οἴκησις, -εως f.	dwelling	οὔτοι	certainly not
*οἶκος, -ου, m.	house	*οὗτος, αὕτη, τοῦτο	this
οἴμοι	alas	*οὕτω(ς)	thus, in this way
οἴομαι	think	ὀφείλω	owe
*οἶος, -α, -ον	such as, of what sort	*ὀφθαλμός, -οῦ, m.	eye
οἰστέος, -ον	having to be carried	ὀφλισκάνω	incur the charge of
οἴστρος, -ου, m.	frenzy	ὄψεις, -εων, f.	eyes
οἰωνός, -οῦ, m.	large bird, bird of prey		
ὄλλυμι (fut. midd.	destroy; (middle) die	πάθος, -ους, n.	suffering
ὀλέομαι, aor. midd.		παίδειος, -α, -ον	of children
ὠλόμην, intransitive		*παῖς, παιδός, m. or f.	child
perf. act. ὄλωλα)		παίω	strike, smite
ὅμαιμος, -ον	related	*πάλαι	formerly, long ago
ὁμαίμων, -ον	related	*παλαιός, -ά, -όν	ancient
*ὅμοιος, -α, -ον	similar	*πάλιν	back, backwards
ὁμορροθέω	flow together	πάλος, -ου, m.	lot cast from a shaken
ὁμόσπλαγχνος, -ον	from the same womb		helmet
ὁμῶς	equally	πάμφλεκτος, -ον	all-blazing
*ὁποῖος, -α, -ον	of what sort	πάνδημος, -ον	of the whole people
ὁπόσος, -η, -ον	as many as	πανουργέω	be a villain
ὅπου	where	πανουργία, -ας, f.	villainy
ὀπτός, -ή, -όν	forged, tempered	παντελής, -ές	complete
*ὅπως	in order to	*παρά	(+ accusative) equal to;
*ὁράω (fut. ὄψομαι,	see		(+ genitive) from
aor. εἶδον, perf.		παράγω (perf. midd.	lead astray
ὄπωπα)		παρῆγμαι)	
*ὀργή, -ῆς, f.	anger	παραλλάσσω	alter
ὄργια, -ων, n.	secret rites	*πάρειμι	be present
*ὀρθός, -ή, -όν	straight	παρεξέρχομαι	slip past
ὀρθόω	set straight	*πᾶς, πᾶσα, πᾶν	all
ὁρίζω	define	*πάσχω (fut.	suffer
ὅρκιος, -α, -ον	belonging to an oath	πείσομαι, aor.	
ὀρκωμοτέω	take an oath	ἔπαθον)	
ὀρνιθοσκόπος, -ον	observing birds	πατέομαι (aor.	taste
ὄρνις, -ιθος, m. or f.	bird	ἐπασάμην)	
*ὅς, ἥ, ὅ	who, which	*πατήρ, πατρός, m.	father
ὅσιος, -α, -ον	holy	πάτρα, -ας, f.	country, native land
*ὅσος, -η, -ον	how great	*πατρῷος, -α, -ον	of a father
*ὅστις, ἥτις, ὅ τι	who, which	*παύω	stop
*ὅταν	whenever	πέδον, -ου, n.	ground, earth
*ὅτε	when, at the time when	*πείθομαι (fut.	obey
*ὅτι	that	πείσομαι)	
*οὐ, οὐκ, οὐχί	not	πέλας	near
*οὐδαμοῦ	nowhere ,	πέλω	be
*οὐδέ	and not, but not, not even	*περί	(+ accusative) around;
*οὐδείς, οὐδεμία,	none		(+ genitive) about
οὐδέν		περισκελής, -ές	very hard
*οὐκέτι	no longer	περισσός, -ή, -όν	excessive
*οὔκουν	not … therefore	περιστέλλω	dress for burial
*οὐκοῦν	therefore	πημονή, -ῆς, f.	trouble
*οὖν	therefore	πιμελή, -ῆς, f.	soft fat
οὕνεκα	since; (+ genitive) for the	πίμπρημι (aor.	burn
	same of	ἔπρησα)	
οὔποτε	never	*πίπτω (perf. part.	fall
οὖς, ὠτός, n.	ear	πεπτώς, -ῶτος)	

*πλείων, -ον	more	πυρόω	burn up
*πλεῖστος, -η, -ον	most	*πῶς	how?
πλεκτός, -ή, -όν	woven		
*πλέω	sail	ῥήγνυμι (aor. pass.	break
πληγή, -ῆς, f.	blow, stroke	ἐρράγην)	
πλῆγμα, -ατος, n.	blow, stroke	ῥοθέω	roar
πλήρης, -ες	full	ῥοῖβδος, -ου, m.	whirring
πλήσσω (aor. pass.	strike	ῥυθμίζω	define
ἐπλήγην)		σάλος, -ου, m.	tossing
πόθεν	from where?	*σαφής, -ές	clear
ποθέω	long for	*σεαυτόν, -ήν	yourself (singular)
πόθος, -ου, m.	desire, longing	σέβας, n.	respect
*ποιέω	make	σέβω	respect, revere
*ποῖος, -α, -ον	of what kind?	σείω	shake
*πόλις, -εως, f.	city	σημεῖον, -ου, n.	sign
*πολίτης, -ου, m.	citizen	σθένω	be strong
*πολλάκις	often	*σιγάω	be silent
Πολυνείκης, -ους, m.	Polynices	σίδηρος, -ου, m.	iron
*πολύς, πολλή, πολύ	much, many	σιωπάω	be silent
πομπός, -ου, m.	escort, guide	σκαιότης, -τητος, f.	awkwardness
*πόνος, -ου, m.	work	σκληρός, -ά, -όν	hard
*πορεύομαι	go	*σκοπέω	consider
πορθέω	destroy	σκοπός, -οῦ, m.	watcher
πόσις, m.	husband	*σκότος, -ου, m.	darkness
*ποτέ	at some time	σμικρός, -ά, -όν	small
*πότερον … ἤ	whether … or?	*σός, -ή, -όν	your (singular)
πότμος, -ου, m.	destiny	σπάω	drag
*ποῦ	where?	σποδός, -οῦ, f.	ashes
*πρᾶγμα, -ατος, n.	deed	στείχω	go
*πράσσω	do, fare	στέλλω (aor. ἔστειλα)	summon
πρέπω	be conspicuous	στέργω	love, approve of
*πρίν	before, until	στερέω	deprive
*προδίδωμι (aor.	betray	*στόμα, -ατος, n.	mouth
προὔδωκα)		*στρατηγός, -οῦ, m.	general
προέχω (fut. προέξω)	(active) prefer; (middle)	*στρατός, -οῦ, m.	army
	offer as pretext	στρέφω (aor. pass.	turn
πρόκειμαι	be established	ἐστράφην)	
προκηρύσσω	proclaim publicly	στυγέω	hate
προμηνύω	denounce beforehand	στύφλος, -ον	hard, rough
πρόνοια, -ας, f.	foresight	*σύ	you (singular)
*πρός	(+ genitive) by	συμφιλέω	love mutually
*πρόσθεν (+ genitive)	before	*σύν / ξύν (+ dative)	with
πρόσκειμαι (fut.	be assigned to	συνέχθω	hate mutually
προσκείσομαι)		συντόμως	concisely
προστίθεμαι (aor.	gain	σφε	him, her, it, them
προσεθέμην)		*σχεδόν	nearly, almost
προσφιλής, -ές	dear	σχέτλιος, -α, -ον	miserable, wretched
προταρβέω	fear on behalf of	*σῴζω (perf. midd.	save
προτίθημι (aor.	appoint	σέσωσμαι, aor.	
προὔθηκα)		pass. ἐσώθην)	
προτίω	honour in preference	*σωτηρία, -ας, f.	safety
προτρέπω	urge forwards		
*πρῶτος, -η, -ον	first	ταλαίπωρος, -ον	suffering, miserable
πτερόν, -οῦ, n.	wing	ταλαίφρων, -ον	of wretched mind
*πύλη, -ης, f.	gate, door	τάλας, τάλαινα,	wretched
*πῦρ, πυρός, n.	fire	τάλαν	

*τάφος, -ου, m. — tomb, burial
*τάχα — quickly, perhaps
*τε — and
τέκνον, -ου, n. — child
*τελευτάω — come to an end
τελέω — fulfil, accomplish
*τέλος, -ους, n. — end, power
τεχνάομαι — carry out skilfully
*τέχνη, -ης, f. — skill
τήκομαι — melt
*τίθημι (aor. act. ἔθηκα, aor. midd. ἐθέμην) — put, make
*τιμάω — honour
*τιμή, -ῆς, f. — honour
*τίς, τί — who? which?
*τις, τι — anyone, anything, someone, something
*τοι — indeed, you know
τοιόσδε, τοιάδε, τοιόνδε — such
*τοιοῦτος, τοιαύτη, τοιοῦτο — such
*τολμάω — dare
*τοσοῦτος, τοσαύτη, τοσοῦτο(ν) — so great
*τότε — at that time, then
τρέφω — nurture
τριβή, -ῆς, f. — delay
*τρίτος, -η, -ον — third
τροφή, -ῆς, f. — nourishment, food
τροχός, -οῦ, m. — wheel
*τυγχάνω (aor. ἔτυχον) — happen to; (+ genitive) meet with
τυμβήρης, -ες — buried
τύμβος, -ου, m. — tomb
τυραννίς, -ίδος, f. — monarchy, tyranny
τύραννος, -ου, m. — king, tyrant
τύφω — produce smoke
*τύχη, -ης, f. — fate, fortune

ὕβρις, -εως, f. — insult, insulting violence
*ὑβρίζω — insult, violate
*υἱός, -ου, m. (dat. pl. υἱέσι) — son
*ὑμεῖς — you (plural)
ὑπεκφεύγω (aor. ὑπεξέφυγον) — flee away
*ὑπέρ (+ genitive) — on behalf of
ὑπερβαίνω — step over
ὑπερδείδω (perf. ὑπερδέδοικα) — fear for
ὑπερμαχέω — fight for
*ὑπέρτερος, -α, -ον — further
ὑπερτιμάω — honour exceedingly

ὑπερτρέχω (aor. ὑπερέδραμον) — run over
ὑπίλλω — restrain
*ὑπό — (+ genitive) by
ὑφίημι (perf. midd. ὑφεῖμαι) — put in secretly; (middle) lurk secretly

*φαίνομαι (perf. πέφασμαι, aor. pass. ἐφάνην) — appear
Φερσέφασσα, -ης, f. — Persephone
*φέρω — carry, tolerate
φεῦ — alas!
*φεύγω — flee
*φημί — say
φθίνω — perish
φθόγγος, -ου, m. — sound
*φθονέω — begrudge, envy
*φιλέω — love
φιλητέος, -ον — must be loved
*φίλος, -η, -ον — loved, dear, friend
φλόξ, φλογός, f. — flame
*φόβος, -ου, m. — fear
φονή, -ῆς, f. — carnage
φόνος, -ου, m. — death
φρένες, φρενῶν, f. — mind, heart
φρονέω — be minded
φρόνημα, -ατος, n. — thought, judgement
φροῦδος, -η, -ον — gone
*φυγάς, -άδος, m. or f. — exile
*φύλαξ, φύλακος, m. — guard
φύομαι (aor. ἔφυν, perf. πέφυκα) — be born, be by nature
φώς, φωτός, m. — man

χαλινός, -οῦ, m. — bit of a horse
χάρις, -ιτος, f. — thanks
*χείρ, χειρός, f. — hand
χέρσος, -ον — dry
χηλή, -ῆς, f. — claw
χθών, χθονός, f. — earth
χοή, -ῆς, f. — libation
χολή, -ῆς, f. — gall, bile
χόω — heap up
*χράομαι (+ dat.) — use
*χρή — it is necessary
χρηστός, -ή, -όν — useful
*χρόνος, -ου, m. — time
χωρίς — separately, apart

ψευδής, -ές — false
ψῆφος, -ου, f. — vote
ψυχή, -ῆς, f. — life
ψυχρός, -ά, -όν — cold

*ὦ	O!	*ὡς	as, when, since, like
*ὧδε	thus	*ὥστε	so that
ὠμός, -ή, -όν	raw, cruel	*ὠφελέω	help

Aristophanes, *Acharnians*

Introduction, Commentary Notes and
Vocabulary by Sarah Harden

A-level: 1–203, 366–92

Introduction

Aristophanes

The ancient evidence for Aristophanes' life is not abundant, but he is generally agreed to have been born around the middle of the fifth century BC (the date 446 BC is most often postulated) and to have died in the 380s. He was a prolific writer of comic plays; eleven out of around forty known compositions survive today. His earliest play was probably the *Banqueters* which was performed in 427 BC and won second prize at the City Dionysia (for details on the dramatic festivals at Athens, see below). The following year he produced the *Babylonians*, also at the City Dionysia, and won first prize but also allegedly got himself into legal trouble. At lines 378–82 of the *Acharnians*, produced the next year in 425 BC, Dicaeopolis suddenly seems to speak in the voice of the poet and refers to being 'dragged into the council-chamber' by Cleon 'on account of last year's comedy'. According to the scholia (ancient commentators) on the *Acharnians*, Aristophanes was prosecuted by one of Athens' leading politicians, Cleon, because he had satirized him so sharply in the *Babylonians*. Cleon is said to have charged Aristophanes with slandering the city in front of foreigners, very many of whom would have attended the City Dionysia each year. His charge does not seem to have been successful, for the scholia report that the council dismissed the case from the court. This anecdote is illustrative of much of the evidence we have about Aristophanes' life, of which almost all comes from his plays or from the ancient commentaries on the plays. We must consider the possibility that the scholia's story was elaborated or even invented to explain the references in the *Acharnians* to Aristophanes' prosecution by Cleon. There is no way of verifying their evidence, and all we can say in the end is that the reference in *Acharnians* wouldn't make a huge amount of sense if there had been *no* public reaction from Cleon, although a full-blown court case may be an exaggeration. It is certainly the case that the comic playwright ruthlessly and savagely satirizes Cleon in many of his plays, and it is not beyond the realms of possibility that Cleon might have been offended by this, but we must exercise due caution in extracting biographical information about their author from the plays themselves, and equal caution is needed in our readings of the ancient commentators, who do not always get things right. At any rate, Aristophanes continued to target Cleon in his plays until the politician's death in 422 BC, so he was evidently not put off by this court case, if it really existed at all.

Aristophanes enjoyed considerable success at the dramatic festivals in Athens, winning first prize at least six times including first prize at the City Dionysia with *Babylonians* in 425 BC and first place at the Lenaea, the other main dramatic festival in Athens, at least three times with *Acharnians* in 425 BC, *Knights* in 424 BC and *Frogs* in 405 BC. The *Frogs* was so popular that Aristophanes was awarded an honorific crown of olive-leaves and the play was ordered to be re-performed at a later festival, a unique honour in a time when plays were usually only performed once.

Dramatic festivals and the theatre

Drama in Athens had a very different place in society from that which theatre holds in our modern world. Tragic and Comic plays were performed not only as entertainment, but as part of civic and religious festivals dedicated to the god Dionysus. There were two main dramatic festivals each year: the City Dionysia was held annually in the ancient month *Elaphebolion* (March–April in the modern calendar) while the Lenaea was held in *Gamelion* (January); both of these festivals took place largely in the theatre of Dionysus which was in the heart of the city on the south slopes of the Acropolis.

The City Dionysia lasted several days and included a religious procession (*pompe*) in which an icon of Dionysus was paraded from the acropolis to a sacred grove outside the city; the procession consisted of a crowd of citizens and other inhabitants, carrying sacrificial offerings, some of whom would also carry large wooden *phalloi* on sticks. It ended in the sacrifice of a bull and hundreds of other, smaller sacrifices. These religious elements were followed by civic ceremonies in the theatre in which honours were given by the state to distinguished citizens; the Athenian allies brought their annual tribute and it was heaped up in the orchestra; there was also a ceremony in which war-orphans were publically paraded, given ceremonial armour and a promise that the state would pay for their keep as a reward for their parents' sacrifice. The dramatic portion of the festival consisted of three tragic trilogies (each followed by a satyr play) and five comic plays (this dropped to three during the Peloponnesian War). It is not known when exactly in relation to the tragedies the comic plays were performed, but it is thought that the comedies either preceded the tragedies on the first day of the dramatic shows or that each tragic trilogy would take place in the morning and one comedy would then be performed in the afternoon. The dramatic performances were a competition with prizes for the best comedy and tragedy. Ten judges were selected by lot from a panel chosen by the Council; it is thought that they would take the mood of the audience into consideration when making their judgements, and that poets would thus attempt to put forward plays which would be popular with the crowd. The prize was a symbolic ivy crown for each victorious poet, who would then be escorted home by a victory parade.

The Lenaea was a smaller festival with a higher focus on comedy, probably restricted to a more local audience than the City Dionysia due to the difficulties of travelling in the depths of winter in the ancient world. We know less about this festival than the larger City Dionysia, but there does seem to have been a parade supervised by the archon before a series of dramatic performances which by the 440s happened in the theatre of Dionysus. There were fewer plays performed at this festival: we have limited evidence for two tragic entrants in the fifth century BC and three comedies.

The theatre of Dionysus had a large seating capacity of 15,000 to 20,000 and there was a fund, started by the Athenian politician Pericles, to ensure that all citizens could afford a seat. Despite this, it is reasonable to assume that wealthier and middle-class citizens were more able to take several days off work to attend and that they may have thus made up the majority of the audience. At the City Dionysia, at least, there would also have been many foreigners in attendance including visiting dignitaries and, from the mid-fifth century BC until the end of the Peloponnesian War, representatives from the Athenian subject states. It is not universally agreed whether women were in attendance at the theatre, as the ancient sources give conflicting evidence on this point. There does seem to have been a strong culture of respectable women staying at home as much as possible which suggests that perhaps only lower-class women would have attended. On the other hand, there is no evidence for any legislation forbidding their attendance and one of the most important senior dignitaries at the festival would have been the priestess of Dionysus, who received the honour of one of the best seats in the house.

Dramatic conventions

The theatre of Dionysus as it survives today has undergone many renovations since the mid-fifth century BC and does not offer much concrete evidence for the design of the stage and set buildings in Aristophanes' time. The chorus would mainly have performed on a semi-circular (or possibly rectangular) area of ground called the *orchestra* in the middle of the theatre with the stage behind them and spectators' seats rising up on a slope on either side and in front of them. Passages for the chorus to enter and exit would have led off the *orchestra* on either side. The stage would have contained a simple wooden building with up to three doors, which often had an upper storey with a window and/or a flat roof so that actors could appear as if 'upstairs'. This is likely to have been a temporary building which was put up and taken down as needed rather than anything more permanent. Flying characters or gods appearing on high could use the crane or *mekhane*, which would suspend them above the stage, while dead bodies or indoor scenes could be brought out and displayed to the audience on a wheeled platform often called the *ekkyklema*.

Actors and costumes

The number of actors was supposedly restricted to three, but many of Aristophanes' plays require four actors on stage at one time, suggesting that the restriction was not rigidly enforced. *Acharnians* in fact appears to require five actors. The rule was mainly bent for very small parts played by children, silent parts (often, in Aristophanes, played by naked women!) and parts such as that of Pseudartabas in *Acharnians* where the actor has only two or three lines. All actors, with the possible exception of the silent 'femme fatale' characters frequently brought on at the end of comic plays, were male and their costumes were deliberately ridiculous. They all wore masks which covered their entire face and often included hair; contemporary vase-paintings make clear that these masks were often grotesque in appearance but we can assume that when a well-known Athenian figure such as Cleon appeared on stage the mask will have been a recognizable caricature of their faces. An anecdote in the miscellany of the third-century AD author Aelian reports that when Socrates appeared as a character on stage in Aristophanes' *Clouds,* the real Socrates was so amused by the appearance of his onstage counterpart that he stood up to let the rest of the audience compare the likeness. Comic actors wore heavily padded body suits with fat stomachs and bottoms, to which a large phallus was attached. The origins of this convention may be linked to the religious parade in the City Dionysia (in which *phalloi* played a part), but it is clear that much humour was derived from this element of the costume (see for instance lines 157–64 of the *Acharnians*).

The chorus

The comic chorus at the City Dionysia was made up of 24 male Athenian citizens, rather than professional actors (who would have taken the main speaking parts); at the Lenaea resident foreigners were also permitted to take part. It is hard to appreciate the extent of their role when reading an Aristophanic play in the classroom: they would have sung and danced some of their lines as choral odes set to music, providing a completely different tone and style from the actors' spoken sections of dialogue and monologue. The chorus in the *Acharnians* sing about a quarter of their lines (the rest are spoken, often in interaction with the actors). This group of highly conservative old men provide the main opposition to Dicaeopolis' private peace-treaty with Sparta: they represent a large group within Athenian society who would have been pro-war.

Directors and producers

Each play was financed by a *choregos*, a rich man who undertook to pay for all the expenses of training the actors and chorus (including musicians to play the music for the chorus), and to pay for masks, costumes and any items needed for the set. He would also be expected to pay for a banquet for the whole cast and crew at the end of the performance. This was his financial contribution to the state, functioning something like the modern taxation system, although the sums of money involved could vary quite widely depending on the needs of the particular production. The *choregos* would come in for some of the praise and glory if his play won a prize, although their award of an ivy crown was obviously entirely symbolic. The hands-on 'director' of the play was called the *didaskalos* (literally, the 'teacher') and this could be the poet himself or a specialized director whom the poet hired for the job: his main role would be to teach the chorus the songs and dances since the actors were usually professionals and would need less instruction than the amateur chorus-members. Aristophanes' earlier plays (including the *Acharnians*) were produced by a man called Callistratus; the poet later began to produce his own plays.

Old Comedy

'Old Comedy' is the name commonly given to the plays of Aristophanes (and other, now fragmentary playwrights) produced throughout the fifth century BC from the first official comic competition at Athens in 486 BC until the end of the Peloponnesian War or just afterwards (c.404–400 BC). It was succeeded by Middle Comedy (of which few examples survive) and finally by New Comedy, best exemplified in the plays of Menander. Most of Aristophanes' surviving plays are of the Old Comic style, although his *Assemblywomen*, produced in 391 BC, is generally considered to be more compatible with the style of Middle Comedy; the fact that the work of a single author spans the two sub-genres of comedy shows that the dividing line between Old and Middle Comedy is not a clear one, however the shift to New Comedy from the late 320s onwards marks a very definitive shift in tone.

Old Comedy is chiefly characterized by its focus on political and topical satire, featuring many contemporary Athenians as characters onstage and lampooning military, political and other public figures with vicious humour. Another defining characteristic of the plays of Old Comedy is their frequent total lack of realism in their plots, characters and premises (one play involves the hero flying to heaven on a giant dung-beetle!); the (sub) genre is also marked by its very frequent use of sexual and scatological jokes. New Comedy, by contrast, is characterized by a shift to very realistic plots dealing with human relationships, with little topical, political or sexual content, deriving humour instead from a kind of 'comedy of manners' where stereotypical figures such as the wily slave, romantic hero or grumpy master interact and are mocked in a manner similar to a modern 'sitcom'.

There is no clear reason for such a strong change in the subject matter and style of Athenian comedy, but it may in some way be related to the stinging defeat the city suffered in the Peloponnesian War and the changes in the city's political and social culture which must have occurred as a result.

Metre

Aristophanes' plays are written in verse in a variety of Greek metres. The spoken sections of the play (i.e. the majority of the lines) are mostly in iambic trimeter, a type of verse intended to imitate the sound of natural speech. The chorus (and occasionally the characters – see Dicaeopolis' iambic song at lines 262–79) also sing songs in Greek lyric metres of various sorts which would have been set to music and accompanied by dance, for instance the iambic song at lines 836ff. The entrance of the chorus (*parodos*) at lines 204–18 (just outside the set prescription for A level) is largely in trochaic tetrameters, a metre suited to rapid movement: the metre is often matched to the action in this way in the choral sections of the play.

The Peloponnesian War

The Peloponnesian War was fought between Athens and Sparta with each state supported by a large group of their allied cities from across the Greek world. The war began in 431 BC after a peace treaty between Athens and Sparta broke down, due in large part to Sparta's anxiety about Athens' aggressive expansion of her empire and her ruthless treatment of Greek city-states who did not do as Athens requested. During the first stage of the war (431–421 BC), Sparta repeatedly invaded Attica (the land around Athens), burning all the crops and destroying olive trees before returning home. The inhabitants of Attica retreated inside the city, leading to massive overcrowding and a devastating plague which wiped out over half of the Athenian population in 430 BC. While Sparta focused on sporadic land attacks on Attica, the Athenians attacked the Peloponnese from the sea, winning a notable victory in 425 BC at the battle of Pylos. The Athenian commanders Cleon and Demosthenes then managed to capture several hundred Spartan hoplites in the battle of Sphacteria only a few weeks later: this proved a vital bargaining chip in later negotiations. Fighting then centred around Amphipolis, an Athenian colony in Thrace which Sparta captured in 424 BC. After several years of skirmishing and a battle in 422 BC in which both the Athenian commander Cleon and the Spartan general Brasidas were killed, Sparta and Athens agreed to make peace. Athens returned the hostages taken in the battle of Sphacteria and Sparta returned some of the cities they had captured in Thrace. After six years of uneasy peace, the war broke out again in 415 BC when Athens decided to invade Sicily and mounted a huge expeditionary force which was humiliatingly annihilated. The Spartans had supported the Sicilians and, after the expedition failed, mounted a new attack on Athens. Sparta was soon supported by the old enemy of Greece, Persia, giving her added momentum in the war. After eleven further years of fighting, Athens was decisively defeated by Sparta in 405 BC and the Long Walls connecting the city to the sea were pulled down to prevent the city from building its naval and trading power again.

The *Acharnians*

The *Acharnians* is the earliest surviving Aristophanic comedy; it was produced in 425 BC at the smaller Lenaea festival where it won first prize. The play is set in contemporary Athens against the backdrop of the Peloponnesian War: the war was in its sixth year when the play was performed and the Athenians had endured several Spartan invasions of Attica in which their farms and crops were destroyed. Although they had access to the sea through the Long Walls connecting the city to the harbour town of Piraeus the, the destruction of crops would have meant considerable financial and emotional hardship for many Athenians, not to mention that many of the citizens from rural demes were now forced to live in cramped, often insanitary conditions inside the city walls.

The major theme of this play is the effect(s) of war on society and the contrasting benefits of peace. The negative impact of the war would have been plain to most Athenians in 426 BC after several years of Spartan raids on their countryside and the resultant shortages of food and space within the city. Dicaeopolis makes clear from the very beginning that peace for him means a return to his countryside home and the pursuits of the country, contrasting the self-sufficiency of an agrarian life with the hustle-and-bustle of the urban market-place (lines 32–6). Aristophanes depicts the city being held to ransom by opportunists such as the ambassadors in the opening scene, drawing extravagant pay and delaying their diplomatic trips abroad to enjoy the luxuries denied to those suffering cramped conditions at home (lines 68–75). Dicaeopolis' market-place (lines 719–970) is a clear display of the advantages of peace over war as he is at once able to access a huge selection of luxury imports (mainly food) forbidden to the rest of Athens. The starving Megarian, so desperate he sells his daughters, adds a potentially darker element to the market-scene: although it must have been intended to be funny, it is nonetheless a barbed comment on the suffering caused by the war even in enemy territories. The presence of informers at the market who try to prevent Dicaeopolis from buying 'enemy' goods is yet another example of the corrosive impact of war on Athenian society, where personal freedom has become curtailed by mean-spirited people profiting from the suffering and deprivation of their fellow-citizens.

The benefits of peace are further exemplified in Dicaeopolis' lifestyle as soon as he receives his 30-year treaty. He is able to celebrate religious festivals involving feasting and drinking (241–79, 1000–6) and is later invited to a very sumptuous supper (1085–1141) where he enjoys plenty of rich food and luxuries while Lamachus, the symbol of the pro-war contingent in Athens, is forced out of his home to fight in snowy conditions on miserable rations (1085–141) and returns badly wounded, loudly lamenting his agony (1174–96). The final scenes of the play show the stark contrast between the two men (and thus, between a life of war and a life of peace) in a tour-de-force of alternating lines in which Dicaeopolis is plainly having the time of his life, having returned from his rich supper drunk and supported by two attractive girls while Lamachus calls piteously for pain-relief and medical treatment for his wound (lines 1190–234).

Lamachus is not the only person who suffers as a result of war in the play, and indeed, his pro-war ideology (ardently expressed at lines 620–3) perhaps robs him of the audience's sympathy when he is eventually wounded. The collateral damage of war is shown by the series of characters who ask Dicaeopolis for help at his Pitcher festival (lines 1018–68): Dercetes has lost his cattle (which are his livelihood) due to raiding and a young married couple each ask for help as they are about to be separated when the groom is called up to the war. Dicaeopolis' refusal to share his peace with Dercetes and the bridegroom may seem selfish, but on the other hand, we have seen the Assembly refusing even to contemplate Amphitheus' offer to make peace with Sparta and so, within the logic of the play, the *men* who suffer due to the war deserve all they get. The fact that Dicaeopolis does help the bride (whom he exonerates of any blame for the war because she is a woman) redeems him from the accusation of being utterly selfish and suggests that he is rather trying to make the point that, in a fully participatory democracy, every man must take responsibility for the decisions of the state.

Most of Aristophanes' surviving plays have a strong political theme and the *Acharnians* is no different. The war which dominates the play is, at its heart, a political issue, as we see from the opening scenes in the Assembly (lines 1–171). Aristophanes depicts the Assembly as utterly gullible, easily deluded both by the various ambassadors who are exploiting their positions and by the foreign representatives who so clearly (to Dicaeopolis and the audience at any rate) have anything but good intentions towards Athens. The Assembly sanctions the rough dismissal of the one man who tries to suggest peace (lines 54–5); it refuses to allow Dicaeopolis to question the King's Eye, preferring to believe in Pseudartabas' false promises of gold (line 125). Anyone who dissents is silenced while the charlatans are rewarded with an honorary dinner in the Prytaneum (lines 124–5). This farcical display mocks an Assembly where good judgement is absent and free speech is only permitted to those who say what the majority want to hear: it makes clear that a large section of the citizenry in Athens is still, despite the hardships of 431–426 BC, pro-war. Such criticism of the political system in Athens is seen later in the play in a stinging criticism of the politicians and generals who personally profit from the war. During the *agon*, Dicaeopolis points out to Lamachus that the ordinary men, the old or the poor never seem to be 'elected' to serve on the profitable diplomatic trips to enemies and allies in war but instead it is the same privileged few (lines 598–619), implying again that the war is being pursued not for ideological reasons but because it benefits those in power at the expense of the ordinary people.

Cleon, a prominent contemporary politician (in fact the leading politician in Athens after the death of Pericles until his own death in the Peloponnesian War in 422 BC) is a target for Aristophanes' satire in this play as he is in many others. In *Acharnians* he is depicted as a bawling censor who attempted to prosecute Aristophanes for satirizing him in a previous play (lines 376–82, 502–3) (see the opening section above for discussion of this accusation); Cleon is also accused of some kind of political corruption for which Dicaeopolis claims he was fined five talents (line 6), the details of this fine are now unknown and the situation is likely highly exaggerated for comic effect but it must have been public knowledge that Cleon had faced some kind of political controversy and punishment for the joke to have worked in the theatre. It is even possible that the political crime and five-talent fine were not real-life controversies but rather well-known elements from a previous *play* of Aristophanes', perhaps even the *Babylonians* itself, but our knowledge of his earlier plays is so scant that it is impossible to determine for certain whether this is the case. It is certainly true that Cleon remained the foremost politician in the Athenian Assembly until his death, which makes a serious political scandal unlikely, and we are left with the possibility that Aristophanes is here exaggerating a minor political faux-pas for comic purposes or referring to one of his own plays in which he had depicted Cleon being caught red-handed in political misbehaviour.

Cleon is not the only Athenian politician to come in for Aristophanes' criticism: Pericles (a very famous Athenian politician who had died in 429 BC in the early years of the Peloponnesian War) is also satirized in *Acharnians* as having caused the war for his own personal reasons (lines 526–34): Dicaeopolis claims that Pericles punished the city of Megara (a former ally of Athens) for the theft of his wife's prostitutes, ultimately leading to war when Megara asked Sparta for help. The claim that a theft from a brothel run by Pericles' wife was a primary cause of the war is patently ridiculous, but there is reason to believe that the trade embargo laid on the Megarians mentioned in these same lines *was*, in part, a cause of the war, so there are some serious political points about Periclean Athens' expansionist attitude and high-handed treatment of allies hidden among the scurrilous gossip.

Another frequent theme in Aristophanic comedy which is important in the *Acharnians* is that of tragic parody. Parody of tragedy in Old Comedy is more properly divided into two separate forms: 'paratragedy' which is defined as generic parody of tragic style and conventions, and 'tragic parody' which is parody of a specific tragedy. Both types of parody are seen frequently in the *Acharnians*: the play is peppered with generic mock-tragic references such as the use of the typically tragic dochmiac metre at lines 358–63 and 385–90, the apostrophe 'Oh city, city!' (line 27) and language such as 'alas for the drachmas' (line 67), 'alas, wretched me!' (line 105): the word '*oimoi*' in the latter two examples is perhaps the most stereotypical of all tragic diction (see the notes on individual lines for further examples). Paratragic references like this are so general and so obvious as to be recognized by any citizen who has seen any Greek tragedy: they do not refer to a specific play or even a specific author, but rather create comedy through the disjunction between the high-flown emotional language and/or poetic techniques of tragedy and the ridiculous situations of comedy. It must be borne in mind that comedy and tragedy were part of the same festivals at Athens and that the *Acharnians* would thus have been performed after the audience had just seen a tragic trilogy or perhaps even several trilogies: thus the majority of the audience would recognize these familiar tragic tropes and appreciate the humour in adapting them to a more light-hearted context.

As well as the frequent low-level paratragedy in the play, throughout the *Acharnians* there is also an extended parody of a specific Euripidean tragedy, the *Telephus*, which is now extant only in fragments. Although the play is largely lost, the general plot-line is known: Telephus, the Greek son of Heracles and rightful heir to the throne of Tegea in Arcadia was exiled in babyhood by his jealous grandfather and ends up as the king of Mysia (a region in Asia Minor). He was then wounded by Achilles in a battle with the Achaeans who stopped at Mysia on their way to Troy. His wound was in some versions also caused by his tripping over a vine sent by Dionysus, who was angry at Telephus' neglect of his cult. Telephus' wound did not heal and the oracle at Delphi informed him that only his attacker could heal it; he must, therefore, convince Achilles to heal his wound. This he did by disguising himself as a beggar and making a speech before the Greeks in Mysia's defence; at some point in the proceedings he held Orestes, the son of Agamemnon, hostage to force the Greeks to listen to him. Telephus is eventually promised a cure and in return offers to guide the Greeks to Troy.

The parody of the *Telephus* is flagged very early on in the opening lines of the *Acharnians* when Dicaeopolis actually directly quotes a line from the play at line 8 ('it was a worthwhile thing for Greece'). There is another direct quotation at lines 440–1 'For I must appear to be a beggar today, to be who I am and yet seem not to be' and at 1188 when the messenger is describing how Lamachus was wounded. These direct quotations would probably have been recognized by only a few of Aristophanes' audience as reading was not yet commonplace in ancient Athens and not all of the citizens would necessarily have seen the play in performance. However, the lines would have sounded tragic in their diction and tone to an audience familiar with tragedy in general, and once the more easily recognized situational parody begins at line 325 the audience will have been on alert for references to the *Telephus* which would have alerted them to the later verbal parodies. In each case the quotation is a means of generating humour: in the prologue it implies that the punishment of Cleon by the Knights was an heroic exploit worthy of a tragic hero; the quotation at line 440–1 draws attention to the link between Dicaeopolis and the hero Telephus, whereupon Dicaeopolis immediately punctures the high-flown tragic language by insulting the chorus; at the end of the play the echo of the *Telephus* serves to emphasize the (mock!) tragedy of Lamachus' wound in contrast to the triumphant Dicaeopolis with his wine and women.

The scene where Dicaeopolis holds a bag of charcoal hostage in order to convince the chorus to listen to him (lines 325–41) is a situational parody of a famous scene from the *Telephus*. The mock-horror of the chorus at this threat to the charcoal (a main export substance from their deme) is a hilarious re-imagining of the genuine horror Agamemnon must have shown on stage when his baby son was held up and threatened by the desperate Telephus. It is likely that most of the audience would recognize this as a parody from Euripides' play and appreciate the transformation of a horrifying and highly emotional scene into a ridiculous farce.

The parody of *Telephus* becomes metatheatrical at line 395 when the playwright Euripides is brought on stage as a character and Dicaeopolis asks him for a costume in which he can gain the pity of the chorus and better persuade them in the *agon*. This type of self-referential humour (in which the play draws deliberate attention to itself as a play) is common in Aristophanes' plays where the chorus regularly addressed the audience in the *parabasis* and characters too involve the audience in the action of the play. Rather than addressing the audience, in this scene Dicaeopolis makes his parody of the *Telephus* explicit by going to visit the playwright Euripides and dressing in the theatrical costume of one of his characters. Euripides' plays are parodied as containing highly erudite and confusing language (line 396) and as frequently portraying 'beggars', a frequent accusation against Euripides in Aristophanes' plays (see also *Peace* 146–8, *Frogs* 842, 1063–4). Both jokes have grounds in reality: Euripides's plays did often contain clever, seemingly paradoxical statements such as 'she lives and she lives not' (*Alcestis* 521) and he did put even noble-born characters on stage in less than heroic dress, such as his versions of Philoctetes, Electra, Ion and of course Telephus himself. Lampooning a tragic playwright in this manner might seem odd to modern eyes, but the public nature of dramatic festivals and the large audience sizes would have meant that Euripides and the other tragic playwrights were well-known public figures much like modern celebrities: the audience would be familiar enough with Euripides's typical style to find these jokes very funny.

However the list of different tragic heroes also emphasizes the wide range of parodies open to Aristophanes and raises the question: why does Dicaeopolis choose to impersonate Telephus in particular? The reason lies in the situation Telephus finds himself in after his wound: he is forced to persuade an extremely hostile audience (the Greeks) that their enemy (the Mysians) were in fact not at fault in fighting them, but in fact only acting as any state would if attacked. So Dicaeopolis must persuade the hostile Acharnians that the Spartans are not entirely to blame for the Peloponnesian War, and that they must accept that Athens' expansionism was also a key reason for the conflict. His defence speech (497–556) is itself thus a parody of the speech in which Telephus managed to convince the Greeks that the Mysians had done no wrong in fighting them. The link is reinforced with verbal parody as Dicaeopolis begins his speech by quoting from the *Telephus* (lines 497–9 'Bear me no grudge, members of the audience, if, although a beggar, I speak before the Athenians about public matters in a comedy' are a close parody of *Telephus* fr. 703 'Bear me no grudge, best of the Greeks, if, although a beggar, I have dared to speak among nobles') and the closing words of the speech are also a quotation from the *Telephus* (lines 555–6 'do we think Telephus would not?', *Tel.* fr. 710). The humour is again derived from the transference of tragic costume, language and character to the comic stage, for instance in the combination of these usually serious elements with ridiculous explanations for how the war started (Pericles' prostitutes again!) or the comically detailed description of the preparations for war at lines 545–56.

It is vitally important that the humour does not fail in this speech, for Dicaeopolis is delivering a message which could potentially have offended a large swathe of

Athenian citizens: the chorus' outrage at the private peace-treaty likely mirrors that of many Athenians whose fields and lands had been destroyed or who had lost family members in battle or to the plague. By dressing his hero up as Telephus, Aristophanes adds credibility (within the world of the play) to Dicaeopolis' case by explicitly citing the precedent of Telephus, who similarly argued that the Greeks should have understanding for the position of their enemy. The humour inherent in the parody (along with other comic devices such as the reference to prostitutes) makes what could potentially have been a radical political message a joke in itself: the very delivery is ridiculous, never mind the content, and ensures that the audience don't take it too seriously and become offended – the last thing Aristophanes would want in a comic competition.

Structure and summary

The play, like all comedies, was structured around a scheme of component parts which could be adapted to suit the individual play while still following a general pattern which is observable across all the surviving examples of Old Comedy. The summary below indicates the scheme as well as the main plot of the play.

Lines 1–42 (*Prologue – usually spoken by a character in the play in iambic trimeters, the metre used throughout Aristophanic plays to mimic speech. It is meant to set the scene and whet the audience's appetite for the action to come.*)
Dicaeopolis is sitting on the Pnyx waiting for the Athenian assembly to begin. He laments the lack of political interest in his fellow-citizens and explains his longing for peace, so that he can leave the overcrowded and expensive city and return to the delights of his rural home.

Lines 43–133: the assembly begins. Amphitheus asks for journey money to go and make peace with Sparta and is immediately dragged off by the Archers (equivalent of modern policemen); the herald announces some Athenian ambassadors who have returned from a long trip to Persia. The ambassadors have not achieved much but have been enjoying their time away at considerable Athenian expense; the ambassador from Persia is a charlatan who has no intention of helping Athens in the war. Dicaeopolis is so disgusted that he sends Amphitheus to make a private peace with the Spartans on his behalf.

Lines 134–73: An ambassador from Thrace has similarly been enjoying luxuries abroad and has brought back some questionable allies who immediately rob Dicaeopolis of his groceries. Dicaeopolis realizes the Assembly are determined not to consider peace and manages to stop the meeting by claiming to have felt a sign from Zeus that the Assembly should not continue (a raindrop).

Line 173–203: Dicaeopolis meets Amphitheus on his way back from Sparta and happily accepts a 30-year peace-treaty. Amphitheus has been chased by the chorus, a group of old Acharnian men, who are outraged that someone is making peace with the enemy.

Lines 204–346 (**Parodos** – *the entrance of the chorus, usually marked with a song and dance, which sets out their identity and characteristics and makes clear their stance on the central issues of the play. They usually vigorously support or undermine the hero, depending on the play.*)

The chorus of old Acharnians (men from the deme Acharnae, north of Attica) enter. They are furious with Dicaeopolis for securing peace and wish to punish him. Their song makes clear their age and their enduring hatred for the Spartans. After expressing their determination to pelt Dicaeopolis with stones, they decide to keep quiet and watch to see what he is up to.

Lines 237–79: Dicaeopolis and his family celebrate a comic version of the rural Dionysia, a fertility festival until they are interrupted by an attack from the chorus.

Lines 280–392: The chorus and Dicaeopolis argue about the peace treaty. Dicaeopolis tries to persuade them to listen to his reasons for making peace and, after many refusals and violent threats, they agree to listen to his speech only when Dicaeopolis makes the (comic) threat to sacrifice a bag of charcoal, an important Acharnian product. Dicaeopolis agrees to speak his defence with his head on a chopping-block, ready for execution if he does not persuade the chorus.

Lines 393–489: An extended digression at the house of the tragic playwright Euripides, whom Dicaeopolis begs for a tragic costume to help him persuade the chorus. This scene is full of tragic parody of Euripides' works.

Lines 490–625 (**'Agon'** – *this is an untypical agon which in some ways starts all the way back at 303 when the chorus first start arguing with Dicaeopolis. More typically the agon consists of two set-piece speeches divided by comment from the chorus; the subject matter is usually the central issue or conflict of the play. When there are two balanced speeches, the first speaker always loses the argument.*)

Here the comic set-piece of the *agon* takes a more unusual form: Dicaeopolis makes a long speech (lines 496–556) defending his private peace which is then followed by an argument with Lamachus, a famous Athenian general who stands for the whole pro-war faction in Athenian society. Dicaeopolis wins the argument and goes off to start a market to trade with all of Athens' enemies.

Lines 626–718 (**Parabasis** – *the parabasis was a longer section of speech and song addressed by the chorus directly to the audience, often used by Aristophanes to reflect on his successes and failures as a poet or the place of poetry in Athenian society more widely. There may be one or two such speeches in a play – there is a second, much shorter, parabasis later in the Acharnians at lines 971–99.*)

The chorus begin their speech in the voice of the poet, accusing the Athenians of being too ready to accept praise at the hands of foreign flatterers; Aristophanes claims to deserve praise for opening their eyes to this practice and for spreading the idea of democracy (presumably through his plays) among the allied states; he presents himself and poets more generally as advisors to the state and gets in a few digs at Cleon. The chorus then sing a short song (lines 665–75) about country pursuits which leads into their second speech, this time addressed from the point of view of old Acharnian men. The theme here is the hardships of old age and the lack of respect for the old in society, despite the contributions the older generation have made in previous wars: this theme is continued into the song at lines 692–702. They finish their speech by demanding a legal reform to allow old men to be prosecuted by old men and the young by the young, to avoid young men deliberately victimizing old and vulnerable people for their own profit.

Lines 719–959: Dicaeopolis establishes a private market-place in which he plans to trade with Athens' enemies; he looks forward to being able to receive foreign imports which have long been banned due to the war. His first trading partner is a starving Megarian who sells his daughters, dressed up as pigs, to Dicaeopolis. An informer spots Dicaeopolis' market and attempts to threaten him, but Dicaeopolis soon sees him off. The chorus sing a song (836–59) indicating how impressed they are with Dicaeopolis' new, exclusive market-place. A second trader arrives, this time from Thebes selling a huge variety of birds and other game. Dicaeopolis manages to trade an informer, Nicarchus, with the Theban in exchange for all his produce and the screaming informer is packed into a box like a piece of merchandise.

Lines 960–69: Dicaeopolis receives the first of several requests for favours from fellow Athenians. Lamachus, the pro-war general from earlier in the play, asks for an eel and some thrushes and is turned down because of his pro-war stance.

Lines 971–99: (*second parabasis*) The chorus directly address the audience in an ode about how clever Dicaeopolis is; they now realize the benefits of peace over war.

Lines 1000–68: Dicaeopolis celebrates a comic version of the *Anthesteria* festival which would have more usually involved private banquets in citizen's own houses with wine drunk from jugs giving the day its name (*choes*). A series of people come to Dicaeopolis asking for a share in the good things he has access to because of his private peace. Dercetes, who has lost his oxen due to the war, asks for his eyes (sore from weeping over the oxen) to be anointed with the wine of the 'peace treaty' but is refused. A bridegroom sends his best man to ask for some of Dicaeopolis's wine so that he can stay at home with his new wife rather than going off to war: he too is refused. The bride, however, who sends her bridesmaid to ask for some of the wine so her husband can stay at home, is granted a share on the grounds that the war is not her fault, as she is a woman.

Lines 1069–1142: Lamachus, the now-familiar general from earlier in the play, now appears in a series of comic contrasts to Dicaeopolis' good fortune. While Dicaeopolis is invited to a fancy dinner, Lamachus is called to war in a freezing location.

Lines 1143–73: the chorus-leader contrasts the fortunes of Dicaeopolis and Lamachus, before launching into an attack on an otherwise unknown individual, Antimachus, who is accused of having deprived a chorus of their dinner.

Lines 1174–234: (***Exodos*** – *the exit of the chorus, usually set to music; often accompanied by feasting and/or drinking or the promise of sexual relations between* *the hero and a female character.*) Lamachus is brought back in, badly wounded from the war, and another series of quick-fire comic comparisons are made between his situation and that of Dicaeopolis. The chorus congratulate Dicaeopolis in a short dialogue and exit, singing. Their *exodos* song is not preserved and is likely to have been a generic one used at the end of many plays rather than a specific one written specially for this play, which is why it is not included in the extant version of the text.

Further reading

The two most useful commentaries on the play are those of Alan Sommerstein (Warminster, 1980) and S. Douglas Olson (Oxford, 2002). The starred items in the list below contain excellent introductions to Aristophanes' works in general as well as specific essays on the *Acharnians*.

General articles on the *Acharnians*

*Douglas M. MacDowell, *Aristophanes and Athens* (Oxford, 1995): 46–79.
*Kenneth J. Dover, *Aristophanic Comedy* (Berkeley, 1972): 78–88.
Angus Bowie, *Aristophanes: Myth, Ritual and Comedy* (Cambridge, 1996): 18–44.
Lowell Edmunds, 'Aristophanes', *Acharnians' Yale Classical Studies Volume 26* (Yale, 1980): 1–41.

On parody of tragedy in the *Acharnians*

Helene P. Foley, 'Tragedy and Politics in Aristophanes', Acharnians' *Oxford Readings in Aristophanes* (ed. E. Segal, Oxford, 1996): 116–142.

On the Peloponnesian War in Aristophanes, with a focus on *Acharnians*

Geoffrey E.M. de Ste Croix, *The Origins of the Peloponnesian War* (London 1972), Appendix XXIX.
Hans-Joachim Newiger, 'War and Peace in the Comedy of Aristophanes', *Yale Classical Studies Volume 26* (Yale, 1980): 219–37.

Text

Δικαιόπολις
    ὅσα δὴ δέδηγμαι τὴν ἐμαυτοῦ καρδίαν,
    ἥσθην δὲ βαιά, πάνυ γε βαιά, τέτταρα·
    ἃ δ᾽ ὠδυνήθην, ψαμμακοσιογάργαρα.
    φέρ᾽ ἴδω, τί δ᾽ ἥσθην ἄξιον χαιρηδόνος;
    ἐγᾦδ᾽ ἐφ᾽ ᾧ γε τὸ κέαρ ηὐφράνθην ἰδών;   5
    τοῖς πέντε ταλάντοις οἷς Κλέων ἐξήμεσεν.
    ταῦθ᾽ ὡς ἐγανώθην, καὶ φιλῶ τοὺς ἱππέας
    διὰ τοῦτο τοὔργον· ἄξιον γὰρ Ἑλλάδι.
    ἀλλ᾽ ὠδυνήθην ἕτερον αὖ τραγῳδικόν,
    ὅτε δὴ ᾽κεχήνη προσδοκῶν τὸν Αἰσχύλον,   10
    ὁ δ᾽ ἀνεῖπεν, "εἴσαγ᾽ ὦ Θέογνι τὸν χορόν".
    πῶς τοῦτ᾽ ἔσεισέ μου δοκεῖς τὴν καρδίαν;
    ἀλλ᾽ ἕτερον ἥσθην, ἡνίκ᾽ ἐπὶ Μόσχῳ ποτὲ
    Δεξίθεος εἰσῆλθ᾽ ᾀσόμενος Βοιώτιον.
    τῆτες δ᾽ ἀπέθανον καὶ διεστράφην ἰδών,   15
    ὅτε δὴ παρέκυψε Χαῖρις ἐπὶ τὸν ὄρθιον.
    ἀλλ᾽ οὐδεπώποτ᾽ ἐξ ὅτου ᾽γὼ ῥύπτομαι
    οὕτως ἐδήχθην ὑπὸ κονίας τὰς ὀφρῦς
    ὡς νῦν, ὁπότ᾽ οὔσης κυρίας ἐκκλησίας
    ἑωθινῆς ἔρημος ἡ Πνὺξ αὑτηί,   20
    οἱ δ᾽ ἐν ἀγορᾷ λαλοῦσι κἄνω καὶ κάτω
    τὸ σχοινίον φεύγουσι τὸ μεμιλτωμένον.
    οὐδ᾽ οἱ πρυτάνεις ἥκουσιν, ἀλλ᾽ ἀωρίαν
    ῥέγκουσιν, εἶτα δ᾽ ὠστιοῦνται πῶς δοκεῖς
    ἥκοντες ἀλλήλοισι περὶ πρώτου ξύλου,   25
    ἀθρόοι καταρρέοντες· εἰρήνη δ᾽ ὅπως
    ἔσται προτιμῶσ᾽ οὐδέν· ὦ πόλις πόλις.
    ἐγὼ δ᾽ ἀεὶ πρώτιστος εἰς ἐκκλησίαν
    νοστῶν κάθημαι· κᾆτ᾽, ἐπειδὰν ὦ μόνος,

στένω κέχηνα σκορδινῶμαι πέρδομαι,   30
ἀπορῶ γράφω παρατίλλομαι λογίζομαι,
ἀποβλέπων εἰς τὸν ἀγρὸν εἰρήνης ἐρῶν,
στυγῶν μὲν ἄστυ τὸν δ᾽ ἐμὸν δῆμον ποθῶν,
ὃς οὐδεπώποτ᾽ εἶπεν, "ἄνθρακας πρίω",
οὐκ "ὄξος" οὐκ "ἔλαιον", οὐδ᾽ ᾔδει "πρίω,"   35
ἀλλ᾽ αὐτὸς ἔφερε πάντα χὠ πρίων ἀπῆν.
νῦν οὖν ἀτεχνῶς ἥκω παρεσκευασμένος
βοᾶν ὑποκρούειν λοιδορεῖν τοὺς ῥήτορας,
ἐάν τις ἄλλο πλὴν περὶ εἰρήνης λέγῃ.
ἀλλ᾽ οἱ πρυτάνεις γὰρ οὑτοιὶ μεσημβρινοί.   40
οὐκ ἠγόρευον; τοῦτ᾽ ἐκεῖν᾽ οὑγὼ ᾽λεγον·
ἐς τὴν προεδρίαν πᾶς ἀνὴρ ὠστίζεται.

Κῆρυξ
πάριτ᾽ εἰς τὸ πρόσθεν,
πάριθ᾽, ὡς ἂν ἐντὸς ἦτε τοῦ καθάρματος.

Ἀμφίθεος
ἤδη τις εἶπε;   45
Κῆρ.   τίς ἀγορεύειν βούλεται;
Ἀμφ.   ἐγώ.
Κῆρ.   τίς ὤν;
Ἀμφ.   Ἀμφίθεος.
Κῆρ.   οὐκ ἄνθρωπος;
Ἀμφ.   οὔ,
ἀλλ᾽ ἀθάνατος. ὁ γὰρ Ἀμφίθεος Δήμητρος ἦν
καὶ Τριπτολέμου· τούτου δὲ Κελεὸς γίγνεται·
γαμεῖ δὲ Κελεὸς Φαιναρέτην τήθην ἐμήν,
ἐξ ἧς Λυκῖνος ἐγένετ᾽· ἐκ τούτου δ᾽ ἐγὼ   50
ἀθάνατός εἰμ᾽· ἐμοὶ δ᾽ ἐπέτρεψαν οἱ θεοὶ
σπονδὰς ποιῆσαι πρὸς Λακεδαιμονίους μόνῳ.
ἀλλ᾽ ἀθάνατος ὤν, ἄνδρες, ἐφόδι᾽ οὐκ ἔχω·
οὐ γὰρ διδόασιν οἱ πρυτάνεις.
Κῆρ.   οἱ τοξόται.
Ἀμφ   ὦ Τριπτόλεμε καὶ Κελεὲ περιόψεσθέ με;   55
Δικ.

ὦνδρες πρυτάνεις ἀδικεῖτε τὴν ἐκκλησίαν
τὸν ἄνδρ᾽ ἀπάγοντες, ὅστις ἡμῖν ἤθελε
σπονδὰς ποιῆσαι καὶ κρεμάσαι τὰς ἀσπίδας.

Κῆρ.   κάθησο, σῖγα.

Δικ.   μὰ τὸν Ἀπόλλω 'γὼ μὲν οὔ,
        ἢν μὴ περὶ εἰρήνης γε πρυτανεύσητέ μοι.   60

Κῆρ.   οἱ πρέσβεις οἱ παρὰ βασιλέως.

Δικ.   ποίου βασιλέως; ἄχθομαι 'γὼ πρέσβεσι
        καὶ τοῖς ταῶσι τοῖς τ' ἀλαζονεύμασι.

Κῆρ.   σῖγα.

Δικ.   βαβαιάξ. ὦκβάτανα, τοῦ σχήματος.

Πρέσβευτης
        ἐπέμψαθ' ἡμᾶς ὡς βασιλέα τὸν μέγαν   65
        μισθὸν φέροντας δύο δραχμὰς τῆς ἡμέρας
        ἐπ' Εὐθυμένους ἄρχοντος.

Δικ.   οἴμοι τῶν δραχμῶν.

Πρ.   καὶ δῆτ' ἐτρυχόμεσθα διὰ Καϋστρίων
        πεδίων ὁδοιπλανοῦντες ἐσκηνημένοι,
        ἐφ' ἁρμαμαξῶν μαλθακῶς κατακείμενοι,   70
        ἀπολλύμενοι.

Δικ.   σφόδρα γὰρ ἐσῳζόμην ἐγὼ
        παρὰ τὴν ἔπαλξιν ἐν φορυτῷ κατακείμενος.

Πρ.   ξενιζόμενοι δὲ πρὸς βίαν ἐπίνομεν
        ἐξ ὑαλίνων ἐκπωμάτων καὶ χρυσίδων
        ἄκρατον οἶνον ἡδύν.   75

Δικ.   ὦ Κραναὰ πόλις—
        ἆρ' αἰσθάνῃ τὸν κατάγελων τῶν πρέσβεων;

Πρ.   οἱ βάρβαροι γὰρ ἄνδρας ἡγοῦνται μόνους
        τοὺς πλεῖστα δυναμένους φαγεῖν τε καὶ πιεῖν.

Δικ.   ἡμεῖς δὲ λαικαστάς γε καὶ καταπύγονας.

Πρ.   ἔτει τετάρτῳ δ' εἰς τὰ βασίλει' ἤλθομεν·   80
        ἀλλ' εἰς ἀπόπατον ᾤχετο στρατιὰν λαβών,
        κἄχεζεν ὀκτὼ μῆνας ἐπὶ χρυσῶν ὀρῶν.

Δικ.   πόσου δὲ τὸν πρωκτὸν χρόνου ξυνήγαγεν;

Πρ.   τῇ πανσελήνῳ· κᾆτ' ἀπῆλθεν οἴκαδε.
        εἶτ' ἐξένιζε' παρετίθει θ' ἡμῖν ὅλους   85
        ἐκ κριβάνου βοῦς—

Δικ.   καὶ τίς εἶδε πώποτε
        βοῦς κριβανίτας; τῶν ἀλαζονευμάτων.

Πρ.   καὶ ναὶ μὰ Δί' ὄρνιν τριπλάσιον Κλεωνύμου
        παρέθηκεν ἡμῖν· ὄνομα δ' ἦν αὐτῷ φέναξ.

Δικ.   ταῦτ' ἄρ' ἐφενάκιζες σὺ δύο δραχμὰς φέρων.   90

Πρ.   καὶ νῦν ἄγοντες ἥκομεν Ψευδαρτάβαν,
      τὸν βασιλέως ὀφθαλμόν.

Δικ.   ἐκκόψειέ γε
      κόραξ πατάξας, τόν τε σὸν τοῦ πρέσβεως.

Κῆρ.   ὁ βασιλέως ὀφθαλμός.

Δικ.   ὦναξ Ἡράκλεις.
      πρὸς τῶν θεῶν ἄνθρωπε ναύφαρκτον βλέπων;   95
      ἢ περὶ ἄκραν κάμπτων νεώσοικον σκοπεῖς;
      ἄσκωμ᾽ ἔχεις που περὶ τὸν ὀφθαλμὸν κάτω.

Πρ.   ἄγε δὴ σὺ βασιλεὺς ἄττα σ᾽ ἀπέπεμψεν φράσον
      λέξοντ᾽ Ἀθηναίοισιν ὦ Ψευδαρτάβα.

Ψευδαρτάβας
      ἰαρταμαν ἐξαρξαν ἀπισσονα σατρα.   100

Πρ.   ξυνήκαθ᾽ ὃ λέγει;

Δικ.   μὰ τὸν Ἀπόλλω ᾽γὼ μὲν οὔ.

Πρ.   πέμψειν βασιλέα φησὶν ὑμῖν χρυσίον.
      λέγε δὴ σὺ μεῖζον καὶ σαφῶς τὸ χρυσίον.

Ψευδαρτάβας
      οὐ λῆψι χρῦσο χαυνόπρωκτ᾽ Ἰαοναῦ.

Δικ.   οἴμοι κακοδαίμων ὡς σαφῶς.   105

Πρ.   τί δαὶ λέγει;

Δικ.   ὅ τι; χαυνοπρώκτους τοὺς Ἴονας λέγει,
      εἰ προσδοκῶσι χρυσίον ἐκ τῶν βαρβάρων.

Πρ.   οὔκ, ἀλλ᾽ ἀχάνας ὅδε γε χρυσίου λέγει.

Δικ.   ποίας ἀχάνας; σὺ μὲν ἀλαζὼν εἶ μέγας.
      ἀλλ᾽ ἄπιθ᾽· ἐγὼ δὲ βασανιῶ τοῦτον μόνος.   110
      ἄγε δὴ σὺ φράσον ἐμοὶ σαφῶς πρὸς τουτονί,
      ἵνα μή σε βάψω βάμμα Σαρδιανικόν·
      βασιλεὺς ὁ μέγας ἡμῖν ἀποπέμψει χρυσίον; [ἀνανεύει.]
      ἄλλως ἄρ᾽ ἐξαπατώμεθ᾽ ὑπὸ τῶν πρέσβεων; [ἐπινεύει.]
      Ἑλληνικόν γ᾽ ἐπένευσαν ἄνδρες οὑτοιί,   115
      κοὐκ ἔσθ᾽ ὅπως οὐκ εἰσὶν ἐνθένδ᾽ αὐτόθεν.
      καὶ τοῖν μὲν εὐνούχοιν τὸν ἕτερον τουτονὶ
      ἐγᾦδ᾽ ὅς ἐστι, Κλεισθένης ὁ Σιβυρτίου.
      ὦ θερμόβουλον πρωκτὸν ἐξυρημένε.
      τοιόνδε γ᾽, ὦ πίθηκε τὸν πώγων᾽ ἔχων
      εὐνοῦχος ἡμῖν ἦλθες ἐσκευασμένος;   120
      ὁδὶ δὲ τίς ποτ᾽ ἐστίν; οὐ δήπου Στράτων;

Κῆρ. σίγα, κάθιζε.
      τὸν βασιλέως ὀφθαλμὸν ἡ βουλὴ καλεῖ
      εἰς τὸ πρυτανεῖον.   125
Δικ.   ταῦτα δῆτ᾽ οὐχ ἀγχόνη;
      κἄπειτ᾽ ἐγὼ δῆτ᾽ ἐνθαδὶ στραγγεύομαι;
      τοὺς δὲ ξενίζειν οὐδέποτέ γ᾽ ἴσχει θύρα.
      ἀλλ᾽ ἐργάσομαί τι δεινὸν ἔργον καὶ μέγα.
      ἀλλ᾽ Ἀμφίθεός μοι ποῦ ᾽στιν;
Ἀμφ.   οὑτοσὶ πάρα.
Δικ. ἐμοὶ σὺ ταυτασὶ λαβὼν ὀκτὼ δραχμὰς   130
      σπονδὰς ποίησαι πρὸς Λακεδαιμονίους μόνῳ
      καὶ τοῖσι παιδίοισι καὶ τῇ πλάτιδι·
      ὑμεῖς δὲ πρεσβεύεσθε καὶ κεχήνετε.

Κῆρ. προσίτω Θέωρος ὁ παρὰ Σιτάλκους.
Θέ
      ὁδί.
Δικ. ἕτερος ἀλαζὼν οὗτος ἐσκηρύττεται.   135
Θέ
      χρόνον μὲν οὐκ ἂν ἦμεν ἐν Θρᾴκῃ πολύν—
Δικ. μὰ Δί᾽ οὐκ ἄν, εἰ μισθόν γε μὴ ᾽φερες πολύν.
Θέ
      εἰ μὴ κατένειψε χιόνι τὴν Θρᾴκην ὅλην
      καὶ τοὺς ποταμοὺς ἔπηξ᾽,
Δικ·   ὑπ᾽ αὐτὸν τὸν χρόνον,
      ὅτ᾽ ἐνθαδὶ Θέογνις ἠγωνίζετο.   140
Θε   τοῦτον μετὰ Σιτάλκους ἔπινον τὸν χρόνον·
      καὶ δῆτα φιλαθήναιος ἦν ὑπερφυῶς,
      ὑμῶν τ᾽ ἐραστὴς ἦν ἀληθὴς ὥστε καὶ
      ἐν τοῖσι τοίχοις ἔγραφ᾽ "Ἀθηναῖοι καλοί."
      ὁ δ᾽ υἱός, ὃν Ἀθηναῖον ἐπεποιήμεθα,   145
      ἦρα φαγεῖν ἀλλᾶντας ἐξ Ἀπατουρίων,
      καὶ τὸν πατέρ᾽ ἠντεβόλει βοηθεῖν τῇ πάτρᾳ·
      ὁ δ᾽ ὤμοσε σπένδων βοηθήσειν ἔχων
      στρατιὰν τοσαύτην ὥστ᾽ Ἀθηναίους ἐρεῖν,
      "ὅσον τὸ χρῆμα παρνόπων προσέρχεται."   150
Δικ. κάκιστ᾽ ἀπολοίμην, εἴ τι τούτων πείθομαι
      ὧν εἶπας ἐνταυθοῖ σὺ πλὴν τῶν παρνόπων.
Θέ   καὶ νῦν ὅπερ μαχιμώτατον Θρᾳκῶν ἔθνος
      ἔπεμψεν ὑμῖν.

Δικ.   τοῦτο μέν γ᾽ ἤδη σαφές.

Κῆρ.   οἱ Θρᾶκες ἴτε δεῦρ᾽, οὓς Θέωρος ἤγαγεν.   155

Δικ.   τουτὶ τί ἐστι τὸ κακόν;

Θέ   Ὀδομάντων στρατός.

Δικ.   ποίων Ὀδομάντων; εἰπέ μοι τουτὶ τί ἦν;
       τίς τῶν Ὀδομάντων τὸ πέος ἀποτεθρίακεν;

Θέ   τούτοις ἐάν τις δύο δραχμὰς μισθὸν διδῷ,
       καταπελτάσονται τὴν Βοιωτίαν ὅλην.   160

Δικ.   τοισδὶ δύο δραχμὰς τοῖς ἀπεψωλημένοις;
       ὑποστένοι μεντἂν ὁ θρανίτης λεὼς
       ὁ σωσίπολις. οἴμοι τάλας ἀπόλλυμαι,
       ὑπὸ τῶν Ὀδομάντων τὰ σκόροδα πορθούμενος.
       οὐ καταβαλεῖτε τὰ σκόροδ᾽;   165

Θέ   ὦ μόχθηρε σὺ
       οὐ μὴ πρόσει τούτοισιν ἐσκοροδισμένοις.

Δικ.   ταυτὶ περιείδεθ᾽ οἱ πρυτάνεις πάσχοντά με
       ἐν τῇ πατρίδι καὶ ταῦθ᾽ ὑπ᾽ ἀνδρῶν βαρβάρων;
       ἀλλ᾽ ἀπαγορεύω μὴ ποιεῖν ἐκκλησίαν
       τοῖς Θρᾳξὶ περὶ μισθοῦ· λέγω δ᾽ ὑμῖν ὅτι   170
       διοσημία ᾽στὶ καὶ ῥανὶς βέβληκέ με.

Κῆρ.   τοὺς Θρᾶκας ἀπιέναι, παρεῖναι δ᾽ εἰς ἔνην.
       οἱ γὰρ πρυτάνεις λύουσι τὴν ἐκκλησίαν.

Δικ.   οἴμοι τάλας μυττωτὸν ὅσον ἀπώλεσα.
       ἀλλ᾽ ἐκ Λακεδαίμονος γὰρ Ἀμφίθεος ὁδί.   175
       χαῖρ᾽ Ἀμφίθεε.

Ἀμφ.   μήπω γε πρίν <γ>᾽ ἂν στῶ τρέχων·
       δεῖ γάρ με φεύγοντ᾽ ἐκφυγεῖν Ἀχαρνέας.

Δικ.   τί δ᾽ ἔστ᾽;

Ἀμφ.   ἐγὼ μὲν δεῦρό σοι σπονδὰς φέρων
       ἔσπευδον· οἱ δ᾽ ὤσφροντο πρεσβῦταί τινες
       Ἀχαρνικοί, στιπτοὶ γέροντες πρίνινοι   180
       ἀτεράμονες Μαραθωνομάχαι, σφενδάμνινοι.
       ἔπειτ᾽ ἀνέκραγον πάντες, "ὦ μιαρώτατε
       σπονδὰς φέρεις τῶν ἀμπέλων τετμημένων";
       κἀς τοὺς τρίβωνας ξυνελέγοντο τῶν λίθων·
       ἐγὼ δ᾽ ἔφευγον· οἱ δ᾽ ἐδίωκον κἀβόων.   185

Δικ.   οἱ δ᾽ οὖν βοώντων· ἀλλὰ τὰς σπονδὰς φέρεις;

Ἀμφ.   ἔγωγέ φημι, τρία γε ταυτὶ γεύματα.
       αὗται μέν εἰσι πεντέτεις. γεῦσαι λαβών.

Δικ.   αἰβοῖ.

Ἀμφ.   τί ἔστιν;

Δικ.   οὐκ ἀρέσκουσίν μ᾽ ὅτι
ὄζουσι πίττης καὶ παρασκευῆς νεῶν.   190

Ἀμφ. σὺ δ᾽ ἀλλὰ τασδὶ τὰς δεκέτεις γεῦσαι λαβών.

Δικ.   ὄζουσι χαὖται. πρέσβεων εἰς τὰς πόλεις,
ὀξύτατον, ὥσπερ διατριβῆς τῶν ξυμμάχων.

Ἀμφ. ἀλλ᾽ αὑταὶ τσί σοι τριακοντούτιδες
κατὰ γῆν τε καὶ θάλατταν.   195

Δικ.   ὦ Διονύσια,
αὗται μὲν ὄζουσ᾽ ἀμβροσίας καὶ νέκταρος
καὶ μὴ ᾽πιτηρεῖν "σιτί᾽ ἡμερῶν τριῶν",
κἀν τῷ στόματι λέγουσι "βαῖν᾽ ὅπη θέλεις".
ταύτας δέχομαι καὶ σπένδομαι κἀκπίομαι,
χαίρειν κελεύων πολλὰ τοὺς Ἀχαρνέας.   200

Ἀμ.   ἐγὼ δὲ φευξοῦμαί γε τοὺς Ἀχαρνέας.   203

Δικ.   ἐγὼ δὲ πολέμου καὶ κακῶν ἀπαλλαγεὶς   201
ἄξω τὰ κατ᾽ ἀγροὺς εἰσιὼν Διονύσια.

204–365: Dicaeopolis and his family celebrate the Country Dionysia, but the chorus attacks him with stones and he tries to explain why he has made peace with the Spartans. They agree to listen to him when he takes hostage a basket of charcoal (the deme's primary export) so he prepares a speech to convince them.

Δικ.   ἰδοὺ θεᾶσθε, τὸ μὲν ἐπίξηνον τοδί,
ὁ δ᾽ ἀνὴρ ὁ λέξων οὑτοσὶ τυννουτοσί.
ἀμέλει μὰ τὸν Δί᾽ οὐκ ἐνασπιδώσομαι,
λέξω δ᾽ ὑπὲρ Λακεδαιμονίων ἁμοὶ δοκεῖ.
καίτοι δέδοικα πολλά· τούς τε γὰρ τρόπους   370
τοὺς τῶν ἀγροίκων οἶδα χαίροντας σφόδρα,
ἐάν τις αὐτοὺς εὐλογῇ καὶ τὴν πόλιν
ἀνὴρ ἀλαζὼν καὶ δίκαια κἄδικα·
κἀνταῦθα λανθάνουσ᾽ ἀπεμπολώμενοι·
τῶν τ᾽ αὖ γερόντων οἶδα τὰς ψυχὰς ὅτι   375
οὐδὲν βλέπουσιν ἄλλο πλὴν ψήφῳ δακνειν.
αὐτός τ᾽ ἐμαυτὸν ὑπὸ Κλέωνος ἄπαθον
ἐπίσταμαι διὰ τὴν πέρυσι κωμῳδίαν.
εἰσελκύσας γάρ μ᾽ εἰς τὸ βουλευτήριον
διέβαλλε καὶ ψευδῆ κατεγλώττιζέ μου   380
κἀκυκλοβόρει κἄπλυνεν, ὥστ᾽ ὀλίγου πάνυ
ἀπωλόμην μολυνοπραγμονούμενος.

νῦν οὖν με πρῶτον πρὶν λέγειν ἐάσατε
ἐνσκευάσασθαί μ᾿ οἷον ἀθλιώτατον.

Χορ.　τί ταῦτα στρέφει τεχνάζεις τε καὶ πορίζεις τριβάς;　　　　385
λαβὲ δ᾿ ἐμοῦ γ᾿ ἕνεκα παρ᾿ Ἱερωνύμου
σκοτοδασυπυκνότριχά τιν᾿ Ἄιδος κυνῆν·　　　　390
ἀλλ᾿ ἐξάνοιγε μηχανὰς τὰς Σισύφου,
ὡς σκῆψιν ἁγὼν οὗτος οὐχὶ δέξεται.

Commentary Notes

1–42

Prologue: Dicaeopolis enters alone and sits down. This opening monologue sets the scene as contemporary Athens and introduces the main themes of the play: war and parody of tragedy.

1–2

ὅσα δὴ δέδηγμαι τὴν ἐμαυτοῦ καρδίαν | ἥσθην δὲ βαιά ... τέτταρα! The mock-tragic opening (the position of ὅσα and the dramatic imagery of δέδηγμαι makes Dicaeopolis' claim to have suffered pain humorously hyperbolic) is punctured with the bathetic, comically specific τέτταρα.

δέδηγμαι: first singular perfect indicitive middle of δακνω – 'I bite'. Commonly used in a metaphorical sense of emotional pain in Greek literature.

ἥσθην: in strong contrast with δέδηγμαι, as βαιά contrasts sharply with ὅσα.

3

ψαμμακοσιογάργαρα: an example of an Aristophanic comic coinage, a humorously long word made up of several other words. Two nouns, ψάμμος (2f) 'sand', γάργαρα (second plural only) 'heaps', are combined with the suffix –κοσιοι which denotes hundreds (e.g. διακόσιοι 'two hundred'), giving us the new adjective 'like sand-hundred heaps'.

4

χαιρηδόνος: χαιρηδών, -όνος, ἡ 'delectation', 'enjoyment' is another Aristophanic coinage based on a set of tragic words which usually have the opposite meaning, e.g. ἀλγηδών 'pain', 'suffering'. This adds to the mock-tragic effect of these opening lines.

5

ἐγῴδ': a colloquial combination of ἐγώ and οἶδα with the final alpha elided.

κέαρ: a poetic, uncontracted version of the epic word τό κῆρ 'heart, soul', continuing the bathos from line 1. This is an accusative of respect with ηὐφράνθην. 'I rejoiced in my heart . . .'.

ηὐφράνθην: εὐφραίνομαι 'I rejoice at, enjoy myself because of' takes ἐπί + dative of the thing at which one rejoices.

6

ταλάντοις: dative after εὐφραίνομαι ἐπί in line 5. τάλαντον, τό 'talent' was a measure of money in ancient Greece. An Athenian talent would have been silver worth 6,000 drachmas: a drachma would have been enough for a family of four to survive on for 1–2 days.

οἷς: the relative ἅ has been attracted into the dative after ταλάντοις.

Κλέων: Cleon was a very prominent Athenian politician and contemporary of Aristophanes and a frequent target for Aristophanes' political satire. The origin of the incident mentioned here is uncertain: there is some (shaky) ancient evidence for Cleon taking a bribe of five talents from some Athenian island subjects in return for reducing their tribute to Athens and Cleon then being forced to give the money up by the Knights (the Knights were a class of men in Athens who were wealthy enough to own a horse and thus made up the Athenian cavalry forces), but Cleon's continued political success until his death makes such a crime unlikely; the ancient sources which mention the crime may simply be attempting to explain this very passage. It is more probable that this reference is not to recent political history but to another Aristophanic comedy, the *Babylonians*, now lost, where Cleon was depicted in this way on stage.

ἐξήμεσεν: ἐξεμέω 'I cough up, vomit up' is a deliberately humiliating and undignified word to use of the politician.

7

ὡς: exclamatory 'how . . .!'

γανόω: literally 'I shine'. In passive 'I am made glad'.

8

ἄξιον γὰρ Ἑλλάδι: 'worthwhile for Greece' a quotation from Euripides *Telephus* fr. 720, continuing the mock-tragic theme.

9

ὠδυνήθην: note the repetition from line 3. Dicaeopolis moves from the general pains he has suffered to one specific pain.

ἕτερον αὖ: 'in yet another way'.

τραγῳδικός: 'tragic', an adjective found only in the plays of Aristophanes. Its use here makes the (mock) tragic tone of the speech explicit and self-conscious.

10

'κεχήνη: elided form of ἐκεχήνη, pluperfect third singular of χάσκω 'I yawn, I gape'.

Αἰσχύλον: Aeschylus, *c.* 524–456/5 BC, the earliest surviving Greek tragedian. He was the only Greek playwright whose plays were given the honour of being re-performed after his death (the main dramatic festivals usually only permitted new plays to be performed). Dicaeopolis' longing for Aeschylus shows his old-fashioned taste for the classics of drama.

11

ὁ δ' ἀνεῖπεν: supply κῆρυξ. An official herald would have announced the plays at each of the dramatic festivals. ἀνειπεῖν is a defective aorist (no present tense exists), translate 'proclaim, announce'.

Θέογνι: Theognis is a minor tragedian mentioned a few times in the plays of Aristophanes where he is often mocked for the 'frigidity' of his poetry. Nothing of his work survives and he is sometimes associated with one of the Thirty Tyrants (leaders of a short-lived oligarchic government 404–403 BC in Athens). He should not be confused with the more famous Theognis of Megara, a sixth-century BC elegiac poet. Here he is a nasty surprise for Dicaeopolis who was expecting a play by the classic tragedian Aeschylus.

12

πῶς . . . δοκεῖς: a humously colloquial rhetorical question.

σείω: (here) I agitate, upset.

13

ἕτερον: 'on another occasion'.

ἐπι + dative (here) 'on the heels of', 'just after'.

Μόσχῳ:· nothing is known of this Moschus except that he is here implied to be a poor musician.

14

Δεξίθεος: nothing is known of this musician either, although the implication here is that he is much better than Moschus.

εἰσῆλθ': (here) 'came on stage'.

ἀσόμενος: future participle of ἀείδω 'I sing'.

Βοιώτιον: 'a Boeotian [song]'.

15

ἀπέθανον: (here) 'I nearly died'.

διεστράφην ἰδών: διαστρέφομαι literally means 'I am twisted, I am turned about'. Translate 'my eyes were tormented'.

παρέκυψε: παρακύπτω 'I come slouching in'.

16

Χαῖρις: a cithara and pipe-player whose name ultimately became proverbial for someone with a good voice. Other comic sources, however, portray him as a very bad lyre-player (cf. *Peace* 951, *Birds* 857).

ἐπί τόν ὄρθιον: 'to sing the Orthian'; ὁ [νόμος] ὄρθιος was a traditional type of song with a very high pitch. Translate 'singing/playing the Orthian'.

17

ἐξ ὅτου: 'from the time when'.

'γὼ: ἐγώ with prodelision of the initial vowel.

ῥύπτομαι: (here) 'I began to wash'. This is a humorously bathetic statement, puncturing the cliché 'since I was a child' with a comic and low-brow specificity.

18

ἐδήχθην: aorist passive δάκνω (here) 'I was stung'.

κονίας: κονία, -ας, ἡ 'dust', 'ashes'. Ash was an ingredient in the soap used in ancient Greece.

ὀφρῦς: accusative of respect with ἐδήχθην. 'Eyebrows' is here used as a poetic equivalent for 'eyes'.

19

κυρίας: 'regular'.

20

ἑωθινῆς: ἑωθινός, -ή, -όν 'early in the morning'.

ἔρημος: a two-termination adjective (i.e. the masculine and feminine endings are the same) in agreement with πνύξ.

πνύξ: 'the Pnyx', a hill in Athens where the Assembly met.

αὑτηί: an intensified form of αὕτη.

21

λαλοῦσι: λαλέω 'I gossip, I babble.'

ἐν ἀγορᾷ: the Agora was the market-place and centre of trade in Athens: it was also filled with religious buildings and a very popular meeting place.

κἄνω καὶ κάτω: και has become blended with ἄνω in crasis. ἄνω καὶ κάτω 'up and down'.

22

μεμιλτωμένον: perfect middle participle of μιλτόω 'I stain red'. Latecomers to the Assembly or those seeking to avoid their civic duty risked having their clothes stained with a red rope carried through the Agora by the Archers, the ancient equivalent of modern policemen. A fine was due from all those with stained clothing – this was to encourage full attendance at the Assembly.

23

οἱ πρυτάνεις: 'the Prytaneis', the 50 men from each Athenian tribe chosen by lot to serve as the rulers of the City Council (βουλή) for a period of 35 or 36 days in each year.

ἀωρίαν: an adverbial accusative, so 'late'.

24

ῥέγκουσιν: 'wheezing' i.e. out of breath from running to try and get the best seats.

ὠστιοῦνται: future of ὠστίζομαι 'I jostle' + dative.

πῶς δοκεῖς: literally 'how do you think . . .' as in line 12, but here better translated as 'certainly' or perhaps 'see how they'll jostle . . .'.

26

εἰρήνη: this is the real theme of the whole play, introduced suddenly here after a litany of humorously minor complaints by Dicaeopolis. The disrupted word order (hyperbaton) emphasises the importance of the word.

ὅπως: + future indicative 'that there should be peace', the normal construction with a verb of precaution, here προτιμάω.

27

προτιμῶσ': προτιμάω 'I prioritise, feel concern about'.

οὐδέν: adverbial with προτιμάω 'they feel no concern *at all* . . .'.

ὦ πόλις πόλις: the apostrophe (direct address to the city) and repetition are paratragic (i.e. parody of tragedy in general rather than a specific tragedy).

28

πρώτιστος: the superlative places the civic Dicaeopolis in strong contrast with the rest of the Athenians babbling in the Agora.

νοστῶν: νοστέω although the verb here means simply 'I come', it has strong connotations of home-coming in particular which would further intensify Dicaeopolis' claim to be an assiduous attender of the *ekklesia*.

29

κᾆτ' = καί εἶτα. Translate 'and then, . . .'.

ὦ: the subjunctive is indefinite after ἐπειδάν (= 'whenever') and indicates that Dicaeopolis often finds himself alone on the Pnyx.

30-1

A comic list of eight verbs with no conjunctions: the asyndeton creates a jerky tone mirroring Dicaeopolis' agitation.

κέχηνα: perfect χάσκω, literally 'I have opened my mouth' therefore 'I yawn'.

σκορδινῶμαι: 'I fidget', 'I stretch'.

γράφω: (here) 'I draw on the ground.'

παρατίλλομαι: 'I pluck out (my) hair.' It is unclear from where Dicaeopolis is removing this hair.

λογίζομαι: literally 'I reckon, calculate', here 'I do my accounts'. Dicaeopolis is calculating his monthly expenses.

32

ἀποβλέπων: confusingly, ἀποβλέπω does not mean simply 'look away from' but more often 'I look longingly at' (at the expense of looking at other things). The citizens of Athens were confined to the area within the city walls at this point in the Peloponnesian War and Dicaeopolis, a farmer, naturally misses his farm and agrarian life. See Introduction for more details.

ἐρῶν: in strong contrast with στυγῶν at the beginning of line 33, as ἄστυ stands in stark opposition to ἀγρόν. στυγῶν is high poetic register and gives this line a paratragic flavour.

33

δῆμον: 'village', in contrast to ἄστυ. The theme of opposition between country and city life is a strong one in the play (and indeed in Old Comedy more generally).

34

ὅς: referring back to the δῆμος.

πρίω: second singular aorist middle imperative of the defective verb ἐπριάμην 'I bought': (the present tense does not exist and the verb is used mainly as the aorist of ὠνέομαι).

36

ἔφερε: 'produced'.

χῶ = καὶ ὁ.

Πρίων: a fake proper noun based on the imperative πρίω and with a pun on the Greek word for saw (πρίων) implying a harsh voice. Sommerstein's translation 'Mr. Buysome!' captures it excellently.

37

ἀτεχνῶς: 'really', 'absolutely'.

39

ἄλλο: 'anything else'.

40

οὑτοιὶ: intensified form of οὗτοι, 'here come' or 'here are'.

μεσημβρινοί: literally 'of noon', here 'at midday', describing the arrival of the Prytaneis.

41

οὐκ ἠγόρευον: a triumphant rhetorical question, 'didn't I tell you?'

οὑγὼ: ὃ ἐγώ.

42

τὴν προεδρίαν: 'the front seat(s)'

43

πάριτ' ἐς τὸ πρόσθεν: 'move forward!'. These words are probably the exact formula used to begin each Athenian Assembly; here they are given prominence by the fact that they are unmetrical (they stand outside the iambic trimeter in which most of the play is composed).

καθάρματος: literally 'the purification', i.e. 'the sacred area' – the area where the Assembly met was ritually purified before each session by the sacrifice of a piglet.

44

ἦτε: second person plural present subjunctive of εἰμί in purpose clause after ὡς ἄν.

45

Ἀμφίθεος: a real Athenian name (although this character is not identifiable as a historical Athenian due to the paucity of our sources) which literally means 'divine on both sides'. The name is chosen for the joke which follows (see line 46).

τίς ἀγορεύειν βούλεται: the usual formula used in the Athenian Assembly to invite contributions from the citizens; in the fully participatory democracy of Athens, any citizen had the right to speak in the Assembly and this freedom was considered one of the most important political institutions in the state.

46

οὐκ ἄνθρωπος: the herald thinks that Amphitheus is using an adjective to describe himself as 'divine on both sides' rather than using the proper name.

47–8

ὁ γὰρ Ἀμφίθεος: i.e. 'the first Amphitheus', 'the original Amphitheus'.
Δήμητρος ἦν ... καὶ Τριπτολέμου: the genitives here mean 'son of'.

48–9

γίγνεται, γαμεῖ: historic presents (the present tense used in a past-tense narrative makes the story more exciting and vivid; translate as past tense.) The genealogy here is rather confused, but some of the names are connected with Eleusis, a town in the west of Attica about 20 kilometres from Athens where there was a very famous cult of Demeter, goddess of the harvest and fertility.

Triptolemus was traditionally a mortal whom Demeter favoured. When she failed to make him immortal due to the interference of his mother she taught him the secret of agriculture. He later became identified as an agrarian god in his own right. Celeus was more usually identified as Triptolemus' human father.

49

Φαιναρέτην: it was socially taboo in Athens to publically name women of the upper and middle classes unless they were dead. Amphitheus here names his grandmother (presumably dead) but avoids naming his mother, who must therefore still be alive.

50

Λυκῖνος: Lycinus was a common Athenian name, as was Phaenarete. Neither is identifiable as a specific Athenian.
ἐκ τούτου: 'because of this'.

52

σπονδὰς ποιῆσαι: a σπονδή is literally a libation, or drink offering; with ποιέω it means 'I make peace', because pouring a libation would be an integral part of a peace-treaty.

53

ἀλλ᾽ ἀθάνατος ὤν: concessive.

54

οἱ τοξόται: vocative, 'Oi, archers!'

55

περιόψεσθέ με;: 'are you going to ignore me?' περιοράω has the sense of 'watch and do nothing about' so, 'ignore', 'allow'.

58

κρεμάσαι τὰς ἀσπίδας: weapons would have been hung up as decoration in the home in times of peace, so this is a clichéd way of indicating a cessation of hostilities.

59

κάθησο: second singular middle imperative κάθημαι 'I sit' – technically a perfect tense, it is used with a present tense meaning.

μὰ τὸν Ἀπόλλω: 'by Apollo . . .!'

60

ἢν = ἐάν.

πρυτανεύσητέ: second plural aorist subjunctive of πρυτανεύω (here) 'I propose a motion for'.

μοι: ethic dative indicating Dicaeopolis' special interest in the action of the verb.

61

παρὰ βασιλέως: παρά + genitive = 'from'.

62

ποίου βασιλέως: a sarcastic rhetorical question (literally 'what sort of king?') which amounts to something like 'What, do you mean, *King*?'

τοῖς ταῶσι: 'peacocks' a recent import to Greece from the East; Dicaeopolis uses them here as a symbol of luxury and corruption in contrast with the simple life of the Greek countryside.

τοῖς τ᾽ ἀλαζονεύμασιν: 'bullshit' or 'fakery'. An ἀλαζων is a liar who exaggerates.

64

βαβαιάξ: an intensified form of the exclamation βαβαί 'Whew!' or 'Wow!'

ὠκβάτανα = ὢ Ἐκβάτανα. Ecbatana was the capital of Media, a region in Persia. It is used here as a kind of expletive expressing surprise at the extravagant appearance of the ambassadors. Persians were stereotyped in Athenian culture as luxurious and elegant dressers – doubtless the ambassadors' costumes reflect this.

τοῦ σχήματος: genitive of exclamation. 'the outfit!'

65

ὡς βασιλέα: ὡς is used + accusative of motion towards a person.

βασιλέα τὸν μέγαν: the Persian king is often referred to in Greek sources as 'the Great King'.

66

δύο δραχμὰς τῆς ἡμέρας: a generous stipend, given that the subsistence pay for a labourer or naval soldier was around half a drachma a day.

οἴμοι τῶν δραχμῶν: 'alas for the drachmas!', οἴμοι + genitive of exclamation.

67

ἐπ᾽ Εὐθυμένους ἄρχοντος: 'in the archonship of Euthymenes', the standard way of dating in Classical Athens was to refer to the eponymous archon for the particular year in question. The ambassadors were sent away in 437/6 BC, (11 years before this play was staged!) and have thus been abroad for a humorously long time, enjoying the luxuries of Persia.

68

ἐτρυχόμεσθα: poetic imperfect first plural middle of τρύχω 'I wear out', best to translate here reflexively 'we wore ourselves out'.

Καϋστρίων: Καύστριος 'of the river Cayster', a river in Lydia.

69

ἐσκηνημένοι: perfect middle participle of σκηνάω = 'camping under awnings'.

70

ἐφ' ἁρμαμαξῶν: ἐπί has become ἐφ' because of the rough breathing on ἁρμαμαξῶν. ἁρμάμαξαι were a special type of covered carriage used by Persians.

71

ἀπολλύμενοι: present middle participle of ἀπόλλυμι 'dying'; an obviously ridiculous and comical statement given the comforts just described.

Dicaeopolis' sarcastic reply makes clear the grim conditions in the city. Many refugees from the countryside around Athens were forced to sleep rough in the city because of overcrowding; it is also possible that Dicaeopolis here refers to the discomforts of evening guard-duty on the walls.

ἐσωζόμην: 'I was safe and sound'; the γάρ adds force to the sarcasm here 'Of course I was absolutely safe and sound then'.

72

ἐν φορυτῷ: 'in a pile of rubbish' φορυτός is anything carried along by the wind, such as straw or other waste. It later came to mean rubbish more generally. Dicaeopolis' poor bed forms a sharp contrast to the luxurious tents and wagons enjoyed by the ambassadors to Persia.

73

ξενιζόμενοι: 'while we were being entertained'. Official ambassadors to Persia would be put up by the satrap (local governors) in the cities they passed through. There were also post-stations on the Royal Roads though Persia where travellers could stay. The hospitality described here is lavish and fits with the Athenian stereotype of the luxurious Persian lifestyle.

πρὸς βίαν: 'by force', 'against our will'. The ambassador pretends not to have enjoyed the luxuries of Persian court life.

74

ἐξ ὑαλίνων ἐκπωμάτων καὶ χρυσίδων: the cups described here would seem wildly extravagant to the Greek audience – glass was a real rarity in Athens during this period and it is here combined with gold, making it even more luxurious.

75

ἄκρατον: the Greeks normally diluted their wine with water – unmixed wine was luxurious and self-indulgent, thus it was often associated with the excesses of barbarians despite the fact that many Greeks enjoyed the beverage this way. The message here is that the ambassadors have been living it large abroad while people at home suffer shortages due to the war.

Κραναά: κραναός, meaning 'rocky' or 'rugged' is a term used of Athens (and, more specifically, of the Acropolis) from the fifth century BC onwards. A mythical king, Cranaus, was invented to explain the name, giving us the mock-tragic address 'O city of Cranaus' here. It is also a pun on the standard Greek verb κεράννυμι 'I mix' implying that while the ambassadors have been drinking their luxurious unmixed wine (ἄκρατον) the Athenians have been diluting theirs (So Olson 2002 ad loc.)

76

καταγέλων: accusative singular of κατάγελως 'derision', 'mockery'.

77

ἄνδρας ἡγοῦνται μόνους: 'they think the only [real] men [are those who . . .]'. ἡγέομαι introduces an accusative + infinitive construction, but the infinitive εἶναι has been left out.

78

πλεῖστα: 'the most'.

φαγεῖν: aorist infinitive ἐσθίω. This plays on the Greek stereotype of the Persians as gluttonous.

79

λαικαστάς: a very obscene term for men who perform oral sex on other men; καταπύγονας is a similarly rude term for men who enjoy receiving anal intercourse. Dicaeopolis is implying that the Athenians think only men who prefer these sexual practices are 'real men'. This type of vulgar sexual humour is extremely common in Aristophanes.

80

ἔτει τετάρτῳ: dative of 'time when'. The expedition has taken an extremely long time – the implication being that the ambassadors have not hurried along the way as they were enjoying the luxurious entertainment so much.

τὰ βασίλει᾽: 'palace', plural used as singular.

81:

the subject 'he' is, of course, the Great King.

εἰς ἀπόπατον: 'to the bog' (ἀπόπατος literally means 'shit'), coarse comic vocabulary.

στρατιὰν λαβών: it is not clear why the King should have taken his army with him to the lavatory, except that it makes the whole situation more ridiculous and thus funnier.

82

κἄχεζεν = καὶ ἔχεζεν. χέζω is another coarse word, meaning something like 'I shit'.

ὀκτὼ μῆνας: a comically long time.

ἐπὶ χρυσῶν ὀρῶν: 'on the golden mountains', there are Greek sources which claimed there were mountains in Persia made of solid gold (which further exemplifies the Greek stereotype of Persian wealth and luxury) but it is more likely that the ambassador here is making a vulgar joke: faeces were thought of as yellow in ancient Greece, so perhaps a better translation is 'the dung mountains'.

83

πόσου . . . χρόνου: 'how long since . . .'.

84

τῇ πανσελήνῳ: the joke transfers well into English given the existence of the term 'mooning' to refer to the exposure of the buttocks in a rude gesture. A similar concept may be at work here.

κᾆτ᾽ = καὶ εἶτα 'and then', 'and next . . .'

85

εἶτ᾽ = εἶτα.

θ᾽ = τε.

παρετίθει: note the imperfect tense, which implies this generosity went on for some time.

85–6

ὅλους ἐκ κριβάνου βοῦς: Persian excess is emphasised yet again, for a κρίβανος was a pottery vessel used as a kind of small bread-oven or loaf-tin set over a fire: this one would need to be massive to contain a whole ox (as Dicaeopolis' disbelief in the next line makes clear).

87

κριβανίτας: (κριβανίτης, -ου, ὁ) something 'pan-baked' or 'cooked in a tin': this is a word used of bread, so its application to a large animal like an ox is humorous as well as incredulous.

τῶν ἀλαζονευμάτων: genitive exclamation 'What bullshit!' (cf. note on ll.62–3).

88

ναὶ μὰ Δί᾽: a colloquial oath 'yes indeed, by Zeus'.

Κλεωνύμου: genitive after τριπλάσιον 'three times the size of Cleonymus'. Cleonymus was a prominent politician in the year this play was staged who may even have been a member of the ruling council. He is known to have proposed three decrees to the Assembly in this year, one of which was an attempt to make the payments of allied tribute to Athens stricter. Aristophanes satirizes him in several of his plays as an obese glutton and a coward who threw his shield down in battle. It is extremely unlikely that the latter accusation is true given his evident political success, but the reference to his size here and in other plays indicates he was probably a large man.

89

φέναξ: 'fooler', 'cheat': the pun comes into force in line 90.

90

ταῦτ': internal accusative with ἐφενάκιζες.
ἆρ ἐφενάκιζες: 'so that's why you were playing the cheat'.
φέρων: 'drawing [pay of]'.

91

Ψευδαρτάβαν: a 'speaking name' (i.e. a name which is chosen deliberately to tell us something about the character that bears it) which seems to mean something like 'False-measure' from the Greek ψευδής (false) and the Persian *artabe* (a unit of measurement). Thus Pseudartabas is marked from the beginning as a deceitful scoundrel who somehow manages to fool everyone except Dicaeopolis.

92

τὸν βασιλέως ὀφθαλμόν: this post really existed in Persia along with the roles of King's Ears, King's Sons and King's Brothers, given to favoured members of the court who were expected to report any serious problems they discovered in the provinces (called satrapies) direct to the King.

92–3

ἐκκόψειέ γε κόραξ πατάξας: optative of wish for the future 'may a crow cut out [his eye] by pecking'.
τόν τε σὸν τοῦ πρέσβεως: 'and your ambassadorial eye too!'.

94

ὦναξ = ὦ ἄναξ.
Dicaeopolis is surprised at Pseudartabas' appearance: we can surmise that he is richly dressed in exotic Persian clothes which probably included brightly coloured or patterned Persian trousers (a typical feature in Greek depictions of Persians) as well as gold adornments and other oriental affectations. His mask seems to have been decorated with gigantic, exaggerated eyes. He is also accompanied by two silent attendants who are also richly dressed and who have large beards.

95

πρὸς τῶν θεῶν: 'by the gods'.
ναύφαρκτον βλεπων: '. . . do you look like a warship?'.

96

ἢ περὶ ἄκραν κάμπτων νεώσοικον σκοπεῖς: Dicaeopolis must be describing Pseudartabas' progress into the theatre as he enters from the wing and turns to face the audience.

97

'I suppose you have leather padding around your lower eye?!'

This line has puzzled scholars and editors for years. There are different schools of thought on what it means: one suggestion is that it refers to the eyes painted on Pseudartabas' mask, which would then be imagined not as beside one another but one on top of the other as the oar-holes would be on an ancient ship), but why these painted eyes should be padded or what the joke is regarding the 'padding' remains unclear. Another suggestion is that the 'lower eye' is Pseudartabas' anus, and that the 'padding' refers to leather trousers (trousers were an item of clothing closely associated with Persian barbarity in Greek thought).

98–9

ἄττα = ἅτινα 'what [things]'. After the imperative phrase ἄγε δὴ σύ 'come on now!' the word order is very fractured – translate in the order φράσον ἄττα βασιλεὺς ἀπέπεμψεν σ᾽ λέξοντ᾽ Ἀθηναίοισιν, ὦ Ψευδαρτάβα.

λέξοντ᾽: future participle in purpose clause after ἀπέπεμψεν.

100

Pseudartabas, despite his exalted position, seems to know virtually no Greek and it isn't possible to make any sense of many of the things he says. This line is particularly difficult. It is likely that these words are deliberate gibberish which *sounds* Persian or Eastern to a Greek ear. It is best simply to transliterate it into English '*iartaman exarxas apisona satra*'.

101

ξυνήκαθ᾽ ὃ λέγει: this question is probably addressed to the whole audience in the theatre. Dicaeopolis' emphatically negative reply makes clear that we are not supposed to understand what Pseudartabas says.

102

πέμψειν: future infinitive in indirect statement (after φησίν).

103

μεῖζον: 'louder'. The ambassador is frustrated with Pseudartabas' poor communication skills.

104

Despite badly mangled Greek, Pseudartabas' meaning is perfectly clear here (and the whole scenario hugely funny to an Athenian audience).

λῆψι = λήψει, second person singular future λαμβάνω.

χρῦσο = χρυσόν.

χαυνόπρωκτ᾽: 'wide-arsed' i.e. they engage often in buggery.

Ἰαοναῦ: a mangled form of 'Ἰᾶον', 'Ionian'. Pseudartabas addresses the Athenian ambassador using a term more properly applied to the Greeks living on the fringes of the Persian Empire along the Eastern shores of the Aegean Sea. The Athenians would take this as an insult, implying that they were from the fringes of the Greek world rather than one of its primary city-states.

105

οἴμοι κακοδαίμων: a comically bathetic exclamation, 'Alas, wretched me!'.
ὡς σαφῶς: supply λέγει.

106

τί δαὶ λέγει: 'But what ever is he saying?' The ambassador hasn't understood
  Pseudartabas' rude statement.

107

ὅ τι: in repetition the direct question-word becomes indirect. 'What [does he say]?'

108

The ambassador wilfully mishears the truth, so keen is he to believe in the vast riches
  available from the Great King. The word he uses, ἀχάνη, sounds similar to the
  opening syllables of the insult χαυνόπρωκτους. An ἀχάνη was a large Persian
  measure; translate 'huge amounts of [gold]'.

110

ἄπιθ᾽: second person singular imperative of ἄπειμι.
μόνος: 'by myself'.

111

πρὸς τουτονί: something needs to be supplied here; the best current suggestion is
  the word 'κόνδυλον' meaning 'fist', given the threat Dicaeopolis goes on to make
  in the next line. Another suggestion is that the missing word is βακτήριον 'stick',
  but this would mean changing the spelling of τουτονί to make it agree with the
  neuter noun. In any case, violence is clearly intended.
πρός: (+ accusative) 'in the presence of'.
τουτονί is the intensified form of τοῦτον.

112

βάμμα Σαρδιανικόν: 'Sardian dye', Sardis was the capital of Lydia which was at this
  time a part of the Persian Empire. It was associated with richly dyed cloth in a vibrant
  shade of red-purple. Dicaeopolis is threatening to give Pseudartabas a bloody nose.
ἀνανεύει: this gesture (throwing the head back from the shoulders) is the Greek
  equivalent of shaking the head to indicate the answer 'no'.

114

ἄλλως: 'just' or 'merely'.

115

Ἑλληνικόν: translate as an adverb, 'the Greek way'.

116

οὐκ ἔσθ᾽ ὅπως: 'there is no way that . . .'
ἐνθένδ᾽ αὐτόθεν: 'from right here'; Dicaeopolis spots that Pseudartabas and his
  two (silent) attendants are strangely familiar with the Greek customs of nodding

(which are a bit different from other cultures). He begins to suspect that something is up and pulls at the men's beards, exposing their disguise.

117

τοῖν μὲν εὐνούχοιν: this is the dual form of the noun (used for two people together) in the genitive 'of the two eunuchs'. Eunuchs would not have beards, but the joke is taken further in the next line where a real (non-eunuch) Athenian of effeminate habits is identified as one of Pseudartabas' followers.

τὸν ἕτερον τουτονὶ: 'this one here'.

118

ἐγᾦδ᾽ = ἐγώ οἶδα.

Κλεισθένης ὁ Σιβυρτίου: 'Cleisthenes son of Sibyrtius'. Cleisthenes is often the butt of jokes in Aristophanic comedy. He is portrayed as weak, beardless and effeminate but there is little evidence outside Aristophanes for his real characteristics. He is likely to have been a very prominent politician in the fifth century BC given the frequency with which Aristophanes attacks him. The reference to Sibyrtius is not giving genuine information about Cleisthenes' father but is a further jibe at Cleisthenes' weak physical condition – Sibyrtius ran a wrestling school, where a man of Cleisthenes' physique would not be likely to thrive. It may also imply that Cleisthenes and Sibyrtius were in a homosexual relationship, with Cleisthenes as the 'passive' partner.

119

ἐξυρημένε: perfect passive participle vocative singular of ξυρέω, 'I shave' with θερμόβουλον πρωκτὸν as accusative of respect – 'Oh you who have shaved your hot-desiring arse'. The implication is that, in line with his beardless face, Cleisthenes has shaved his backside in order to be more attractive to male lovers. Pubic depilation was a definitely feminine pursuit in Classical Athens so this would be extremely funny to a male audience. The tone of the address is paratragic.

120

ὦ πίθηκε: 'you monkey'; this is a parody of a story in Archilochus, an archaic Greek iambic poet, about a fox who outwits a monkey. The fox mocks the monkey's brightly coloured bottom and suggests that this ridiculous body part makes him unfit to rule over the animals. Dicaeopolis here suggests that Cleisthenes' ridiculous appearance makes him unfit for his prominent role in the Assembly.

τὸν πώγων᾽ ἔχων: Dicaeopolis holds up the fake beard that he has removed from Cleisthenes as he speaks here.

121

ἐσκευασμένος: 'dressed up as' (perfect participle middle masculine nominative singular σκευάζω).

122

όδὶ: the intensified form of ὅδε.

τίς ποτ᾽: 'who on earth'.

Στράτων: Strato was another Athenian whom Aristophanes mocks for being effeminate and beardless. We know very little about him except for the jokes made about him in Aristophanes' own plays.

123
this line is outside the metre.

124
The βουλή was the ruling Council of the Assembly made up of 50 men from each of the ten tribes of Athens. They were elected by lot and served for one year. The βουλή was managed by the Prytaneis (50 men elected each month from the total of 500 on the Council).

125
εἰς τὸ πρυτανεῖον: the Prytaneum was the magistrates' hall where the Prytaneis lived during their service. It was also used, as here, to entertain foreign dignitaries and to give honorary dinners to outstanding citizens such as Olympic victors.

ἀγχόνη: literally 'isn't this a hanging?!' i.e. 'isn't this enough to make you choke [from rage]?!' Dicaeopolis is disgusted as he watches the liar Pseudartabas and his false cronies, the 'eunuchs', leave for a fancy dinner.

126
κἄπειτ' = καὶ ἔπειτα 'in that case'.
ἐγώ: highly emphatic.
ἐνθαδὶ: strengthened form of ἐνθάδε.

127
a difficult line. Take θύρα as the subject and supply 'anyone' as the object of ἴσχει. τοὺς δὲ ξενίζειν is dependent on ἴσχει 'from entertaining *that lot*' (i.e. Pseudartabas and company) 'Never does a door restrain [anyone] from entertaining *them*' i.e. 'the door's never closed to *them*!'.

129
μοι: ethic dative of person interested.
οὑτοσὶ: Amphitheus talks about himself in the third person, as is frequent in poetry. Translate 'Here I am!' or 'I'm right here!' Note the final iota (deictic iota) which should now be familiar as an intensifier.

130
ἐμοί: note the emphatic position: Dicaeopolis is making peace for *himself* alone.
Dicaeopolis is not bribing Amphitheus but offering him the journey-money which the Assembly had denied to him.

131
ποιῆσαι: the infinitive is used here for the imperative, another common poetic feature.

μόνῳ: in agreement with ἐμοὶ at the beginning of the previous line. The hyperbaton (= disrupted word order, here the separation of noun/pronoun and adjective) emphasizes the exclusivity of this peace which is only for Dicaeopolis and his family, not the Athenians as a whole.

133

ὑμεῖς: Dicaeopolis 'breaks the fourth wall' and addresses the audience.

πρεσβεύεσθε: present middle imperative with iterative force 'keep on sending embassies'.

κεχήνετε: second plural perfect active imperative χάσκω with -ετε here for the more normal -ατε.

134

προσίτω: third singular imperative πρόσειμι.

παρὰ Σιτάλκους: παρά + genitive of person frequently refers to royalty – 'from the court of Sitalces'. Sitalces was a Thracian king with a substantial empire of his own. The Athenians were hoping he would help them in the Peloponnesian War by sending cavalry fighters (Thrace was famed for the quality of its horses), but this did not happen before Sitalces himself was killed in in a local war.

ὁδί: like Amphitheus, Theorus speaks of himself in the third person. Translate 'here I am!'.

136

χρόνον … πολύν: the hyperbaton emphasizes the sheer length of time they have been away – these ambassadors, like the ones to Persia, have been enjoying themselves a little too much at state expense.

ἂν ἦμεν: past counterfactual 'we would not have been . . .'.

137

μὰ Δί᾽ οὐκ ἂν: supply ἦσθα 'no, by Zeus, you wouldn't have been . . .!'.

εἰ μισθόν γε μὴ 'φερες πολύν: presumably these ambassadors, as at lines 65–7, are also on the very generous pay-packet of two drachmas a day. Dicaeopolis supples a humorous protasis for the ambassador's apodosis.

138

εἰ μὴ κατένειψε χιόνι τὴν Θρᾴκην ὅλην . . .: Theorus ignores Dicaeopolis and completes his own counterfactual conditional statement with an exaggerated account of the bad weather on the journey. The Assembly will likely believe Theorus as the extreme winters and bad snow in Thrace were well-known in Athens at this time.

κατένειψε: impersonal 'if the weather hadn't covered the whole of Thrace in snow'.

139

ἔπηξ᾽: impersonal from πήγνυμι with ποταμούς as object.

ὑπ᾽ αὐτὸν τὸν χρόνον: 'about the same time as'.

140

Θέογνις: see notes on lines 10–11.

ἠγωνίζετο: (here) 'was contending for the tragic prize'. The joke is that Theognis' tragic style was generally criticized as 'frigid', a style marked, among other things, by a fondness for complicated vocabulary and odd metaphors.

141

τοῦτον . . . τὸν χρόνον: accusative of time how long 'for all this time . . .'.

143

ἐραστὴς: this language implies a homosexual relationship in which the Athenians take the passive role, as the ἐραστής was the older, more experienced lover in this type of affair.

ὥστε: a result clause.

144

τοῖσι =τοῖς the final iota is a feature of the epic and Ionic dialects and is thus often used in poetry.

ἔγραφ': imperfect tense, implying that this is a habitual action.

Ἀθηναῖοι καλοί: this is an adaptation of a standard phrase 'X is beautiful' used in homosexual flirtation and courtship, of which we have much evidence from epigraphy, graffiti and Greek vase-painting.

145

ὃν Ἀθηναῖον ἐπεποιήμεθα: One of the Athenians' gambits to persuade Sitalces to help them was to make his son Sadocus an Athenian citizen, a status which brought considerable benefit in the fifth century BC. ἐπεποιήμεθα is the pluperfect indicative middle of ποιέω 'I make, do'.

146

ἤρα: third singular imperfect active ἐράω 'I long (for), desire'.

ἐξ Ἀπατουρίων: ἐκ here 'at'. The Apaturia was a religious festival celebrated in the Greek month Pyanepsion (which spanned parts of the modern September and October) in which children and other new citizens would be welcomed into the phratries. Phratries were kinship-groups within Athenian society of people believed to share a common ancestor – membership of one of these was essential for full Athenian citizenship.

147

ἠντεβόλει: third singular imperfect indicative active ἀντιβολέω with a double augment.

πάτρα: a word from the high epic and tragic tradition, used here not primarily in a parody of a tragedy (as would be expected) but as part of a pun with πατέρ' earlier in the line. The irony is, of course, that Sadocus' fatherland is *really* Thrace, and that his father never did help Athens. There may also be a flavour of humorous tragic melodrama in Sadocus' plea here.

148

ὁ δ᾽: i.e. Sitalces.

ὤμοσε: ὄμνυμι + future infinitive introduces a sworn promise.

ἔχων: take with στρατιὰν τοσαύτην in the next line.

149

ὥστ᾽ Ἀθηναίους ἐρεῖν: result clause with future infinitive 'that the Athenians would say'.

ἐρεῖν: a defective verb with no present tense. ἐρῶ is regularly used as the future of λέγω.

150

ὅσον τὸ χρῆμα: a colloquial phrase 'what a lot of . . .'.

παρνόπων: locusts, as already in biblical times, were strongly associated with huge swarms. This analogy is double-edged – although on the one hand it suggests that Thrace will send huge numbers to help Athens, on the other, locusts were known for their voracious destruction of the land on which they swarmed. The implication is that the Thracians will consume everything in their path, and indeed they do steal Dicaeopolis' garlic at lines 164–5.

151

κάκιστ᾽ ἀπολοίμην, εἰ . . .: a colloquial way of denying the truth of something that has just been said 'May I die most wretchedly if . . .', i.e. 'I'll be damned if . . .' (so Sommerstein 1980, Olson 2002 ad loc.). ἀπολοίμην is first singular aorist middle optative of ἀπόλλυμι (NB that the middle of this verb means to die, the active meaning is 'to destroy'). κάκιστ᾽ is the superlative adverb.

τούτων: partitive genitive with τι 'any of that'.

πείθομαι: 'I trust, believe'.

152:

ὧν = ἅ, attracted into the genitive because it refers back to τούτων.

εἶπας = εἶπες.

ἐνταυθοῖ: 'here' rather than, as usually, 'hither'.

πλὴν τῶν παρνόπων: Dicaeopolis clearly suspects the worst of the 'locusts' and does not at all believe that Sadocus or Sitalces wishes to help Athens.

154

μέν γ᾽: draws attention to what Dicaeopolis is saying 'Well, *that* is clear now at least!'

156

τουτὶ = τοῦτο.

Ὀδομάντων: the Odomantians, a tribe in Thrace who lived near Mount Pangaeum, east of the river Strymon. It is clear that Aristophanes thought that they were under Sitalces' rule, but they were, in fact, an independent tribe.

157

ποίων Ὀδομάντων: see note on 62.

158

ἀποτεθρίακεν: third singular perfect indicative active ἀποθριάζω (literally I remove leaves from) here 'I circumcise'. It is unclear what exactly Dicaeopolis means by this, as it is very unlikely that the Odomantians are really circumcised. Their phalloi (see Introduction) are probably visible and perhaps they are costumed as if in a state of sexual arousal. In any case some kind of vulgar joke is clearly intended.

159

διδῷ: third singular present subjunctive active δίδωμι. Two drachmas per day was a ridiculously high sum for a soldier to be paid in this period.

160

καταπελτάσονται: third plural of the middle future indicative of καταπελτάζω 'I over-run with peltasts'. Peltasts were lightly-armed Thracian soldiers who carried a shield called a πέλτη.

Βοιωτία: Boeotia was an area in central Greece on the Spartan side in the Peloponnesian War.

161

ἀπεψωλημένοις: dative masculine plural perfect participle passive of ἀποψωλέω. Supply 'give' from line 159 'give two drachmas to those circumcised freaks?!'.

162

μέντἄν = μέντοι ἄν. μέντοι here indicates Dicaeopolis' outrage.

θρανίτης: 'top-bench' people, those who rowed on the highest bench in a trireme. We have evidence that these rowers were paid a high rate of one drachma a day in 415 BC during the Athenian expedition to Sicily, presumably because their work was considered more skilful or more risky.

163

οἴμοι τάλας: 'alas, wretched me!' a common phrase from Greek tragedy indicating extreme despair – clearly mock-tragic here.

ἀπόλλυμαι: probably the passive here 'I am being killed!' as the Odomantians charge Dicaeopolis and steal his food.

164

τὰ σκόροδα πορθούμενος: 'being robbed of my garlic'.

165

οὐ καταβαλεῖτε: 'will you not ...' – this question has the same force as an imperative.

μόχθηρε: μοχθηρός, -ά, -όν – 'wretched' (often used in vocative as an insult).

166

οὐ μὴ πρόσει: οὐ μή + future indicative is used as a prohibition with the same force as μή + aorist subjunctive. 'Don't go near them . . .!'

ἐσκοροδισμένοις: dative masculine plural perfect participle passive σκοροδίζω 'I dose with garlic' so '[when] they've been dosed with garlic'. Fighting cockrels were given garlic in their food in ancient Athens as it was believed to make them more aggressive. The Odomantians, already formidable, are assumed to be even more bloodthirsty after eating Dicaeopolis' garlic bulbs.

167

ταυτὶ = intensified ταῦτα.

περιείδεθ᾽: second plural aorist indicative active of περιοράω 'I ignore' with the final epsilon elided and the tau aspirated due to contact with the rough breathing in οἱ. The aorist here should be translated as a present tense with the vocative οἱ πρυτάνεις 'You Prytaneis, are you ignoring . . .'.

168

ἐν τῇ πατρίδι: Dicaeopolis is outraged to have been treated badly in *his* own fatherland by barbarians.

καὶ ταῦθ᾽: 'and moreover'.

169

ἀπαγορεύω: note the redundant μή, regularly found with the infinitive after verbs of preventing, prohibiting or denying; here μὴ ποιεῖν ἐκκλησίαν means something like 'to continue holding an Assembly' (so Sommerstein 1980 and Olson 2002 ad loc.).

170

τοῖς Θρᾳξὶ: dative of interest '[pay] for the Thracians'.

171

διοσημία: the Assembly stopped the meeting if there was a sign from Zeus that the gods disapproved, such as an earth tremor or a storm.

'στὶ = ἐστί.

βέβληκέ: third perfect indicative active βάλλω 'has struck [me]'.

172

ἀπιέναι, παρεῖναι: infinitives with the force of imperatives – a formal usage which suits this official pronouncement.

εἰς ἕνην: 'the day after tomorrow'.

Scholars disagree as to whether there is a scene-change here. Olson (2002) argues that Dicaeopolis remains where he is on the Pnyx while Sommerstein prefers to have him walking home when Amphitheus enters. It seems likely to me that he can't have gotten very far at least, so that Amphitheus is able to find him.

174

μυττωτὸν: μυττωτός was a paste or pate made primarily of garlic with the addition of other condiments and vegetables such as leeks, onions and honey, very similar

to the modern Greek speciality *skordalia*. It was used to flavour other foods such
as fish.

ὅσον: as at line 150, this is a colloquial usage meaning 'what a . . .!'.

ἀπώλεσα: ἀπόλλυμι here means 'lose' rather than 'destroy'.

175

ἀλλ' ἐκ Λακεδαίμονος γὰρ Ἀμφίθεος ὁδί: it is, of course, an impossibility for
Amphitheus to have travelled to Sparta and back in a matter of minutes, but such
practicalities have no place in an Aristophanic comedy.

176

χαῖρ' Ἀμφίθεε: χαῖρε is the standard Greek greeting (to one person, χαίρετε
to more than one person) but it is literally translated 'rejoice!' (present second
person singular active imperative from χαίρω). Amphitheus takes Dicaeopolis
literally here and refuses to 'rejoice' as he is being chased by a crowd of angry old
men.

πρίν <γ> ἂν στῶ τρέχων: indefinite construction following πρίν after a negative.
στῶ is first singular strong aorist subjunctive active of ἵστημι, literally 'not until I
stand as I run' i.e. 'not until I stop running'.

177

φεύγοντ' ἐκφυγεῖν: not redundant repetition, as it may seem at first glance.
ἐκφυγεῖν has the more specific meaning 'to escape', so translate 'for I must flee
and escape the Acharnians!'.

Ἀχαρνέας: the Acharnians or men of Acharnae, a deme (region) north of
Athens. Demes were important administrative sub-divisions within the *polis*
and there was a strong sense of deme-loyalty and pride among the members of
each division. Acharnae was the largest of all the demes and their farms had
suffered especially badly from the Spartan slash-and-burn policy in 431 BC (see
Introduction for more details). The Acharnians were thus rabidly anti-Spartan
and wished to seek revenge though continuing the war rather than for a peace-
treaty.

178

τί δ' ἔστ': 'What's up?', 'What is it?'

σπονδάς: in the scenes which follow, humour arises from the deliberate confusion
between σπονδή 'wine-offering' and σπονδαί 'peace-treaty', with Amphitheus
offering Dicaeopolis a selection of fine (and not-so-fine) *wines* for him to try, each
standing for a different type of peace agreement.

179

ὤσφροντο: 'caught the scent of' i.e. they could smell the bouquet of the different
wines.

180

στιπτοί: literally 'trodden-down', 'compacted' and therefore 'tough'.

πρίνινοι: 'made of holm-oak', a very hard wood.

181

Μαραθωνομάχαι: 'Marathon-fighters', the battle of Marathon in 490 BC was the turning point in the first Persian invasion of Greece in which the Athenians, with help from the Plataeans, decisively defeated the Persians. If the chorus had really fought at Marathon they would now be in their eighties by the time of this play (426/5 BC). However, as often in comedy, precise accuracy is sacrificed in order to create a strong impression: here, the men are characterized as a) very old indeed and b) that they have heroic deeds under their belt and are formidable foes.

σφενδάμνινοι: 'men of maple-wood', the maple was also known for its toughness.

183

τῶν ἀμπέλων τετμημένων: genitive absolute 'when our vines have been cut down'. τετμημένων is genitive plural feminine perfect participle passive of τέμνω 'I cut'. The Spartans had deliberately destroyed the crops and farms of Attica during the war. Vines were one of the most important crops to the Athenian economy so their destruction would be a harsh blow to the farmers.

184

κἀς = καί εἰς.

τρίβωνας: a τρίβων was a rough cloak worn by the poorer classes.

ξυνελέγοντο τῶν λίθων: supply τινας with τῶν λίθων 'some stones'. ξυνελέγοντο is third plural imperfect indicative middle of συλλέγω (σ has become ξ).

185

κἀβόων = καί ἐβόων.

186

οἱ δ᾽ οὖν βοώντων: οἱ δ᾽ οὖν is scornful 'Well, let them shout!' βοώντων is third plural present active imperative of βοάω.

187

ἔγωγέ: intensified form of ἐγώ 'I at least'.

φημί: literally 'I say', i.e. 'I do indeed!'

188

αὗται μέν εἰσι πεντέτεις: supply σπονδαί. πεντέτεις: 'five-year'. Vintage wine was appreciated in ancient Greece as it is now, so the joke works on both levels – Dicaeopolis eventually chooses the longest peace-treaty and the finest wine.

γεῦσαι: second singular aorist imperative of γεύομαι 'I taste'.

189

αἰβοῖ: a non-verbal cry of disgust.

οὐκ ἀρέσκουσιν: supply σπονδαί as the subject.

190

πίττης: Dicaeopolis can smell the preparations for war (pitch, used for caulking naval ships) on the bouquet of the 'wine' and does not like it much; wine-jars were also proofed with pitch, but the end of the line makes clear it is naval preparations he is worried about. πίττης and παρασκευῆς are genitive depending on ὄζουσι 'they smell of . . .'.

191

δ᾽ ἀλλά: 'Well then', offering Dicaeopolis an alternative (so Olson 2002 ad loc).

δεκέτεις: 'lasting ten years'.

192

χαὖται = καί αὗται [σπονδαί].

πρέσβεων: genitive after ὄζουσι. The embassies in question are probably not those to other Greek cities in case of a Panhellenic war; rather, given what Dicaeopolis says in the next line, they are likely to be embassies to Athens' subject states asking for supplies for the war-effort.

193

ὀξύτατον: 'very sharp', superlative adjective used adverbially.

διατριβῆς τῶν ξυμμάχων: '[it smells of] the allies being hard-pressed'.

194

αὑταιι: note the now-familiar intensifying final iota.

τριακοντούτιδες: 'lasting 30 years'. A 30 year peace had been made between Athens and Sparta in 446 BC but it did not last long – the Peloponnesian War began in 431 BC.

195

κατὰ γῆν τε καὶ θάλατταν: this is the standard formula used in official documents regarding peace and war between Greek states.

ὦ Διονύσια: Dicaeopolis probably refers to the rural Dionysia or Anthesteria, two countryside festivals which he would not have been able to celebrate for some years because of the war.

196

ἀμβροσίας καὶ νέκταρος: ambrosia and nectar are the food and drink of the gods. Not only do they smell exquisite, but they symbolize life, the opposite of the death-dealing war he could smell in the other samples.

197

μὴ 'πιτηρεῖν = τοῦ μὴ ἐπιτηρεῖν, an articular infinitive working as a noun (with the article missing!) 'and [it smells] of not keeping watch . . .'.

σιτί' = σιτία. Three day's rations was the standard allocation of food troops were expected to bring with them to war.

198

κἀν = καί ἐν

βαῖν᾽ ὅπη θέλεις: 'go wherever you want', Dicaeopolis, like many Athenians from the demes outside the city, has been trapped inside the city due to the war: we saw his claustrophobia and longing for his country home earlier in the play at lines 32–3.

199

σπένδομαι: I make peace (pour a libation for peace).

κἀκπίομαι = καί ἐκπίομαι future tense of ἐκπίνω.

200

χαίρειν κελεύων πολλά: χαῖρε πολλά = 'a hearty hello/farewell'. Dicaeopolis bids a firm goodbye to the war-mongering Acharnians and sets off for his own farm.

201–365

The chorus enter, furious with Dicaeopolis and determined to punish him for making peace with Sparta; they wish to seek revenge on Sparta for the destruction of the Athenian countryside. As the chorus look on, Dicaeopolis and his family celebrate the Country Dionysia, a religious festival involving sacrifice and a procession. Just as Dicaeopolis sings a bawdy song (a comic replacement for the religious hymn that would have been sung at a festival) the chorus attack him with stones. Dicaeopolis tries to explain to them why he has made peace with the Spartans, but his attempts only enrage the Acharnians further. Realizing that they will never listen to him, Dicaeopolis takes a basket of charcoal 'hostage' and threatens to cut its 'throat' if the Acharnians won't hear him out. As charcoal is the primary export of the deme, they react with horror to this threat and immediately agree to listen. Dicaeopolis prepares to persuade them and is so sure he will succeed that he agrees to speak with his head already on the executioner's block (ready to be killed if he fails to convince the chorus).

366–7

ἰδού: [see] there! θεᾶσθε adds a specific element of *looking* to the command.

τὸ μὲν τοδί ... ὁ δ᾽ οὑτοσί: 'here's ... and here's ...' τοδί = intensified τόδε.

τυννουτοσί: τυννοῦτος, -ον literally 'so small, so little' (the additional iota makes it more demonstrative); translate 'here's little old me' with οὑτοσί.

ἐπίξηνον: Dicaeopolis carries a chopping-block out of his house and places it on the stage.

367

λέξων: future participle of λέγω (more usually supplied by ἐρῶ).

368

ἀμέλει: originally the imperative from ἀμελέω, it becomes a colloquial phrase used at to mean 'don't worry'.

ἐνασπιδώσομαι: future of ἐνασπιδόομαι 'I won't hide behind a shield' i.e. 'I won't just try to save myself'.

369

ἁμοί δοκεῖ: 'What seems good to me', 'What I think'; ἁμοί = ἃ ἐμοί.

370

δέδοικα: perfect δεῖδω used with present meaning, 'I fear'.
πολλά: adverbial 'greatly'.

371

οἶδα χαίροντας σφόδρα: participial indirect statement after οἶδα, χαίροντας refers to the ἀγροίκων, but has been attracted into the accusative by αὐτοὺς in the next line. Dicaeopolis is concerned that the Acharnians won't want to hear what he has to say because it isn't pleasant.

372–3

τις: take with ἀνὴρ ἀλαζὼν in the next line 'some fraudster'.

373

καὶ δίκαια κἄδικα: literally accusative with εὐλογῇ, i.e. 'whether justly or unjustly'.

374

κἀνταῦθα: καί ἐνταῦθα, 'and then'.
λανθάνουσ': + participle 'they don't realize that'.

376

βλέπουσιν: βλέπω + infinitive literally 'I look to X' i.e. 'I care about X', 'I focus on X'.
ἄλλο: 'else'.
ψηφῳ δάκνειν: 'injuring [people] with their voting-ballots'. Greek juries were paid a low sum of two obols a day and thus tended to be staffed by older men who couldn't work in a more physical job. In the fifth century BC jurors voted by putting a pebble into one of two urns, one urn for a guilty verdict and one for acquittal.

377

ἅπαθον = ἃ ἔπαθον.

377–8

αὐτός τ' ἐμαυτὸν ... ἐπίσταμαι: literally 'I myself know myself' translate 'I certainly know what I myself ...'. Dicaeopolis is now speaking in the voice of the poet, Aristophanes, something which more usually happens in the *parabasis*. For Cleon see note on line 6.

378

διὰ τὴν πέρυσι κωμῳδίαν: probably a reference to Aristophanes' *Babylonians* which had been produced at the City Dionysia in 426 BC. Cleon was apparently satirized in this play and accused Aristophanes in the City Council of bringing the city into disrepute in front of foreigners (there were usually guests from the Athenian allied states at the big dramatic festivals). The case seems to have been dismissed, indicating that the Council did not agree with Cleon's interpretation of the play as damaging the city.

380

διέβαλλε: the imperfect tense implies a litany of slander.

ψευδῆ κατεγλώττιζέ μου: καταγλωττίζω means here 'I french-kiss' so 'he licked me with falsehoods' or similar. The verb is used to suggest Cleon should be lampooned for his sexual preferences as well as for being a liar.

381

κἀκυκλοβόρει = καί ἐκυκλοβόρει 'and he roared like Cycloborus', a stream near Athens which was famous for the loudness of its roar.

κἄπλυνεν = καί ἔπλυνεν literally 'he bathed [me]', i.e. 'he drenched me in abuse'.

ὀλίγου πάνυ: 'almost completely'.

382

μολυνοπραγμονούμενος: present participle middle masculine nominative singular of μολυνοπραγμονέομαι 'I get into filth[y trouble]', a comic word made up based on the words μολύνω 'I make dirty' and πολυπραγμονέω 'I make myself busy'.

383

πρὶν λέγειν: 'before I speak'.

ἐάσατε: + accusative and infinitive allow X to Y.

384

ἐνσκευάσασθαί μ': aorist middle infinitive 'to dress myself up'.

οἷον ἀθλιώτατον: 'as a most wretched sort of person'. It was apparently a common technique in Athenian law courts for the accused to dress in rags to get the pity of the jury.

385

ταῦτα: an internal accusative with both verbs, best translated 'in this way', 'thus'. There is a change into lyric (sung) metre here from the spoken iambic trimeter verse used for speech in Aristiphanic comedy. This is the antistrophe corresponding to the strophe sung at lines 358–63. The metre is dochmiac and characteristically marks scenes of high tension in tragedy: its use in this scene is mock-tragic, as Dicaeopolis is obviously never in real danger.

στρέφει: middle, 'turn yourself about', i.e. 'wriggle around'.

386

πορίζεις τριβάς: 'invent delays'.

387

ἐμοῦ γ' ἕνεκα: literally 'on account of me', i.e. 'as far as I am concerned'.

388

Ἱερωνύμου: Hieronymus, a tragic and dithyrambic poet who was criticized for using melodramatic plots and horrible masks. The point here is that he had very long hair, which he hid behind.

389

σκοτοδασυπυκνότριχά: 'dark with shaggy thick hair', a ridiculous compound adjective which fills the whole line. It agrees with κυνῆν in the next line.

390

Ἀΐδος κυνῆν: Hades' cap traditionally made him invisible, his special gift which was aligned with Zeus' thunderbolt and Poseidon's trident.

391

μηχανὰς τὰς Σισύφου: 'your Sisyphean tricks'. Sisyphus was a mythical Corinthian king famed for his cunning. He traditionally managed to trick his way out of the underworld, escaping death.

392

ὡς: 'because', 'for'.
σκῆψιν: 'plea for exemption'.
ἀγὼν = ὁ ἀγών.

Vocabulary

While there is no Defined Vocabulary List for A-level, words in the OCR Defined Vocabulary List for AS are marked with * so that students can quickly see the vocabulary with which they should be particularly familiar.

*ἀγορά, ἡ	market-place	ἀνεῖπον (aor. only)	I announced
ἀγορεύω	I say, speak	*ἀνήρ, ἀνδρός, ὁ	man
ἄγροικος, -ον	rustic	ἄνθραξ, -ακος, ὁ	charcoal
*ἀγρός, ὁ	field	*ἄνθρωπος, ὁ	man
ἀγχόνη, ἡ	a hanging, a strangling	ἀντιβολέω	I beg
*ἄγω (aor. ἤγαγον)	I lead	(+ acc. person)	
*ἀγών, -ῶνος, ὁ	contest, trial	ἄνω	up(wards)
ἀγωνίζομαι	I contend for a prize	*ἄξιος, -ία, -ιον	worthy of
*ἀδικέω (+ acc.)	I do wrong to	ἀπαγορεύω	I forbid
*ἄδικος, -ον	unjust	ἀπαλλάσσω	I set free from
*ἀεί	always	(aor. ἀπηλλαχθην)	
ἀείδω (fut. ἄσομαι)	I sing	ἀπεμπολάω	I sell (pass. I am betrayed)
ἀθάνατος, -ον	immortal	ἀπέρχομαι	I go away
*Ἀθηναῖος	Athenian	ἀποβλέπω	I look longingly on
ἄθλιος, -α, -ον	wretched	*ἀποθνησκω	I die
ἀθρόος, -α, -ον	gathered, together	(aor. ἀπέθανον)	
αἰβοῖ	yuck!	ἀποθριάζω	I circumcise (lit. strip of leaves)
Ἅιδης, -ου, ὁ	Hades		
αἰσθ ἀνομαι	I perceive	*ἀπόλλυμι	I destroy, lose (pass. die)
ἄκρατος, -ον	unmixed	ἀπόπατος, ὁ	toilet, bog
ἄκρη, ἡ	headland	ἀποπέμπω	I send away
ἀλαζόνευμα -ατος, τό	fakery, bullshit	*ἀπορέω	I am in despair
		ἀποψωλέω	I draw back (someone's) foreskin
ἀλαζών, -όνος, ὁ	a liar, charlatan		
*ἀληθής, -ές	true	*ἄρα	then
ἀλλᾶς, -άντος, ὁ,	sausage	*ἆρα	= a question
*ἀλλήλους	one another	ἀρέσκω	I please (+dat.)
*ἄλλος, -η, -ο	another, other	ἁρμάμαξα -ης, ἡ	covered carriage
ἄλλως	otherwise, differently	*ἄρχω	I rule
ἀμβροσία, ἡ	ambrosia	ἄσκωμα, -ατος, τό	leather padding
ἀμέλει	never mind	*ἀσπίς, -ίδος, ἡ	shield
ἄμπελος, ἡ	vine	*ἄστυ, τό	city
ἀνακράζω	I shout out	ἀτέραμνος, -ον	stubborn
(aor. ἀνέκραγον)		ἀτέχνως	really, absolutely
ἀνανεύω	I shake my head (indicating no)	*αὖ	again
		αὐτόθεν	from the very spot
ἄναξ, ἄνακτος, ὁ	lord	*αὐτός, αὐτή, αὐτό	self, same

ἀχάνη, ἡ, (+ gen.)   a large dry measure, a large amount of

ἄχθομαι   I hate (+ dat. of thing hated)

ἀωρία, ἡ   the wrong time

βαβαιάξ   wow!, whew!

*βαίνω   I go

βαιός, -ά, -όν   little, small

*βάλλω (aor. ἔβαλον)   I throw

βάμμα -ατος, τό   dye

βάπτω (fut. βάψω)   I dye

*βάρβαρος, -ον   barbarian

βασανίζω   I examine closely

βασίλειον, -ου, τό   palace

*βασιλεύς, -έως, ὁ   king

βέβληκα   perf. of βάλλω

*βία, ἡ   force

*βλέπω   I look

*βοάω   I shout

*βοηθέω (+ dat)   I help

βουλευτήριον, τό   council chamber

*βουλή, ἡ   council

*βούλομαι   I want, am willing

βοῦς, βοός, ὁ   cow, ox

*γαμέω   I marry

γανόω   I make bright (pass. I am gladdened)

*γάρ   for

*γε   at least, at any rate

*γέρων, -οντος, ὁ   old man

γεῦμα, -ατος, τό   taste, sample

γεύω (aor. ἔγευσα)   I taste

*γῆ, ἡ   land

*γίγνομαι   I happen, become

*γνώμη, ἡ   wit, understanding

*γράφω   I write

δάκνω (aor. ἔδακον)   I bite, I injure

δέδοικα   I fear

*δεῖ (+acc.)   it is necessary (+ acc. + inf.)

*δεινός,-ή, -όν   terrible, clever

δεκέτης   of ten years

*δεῦρο   here

*δέχομαι   I receive, accept

δῆμος, ὁ   deme

*δήπου   surely, certainly

*δῆτα   certainly, to be sure, of course

*διά (+acc.)   because of

διαβάλλω   I slander

διαστρέφω   I turn different ways, twist around

διατριβή, ἡ   a grinding down

*δίδωμι   I give

*δίκαιος, -α, -ον   just

Διονύσια, τά   Dionysia, festival of Dionysus

Διοσημία, ἡ   a sign from Zeus

*διώκω   I pursue

*δόκει (+ dat.)   it seems good to X

*δοκέω   I think, suppose, imagine

δραχμή, ἡ   a silver coin worth six obols

*δύναμαι   I am able to (+ inf.)

δύο   two

*ἐάω (poet. aor. ἐάσω)   I allow

*ἐθέλω   I am willing

*ἔθνος, -εος, τό   tribe

*εἰρήνη, ἡ   peace

*εἰς (+ acc.)   into

εἰσάγω   I lead in

εἰσδέχομαι   I admit, allow

εἰσέλκω   I drag into

εἰσέρχομαι   I go into

εἰσκηρύσσω   I summon by herald

εἶτα   then, next

*ἐκεῖνος, ἐκείνη, ἐκεῖνο   that (man, woman, thing)

*ἐκκλησία, ἡ   assembly

ἐκκόπτω   I cut out

ἐκπίνω   I gulp down, drink dry

ἔκπωμα, -ατος, τό   cup, beaker

*ἐκφεύγω   I escape

ἔλαιον, τό   olive-oil

Ἑλληνικός, -ή, -όν   Greek

ἐμαυτόν   myself (acc.)

ἐμαυτοῦ, ἐμαυτῆς   of me, of myself

*ἐμός, -ή, -όν   mine

ἐνασπιδόομαι   I hide behind a shield

ἐνδέχομαι   I admit, allow of

ἔνδον   inside

*ἕνεκα (+gen.)   on account of

*ἐνθάδε   here

*ἐνθένδε   from here

ἐνσκευάζω   I dress in

*ἐνταῦθα   then, here

ἐνταυθοῖ   to here, here

ἐντός (adv.)   inside, within

ἐξανοίγω   I open, reveal

*ἐξαπατάω   I trick, deceive

ἐξεμέω   I vomit up

ἔπαλξις, -εως, ἡ   battlements, walls

*ἐπειδάν   whenever

*ἔπειτα   then, next

*ἐπί (+ gen.)   upon, on

ἐπινεύω   I nod (assent)

ἐπίξηνον, τό	chopping-block	*κακός, -ή, -όν	evil, bad
*ἐπίσταμαι	I know	*καλέω	I call
ἐπιτηρέω	I watch out for	*καλός, -η, -ον	beautiful
*ἐπιτρέπω (+ dat.)	I entrust to	κάμπτω	I bend, turn
ἐραστής, -οῦ, ὁ	lover	καρδία, ἡ	heart
ἐράω (impf. ἤρων)	I desire	καρτερός, -ά, -όν	strong
*ἐργάζομαι	I work, I do (a deed)	καταβάλλω	I set down
*ἔργον, τό	deed	κατάγελως, -ωτος, ὁ	derision (acc.
*ἔρημος, -ον	empty, deserted		καταγέλων)
*ἔρχομαι (aor. ἦλθον)	I come	καταγλωττίζω	I French kiss
ἐρῶ	I will say	κατάκειμαι	I lie down
ἐς	see εἰς	κατανείφω	I cover with snow
*ἐσθίω (aor. ἔφαγον)	I eat	καταπελτάζω	I overrun with light-
*ἕτερος, -α, -ον	one or the other [of two]		armed troops
*ἔτος, -εος, τό	year	καταπύγων, -ονος, ὁ	a 'passive' homosexual
εὐλογέω	I praise	καταρρέω	I rush down
εὐνοῦχος, ὁ	eunuch	κάτω	down(wards)
εὐφραίνω	I cheer, gladden	Καΰστριος	of or from the river
ἐφόδιον, τό	travelling expenses,		Cayster (in Lydia)
	journey money	κέαρ, τό	heart
*ἔχω	I have	*κελεύω	I order
ἑωθινός, -ή, -όν	early in the morning	κονία, ἡ	dust
		κόραξ, -ακος, ὁ	crow
		κραναός, -ή, -όν	rugged, rocky
*Ζεύς, Διός, ὁ	Zeus	κρεμάννυμι (aor.	I hang up
		ἐκρέμασα)	
*ἡγέομαι	I consider	κριβανίτης, -ου, ὁ	baked in an oven
*ἤδη	already, now	κρίβανος, ὁ	oven
*ἥδομαι (aor. ἥσθην)	I enjoy myself	κυκλοβορέω	I brawl like the torrent
*ἡδύς, ἡδεῖα, ἡδύ	sweet		Cycloborus
*ἥκω	I have come	κυνῆ, ἡ	cap
*ἡμέρα, ἡ	day	κύριος, -α, -ον	having power, being in
ἡνίκα	when		authority
		κωμῳδία, ἡ	comedy
*θάλαττα, ἡ	sea		
θεάομαι	I see	λαικαστής,-οῦ, ὁ	one who performs oral
θέλω	I want, I am willing		sex on men
*θεός, ὁ	god	*Λακεδαιμόνιος, ὁ	Spartan
θερμόβουλος, -ον	hot-tempered	Λακεδαίμων, -ονος, ἡ	Sparta
Θρᾴκη, ἡ	Thrace	λαλέω	I gossip
θρανίτης, -ου, ὁ	rower on the topmost	*λαμβάνω (aor.	I take
	bench in a ship	ἔλαβον)	
Θρᾷξ, Θρᾳκός, ὁ	a Thracian	*λανθάνω	I escape the notice of
*θύρα, ἡ	door	*λέγω (aor. εἶπον)	I say
		λεώς, -ω, ὁ	people
Ἰάων, -ονος, ὁ	Ionian	*λίθος, ὁ	stone
ἰδού	see there!	λογίζομαι	I count, reckon
*ἱππεύς, -έως, ὁ	horseman, knight	λοιδορέω	I abuse
*ἵστημι	I stand, make to stand		
ἴσχω	I restrain, stop	μά	by . . .! Exclamation
			invoking a deity (+
			acc. of deity invoked)
κάθαρμα -ατος, τό	sacred enclosure	μαλθακός, -ή, -όν	soft
κάθημαι	I am seated	Μαραθωνομάχης,	Marathon fighter
*καθίζω	I sit down	-ου, ὁ	
*καίτοι	and further, indeed	μάχιμος, -η,-ον	warlike
κακοδαίμων, -ον	unlucky		

*μέγας, μεγάλη, μέγα great, big
*μέντοι however
μεσημβρινός, -ή, -όν noontide, belonging to noon
*μετά (+ acc.) after
*μετά (+ gen.) with
μήπω not yet
μεις, μηνός, ὁ month
*μηχανή, ἡ trick
μιαρός, -ά, -όν foul, corrupt
μιλτόω I make red, redden
μισθὸν φέρω I draw pay, take a salary
*μισθός, ὁ pay, salary
μολυνοπραγμονέομαι I get into dirty quarrels
*μόνος,-η, -ον alone
μοχθηρός, -ά, -όν wretched
μυττωτός, ὁ savoury mash

*ναί (adv.) yes, verily (expresses strong affirmation)
*ναῦς, νεώς, ἡ ship
ναύφαρκτος, -ον like a warship, ship-fenced
νέκταρ, -αρος, τό nectar
νεώσοικος, ὁ ship-shed
νοστέω I return (home)
*νῦν now

ξενίζω I receive (pass. I am received as a guest)
ξύλον, τό (here) seat
ξυμμάχων see συμμαχος
ξυρέω I shave

*ὅδε, ἥδε, τόδε this (man, woman, thing)
ὁδοιπλανέω I roam about, wander
ὀδυνάω (aor. ὠδυνήθην) I suffer pain
ὄζω I smell
*οἶδα I know
*οἴκαδε homewards, towards home
οἴμοι alas!
*οἶνος, ὁ wine
*οἷος, οἵα, οἷον of such a sort
οἴχομαι, impf. ᾠχόμην I go
ὀκτώ eight
*ὀλίγος, -η, -ον little, small
ὅλος, -η, -ον whole
ὄμνυμι (aor. ὤμοσα) I swear (an oath)
*ὄνομα, -ατος, τό name
ὄξος, -εος, τό vinegar
*ὀξύς, -εῖα, -ύ sharp
ὄπῃ to wherever

ὁπότε when
*ὅπως (+ fut. ind.) that, how
ὄρθιος [νόμος] the 'Orthian', a high-pitched song
ὄρνις, ὄρνιθος, ὁ bird (acc. sg. ὄρνιθα and ὄρνιν)
*ὄρος, -εος, τό mountain
*ὅσος, -η, -ον how great! What a big . . .!
ὅσπερ, ἥπερ, ὅπερ the very man
ὅστις, ἥτις, ὅτι anyone who
ὀσφραίνομαι (aor. ὠσφρόμην) I smell
*ὅτε when
*ὅτι that, because
*οὐδείς, οὐδεμία, οὐδέν no one, nothing
*οὐδέποτέ never
οὐδεπώποτε and not yet ever
*οὖν therefore
*οὗτος, αὕτη, τοῦτο this (man, woman, thing)
*οὕτω(ς) thus, in this way
*ὀφθαλμός, ὁ eye
ὀφρύς, -ύος, ἡ eyebrow

παίδιον, τό little child
*παῖς, παιδός, ὁ child, slave
πανσέληνος, ἡ the full moon
πάνυ completely
παρά (+ acc.) beside, by (with verbs of rest)
παρά (+ gen.) from
παρακύπτω I stoop sideways
*παρασκευάζω I prepare
παρασκευή, ἡ preparation
παρατίθημι I serve up, dish up
παρατίλλω I pluck the hair
*πάρειμι I am present
πάρνοψ, -οπος, ὁ locust
*πᾶς, πᾶσα, πᾶν all
*πάσχω (aor. ἔπαθον) I suffer
πατάσσω (aor. ἐπάταξα) I beat, smite (here) peck
πάτρα, ἡ fatherland
*πατρίς, -ίδος, ἡ fatherland
*πεδίον, τό plain
*πείθω I persuade (mid. I obey, I believe in)
*πέμπω I send
πέντε five
πεντέτης, -ες of five years
πέος, -εος, τό penis
πέρδομαι I fart
*περί (+ acc.) around
*περί (+ gen.) about

περιοράω	I ignore, allow
πέρυσι	last year
πήγνυμι (aor. ἔπηξα)	I stick, freeze
πίθηκος, ὁ	monkey
*πίνω	I drink
πίττα, ἡ	pitch
πλᾶτις, -ιδος, ἡ	wife
*πλήν (+ gen.)	except
πλύνω	(here) I abuse, tell off
πνύξ, gen. πυκνός (v. infr.), ἡ	Pnyx
ποθέω	I long for, desire
*ποιέω	I do, make
ποιέω σπονδάς	I make peace with (+ προς + acc.)
*ποῖος, -α,-ον	of what kind?
*πόλις, -εως, ἡ	city
*πολύς, πολλή, πολύ	many
πορθέω	I plunder, rob
πορίζω	I bring
*ποσός, -η, -ον	(of time) how long . . .?
*ποταμός, ὁ	river
*ποτέ	ever, once
*που	I suppose
*ποῦ	where
πρεσβύτης, -ου, ὁ	old man
πρεσβεύομαι	I send ambassadors, embassies
*πρέσβυς, -εως, ὁ	old man, ambassador
*πρίν	before, until
πρίνινος, -η, -ον	made of holm-oak
πρίω	'buy!' (imper. of defective vb ἐπριάμην)
προεδρία, ἡ	front seat
πρός (+ gen.)	by [the gods]
προσδοκάω	I expect
πρόσειμι	I come forward
πρόσειμι (+dat.)	I approach
προσέρχομαι	I approach
πρόσθεν	(with verbs of motion) forward
προτιμάω	I care, take heed that
πρυτανεῖον, τό	the *Prytaneion* or town hall
πρυτανεύω	I decide, put a motion about
πρύτανις, -εως, ὁ	member of the Prytany
πρωκτός, ὁ	anus
*πρῶτον	first of all
πώγων, -ωνος, ὁ	beard
πώποτε	ever yet
πῶς	how?
ῥανίς, -ίδος, ἡ	drop, rain-drop
ῥέγκω	I wheeze

*ῥήτωρ, -ορος, ὁ	orator
ῥύπτω	I wash
Σαρδιανικός, -ή, -όν,	Sardian
*σαφής,-ές	clear
σείω	I shake
*σιγάω	am silent
σιτίον, τό	food, rations
σκευάζω	I prepare, dress up
σκηνάω	(in middle) I encamp, I lie under a tent
σκῆψις, -εως, ἡ	excuse
*σκοπέω	I look
σκορδινάομαι	I stretch my limbs
σκοροδίζω	I feed garlic to, dose with garlic
σκόροδον, τό	garlic
σκοτοδασυπυκνόθριξ	dark with shaggy thick hair
σπένδω	I pour a libation
σπεύδω	I hurry
*σπονδή, ἡ	drink-offering, peace treaty (pl only)
στένω	I groan
στιπτός, -ή, -όν	tough, sturdy
*στόμα, στόματος, τό	mouth
στραγγεύομαι	I hang about, dawdle
*στρατιά, ἡ	army
*στρατός, ὁ	army
στρέφω	I turn
στυγέω	I hate
συλλέγω	I gather
*σύμμαχος, ὁ	ally
συνάγω	I bring together, I close
συνίημι	I understand
σφενδάμνινος, -η, -ον	made of maple-wood
σφόδρα (adv.)	exceedingly, absolutely
σχῆμα, -ατος, τό	fashion, clothing
σχοινίον, τό	rope
σώζω	I save
σωσίπολις, -ιδος, ὁ	city-saviour
τάλαντον, τό	a talent (large sum of money)
τάλας, τάλαινα, τάλαν	wretched
ταώς -ω, ὁ	peacock
*τέμνω	I cut
τέταρτος,-η, -ον	fourth
τέτμημαι	perf. mid./pass. τέμνω
τέτταρες, -ων	four
τεχνάζω	I use subterfuges
τήθη, ἡ	grandmother
τῆτες	this year
*τις, τι	anyone, anything
*τίς, τί	who?, what?

τοιόσδε,-άδεόνδε — such as this
τοῖχος, ὁ — wall
τοξότης, -ου, ὁ — archer
*τοσοῦτος, -αύτη, -οῦτο — such large, so great
τραγῳδικός, -ή, -όν — tragic
τρεῖς, τρία — three
*τρέχω — I run
τριακονταετής — 30 years old
τριβή, ἡ — delay
τρίβων, -ωνος, ὁ — cloak
τριπλάσιος, -α, -ον — three times the size of (+ gen.)
*τρόπος, ὁ — way, habit
τρύχω — I waste (pass. to be worn out)
τυννοῦτος, -ον — so small, so little

ὑάλινος, -η, -ον — of crystal, of glass
*υἱός, ὁ — son
*ὑπέρ (+ gen.) — on behalf of
ὑπερφυῶς — marvellously, excessively
*ὑπό (+ gen.) — at the hands of, by
ὑποκρούω — I interrupt
ὑποστένω — I groan

φενακίζω — I lie, cheat
φέναξ, -ακος, ὁ — fooler, cheat
*φέρω — I carry, produce
*φεύγω — I flee

*φημί — I say
φιλαθήναιος, -ον — in love with Athenians
*φιλέω — I love, like
φορυτός, ὁ — rubbish
φράζω (aor. ἔφρασα) — I tell, speak

χαῖρε — hello!
χαιρηδών, -όνος, ἡ — delectation
*χαίρω — I rejoice
χάσκω — I gape, yawn (perf. κέχηνα)
χαυνόπρωκτος, ον — wide-arsed
χέζω — I relieve myself, go to the toilet
χιών,-όνος, ἡ — snow
χορός, ὁ — chorus
χρῆμα, -ατος, τό — crowd, heap
*χρόνος, ὁ — time
χρύσεος,-η,-ον — gold
χρυσίον, τό — gold, gold piece
χρυσίς, -ίδος, ἡ — gold vessel
*χρυσός, ὁ — gold

ψευδής, -ές — false
ψῆφος, ἡ — voting pebble
ψυχή, ἡ — spirit

ὥρα, ἡ — hour
*ὥσπερ — just as, like
ὠστίζομαι — I jostle